About the authors

Dr Jacques M. Chevalier, Professor of Sociology and Anthropology at Carleton University, Ottawa, has been part of the IDRC (International Development Research Centre) co-operative research project on sustainable development in the Sierra de Santa Marta, Mexico, since 1990. His scholarly interests have also included economics and kinship in native Latin America and semiotics as applied to a variety of disciplines, most recently to scriptural mythology. Among his publications are *Civilization and the Stolen Gift: Capital, Kin, and Cult in Eastern Peru* (Toronto University Press, 1982) and *Semiotics, Romanticism and the Scriptures* (Mouton de Gruyter, 1990).

Dr Daniel Buckles is a Senior Scientist at the International Maize and Wheat Improvement Center (CIMMYT) in El Batan, Mexico. He was formerly a professional artist, and his current work as an agricultural anthropologist has led him to deal with such topics as the development of sustainable agricultural systems, rural extension and policy analysis for natural resource management. He too is a co-founder of the IDRC-funded project in the Sierra de Santa Marta with his co-author Dr Chevalier and with Dr Luisa Paré. He has recently completed a study of agricultural innovation entitled *The Green Manure Revolution in Atlantic Honduras*.

A Land without Gods

*Process theory, maldevelopment and
the Mexican Nahuas*

JACQUES M. CHEVALIER
AND DANIEL BUCKLES

Zed Books
LONDON AND NEW JERSEY

Fernwood Publishing
HALIFAX, NOVA SCOTIA

This book has been published with the help of a grant
from the Social Science Federation of Canada, using funds
provided by the Social Sciences and Humanities Research
Council of Canada.

*A Land without Gods: Process theory, maldevelopment
and the Mexican Nahuas* is published in Canada by
Fernwood Publishing Co. Ltd, PO Box 9409, Station A,
Halifax, Nova Scotia, Canada B3K 5S3
and in the rest of the world by Zed Books Ltd,
7 Cynthia Street, London N1 9JF and 165 First Avenue,
Atlantic Highlands, New Jersey, 07716, USA in 1995.

Cover designed by Andrew Corbett
Frontispiece: Monument No. 1, 'El Señor del Cerro',
San Martín, Papajan, drawing by Daniel Buckles
Cover photograph by Daniel Buckles

Set in Monotype Plantin by Ewan Smith, London
Printed and bound in the United Kingdom by
Redwood Books, Trowbridge, Wiltshire

A catalogue record for this book is available from the
British Library

US CIP is available from the Library of Congress

Canadian Cataloguing in Publication Data

    Chevalier, Jaques M., 1449–

       A land without gods

       Includes bibliographic references.
       ISBN 1-895686-52-0

       1. Nahuas—Social conditions.   2. Indians of
    Mexico—Mexico—Pajapan—Social conditions.
    3. Pajapan (Mexico)—Social conditions.
    I. Buckles, Daniel. II. Title.

    FI221.N3C43 1995   972´.62´004974   C95-950062-6

ISBN 1 85649 325 3 hb
ISBN 1 85649 326 1 pb

Fernwood Publishing Co. Ltd, Canada
ISBN 1 895686 52 0

FTW
AHH 7014

CONTENTS

FIGURES, PLATES
AND MAPS

Figures

Plates

Maps

GLOSSARY

acaual: fallow land covered with secondary forest vegetation

Agrarian Ejido Committee: local committee petitioning the federal government for the creation of an *ejido*

alcalde: town mayor

cabecera: administrative center of a municipality, usually the largest and most populous village

cacique: a local or regional political boss

certificado de inafectabilidad: legal document issued by the federal government protecting property and land against expropriation

chaneques: dwarf-like spirits of the underworld, owners of animals and fish

CNPA (*Congreso Nacional del Plan de Ayala*): National Congress of the Plan de Ayala, a national organization of independent peasant groups

CNPI (*Coordinadora Nacional de Pueblos Indigenas*): National Network of Indigenous Peoples

cofradia: civil religious organization formed around community saints (also known as *hermandades*)

columna volante: State Security Force used as rural police

comisariado: a council responsible for the administration of collective works and communal or *ejido* lands (and other resources), elected by a general assembly and comprising a president, a secretary and a treasurer, each with a replacement in case they cannot fulfil their duties

compadrazgo: fictive kinship ties established through Christian rituals such as baptism

comunero: holder of right of access to communal land

comunidad agraria: agrarian community comprising all holders of communal land rights

condueñazgo: land co-ownership

consejo de vigilancia: administrative body elected by the general assembly of *comuneros/ejidatarios* to monitor the *comisariado*

derechoso: holder of right of access to collective land (*ejido* or communal)

ejido: a common land owned and used by *ejidatarios* forming an association of independent producers with usufructuary rights over individual parcels of land

faena: collective work party

FCIP (*Frente Civico Indigenista de Pajapan*): Indigenous Civic Front of Pajapan

FIFONAFE (*Fideicomiso Fondo Nacional de Fomento Ejidal*): National Ejido Trusteeship Fund

FONDEPORT (*Fondo Nacional para el Desarrollo Portuario*): Port Development National Fund

FREPOSEV (*Frente Popular del Sureste de Veracruz*): Popular Front of Southeastern Veracruz

fundo legal: land trust used to establish a town site or village

Gulf Nahuas: native Nahua-speaking inhabitants of southern Veracruz

Hacienda del Estado: State Revenue Office

hermandad: religious brotherhood

INI (*Instituto Nacional Indigenista*): National Indigenous Institute - a federal state agency responsible for Indian people in Mexico

jefe de lote: administrator representing all those who have rights of access to land located within a given lot

lote: a communal lot under the administration of a *jefe de lote*

mayordomo: man holding a civil-religious office associated with a particular saint

media: agreement between rancher and peasant involving cattle raised on a share basis

mestizo: the offspring of a Spaniard and an American Indian

milpa: a maize plot

nortes: heavy drizzle and strong, cool winds blowing from the north from October until early March

Olmecs: a Mixe-Zoque people that developed a complex culture between 1200 BC and AD 300

PEMEX (*Petróleos Mexicanos*): Mexico's state-owned national oil company

PFCRN (*Partido Frente Cardenista de Reconciliación Nacional*): Cardenista National Reconciliation Front Party

peon: an unskilled worker (formerly an agricultural person forced to work off a debt)

porfiriato: period of Mexican history (1876–1910) under the rule of president and dictator Porfirio Diaz

prestanombre ("loaned name"): land ownership by proxy

PRI (*Partido Revolucionario Institucional*). Institutional Revolutionary Party (formerly the *Partido Nacional Revolucionario*), in power since the Mexican Revolution (1910–17)

PSUM (*Partido Socialista Unificado de México*): Unified Socialist Party of Mexico, founded in 1981

ranchería: small ranch settlement

SAHOP (*Secreteriá de Asentamientos Humanos y Obras Públicas*): Department of Human Settlements and Public Works

SARH (*Secretaría de Agricultura y Recursos Hidráulicos*): Department of Agriculture and Water Resources

SCT (*Secretariá de Comunicaciones y Transportes*): Department of Transport and Communications

SEDUE (*Secreteriá de Ecología y Desarrollo Urbano*): Department of Ecology and Urban Development (formerly SAHOP)

Sintiopiltsin: Corn-God-Child

SRA (*Secretariá de Reforma Agraria*): Department of Agrarian Reform (formerly DAAC)

SSMP: Sierra Santa Marta Project

tagatauatatzaloyan: literally "the land-where-men-are-dry", mythical burying place of the corn-god's father

talogan: underworld paradise ruled by *chaneque* spirits

tapachole: dry-season maize planted in November and harvested between March and April

temporal: wet-season maize planted in June and harvested between November and January

tierras afectadas: local expression denoting communal lands expropriated by the federal government

títulos primordiales: "primordial titles" of land ownership (in the case of Pajapan, dating back to 1765)

INTRODUCTION

Anthropology and the Gulf Nahuas

For more than three thousand years the Olmec statue of the Maize God sat undisturbed in the thick cloud forest atop the volcano San Martín Pajapan. In 1968 this 3-ton statue was dragged down the slope and transported to the Museum of Anthropology in Xalapa, Veracruz, where it now sits on a marble pedestal. Without the power of the Maize God, agricultural yields in Pajapan have fallen, rains are no longer sufficient and the land has dried. This is the belief of native villagers who associate the removal of the statue with the decline of *milpa* cultivation and the period of rapid growth in the local cattle industry when forests were destroyed and farmers pushed off the land by grazing cattle.

This act of archaeological rescue highlights a basic contradiction in Mexican society and in the Western world as well: the relentless pillage of native territory, labor and wealth combined with a romantic idealization of an Indianness frozen in time and confined in museums, in glorified cemeteries of history and storage rooms of colonial spoils. This book is not a romantic account of native culture and history. Like most other aboriginal populations of the late 20th century, the Gulf Nahuas cannot be portrayed as a people living in a pristine state of social and natural unity, the kind that heirs of Rousseau will use as a moral exemplar to critique the many evils and disenchantments of modern life. Noble savages are lifeless puppets of romantic rhetoric. However fascinated they may be by unfamiliar modes of life, students of other cultures should know that native societies have never been immune to the tragic in life and have generated tensions, struggles, inequalities and conflicts of their own. Ethnicity is never simply the world of sharing (ideas, values, resources) it is made out to be: collective identities thrive on the constant production of both internal differences (genders, age groups, kin positions) and external interactions and claims directed against other groups (Stephen 1991; Urban and Sherzer 1991). Also, anthropologists should remind themselves and others that first peoples have been radically transformed by centuries of incorporation into broader domains ruled by capital, state and church. Indianness has been defined and manipulated for 500 years by outsiders: religious orders, colonial officers, landlords, legislators, bureaucrats, tourist agencies, intellectuals and academics.

These lessons of history, however, should be qualified lest we reinforce another abiding legacy from Romanticism: the commonplace imagery of a tragic fall from grace. As Clifford (1988: 333, 341–4) and Sahlins (1985) have argued, the either/or logic of assimilation vs survival does little justice to the complexity of native history. While exploited through state and market mechanisms, the Indians of today have not turned into ethnic classes fully absorbed by capitalist society, let alone ethnic groups integrated within the pluralist state.[1] Nor are they victims of history that have become "our Indians" at best, counterfeit images or pale reflections of the authentic "others" they used to be (see Bonfil Batalla 1991: 125). Although anthropologists should eschew the temptation to portray first peoples as living fossils of a glorious past, they should be wary of the opposite strategy, which is to treat current manifestations of Indianness as false appearances, vestigial claims marred with problems of authenticity. Our case-study speaks to the profound changes that have affected Gulf Nahua society since conquest, yet we also take care to document the resilience of this southern Veracruz population and their active resistance to full incorporation into broader domains.

There is another legacy of Romanticism that keeps haunting the discipline: the confession of ethnocentric guilt. Anthropologists constantly fear viewing other cultures through terms and concepts that are too familiar, hence language fashioned by their own surroundings. Objective science was an answer to ethnocentric assumptions haunting the discipline. In recent decades, however, ethnographers have challenged the scientific approach to anthropology, pointing out that science is also a value-loaded product of Western history, a discourse that cannot be applied to other knowledge systems and ways of life without imposing our own modes of thinking. Post-modern ethnography offers an alternative to the scientific approach, a radically new perspective involving a de-centered, self-critical and anti-authorial exchange between informants, writers and readers. The basic implication of this new anthropology is that human experiences are so diverse they can never be transcended through grand theoretical syntheses, objective representations of reality, or any other similar exercise of scientific authority (Clifford and Marcus 1986).

The exploration of alternative literary genres, less analytical and more intersubjective, is an important contribution to anthropology. But when pitted against all other modes of discourse, post-modern ethnography can reduce a highly varied corpus to a few outdated tropes: visual perspectivism, the classic Polynesian arrival scene, the realist scientist-was-here rhetoric, the holistic organism imagery, the deep structure metaphor, and so on. With post-modernity, cultural masochism becomes second nature for a discipline that turns intolerant of its own origins and shows guilt for having chosen premises of its own – for having pursued sound knowledge, the right to speak the truth, and the obligation to do it with discipline. When pushed too far, this new attempt at freeing the ethnographic enterprise from habits of Western speech amounts to no more than a will to listen to all possible voices coupled with a verbose will to speak no more. The polyphonic acceptance of all voices that clamor for expression suggests a reversion to Rousseau's all-too-familiar herd instinct: an absolute democratization of all possible worldviews, hence truths that are so interchangeable as to become an object of supreme indifference to all parties concerned.

This book is not a post-modern exercise in ethnographic dialogue mixed with an overdose of self-distrust. Cognizant of the controversial nature of the issues we wish to raise, we have chosen to take our own stand on central questions such as the impact of state and capital on native society and the environment. These questions cannot be addressed through individual life stories and personal anecdotes, nor can they be resolved in a falsely dialogical style that reflects the interests of all parties concerned. Our research is informed by the work of other social scientists and by countless discussions with natives from all segments of Gulf Nahua society. All the same, we do not wish to present our findings as anything but our views on the subject. Nor do we wish to apologize for the biases built into the analyses offered throughout the book. Actually, our intention is to make these biases as compelling as can be to convince the reader of what we think to be the causes and deplorable effects of underdevelopment and unequal power relations in contemporary Gulf Nahua history. With this end in view, we have collected and processed field observations, made use of specific analytic methods, and developed conceptual frameworks that may contribute to the pressing debates raised throughout the text. Although dialogical theorists may view authorship as an authoritative institution in its own right, we consider ourselves to be personally accountable to the Gulf Nahuas, our readers and colleagues for the information, methods and arguments presented below.

On the theoretical plane, we have drawn on the contributions of different schools of thought to state theory, underdevelopment studies, ecology, gender analysis and semiotics. In our view, however, there is more to interdisciplinary research than the total sum of disparate perspectives and fields of investigation applied to one particular population or subject matter. Some analyses are more convincing than others, and some arguments will not let themselves be peacefully juxtaposed within a loosely written, multi-sided text. Faced with an array of theories and models that often ignore one another or that may be irreconcilable, anthropologists must exercise their own judgment and select or develop those analyses and levels of generalization that can combine to produce a higher-order approach to social phenomena. The final product need not be a dialogically eclectic language but rather a mode of discourse that breaks new ground within the discipline, a contribution to an ongoing "argument between styles of language" or "struggle among sociolinguistic points of view" (Bakhtin 1981: 76, 273). To paraphrase Heidegger (1968: 178), dialogue between disciplines and perspectives is worth pursuing only if it leads speakers into the unknown and the unspoken.

Before we sketch out the methods and theories developed in this book, more should be said about our case-study. The present-day people of Pajapan are all Nahua speakers. They inhabit a remote corner of southern Veracruz wedged between the Gulf of Mexico and the massive petro-chemical complex of Coatzacoalcos and Minatitlán (see Map 1). Their territory is part of the Olmec heartland, a hot, humid region where Mesoamerica's Mother culture developed between 1200 and BC. The Pajapan village is the administrative center (*cabecera*) and l village in the municipality (*municipio*) of Pajapan.² It is also the center for an agrarian community whose members live mostly in the *cabecera* but also in the nearby village of San Juan Volador and the hamlets of Jicacal, El Mangal, Palma Real, and Tecolapa. While some 8,000 people live in these congregations, the *comuneros* form a much smaller group that holds title to 19,158 hectares of land between the Laguna del Ostión and the peak of the volcano San Martín Pajapan.³ Together with their Mecayapan neighbors, the people of Pajapan are among the last of a large group of Nahua speakers in southern Veracruz, many of whom were displaced from the best agricultural land in the region and gradually absorbed into the wider mestizo society. The Gulf Nahua language is a variant of the language once spoken by the Aztecs and the people refer to their own dialect as *Mexicano*. Similar variants of the Gulf *pipil* or eastern Nahua dialect are spoken throughout southern Veracruz and eastern Tabasco (García de León 1969: 280). Sierra Popoluca, a Mixe-Zoquean language, is spoken by the neighboring people of Soteapan. All in all, the Gulf Nahua and Popoluca population numbers some 30,000 scattered in small communities in the mountainous area known as the Sierra de Santa Marta.

Beyond the Gulf Nahua area lie the cities of Coatzacoalcos, Minatitlán and Jáltipan which have a total population of over one million. These cities have grown rapidly in the past 30 years as a result of their strategic position between the oil-producing southeast and the industrial Valley of Mexico. They are ideally located on the narrow isthmus that divides the Gulf of Mexico and the Pacific Ocean. Some 70% of Mexico's petrochemical industries are concentrated there. To the west of this massive and highly polluted urban industrial complex lies the bustling cattle ranching and commercial city of Acayucan. The cattle industry has a long history in the region and is the economic mainstay in rural areas. Stimulated in recent decades by favorable national policies and growing national demand for low-quality beef, this land-extensive cattle economy has expanded rapidly, encroaching upon tropical rain forests and agricultural land and causing countless violent confrontations in the countryside. Thousands of peasants have lost their land, forced out of agriculture into unemployment or other poorly paid sectors of the rural and urban economy. As we shall see, the story of Pajapan is an illustration of the ravages of modern economic history on rain forest environments and Mesoamerican native society.

The expansion of state and capital profoundly altered the slash-and-burn subsistence economy and the rain forest environment that used to support it. It also brought radical changes to the native government process and traditional family structures. In order to understand such critical transformations, it is important that we look back over past events and broader forces that have shaped modern Gulf Nahua society. These factors are discussed in Chapter 1. They include land settlements of the colonial era, municipal divisions and the lot system created in the 19th century, the PRI apparatus established after the Revolution, the collective landholdings promoted under Cárdenas, and the post-war expansion of

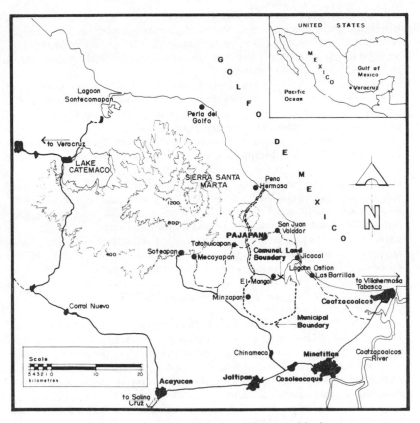

Map 1 Study area in southern Veracruz, Mexico

a cattle industry controlled by the powerful *caciques* (political bosses) of southern Veracruz.

Set against this background, municipal politics and the concentration of wealth in land and cattle in 20th-century Pajapan are explored in Chapters 2 and 3. Our account of Gulf Nahua economics and politics is informed by a theoretical approach that recognizes the convertibility of the two forms of power: authority over land has been used to acquire wealth, and wealth in cattle to achieve positions of authority. These conversions, however, have been performed within limits and under conditions that have varied through history. Even when controlled by a dominant bloc, wealth and office are never fused into a single system and continue to be managed through different institutional arrangements, those of capital and state. Moreover, the concentration of formal power in the hands of the few is offset by divisions between dominant groups and struggles launched against the ruling interests. Finally, power is exercised under conditions that are liable to change: the analysis shows how connections between power systems change over time. In Pajapan, the dominant regime has evolved from a brutal exercise of PRI rancher hegemony prior to the 1980s to an ethno-popular coalition of peasants and ranchers struggling against state capital in the early 1980s and a recent outburst of factionalism.

In Chapters 4 and 5, we address issues of agricultural economics and rain forest ecology. The analysis shows how Indian peasants have been divided and exploited through an unequal distribution of the factors of production (land, cattle) and the returns of labor. Our case-study stresses the various ways in which peasants and their rain forest environment have been exploited and impoverished by ranching capital, through means other than outright proletarianization and industrialization. But while ranching activities have radically altered previous relations and forces of production, they have fallen short of taking over the whole economy. Some older patterns of slash-and-burn farming and subsistence production have survived. Two important factors account for this distorted reproduction of older productive patterns: the weaknesses of local capital and peasant resistance. We argue that the local property system and the overall conditions of production have been shaped by struggles over land and a whole range of peasant survival strategies, from modifications of *milpa* agriculture to the intensification of complementary subsistence activities (e.g., lagoon fisheries).

Finally, we demonstrate the inefficiency and shortsightedness of Pajapan's hinterland ranching industry, a poorly managed breeding economy harnessed to urban-based operations controlling the more profitable processes of finishing and commercialization. Cattle ranching in the Santa Marta area creates few jobs and imposes poor-quality pastures on diverse rain forest ecosystems. The industry has had a negative impact on *milpa* productivity, causing a loss of food self-sufficiency. A highly constrained pastoral economy has spoiled the area of its natural riches and undermined long-term prospects for sustainable agricultural production in Pajapan.

Capitalism is adaptable and aggressive but it is also a stupid machine bent on creating obstacles to its own growth. In Pajapan, the expansion of the regional cattle industry has depleted resources and created poverty, unemployment and economic stagnation. These deplorable effects of capital accumulation in agriculture reflect chronic problems of mismanagement costly to the current profitability and future prospects of local and regional capital.

Our claim that older relations of production have survived the growth of the cattle economy is made in Chapter 6. Kin-based power and exchange relations continue to play a key role in current forms of Gulf Nahua adaptation to the rain forest environment and the market economy. Productive activities and the allocation of wealth are still founded on divisions and struggles of gender and generation that escape the control of broader domains. Actually these customary relations form a domain of their own, a bilateral descent system consisting of nuclear households governed by patrimonial rules of residence, marriage and inheritance (polygyny, brideservice, male ultimogeniture). Unlike the state and the market economy, patrimonial organization is highly decentralized, centered as it is on nuclear family activities. But it is also subject to broader requirements of reciprocity mixed with a strong dose of social hierarchy, the kind that favors men, older generations and wife-givers. Finally, the system is dynamic, a terrain of struggles, strategic actions and cyclical changes that create important differences and shifts in the domestic economy. Variations in household organization are the outcome of negotiations between genders and age-groups and also the transformation of power relations and productive activities linked to the market economy.

From the patrimonial domain emerges a particular view of relations between humans and the universe, a worldview conveyed through narrative discourse. Chapter 7 explores this subject matter through a close reading of the story of the Corn God known as Sintiopiltsin. Interactions between men and women, the old and the young, are thus situated against the background of native discourse on problems governing all life forms, including plant spirits. The analysis shows how native myths address two basic questions: the exigencies of hierarchy, but also the obligations of reciprocity and self-sacrifice that life places on human, animal and plant spirits alike. The concept of death as a condition of reproduction is central to this discourse and touches on all aspects of Nahua culture. While echoing prehispanic notions of asceticism, images of the offerings of life imply a native *Weltanschauung* that goes beyond Aztec sacrificial rites performed with a view to reinforcing structures of domination (Séjourné 1957: 35; González Torres 1985: 37), limiting population growth (Cook 1971), feeding the gods (Seler 1963, 1: 155; Caso 1953: 22), or providing protein food for humans (Harner 1977). We shall see that folk tales also ponder the ravages of modern history, external forces robbing the land of its gods and natural riches. The Maize God, underworld *chaneques* and the plumed servant have suffered yet they will not let the land, the waters of life and their native custodians be pillaged with impunity. In the long run, all segments of society and the universe lose from humans who refuse to behave ascetically and with regard for all those reciprocities that feed into the web of life.

The Conclusion specifies the common denominators underlying our discussion of agrarian politics, hinterland capitalism, rain forest ecology, gender relations and the narrative process. The conceptual frameworks and methods of analysis applied to different aspects of Gulf Nahua history converge on what we call the *processual* nature of social reality. The term "process" is often used to evoke changes occurring over time. Accordingly, our case-study speaks to the dynamics of native politics, economics, kinship and symbolling. A process-oriented view of history, however, must also speak to the question of order and established methods of doing things in society, whether they be habits of family life, a narrative tradition, a mode of production or a government process. Not that these "orderly processes" are invariable and unchanging. As readers will soon realize, our intent is to emphasize the variable properties and internal contradictions of each process: some degree of indeterminacy and irrationality is built into all rules of social activity. In keeping with these comments, the term "process" is used to imply a battle over rights. Social life is a power struggle involving the imposition of a ruling order (capitalism, *caciquismo*, patrimonialism, asceticism), an unequal distribution of the proceeds of social activity, and the confrontation of classes, kin groups and signs – forces constantly "serving a process" on each other.

Research methods and data base

Our exploration of Gulf Nahua society began in 1984 with a three-month stay in the fishing village of Jicacal. The research project was eventually supported by the Social Sciences and Humanities Research Council of Canada. The purpose of the project was to gather and analyze detailed information on the impact of the Mexican cattle-raising and petro-chemical industries on both the economy and the socio-cultural fabric of the Indian population located in the Santa Marta area. Following this initial plan, a wide range of information was collected by ourselves (with the help of Dominique Caouette and local field assistants)[4] every year since 1984. Stays in Pajapan and nearby villages were frequent and extended from several weeks to three months at a time. Daniel Buckles (1989) developed a PhD dissertation and Dominique Caouette (1989) an MA thesis from this material.

The analyses presented in this book are based on information gathered in the Pajapan area, the state capital Xalapa and Mexico City. Data were obtained through a variety of methods: surveys, interviews, archival research and participant observation. One key source of information consists of a general household survey conducted in 1986 following several months of informal interviews. The survey deals with household composition, access to land, property in cattle and occupational profile based on a random sample (N 592) of people in the village of Pajapan and surrounding hamlets. A team of ten local assistants did the interviews in the Nahua language under close supervision by the researchers. Additional interviews with peasants, fishers and Indian ranchers were carried out over the course of several years. Twelve case-studies provided supplementary information on cattle ranching enterprises and 50 structured interviews with farmers covered in greater detail aspects of local farming practices not examined in the general survey. Sales statistics obtained from the local Rancher Association dating back to the early 1960s allowed us to add some historical depth to our quantitative analysis of Pajapan's cattle industry. A census of all households in the fishing village of Jicacal (N 74) was also undertaken in 1984 along with a survey of fishing activities involving over 200 lagoon fishers from Pajapan, San Juan Volador and Jicacal. Through participant observation and numerous discussions with native informants, information was collected on the labor process in most sectors of the local economy and on general features of local soil, water, land and forest resources. Finally, a census of all stores in Pajapan, lengthy interviews with eight store-owners in the village, several studies of petty trade in fish and fruit and a series of discussions with key informants on the history and concrete conditions of commerce in the area form part of the ethnographic material amassed over the years. Other data include interviews of craft workers, construction laborers, taxi drivers, carpenters, butchers, bakers and midwives.

Our history of politics in Pajapan is the product of extensive archival research and countless discussions by Dominique Caouette and ourselves with peasant leaders, Indian ranchers in Pajapan and outside bureaucrats as well. The researchers were present in the village during some important political events. Many government documents and published materials referring to Pajapan were also collected. Archival material includes Pajapan's primordial land titles stored in a wooden chest held by a village elder. The primordial titles are copies, hand-made in the mid-1880s, of documents dating back to 1605. Correspondence from 1932 to 1992 between the village of Pajapan and government officials, contained in the communal chest and various national archives, details local struggles between peasants and ranchers for control over land and the local land commission. We also consulted all the letters exchanged over the last 60 years or so between the village of Pajapan and the Office of the President of Mexico, letters full of rhetoric and description of land conflicts prevailing in the municipality.

Another aim of the project was to obtain primary data on the cultural and social aspects of life among the Gulf Nahuas, with a view to exploring the relationship between economy, society and culture in the Santa Marta area. The material collected over the years touches on household budgets (19 cases), the sexual division of labor, rules of descent and inheritance (six cases), patterns of marriage and residence, and fluctuations in brideprice from the 1940s onwards. Demographic trends were reconstructed with the use of our own 1986 survey and national census statistics published by the Mexican government from 1900 onwards. As for the cultural side of things, lengthy interviews were carried out with two local healers. Linguistic material of a semantic nature (Nahua words and meanings related to the imageries appearing in the corn myth) was also collected in May 1991 with the help of two local informants.

We have consulted and referenced all the secondary sources that contain information about the Gulf Nahuas. The works of Stuart, García de León, Nahmad and native researchers of Culturas Populares were helpful in filling gaps in our own data base. Some recent findings of the Sierra Santa Marta Project, an interdisciplinary research team initially launched in 1989 and funded by the International Development Research Center, are reported.

During our many trips to Pajapan we were always received by the local population with hospitality. Our interest in the language was an important factor facilitating our rapport with villagers. Most people we met did not perceive us as a threat to local interests and spoke with us very frankly, even about delicate issues. The absence of any affiliation with local, regional or national interest groups also made it easier for us to conduct interviews with peasant organizers, municipal politicians and government bureaucrats. Over the years, however, our involvement in the Sierra Santa Marta Project (see Conclusion) has changed our personal relationship to people in the region. While permanently residing outside the area, we are actors firmly committed to supporting local and regional efforts to resolve problems of poverty and resource depletion in the Santa Marta highlands. Our research has played a useful role in orienting some local initiatives; moreover, support for these actions has directly influenced our research process and the analyses presented below. Our sincere hope is that we continue to have this opportunity.

Notes

1. Authors who subsume Indianness under class include Harris (1964), Stavenhagen (1965), Pozas and Pozas (1971), Herbert, Guzmán and Qan (1972). In recent years, Mexicanists have preferred to emphasize the interplay of class and ethnicity (Stavenhagen 1979; Campbell 1989; Schryer 1990).

2. The municipality includes numerous hamlets and *congregaciones*: San Juan Volador, Minzapan, Coxcapa, José María Morelos (founded in 1960, an *ejido* since 1974), Benito Juárez (founded in 1971, an *ejido* since 1973), Lázaro Cárdenas (founded in 1975, an *ejido* since 1981), San Miguel Temoloapan, Ursulo Galván, Lorenzo Azúa Torres, El Mangal (1950s), Batajapan (1957, annexed to the *cabecera* in 1982), Jicacal (1970), Palma Real, El Pescador (1980) and Tecolapa (1940).

3. Throughout this book, reference will be made to three main groups: Indian peasants, Indian ranchers and mestizo ranchers. While the Indian ranchers live in Pajapan, mestizo ranchers live in urban centers. Only Indians (but not all of them) living in the municipality are *comuneros*, i.e., holders of communal land rights in Pajapan.

4. Gustavo Antonio, Chabelo Antonio, Adelina Jaúregui, Saturnino Hernández, Francisco Salas, Leonardo Salas and Roberto Salas.

CHAPTER I

FROM COLONIALISM TO REVOLUTION

Commonplace notions of aboriginal communal land tenure systems dating back to the prehistoric era and preserved through native traditions and post-revolutionary agrarian reforms, do little justice to the complex history of land politics in Mexico. This chapter shows how the Gulf Nahua land tenure system has assumed various legal forms and land-use patterns over time. In the colonial period, conglomerations of kin-based *calpolli* governed by regional *caciques* were dismantled through outright dispossession or reduction of aboriginal settlements by the Spanish Crown, giving way to large estates and the extraction of tribute by the Spaniards. In 1765, the people of San Francisco Minzapan (Pajapan's ancestral village) nevertheless purchased collective titles to a local territory to be used by all community members within the confines of the communal "reserve". Toward the end of the 19th century, private property reforms of the Porfiriatio converted these lands into a semi-private *condueñazgo* – lands divided into lots owned by local administrators (*jefes de lote*) and private peasant associations. This legal regimen, the Mexican revolution and agrarian reforms that followed favoring the recognition of native collective landholdings had little impact on local land use patterns involving family-based, universal and flexible forms of access to land within the communal reserve.

Coatzacoalcos, a prehispanic state

When Hernán Cotés explored the Gulf coast of Mexico in 1520, he found a land divided into many political territories. Coastal states, including Tlacotalpan, Acuezpoltepec and Tuxtla, were dominated militarily by the Aztec Empire and paid tribute to the leaders of Tenochtitlán. Coatzacoalcos, a large geopolitical unit including much of present-day southern Veracruz and parts of Tabasco, Chiapas and Oaxaca, was an exception; the inhabitants repelled invading Aztec forces in the late 15th century, thereby maintaining political independence (Cruz Martínez 1991: 48-9). There were, however, important trade links with Tenochtitlán. Safe passage was granted to *pochtecas*, Aztec merchants that traded with the Maya in the Yucatan and Central America. The people of Coatzacoalcos traded cacao, emeralds, shells, birds, jaguar skins and feathers for obsidian and pottery from the high valley of Mexico.

At the time of the Spanish invasion, approximately 50,000 people lived in 76 small, agriculturally-based villages scattered throughout the

os region (García de León 1976: 11–16). The *Espíritu Santo*
580 mentions that the heaviest populations lived "in the area
m the southern slopes of the Sierra San Martín south-
to Río Coatzacoalcos and on the lower course of this river"
(Stuart 1978: 22). Each village governor acted under the authority of the
cacique of Coatzacoalcos, the political leader of a large village located at
the mouth of the Coatzacoalcos River. Both men and women occupied
positions of political leadership in Coatzacoalcos, a practice shared by
the Totonacas but not by the Aztecs. *Caciques* received tribute of cacao
beans (also used as money, see Lockhart 1992: 178), cotton, maize, wild
birds, honey, copper axes and small quantities of gold from the village
population, and passed their rights to rule on to sons and daughters.

The region was culturally diverse. Most of the population probably
descended from the Olmecs, a Mixe-Zoque-speaking people that built a
complex culture between 1200 BC and AD 300. The region was influenced
later by Nahua-speaking people from the high valley of Mexico who
scattered throughout southern Mexico and Central America following
the collapse of the cities of Teotihuacán and Tula in the 9th century.
These people imposed the Nahua language on the aboriginal population
of the Coatzacoalcos region; García de León (1976) argues that the
ancestors of Pajapan originally spoke Mixe-Zoque and adopted the Nahua
language under the influence of migrants from central Mexico. Soteapan
is one of only a few villages in the region that retained the Mixe-Zoque
language.

Regional dominance of the Nahua culture extended beyond the use
of language. The gifts sent from Coatzacoalcos to Tenochtitlán for the
consecration of the *Templo Mayor* in the mid-1400s suggest that the two
regions shared a similar religious system (Cruz Martínez 1991: 51). Both
peoples practiced ritual warfare with neighboring villages and were known
to cannibalize prisoners. These similarities were not due to the influence
of the Aztec Empire, a newcomer on the military and cultural scene.
Rather, they reflect common inspiration in the Nahua-speaking civiliza-
tions of Teotihuacán and Tula from which the Aztecs drew heavily.

The Gulf Nahuas of prehispanic times lived under a patrimonial
domain where control over office, land and wealth was exercised through
a blend of kinship, religious and military forms of organization. As
suggested by Wolf (1966: 50), the rights assigned within a patrimonial
domain can be pyramided, "with lords of a higher order exercising
inherited rights over lords of a lower order, and lords of the lower order
exercising domain over the peasants who work the land. The peasant is
always at the base of such an organizational pyramid, sustaining it with
his surplus funds." A patrimonial domain, however, is not historically
uniform; the profile of any given society is shaped by the way power-
holders use the domain (Wolf 1966: 56). In prehispanic Coatzacoalcos,
surplus production was delivered mostly in the form of labor and goods
rather than money. Geographic isolation, low population density and the
prevalence of semi-autonomous subsistence economies severely limited
military domination, land concentration and the extraction of surplus

funds. Regional geo-political fragmentation produced tensions between competing patrimonial domains and permitted a high degree of autonomy among various domain holders. Just as the state of Coatzacoalcos succeeded in maintaining political independence *vis-à-vis* the Aztecs, so too peasant villages of different ethnic backgrounds preserved part of their own social fabric against outside forces, including the lordlike *cacique* of Coatzacoalcos.

There is little information on the prehispanic land tenure system of the Coatzacoalcos area. However, given the regional dominance of Nahua linguistic, political and religious traditions, it is likely that there was much in common with the land tenure system of the Aztecs, about which much more is known.[1] Land tenure amongst the Nahuas was associated with the *altepetl*, a territorial kin-based conglomeration consisting of several *calpolli*, governed by a dynastic ruler or *tlatoani*, and subjected to the imperial regime through tribute and levy exacted on a rotational basis. These corporate multi-ethnic entities took over lands that were conquered or abandoned, they controlled residual rights to all lands, and they sanctioned the allocation of tillable plots, usually through community consultation.

By and large, however, individuals and households held arable land on a long-term basis, as in Europe. They worked various scattered plots obtained mostly through inheritance but also through corporate allocation and outright purchase (Lockhart 1992: 15–18, 27, 142, 147ff., 152–65). Households had access (with certain restrictions) to the resources of untilled areas within the *altepetlalli* such as hunting grounds, timber lands, grasslands used for gathering construction materials, rock quarries, etc. Other lands of the *calpolli* included plots worked with community labor for the maintenance of the *cacique* and special visitors, the payment of tribute to military and religious institutions, and the undertaking of wars. The size of the individual and public plots and the common untilled areas varied depending upon the amount of land controlled by the *calpolli*, the number of households in the kinship group, the amount of tribute owed, and agronomic factors such as the quality of the soil and the supply of water. Ideograph records were kept of the various uses of *calpolli* lands and landmarks such as low stone walls, rows of bushes and drainage or irrigation canals formed boundaries dividing *calpolli* from *calpolli*.

According to Lockhart (1992), the Spaniards converted the *altepetl/calpolli* system into an area with a city (*cabecera, pueblo*) and its *cacique* ruling outlying hamlets (*sujetos*). After they had destroyed the imperial structure, the Spaniards dealt directly with *altepetl* authorities, shaped *encomiendas* around the traditional *caciques*, took advantage of the older cacao currency system to exact money tribute, and developed a mixed system of local government that lasted until the early 19th century. Through adaptation, indigenous modes of organization thus survived long into the post-conquest period (Lockhart 1992: 4, 20, 27f., 52, 55, 133, 180). Although large units initially meant lucrative and easily-administered *encomiendas* and *repartimientos*, the colonial period none the less witnessed their gradual dismemberment and the formation of independent *cabeceras* embodying indigenous units that had existed since remote times. "The principles of microethnicity, small unit self-containedness, and the separate representation of subunits held the possibility of a progressive fragmentation that in fact began very early in the postconquest period and gained momentum in the seventeenth and eighteenth centuries" (Lockhart 1992: 48, see 53–7, 175). A movement in the direction of a more individualized land tenure system also developed over time.

McBride (1923: 117) rejects egalitarian characterizations of the land system in Aztec Mexico, arguing that "certain modifications had been introduced which were gradually destroying whatever equality had formerly existed in the distribution of the land and in the social organization that was based upon it." The term *altepetlalli* or village lands shows that "the village itself, as distinguished from the individual *calpolli* composing it, had already become a recognized territorial division" (McBride 1923: 114). In addition to the *calpolli* there were estates belonging to Aztec nobility with tenants bound to the land who cultivated subsistence plots and the fields of the landlord and provided personal service to the landlord's household. These estates were passed on within certain families from generation to generation and could not be transferred to households living on *calpolli* lands. Individuals occupying public offices also controlled estates that were passed from father to son (and in Coatzacoalcos to daughters) along with the office. Thus, the distribution of land in areas where the Nahua culture dominated was unequal, as was the distribution of social and political power. Other aspects of the Gulf Nahua version of patrimonial politics such as kinship relations (alliance, descent) and religious practices (shamanic) have survived until the present day, albeit not in their original form. We shall return to the particulars of Gulf Nahua society and culture later.

The colonial period

The new province of Coatzacoalcos was divided by the Spanish into ten *corregimientos* and many *encomiendas* (Cruz Martínez 1991: 83). The *corregimientos* were specific territories and tribute obligations on the aboriginal population controlled by the Spanish Crown while the *encomiendas* were similar designations granted to Spanish soldiers who aided in the invasion, a reward system dating back to the Spanish Reconquest (Chevalier 1963: 310). Many of the most important figures in the Spanish invasion received *encomiendas* and established their own plantations or cattle ranches in the area. Cortés laid claim to a vast cotton-producing area in the Tuxtlas while Captain Luis Marín was appointed the first governor of the Villa Espíritu Santo at the mouth of the Coatzacoalcos River and granted under his *encomienda* Acayucan, Jáltipan, Tequecistepeque and Chacalapa, among other villages.

It is often said of the Spaniards that they did not change prehispanic forms of domination but rather substituted one ruling class with another.

The territorial and tribute divisions of the *corregimiento* and *encomienda* were thus based on the prehispanic tribute system, modified in light of Castilian legal traditions. The system, however, was abused by the Spaniards. Hardships imposed by excessive tributes and epidemic diseases devastated the regional population as thousands died and others moved to more isolated areas. The population of Coatzacoalcos declined from 50,000 to only 3,000 between 1522 and 1580 (Cruz Martínez 1991: 46). This undermined the tribute system adopted by the Spanish, forcing the Crown to consider other means of exploiting the population and land resources.

By the early 1600s, the prehispanic patrimonial regime had given way to a mercantile hacienda economy (plantations, cattle ranching) combined with a prebendal rule based on the granting of permanent estates to officials (administrative, military, ecclesiastical), at the expense of the Indians and their subsistence economy. In keeping with Spanish villa traditions, land was divided into collective and individual property, the inalienable and the alienable (exchangeable for money). Government was centralized and standardized: it became the sphere of the public and the civil-religious (Catholic *cofradias*), as distinct from the kinship domain. The new regime imposed an official language (Spanish) and created new socio-political categories; the *Indios* treated as colonial subjects of the Spanish Crown and the Ladino rulers.

The *encomienda*, a temporary concession at any rate, was almost entirely replaced by *mercedes*, permanent land grants to Spanish soldiers that did not involve tribute from the resident population. In an attempt to slow the rapid decline of the aboriginal population, royal decrees (*cédulas reales*) called for the concentration of populations into Indian *pueblos*. Dehouve (1984) shows how these *pueblos* comprised a variety of administrative and ecclesiastical centers: i.e., places of residence of governors (*cabecera de república*), mayors (*cabecera agraria* or *cabecera de alcadía mayor*), teachers (*pueblo con escuela*) and parish fathers (*cabecera de curato*). Each center controlled particular offices and resources, interacted with church and colonial authorities, and extracted tribute or services from satellite settlements (*sujetos, barrios*) located within its jurisdiction. These hierarchical divisions favored a regional concentration of indigenous government power, at the expense of the Spanish Crown. They also produced constant tensions and struggles between neighboring *pueblos*. As a result, the regime was eventually replaced by a more fragmented and decentralized "Indian community" system (so dear to anthropologists).

Each *pueblo* was composed of a town site, or *fundo legal*, and an *ejido* comprised of individual agricultural plots and a common untilled area of forest and pastures. These lands were administered by town councils and could not be alienated from the *pueblo*. The collective and inalienable land title applied to the aboriginal *pueblo* had its legal foundations in the *ejidos, propios, montes* and *pastos comunes* of Castilian landholding villas.[2] While paralleling some features of the *calpolli* system, this form of land tenure had more in common with the landholding villas of Spain than the Aztec *calpolli*. The kin-based *calpolli* polity gave way to a place designation and village council similar to the local government of Spanish villas.

While designed to establish an Indian land base, few aboriginal settlements obtained formal recognition of their collective landholdings in conformity with Spanish law. This did not mean, however, that they retained prehispanic forms of land tenure. The dramatic decline in aboriginal population undermined the traditional kinship structure and the authority of *caciques* was gradually usurped through the introduction of a parallel Spanish administrative structure (the *alcalde* or town mayor), often controlled by *hacendados* and regional officials. Meanwhile, the haciendas expanded *mercedes* provided by the Spanish Crown, often at the direct expense of aboriginal settlements without legal title. The land base of many aboriginal *pueblos* was reduced while other settlements were completely absorbed by the haciendas. Deprived of land, aboriginal peoples in many parts of Mexico were forced to work on the haciendas as wage laborers or rentiers, indentured through debts they could never repay.

Despite these transformations, the colonial state administration was plagued by problems of underpopulation and weak regional economies. Patrimonial rules of government and land allocation were not eradicated in all areas by the colonial regime. The forefathers of Pajapan continued to cultivate their land and, to some extent, govern themselves through institutions of their own. Moreover, colonial policies allowed the Gulf Nahuas to use legal mechanisms to gain ownership of the lands they occupied. As we shall see, the people purchased the titles of the lands they possessed, a strategic move that marked the course of local history.

As with peasants of Otumba and the Guadalajara region (Charlton 1991: 231; Van Young 1981: 295), the colonial history of the people of Pajapan is an intricate story of claims and counterclaims made by competing Spanish *hacendados*, a story of forced migrations and legal proceedings to regain lost lands. The ancestral village of Pajapan was San Francisco Minzapan, located near the Laguna de Minzapan, on the southern bank of what was then the Nancinapa river (see Map 2). The Nancinapa is now called the Metzapa (Nahua origin of Minzapan) and the Laguna de Minzapan has been renamed the Laguna del Ostión. The old village site is known locally as Minzapan Viejo or Casas Viejas. A ranch in the area retains the name Nanchital, a variation on Nancinapa.

Following the Spanish invasion, the villages of the area, including San Francisco Minzapan, became part of an *encomienda* (Bouysse-Cassagne 1980: 13). At the turn of the 17th century, people living in different hamlets were forced to relocate to the village of San Francisco Minzapan in compliance with the decrees creating Indian *pueblos*, thereby releasing lands for claims by Spanish *hacendados*. In 1611, the people of San Francisco Minzapan became embroiled in a dispute between two Spaniards attempting to claim lands left vacant by the local Indian population. The legal battle is documented in a bound book held by a village elder transcribed in 1884 from original documents of the early

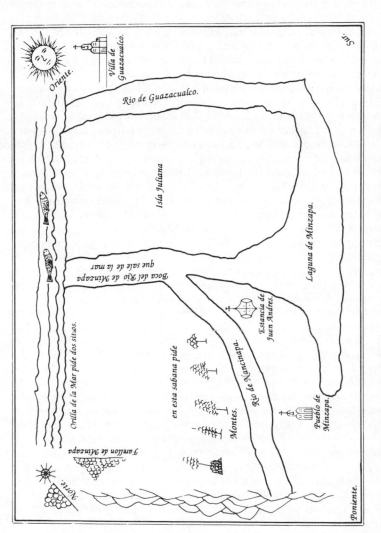

Map 2 The village of Minzapa (later Paiapan) and Laguna de Minzapa (later del Ostión), 1605 (copy made in 1880)
Source: Archives of the Comisariado Comunal

17th century. According to these primordial titles, Francisco Dávila Varaona, a powerful *hacendado* with extensive landholdings in the region (cattle ranches totalling 50 *sitios*), requested a *merced* of two *sitios* between the Laguna de Minzapan and the Farellón de Minzapan, a point of land that refers to present-day Peña Hermosa. A counterclaim was made by Mariana de Ojeda, the widow of Juan Andrés Coronada and owner of the Hacienda San Miguel Temoloapan located near the village of San Francisco Minzapan. The hacienda had been using the land to graze cattle and the *hacendado* objected to the *merced* requested by Dávila.[3]

The primordial titles of Pajapan indicate that on February 2, 1611, a hearing was convened in the village of San Francisco Minzapan by Matías de Gama, chief justice of Coatzacoalcos. Testimony was presented by *criollo* ranch hands and Indians of San Francisco Minzapan that the lands from the Laguna de Minzapan to the Farellón de Minzapan were vacant (*baldío*) and could be granted as a *merced* without prejudice to the Indians. The testimony reflects the legal requirement that claims to land not be contested by aboriginal *pueblos*. Sebastián Gómez, a criollo ranch hand and *compadre* of Francisco Dávila, testified before the judge that for over a decade Indians had not planted maize in the contested area as the lands were being grazed by the cattle of the Hacienda Temoloapan. He stated that the *merced* requested by Dávila would not deprive the Indian population of access to land as they had already gone elsewhere. A separate document from 1593 notes that Juan Andrés Coronado was summoned by the court of Coatzacoalcos to reimburse the native population for damages to their crops caused by his cattle, possibly on these same lands (Melgarejo Vivanco 1960: 83–4). As we shall see, similar methods of occupying Indian lands were to be used by ranchers centuries later.

Further testimony was provided at the hearing by Juan Pérez, a native and treasurer of San Francisco Minzapan. He stated that while in the past local Indians had planted maize on the requested lands, they had been abandoned because they were too far from the current village. Testimony that the lands had no current owner was also given by the Indian *Gobernador* of the village, Don Francisco Hernández, and two *Alcaldes Ordinarios*, Gregorio Gerónimo and Juan García. These and other Indian witnesses noted that the lands requested by Dávila were far from the village and did not have forest vegetation (*monte*) suitable for *milpa* cultivation. Various references to the absence of *monte* on the disputed lands suggest that at least some of the territory was comprised of natural savannas. The Chief Justice ruled in favor of Francisco Dávila and the lands were granted to him in 1613 under orders from Don Diego Fernández de Córdova, the Viceroy of New Spain. The Alcalde of Coatzacoalcos, acting on the orders of the Viceroy, pulled out grass and presented it to Dávila as a sign of possession. Mariana de Ojeda continued to protest the *merced* for several years but to no avail.

The concentration of land and the growth of the cattle economy in southern Veracruz in the 18th century directly affected the livelihood of native populations such as San Francisco Minzapan. Some seven haciendas and 37 ranches located within the jurisdiction of Acayucan were providing the cities of Coatzacoalcos and Minatitlán with 4–5,000 bulls per year (Melgarejo Vivanco 1980: 130). In 1759 the people of San Francisco Minzapan requested the lands of the Hacienda Pajapan,[4] the original *merced* granted to Francisco Dávila, arguing that they had "nowhere to plant maize or to feed their cattle" (Bouysse-Cassagne 1980: 15). However, the pressure of haciendas and the cattle industry on aboriginal land was probably not as great on the southern coast of Veracruz during the 18th century as in many other parts of Mexico. Villa de Espíritu Santo and other Spanish communities along the Gulf coast of Mexico were forced to move inland by epidemic diseases and the frequent attacks of pirates in the late 1700s, thereby reducing Spanish pressure on land resources. In 1765 the villagers of San Francisco Minzapan were able to purchase four *sitios* of land corresponding to the Hacienda Pajapan for the sum of 300 pesos in gold. The boundaries of the land extended from the Laguna de Minzapan to the Sipaquiapa River where it emptied into the Gulf of Mexico at the Farellón de Minzapan. In the presence of the Mayor of Coatzacoalcos, the *Gobernador* of San Francisco Minzapan (Jose Martín) opened and closed the doors of hacienda buildings and threw grass and soil in the four directions as a sign of possession.[5] This gesture and the titles granted under the seal of Carlos III established the claim that was to be used two centuries later by Pajapeños struggling to preserve their territory.

The liberal land policies

Independence from Spain and the liberal revolution that followed intensified the monetarization and privatization of land and labor. By the end of the 19th century, land and colonization policies had displaced peasants and Indians, forcing them into wage-labor. The mercantile hacienda economy of previous centuries gave way to the industrial revolution based on a private property regime intolerant of aboriginal claims to communal land. On the political level, local governments became instruments of tax collection for state revenues, a tendency that undermined the autonomy and sustainability of patrimonial societies such as Pajapan. The early industrial transformation of prebendal and mercantile domains in southern Veracruz, however, was not without limits – constraints of capital and state that allowed the community of Pajapan to reproduce some of its own political institutions while retaining effective possession and partial ownership of property in land.

Political instability following the struggle for independence (1810–21) created economic stagnation in much of Mexico. Legislators inspired by the liberal ideals of laissez-faire and private property attempted to address some of the national and regional economic problems by challenging the remaining collective landholdings of aboriginal settlements. Federal and state government legislation against collective ownership of land was introduced and enforced to varying degrees throughout the 19th century (Florescano Mayet 1984: 24–6). Aboriginal villages that refused to divide their communal lands into individual properties were threatened with legal actions and the loss of all land rights.[6] Land policies aimed at breaking up the aboriginal communities were accompanied by legislation to promote the colonization of Mexico's humid tropics and arid north (Revel-Mouroz 1980: 147–57; Asaola Garrido 1982: 56–72). European colonists were sponsored by the Mexican government in the 1820s but in most cases these experiments ended in failure. In the Coatzacoalcos area, French immigrants established a colony that was abandoned after only a few years because of outbreaks of disease and poor support services (Maison and Debouchet 1986).

In the 1820s, San Francisco Minzapan and the surrounding area became a municipality. The population had increased from 178 Indians and one Spanish family in 1803 to 773 people in 1831 (Blom and La Farge 1926; Iglesias nd: 65–6). The natives grew corn, beans and tobacco and the land was of good quality for agriculture and ranching. The community had a mayor, a deputy, a syndic, and a primary school affiliated to the mission of Chinameca. Unlike neighboring communities such as Mecayapan (Velázquez 1992a, 1992b), San Francisco Minzapan had legal title to their land; five leagues extending from Las Barrillas to El Farallón, including the slopes of the San Martín volcano. No mention is made of haciendas in the area.[7]

The population and administrative center of the Gulf Nahuas shifted from San Francisco Minzapan to the current village of Pajapan during the mid-1800s following aggression committed during the French Intervention. In 1869 the village of Pajapan had a total population of 263 compared to 686 for Minzapan. Between March and November of the following year, population figures for the two areas changed drastically: Pajapan rose to 817 while Minzapan fell to 469. The corresponding population figures for the 1870s are: 817 and 440 (1871), 913 and 517 (1873), 1,035 and 542 (1878). By the mid-1880s, Pajapan (921 people) was more than twice the size of Minzapan (441 people). Administrative boundaries also changed during this period. Records show that sometime during the 1860s Pajapan became a municipality. In 1869 it had a civil registry and a rural police officer. A year later, positions of authority in Pajapan included a syndic, a justice of the peace and an assistant, two aldermen and a sub-alderman, outnumbering those of Minzapan. By 1873 Pajapan had a school with ten pupils compared to eight in Minzapan. Local politics were apparently controlled by the regional *jefe político*, General Eulalio Vela, and the local Martín family (Eduardo as mayor, Lorenzo as alderman, Prisciliano as syndic; see Cruz Martínez 1991: 45). San Juan Volador joined the municipality of Pajapan in 1886. In 1889, following a conflict between Pajapan and Mecayapan, the Agachapa River was established as the dividing line between the two municipalities and between the Cantón of Minatitlán and the Cantón of Acayucan. The municipality of Minzapan was later reduced to the village of Minzapan and finally annexed to the municipality of Pajapan in 1898.

Oral history of the migration from San Francisco Minzapan to Pajapan differs from the archival record in one important aspect. Villagers report that pirates attacked the village of Minzapan Viejo and raped women while the men were working in the fields, precipitating the massive relocation. The community apparently divided into two, one group moving inland to create the current village of Minzapan (see Map 1) and the other moving up the Metzapa (Nanchinapa) River to join families already living in Pajapan. The population figures for Minzapan from 1870 onwards probably refer to the village at its new site, not the original site of San Francisco Minzapan. According to oral tradition, the exodus involved the transfer of images of Catholic saints; to this date the celebrations of the village patron saint, San Juan de Dios, involve the ritual transfer of his image from Minzapan to Pajapan. Furthermore, the site of the first houses in Pajapan is still marked in the village with a cross. While much of this account is probably accurate, the identity of the attackers is not. Oral traditions in the region confuse 17th-century pirates (especially Laurens de Graff alias Lorencillo) with French soldiers who attacked Cosoleacaque in the 1860s during the French Intervention (García de León 1976).

The excesses and limits of the Porfiriato

The prospects for economic development in southern Veracruz improved during the Porfiriato (1876–1910). In the 1870s, a sawmill was established in Minatitlán by an American company to process mahogany, caoba and other precious woods. The port of Coatzacoalcos (the Villa del Espíritu Santo or Puerto México, renamed Coatzacoalcos in 1936) also developed rapidly when foreign-owned plantations in central Veracruz began exporting sugar to Europe. The opening of a trans-isthmic rail link in 1894 between Coatzacoalcos and Salina Cruz on the Pacific Ocean further stimulated the regional economy. The discovery of oil during the construction of the railway led in 1909 to the establishment of an oil refinery in Minatitlán by Lord Cowdray, a British partner in the construction of the railway. By 1910, Coatzacoalcos and Minatitlán were thriving, eclipsing Acayucan and Catemaco as commercial centers of the region (Salamini 1971: 5; Nolasco 1980: 133–5). Fuelled by the economic boom, the regional population grew from seven inhabitants per square kilometer in 1878 to 25 in 1910.

Colonization policies took a new direction as well with the *Ley de baldíos* of 1883, legislation that declared all lands without formal title and specific boundaries properties of the state. The legislation gave land companies the right to survey and appropriate "abandoned" lands for resale, on the condition that they promote colonization. This was followed by the *Ley sobre la subdivisión de la propiedad territorial*, passed in 1889 by the state governor Juan de la Luz Enríquez with a view to dividing collective lands into private property. Porfirio Díaz strengthened the hand of surveying companies in 1894 by lifting all limits on the amount of land they could own and weakening the obligation of companies to colonize the land (Tannenbaum 1968: 12–13).

The economic prosperity and future prospects of southern Veracruz led to a flurry of land speculation. Romero Rubio, the father-in-law of Porfirio Díaz, acquired some 149,404 hectares of land in the districts of Acayucan and Minatitlán, including most of the communal lands of Soteapan and Mecayapan. These lands were later sold to Lord Cowdray, becoming part of a land empire totalling 177,110 hectares held by various companies such as the Veracruz Land and Cattle Company, Mexican Real Estate Company, and El Aguila, the petroleum company. Other foreign beneficiaries of the land policies of the Porfiriato were William Randolph Hearst (106,000 ha.) and Carlos David de Ghest (56,690 ha.). The Sanbourn family of Mexico City also owned large haciendas in the area. Asaola Garrido (1982: 104–16) estimates that half the District of Acayucan, 295,551 hectares of a total surface area of 594,000, was in the hands of four families living in the area and four foreign companies. Approximately 532,050 hectares or almost half of the District of Minatitlán was owned by eight foreign companies and six Mexican families. A large portion of the remaining lands were controlled by medium-sized haciendas with between 1,000 and 10,000 hectares dedicated to cattle ranching and plantation agriculture. These *latifundistas* controlled the best quality lands as well as regional commerce and transportation.

The concentration of land under the control of large and medium-sized haciendas resulted in extreme poverty in the rural areas. Some 94% of the population of the state of Veracruz had no land of their own and worked for very low wages as woodcutters or as day laborers on plantations. Many lived on haciendas as indentured *peones* tied to the hacienda through a system of debt-peonage: they had access to a small plot of land for cultivating corn in exchange for free labor. Indians living in more isolated areas claimed by haciendas were forced to pay exorbitant rents to farm the land or face deportation to distant areas. Those who could not cancel their debts with money paid with agricultural produce or labor on the hacienda (Martínez Hernández 1982). Peasants displaced from their land migrated in massive numbers to urban centers and villages along the railway where they worked for low wages in construction and services. The oil refinery at Minatitlán and the docks of Coatzacoalcos were surrounded by shantytowns of their makeshift homes.

Historians should be careful, however, not to exaggerate the impact of 19th-century land policies and the Porfiriato regime on native communities in Mexico. Urias Hermosillo (1987: 29) and Florescano Mayet (1984: 16) note that the application of the reform laws against communal land during the early and mid-19th century was weak in many parts of Veracruz because of the political instability of the period. Ducey (1992) warns against the legal emphasis in histories of peasant social movements in 19th-century Mexico and the assumption that the frequent rebellions of the era were an effect of land dispossession facilitated by the liberal land reforms (e.g., Tutino 1986: 274–6; 1988: 118–23). He argues that the liberal land laws ordering the privatization and division of community land into individual plots were greatly modified in practice. Between 1821 and 1880 many Indian communities in northern Veracruz (and possibly elsewhere) actually increased their land base during the chaos of liberal rule by modifying the implementation of the land tenure legislation in their favor (Schryer 1990: 107). Communities purchased lands from credit-poor *hacendados*, won title to land in regional legal battles and occupied land forcefully. Communities that participated in the defense of the *República Restaurada* against foreign invasions and competing national factions received concessions in the courts and from the regional *jefe político* (Ducey 1992). In a context of economic stagnation and weak governments, *hacendados* calculated the potential profit from disputed land considering legal costs of land settlement procedures and the related problems of policing land and collecting rent. Ducey concludes that the many 19th-century rebellions in the area were not the result of recent land appropriations by *hacendados*, as is commonly thought, but rather the response of Indian communities to an historical opportunity favoring an increase in their own land base.

While legal title to vast areas of southern Veracruz passed into the hands of land speculators and developers, in many cases the aboriginal population was not expelled from the land or subject to direct economic exploitation. Thus, it was not until Soteapan and Mecayapan began to divide their communal lands into individual properties in the 1890s that they realized the full extent of their loss to Romero Rubio, one of the principal land speculators of the region. Legally, communal lands (*las Repúblicas*) were administered by municipalities dominated by mestizos; this rule, however, did not apply in Indian communities such as Pajapan. Moreover, few plantations were established in the region and both forestry and cattle ranching activities were confined mainly to the most accessible areas near major rivers and urban centers. Extensive natural pastures in the Coatzacoalcos area favored the cattle industry but production was limited by very low population densities and poor transportation to central Mexico. Despite an abundance of good agricultural land, a shortage of labor restricted the development of plantation agriculture. Cotton production, an important activity in southern Veracruz prior to the 1820s, had already shifted to La Laguna and the United States where a large labor force provided comparative advantages (Urias Hermosillo 1987: 28; Asaola Garrido 1982: 40). Oil production was concentrated in the cities of Minatitlán and Coatzacoalcos. As a result of these weaknesses in the regional economy, land legally held by speculators was often not utilized by them but rather remained under the *de facto* control of the aboriginal population. Pajapan is a case in point: like many other Nahua-speaking villages of Veracruz and other Mexican states (Schryer 1990: 99), the peasants of Pajapan continued to cultivate the land and were not greatly affected by land rents. Some degree of autonomy was also retained in the legal-political sphere through the lot system, to which we now turn.

The lot system

The village lands of Pajapan survived reforms of both the liberal era and the Porfirio regime by converting the land into a co-ownership system (*condueñazgo*) or disguised collective property with legally recognized title. The *títulos primordiales* issued to the people of San Francisco Minzapan in 1765 were used and modified in the 1880s to protect native lands against the neighboring municipality of Mecayapan and legislation favoring non-native land speculators. Documents currently held by the Communal Land Commission of Pajapan describe how communal lands (15,932 ha.) were divided in 1884 into five lots in accordance with laws requiring the division of communal properties (see Map 3). The divisions were carried out with the assistance of a government engineer and made official by the local syndic (Francisco Gabriel) in 1888. Lots 1, 2, 3 and 4 comprised 3,070 hectares each while lot 5 had 3,629 hectares. These five lots were delimited by trails linking Pajapan to the Farellón (north), Minzapan (south), San Juan Volador (east) and Tatahuicapan (west). Local informants indicate that four of the five lots were administered by the village of Pajapan while the fifth was the responsibility of the neighboring village of San Juan Volador.

The title to each of these lots appears under the name of a lot administrator (*jefe de lote*) representing the interests of a larger group consisting of 55 to 60 *comuneros*. The titles to lots 1, 2 and 4 were assigned to Anastasio Santiago, Basilio Martín and Pascual Martín, who represented 57, 59 and 57 right-holders (*derechosos*), respectively. The documents for lots 4 and 5 have been lost. The inclusion of right-holding groups in the title document suggests that while the reform laws called for the division of communal lands into individual properties, concessions were made to the collective rights of the aboriginal population by permitting the creation of private associations wherein the community members were granted *acciones*. Similar arrangements were made in the villages of Oluta, Texistepec, Soconusco, Cosoleacaque, Ixhuatlán, Moloacán, Jáltipan and Zaragoza (Baez-Jorge 1973: 75).

The willingness of government authorities to recognize forms of co-ownership of village lands reflects practical and political limitations on the state's ability to impose a private property land tenure regime. Ducey (1992) notes that in many municipalities controlled by mestizos the local authorities could not collect taxes on lands formerly belonging to native *pueblos* because they did not know who was actually farming the land. By allowing Indian communities to administer their lands as a *condueñazgo*, the state facilitated the collection of land taxes via local representatives of the farming population.

The division and titling of Pajapan's village lands in 1884 resulted in the creation of a new land administration system in the community, a regime based on a combination of private property and native polity. The lot administrator, a position held for life by a senior member of the community, was responsible for maintaining legal collective title and protecting the land from market speculation. In addition to representing the village as the principal landowner, the lot administrator was respons-ible for organizing a *faena* or collective work party to clear the lot line bordering on neighboring landholders (Tatahuicapan and the hacienda Temoloapa). Once a year, the lot administrator, municipal president,

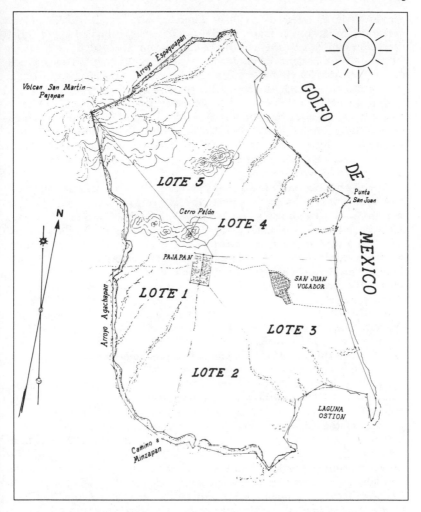

Map 3 Communal lands of Pajapan, showing five lots created in 1884
Source: Archives of the Comisariado Comunal

alderman and a drummer led a team of *comuneros* as they cleared the outer boundary of their particular lot, thereby defining the limits of the village lands.

Some Pajapeños recall that the *jefes de lote* were elected by male household heads. Others suggest that the candidates were approved or even designated by the municipal president (García de León 1976). According to Nahmad (nd: 20, 22), *mayordomos* and members of *cofradías* or *hermandades*, formed around community saints and dating back to the 18th century, occupied or selected candidates for administrative positions (mayor, syndic, parish council, lot administrators, deputies).[8] The close relationship between civil and religious offices was embodied in the ritual staff of authority, a *bastón* held by the village council and used by religious officers during Easter celebrations up until the 1960s.[9] The village council was responsible for church *faenas*, such as the one held in the mid-1970s to rebuild the church destroyed by an earthquake in 1973. Pajapan's civil-religious hierarchy was also governed by relations of Nahua kinship; two out of the three lots for which we have information were assigned to the Martín family (Basilio and Pascual). Eduardo Martín was Pajapan's municipal president in 1882, assisted by alderman Lorenzo Martín and syndic Prisciliano Martín. Another member of the Martín family served as secretary in Minzapan.

Pajapan's lands included a *fondo legal* or village area for houses and *tierras de trabajo*, the lands worked by individual farmers.[10] Four lots corresponded to a particular *manzana* or neighborhood within the village; lot 1 belonging to *manzana* 1, lot 2 to *manzana* 2, etc. Each *manzana* also had a leader (*jefe de manzana*, *piceros*) who was selected for a term by the municipal president. These individuals collected taxes from all independent household heads (above the age of 14), including a land tax paid collectively in the name of the *jefe de lote* to the government (*Hacienda Federal*) in Chinameca and a musicians' fund for the village *fiesta*. Each household head was charged two and a half pesos per year for access to communal land. Taxes paid to the state were believed by locals to be land rent paid to the Spanish Crown (this view was held till the 1940s; Nahmad nd: 22–3). The *jefe de manzana* was also responsible for maintaining the boundaries of household lots (*solares*) and for organizing *faenas* to open roads, bridges and paths within the neighborhood and collective works for the community as a whole.[11] Individuals working land in one lot paid taxes for the corresponding lot and assisted in the clearing of the lot border. Villagers had rights to land in one lot only, although they could change lots at will and live in any of the four *manzanas* provided that they fulfilled their tax and work obligations for the lot where they worked. Thus, the rigid connection between residence and land rights of the prehispanic *calpolli* did not apply in 19th-century Pajapan. This was probably a function of the small population and lack of any real competition within the village for access to land.

According to Chance and Taylor (1985), *cofradías* created in the colonial era with the purpose of collecting tribute and administering community wealth for religious purposes were replaced in the liberal private-property era by *mayordomías* based on the individualization and alternation of religious and civil posts. Religious brotherhoods gave way to individual household heads forming community assemblies, occupying civil-religious *cargos* and using their personal wealth to sponsor village feasts. These developments occurred in Pajapan not until the second half of this century when lot administrators lost control over communal property and when land and wealth in cattle began to concentrate in the hands of the few.

To conclude, the lot system brought together two sets of institutions:

native principles of kin-based patrimony and Mexican agrarian law, territorial government and taxation system. Local authorities acted as brokers between Nahua Indians and agents of the state. The native principles of organization involved the collective ownership and flexible administration of communal lands, the individual use of small plots available in relative abundance, and a civil-religious government controlled by old men (in keeping with the prehispanic age system; see Greenberg 1981: 61–6). This system emerged during the Porfiriato and survived the events of the Mexican Revolution.

Pajapan and the Mexican Revolution

The Mexican Revolution (1910–21) joined the economic discontent of a rising class of professionals and progressive capitalists with the misery of the rural and urban poor. A movement led by Francisco Madero forced Porfirio Díaz to flee the country, initiating a long period of social upheaval. Southern Veracruz was the scene of an important harbinger of the national uprising. In 1906, Indian peasants from Soteapan, led by a few mestizo workers from urban centers, launched attacks on Acayucan. The leaders were members of the Mexican Liberal Party formed by the anarchist Ricardo Flores Magón committed to the armed overthrow of the dictatorship of Porfirio Díaz. The revolt mobilized many peasants but failed militarily because of a lack of arms. The rebels were pursued into the Sierra de Santa Marta and many were captured or killed. Soteapan was burned to the ground. Politically, the uprising none the less played an important role in that it allied peasants, workers and the middle class against the Porfirio regime and signalled to diverse groups around the country that armed struggle had begun.[12]

Pajapan was to be the point of departure for an attack on Coatza- coalcos that was called off when it was learned that the storming of Acayucan had failed. The rebels who entered Pajapan with banners and calls of "victory for the rebels and death for Porfirio Díaz" fled into the hills to avoid being captured by federal troops (Asaola Garrido 1982: 157–8). Both Martínez Hernández (1982) and Asaola Garrido (1982: 288) note that a number of Pajapeños were involved in the uprisings of the period but there is little other recorded evidence of their role in the Mexican Revolution or in regional political struggles of the period.[13]

Compared to Soteapan, Pajapan was only marginally involved in the uprising of 1906. The two communities were in different situations vis- à-vis broader domains. Pajapan, armed with titles purchased in the mid- 1700s, had been able to obtain a condueñazgo arrangement from the Porfirio administration, thereby avoiding being expropriated by Romero Rubio and other land speculators of the early 1900s. San Miguel Temoloa- pan was the only hacienda located within the municipal boundaries of Pajapan (Melgarejo Vivanco 1980: 187). By contrast, the Zoque-Popolucas of Soteapan had still not gained clear titles or subdivided their lands into lots by the time the land speculation boom began. This left the Zoque- Popolucas open to declarations that their lands were baldío (uncultivated) and available for expropriation. As a result, Soteapan lost most of its territory to Romero Rubio.

Elders of Pajapan remember the Mexican Revolution as a time of great hardship.[14] The village was raided on a number of occasions by roaming bands of revolutionaries and counterrevolutionaries who forcibly recruited young men into their ranks, raped native women, stole animals to feed themselves and left behind them depleted stores of grain. Some of these rebels, armed with muzzle-loading rifles, bows and arrows, may have been *serranos* from Soteapan. Villagers lived on wild roots and fruits. According to Nahmad (nd: 27), Pajapan was virtually abandoned during these years. Florentino Gracio who served as *alcalde* during this period was forced to flee when the rebels arrived (Asaola Garrido 1982). The village was also severely affected by a smallpox epidemic in 1916 and was pacified by the constitutional army and resettled in the early 1920s.

Although a source of hardships at the local level, the civil war had no immediate impact on local land and government institutions. Pajapan's semi-autonomous position *vis-à-vis* outside forces was maintained throughout this period of great unrest. One of Stuart's informants recalls his parents' description of Pajapan as a prosperous community "with many cattle and pigs" (mostly for local consumption) and with no *patrones* (bosses). Spanish was rarely spoken, and the natives produced most of what they needed to subsist. They travelled a day's journey along the beach to sell small quantities of produce in Puerto México (Coatzacoalcos), in exchange for the money needed to buy machetes and other tools (Stuart 1978: 24).

While the Mexican Revolution had little impact on Pajapan, it relegated aboriginal land titles to a state of juridical limbo. Paradoxically, the main effect of a revolution aimed at redressing the inequities of the Porfiriato dictatorship was to undermine the foundations of Pajapan's delicate land tenure system based on the "communal" ownership and management of "private" lots. The agrarian law of 1915 and the Ejido law of 1920 favored the dismantling of large, privately-owned estates, yet there was no guarantee that the new agrarian code and federal land agencies would quickly recognize local land titles. With the Revolution, Pajapan's titles lost their validity; legally, the Gulf Nahuas were back to square one. What is more, the Mexican Revolution meant that the political institutions and powers emerging after the war could infringe on the authority vested in senior members of the community who controlled the lot system. Thus began a new struggle for land and government in Pajapan.

PRI institutions, agrarian law and the cattle industry

Basic features of human geography in Pajapan are the outcome of colonial land settlements combined with migratory movements, new municipal divisions and the lot administration created in the 19th century. The current Gulf Nahua land tenure regime, however, has also been shaped by the political and economic transformations wrought by the Mexican

Revolution and the growth of agribusiness and the oil industry in the state of Veracruz. The material that follows highlights the breadth of changes observed at the national and state levels following the Mexican Revolution. It also shows how a revolution in the Mexican land tenure system has favored the expansion of the cattle industry in southern Veracruz. In the next two chapters, we discuss the impact of these broader forces on Pajapan society and the local land government process. The analysis is set against the background of general issues regarding the role of the state and the relationship between economy and polity in modern history.

PRI institutions

Following the Mexican Revolution, the creation of new federal, state and municipal institutions and electoral bodies governed by a strong presidential office and a highly centralized party (the Institutional Revolutionary Party) transformed Gulf Nahua municipal politics and reduced Pajapan's already limited autonomy vis-à-vis the outside world. The new order entailed the rise of a powerful and highly bureaucratized federal land agency responsible for the settlement of land claims and the implementation of land reform (DAAC/SRA). Civil associations representing the class interests of ranchers and peasants (peasant leagues, rancher associations) were formed, regulated and co-opted, a process that put an end to a brief post-revolutionary period of independent political and paramilitary activism.

The Constitution of 1917 provided for local representative governments organized as "free municipalities", a body modelled after the Spanish ayuntamiento but with fewer powers. Municipal governments are currently responsible for the collection of taxes, for conserving natural resources, and for the administration of justice and public security, elementary schooling and public health work, the civil registry, roads and public utilities. The president and aldermen of the municipal council are elected for two to three years and may not be re-elected at the end of their term. Individuals must be literate in order to be eligible for office. The council appoints a syndic, a secretary, a treasurer, representatives of smaller villages, police officers and a justice of the peace (usually a man of means without legal training, someone to handle minor civil and criminal cases). The secretary is the chief administrative officer: he signs all correspondence, maintains archives and civil records, hears complaints and gives advice about state law. The syndic is responsible for protecting communal resources, investigates violations of state law, and has authority to use local police.

Municipal government has become an appendage of a highly centralized corporative polity dominated by the President of Mexico and the federal bureaucracy. Although a nominally democratic country, Mexico was and still is a republic largely ruled from Mexico City and the Office of the President; peasant demands for land are frequently forwarded directly to the President of Mexico. Moreover, most taxes collected go to the federal bureaucracy; state governments receive little and the municipalities even less. Lower government divisions are dependent upon federal subsidies and have few resources of their own.

The PRI government has considerable control over the electoral process at all levels and frauds are commonly reported. Laws passed from 1946 to 1977 made it very difficult for new political parties, especially the larger ones, to receive official registration from the Federal Electoral Commission headed by the Minister of the Interior. In reality, Mexico's political regime is a modified one-party system legitimized by the presence of weak opposition parties, of which more later. The most influential members of the party nominate candidates that are simply rubber-stamped with their approval by the voters. The party apparatus is largely controlled by a small oligarchy of party officials forming the National Executive Committee (Story 1986: 80). State and municipal assemblies of the PRI also elect their own Executive Committees; the distinction between local government and the official party organization is often blurred. PRI officials make abundant use of revolutionary rhetoric and the party acts as an indispensable source of political legitimacy within the country as well as abroad.

The interaction of sectors and interest groups within the PRI and the government is a form of political participation more significant than the actual elections. Personal ambitions and a host of political demands, grievances and policy choices are addressed within the party apparatus. Although controlled by the President and the national Executive Committee, the PRI functions as a corporative machine supporting those exercising power at all levels of Mexican society. The party has a built-in membership in that various interest groups are incorporated into the party through three sectors: the agrarian sector, labor (includes all PRI-affiliated unions), and the popular sector (professionals, intellectuals, civil servants, bank employees, small entrepreneurs, artisans, co-operative members, neighborhood associations, youth and women's groups). The agrarian sector includes the National Peasant Confederation (CNC), an umbrella group for peasant organizations created by Cárdenas in 1938 and affiliated to the party. All *ejidatarios* are members of the CNC, and hence the PRI, and many peasants depend on the CNC for access to state-subsidized resources such as seeds, fertilizers, credit and so on. Loyalty to the party is rewarded by the government through patronage (Story 1986: 83). Given this system of corporative co-optation, conflicts of power and interest are never fully resolved; rather they are managed, finessed, postponed, denied, assuaged, overborne (Needler 1982: 71).

Agrarian law

One crucial legacy of the Mexican Revolution and the PRI politics that followed is the federal agrarian code. The great innovation of the land tenure system outlined in the Mexican Constitution of 1917 and developed in subsequent land reform legislation is its flexibility. Article 27 of the Constitution states that ownership of land and waters within the national territory is vested originally in the Nation. As noted by Tannenbaum (1950: 102f.), it provides the state with extensive rights over the form, content and amount of property that may be transferred to private persons or corporations, rights which give the government "a legal instrumentality for molding private real property in any manner it considers desirable". Property "can be made to mean many sorts of different things, and may be defined differently for different purposes."

The juridical principle upon which this article is based can be traced to the Spanish colonial dominion. The American possessions of the Spanish kings were held as personal property that could be granted to individuals and corporations as a *merced*, a gift from the king. The *estancias* and the *encomiendas* were also temporary trusts subject to reversion at the will of the Spanish Crown, only later converted into permanent private property. Similarly, the modern Mexican state, by virtue of its original ownership of all national territory, may grant the right of usufruct to individuals and corporations. The state reserves sub-surface rights, limits property rights to the use of the land (without the right to sell, rent or mortgage) and expropriates property "for the public good". Thus, "ownership of property has become conditional, subject to use and to the requirements of public interests, and variable in form and content" (Tannenbaum 1950: 122). This is a radical departure from the legal property traditions established in modern Europe, North America and during the liberal reforms of 19th-century Mexico.

The protean rights of property are clearly illustrated by the varied forms of property in land that have developed and changed over the years since the Revolution of 1910. The *ejido* and the *comunidad agraria* have been promoted at different times and in different ways by the Mexican state. Collective forms of property represent some 50% of the national territory and 60% of the farmers. National statistics indicate, however, that 74% of these collective lands consist of natural pasture or forest unsuitable for crop cultivation. Although not individually owned, most of the remaining lands have been broken up into parcels assigned to individual right-holders. The vast majority of peasants living on collective lands have parcels of less than 2.5 hectares and either fail to produce enough foodstuffs to meet their subsistence needs (65%) or produce barely enough (25%) (Oswald Spring 1992: 46).

The *ejido* is by far the most important form of collective land tenure.[15] It is both a specific territory and an association of independent producers with rights to use lands owned permanently by its members. When the *ejido* is parcelled, *ejidatarios* have exclusive rights to use of specific parcels of land and, where they exist, to common untilled lands (usually forests). About 92% of the 28,958 collective landholdings of Mexico (totalling 95,108,066 ha.) are *ejidos*, virtually all of which have been divided into individual parcels.[16]

By contrast, the *comunidad agraria* is a regimen of communal land title without any specified method of distribution or use. This system typically applies to isolated indigenous communities that were not displaced from their land prior to the Mexican Revolution, that did not adopt the *ejido* system and that applied to state agrarian authorities for the titling of their *tierras comunales*. Unlike the *ejidatarios, comuneros* may use untilled lands in any part of the collective territory in accordance with local custom. Also, while an *ejido* is established by a land grant, the prior land rights of an agrarian community are merely recognized by the state. The Mexican state has tended to favor the granting of *ejidos* as they are subject to greater administrative control than the 2,000 *comunidades agrarias* currently recognized by the federal state (Binford 1985: fn. 28; Oswald Spring 1992: 46).

All collective landholdings are regulated by legal procedures and constitutional guarantees defining land rights and administrative structures. At the time of the petition for *ejido* lands or for the titling of communal lands, a census of members of the group is conducted by state authorities, identifying the individuals who will receive agrarian rights. When established by presidential decree, agrarian rights are granted to the original group of solicitors identified in the census or their legal descendents, with one right to an unspecified unit of land being assigned to each *ejidatario* or *comunero*. Membership in the collective is restricted to the head of household, typically the male member of a family. Women who are heads of household are eligible and in cases where they marry men who are also members of the collective, both can retain their agrarian right. Otherwise, only one agrarian right can be held by each nuclear family. Membership in the collective can be passed from one family member to another, the main legal criterion being residence in the community, a commitment personally to work the land and possession of less than 20 hectares of private property. In principle, members can lose their rights to land if they or their family do not personally work the land for two consecutive years or more. As communities and *ejidos* grow and new households are established, distinctions develop between individuals with agrarian rights and those without.

The administrative structures of the *ejido* and the agrarian community are basically the same. The general assembly makes democratic decisions concerning the form of exploitation of land, collective works and other major plans. It elects the *comisariado,* an administrative council comprised of a president, a secretary and a treasurer, each with a replacement in case they cannot fulfill their duties. These *comisariados* represent the collective before outside authorities, oversee the division of land into parcels and administer communal lands and other collective resources such as waters, forests and natural pastures. They enforce decisions taken by the general assembly and may resolve conflicts between members. Their powers are tempered by a third administrative body within the collective, the *consejo de vigilancia*. This council of three members and their replacements monitors the *comisariado,* audits the accounts and denounces the failings of the *comisariado* to state agrarian authorities if need be.

The rate at which petitions for *ejido* land grants and recognition of agrarian communities pass through the various stages in the legal process varies considerably. In principle, the original petition and the final

Presidential Resolution should take a few years or less. More typically, petitions linger for 20 years or more, delayed by the legal actions of property owners, the inefficiencies of the bureaucracy and the political agenda of the President of the Republic, the final arbiter in agrarian reform. These long delays and complex bureaucratic procedures impose severe limits on the effective redistribution of land. Also the norms establishing the size of individual parcels held by *ejidatarios* are the exception rather than the rule. By law, the minimum land grant is 10 hectares for irrigated lands and the maximum is 20 hectares for non-irrigated lands. In arid and mountain regions larger parcels may be granted. Nevertheless, natural increases in the farming population and the arrival of other peasants between the time of the original petition and the final Presidential Resolution often require the distribution of parcels much smaller than the legal norm. The average *ejido* parcel in Mexico is less than 3 hectares.

The counterreform

Agribusiness in southern Veracruz has never been seriously hampered by the collective landholding regimes promoted after the Mexican Revolution. The industry actually received support from the government through legislation favorable to medium and large-scale ranches. New laws allowed ranchers to delay and thwart the implementation of agrarian reform policies. Initially, article 10 of the Constitution of 1917 was used to seek court injunctions protecting land from presidential land grants to *ejidos* issued under the Agrarian Code. While technically these injunctions delayed expropriations for up to one year, the Secretariat of Agrarian Reform was flooded by so many that even longer delays were common. In 1931 the law was changed as the system could no longer handle the numerous requests. Six years later it was replaced by legal provisions limiting the petitions of landless peasants. President Cárdenas introduced the *certificados de inafectabilidad* protecting ranchers from expropriation on the grounds that Mexico was faced with underproduction problems in the cattle sector and that the conversion of private ranches into *ejidos* would deepen the crisis. Between 500 and 800 "immunity certificates" with a duration of 25 years and totalling between 6 and 9 million hectares were issued to ranchers. The certificates legally perpetuated some *latifundios,* in direct violation of the Agrarian Code (Rutsch 1984: 35).

Cárdenas also introduced counterreform legislation giving exclusive state recognition to three levels of ranchers' organizations: the National Rancher Confederation, Regional Rancher Unions and Local Rancher Associations. Ranchers could not organize outside these associations. While the division and co-optation of the peasant movement weakened the voice of peasants at the regional and national levels, the unification of rancher associations created a monopoly that was easily dominated by medium and large ranchers opposed to the creation of ranching *ejidos* and the proliferation of small-scale ranches. The associations became an instrument of the *neolatifundios* in the fight against land reform and an exclusive channel for credit and other economic subsidies provided by the state for the the cattle industry. Rutsch (1984: 33–34) notes that between the certificates of immunity and the law of ranching associations "the principles of the revolution took a step back during the regime of General Cárdenas, contrary to the overall image of this period that has been popularized". While Cárdenas redistributed more land to peasants than any other Mexican President (mainly in central Mexico), he countered these reforms by favoring the creation of private property and the development of large-scale cattle ranching in northern Mexico and along the Gulf coast.

Anti-agrarian legislation continued under Cárdenas' successor, President Avila Camacho, and reached its peak when Miguel Alemán, the ex-governor of Veracruz, became the President of Mexico. Michaels and Bernstein (1973: 705) note that Alemán embarked "on an openly capitalist development program emphasizing economic growth and capital accumulation with virtually no challenge or protest". Amendments to the Constitution were introduced in 1947 allowing landowners to protect themselves from expropriation orders and from petitions by peasants seeking to establish *ejidos*. The law reasserted the right of landowners to seek a federal court injunction against expropriation pending a legal investigation and resolution of the case, a process that on average took 15 years to complete. By 1969 there were more than 1.5 million hectares of land frozen by these *amparo* injunctions. Based on articles 103 and 107 of the Mexican Constitution, this legal measure has no equivalent in Anglo-Saxon jurisprudence (Revel-Mouroz 1980: 304; Tucker 1957: 118; Levy and Székely 1987: 59).

The principle of immunity established by Cárdenas was also strengthened by Alemán. The 1947 amendments to the Constitution provided for the creation of "small ranching properties"; their legal limit was established as the amount of land required to support a herd of 500 head of cattle in any given environment. The extensive system of animal grazing characteristic of Mexico at the time required the creation of very large "small ranching properties". The Secretariat of Agriculture determined that a small property dedicated exclusively to cattle-raising could be up to 300 hectares if it were located on good quality land and up to 50,000 hectares on arid land. This provision increased dramatically the amount of land one person could legally own. In concert with the court injunction, it was used to protect land from reform and convert *latifundios* into private properties with permanent immunity (Rutsch 1984: 43–6; Sanderson 1986: 129–30; Revel-Mouroz 1980: 188, 309; Siemens 1964).

The amendments to the Constitution introduced by Alemán complemented the "Law of Colonization" also promulgated during his term. In the years following the Revolution, the large *latifundios* owned by the railway companies, oil industry and foreign capital were expropriated and redistributed. A program of colonization of these vast, "unoccupied' areas of *tierra caliente* was launched by Presidents Avila Camacho and Miguel Alemán under the banner "March to the Sea". National land was made available at very low cost to individuals and collectives for the purpose of colonization. While colonization was often hailed as a land policy for the poor, in many cases it was the rich who benefited, as in the 1920s under Calles (Falcón Vega 1977). The lands of Lord Cowdray were expropriated by PEMEX, the newly created national oil company, and remained frozen as national lands for many years. Revel-Mouroz notes that

> the new law opened the possibility of creating 'small properties' (of 300 hectares!) on national lands, while the *ejidatarios* of the 'New Centers of Ejido Population' only had rights to parcels of 20 hectares ... The law of colonization was used to withhold the *latifundios* from Agrarian Reform so that instead of being redistributed in *ejidos* they could be colonized as small properties. (Revel-Mouroz 1980: 164)

Many haciendas in southern Veracruz were divided into "small ranching properties", each in the name of a different family member or *prestanombre* (name "loaned" to ranchers for legal documents). Ranches of 300 hectares or more were grouped together by a single administrator into haciendas of several thousand hectares, with complete protection from the reform laws. Government officials and merchants living in the cities also got title to land through illegal manipulation of the law of colonization (Revel-Mouroz 1980: 128, 132, 164f., 187f.).

Peasants made some gains from land reform but in many cases could not fully benefit from their new-found position as landowners. Land reform legislation and the law of colonization resulted in a significant increase in the number of properties of less than five hectares. Many of these *minifundios*, however, were established on land unsuitable for intensive cultivation or were too small to support viable agricultural enterprises. Thus they were often sold to ranchers and converted to pasture. Land received by peasants was cleared of forest vegetation, cultivated for a few years and then converted into pasture for use by ranchers. *Colonos* who received lands on forested hill tops in the Acayucan area found that after a few years the land could not support agriculture (Siemens 1964). In the lower Papaloapan, forested land declined by some 138,000 hectares between 1950 and 1960 (Revel-Mouroz 1980). Rutsch's (1984: 101) data indicate that more than 40% of the forested areas in the humid zone along the Gulf of Mexico were felled between 1950 and 1970. Most of this land was eventually diverted to pasture production, often by peasants later displaced by ranchers.

A prosperous cattle industry

Although inspired by the pro-peasant ideals of the Revolution, Mexico's collective landholding legislation has never posed a sustained threat to the growth of agribusiness and the concentration of arable land in the hands of the few. Unlike other sectors of the national economy, cattle ranching activities continued to prosper after the Revolution. The Mexican economy was severely weakened during the years of revolutionary unrest and recovered only slowly during the 1920s and 1930s. Veracruz was particularly hard hit when the price of sugar dropped sharply during the 1920s and when international markets for tropical forest and agricultural products softened in response to the development of synthetic substitutes. Foreign investment declined dramatically and even the oil industry, an island of relative stability during the Revolution, faltered from 1922 to 1937 as a result of labor unrest and the world economic crisis. Only the cattle ranchers, with their very low labor costs, extensive landholdings and gradually expanding urban markets, managed to hold their own economically (Revel-Mouroz 1980: 126, 131, 189; Nolasco 1980: 136).

The Second World War initiated a long period of national industrialization known as the "Mexican miracle". Mexico's economic profile as a producer of primary materials for the international market was gradually altered by the development of a strong agro-export industry and new manufacturing industries oriented toward national demand. In 1940, Veracruz occupied an important position within the national economy, mostly as a producer of raw materials for export (sugar, coffee, sulphur, petroleum) and internal markets (petroleum, cattle). The capital-intensive petroleum industry was the largest sector in the state economy (23% of total production), providing some 90% of Mexico's oil production. Cattle production in Veracruz went through a period of rapid growth (15% of total state economic production, 16% of national cattle production; Bravo Garzón 1972: 17–18).

The national economic boom continued throughout the 1950s and · 1960s, buoyed by state-led industrialization policies and state investment in electric power, petroleum, transportation and communications. The growth rate exceeded 7% during the 1950s, one of the highest in the world (Michaels and Bernstein 1973: 706). State investments and import substitution policies were initially based on national financing of public debt. From the late 1950s onwards, however, public finances drew increasingly on external sources (Gollas and García Rocha 1973: 411). National foreign debt has grown steadily ever since. Despite a strong bias in public investment toward industrial activity, the agro-export sector expanded rapidly from 1940 to 1965 (5% annually), mainly in the north of Mexico where extensive irrigation projects were initiated. The country reached self-sufficiency in grain production.

One major effect of the so-called Mexican miracle was to increase the income gap between the wealthy and the poor. Population explosion, rural depopulation and agricultural underdevelopment resulted in high levels of unemployment and poverty at both regional and national levels. Economic growth also meant increasing dependence on US markets, tourism and remittances from Mexican *braceros* (Teichman 1989). The state of Veracruz continued to supply raw materials for export and national markets. Its economy depended on the petroleum industry of southern Veracruz which was becoming increasingly urbanized (Saldana and Juárez Sánchez 1972: 322). The state nevertheless lagged behind in other sectors of industrial growth and in national urbanization trends: 61% of its population lived in rural areas in 1961 compared to 50% for the country as a whole. The relative self-sufficiency of the rural population and the low labor demand in the state's major industries (petroleum, cattle) produced only slow growth in consumer demand and commerce in general.

The cattle industry suffered a sharp decline in the 1950s both regionally and nationally. The shift was caused by the spread of animal diseases and the closure of US markets for Mexican beef. The industry eventually recovered in the 1960s, once again occupying second place in the economy of Veracruz (after petroleum). The growth of cattle ranching activities was facilitated by improvements in market conditions and techniques of production. More specifically, ranchers increased the proportion of zebu, a cattle species better suited to the tropics than the traditional criollo. New varieties of pasture facilitating increases in stocking rates were also introduced. Meanwhile the demand for beef and milk in central Mexico increased rapidly and new roads were constructed to connect Coatzacoalcos, Minatitlán and Acayucan with them. A road to Soteapan completed in 1964 opened the uplands of the Sierra de Santa Marta to the expansion of the cattle industry. Ranchers responded to these technical and commercial opportunities by expanding herds and increasing the amount of land under production. From 1930 to 1960, the number of cattle in the state of Veracruz increased by 62% and the amount of pasture by 89% (Revel-Mouroz 1980: 345).

The cattle industry of southern Veracruz expanded both in total herd and total area under pasture. The region as a whole nevertheless remained a relatively undeveloped sector of the national industry, supplying beef on the hoof for industrial processing in Mexico City. Within the region, production was divided along dual lines. On the one hand, small and medium-scale Indian and mestizo producers located on marginal lands with limited access to pasture (especially during the dry season) raised immature calves with few inputs and low levels of productivity. These calf producers absorbed the greatest risks associated with the cattle industry. On the other hand, large-scale ranchers or regional merchants financed local buyers who purchased calves. The buyers arranged transportation to lowland ranches where improved pastures provided stable year-round grazing, hence greater control over the health and development of the animals. This situation favored a few large ranchers who controlled better lands, trucking companies and sufficient capital to buy calves and resell full-grown steers directly to slaughterhouses in Mexico City, Puebla and Veracruz.

To sum up, the expansion of markets and improvements in transportation and ranching technology facilitated the expansion of the cattle industry in southern Veracruz. The commercialization of cattle was monopolized by a handful of the largest ranchers who owned slaughterhouses and controlled transportation networks. Wealth in cattle and land, usually the best, was accumulated with the support of state legislation and with the use of corruption and violence. Large ranches escaped the agrarian reform through legislation such as the *amparo* and *certificado de inafectabilidad* and through illegal means ranging from collusion with state officials to the use of *prestanombres*. In the end, the land reforms introduced during the period did little to stop the formation of large properties and the proletarianization of a peasantry forced to sell, rent or give up their land to local and regional *caciques* controlling both the regional PRI apparatuses and the cattle industry.

In the next chapter, we discuss the rise of PRI rancher *caciquismo* in Pajapan, a new ruling order that brought major transformations in all areas of Gulf Nahua society. To this day, however, the political economy of Pajapan has also retained legacies of older regimes: i.e., land titles dating back to the 16th century, municipal divisions of the pre-revolutionary era, kin-based forms of patrimonial organization, and the lot administration instituted during the Porfiriato.

Notes

1. See McBride (1923: 103–38); Tannenbaum (1968); F. Chevalier (1963); Lockhart (1992).
2. Castilian *villas* held various kinds of public lands. The *ejidos* were relatively small areas of collective lands located just outside the city gates used as public threshing floors, pounds for stray cattle, public rubbish heaps and the village slaughter pen. *Propios* were village lands rented to individuals from year to year. *Montes* were woodlands open to the regulated use of the community. *Pasto comunes* were lands possessed for the common pasturage of flocks and herds (McBride 1923: 106–7; see also Florescano Mayet 1984).
3. Primordial Titles of Pajapan, Comisariado Comunal; AGN, Vol. 3030, No. 1.
4. AGN, Vol. 3030, No. 1, p. 103.
5. Primordial Titles of Pajapan, Comisariado Comunal; AGN, Vol. 3030, No. 1.
6. The best known of these measures taken against communal landholdings is the "Ley Lerdo" of June 25, 1856.
7. "Los minzapeños tienen la propiedad de tierras muy buenas de labor y pastos, bosques de madera de construcción, que se extienden según sus títulos desde la Barrilla hasta el Farallón, y de aquí toda la falda de la cerranía hasta dicho pueblo, que son sobre 5 leguas" (Iglesias nd: 64–6).
8. The *Cofradía del Señor de la Salud* was founded on May 12, 1745, and the Brotherhood of San Antonio in July 1777 (Cruz Martínez 1991: 12–13).
9. In Mecayapan, the incoming municipal president had to go on a lengthy 'sexual diet' prior to receiving the staff (Velázquez 1992b: 33). For a discussion of the *cofradía* system and its relationship to the civil administration, see R.E. Reina 1966: 97–165. Writing about the civil-religious hierarchy amongst the highland Mayas of Guatemala, Hill and Monaghan (1987: 15) point out that "people alternate between the *cofradías* and the *alcaldía*, slowly advancing up the ladder of offices, all the while gaining in prestige and authority. Ultimate authority in the institution is concentrated in the hands of those who have passed through all its offices."
10. Interview with Pascacio Silvestre, May 18, 1990.
11. Interview with Pascacio Silvestre and Simón Antonio, May 1990. See Martínez Lorenzo et al. 1981. According to Nahmad (nd: 7), these *manzana* divisions were also used in the electoral system.
12. See Salamini (1971: 11); Asaola Garrido (1982: 117). For a different view of the 1906 rebellions, see Knight (1985).
13. Interview with Pascual Hernández Antonio, elder of Pajapan, June 2, 1990.
14. Ibid. Interview with Andrés Martínez, May 15, 1986. See also Stuart (1978: 25).

15. National statistics do not distinguish between *ejidos* and *comunidades agrarias*. In the early 1970s, about 1,915 *comunidades agrarias* held some 5% of all surveyed land in Mexico, mainly forests and natural pasture (R. Bartra 1974: 106).

16. Collective *ejidos* were first established by President Cárdenas in the 1930s. They differ from the individual *ejido* and agrarian community in that all lands and capital are owned and worked collectively by the members of the *ejido* instead of being distributed to individual members. They are modelled on the collective farms envisaged in the communist model. *Ejidos* and communal landholdings, a legacy of the Spanish and colonial land tenure systems, however, are rarely based on collective work organizations: only 18% of them involve collective forms of agricultural labor. It should be mentioned that in its original Castilian meaning, the term *ejido* denoted areas of collective land, not the individual parcels it has come to be associated with. See *Encuesta Nacional Agropecuaria Ejidal 1988*. Vol. 1. Instituto Nacional de Estadística Geográfica e Información, 1990.

CHAPTER 2

STATE THEORY AND NATIVE
HISTORY (1930–68)

Pajapan society of today is the outcome of two intertwined histories: on the one hand, a kin-based patrimonial system transformed over time, and, on the other hand, a broader power system driven by the colonial and post-colonial actions of state polity and the market economy. Our objective is to examine the internal dynamics of each system while also accounting for the day-to-day interplay of kin relations, market forces, and the government process. In Chapter 6, we shall see that the patrimonial domain dating back to the prehispanic era and its transformation over time have affected native divisions between genders and age groups observed in present-day Gulf Nahua society and economy. In this chapter and the next, however, we leave the patrimonial domain aside and focus our attention on money and government authority, or municipal land politics and the accumulation of wealth in land and cattle in 20th-century Pajapan.

Our study of native politics and economics requires a close examination of the history of local land tenure systems and the cattle industry. Recent struggles over land have been affected by land titles acquired in the colonial era, municipal divisions and the lot administration created in the 19th century. Land politics have also been molded by the centralized PRI institutions developed after the Revolution, the agrarian laws and the *ejido* regime promoted under Cárdenas, and the post-war growth of a hinterland cattle industry controlled by the *caciques* of southern Veracruz.

Before we say more about these processes, however, there are some basic theoretical problems that must be addressed concerning the relationship between the political and economic determinations of social history – the extent to which capital and state are autonomous from one another and convertible forms of power. The theoretical approach outlined below is applied to the analysis of struggles for land and office spanning three periods of Gulf Nahua history. As we shall see, each period involves a particular correlation of political and economic forces. From the 1940s to the late 1970s local and regional *caciques* rose to power; PRI ranchers controlled wealth in land, cattle and the local government process. The second period revolved around an ethno-popular front formed in the early 1980s and directed against the state-owned oil industry moving into the lowlands of communal Pajapan. The last period started with the cancellation of the PEMEX port project in 1984, an event that put an end to both *caciquismo* and ethno-populism and brought about a general crisis in the local power system. The recent history of Pajapan is one of outright factionalism, i.e., a fragmentation of classes and politically-constituted groups competing over issues of land and office.

From class politics to political classes

Our account of the struggle for land and office in Pajapan is informed by a theoretical approach that revolves round three principles. First, the analysis acknowledges the specificity of the body politic *vis-à-vis* the productive system and, more importantly, the *relational differences instituted* between and within private and public business. Second, we discuss the *partial convertibility* of money into authority, or the impact of class relations on the management of state power (and vice versa). Three, Gulf Nahua politics involve the struggle of *political positions* that have unequal access to the legal, administrative, bureaucratic and coercive organizations of the state. By position we mean a particular location within the state system but also a set of *propositions* put forth for political consideration, an active stand taken in regard to the disputes and struggles inherent in the government process. The latter concept implies group actions designed to overcome difficulties but also fraught with problems of their own, subject as they are to the contradictions, crises and uncertainties of political history.

Polity – from relative autonomy to relational differences

Although conditioned by the process of production, divisions of authority and relations established between governments, state and citizen, the elected and the electorate, the military and the civilian, are different from those of capital and labor. To argue that a government, an army or a legal apparatus serves or counters the interests of capital, one must acknowledge the distance that lies between legal-political organizations and the sphere of production and market circulation proper. A Pajapan rancher can be elected to local presidential office as a means to securing his and other ranchers' monopoly over land, yet a rancher is not by definition a municipal president, nor is the president a rancher by law. The two positions may be occupied by the same person, but they are still distinguishable in that they entail the appropriation and distribution of different resources and the establishment of different power relations, each with their own activities and institutional materiality.

Our history of Pajapan politics recognizes the institutional specificity of the political domain *vis-à-vis* the economic sphere, the activities of government *vis-à-vis* the process of capital accumulation, or the battle for democracy *vis-à-vis* class struggle. This is not to say that we consider the two institutions as fully autonomous. The notion of specificity differs from that of neutrality or even autonomy understood as "the ability of the state to act for ends antagonistic to dominant class interests" (Hamilton 1982: 13; see Zeitlin 1980: 16–17). The issue of causal over-

determination, i.e., what the state does to a class economy and vice-
versa, should be distinguished from the question of *structural effectivity* –
what the state actually is and how the government process actually
functions.

Even when concerned with the specificity of the state *vis-à-vis* capital,
neo-Marxist theory tends to reduce political institutions to their economic
effects. The government process reproduces the class system by securing
the interests of capital and keeping its contradictions in check (Carmona
1982; Labra 1982; Guerrero 1979; R. Bartra et al. 1975). Or it is an
extension of the class struggle into the political arena proper (Alavi
1982: 293; Otero 1980: 55; Rello 1982)? As noted by Skocpol (1985: 5),
the tendency for neo-Marxists has been to reinforce society-centered
assumptions about the state, some regarding it "as an instrument of
class rule, others as an objective guarantor of production relations or
economic accumulation, and still others as an arena for political class
struggle."[1]

By contrast, structuralists argue for a regional theory of the political
field, a discipline made possible by the differentiation of economy and
polity in capitalist society.[2] The implication is that "states conceived as
organizations claiming control over territories and people may formulate
and pursue goals that are not simply reflective of the demands or interests
of social groups, classes, or society" (Skocpol 1985: 9). The regional
approach to politics represents a challenge to all instrumental conceptions
of the state, liberal and Marxist alike. In the words of Shanin (1982:
316), what this approach brings into question is the notion of an epi-
phenomenal state, "a reflection of underlying class forces, local and
foreign, or the setting for their interplay – a conceptual equivalent of the
class-neutral state of pluralist theories of society, which acts as a management computer; alternatively, the state is seen as an expression of the
structural needs of capital accumulation only."

Our case-study is an exercise in the regional analysis of politics, one
that recognizes the institutional difference that lies between market
activities and the government process. To this notion of "institutional
difference", however, we have added a good dose of anthropological
relativity. There is no such thing as an absolute difference between
institutions that have interacted so extensively as to become enmeshed in
one social fabric. The distinction between state and class power is only
relative. Although demarcated, the two systems share certain characteristics that are indicative of a determinate mode of social existence. Briefly,
polity and economy in recent Gulf Nahua history are both secularized,
freed from direct ecclesiastical control. All corresponding activities are
treated as impersonal, hence partly removed from the sphere of personal
domestic life. The activities of the state and the market also share the
rhetoric and claims of contractual freedom, i.e., peoples' freedom to
engage in commodity transactions and to govern themselves through
mechanisms of electoral representation. The enfranchisement principle
and the monetarization process presuppose in turn the measurability of
material value and political power, hence mechanisms of pricing and

voting. Power is exercised through a monetary and electoral calculus designed to reflect determinate quantities of economic value and political will. Finally, despite their institutional differences, both private business and the public sector employ labor-power in exchange for money.

The institutions of state and capital are relatively different. The problem with the "relative difference" notion, however, is that it is purely comparative and somewhat static. A better concept to account for the division between polity and economy is that of *relational differentiation*, a process involving not only a dislocation between private and public business but also the development of complex relations between and within the two spheres. Far from engendering a simple separation of one domain from another, the process of institutional fragmentation so typical of modern regimes is inherently *relational*: linkages established between the two power structures constitute each system in relation to the other. Thus state formation is an essential "dimension of how both capitalist civilization was made and how it is held together; the central means, to repeat, of its organization" (Corrigan and Sayer 1985: 200). It is through bourgeois law that commodity and wage-labor exchanges are construed as contractual transactions between free owning subjects, rational equals before the law (Corrigan et al. 1980: 15). Extra-economic effects of bourgeois law are not added on to capitalism *ex post facto*, like a super-structure designed to reproduce capital from the outside. Rather, legal dispositions are built into the property system, the relations of production and the market operations of capitalism from the start. State apparatuses are essential ingredients of a bourgeois economy; they create the necessary conditions for private business to develop without the state actually taking full control over all economic activities.

The inverse relationship is also true. Just as capitalist relations of production and exchange are inherently *juridified*, so too the bourgeois state is *commodified*. In addition to legitimating the market economy, the state is responsible for issuing and controlling the flow of money and for managing public revenue through infrastructural expenditures, subsidies to the private sector, investments in state-owned industries, public wage-labor employment, educational and welfare services to the labor force, etc. As argued by Offe (1984: 122), these activities require the decommodification of material resources withdrawn from the market but also the administrative recommodification of public wealth, feeding it back into the process of capital accumulation and securing the general conditions for market production and exchange.

Our book is premised on this two-way relationship between economic structure and the process of government, between class conflict and the struggle for democracy. While differentiated, the two power structures are systematically intertwined and have direct effects on each other's history. As Shanin (1982: 316) puts it, "while states can be shown to be shaped, produced, and determined by class interests and action, they have also produced class structures, transformed them, or made them disappear."

Politics must be understood *in relation* to economics and vice-versa.

But the political process is also a *relational* system in its own right. To understand this process, analysts must delve into the internal linkages operating within civil society (Lat. *civis*, a citizen), within a community of citizens, their territorial government and their political interrelations regulated by law. Far from being a centralized unified body, the state creates and regulates competing interests within civil society, divisions that interact but do not coincide with class relations proper (Sorj 1983: 187–90).[3]

Even when supporting capitalist economies, modern state regimes allow for a wide range of legal forms and localized politics that require careful investigation.[4] Our discussion of Gulf Nahua politics takes these historical variations into account. The analysis explores the change of authority structure resulting from the Spanish Conquest and other transformations that affected local political institutions from the colonial rule to the liberal era, the Porfiriato and the post-revolutionary regime. We also discuss the impact of pre-Columbian forms of organization on local politics: more precisely, the patrimonial domain, a kin-based regime comprising elements of reciprocity and hierarchy instituted through native rules of descent, marriage, residence and inheritance. These native rules vest older men and wife-givers with rights not granted to women, wife-receivers and younger men. The dynamics of government and state power in Pajapan must therefore be understood against the background of Indian forms of political organization and broader changes in national Mexican history.[5]

In the analyses that follow, special attention is paid to questions of administrative authority over property in land. As in the works of Binford (1985) and Schryer (1986: 309; 1990: 9), we shall delve into the intricacies of Mexican agrarian law with a view to understanding the discursive effects, the social divisions and the potential for economic and political struggle created through the legal apparatuses. These agrarian laws have varied considerably throughout the 20th century and have generally served the interests of local, national and foreign capital (Gutelman 1974). Still, legal dispositions are not reducible to economic determinations alone, to a fetishistic creation of subjects of legal ownership and exchange, an instrument of bourgeois domination manipulated by the powers that be (so Pashukanis 1978: 109–29; Collins 1982: 17–34; Wells 1981: 128–34). There is more to law than an instrument of the normative order that keeps society together, or the power system that pits dominant classes against the subordinate. While fulfilling vital functions in society, the legal system exhibits a certain degree of autonomy from other functions of government and the economy as a whole. As argued by E.P. Thompson (1975: 267) and others (Jessop 1987; Hall 1986: 154–5), laws have an effectivity of their own. They create divisions and social conflicts that are constitutive of civil society and that revolve round the control exercised over a body of citizens defined as members of a state, free individuals subject to particular obligations and entitled to certain rights, including private property, equality before the law and the power to be represented in government.

Just as capital exists by virtue of its separation from labor, so too state power is but one side of a basic equation,[6] with the community of governed citizens on the other (E.P. Thompson 1977: 163).[7] Both relationships, those of capital/labor and state/citizens, have had profound effects on Gulf Nahua social history. Practical divisions instituted between and within the market economy and the government process (as opposed to church activity and family life) have broken up an older power structure of prehispanic origin, reducing native society to fragments of its former self (Boege 1988: 55–6, 283–8). Although still operative in some respects (see Chapter 6), Pajapan's kin-based patrimonial domain has lost ground to the political institutions of the colonial and post-colonial eras, systems of power differentiated from market forces proper. Triggered by an expanding cattle industry, the struggle over land in 20th-century Pajapan has been associated with an increase in state forms of government intervention and bureaucratic control. At the same time the latter process has generated a struggle to achieve greater democracy in the political sphere via mechanisms of representation and popular participation, towards a community ruled by the ruled. Our aim is to reflect on the role of Western political institutions and struggles in native history, without ever reducing issues of polity to class analysis alone.

The approach to law, government and civil society outlined above implies a neo-institutional perspective that focuses on organized politics rather than power relations broadly defined as multiple and mobile fields of force relations, as followers of Foucault and Bourdieu would have it. As anthropologists, we recognize the importance of looking at the manipulative powers of discourse and all the tactics of local domination constituted through everyday practices and dispersed systems of micropower. In the last two chapters of this book, we discuss these issues at length, in light of Pajapan's patrimonial domain and the disciplinary powers of Nahua symbolling. These local analyses, however, do not preclude studies of centralized forms of power or global strategies of domination vested in capital or the state. In the words of Smith (1989: 218), "studies of the minutiae of a people's culture not firmly situated within the context of economic and political relations of exploitation and domination, at regional, national, and international levels simply obscure the essential elements of struggle and resistance inherent in cultural production." The two levels of regulation and domination, local and global, are both constitutive of society and coexist in everyday life. Actually, this book is an anthropological contribution to our understanding of the complex relations that exist between all forms of power, whether they be economic or political, domestic or public, practical or symbolic.

Conversions of power: polity and politics

The institutionalization process creates divisions and relations within and between the two spheres of power, the political and the economic, each having its own effectivity and producing conditions necessary for the other domain to exist. The effects of state and capital, however, become all the more complex when viewed interactively, subject as they are to interferences from all exercises of power: wealth can be used to reinforce a particular political regime, and authority to secure particular conditions of capital accumulation. We now turn to this issue of correlations of forces, or the question of causal overdetermination defined as conversions of power from one institution to another.

Prior to the 1980s, ambitious individuals had to have wealth in cattle to occupy key political offices in Pajapan. Also the rancher class had to control the local PRI government to increase and maintain their control over arable land. Capital was a condition to attain positions of authority, and authority to accumulate capital. Money and office complemented one another and were mutually convertible (see Dow 1977). Although embedded in different institutional forms, power tends to be mobile. Wealth in money can be expanded through diversification or transfers between branches or fractions of capital. The internal conversion mechanism applies to political relations as well, in that access to one position (head of PRI party) may be a stepping stone to other government offices (municipal president). More importantly, investments in wealth can be converted into political capital, and political clout into economic benefits. A regional analysis of politics does not rule out a close examination of this basic conversion process, from authority into capital and vice-versa.

This chapter pays as much attention to issues of *polity*, by which we mean the structuring of political offices in Pajapan (and in relation to external political agencies), as to questions of *political economy* – the concrete ways in which the government process directly affects and is affected by the expansion of capital. To use another terminology, the analysis considers the causal linkages between economy and polity, forces and factors from one sphere that "overdetermine" the history of power relations within the other (Chevalier 1982: 52).

But we also consider the limitations imposed on interchanges of money and authority, on movements of power across institutions. For one thing, the conversion concept should not be confused with that of exchange: wealth that leads to political office does not mean wealth given up in exchange for office. Power held in one sphere can be used to attain power in another field provided that the two systems are not one and the same, provided that they never become perfectly interchangeable. The mobility of power is also limited by the many rivalries that exist between fractions of capital (ranchers vs oil industry), between modes of government, geopolitical divisions and spheres of authority, the state holding class and private business (or foreign capital, see Alavi 1982: 299). Concrete examples of clashes between power-holders will be discussed at length. A close examination of divisions and crises of power is all the more important as it allows us to avoid a purely functional, static and monolithic view of the power structure prevailing amongst the Gulf Nahuas. Our analysis will thus address the uneven distribution of power in Pajapan and the chronic weaknesses of local forms of power in relation to external forces.

Studies of the bourgeoisie as a unified bloc or a conglomerate ruling class rarely do justice to the complexity of state and class systems, both of which are more often than not unevenly developed, conflict-ridden and crisis-prone (Offe 1975). Power is never simply unified or concentrated, nor does it tend to disperse evenly as in elite analysis or to mushroom everywhere and at random as in Foucaultian theory. To avoid these unrealistic conceptions of power, we shall speak of (a) the centrality of certain key positions within the class structure and the political system (e.g., PRI leadership, the Executive; see González Casanova 1970: 20); (b) the dominance of money (ranching capital) over authority in local and regional history; and (c) the chronic limitations of both forms of power vis-à-vis external agents of capital and state. These effects of positional centrality, institutional dominance and chronic underdevelopment are expressed in ways that must be uncovered through concrete analysis, not through constructions of abstract theory.

Lastly, the mobility of power is subject to limitations imposed by subordinate groups engaged in struggles for a classless society and for democracy, battles pursued through organized resistance and alliance with progressive factions of government and society. The recent history of politics in Pajapan illustrates the success (if only partial) of peasant movements in exploiting the weaknesses and internal divisions of the powers that be, thereby curbing the concentration of power in the hands of ranchers, politicians and bureaucrats.[8]

To sum up, the convertibility and concentration of political and economic forms of power will be dealt with from two complementary angles: the functional interchanges between office and wealth, and the constraints on the convergence of authority and money. These constraints result from the externality of the body politic vis-à-vis class relations, the uneven distribution of power controlled by the ruling interests, and the struggle of subordinate groups against domination by state and capital.

Political positions and land tenure propositions

Although conditioned by class forces, the government process consists of particular relations established between politically constituted positions, social ranks involving government authorities and levels of bureaucracy, parties and presidents, elected representatives and their constituencies, etc. By definition, these positions entail unequal access to the "fourth factor of production", i.e., the administrative, legal, bureaucratic and coercive organizations of the state (Hodges and Gandy 1979: 87–8). Comuneros in Pajapan are a case in point. They comprise all community members who have rights of access to communal land. They exclude from their ranks non-residents of Pajapan and community members who were not listed in the original comunero census or inherited land rights since then. Since they include ranchers, merchants and peasants, the comuneros of Pajapan are not a homogeneous group or class, yet as a legal formation they constitute an important political body. All of them hold a position of landholding citizens with specific corporate interests, one that ranchers, local authorities and government agencies must reckon with in their effort to secure their control over the local economy and the local government process. Similar comments apply to other politically-constituted formations such as the municipality, local authorities and formal committees, leaders of the PRI party, PEMEX bureaucrats, formal peasant and rancher associations: all of these groups and organizations wield unequal quantities of material resources, bureaucratic influence and legal authority.

The concept of *political position* implies a place within a system of divisions pitting the ruling interests against the subordinate groups. Political relations are no less structured than class relations. What we wish to avoid here is a structural view of economic classes defined as fixed locations in a system of production, to which can be added a conjunctural analysis of the struggles carried out in the political arena. Although well intentioned, this dialectical synthesis of class structure and class struggle, the economic system and the political process (R. Bartra 1974; Beaucage 1973; Durand 1975; Paré 1979), ignores the structural features governing the political process (and the on-going struggles built into economic forms). As in recent studies of peasant politics and agrarian conflict in Mexico and Central America,[9] the tendency prevailing in this dialectical literature is to "look first to economic issues and then, in varying degrees, to the ways that those issues are mediated politically" (Fowley 1991: 218).

The notion of political position, however, should not be used in a static way, as a fixed location within an immutable structure. Rather the term presupposes a process of historical differentiation (political positions emerge, expand, and are transformed) and of relational interaction as well (between the electorate and the elected, the state and the munici-pality, etc.). Moreover, each *position* involves an active stand taken in regard to the disputes inherent in the structure, a set of *propositions* put forth for political consideration. This is a crucial point. A political position is not only a site within a system but also a set of habits or dispositions to act in ways that inhere to that position, a propensity to defend certain propositions against alternative plans. These inclinations to act in parti-cular ways correspond to the powers and resources that the position-holder wields or seeks to obtain within a broader structure. This approach is in keeping with Bourdieu's post-structural notion of habitus, save that it does away with Bourdieu's distinction between structural position, actional disposition, and discursive rationalization (Bourdieu 1977). In our view, a position and its habitus are one and the same thing. Actually, all political dis-positions entail four basic attributes, the unity of which implies a theory of practice that dispenses with the usual distinctions drawn between structure, agency and history, or between the logic and contradictions of social history.

First, the behavior characteristic of a political position must be situated within a system of inequalities rife with tension and manipulative conflict. As with collective action analysis, studies of political behavior require "a model of interaction with multiple actors rather than a single-group model" (Tilly 1985: 737). Far from being reflections of group attributes, political positions are intrinsically interactive. For instance, the *comuneros* of Pajapan form a legal landholding group inclined to protect their land titles against outsiders, the state, land-hungry ranchers and landless peasants as well. They can put forth particular land tenure propositions and defend their interests through actions and mechanisms assigned to them by agrarian law: formal petitions, general assembly meetings and resolutions, representational delegations, communal rhetoric, etc. As observed by Schryer (1990: 9), "the law can serve as a class weapon for militant peasants in their fight for access to more land and greater control over the productive process."[10] The collective of landholding *comuneros*, weak as they may be, are a group in action constantly interacting with other groups and employing individual and collective action and legal means at their disposal to promote their own interests — *means and processes that are constitutive of the position they occupy at any given moment in time*. Political group positions thus transcend all rational economic measures that individual peasants may take daily to counter their vulnerability *vis-à-vis* dominant classes, measures otherwise correctly emphasized by moral economists and rationalists alike.[11]

Second, political dis-positions are meanings in action, material positions and active *propositions* made regarding values pursued in society. Approaches that stress the dialectical interaction between the realms of belief and action (e.g., Murphy 1971; Medick 1987: 97) – between ideas and the material or practical conditions of social life – presuppose that elements of culture and social structure can be distinguished, if only for analytic purposes. In our view, however, these distinctions are problematical. To use the example introduced above, the communal system is not an ideology acting as a legal superstructure, or an element of cultural identity intervening in the sphere of class relations, as Sider (1986) and Smith (1989) would have it. Rather, the communal system denotes practices ranging from a collective government and control over land to a distinctive agrarian discourse, a mode of speech with a legal effectiveness of its own, all of which form an integral part of Mexican cultural-political history. To be a *comunero* is to have legal rights to the use of land, a voice in discussions and deliberations carried out by the collective, and, one hopes, a parcel at one's disposal for agricultural use. The *comunero* position implies a particular distribution of power and material resources, or *claims to that effect* as expressed through communal discourse and the corresponding forms of representation.

Third, it follows from what we have just said that a "position" is not a static place occupied by a group within a fixed structure. As Smith writes (1989: 223), structural determinants hold no primacy "over agency of actors engaging in political struggle". By definition, a position implies a site of actions and calculations, strategic allocations and allocutions generated by a group exploiting its own resources, legal entitlements, cracks in the system, potential alliances with or divisions between other groups, all with a view to promoting particular government propositions. For instance, a majority of *comuneros* can mobilize internal and external support (the media, peasant organizations, pro-Indian state agencies) to protect their land against expropriation by the state-owned oil industry. They may proceed through elections, party politics, delegations, public assemblies and demonstrations, declarations and legal suits. The actual position adopted will entail a group's active effort to manipulate social forces (rights and commodities, the government process, the powers of speech) to achieve its own ends, toward a formal protection of their land base.

Fourth, political positions are subject to constraints, crises and contradictions, uncontrollable forces and unintended consequences of social interaction – forces that tend to be neglected in studies of peasant politics in Mexico and Latin America.[12] Disruptive effects of all kinds introduce elements of unpredictability and irrationality into social life, unstable elements that cause group positions and propositions to undergo important shifts over time. Problems of irrationality may result from inadequate material and organizational resources or from external imponderables such as the environment or fluctuations in broader-level politics. A group's failure to behave according to its interests and achieve its ends may be caused by sheer miscalculations or aggregate actions that cannot be reconciled (short-term vs long-term objectives). Policies implemented by the state-holding classes are a case in point: "official initiatives can be stupid or misdirected, and autonomous initiatives may be fragmented and partial and work at cross-purposes to one another" (Skocpol 1985: 15; see Alavi 1982: 296).

Political struggles represent another risk factor, for they imply that one group strategy will always be met with resistance and opposition. Intra-group divisions also impose limits on the ability of legally formed groups to act corporatively and rationally. Since a group may be fragmented (*comuneros* without a communal organization) and since its members may have different class affiliations (peasants, ranchers), their capacity to form a united front and to act on other groups (state officials) with some effectiveness (toward recognition of land titles) depends on how successful groups are in containing their internal differences and in manipulating collective actions, resources (wealth, authority, discourse) and coalitional opportunities to gain their objectives. As emphasized by Schryer (1990: 318–19), the conditions of collective mobilization and the connection between the active group and the base population will vary from one group to another, from one period of history to the next. A collective action may be proposed without its members being able to act on it, or it may be undertaken without expressing the common interest of a fully formed group (Tilly 1985: 731). More recently, while they can serve to contain opposition or to resolve crises, alliances struck between groups can create instability and a whole series of compromises, concessions and shifts in power that will limit the potential of any particular group or system for rational action and stable reproduction over time. While essential, macro-studies of peasant rebellions (B. Moore 1966; Wolf 1969; Migdal 1974; Paige 1975; Skocpol 1985) rarely capture the degree to which political struggles can be limited by these intra-group divisions and the volatility of alliances observed at the micro-level.

This concludes our outline of the theory informing our understanding of Gulf Nahua political history. The narrative genre adopted below, i.e., following a chain of events involving precise actions, subsequent reactions and their consequences within a larger story, is in keeping with a view of the political process based on concepts of strategic action, irrationality and social speculation. History, as Ricoeur (1984: 181) puts it:

> remains historical to the extent that all of its objects refer back to first-order entities – peoples, nations, civilizations – that bear the indelible mark of concrete agents' participatory belonging to the sphere of praxis and narrative. These first-order entities serve as the transitional object between all the artifacts produced by history and the characters of a possible narrative. They constitute quasi-characters, capable of guiding the intentional reference back from the level of the science of history to the level of narrative and, through this, to the agents of real action.

This approach to social life requires that we struggle against the illusion of fatality resulting from strict causal analysis and that we preserve for the past all the uncertainties and potentialities that were once assigned to the future. Our aim is to restore to Gulf Nahua history all those calculations and decisions, uncertainties and probabilities, hopes and fears that the actors of Pajapan society have invested in their own final causes – causes they have chosen to struggle for and that were never sure of success.

The Gulf Nahuas and the new order

Money and authority are convertible but not perfectly interchangeable. Even when highly centralized, the two forms of power are embedded in distinct institutions that never merge into a uniform domain. Moreover, the concentration of political and economic power may be offset by confrontations between the powers that be and struggles launched against dominant groups. These inter- and intra-group conflicts impose limits on interchanges between wealth and office and the formation of a ruling bloc. Moreover, obstacles to the development of hegemonic coalitions vary from one context to another and from one period of history to the next. The latter point can be illustrated by a close examination of modern Gulf Nahua history. As already mentioned, economics and politics in 20th-century Pajapan have gone through three different phases: *caciquismo* (1940–79), ethno-populism (1980–84), and factionalism (1985–). Gulf Nahua *caciques* formed a dominant bloc exercising strict control over local capital and government institutions, a ruling order sanctioned by broader market forces and the state bureaucracy. By contrast, the ethno-populist movement of the early 1980s implied a local interclass alliance pitting the citizens and authorities of Pajapan against the federal government and the state-owned oil industry. This brief period was marked by an open conflict between internal and external agents of capital and the state, a confrontation that brought two things to the fore: the "relative autonomy" of geopolitical conflicts (Pajapan vs PEMEX) *vis-à-vis* class struggle, and the divisions between branches of capital (cattle economy vs oil industry) and levels of government (local vs federal). Finally, *caciquismo* and ethno-populism have given way to local factionalism, a highly fragmented power system marked by the proliferation of inter- and intra-group rivalries over wealth and office.

While the domination exercised by capital and the state has marked all periods of modern Gulf Nahua history, the concentration of political and economic power in the hands of PRI ranchers decreased after the 1970s. We now turn to a detailed discussion of this general historical process, starting with the early development of PRI institutions and the cattle economy in Pajapan and the rise of PRI rancher *caciques* to power – a hegemonic rule that reached its peak in the 1970s.

The Mexican Revolution and the reforms that followed brought about a new social order, a radically different set of political institutions, administrative structures and legal dispositions that allowed public business to expand well beyond the state structures and activities of the Porfiriato regime. All of this occurred in conjunction with the development of the cattle economy and the petro-chemical industry in southern Veracruz. As we shall see, the political economy of Pajapan retained legacies of older patrimonial, colonial-prebendal and liberal-mercantile regimes. These older regimes, however, were weakened and transformed by the industrial revolution, the expansion of a capitalist domain over land, and a tight administrative rule exercised by government and the federal bureaucracy. From the 1930s to the late 1960s, power was to be gradually concentrated in the hands of a few local and regional *caciques* controlling both the cattle economy and the PRI institutions. PRI ranchers, however, were able to exercise their hegemonic rule within certain limits only, those imposed by weak branches of the cattle industry and the PRI state. Also, the period witnessed important struggles and shifts in local land politics, resulting in the creation of a new legal entity: the *comuneros* of Pajapan.

The hegemonic rise of PRI ranchers

The two major institutions in Pajapan at the time of the Mexican Revolution were the municipal government and the lot administration inherited from the Porfiriato. The municipal government included an elected president, treasurer and alderman as well as an appointed secretary and justice of the peace. These individuals mediated between the community and outside authorities on all matters of taxation, legal representation and the provision of services to villages and hamlets throughout the municipality. In 1923, local representatives of the National Revolutionary Party (PRN) were elected to form the first post-revolutionary municipal government in Pajapan, ending a 20–year political vacuum. This party, later renamed the Partido Revolucionario Institucional (PRI), has dominated politics ever since.

In 1925, a general assembly was called to select a senior member (*persona de edad*) of the community as mayor. There were neither elections with secret ballots nor campaigns involving personal or party expenditures. Once the mayor had been selected, a document was forwarded to Minatitlán and then returned to the village. The transfer of power was performed with great pomp, by means of a procession involving civil authorities (carrying the municipal archives in a box), *mayordomos* and *comuneros* accompanied by flutes and drums (Martínez Morales et al. 1982: 19). Individuals aspiring to positions of authority (*secretario, síndico, regidor*) typically began as low-level officials such as police officers.[13]

Because of its relative isolation from the centers of power, Pajapan and other neighboring villages (Velázquez 1992b: 33) initially managed to adapt Mexico's political institutions to its traditional mode of government, a patrimonial polity based on assemblies of male heads of family and a system of civil-religious authority vested in elders acting as government officers and lot administrators. As the cattle industry and state agencies made inroads into the municipality, however, the Gulf Nahuas yielded to the rise of PRI rule within their own territory. The new regime resulted in a full separation of civil and ritual posts, reducing the responsibilities assigned to religious brotherhoods and senior community members acting as protectors of communal lands and brokers between village interests and the Mexican state. The patrimonial *cofradia* institution gave way to a *mayordomia* system involving religious feasts financed by wealthy PRI individuals, hence Indian *caciques* redistributing small portions of their personal wealth to gain prestige and legitimacy in a context of increasing village stratification and potential conflict developing along class lines (see Chance and Taylor 1985; Wasserstrom 1983).

Three distinct groups have emerged from the new political order to fashion the history of land use in 20th-century Pajapan: (a) outside PRI leaders and government officials (the Presidency, DAAC/SRA bureaucrats, national and regional party officials); (b) Indian authorities comprising the municipal government, the PRI party, the lot administrators, the Rancher Association, and the petitionary Communal Land Committee; and (c) the people of Pajapan (the electorate, natives with claims to communal land titles) and the petitionary Agrarian Ejido Committee. These groups have changed over time, subject to internal divisions and conflicts between political factions, spheres of authority, levels of government and neighboring geopolitical entities. They are none the less recognizable group formations that have had unequal access to public resources and authority and that have played major roles in the struggle for land and political power in the municipality. The struggles recounted below center on the role of state government officials, the municipal PRI government and other local authorities in preserving the material and political interests of regional and local *caciques* against pressures to redistribute the land through an *ejido* reform.

Different segments of Gulf Nahua society have held conflicting positions regarding issues of land administration. They have put forth competing propositions as to how the lands of Pajapan should be legally defined and actually distributed. Politics in Pajapan from the 1930s to the late 1960s involve a struggle over three possible land government systems: the old lot administration, the communal land system, and the *ejido* regime. The lot system instituted during the Porfiriato was administered locally by the municipal government in conjunction with lot administrators accountable to federal land agents (DAAC/SRA). With the revolution, however, the lot system lost its legal status. Meanwhile, the revolutionary ideals in matters of land were instituted through the creation of collective landholding bodies of democratic, self-governing *comuneros* and *ejidatarios*, exclusive corporate groups with equal individual rights to communal or *ejido* land subject to the authority of Mexican agrarian law.

As already mentioned, the communal and ejido systems are different in a few important respects. The communal regimen has an administrative organization of its own, a system regulated by federal law and, in principle, independent of the municipal government. *Comuneros* must follow democratic rules when deciding how land is to be distributed and used (individually or collectively). Until communal land is recognized by the state government and the Presidential Office and regulated by the Agrarian Code, federal laws and agencies cannot intervene in the distribution of land among members of the community. The *ejido* is also a collective landholding body recognized and monitored by the state, with its own democratic organization. Unlike the *comuneros*, however, *ejidatarios* typically form an association of independent producers with usufructuary rights over individual parcels of land. Legal procedures to obtain a collective landholding regime must be channelled through the appropriate committee (see Chapter 1).

As pointed out by Schryer (1990: 232–3), "the status of communal land tenure in Mexico is much more flexible in terms of how such land is actually allocated to community members"; as a consequence, ranchers tend to prefer the communal system while peasants are inclined to fight "for a change in legal status from communal to *ejido*". In Pajapan, while the wealthier ranchers have either maintained the old lot administration or supported the communal land proposal, politically active peasants have fought for an *ejido* reform, with little success. As shown below, the control that ranchers have exercised over the municipal government process has given them all the power needed to block the *ejido* reform movement in Pajapan. From this confrontation emerged a compromise solution, if only at the legal level: the communal status formally recognized in 1968.

Before the cattle industry made inroads into the municipality, local authorities were favorable to the *ejido* regime promoted under Cárdenas. In 1930, Fidencio de la Cruz, the Municipal President (1929–31), organized the first Agrarian Ejido Committee in Pajapan, with a view to protecting the local land base from external threats. It was modelled on the radical agrarian policies of the State Governor, Adalberto Tejeda, and the Veracruz Peasant League that was actively organizing peasants throughout Veracruz.[14] The committee requested that the Departamento de Asuntos Agrarios y Colonización (DAAC), the federal land authority, authorize the creation of an *ejido* in Pajapan.

There are two methods of providing communal or *ejido* land titles to landless villages: donation or restitution based on proof of prior ownership. Most *ejidos* in Mexico were created from the division of haciendas following the Mexican Revolution. Paradoxically, communities that had no titles to the land could gain more from the Mexican Revolution than those that had retained some ownership of land. In the case of Pajapan, the objective of the *ejido* request was not to provide a land base for peasants or to change the structure of land use within the community but rather to protect their existing claims from external threats. As already noted, land conflicts from within Pajapan were relatively minor since land was distributed on the basis of actual use by families with very similar economic and social profiles. External threats, however, were more pressing. Blom and Lafarge (1926) report that in the early 1920s Pajapan and the neighboring Nahua village of Tatahuicapan were in conflict over a coffee plantation located between the two communities. Tatahuicapan had made a request for an *ejido* and would have gained the upper hand in the border dispute if Pajapan had not followed with a similar request. The border between the lowlands claimed by Pajapan and the Hacienda Temoloapan was also in dispute. Juan Porfirio and Juan Silva, two leaders of the Agrarian Ejido Committee, were also the administrators of the two lots affected by the dispute, those bordering Tatahuicapan and the Hacienda Temoloapan.[15]

The promotion of an *ejido* in Pajapan by the Agrarian Ejido Committee was strongly resisted by ranchers from Coatzacoalcos. Just prior to the 1932 *ejido* request, F. de la Cruz, the Municipal President of Pajapan, was assassinated by the *guardias blancas* of mestizo ranchers as was A. Martínez, Municipal President from 1933 to 1934. Both leaders had strongly supported the committee and forged an alliance between local municipal and land authorities to promote the establishment of an *ejido*. The Municipal President to follow Martínez (Pascual Bruno, 1934–37) was appointed by the State Governor and later assassinated.[16] Some members of the Agrarian Ejido Committee were put in jail and by 1936 the movement for an *ejido* faltered. The committee in Pajapan (headed by Rosalino Martínez from 1936 to 1943) was reactivated in 1943 and its new president (Moisés Hernández) ran for Municipal President but was defeated. At the state level, support for *ejido* requests was also weakened when Miguel Alemán became State Governor and stripped the Veracruz Peasant League of its power. The hired guns of powerful ranchers operated with impunity during this period in many parts of Veracruz. These violent confrontations eventually disappeared as regional *caciques* developed the local ties needed to gain ascendency over the local government, which they did from the 1940s until the late 1960s.

Prior to the 1940s, Pajapeños lived primarily on subsistence agriculture. Money was obtained through the cultivation and sale of sugar cane planted on communal lands or through wage labor contracted at the sugar refinery of Huazuntlán or San Miguel Temoloapan (Coscapa; the refinery burned down in 1938).[17] Peasants also travelled to Coatza-coalcos by foot to sell corn, beans, pigs, chickens, eggs, mangos and papayas, articles sold in exchange for the money needed to buy salt, petrol, soap, fabric and other industrial goods. Pig merchants came from Coatzacoalcos to purchase as many as 100 pigs at a time, transported in herds along the beach to markets in the urban center.[18] Although on a limited scale, these market transactions caused a gradual separation of agriculture from manufacture and allowed some individuals, especially pig farmers, to accumulate enough money to purchase a few head of cattle from mestizo ranchers or cattle thieves. A handful of peasants had small herds of fewer than ten animals, used mostly as savings against future subsistence needs.

As in Chiapas (Wasserstrom 1983: 181; Benjamin 1989: 233) and northern Veracruz (Schryer 1990: 152), the expansion of beef markets and new ranching technology allowed the cattle economy of southern Veracruz to grow steadily during the 1920s and the 1930s and more rapidly from the 1940s onward. The growth of the cattle industry, from the lowland Coatzacoalcos area to the Sierra de Santa Marta, changed the Gulf Nahua economy. Ties between Pajapan villagers and outside mestizo ranchers started to develop in the 1940s, causing greater internal opposition to the *ejido* request. Arrangements (called *a media*) were made between individuals in Pajapan and ranchers from Coatzacoalcos to rent natural grasslands on the lowland near the lagoon. Individuals were provided with wire for fencing and in some cases with cattle to be raised on a share basis. Initially, fenced areas were moved around by the ranchers as the pastures were grazed. As the herds increased and more pasture was required, larger parcels of temporarily abandoned land were fenced and a few Indians began to acquire herds of their own. Caballero, a powerful rancher from Coatzacoalcos, provided some natives in Pajapan with their start in the cattle industry as did Don Félix Martínez (alias El Negro) of Coatzacoalcos and Eulogio Lagunes, a wealthy rancher from La Perla del Golfo. One Indian rancher recalled how his father went to Las Barrillas in 1945 to care for the cattle of Cruz Izquierdo, a mestizo rancher with over 200 head of cattle, and returned to Pajapan a few years later with 36 animals of his own.[19] Another Indian rancher established his herd with a cow and calf purchased in Chacalapa with earnings obtained from the sale of corn, beans and a pig.[20]

As observed by Schryer (1990: 101), "informal alliances between Mestizo landowners and the wealthy Indians who controlled their own communities could serve the economic interests of an emerging ranchero elite." As outside mestizo *rancheros* intervened in the production sphere, local agricultural capital developed and land was concentrated in the hands of a few Indian ranchers. These changes undermined the kin-based subsistence activities that had prevailed during previous centuries. Communal land acquired a different value; although inalienable by law, it became a commodity and the object of competition between munici-palities, peasants and ranchers. The new economy brought about changes in the political sphere as well. PRI institutions established in Pajapan (the party, municipal offices, the rancher association) fell under the control of Indian and regional mestizo *caciques*, "political intermediaries who effectively monopolize the distribution of public resources in the countryside" (Paré 1990: 82). These "bosses" dominate local politics, controlling the electoral process and access to public office. They play a central role in maintaining the corporatist state system and PRI hegemony in rural areas of Mexico.

The most powerful of the southern Veracruz *caciques* was Amadeo González Caballero, a cousin of President Alemán. During the 1940s, 1950s and 1960s he acquired numerous ranches in the names of different family members. In addition, he gained access to land through special arrangements with small property owners, *ejidatarios* and *comuneros* throughout the Sierra and along the coastal plain. In exchange for a share of new calves and milk, a few *comuneros* in Pajapan grazed and cared for Caballero's cattle on village communal land. In this way Caballero was able to increase his herd without assuming the costs of land ownership or cattle management. When the *comuneros* eventually established ranches of their own, they became suppliers for slaughter-houses and cattle brokerages owned by Caballero. His empire included trucking companies and many other businesses in urban centers. Caballero occupied many political positions including Municipal President in Coatzacoalcos, state deputy, and director of the regional cattle ranching association. He exerted considerable influence over key politicians in Coatzacoalcos, Acayucan, Jáltipan, Minatitlán, Cosoleacaque, Moloacán and other municipalities. The political and economic power of Caballero was unrivalled in southern Veracruz until his death in 1970 (Mendoza Neri 1982: 53, 55).

Given the tight control they exercised over political offices, local and regional *caciques* managed to preserve the traditional lot system against pressures to convert lands into an *ejido*. Ranchers preferred the traditional lot system over the *ejido* as it provided them with ready access to land – access not available in areas of southern Veracruz where private properties and *ejidos* predominated. Since the land in Pajapan was not parcelled, villagers could claim unused land as their own. Indian ranchers allowed their cattle to graze freely on the natural lowland savanna, often into the corn fields of peasants. The violent conflicts that sometimes erupted between peasants and ranchers were used by ranchers to justify the erection of fences and claims to larger areas of second growth on "abandoned" corn fields. Peasants who cultivated land within the fenced areas were not compensated for damage to their crops.[21] Those who objected to the loss of their plot received little support from local authorities who were often themselves engaged in cattle-raising. In some cases, peasants were offered a small amount of money by individuals who wanted their land. The money was to encourage them to clear a new field elsewhere. Usury forced indebted peasants to sell their land. Since land was relatively abundant during the early years of ranch expansion, peasants had alternatives to confrontations with Indian and mestizo ranchers.

The strategy of land concentration developed by ranchers was promoted by Guillermo Salinas Mendoza, a mestizo sent to Pajapan from

Coatzacoalcos in 1948 as a representative of the PRI, the ruling political party. His official status was as a school teacher but he also organized the successful campaign of W. Martínez Corsiano, who took office as Municipal President in 1949. Salinas was appointed municipal secretary and justice of the peace. The man's ability to read and write was an important asset in a community where very few people were literate, less than 5% up until the mid-1940s and less than 10% in 1960. He later organized the local chapter of the Rancher Association (founded in 1951, with 47 members owning fewer than ten animals each) where he incessantly promoted the development of cattle ranching; 14 chapters (out of 22) of the powerful southern Veracruz Rancher Association had been founded by 1947. According to one peasant, when Guillermo Salinas became the municipal secretary, he allied himself with those who had more money and told them to fence their land. People with small *milpas* increasingly lost their land. Mendoza Salinas told the ranchers, "Bring the poor to drink, buy them beer in exchange for their parcels." He justified the appropriation of lands by ranchers with the use of such revolutionary rhetoric as *la tierra a quien la trabaja*, the land to those who work it.

The tax system traditionally controlled by the lot administrators was also used to dispossess peasants of their land. When land rental to outside mestizo ranchers began in the late 1940s, the land tax on each household was changed by the local authorities to a tax per hectare of land used by ranchers; cattle-raisers began paying 5 pesos per hectare while peasants continued to pay a total of 5 pesos per year. By fencing land and paying taxes to the local lot administrators, native allies of wealthy mestizo ranchers claimed larger parcels of land.[22] In 1951 a special land tax of 22 pesos was demanded of every family in Pajapan, followed a year later by an additional 20-peso tax. The taxes were denounced by local and regional branches of the Agrarian Ejido Committee.[23] According to the lot administrators and the municipal government, the purpose of these taxes was to raise money to lift an embargo on Pajapan land imposed by the state for non-payment of federal taxes and to initiate the procedures required for the recognition of communal land titles.[24] While the taxes were eventually paid and the embargo was lifted, shrewd ranchers took the opportunity to increase their landholdings by paying taxes on land claimed by peasants unable to pay.

Municipal government and lot administrators also allied themselves with mestizo and Indian ranchers to oppose an *ejido* request to restrict the expansion of ranches. Divisions developed within the Agrarian Ejido Committee when one member of the executive joined the municipal authorities in denouncing the *ejido* reformers for undermining the village traditions. He was later assassinated. When officials of the state land commission arrived in Pajapan during the early 1950s to undertake surveys of the land in response to a request submitted by the latter committee, the rancher-dominated municipal government was uncooperative and in one incident put a surveyor in jail for several days.[25]

In 1952, the municipal authorities rallied ranchers to block the *ejido* request and initiate an application for presidential recognition of an agrarian community and *tierras comunales* in Pajapan. Documents from 1765 and 1884 were brought to Mexico and a request submitted by the newly-formed Communal Land Committee to DAAC via the General Direction of Indigenous Affairs (Oficio No. 105–00045). As already pointed out, the *ejido* system allows for the division of land into plots of equal size distributed to all *ejido* members. By contrast, the communal land tenure system leaves the use and administration of the land up to a General Assembly of *comuneros* and an elected Communal Land Commission. Communal tenure was similar in many respects to the traditional lot administration system except that it had legal status under modern Mexican agrarian law, a status that did not apply to the pre-revolutionary lot system.

Ranchers preferred the status quo to a clear definition of land boundaries which would uphold the rights of villagers to land in Pajapan, but a communal land regimen was more desirable than an *ejido* with individual parcels. In the absence of an officially recognized land tenure system, ranchers felt compelled to counter the *ejido* request with a land tenure proposal more favorable to their interests and over which they could exercise greater control. By building on the traditional lot administration system they controlled, ranchers were able to claim that they were acting in the interests of all villagers as they were protecting the traditions of local land tenure. The communal rhetoric was being used to attain purely personal goals and give the ranchers' position greater legitimacy in the eyes of outside agents.

Power-holders worked toward the integration of the local economy into broader markets dominated by capital. In spite of this, they made abundant and effective use of the rhetoric of communal tradition and autonomy to legitimate the old lot system under attack by landless members of the community. The lot administrators played an important role in this regard as they represented legitimate holders and protectors of communal lands. Their voice was co-opted by the local PRI government and eventually displaced by the petitionary Communal Land Committee also controlled by the PRI.

The struggle for land and the communal compromise

Political positions do not coincide with classes formed in the private sector. Nevertheless, they do respond to class relations of production and exchange. Power is transmutable. Wealth is convertible into authority and authority into wealth; the greater the concentration and the conversion of one form of power into the other, the more despotic the regime is. In Pajapan, wealthy ranchers acquired the land needed to expand their operations by exercising strict control over the local government process. All the Municipal Presidents elected between 1948 and 1968 were ranchers and members of the local Rancher Association.

By and large, Indian and mestizo ranchers upheld the lot organization, a system that allowed them open access to the land needed to increase their herds. Alternative land tenure systems were promoted in word only. As we are about to see, Indian and outside mestizo ranchers maintained the old land tenure system until the late 1960s by means of force (hired guns), pressure channelled through rancher associations and, most importantly, tight control over the local PRI, the municipal presidency and secretariat, the lot administration and the Communal Land Committee. Ranchers attained a hegemonic position in local affairs through a constant manipulation of communal rhetoric and through direct political representation or by proxy. In their effort to silence all forms of opposition, municipal authorities subservient to the rancher class mobilized political support and influence at higher levels of government (federal agents and state government delegates of DAAC/SRA) and delayed procedures to resolve communal land claim settlements or to establish an *ejido*.

The power exercised by PRI ranchers was nevertheless limited at both the economic and the political levels. The penetration of the Gulf Nahua economy by the cattle industry and the money medium did not destroy a peasant economy based on shifting cultivation, a kin-based division of labor, a low population density and the individual use of communal lands. Pajapeños continued to rely on the cultivation of food plants, hunting, fishing and small-scale commercial livestock production (pigs) to provide for their needs. In many ways the strength of subsistence and petty commodity activities reflected the weaknesses of the cattle industry. As in the Huasteca region (Schryer 1990: 153), cattle production in the San Martín highlands involves low costs in labor and a non-mechanized use of large tracts of forest land converted to pasture, conditions of land and labor management that threatened the long-term sustainability of the peasant economy. Prior to the 1970s, however, ranching had not expanded to the point of appropriating all the land available for cultivation. The growth and concentration of agricultural capital in Pajapan was offset by insecure land titles and pasture and herds of poor quality. Poverty and the isolation of Pajapan country also meant that Indian ranchers were chronically dependent on urban-based markets in money and cattle. Given their poor access to capital, credit and technology, Pajapan ranchers provided a cheap and limited source of immature calves for larger ranching and cattle brokerage operations controlled from the lowland centers of Coatzacoalcos, Minatitlán and Acayucan.[26] Production on a small scale meant a proliferation of Indian ranching operations and the fragmentation of land use, a tendency that further reduced Pajapan's potential for capitalization and wealth accumulation.

On the political level, the power marshalled by local PRI authorities has never been absolute. For one thing, the local government often intervened merely to sanction the rule of powerful ranchers maintained through patronage and paramilitary force. Moreover, the *municipio* was and still is a dependent and chronically weak branch of the Mexican political system, with few resources, administrative capacity and legislative powers. And while PRI institutions have suppressed opposition and promoted the formation of capital in agriculture, they have channelled manifestations of conflict over land and political office. The political structure prevailing in Pajapan was never so homogeneous as to leave no room for rivalries between different interest groups vying for power. The ruling order was affected by intra- and inter-class battles over state-regulated access to office and land – conflicts between mestizo and Indian ranchers and between Indian ranchers themselves. Finally, authorities had to contend with manifestations of opposition from agrarian reformers organized into civil committees.

Struggles were fought on all fronts: paramilitary but also legal, administrative and electoral. The latter battles suggest that the Mexican laws in matters of land and government are not infinitely manipulable. Although serving the dominant economic interests, they impose real constraints on the land tenure system, the distribution of authority and the operations of government. Peasants struggling against the concentration of land in the hands of ranchers persistently denounced the status quo and promoted the *ejido* system through procedures (committee petitions, requests, formal protests) instituted by the federal state. By and large, subordinate groups exploited two major cracks in the ruling order: the tension between Indian and federal authorities and the competition for land between ranchers. They defended themselves through initiatives of the Agrarian Ejido Committee and the Communal Land Committee and through formal appeals to the federal land agency, the State Governor and the President of Mexico. Without support from the PRI machine and state officials, however, politically active peasants and *ejido* reformers failed to take control of the local government and the administration of land. By the late 1960s they had not been able to stop Indian cattle-raisers from gaining access to all the land they needed to expand their ranches. Nevertheless, peasants gained some legal control over the land (converted into *tierras comunales*) and a voice in the government process as well.

The early 1950s saw the first expression of divisions emerging within the PRI rancher class in Pajapan. Salinas Mendoza and the Municipal President W. Martínez were popular with the majority of ranchers but peasant resentment over the land tax cost them the municipal elections of 1952. The winner was Juan Martínez, a wealthy Indian rancher who gained peasant support by criticizing the previous municipal government for not supporting the Agrarian Ejido Committee and for taxing land and imposing collective work (*faena*) on the villagers. During his term, the Agrarian Ejido Committee (headed by Rosalino Lara from 1952 to 1962) became a political tool in the struggle between competing groups of Indian ranchers for the support of the majority peasant population. The objective of Juan Martínez was to promote an alternative resolution of the land tenure conflict favorable to a few select ranchers. Archival data and interviews with Martínez confirm that he and a few other Indian ranchers wanted to create an *ejido* on the poorer lands near the volcano and establish private properties on the fertile lowland below the village. In a complete reversal of the ecological facts, Martínez claimed that the lowland "is not good for maize. Let us work this land with cattle. For pasture, the land is fertile, for maize it is not."[27] This approach to the land tenure question was also being promoted by Guillermo Caballero, the powerful mestizo rancher from Coatzacoalcos. Caballero owned land bordering the communal land of Pajapan and in the absence of clear survey lines could claim some of Pajapan's land as his own. As a member of the State Electoral Committee of the PRI, he arranged for Juan Martínez to take the position of PRI candidate, accompanying him on the day of the municipal elections. Juan Martínez informed us that shortly after he was elected, Caballero told him, "I put you in as municipal president to keep the community calm. If the community complains to me, I will punish you."[28]

The position of Juan Martínez regarding land tenure was denounced by some Indian ranchers who knew they would not benefit from the creation of private properties controlled by a few individuals. In a masterful use of communal rhetoric, the Communal Land Committee dominated by the land-hungry Indian ranchers wrote to the State Governor that "Mr. Juan A. Martínez, a big rancher, and his relatives are trying to mislead the State administration by affirming that these lands are private properties. Mr. Governor, in this community *nobody is land-owner*, there is no private property available for the creation of an *ejido*."[29]

The concerns of the Communal Land Committee were confirmed when an associate of Caballero and owner of the ranch El Moral located on the lower border of Pajapan claimed 164 hectares of land traditionally considered to be part of the communal lands of Pajapan. Other conflicts over the boundaries of the communal land also arose when DAAC gave orders for the establishment of an *ejido* in Tatahuicapan, a neighboring Nahua community. Pajapeños feared they could lose some of their land to Tatahuicapan or El Moral if they did not clarify and confirm their land rights.

Outside threats and internal struggles over land incited ranchers favoring the communal system to regain complete control of local political institutions including the local office of the PRI, the municipal government, the Communal Land Committee and the lot administration. An Indian rancher from San Juan Volador was selected as the PRI candidate for the municipal presidency, a decision which in the absence of any organized opposition guaranteed his election to office in 1955. Salinas Mendoza was once again appointed municipal secretary and the lot administration was used to reactivate the request for communal land tenure status.[30] In 1956 a Mexico City lawyer working in close association with the CNC (National Peasant Confederation) was hired to represent the Communal Land Committee and promote the request with DAAC, the federal government land authority.[31]

The actions of the ranchers met with a rapid response from national authorities. In January of 1957 the DAAC sent an engineer to complete the technical work needed to recognize communal title. He was followed later by two other engineers who confirmed his findings that the communal land included 19,158 hectares with no border disputes with neighboring *ejidos* (Tatahuicapan and Minzapan). He also concluded that there was no private property within the boundaries of the communal land. A census identified 1,222 heads of household. He made no mention, however, of the numerous disputes between peasants and ranchers over land or the formal complaints of land invasion that flooded the offices of DAAC and the office of the Mexican President throughout the 1950s.

The deepening conflict between land-hungry Indian ranchers who were expanding their landholdings and peasants displaced from the land resulted in the reorganization of the Agrarian Ejido Committee in Pajapan and the formation of a similar committee in San Juan Volador. While the committee had been controlled in previous years by Juan Martínez, the new committees were controlled by peasants with more forceful demands. In Pajapan they totalled some 150 heads of households and in San Juan Volador another 25. In separate letters, these two committees denounced the municipal authorities for evicting peasants from their lands, allowing mestizo ranchers from Coatzacoalcos to use community lands, illegally appointing the lot administrators and threatening peasants with fines, jail and death. They also requested that an *ejido* be established in the community on Lots 1, 2, and 3, the best lands in Pajapan.[32]

At that time, applications for communal and *ejido* status were handled by different branches of the DAAC and for each, a separate set of surveys and census data were needed to process the request. Data had already been collected for the area by the office of communal requests. The agrarian authorities responsible for *ejido* requests responded to the petitions of the agrarian committees of Pajapan and San Juan Volador by sending an engineer of their own in 1958 to conduct a census of Pajapan and survey the land. This was followed in 1960 by a survey of San Juan Volador that was never completed as Indian ranchers supported by the municipal government confiscated the technician's equipment. Other actions taken by Indian ranchers against the *ejido* request included letters from the lot administrators and the Communal Land Committee to the state governor, important politicians in Coatzacoalcos, the Agrarian League, and the Revolutionary Federation of Workers and Peasants (CROC) denouncing the actions of the Agrarian Ejido Committee. These letters claimed that all the land in Pajapan was communal and that no private property was available for an *ejido*. The Mexico City lawyer representing the Communal Land Committee and the regional representative of the CROC also wrote letters to the governor calling for rejection of the *ejido* request in favor of the communal land proposal. These groups and individuals made frequent references to the communal traditions of Pajapan including land tenure and collective labor for community projects.[33]

Ranchers had no interest in resolving the land tenure question but rather in prolonging the ambiguity of land rights. The municipal authorities did little to pressure state authorities to settle the dispute between the Agrarian Ejido Committee and the Communal Land Committee. Indian ranchers feared that marking the boundaries of the communal land would make it difficult for them to continue the lucrative practice of renting land to outside mestizo ranchers with land bordering on the communal area. Thus the regional *cacique* González Caballero had acquired the disputed area claimed by the ranch El Moral and was using up to 500 hectares of Pajapan's best land to graze his cattle. This was sanctioned by the municipal authorities under Salinas who received payment in the form of "taxes". Caballero also purchased cattle raised on the pastures of Pajapan through his *dedo* ("finger") Enrique Domínguez, a native of Pajapan residing in Coatzacoalcos.[34] Another reason why Indian ranchers wanted to delay the resolution of the tenure conflict was that they controlled *de facto* use of most of the communal land. An investigation into the distribution of land and the number of peasants with land rights would have revealed the high concentration of land ownership, providing peasants with a basis for demanding land reform. The absence of clearly recognized rights to the land was used by ranchers to discredit peasant claims and assert their own, often through the use of force with the full support of the municipal authorities.

Since the rancher-dominated municipal government was not committed to the communal position, a split resulted between them and the Communal Land Committee. Indian ranchers could no longer control the committee they had launched against the *ejido* request. Support for a communal land tenure system developed among peasants who opposed threats to the land base posed by Caballero and other mestizo ranchers. The committee was also supported by peasants with small parcels of land who wanted their *comunero* rights formally recognized so that they could protect their land from the expansionist tendencies of ranchers. Protests to the President of Mexico were launched against the municipal authorities for supporting land invasions in Pajapan and the Director General of the Communal Lands branch of DAAC for subverting and delaying the procedures for recognition of the communal lands. Between 1965 and 1968 three trips were made by the Communal Land Committee to Mexico City to promote their cause.[35] The Regional Agrarian Committee wrote several letters to DAAC in support of the communal request as did the Mexico City lawyer employed by the committee. The lawyer argued that the Director General of Communal Lands was unduly influenced by Indian and mestizo ranchers opposed to the resolution of Pajapan's land tenure struggle.

A turning point in these struggles occurred in 1965 when the state Land Commission once again sent an engineer to undertake an *ejido* census and survey. The engineer was met with massive opposition in Pajapan and a general village assembly was convened to decide the fate of the *ejido* plan. Indian ranchers overwhelmingly opposed the *ejido* as did peasants working as *peones* for the ranchers and a growing number of peasants who supported the communal land request. During the assembly, the *ejido* request was struck down and several decades of struggle between promoters of the two land tenure systems ended.

In 1967 a peasant leader supportive of the communal land request was elected Municipal President. Shortly afterwards, Salinas was chased out of town by a large group of peasants who objected to local authorities renting lands to regional *caciques*; Salinas never returned to the community. The lot administration and Communal Land Committee adopted a more aggressive position toward land conflict and invasions by mestizo ranchers. This shift in local political orientation forced the DAAC to proceed with the communal land petition.

The struggle over land tenure initiated by peasants in the 1930s and commandeered by ranchers since the 1940s culminated in March 1968 with official recognition of Pajapan's communal property and status as an agrarian community. After years of procedures and delays, President Díaz Ordaz signed a Presidential Resolution which recognized the rights of the community of Pajapan to the 19,158 hectares of land included in the primordial titles and identified 905 household heads or *comuneros* with land rights. The list was based on a census that was conducted in the village in 1967 and that excluded women, migrants who had left the village, and all those who failed to sign up because misinformed; ranchers spread rumors that only those who were actually farming the land were eligible and that registered *comuneros* would have to pay taxes (Vázquez García nd). The resolution called on the community to organize a General Assembly of *comuneros*, a Communal Land Commission and a Vigilance Council. These administrative bodies replaced the lot administration and the Communal Land Committee which had originally requested recognition of the communal land.

The Presidential Resolution coincided with a decision on the part of the Díaz Ordaz administration (1965–70) to hand out about 25 million hectares of mostly marginal, rain-fed land to Mexican agricultural workers. It reflected broader developments in Mexican land reform policies and represented an important gain for the peasants of Pajapan. And yet the struggle over land was by no means over. As we shall see, Indian ranchers could still put obstacles in the way of the communal administration and the effective implementation of agrarian laws. Nor were peasants about to stop fighting for individual rights over parcels of their own.

The growth of ranching activities forced peasants to establish smaller settlements in remote corners of the municipality. Most of these *rancherías* and *ejidos* were created between 1945 and 1975 by landless peasants from Pajapan, San Juan Volador, Minzapan and Coscapa. By the late 1960s, however, the cattle industry in Pajapan was still operating on a small scale and awaiting better market conditions to expand. Although modern utilities were being installed in the village (running water in 1966, electricity in 1970), the local economy was dominated by subsistence and petty commodity production. Few adults worked for wages; according to the 1950 census, fewer than 250 adults engaged in full-time wage work in agriculture. Herds of more than 100 head of cattle were rare and the total herd numbered less than 2,500.

In spite of the land reform promulgated in the Cárdenas era, the whole of southern Veracruz by 1950 had already become the property of a few wealthy ranchers: 4% of all landholders owned 79% of private property in land (Siemens 1964: 143). In Pajapan, however, it is only with the 1970s that the cattle population and the power vested in the rancher class expanded to the point of radically transforming the livelihood of the people of Pajapan.

Conclusion

Agrarian reformers fully committed to the *ejido* system never controlled municipal government after the 1930s. Yet the procedures advanced by the Agrarian Ejido Committee during more than three decades were not in vain. Their actions eventually forced municipal authorities traditionally committed to the lot system to counter the *ejido* movement with an alternative proposal: a formal request to the federal state for presidential recognition of Pajapan's communal land titles. The proposal met with the approval of many Indian ranchers and the municipal authorities who were vying with mestizo ranchers for control over communal lands. It was indicative of broader developments in the cattle industry as well: the tendency for Indian ranchers to specialize in the production of immature calves sold at cheap prices on a regional market controlled by mestizo cattle-brokers. Regional *caciques* could convert the Pajapan economy into a dependent branch of the cattle industry without ever expropriating Pajapan villagers (mostly Indian ranchers) of their land.

It should be emphasized that Indian and mestizo ranchers defended first the collective lot system and later the legal communal land regimen not because of a commitment to native values of a closed corporate community but rather as the most effective means of maintaining their *de facto* control over the local administration of land. This raises serious problems concerning the functions of the "closed corporate community", a concept originally developed by Wolf (1955; 1957; 1966: 86) to denote collective landholding communities characterized by "an enduring organization of rights and duties held by a stable membership" and equipped with various mechanisms designed to level differences between members. In her analysis of Indian communities in the Sierra of Puebla, Chamoux (1981: 370) observed that while the local economy was increasingly integrated into broader markets, political and symbolic practices continued to reflect basic corporate community features. Both Schryer (1990) and Chamoux have suggested, however, that the institutions and practices of corporate peasant communities are flexible and can be used by different social classes to promote their own interests (see also Stern 1983: 24). In light of contemporary works on Mesoamerica and Peru,[36] Wolf (1986) has finally reassessed his concept to emphasize the relationship between the process of internal differentiation and the manipulation of redistributive mechanisms such as the *cargo* system. Our own case-study is a contribution to this important literature.

In Pajapan, the communal regimen was made legal for reasons that had little to do with traditional land distribution practices or the preservation of native values. The election in 1967 of a peasant leader supportive of the communal land request and pressure exerted by official peasant organizations forced the federal land agency to proceed with the petition, a land survey and a census of local *comuneros*. A Presidential Resolution recognizing the land titles of Pajapan soon followed. The whole process resulted in the creation of a new political body with its own organization: the *comuneros* of Pajapan. From an illegal market commodity, land became not a collective use-value but rather a "state commodity" partly controlled by the administrative domain: a factor of production under the jurisdiction of a communal body created by the state and administered as a scarce resource, internally divisible and transferable under conditions specified by agrarian law.

This new communal group sanctioned by the state had no immediate impact on the internal use of land, save to exclude outsiders from claiming access to the land. The assembly of *comuneros* substituted for the lot administration was a legal voice in a government process and land tenure system otherwise ruled by official representatives and allies of the Indian PRI rancher class. This is to say that events of the 1960s did not hinder the full concentration of political and economic power in the hands of the few. As we are about to see, the 1970s witnessed a full-blown development of *caciquismo* in Pajapan. The Gulf Nahuas had to wait another dozen years or so for the legal body of *comuneros* to take possession of their land.

Notes

1. The same comment applies to the state derivation school. For Holloway and Picciotto (1978: 14), the economy–polity division is duly recognized, but their objective is still to "derive the state (or the separation of economics and politics) from the category of capital". Thus the question is "why bourgeois society, the reproduction of which is apparently regulated in the apparently material (economic) mediation of the law of value, requires an external relationship between politics and economics" (Blanke et al. 1978: 121; see also Hirsch 1978; Clarke 1991: 9–16). On neo-Marxist approaches to state theory, see Hindess (1983: 40) and E.P. Thompson (1978: 48).

2. See Cohen (1983: 103); Poulantzas (1978); Laclau (1977: 27); Habermas (1987: 338); Skocpol and Trimberger (1978: 127–8).

3. Although simple enough, the argument presupposes that we move beyond analyses of the state and government officials viewed as "weighty actors" affecting "political and social processes through their policies and their patterned relationships with social groups" (Skocpol 1985: 3). The government process cannot be reduced to a special class of state officials intervening in a civil society otherwise governed by capital and wage-labor relations. The latter approach reflects one common acceptation of the term state, defined as the sphere of highest governmental authority and administration (so Mann 1986: 112). Its weakness lies in its monolithic view of the body politic, in its failure to address the complex divisions and relations that lie between and within nation-states – between geopolitical formations, the elected and the electorate, officials and citizens, organized parties and the government, branches of bureaucracy and spheres of authority.

4. To say that the state plays a key role in securing the reproduction of capital (Holloway 1991: 241; Clarke 1991) is not to say that state and capital must take predetermined forms and that the issue of capitalist reproduction is unproblematic. The notion that some correspondence is bound to exist between economic and political domains makes sense only as a question mark that must be answered through a close analysis of the historical conditions and limitations affecting the interaction of money and authority, economy and polity. As argued by Jessop (1990: 19–21, 221–3) and Harrison and Mort (1980: 108), the correspondence that

may exist between economic and political institutions is the subject matter of history, not of deductive logic or grand metatheory.

5. In the words of Fowley (1991: 237), "the explanation of conflict must be context-specific, and if this demand entails attention to large-scale economic and political tendencies, it also requires that analysis look ever more closely at the evolution of conflict and the process of mobilization 'on the ground'." See also Stern (1987), Orlove et al. (1989).

6. Depending on the context, the term capitalism can refer to either the system as a whole or to one part of the system only, i.e., owners of capital seeking profits. Likewise, the notions of state and civil society lend themselves to maximal and minimal definitions. When viewed "macroscopically", both concepts refer to a body of citizens and their overall mode of government. When used more narrowly, however, the two terms apply to opposite parts of the body politic: holders of state power and citizens under their rule, respectively.

7. Civil society should not be treated as an amorphous lifeworld, a conceptual glory-hole that accommodates an undetermined and pluralistic sphere outside of politics and economics. The concept of civil society is of little use when equated with all social relations and struggles not strictly determined by capital or state, whether they be based on gender, sexual orientation, race, ethnicity, religion, generation or nationality (Cohen (1983); Urry (1981); Pierson (1984: 569); Harrison and Mort (1980)). Although they affect all aspects of social life, the legal regulations of civil society are but one field of domination, a domain founded on relations between citizen and government, divisions between jurisdictions, spheres of authority and branches of bureaucracy, categories of citizens and non-citizens. Civil society is an "institutionally specific complex of organizations and agents, discourses and practices" (Hirst (1980: 62); see also 1985), a system that creates discursive and socio-political divisions and that produces conflicts and competing claims over material resources under private or public control.

8. For an overview of the recent history and achievements of regional and national peasant organizations in Mexico, see A. Bartra et al. (1991).

9. See Barry (1987); Brockett (1988); Eckstein (1989); Díaz (1986); Flores Lúa et al. (1988); Gordillo de Anda (1988); Greenberg (1989); Pearce (1986); and Rubio 1987.

10. Agrarian laws of the federal government have been the site of constant conflicts between the powerful and the powerless. The legal system served neither as the revolutionary handmaiden of a classless society nor as a simple instrument of land concentration in the countryside. More accurately, legal dispositions pertaining to land have resulted in the promotion of collective land tenure systems (of colonial inspiration) combined with an even more effective deployment of counterreform legislation allowing for the formation of large private agricultural properties in all parts of Mexico. Our account of conflicts in Pajapan is reconstructed against the background of such contradictions and complexities in Mexican agrarian legislation and actions channelled through the state.

11. See Scott (1976, 1985); Popkins (1979); Bates (1978); Schryer (1990: 44–5). For a critique of the moral economy school, see Evans (1986).

12. See Mallon (1983); Mitchell (1991); Sandstrom (1991); Sheridan (1988); and Tutino (1986).

13. Interview with Pascacio Silvestre, Pajapan, May 18, 1990.

14. The Veracruz Peasant League was at the head of a radical peasant movement that swept Veracruz during the 1920s and 1930s (Salamini 1971; Domínguez Pérez et al. 1992). Juan Porfirio, a leader of the new Agrarian Ejido Committee in Pajapan, was a member of the Agrarian League of Minatitlán and the Mexican Communist Party. ACAM, Expediente No. 1860, Pajapan.

15. ACAM, Expediente No. 1860.

16. AGN, Rama Presidentes, Rodríguez, 515.5/25–93.

17. Interview with Pascual Hernández Antonio, elder of Pajapan, June 2, 1990.

18. Interviews with Pascacio Silvestre and Andrés Martínez, May 12, 22, 1990.

19. Interview with Simón Antonio, February 1, 1988.

20. Interview with Pascacio Silvestre, May 12, 1990.

21. Interview with Simón Antonio, February 1, 1988.

22. The lot administrators in 1951 were Juan Silva (lot 1), Juan Porfirio (lot 2), Primo Martínez (lot 3), Ernesto Montiel (lot 4) and Martiano Martínez (lot 5).

23. ACAM, Expediente No. 1860. Letter, 1952. Alvaro Ciriaco acted as president of the Agrarian Ejido Committee from 1947 to 1952.

24. ASRAM, Letters of July 2, 1951, and February 28, 1952.

25. ACAM, Expediente No. 1860.

26. Sheridan (1988: 83–103) makes similar comments with respect to cattle ranching operations in a village of northwestern Mexico.

27. Interview with Juan A. Martínez Jáuregui, September 29, 1987. ACAM, Expediente No. 1860. See also Nahmad (1984).

28. Interview with Juan A. Martíncz Jáuregui, September 29, 1987.

29. ASRAM, Letter, October 18, 1958 (their emphases).

30. ASRAM, Letter, April 23, 1956. On the 8th of June and the 23rd of July, 1956, the authenticity and validity of Pajapan's *Títulos Primordiales* were confirmed by DAAC officials. ASRAM, Dictámen Positivo, November 28, 1967.

31. AGN, Rama Presidentes, Cortínez, 404.1/471. Letter, 1958.

32. ASRAM, Letter, September 2, 1957.

33. See ASRAM, Letters of September 30, 1966, from CROC; May 10 and June 15, 1967, from the Agrarian League of Veracruz; August 16, 1967, from the National Peasant Confederation.

34. Archives of the Local Rancher Association, and Interview with Simón Antonio, February 1, 1988.

35. Interview with Santos Martínez, May 20, 1990.

36. See Cancian (1965); Taylor (1972); McLeod (1972); Murra (1975); Dow (1977); Greenberg (1981); Carmack (1981); J.M. Chevalier (1982); Stern (1982); Mallon (1983); Wasserstrom (1983); Spores (1984); Farris (1984); and Spalding (1984).

CHAPTER 3

OIL AND CATTLE POLITICS

Coauthored with Dominique Caouette

In this chapter we examine major shifts in recent Gulf Nahua politics and economics, using the general concepts introduced in the preceding chapter and applied to the formative years of PRI rancher *caciquismo* in Pajapan. Politics shifted from a centralized power system to weaker forms of local domination – from Indian *cacique* rule in the 1970s to the ethnopopular front of the early 1980s and the outburst of factional conflicts in subsequent years. Each period of local politics is situated against wider trends affecting the region of southern Veracruz and the whole of Mexico. The chapter ends with a brief discussion of broader anthropological contributions to our understanding of *caciquismo*, ethno-populism and factionalism in Latin America.

PRI rancher *caciquismo* and the struggle for land

During the 1970s, class inequalities between wealthier landholders, peasants cultivating marginal lands and the landless in general were on the increase throughout Mexico (Hansen 1973: 391). Although aimed at containing rural discontent, the neopopulist politics of President Luis Echeverría favored the active mobilization of peasants struggling for access to land: in 1973, 600 land invasions were reported in three states alone. Peasants demanded control over natural resources, the settlement of long-standing land rights, the democratization of municipal political institutions and the establishment of regional fronts and national organizations independent of the ruling PRI party. These struggles rapidly produced a division between official and independent peasant organizations, a split that introduced important cleavages within the peasantry and undermined the credibility and hegemony of PRI corporatist institutions in the Mexican countryside (Paré 1990: 83–5). Similar trends could be observed at broader levels of Mexican society. The social turmoil that hit the country in 1968 signalled broad-based discontent *vis-à-vis* major national institutions and a loss of elite self-confidence that may have heralded the end of Mexico's modern history (Michaels and Bernstein 1973: 710). Factors that contributed to Mexico's political legitimacy crisis include a growing middle class with limited mobility and a wealthy upper class increasingly out of touch with the social and economic realities of Mexican society. Although important transformations marked the 1970s, discontent was contained by effects of economic growth and adjustments to a PRI regime showing resilience.

While the national and state level oil industry boomed throughout the 1970s, agriculture in the north of Mexico continued with its green revolution based on improved seeds, irrigation, chemical inputs and modern machinery. In other parts of the country, however, the agricultural sector stagnated and rural discontent mounted. From 1963 to 1972 the market witnessed a loss of about 25% in the value of maize. By the early 1970s the total area dedicated to corn cultivation had fallen by one million hectares. Total production failed to keep up with population growth and the country as a whole lost self-sufficiency in maize production. This trend continued throughout the 1970s and the 1980s (Barkin and Suárez 1985; Sanderson 1986). The growth of the cattle industry was largely responsible for these losses in corn production. In the state of Veracruz the area under pasture grew from 1.6 million hectares in 1940 to as much as 3.4 million hectares in 1985, representing about 41.5% of the state. The number of hectares dedicated to corn and beans was reduced by 50% and 80% (respectively) over the last two decades. The Santa Marta highlands were no exception to the rule: corn production (measured in hectares) fell by 36% over the 1970s. The corresponding figure for municipal Pajapan is 63% (from 3,850 to 1,415 ha.).[1]

The cattle industry in Pajapan grew rapidly in the 1970s in response to demand for meat in the urban areas of Mexico and a shortage of pasture in Veracruz. New linkages also facilitated the integration of the Gulf Nahua economy into wider markets. In 1976 a dirt road suitable for vehicles was constructed from Tatahuicapan to Pajapan and the lowland Laguna del Ostión. The Sotavento Bus Company started operating locally two years later.

The growth of herds and pressure to occupy more land in Pajapan made it important for Indian ranchers to block the land reform movement and maintain control over local political institutions. Ranchers were successful at expanding their property in cattle and land, in spite of presidential recognition of Pajapan's status as an agrarian community with communal property. Much of the newly occupied territory was converted directly from forest into pasture. Our survey data indicate that by the late 1970s, 61% of all households had no land of their own. Small parcels of land were loaned by ranchers to peasants in exchange for labor or a portion of the crop and as a means of clearing land for the expansion of pastures. Meanwhile an estimated 3% of the population controlled half of the arable land.[2] They comprised some 40 families living in Pajapan and neighboring hamlets, with an average of 235 hectares each and a maximum property of 800 hectares. Of a total herd of 9,000 animals, 84% was owned by these 40 families with average herds of 190 head of cattle. Only 19% of all households owned cattle.[3] Statistics obtained from the local Rancher Association indicate that sales of local cattle (within or outside Pajapan, usually one animal sold at a time) went up from between 500 to 1,000 per year in the 1960s to 1,612 in 1971 and about 3,408 in 1978.

These developments brought about important transformations in Gulf Nahua society. On the economic level, the expansion and concentration of capital in land and the cattle industry, not a labor-intensive sector of the regional economy, resulted in the rise of a wealthier and more powerful class of Indian ranchers, a marked decline in subsistence production, and the outmigration and proletarianization of landless peasants seeking non-skilled jobs (mostly construction and petty trade) in Coatzacoalcos and Minatitlán. On the political level, the power exercised by PRI ranchers reached full hegemonic proportions. To use the language introduced in the preceding chapter, conversions of property and authority continued to function in basically the same way: access to political office and influence was converted into the possession of land and the expansion of wealth in cattle (and vice-versa). The power marshalled by the rancher-dominated authorities enabled the dominant group to prevent the legal landholders of Pajapan from converting their newly-gained status of *comuneros* into effective property. Power-holders maintained their positions of authority through clientelistic practices, legitimating their power through measures of co-optation. They took advantage of the increasing dependence of peons *vis-à-vis* their local employers and of all villagers *vis-à-vis* PRI government officials; PRI votes were traded for villagers' access to jobs, land and public services. PRI ranchers also made the most of geopolitical divisions emerging between members of the same class: between *comuneros* and non-*comuneros*, rural workers and urban (unionized) wage-earners.

Despite this, rivalries between Indian ranchers competing for land and peasant electoral support and between the oil industry and ranchers vying for a cheap labor force made it difficult for the rancher class to act as a unified and unopposed bloc controlling the local political apparatus. The hegemony of the PRI rancher class was also countered by the emergence of alternative political parties and the direct involvement of the Communal Assembly and the Communal Land Commission in local land politics. Finally, the decade witnessed the proliferation of geopolitical divisions and conflicts over issues of wages, land and office (village vs hamlets, *comuneros* vs Pajapeños without land rights, local ranchers vs state-owned urban industry, rural workers vs urban unions). As we shall see, these tendencies laid the ground for even more profound transformations in the early 1980s.

Struggles of the 1970s revolved round the organization of political opposition outside the PRI and the effective implementation of the communal land tenure system in Pajapan. The powerless and the landless fought to gain access to land and office through physical occupation, electoral opposition, representations of the Communal Assembly and the Communal Land Commission and alliances with progressive Indian ranchers and authorities at the municipal or national level. These actions, however, resulted in few gains. Power-holders successfully countered these subversive movements by using political influence and by taking advantage of divisions within subordinate groups and their dependence *vis-à-vis* their employers and the PRI government. By and large, they kept control over all local offices, including the municipal presidency and the Communal Land Commission, using them as instruments of communal representation and political legitimation. In short, the material presented below shows how the rapid expansion of local cattle ranching operations was made possible by the dominance of rancher interests in the sphere of government.[4]

Elections of 1970 and the Enrique Cruz movement

The formal recognition of Pajapan's communal land titles diffused peasant mobilization around the land issue. As one prominent rancher noted, "the people quietened down a lot after the Presidential Resolution."[5] Peasants felt that the formation of an agrarian community and granting of communal titles would be followed by real changes in land use, changes implemented by DAAC. Although Indian ranchers could not stop the legal redefinition of Pajapan's land tenure system, they used this lull in peasant political activity to delay state intervention in land distribution and continue controlling *de facto* access to land.

Although the political power of ranchers had been weakened in 1967 by the election of peasant leaders to positions of local authority, ranchers continued to dominate the local PRI committee, the local Rancher Association, and the office of municipal secretary.[6] Indian ranchers also counted on the political support of mestizo ranchers and political organizations including the regional office of the SRA in Chinameca, the state delegate of the SRA in Xalapa, the regional office of the PRI, the state ranching division, and the regional union of ranchers. As informants noted, "the *caciques* had contacts in the SRA offices of Acayucan, Chinameca and Coatzacoalcos. They had access to privileged information."[7]

When elections were called in 1970 to form the Communal Land Commission, the Vigilance Council and a new municipal government, ranchers were once again able to diffuse peasant demands and gain the support of enough peasants and dayworkers to win the election. As shown in Table 3.1, ranchers occupied all of the important positions within the newly-formed Communal Land Commission, the municipal government and the local PRI committee. Many of them had held positions within the previous administration and simply transferred from one office to another. Thus P. Silvestre Martínez, the Municipal President from 1964 to 1967, became the Communal Land Commission's treasurer in 1970. The president of the PRI committee, a literate man and son of Juan Grande (Municipal President, 1952–55), was the former secretary of the Rancher Association and the municipal government elected in 1967.

The transfer of power to the new authorities did not go without resistance. Enrique Cruz Antonio, a former member of the Agrarian Ejido Committee, began to organize the peasant struggle for land. According to the peasant leader, there was in 1970,

Table 3.1 Individuals in political positions, 1970

		Prior positions	
Communal Land Commission			
President	J. Martínez Alvarez	–	Small rancher
Secretary	A. Osorio Hernández	–	Small rancher
Treasurer	P. Silvestre Martínez	Municipal President 1964–67	Large rancher
Vigilance Council			
President	N. Antonio Antonio	Municipal President 1961–63 PRI President 1967–70	Large rancher
Secretary	W. Morales Hernández	Communal Land Committee	Large rancher
Treasurer	–	–	–
Municipal Government			
President	R. González Cruz	–	Large rancher
Substitute	J. Martínez Encarnación	Syndic 1949–52	Small rancher
Syndic	P. Martínez C.	–	Large rancher
Substitute	A. Cruz Salas	Lot Treasurer No. 5	–
Alderman	M. Hernández R.	–	–
Substitute	G. Lorenzo de Silvestre	–	Large rancher
PRI Committee			
President	S. Martínez Alemán	Municipal Secretary 1968–70	Large rancher

Note: A dash (–) indicates missing information. The "small rancher" category refers to individuals with fewer than 50 head of cattle. The "large rancher" category refers to individuals with more than 50 head of cattle.
Sources: Interviews with Juan A. Martínez Jáuregui, Esteban Martínez Bautista, Sergio Martínez Alemán and Nicanor Trujillo, Pajapan, September 14, 17 and 23, and October 1, 1987; Antonio Hernández, 1979; ASRAX, "Informe sobre la comunidad Pajapan (antecedentes)," July 7, 1976; Bouysse-Cassagne 1980; Gaceta Oficial, Vol. CIX, No. 139, November 19, 1973; Chevalier and Buckles, Genealogical Field Notes, 1986.

Table 3.2 Individuals in political positions, 1973

		Prior positions	
Communal Land Commission			
President	S. Vargas Lorenzo	–	Large rancher
Secretary	R. Hernández Martínez	–	Large rancher
Treasurer	P. Antonio Antonio	–	Small rancher
Vigilance Council			
President	S. Antonio Hernández	Syndic	Large rancher
Secretary	D. Villanueva de la Torre	–	–
Member	A. Martínez Martínez	–	–
Municipal Government			
President	A. Hernández Martínez	Comm. Land Commission Pres. 1970–73	Large rancher
Substitute	J. Martínez Álvarez	–	Small rancher
Syndic	S. Martínez Morales	Vigilance Council	Large rancher
Substitute	S. Antonio Hernández	–	Large rancher
Alderman	A. Hernández Martínez	–	Small rancher
Substitute	S. Hernández Martínez	–	Small rancher
PRI Committee			
President	R. Martínez Nepumoceno	–	Large rancher

Note: A dash (–) indicates missing information.
Sources: As Table 3.1.

a group of 520 peasants who did not have any land. We went to
Mexico to ask the SRA to send an engineer to divide the land into
two parts; one part for the peasants, another part for the ranchers.
When the engineer arrived, the communal land president accused
me of improperly acting on his behalf and put me in jail. The
ranchers let the engineer work in the upper part of the communal
land but when he reached the lagoon, the problems started. Then
they paid him and he left Pajapan.[8]

The same informant commented that the peasants were neither able nor
willing to pay for the services of engineers in Pajapan.[9] Another peasant
noted that "the ranchers took the engineer to Modesto Pérez's bar in
Coatzacoalcos. He never came back to Pajapan. He even left his equipment here!"[10]

Peasant requests for state intervention in land distribution, combined
with indications that the SRA would respond to the demands, once
again forced ranchers to take the offensive. In a letter to the state delegate
of the SRA, the rancher-dominated Communal Land Commission denounced the peasant leader who had initiated the request for usurping
the official functions of the commission.[11] Shortly afterward they initiated
a petition of their own against a local rancher, the father of the local
PRI president. The commission claimed that Don Guadalupe, a wealthy
Indian rancher who had fought earlier for the recognition of communal
titles,[12] was controlling 232 hectares of land within the communal land
area and was demanding private title to this land. They announced that
the General Assembly had rejected the rancher's claim and redistributed
his land among landless *comuneros*. In fact, no such redistribution occurred and while the actions of the commission were partly directed at
controlling the expansion of this rancher they were also intended to give
the SRA in Mexico City the impression that the commission was acting
on behalf of the majority of the *comuneros*, in conformity with the legal
responsibilities assigned to communal land representatives.[13] The rhetoric
of communal traditions was used by some ranchers against others to
legitimize their own political power.[14]

The Acayucan Regional Peasant Committee of the CNC, the national
peasant council, supported the petition of peasants for implementation
of the Presidential Resolution and for a survey of communal land
boundaries. They met with local peasant leaders and brought the case to
the attention of the general secretary of the CNC who in turn requested
support from the national office of the SRA. Over a period of several
years, the SRA in Mexico City ordered the state delegate (regional
representative of the SRA) to intervene in the distribution of communal
land at least five times. The state delegate claimed that they lacked the
personnel needed to implement the order and nothing was done; local
peasants argued that he was pressured by ranchers through the Southern
Veracruz Rancher Association into not acting.[15]

By the time elections were organized for land and municipal authorities
in 1973, no action had been taken in response to pressure exerted by the
national office of the SRA. Ranchers dominated again the slate of PRI

candidates and formed a new commission and municipal government. For another three years, the land distribution problem remained unaddressed.[16] Table 3.2 shows the strong control ranchers exercised over local authorities and how some members of the 1970 administration continued to occupy political offices in 1973.

Land invasion by a mestizo rancher

In 1976, when some of the communal lowlands were invaded by an outside mestizo rancher, Pajapeños once again rallied to demand a *comunero* census update and land redistribution.[17] Pedro Florentino, a large rancher from Coatzacoalcos, was denounced by the Communal Land Commission for occupying a tract of communal land near the Laguna del Ostión. The CNC was informed of the invasion as was the director general of Inspection and Complaints of the SRA in Mexico City.[18] Peasants in Pajapan took matters into their own hands by planting corn on the disputed land. The *columna volante* of Coatzacoalcos was called in by the rancher and two peasants were arrested. Before they could be removed from the area a large band of peasants armed with machetes and wooden sticks attacked the police. One Pajapeño reported that "the *columna volante* first shot in the air but then they started shooting people."[19] The confrontation ended tragically with three peasants killed and three others wounded.

The peasants involved in this action continued to occupy the disputed land and built a corral to keep 113 head of cattle taken from Florentino's ranch. It took almost two years of negotiations before an agreement was reached in which Florentino paid a small amount of money to the widows and the wounded in exchange for his cattle. The incident was significant for the long-term struggle for land in that it galvanized the resistance of peasants and provided a catalyst for peasant action on a number of fronts.[20]

Peasant resistance to land invasions once again forced Indian ranchers controlling the local land and municipal authorities to take an aggressive pro-peasant position if only to maintain a degree of legitimacy with the local population and outside authorities. The most active of these rancher leaders was Sixto Vargas, the Communal Land Commission president. He supported peasant demands for a census update required to transfer the rights of *comuneros* who had died or were living outside Pajapan to the landless. Although he was a rancher, he supported the peasant position against mestizo ranchers in the hopes of maintaining political power and influencing the outcome of peasant demands.

In response to the peasant demands and their uprising against the land invasion, the SRA conducted a thorough investigation of land issues in Pajapan. In 1976, the SRA confirmed and formalized the communal land boundaries while also providing title to the communal property. Officials conducted a census update and submitted a report indicating that most of the communal land of Pajapan was under the control of some 33 families with properties ranging between 80 and 1,300 hectares each.[21] The federal land agents organized a General Assembly of *comuneros* at which it was resolved that a parcel of land would be given to each registered *comunero*. These were the most significant steps taken toward the redistribution of land since inequalities in land use had developed in the community in the 1940s.[22]

While the actions of the SRA seemed definitive, Indian ranchers were once again able to block all of them (except the resolution of communal land boundaries) by lobbying the SRA and the CNC in Mexico City and Xalapa, the state capital. In addition to letters and meetings with officials from these agencies, 30 ranchers went to Xalapa to testify before the governor that there were no land problems in Pajapan and that no census update was required. A letter to the President of Mexico signed by 203 *comuneros*, including Indian ranchers and their day laborers, denounced the investigation conducted by the SRA and the Communal Land Commission president in Pajapan, Sixto Vargas. Ranchers accused Vargas of occupying his office for more than the legal period of three years and of not paying land taxes to the municipal treasurer and the State Revenue Office (*Hacienda del Estado*). Finally, they claimed that the majority of the *comuneros* did not want to parcel the *tierras comunales* or to change the current distribution of land in the community.[23]

Ranchers also pressured Sixto Vargas into withdrawing his support for the census update and land redistribution. As one Indian rancher candidly acknowledged:

> We felt that a land redistribution was coming, we knew we were wrong but we decided to fight until the end. It was going to be the last fight. To stop the census we had to pressure the Communal Land Commission president, Sixto Vargas, into supporting our position and calming the people. ... Since he was supporting the small peasants and landless workers we had to bring him on to our side. We threatened him so that he would start supporting us. We also had a lot of support from the Southern Veracruz Ranchers Union and the Veracruz State Ranching Division. We had contacts all over. ... We went and talked to the *comuneros* to calm them. We were able to calm the *comuneros* for a year. However, I believed that the situation would not last much longer. I felt that the 905 *comuneros* had to be able to use the land also.[24]

Sixto Vargas himself noted that under considerable pressure from ranchers opposed to the census update, "I decided to stop fighting and I said, it is better not to do anything."[25] As a result of the protests of Indian ranchers, the SRA disallowed the census update and took no further action to redistribute land. Once again, the politically well-connected Indian ranchers were able to thwart peasant demands and delay an equitable solution to local land problems.

The emergence of alternative political parties

Municipal politics in Pajapan were dominated by the PRI from the 1920s onward. PRI candidates were selected by the rancher-led local PRI office and election to power was assured by the absence of a local alternative and by a well-funded campaign replete with food, drink and radical rhetoric. When municipal elections were organized in 1976, Indian ranchers once again proposed their own slate of PRI candidates and, while they won the presidency and other major positions, an opposition candidate received enough votes to win the position of alderman. Pascual Pablo Martínez ran for office with the support of a recently established chapter of the Partido Popular Socialista (PPS), a national party with a regional office in Coatzacoalcos.[26] Table 3.3 indicates the results of the municipal elections of 1976 and the movement of peasants into positions of political power. Ranchers nevertheless held the main offices and continued the practice of transferring from one position in the previous administration to another in the new administration.

Although elections for municipal authorities were held at the end of a three-year term as required by law,[27] the Communal Land Commission led by Sixto Vargas did not call elections for a new commission and Vigilance Council when they were due. In protest, the Partido Auténtico de la Revolución Mexicana (PARM), an opposition party founded in 1952 by retired army generals alienated from the PRI, began pressuring SRA's regional and national delegates for a change in the local land authorities. PARM denounced Sixto Vargas for remaining in office beyond the period of his mandate and for defrauding *comuneros* of $1.6 million pesos in taxes owed to the Federal Revenue Office in Coatzacoalcos. They also organized a peasant defense committee to denounce a Pajapan rancher for invading the land of peasants. In a letter to the state delegate of the SRA, the defense committee claimed that "a land invader from Pajapan forced six peasants off three hectares of cultivated land. The regional agrarian office headed by Mr. Carrioza has not paid any attention to our demands. If justice is not done, there will be violence in Pajapan."[28] This action was part of a general plan to remove the commission president and to divide the land into individual parcels, in agreement with the resolution passed by the General Assembly of *comuneros* in 1976.[29]

After almost three years of protest by the PARM to the regional and national offices of the CNC and several attempts to organize a General Assembly, elections for the Communal Land Commission were finally held in Pajapan in 1979 by the SRA. The only party to present a panel of candidates was the PARM, which won the election by acclamation. Nevertheless, neither the previous commission nor the municipal authorities were willing to sign the election act and the election was eventually voided.[30] When new elections were organized several months later, the rancher-dominated PRI forwarded a panel of its own and won. According to one peasant, "on the day of the elections the *caciques* killed several bulls to get votes for the PRI. Since many people were hungry they supported the PRI candidate." Another indicated that ranchers pressured their dayworkers to vote for their candidate, a co-optative patron–client practice often observed in rural Mexico.[31]

Following the election of the Communal Land Commission, the leaders of the PPS and the PARM joined forces to denounce the

Table 3.3 Individuals in political positions, 1976

		Prior positions	
Communal Land Commission (same as in 1973)			
Vigilance Council (same as in 1973)			
Municipal Government			
President	E. Trujillo Antonio	–	Large rancher
Substitute	R. Hernández Martínez	Secr. Communal Land Commission	Large rancher
Syndic	E. Matías Martínez	–	Large rancher
Substitute	M. Pereyra Martínez	Agrarian Ejido Committee	Peasant
Alderman	P. Pablo Martínez	Leader Partido Popular Socialista	Peasant
Substitute	L. Palomino Patraca	–	–
PRI Committee			
President	S. Antonio Hernández	Vigilance Council	Large rancher

Note: A dash (–) indicates missing information.
Sources: As Table 3.1 and Gaceta Oficial, Vol. CXV, No. 143, November 27, 1976, p. 158.

Table 3.4 Individuals in political positions, 1979

		Prior Positions	
Communal Land Commission			
President	R. Hernández Martínez	Communal Land Commission	Large rancher
Secretary	G. Domínguez Hernández	–	Small rancher
Treasurer	C. Ciriaco Martínez	–	Large rancher
Vigilance Council			
President	P. Martínez Tino	–	–
Secretary	E. Cruz Reyes	–	–
Treasurer	W. Martínez Osorio	–	–
Municipal Government			
President	A. Hernández Martínez	–	Large rancher
Substitute	S. Martínez Alemán	Mun. Secretary/PRI President	Large rancher
Syndic	P. Martínez Vargas	–	Bilingual teacher
Substitute	S. Silvestre Morales	–	Large rancher
Alderman	S. Hernández Martínez	PPS/Substitute Alderman	Small rancher*
Substitute	A. Martínez Osorio	PPS	Large rancher*
PRI Committee			
President	E. Trujillo Artonio	Municipal President	Large rancher

Note: A dash (–) indicates missing information.
Sources: As Table 3.1, and Gaceta Oficial, Número Extraordinario, Vol. CXXI, No. 142, November 27, 1979, pp. 120–1.
*Alejo Martínez Osorio and Santos Hernández Martínez were among a small group of ranchers supporting the PPS.

monopolization of land in Pajapan by Indian ranchers and to request a redistribution of communal land. They sent a letter of protest to the President of Mexico signed by 151 *comuneros* (including some Indian ranchers) and 128 other villagers without land rights. They also took legal steps to protect Pajapan peasants from arrest and harassment by ranchers.[32]

Table 3.4 shows once again the dominance of Indian ranchers over political positions within the municipal government, the Communal Land Commission and the local PRI committee. Some of these ranchers had held positions of authority in the 1976 administration.

While inexperience and possibly fraud had cost them the previous elections, the PPS defeat in 1979 was partly due to a lack of political organization in the villages and hamlets outside Pajapan. According to a leader of the PPS:

> The PRI received the majority of the votes (1,000 vs 530) because only the villagers of Pajapan voted for the PPS while hamlets such as Chacalapa, Benito Juárez and Minzapan voted for the PRI. These hamlets were not aware of the struggles for land redistribution in Pajapan. Some of the hamlets are *ejidos* unconcerned with land redistribution, so they supported the PRI.[33]

Divisions between communal land villagers and those living in the rest of the municipality weakened the political position of peasants. The 1979 election, however, was probably influenced by a new external factor. During the election period, the Mexican government announced that it was going to expropriate part of the communal land to make way for the construction of an industrial port. According to one peasant leader, "the people felt that they should go with the PRI to protect their interests [against the industrial port]. As a result, the PPS lost the municipal election."[34]

In summation, the period following the Presidential Resolution (1968) and leading up to the expropriation of land for an industrial port (1980) was characterized by a constant and sometimes violent struggle between peasants and ranchers over access to communal land. Presidential recognition of communal property implied a potentially equitable distribution of land that was not forthcoming under the rule of the ranchers. Ranchers used their control over local political institutions and connections with regional and state-level organizations to avoid state intervention in land distribution and retain *de facto* control over the communal land. Although they mobilized under the banner of an opposition party to present their own slate of candidates for municipal and land administration offices, peasants were without sustained support from outside agencies and their actions were undermined by politically more powerful Indian ranchers.

A labor dispute

Before we turn to the 1980s, mention should be made of a labor dispute unrelated to land conflicts that occurred in 1975 and that involved ranchers attempting to block worker access to the higher wages offered by urban industry. The dispute illustrates the advantages ranchers gained from access to land and from the cheap labor provided by peasants who maintained their pasture. But the incident also points to tensions emerging between cattle ranchers and the state-owned oil industry competing for the same resources: labor and land. Although the events described below had no significant impact on Pajapan society, they did announce broader developments that would eventually transform Gulf Nahua economics and politics.

The incident began when port authorities in Coatzacoalcos sent an engineer to Pajapan to supervise the extraction of rocks to be used in the construction of new port facilities. The natural resources of the San Martín highlands and the labor power needed to extract them were of increasing interest to an expanding urban economy. Workers from Pajapan were offered 50 pesos a day, more than three times the salary offered to day workers by ranchers and other employers in Pajapan. The rancher-dominated municipal authorities strongly objected to this arrangement and shortly after the project began, they jailed the project supervisor and pressured him to sign blank sheets of paper intended for false declarations. They then announced that half of the salary paid would be added to the municipal treasury for "collective" work projects.

These actions caused a strong reaction from peasants who gathered around the office of the Communal Land Commission in preparation for an assault on the municipal palace. A bloody confrontation between peasants and the municipal authorities was prevented by the arrival of the *columna volante,* the rural police force dispatched from Minatitlán. The peasants were assured by the police captain that the Governor would be informed of the incident and that the Municipal President would be removed for abuse of power. The peasants dispersed but several days later reorganized to occupy the municipal palace, which in turn brought back the *columna volante.* Finally, a week or so after the incident started, a state government deputy arrived in Pajapan with orders from the Governor to dismiss the Municipal President and replace him with the substitute president (the former Communal Land Commission president) for the remainder of his term of office. Meanwhile, the rock extraction contract was cancelled and the non-unionized workers from Pajapan were banned from further employment on the construction of the new port by the Union of Construction Workers of Coatzacoalcos. The incident marked the first collective violent peasant action since the beginning of land conflicts.[35] It also revealed the weakness of the local rancher class *vis-à-vis* the expanding interests of a much broader domain: the state-controlled oil industry.

From hegemony to ethno-populism

The oil boom

The 1970s in Mexico were heralded as the era of economic prosperity for all, fuelled by the riches of the oil industry. Political leaders promised to redress the imbalances of Mexico's social and economic development suffered during the 1950s and 1960s by investing oil revenues in other sectors of the economy and improving rural and urban standards of living. The origin of these ambitious and ultimately unsuccessful plans can be traced to the early 1900s when the discovery of oil in southern Veracruz catapulted Mexico into the forefront of the 20th century's key industry. From 1911 to 1922, following initial oil discoveries, the production of oil boomed, placing Mexico in second place among the world's oil-producing countries (after the United States).

During the 1920s, however, the multi-national oil companies reduced levels of production in Mexico. Government limitations on the ownership of new oil fields and more effective taxation of the oil companies led them to shift their focus to Arab countries and Venezuela. Mexican production stagnated in a context of world economic crisis, low oil prices and increasing competition from other producers. By 1934 Mexican production had dropped 20% compared to levels attained in 1921. The situation began to change when prices improved during the late 1930s in anticipation of the Second World War. Mexico would probably once again have retained prominence on the world oil market had not tensions between the oil companies, labor and the Mexican government dramatically changed the course of events for the oil industry and the nation as a whole. In 1938 the government of Lázaro Cárdenas shocked the nation and the world by expropriating the oil industry and creating a state-owned national oil company known as PEMEX (Colmenares 1982: 51-2).

The nationalization of the oil industry and the formation of Petróleos Mexicanos (PEMEX) was followed by a major crisis in the industry. Oil refineries and production facilities were sabotaged by the vacating companies and a boycott by the United States, Britain and the oil companies made it difficult to sell oil offshore or purchase spare parts. The new state-owned company also lacked skilled personnel to run the plants. Levels of production declined dramatically and remained low throughout the war years.

The basic structure of the labor force was not significantly altered by the nationalization of the industry. Nolasco (1980: 139) points out that the enclave of elite foreign employees was replaced by an elite of national administrators, bureaucrats and technicians recruited from Mexico City and other major centers. In cities such as Coatzacoalcos and Minatitlán they occupied company housing and reaped the benefits of services supplied by PEMEX and, increasingly, by the union itself. Divisions within the union were enhanced by stronger distinctions between *trabajadores de planta* (permanent employees) and temporary workers with little security and few benefits. Meanwhile, the flood of unskilled workers arriving in the cities built their homes on the sand dunes and swamps surrounding the industrial facilities, creating "lost cities" without basic sanitation or other services.

The oil industry experienced slow but steady growth throughout the 1950s and 1960s. When the price of oil increased sharply on world markets in the early 1970s (due to instability in the Middle East and a stronger OPEC), the state-owned oil industry responded by borrowing money from international banks and increasing investments. The loans and investments were facilitated by the discovery of vast reserves of oil in Tabasco and offshore in the Sonda de Campeche in the Gulf of Mexico. Exploration and drilling programs were expanded, new refineries were built and port facilities were developed to export the increased production.

By the late 1970s oil production accounted for two-thirds of national exports. PEMEX absorbed some 19% of total para-state expenditure (Teichman 1989: 8) and was responsible for 17% of the national debt. Overall, PEMEX carried a negative commercial balance as the industry depended on imports for 75% of its technology and materials (Zavala de Cosío 1985: 21). By 1982, PEMEX had received US$5,360 million in loans from international financial markets, most of it to purchase foreign technology (A. Toledo 1982a: 49). Private investment in petro-chemicals increased rapidly.

Southern Veracruz was a major focal point for developments in the oil industry. In 1957 a new refinery, storage facility and port were constructed near Coatzacoalcos and within a few years several plants began processing basic chemicals derived from petroleum. In priority areas such as Coatzacoalcos companies received a 30% discount from PEMEX on energy and primary materials. The refinery at Minatitlán was expanded and new petro-chemical industries were established in the nearby Indian village of Cosoleacaque. The regional boom drew thousands of people from all over Mexico, doubling the population between 1950 and 1960. The location of Coatzacoalcos on the Isthmus of Tehuantepec and the concentration of petro-chemical industries established in the region prompted the national government to designate the area a priority zone for future developments. Several major projects were planned including a huge new oil refinery (Morelos) and the development of trans-isthmic transportation services for ship containers.

By the early 1980s, approximately 70% of basic petro-chemical production occurred in the region and the system of pipelines, shipping facilities and storage tanks handled 90% of the crude oil and 80% of the natural gas produced in Mexico. The refinery Lázaro Cárdenas in Minatitlán, originally constructed in 1909 by Lord Cowdray's company El Aguila, processed 16% of the nation's crude oil. The terminal of Pajaritos on the outskirts of Coatzacoalcos was the largest port facility in the country, capable of loading 6 million barrels of oil a day. The industrial plant at Cosoleacaque became the largest producer of ammonia in the world and plants in Jáltipan began providing a major share of the world's sulphur. Regional plants owned by some of the largest companies in Mexico produced plastics, fertilizers, cement and a host of other industrial products (Zavala de Cosío 1985: 18; *Estrategia* 1986: 59–63).

Urban growth and industrial development have created an ecological nightmare of unparalleled dimensions in southern Veracruz. The Coatzacoalcos watershed is considered one of the most contaminated regions in the world. Urban garbage and sewage is dumped into rivers and wetlands, contaminating drinking water during the wet season and creating a very high risk of epidemic disease. Industrial wastes have virtually destroyed all life in the lower Coatzacoalcos river, surrounding lagoons and wet-lands. Oil, alkalis, sulfites, heavy metals and other toxic substances are dumped into the ecosystem almost without control. Extensive areas of swamp are covered or crisscrossed with roads and pipelines, interfering with the natural system of drainage, the movement of aquatic life and the habitat of numerous species of migratory birds (A. Toledo 1982b: 55–62). The coastal waters have suffered from numerous oil spills, the most notorious of which occurred in 1979 when the offshore oil platform Ixtoc blew out and for months spilled massive amounts of oil into the Gulf of Mexico. More routinely, tankers approaching the port of Coatza-coalcos illegally dump bilge water contaminated with oil and other substances into the Gulf of Mexico and spill crude into the river because of faulty valves at the port facility.[36]

But the oil industry meant jobs, the proliferation of private businesses and important revenues for the federal state. The urban construction industry and the service sector grew rapidly in response to the oil boom. The local bourgeoisie comprised of ranchers, landowners and merchants invested in storage facilities, hotels, transportation companies, car dealer-ships, clothing stores and a myriad of other services. Although large construction companies from Mexico City such as ICA and Protexa were contracted to build the major installations, many other smaller construction companies financed with local capital built houses, small factories and public buildings.

Attracted by the prospect of urban employment, thousands of unskilled workers arrived from Oaxaca, Chiapas and other parts of southern Mexico where the agrarian crisis of the 1970s and population increases under-mined the viability of rural life. The population of Coatzacoalcos quad-rupled and Minatitlán tripled. The regional population reached more than a million, with approximately 28% consisting of recent immigrants. Very few of the newly arrived were employed directly in primary in-dustries. An estimated 83% of the working population was employed in unstable and low-paying jobs in construction, retail and petty trade servicing the oil enclave (Nolasco 1980: 144). Even at the height of the oil boom, about a quarter of eligible workers were unemployed or underemployed. While the region had the greatest concentration of oil workers in the country, the majority were classified as transitory workers with relatively few benefits or job security. Most permanent PEMEX employees were "imported" from Mexico City and other major centers in central Mexico where the main technical and administrative institutions are located. This elite enjoyed company housing, hospitals and stores while the masses inhabited spontaneous settlements in the swamps surrounding the industrial complex. Toledo (1982b: 61) estimated that 40% of urban families lived in one-room houses, with an average of five people per room. Among the urban poor, Nolasco (1980: 144) found that the average family income fell below the cost of the basic food basket; approximately 85% of the family income went to buy food only.

Another study demonstrated that in Cosoleacaque 80% of the population had no running water, 90% had no drainage and only 23% had electricity (Závala de Cosío 1985: 25). Urban transportation and medical services for the majority of the population were and continue to be inadequate (Colmenares 1982: 197; *Estrategia* 1986: 65).

During the 1970s, the oil workers' union became increasingly influential not only because of the large population it represented but also because of the economic resources at its disposal. Among the services provided to employees by the Union of Mexican Oil Workers were stores, schools, hospitals and insurance services. Legal provisions introduced by President Alemán gave unions and their leaders a great deal of power in determining who could join the union and which companies would undertake sub-contracts for a wide range of services not directly supplied by the union. Corruption involving the sale of union jobs and the purchase of sub-contracts became widespread. Strong union leaders also enhanced their political power by demonstrating their control over the labor force and loyalty to PEMEX: the region has had no major strikes in over 15 years. Union bosses amassed personal fortunes and established themselves as regional *caciques*, entering into direct conflict over political territory with established ranching interests. Leadership in political parties, municipal governments and other political institutions was hotly contested by union bosses and the local bourgeoisie. While the oil industry boomed, cattle production in the state economy declined (Bravo Garzón 1972: 29) and so did the regional political hegemony of cattle-raisers and merchants who had traditionally controlled municipal politics and many regional institutions.

Given Pajapan's proximity to Coatzacoalcos, the regional clash between the oil industry and the cattle economy was bound to have a direct impact on Gulf Nahua history. The clash took the form of a federal government expropriation decree, a measure required for the development of a mega-industrial port project to be built in the lowland area of Pajapan.

Oil versus cattle

The 1970s in Pajapan witnessed the rapid expansion of the cattle industry and the decline of the Indian peasantry. Hundreds of landless Pajapeños were forced to leave the community and join the ranks of the unemployed, the petty traders and the poorly-paid unskilled workers of Coatzacoalcos and Minatitlán. As in other areas of southern Veracruz, peasants expelled from their land became a source of cheap labor for urban industry. As the urban population grew, the regional demand for beef also increased, thereby sustaining nearby hinterland ranching activities. Prior to the 1980s, the urban-based oil industry and Pajapan's cattle economy thus complemented one another. Quite unexpectedly, however, the two central tendencies of previous decades – the growth of urban industry and the concentration of land in the countryside – entered into conflict in the early 1980s with the announcement of an industrial port project to be located in the Pajapan area. The short-term interests of the Indian rancher class were no longer compatible with the growth of the state-owned oil industry, nor was the Indian rancher class in a position to foil federal state plans to expand oil industry operations in southern Veracruz. Given the basic weaknesses of cattle operations in Pajapan, the state could afford to dispossess the local *caciques* of their land base without incurring any major cost. In the early months of 1980, the Mexican state expropriated the rancher-controlled lowlands of Pajapan as part of its megaproject. The expansion of a weak branch of agricultural capital gave way to the imperatives of industrial growth in both the private and public sectors of the national economy.

Local conversions of authority and land property were suddenly overruled by the exigencies of capital and the broader administrative domain. State and PEMEX officials used their authority to appropriate by eminent domain the lands needed for the port project. Ranchers and local authorities could no longer count on the state's active support (or administrative inaction) to maintain their position of hegemony within the local power system. This clash of interests between ranchers and state capital affected local politics in two contradictory ways. First, it highlighted the division between Indian ranchers, most of whom opposed the expropriation, and the landless peasants who had nothing to lose from the port project, save their hopes for just financial compensation, better livelihoods in urban industry, and the state's intervention in the allocation of non-expropriated lands. Second, manifestations of class conflict provoked by the expropriation soon gave way to a popular alliance between Indian ranchers and peasants, local PRI authorities and opposition groups against PEMEX and the state bureaucracy. Having lost their hegemonic control over the Pajapan economy and land administration process, ranchers and local authorities struck an antigovernment, ethno-popular alliance with peasants, opposition parties and outside agencies (bureaucrats, courts, lawyers, regional and national media) favorable to native demands. Subsequent struggles were couched in ethnic and geopolitical terms: the native people of Pajapan versus the government of Mexico.

This popular front made use of legal injunctions, lobbying, strikes, mass media coverage and communal–Indian rhetoric with a view to obtaining three things: compensation for the Indian ranchers' loss of lowland property, the redistribution of the unexpropriated lands among all *comuneros*, and the improvement of state services and public works in Pajapan. The state countered the movement with administrative inaction, legal measures and the use of force. Planned investments in the port project and expected returns, however, were so great that obstacles in the way of the project had to be removed and concessions made to the people of Pajapan. Within two years of the expropriation, many of the demands made by Pajapan had been met. Large sums of money were invested by the state in local infrastructure, public services, schools, a municipal palace, etc. Peasants were given parcels of land of their own: that is, communal lands controlled by Indian ranchers were regrouped into collectively administered lots and divided into *ejido*-like parcels assigned to individual *comuneros*, a legal superstructure meant to preserve the communal character of Pajapan's land tenure system or appearances to that effect. As for the ranchers, they received large amounts in compensation from the government, sold their cattle and reinvested their capital in small businesses that would profit from the development of industry and the urban economy.

Expropriation and land redistribution 1980–82

The strategic location of Coatzacoalcos on the Isthmus of Tehuantepec prompted the López–Portillo government to designate the area a priority zone for future developments. One of the major projects planned for the Coatzacoalcos area was the construction of a new industrial port on the coast 15 kilometers northwest of the city, to be called El Puerto Industrial Laguna del Ostión. Although the Laguna del Ostión was initially selected because of its potential as a natural harbor, studies soon revealed it was underlaid with a rock shelf and the site of the port was moved a few kilometers toward Coatzacoalcos. Plans were made to construct huge piers and conduct a massive dredging operation to create a sheltered port along an uninterrupted strip of coastline.

The industrial port was to cover an area of approximately 20,000 hectares and required the expropriation of 11,907 hectares including territory held by the community of Pajapan, the mestizo *ejido* Las Barrillas and private land-owners (see Map 4).[37] The project called for the construction of 1,900 meters of docks and a deep-water zone capable of handling boats of up to 100,000 tons. A large industrial park was also to be constructed for basic and secondary petro-chemical plants, agro-industries, mining and service industries. The plants were to produce vinyl chloride, benzene, dichloride, polyethylene, toluene, polyester fabric, reinforced plastics, flour, vegetable oil, aluminum sulfate and rock salt. A railway link to the main line from Coatzacoalcos was to be constructed along with a network of roads and a bridge spanning the mouth of the Laguna del Ostión. An urban complex with a projected population of one million people by 1990 was also planned as was the creation of an ecological reserve around the lagoon that would include some of the mangrove forest. These developments supported by foreign investments were to cost an estimated three billion pesos in their initial phases and several billion more until completion of the project. Thousands of workers were expected to gain temporary or permanent employment.[38]

The first time that the people of Pajapan heard of this mega-project was in October 1979 when government officials met with communal land administrators and residents of Jicacal, a fishing village on the shores of the Gulf and the Laguna del Ostión. Although "nobody even knew what an expropriation was", those attending the meeting responded favorably to the news, as everybody felt "they were going to receive a lot of money" and jobs as well.[39] The reactions in Pajapan were not as positive. *Comuneros* and Indian ranchers resented the fact that the meeting

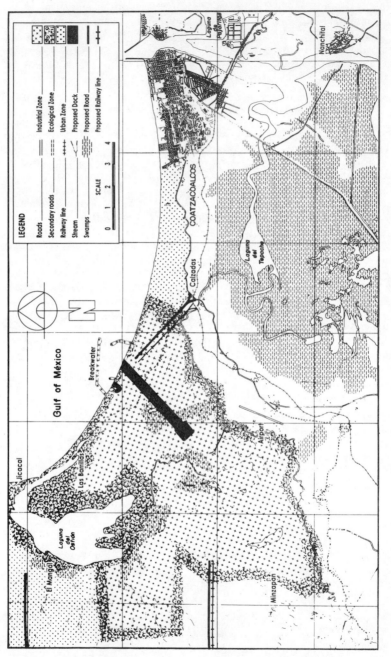

Map 4 Proposed industrial port, Laguna del Ostión, 1981

had not been held in Pajapan and that the president of the Communal Land Commission had apparently signed papers without consulting anyone. In January 1980, government agencies responsible for the industrial port project met with the *comuneros* of Pajapan in a General Assembly to inform them of the project and the planned expropriation of 5,154 hectares of communal land.[40] Officials assured the villagers they would receive compensation for land and private goods according to regional market values. They also affirmed that the project would create many short- and long-term jobs for the people and the youth of Pajapan and that government agencies would construct a secondary school, a municipal palace, a public market, public utilities and paved streets for the village. Only one villager attending the meeting expressed a negative reaction to the news:

> Imagine, for every hectare of watermelon or bananas I plant, I make more than 60,000 pesos. What they'll give me for the land, 15 pesos per square meter, doesn't add up to half of what I get ... The land is like our mother, she gives us everything, she protects us, she feeds us, and to be without her is like being an orphan. We're told that they're going to give us money, that they'll employ us in factories, but many of us are not prepared, the money will run out, we'll be without land and in no time we'll be thrown on the beaches, in federal lands, at the outskirts of the industries (quoted in Bouysse-Cassagne 1980: 28).

The meeting was attended by a representative of the Coordinadora Nacional de Pueblos Indígenas (CNPI), a national umbrella organization for Indian people. He called on the Pajapeños to resist the expropriation, arguing that the people of Pajapan would be excluded from the skilled jobs in urban centers. The project was endorsed, however, by a prominent rancher in Pajapan, Sergio Martínez Alemán. He presented a list of 21 demands in exchange for support of the project, including guarantees that villagers would have access to employment, schools in Pajapan to prepare them for work in industry, provisions for resettlement in urban areas with electricity, sewers and drinking water, etc. He was supported by a few prominent rancher-politicians who recognized that the project could not be stopped but hoped to derive maximum benefits from its realization.

The community was divided along class lines over the expropriation issue. While some Indian ranchers closely associated with local land and municipal authorities expressed conditional support for the expropriation, the majority opposed it as it implied the loss of control over the fertile lowland near the lagoon. According to local informants, about 250 ranchers and their day workers attending the assembly opposed the project and voted against it. However, the majority of the population comprised of landless workers and peasants approved the government proposal. Since virtually all of the land to be expropriated was controlled by ranchers, they had little to lose. Peasants also hoped to get cash compensation for the land and access to steady wage employment. As one peasant informant noted, "there were only ranchers occupying the expropriated lands. The expropriation did not directly affect the peasants." Another peasant pointed out that "many people were happy about the industrial port because they thought that they would be able to get a job."[41]

The decree signed by the President of Mexico in 1980 expropriated 5,154 hectares of communal land belonging to Pajapan and specified the amount and method of compensation. Some 8,500 pesos per hectare totalling $43,801,193 were offered in payment for the land with a further $8,626,708 for 182 comuneros with private goods on the affected land (rolls of wire, fence posts, fruit and palm trees, wells and buildings). The amount offered to each comunero ranged from as little as 150 to half a million pesos. Fifty-one comuneros were to receive more than 50,000 pesos each, half of whom were Indian ranchers. The decree proposed that the payment for land be deposited in the Bank of Mexico in the name of the community and that the payments for private goods be paid directly to the 182 comuneros affected. It also offered them two lots each in the urban zone of the industrial port.[42]

The public release of details of the expropriatory decree had a great impact on ranchers' and peasants' attitudes toward the expropriation. First, the amount of money offered per hectare was much lower than expected: 0.85 pesos in lieu of 15 pesos per square meter. Second, comuneros feared that they would not benefit personally from money deposited in the Bank of Mexico in the name of the community as a whole. The experience of villagers with official corruption and the self-interested actions of local authorities did not inspire confidence in a system of compensation administered by these same officials. Third, many villagers had been excluded from the list of 182 (mainly ranchers) who would receive urban lots and compensation for private goods in the expropriated zone.

The objections of peasants and ranchers to the expropriatory decree were first aired publicly at a General Assembly in June 1980, convened to discuss the reallocation of land to comuneros who never had land of their own or stood to lose land in the expropriated zone.[43] The chief of the regional agrarian office of the SRA attended the assembly and proposed that the list of 905 registered comuneros be updated to allow approximately 100 new comuneros to replace those who had died or left the community. All registered comuneros would then have collective access to the communal land not affected by the expropriation.[44] The Municipal President made a similar proposal and added that the money given for the expropriated land should be shared equally among all comuneros. The local representative of the PPS, however, countered with a proposal that the 182 comuneros be paid for both their share of the land and the private goods, after which they would forfeit their agrarian rights. With this proposal the PPS hoped to expel lowland ranchers from the communal landholding body. When a vote was called, some comuneros interrupted the assembly with cries that they were "tired of being misled and cheated by the land and municipal authorities". They demanded that the land unaffected by the expropriation be divided into equal plots for the 905 *comuneros* (including ranchers) by representatives of the SRA. Peasants feared that without the division of land into equal parcels and the direct intervention of the SRA in the redistribution of land, ranchers would once again undermine their demands and retain *de facto* control over the land.

No decision was taken by the Assembly but the SRA representative assured them that he would voice their demands to the state delegate in Xalapa. However, in a decision by the state delegate, SRA refused to parcel the land on the grounds that such a provision was not specified in the original Presidential Resolution of 1968. The bureaucrat failed to note that agrarian law does permit the parcelling of communal land when requested by the majority of the *comuneros*.[45] While no evidence of influence by ranchers on the state delegate is available, the decision clearly benefited Indian ranchers by blocking a definitive redistribution of land.

Although ranchers could do little to stop the expropriation, they tried to delay peasant demands and maximize compensation for the loss of access to the lowland area. Following the June General Assembly, ranchers organized a strong lobby to protest the exclusion of 100 *comuneros* from the list of 182 who claimed they had private property in the expropriated zone. On their behalf, the CNC in Mexico City pressured SRA to undertake a new inventory of private property owned by 100 *comuneros* excluded from the decree.[46] According to one peasant, in addition to the lobby for compensation for private property, "the ranchers went to the different government agencies and asked them to oppose the expropriation. During a meeting at the local Rancher Association they collected money from each rancher to pay the state delegate of the SRA to oppose the expropriation."[47]

Meanwhile, peasants continued their struggle against local ranchers and the federal state as well. Frustration over peasant demands for land redistribution and equitable compensation for the expropriation exploded in August 1980 when 500 peasants stormed the municipal palace in Pajapan and demanded the resignation of the Municipal President and Communal Land Commission. The action was organized by leaders of the PPS (Pascual Pablo and others) and temporarily supported by a small number of Indian ranchers who opposed the redistribution of land but were none the less dissatisfied with the compensation arrangements. Ranchers controlling the local authorities requested the intervention of the *columna volante* who repelled the attacking peasants with tear-gas. When two protesters were arrested and sent to jail in Coatzacoalcos, the peasants countered by blocking all roads to and from the village and informing the national press of the uprising.[48] Extensive regional and national media coverage of this rebellion brought federal and state-level representatives of the SRA to Pajapan where they assured the protesters they would free the prisoners, remove the *columna volante* from the municipal palace, and support their demands for land redistribution and equal individual payments for the expropriated land. The August rebellion was a major advance toward land redistribution. For the first time representatives of the federal government were forced to sit with the pro-peasant formation and negotiate. It also made it abundantly clear to the Indian ranchers that their traditional lines of communication with regional and state-level representatives of government agencies were no longer working and that alternative methods of control and manipulation were needed.

As already noted, the Coordinadora Nacional de Pueblos Indígenas (CNPI) was represented in Pajapan during the first meetings between Pajapeños and government agencies responsible for the industrial port. According to a regional CNPI organizer, local land and municipal authorities requested advice from the CNPI on the impact of the project on their community. For the CNPI, this was an opportunity both to extend its influence into a new area and raise its profile on an issue that was receiving national attention from academics and the press.

The national status and legal expertise of the CNPI provided the leaders of Pajapan a new forum in which to voice their demands. At meetings between the CNPI and the municipal authorities, it was decided that the community would seek a court injunction (*amparo*) protecting their land from expropriation. We have seen that similar legal actions have been taken by ranchers and landowners throughout Mexico to protect their lands from land reform and to negotiate better terms of expropriation for themselves. In the case of Pajapan, three articles of the Mexican Constitution (14, 16 and 27) were used to denounce the Office of the President of Mexico and eight other government agencies for not compensating an additional 176 *comuneros* who had private property in the expropriated area and for not offering the true market value of the land expropriated. The legal action also demanded the suspension of construction activities by the industrial port authority until all issues were resolved. A judge in Coatzacoalcos accepted the request and a temporary injunction was granted. Counterclaims were presented by the government, initiating a complex and lengthy legal process.[49]

The public image of the conflict presented by local leaders to the outside was of an Indian community being exploited by the heavy hand of PEMEX and the national government. Ranchers downplayed internal divisions within the community by focusing the attention of the media and academics on threats to communal land tenure, traditional Indian culture, religion and language.[50] They emphasized the romantic image of an Indian culture being crushed beneath the wheels of progress.

Peasant mobilization during the August rebellion convinced local leaders that land reform could not be delayed any longer. At a General Assembly a month after the legal action was launched, Sergio Martínez, an Indian rancher and key political leader in the community, called on peasants to join in the struggle for better expropriation compensation in exchange for rancher support of land redistribution. In his words:

> Two or three days before the Assembly, we recognized that we had to give up the land. At the assembly I asked the peasants what they wanted, the land redistribution or the payment of compensation. They answered that they wanted the land redistribution. So I told them, first let's fight for land redistribution and then for the payment of compensation. From then on, the people supported me.[51]

The local political leaders' concession to a land reform became all the more necessary as their credibility was at an all-time low. Peasants acted independently of the ranchers and received considerable attention from state authorities and the media. Since land redistribution was inevitable, Indian politicians made concessions to the peasants in exchange for support for a reevaluation of compensation payments that would mainly benefit ranchers. In addition, the position taken by the municipal authorities received strong support from Indian ranchers who had lost most or all of their land in the expropriated area and wanted to gain access to land in the unaffected area. During a General Assembly in November 1980, the majority agreed to a new inventory of private property in the expropriated zone, a census update to a maximum of 905 *comuneros* and the parcelling of unexpropriated land. While similar agreements had been reached in the past, this time it had the support of the municipal government, the Communal Land Commission and a majority of ranchers.

The struggle did not end with the agreement made among peasants, ranchers and local political leaders. It took another two years of constant pressure and violent confrontations to bring about an implementation of the land reform and compensation payment. In the weeks following the General Assembly, members of the PPS began to divide land into individual parcels of about 14 hectares each. The action was halted in February 1981, however, when a day worker employed by several powerful Indian ranchers shot and wounded Tomás Martínez Encarnación, one of the people involved in the redistribution. According to local peasants, this incident forced the Secretaría de Reforma Agraria (SRA) and the state government to take decisive action.

At the state palace in Xalapa a meeting was convened on February 6, 1981 to bring together the key actors involved in the struggle: the municipal government of Pajapan, the Communal Land Commission, the state government, the SRA, the Fondo Nacional para el Desarrollo Portuario (FONDEPORT), the Secretaría de Comunicaciones y Transportes (SCT), the PRI, the Partido Popular Socialista (PPS) and the Coordinadora Nacional de Pueblos Indígenas (CNPI). The participants at this meeting agreed to delineate the communal lands of Pajapan, divide the unexpropriated land into individual parcels and make a complete inventory and re-evaluation of private goods eligible for compensation, including the property of those 155 *comuneros* not listed in the initial proposal. Several months later, the agreement was formalized in a contract signed by the Communal Land Commission and senior representatives of government agencies responsible for the expropriation. In exchange for the reform and compensation payments, *comuneros* agreed to withdraw the legal action they had launched against the expropriation.[52]

The government agreed to the demands of peasants and ranchers, for it wanted to remove a bothersome impediment to the resumption of an important state-sponsored project. While construction had not been completely stopped by the legal action of Pajapeños, the violence associated with the land conflict and the attention the expropriation was

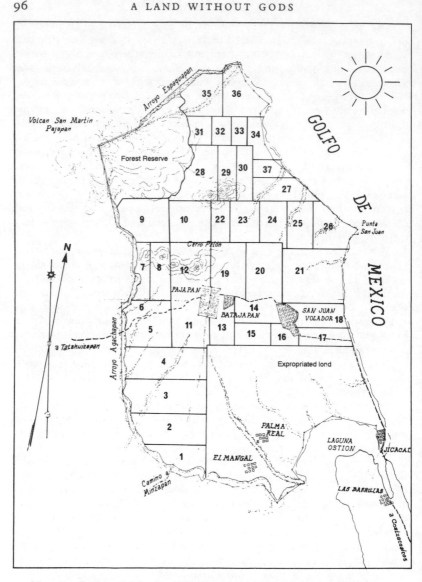

Map 5   Communal lands of Papajan, 1981, showing expropriated area
and division into 37 lots

receiving from the national media was a political embarrassment for the
Mexican government.[53]

It demanded an immediate solution. As one senior government official
noted, "the need to pacify the community was the main reason for the
land redistribution. ... When needed, the Secretaría seeks political solutions, even if they are not written in law."[54]

In May and June of 1981, SRA engineers marked the boundaries of the communal land and divided the unexpropriated area into 36 lots of 300 hectares each and one lot of 60 hectares (see Map 5). Peasants and ranchers in turn formed 36 groups of 25 *comuneros* and one group of five *comuneros*, with each group assigned to a lot modelled after the traditional lot system. Unlike the older system, however, *comuneros* sub-divided the large lots into parcels of 12 hectares each distributed to individual *comuneros*. The decision to divide the land as if it were an *ejido* was technically legal, yet it contravened the convention of communal property and collective labor promoted by the SRA in agrarian communities. In order to resolve this problem, an agreement was reached to divide the land into large lots worked by groups of *comuneros*, thereby promoting communal methods of production and organization, *or at least legal appearances to that effect.* The redistribution thus created an *ejido*-like structure within an agrarian community. A census update was carried out using the list of *comuneros* struck in 1967 and replacing the names of the 290 *comuneros* who had died or left the community since then by their sons or widows (40 of them; see Vázquez García, nd).

Ranchers attempted to make the best of a bad bargain. More than half of the newly-appointed lot administrators were Indian ranchers and/or *comuneros* occupying local political offices, positions used to their advantage. With the support of the Communal Land Commission, ranchers claimed the best lands in the unaffected area. They also grouped their day workers in parcels around their own property, thereby retaining access to a number of parcels. Since no surveying equipment was used, the politically and economically more powerful fenced in more than the 12 hectares to which they were entitled.[55]

Formal agreement on compensation for both land and property was followed quickly by payments to the ranchers for losses in property. Land payments did not come till later. The local Rancher Association appointed Emiliano Trujillo, the former president of Pajapan, to oversee the inventory of private properties in the expropriated zone.[56] A team of engineers conducted a new inventory that increased the number of beneficiaries from 182 to 364 and the total amount of compensation from US$28,756 to US$185,250.[57] Since no revision had been brought to the value of land, the compensation for private property in the expropriated area owned mainly by ranchers now totalled more than the money offered to *comuneros* for the land itself! The agreement prepared by government officials and signed by the communal land administrators and the *comuneros* attending the meeting held on May 7 (only 216 of them) included a promise from the community to withdraw the court injunction on the PEMEX port project and take no further legal action against the expropriation.[58]

The CNPI was instrumental in developing the legal action against expropriation, with support from land and municipal authorities. But when an agreement was made with federal and state agencies to withdraw the court injunction, a split developed between local authorities and the CNPI. Local members and national representatives of the *Coordinadora* continued to protest the expropriation and denounced the parcelling of communal land, the large sums of money given to some *comuneros* (Indian ranchers), and the inadequate payments made to all *comuneros* for the expropriated land (0.85 pesos per square meter). They warned Pajapeños that urban developments and the industrial port installations located near the Laguna del Ostión would jeopardize their access to lagoon fisheries and damage the local ecosystem. Also, many *comuneros* would stand to lose land, either because they were landless peasants not included in the census or because the land they held (as ranchers) prior to the redistribution exceeded the new limit of 12 hectares imposed by the reform. The CNPI's bid for a census update and the cancellation of the industrial port project continued to receive support from a few ranchers and middle peasants who had land in the non-expropriated zone and were going to be adversely affected by its redistribution. In April 1982, however, CNPI members were threatened by crowds of angry Pajapeños and put in the local jail. CNPI actions were vehemently denounced by leaders of the PPS, the new lot administrators, the Communal Land Commission and the municipal authorities. Despite their formal protests and efforts in popular education, this relatively small group (50 local members) had little influence on federal officials and the final resolution of land issues in Pajapan.[59]

Despite CNPI's loss of credibility, delays in land compensation payments prompted the Communal Land Commission to reinstate the court injunction in June 1982 and foster other protests. In October of the same year, two unions formed in Pajapan in anticipation of the construction phase of the industrial port joined with the commission and municipal authorities in their efforts to stop road works undertaken by the *Constructora General del Norte*. The strike lasted for three weeks. They demanded payment for the expropriated land and other actions promised by PEMEX such as schools, a market, paved roads, etc. They also asked that PEMEX and sub-contractors respect the rights to employment of union members in Pajapan.[60]

Once again, the protests of Pajapeños forced the authorities to respond or face further delays in the project and bad publicity from the national press. Representatives of the SAHOP, the federal agency responsible for the expropriation, arrived in Pajapan in November 1982 to pay for the expropriated land. To each *comunero* listed on the updated census they issued a cheque of US$303 (91,000 pesos), twice the amount originally established in the presidential decree (due to added interest payments). With the money "some bought cattle, others built a house in block, others drank it all." One rancher sold all of his cattle and built a small hotel. Local demands formulated during the strike were all accepted and work was immediately begun on a secondary school in Pajapan. This sudden influx of cash and wage work in the community inflated local wages and the cost of living at the municipal level as well.[61]

By the end of 1983, 2,189 million pesos had been invested in the project: two-thirds of the money had gone into harbor infrastructure and road works, 19% into water works, and only 13% into compensation

Table 3.5 Villagers occupying official positions in the early 1980s

Communal Land Commission (led by Aniceto Hernández)		
President	L. Antonio Gracía	PRI
Secretary	G. Hernández Antonio	PRI
Treasurer	A. Martínez Lorenzo	PRI
Communal Land, Vigilance Council		
President	J. Pereyra Fonseca	PPS, PSUM
Secretary	V. Martínez Reyes	PSUM
Treasurer	C. Martínez Martínez	PSUM
Municipal Government		
President	S. Martínez Alemán	PRI
Substitute	E. Trujillo Antonio	PRI
Syndic	E. Marcelino Prisciliano	PPS
Substitute	A. Huervo Abad	
Alderman	T. Martínez Encarnación	PPS
Substitute	J. Pereyra Fonseca	PPS, PSUM
PRI Committee		
President	E. Trujillo Antonio	

payments, relocation costs and the building of a secondary school in Pajapan. Major works undertaken or completed prior to the cancellation of the port project included residential lots for the *ejidatarios* of Las Barrillas (a nearby mestizo village also affected by the expropriation), 30% of the dredging for the interior harbor, 85% of the dredging for the service access canal, 80% of the secondary piers and more than half of the access gravel roads and railway tracks.

A temporary floating bridge was built across the mouth of the Laguna del Ostión. The bridge established a direct link between Pajapan and Coatzacoalcos, with an immediate impact on local petty commercial activity and the development of tourism in Jicacal, a small village of fishers located between the lagoon and the Gulf of Mexico. Other public works completed during this period at no cost to Pajapan included the municipal palace, a kindergarten, 20 primary school classrooms, three sport fields, the installation of a new potable running-water system, a market place, eight small bridges, a huge unfinished bridge in Jicacal, a new road from Tecolapa to Batajapan and 26 kilometers of road maintenance in Pajapan. The port project and compensation payments poured into the village also introduced new employment opportunities into an economy that had been dominated by a cattle industry based on the exploitation of land rather than labor.[62] The rancher Sergio Martínez elected to municipal office in 1982 negotiated many of these investments, becoming a prestigious actor in local politics. He was perceived by many as the first municipal president in Pajapan to act in the interests of the community rather than his own, by contributing to the improvement of the village with money obtained from the federal government.[63]

Post-reform elections of 1982 and 1983

Expropriation payments and redistribution of the remaining lands among all right-holding *comuneros* marked the end of a three-year protest movement which had mobilized not only the people of Pajapan against the federal state but also the peasant population against the most powerful elements in the Indian rancher class. During the period of relative calm that followed the concessions made to peasant demands, ranchers moved quickly to re-establish control over local political institutions. They co-opted the leadership of the peasant- and CNPI-backed PPS by inviting them to join the PRI and promising them positions in the next municipal government. In municipal elections of late 1982, shortly after the land payments were made, the PRI candidate won the majority of votes, with the PPS candidate a strong second. The elected Municipal President, Sergio Martínez, was a well-established rancher and an experienced politician who had occupied the positions of municipal secretary, secretary of the local Rancher Association and president of the PRI municipal committee. His success as an intermediary between the population and outside authorities during the expropriation contributed to his success in the municipal campaign. As for the PPS candidate (Tomás Martínez Encarnación), he won enough votes to ensure him a position as alderman in the new municipal government; two other *comuneros* associated with opposition parties also joined the municipal government.[64]

Control of the Communal Land Commission was also a vital issue to ranchers following the land redistribution. While supporting the ranchers' claims to financial compensations, the communal land commissioners had led peasant demands for an *ejido*-like reform. They oversaw the distribution of individual parcels and used their power to resolve disputes between peasants. They accommodated the ranchers' interest in acquiring the best land available in the redistributed area, often in excess of the 12 hectares legally available to each registered *comunero*. Once this process of accommodation was complete, the commission continued to serve as a vital instrument of control over land disputes and a channel for competing ranchers and peasants.

The commissioners failed to call elections in 1982, as required under agrarian law. They did not do so until the CNPI and the recently-formed PSUM (Partido Socialista Unificado de México, founded in 1981, successor to the PCM, the Mexican Communist Party) had lodged formal complaints against it and until the state agrarian authorities instructed them to abide by the law. The elections were finally held in May 1983. In a bid to establish its own panel of candidates, the PSUM rallied peasants who had supported the PPS during the 1982 municipal elections and whose leaders had been partly absorbed by the PRI. The PSUM was probably drawn to the political scene in Pajapan by the publicity land conflicts in the municipality received in the regional and national press and by hopes of extending their influence into the region. Peasants opposed to the PRI welcomed the organizational expertise of the PSUM activists and presumably found no objection to its socialist orientation, a radical rhetoric shared by virtually all parties in Mexico.

The PRI panel for the Communal Land Commission was not selected by the ruling group of ranchers in Pajapan but rather by a rival faction. Although he did not run for office, Aniceto Hernández organized a PRI panel of candidates with a view to blocking out the rancher Emiliano Trujillo and "his people". Like his father and older brother,[65] Aniceto was a wealthy rancher who had been in direct competition with Emiliano Trujillo, the PRI committee president, former Municipal President and active defender of the ranchers' financial interests at the time of the land reform. Since the dominant rancher faction knew that it had limited support in the community, little struggle seems to have occurred around this shift in control over the PRI apparatus. The PRI panel led by Aniceto won the 1983 elections supervised by the SRA with 64% of the vote, an unimpressive victory given the organizational experience of the PRI. As the minority panel, the PSUM candidates formed the *Consejo de Vigilancia*, in keeping with article 40 of the Agrarian Code.

The main issue of the election, round which subsequent actions were organized, was raised by the PSUM panel who demanded that more be paid for the expropriated land or that it be returned to the community. The newly elected Communal Land Commission (PRI) took up this call and proposed an alliance with the *Consejo de Vigilancia* (PSUM) to promote the idea. Since the traditional connections with the regional PRI power structure were of little use in the struggle against a PRI-sponsored project, the political influence and connections of the PSUM became highly valued in the community by ranchers and peasants alike. In spite of their differences, the local PSUM and PRI both played a key role in assisting the Communal Land Commission in its struggle against the federal state over the expropriated land.

The satisfaction of villagers with Sergio Martínez's PRI municipal administration coupled with the activism of the PSUM facilitated a political consensus in Pajapan round a central objective: fair payment for the expropriated land. A coalition re-activated the injunction against the port project immediately after payment for the expropriated land was made, with the active support of the local PRI and the assistance of a PSUM alderman from Coatzacoalcos. While virtually all of the *comuneros* had signed an agreement to suspend the court injunction when receiving their cheques, the president of the Communal Land Commission had not, which meant that the injunction was withdrawn without his formal approval.[66] The lawyer hired to re-activate the injunction on behalf of the newly-elected communal land authorities argued that the *comuneros* of Pajapan had been unduly pressured to sign the agreement and had not been given due process in the evaluation of the expropriated lands.[67] The reaction of the judge in Coatzacoalcos was favorable: he reinstated the injunction and agreed to hear the case. Two new evaluations (*peritaje*) of the lands were carried out, one on behalf of the *comuneros* and the other at the request of the judge. The data presented by the plaintiff showed that the original evaluation had ignored not only the actual quality and productivity of the land but also price changes in the market for land (after the announcement of the port project), the real value of the orchards and improved pastures, and the economic worth of the lagoon and surrounding lands for fishing and tourism. The first evaluation concluded that the *comuneros* had received only 6% of what their lands were worth; the second, 18%.[68]

In July 1984, the judge ruled that another 68 individuals recognized as *comuneros* by the Presidential Resolution of 1968 had not been included in the expropriatory decree or paid. This was sufficient grounds to review the entire process, including the land evaluation.[69] The decision was immediately appealed by SEDUE officials (Secretaría de Ecología y Desarrollo Urbano, former SAHOP) and, as with most injunction procedures, the case went to the Supreme Court of Mexico. Lawyers representing the government claimed that all *comuneros* had been duly compensated. On February 6, 1986, the Supreme Court finally rescinded the lower court decision and cancelled the court injunction on the grounds that all peasants had been given due process and that the expropriation was legal and effective.[70]

Factionalism on the rise

The national crisis

Economic growth and industrial expansion in southern Veracruz and in Mexico as a whole came to a sudden halt in 1982 when the price of oil plummeted and interest rates tripled in a few months (to counter the flight of capital). Mexico had been borrowing over the previous decade from international banks and governments at a higher rate than any other country in the world, thereby accumulating one of the largest debts in Latin America. Lower revenues from the oil industry and the massive debt threw the national economy and government into its worst economic crisis since the Great Depression (Teichman 1989: 1). By the end of 1982, construction on the industrial port near Pajapan ground to a halt. Other industrial port projects in Lázaro Cárdenas and Altamira were more advanced than the Pajapan project and were favored when cuts became unavoidable. Serious concerns had also been expressed about the technical feasibility of the southern Veracruz project.[71] This period corresponded to the end of President López Portillo's mandate, a time when difficult choices are often made to provide the incoming President with a clean slate. Rumors that the Laguna del Ostión project could be cancelled were already circulating.[72]

In April 1983 some 750 urban lots were made available in the expropriated zone for the relocation of Pajapeños affected by the project. This was in response to pressure exerted by some residents of Jicacal. The residential lots were allocated in the hope of removing the population from the land so as to proceed with the construction work.[73] A few months later, however, the director of PEMEX announced the indefinite suspension of construction on the port facility. The initial reaction in Pajapan was made known through an anonymous pamphlet circulating in the village; it was negative and also critical of PRI-affiliated ranchers occupying large tracts of land in the expropriated zone.[74] After years of uncertainty, the cancellation of the port project was finally announced in October 1984 by President Miguel de la Madrid during a visit to Coatzacoalcos. The President declared that the expropriated lands of Pajapan would be returned to their former owners, the *comuneros* of Pajapan.[75]

The crisis in the oil industry in southern Veracruz devastated the regional construction industry. While primary and secondary production continued at the same or slightly lower levels, the cancellation of new projects left construction companies with little work. Many small businesses went bankrupt while others scaled down or moved elsewhere. Vast numbers of unskilled workers continued to flood into the cities from depressed areas around the country but more than ever they were left without employment or forced to earn a meager living as underemployed petty traders and occasional laborers. While at one time construction work provided a tenuous link between urban industry and the peasant economy, its potential to fulfil this role was seriously eroded by the economic crisis.

The agricultural sector, both regionally and nationally, was hard-hit by the crisis, with reductions of 74% in the budget of SARH between 1981 and 1987, a drop in coffee prices and, under pressure from the IMF, changes in long-standing policies of price guarantees. The extension service of SARH was virtually eliminated in 1992. The terms of trade between the agricultural sector and the rest of the economy declined by 30% between 1981 and 1987. The food deficit, already severe during the 1970s, worsened forcing ever greater imports of basic grains and a reversion to subsistence agriculture as well (Robles and Moguel 1990: 7; Hewitt de Alcántara 1992: 25, 36, 49).

Despite a general decline in support to agriculture, new policies favored the cattle sector through increases in milk prices, government expenditures (twice the amount assigned to agriculture), incentives to convert agricultural land into pasture and pledges of *certificados de inafectabilidad*. In 1992 Mexico's current president, Salinas de Gotari, accelerated the legalization of large landholdings by granting *certificados* to 30,000 ranchers in the state of Veracruz, more than all the *certificados* previously granted in the history of the state. Ironically, he combined this strong endorsement for the cattle industry with declarations against the environmental costs of extensive cattle ranching.[76] Agrarian reform, declared over first by President López Portillo and again by Salinas de Gotari, came to a halt and the legal ground work for the dissolution of the *ejido* in favor of private property in land was laid. Paré (1990: 80) points out that revisions to the *Ley de Fomento Agroindustrial* allow for private farms producing basic grains of up to 800 hectares, essentially

legalizing the *neolatifundio*. Revisions to article 27 of the Mexican Constitution made law by the Salinas government permit the conversion of
ejido lands into private properties and facilitate private investment in
ejido lands. The implications for rural villages are far-reaching; disparities
in wealth within *ejidos* will increase as wealthier members purchase land
from poorer members. Land concentration and the expulsion of the
rural labor force into the cities will develop new momentum as agro-
industry invests in the most profitable branches of the agricultural sector
while peasants on marginal lands languish (A. Bartra 1991). The ranchers
of Pajapan, however, may benefit only partially from the reforms; agrarian
communities are explicitly excluded from reforms permitting the sale of
collective lands.

On the political front, the crisis of the 1980s renewed the struggle for
democracy at all levels of Mexican polity. Since the mid-1970s, agrarian
struggles have gone hand in hand with electoral struggles to defeat the
rule of *caciques* in rural municipalities and *ejidos*. With the fiscal crisis of
the 1980s and the repression of union demands, the political returns of
caciquismo were further reduced as the government could no longer count
on patronage to bring out votes via PRI-affiliated unions and peasant
organizations (Teichman 1989: 23–5). In recent years, the hegemony of
PRI institutions in Mexico has been challenged by the Cardenista
movement, a broad-based left-wing opposition front headed by the son
of Lázaro Cárdenas. Meanwhile, peasant movements have continued to
free themselves from the organizational control of PRI apparatuses. The
National Congress "Plan de Ayala" (CNPA) consisting of independent
peasant groups has broadened the national base of peasant movements
by introducing a new style of mobilization based on principles of decentralization and regional group autonomy (Paré 1990: 88, 91).

The power-holders reacted to these new developments in several ways.
One response has been to use force: according to the national press, 705
peasants have been assassinated as a result of social conflicts between
1982 and 1987. Moreover, the few gains made by opposition parties in
the 1988–89 municipal elections were offset by massive fraud and problems of abstentionism (between 70% and 90% in Veracruz). It is widely
recognized that President Salinas de Gotari lost the 1988 presidential
election to Cuauhtémoc Cárdenas. Many more state-level and municipal
elections (Michoacán, Estado de México, Yucatán, San Luis Potosí) were
marred by electoral irregularities and other indications of fraud. The PRI
regime has attempted to regain legitimacy by confronting local and
regional power structures with a view to unseating corrupt officials and
promoting a limited democratization of the party. However, in the absence
of local allies other than the *caciques*, the federal government continues
to tolerate, with few exceptions, those traditional power-holders it
apparently tries to displace. Finally, recent years have witnessed the
emergence of a neo-corporatist ideology based on principles of class
cooperation. The Salinas government recognizes independent organizations as valid representatives of workers and peasants, treating them
as partners in joint efforts to resolve problems of democracy and wealth

distribution. One aim of this government strategy, however, has been to avoid negotiations with powerful national organizations, in favor of local and regional pressure groups that are more easily rejected when their demands get out of control (Paré 1990: 88–92).

The political and economic crisis affecting Mexico in the 1980s also reached the Gulf Nahuas. The analyses presented below show that the second half of the 1980s was marked by critical shifts in the government process, from an ethno-popular front to a proliferation of factional divisions in Gulf Nahua society. The anti-government alliance formed between dominant and subordinate groups in the early 1980s was followed by a reduction in direct state intervention in local affairs and a fragmentation of political and economic class interests.

Once the port project was cancelled, it was no longer in the interest of a federal state crippled with debts to invest more money in satisfying local peasant demands. Nor was it necessary to intervene further in local struggles over land. The withdrawal of federal state agencies from the local economy and land tenure politics put an end to the popular, inter-class and anti-state alliance formed in the early 1980s. As a result, the second half of the 1980s witnessed a partial recuperation of the Indian ranchers' control over communal land: ranchers recuperated some of their losses in land by exercising control over the new lot administration or through rental and illegal purchases of land. Nevertheless, the local class structure and related conditions of material livelihood had already undergone major transformations. The influx of state subsidies into public works, the expropriation of the lowlands and the effective redistribution of other communal lands caused a decline in cattle ranching activities, the proliferation of small businesses, and a reversion to subsistence agriculture combined with small-scale ranching and cash crop production (see Chapter 4).

The 1980s also witnessed a marked fragmentation of political and economic class interests in Pajapan. The recent history of Pajapan is one of competition over the expropriated land pitting ranchers against ranchers, comuneros against the landless (especially those living outside the main village), and the ruling PRI authorities against opposition groups – conflicts exacerbated by problems of overpopulation and economic stagnation. As shown below, dominant groups maintained themselves in power throughout the decade, yet they were increasingly faced with internal divisions and external opposition over issues of land, local government offices and outside political support, thus failing to re-create either the stable hegemonic rule that used to prevail locally prior to the land reform or the popular front of the early 1980s. Finally, local PRI ranchers had to cope with pressure groups and alternative political parties that had been absent from previous village history.

Divisions between hamlets and the village of Pajapan

The cancellation of the port project in October 1984 marked the beginning of a new land struggle in Pajapan. The President of Mexico entrusted the expropriated lands to the Fideicomiso Fondo Nacional de Fomento Ejidal (FIFONAFE), with the understanding that they be returned to their former owners.[77] Three groups, however, were already actively vying for use of the *tierras afectadas*: local ranchers, the *comuneros* of Pajapan, and peasants living in smaller villages within the expropriated area. First, Indian ranchers such as Emiliano Trujillo had not removed their cattle from the disputed area and continued to occupy the largest proportion of the expropriated zone. Other ranchers began occupying the zone as soon as rumors began that the project might not go ahead. They used local political offices under their control to delay the formal return of the lands to the community, much as they delayed the formal creation of an agrarian community in previous decades. Second, the *comuneros* of Pajapan decided during a General Assembly to divide the expropriated land into 6-hectare parcels for each communal landholder. This idea was initially promoted by the *comisariado comunal*'s lawyer as a means of strengthening their case for a re-evaluation of the land, and it gained force among the *comuneros* of Pajapan following cancellation of the port project. Third, peasants living in El Mangal, Palma Real and Jicacal located on the expropriated lands petitioned for the creation of three new *ejidos*, completely independent from the agrarian community of Pajapan. The confrontations resulting from these competing claims were very bitter as the disputed land was and still is the best agricultural land in the community.[78]

Struggles over land between Indian ranchers and peasants were partly transformed by the emergence of a new faction within the municipality: peasants living in the hamlets of El Mangal, Jicacal and Palma Real (see Map 5). As in the region of Huejutla, in northern Veracruz, "local class conflicts can take the form of factional disputes within the same village or disputes between Indian town centers and their surrounding hamlets" (Schryer 1990: 49). The population forming the hamlets was composed of two groups: registered *comuneros* with rights to 12-hectare parcels, and sons of *comuneros* from various Gulf Nahua villages (including Pajapan) who had no land rights at all. When the lands unaffected by the expropriation were redistributed in 1981, registered *comuneros* living in the hamlets had almost without exception received very poor-quality parcels located on the upper slopes of the volcano, more than six hours' walking distance from their homes. These *comuneros* had no legal land base where they lived within the expropriated area and were both physically and politically marginal to the land redistribution process.[79] The other group in the hamlets were landless sons of *comuneros* who had occupied small parcels of land in the expropriated zone left vacant by ranchers following the expropriatory decree. Some landless peasants from Pajapan established homes in Palma Real, a ranch that grew from a few houses to several dozen during the period. A few landless peasants from the *ejidos* of Benito Juárez and Tatahuicapan also moved to Palma Real. Both these groups had been working and claiming rights to the expropriated land since 1981.

The three hamlets formed a loosely organized front called the

Indigenous Civic Front of Pajapan (FCIP, Frente Cívico Indigenista de Pajapan).[80] The FCIP worked within a larger regional organization called the Popular Front of Southeastern Veracruz (FREPOSEV) also affiliated at the time with the National Congress Plan de Ayala (CNPA), a national organization of independent peasant groups. Their activity drew heavily on Christian Base Communities (*Comunidades Cristianas de Base*) promoted by the Jesuit order as part of a broader reform influenced by the teachings of liberation theology.

Struggles over the use and legal definition of the expropriated lands produced many violent clashes throughout the late 1980s and into the 1990s. While ranchers occupying much of the land adopted a strategy of delay and subversion, other groups developed detailed proposals for resolving the conflicts. Peasants in El Mangal and Palma Real fenced lands near their hamlet in the expropriated zone in an effort to create a separate *ejido*, an action interpreted by the *comuneros* of Pajapan as an illegal land invasion. The communal land authorities of Pajapan responded by putting several people in jail, thereby protecting the vested interests of the landholding peasants of Pajapan and ranchers as well. After three days the prisoners were freed when a group of peasants bearing machetes demanded their release. As in Schryer's study of Huejutla, the eruption of fierce conflicts between the hamlets and the *comuneros* of Pajapan was "an indication that the level of internal differentiation, combined with an extremely ambiguous and contradictory land tenure situation, had reached a breaking point in such Nahua villages" (Schryer 1990: 223).

In response to the actions of the hamlets, a General Assembly of *comuneros* resolved to request the return of the expropriated lands, offering FIFONAFE a payment of 1,000 pesos per hectare.[81] The hamlets countered with detailed proposals for the creation of several *ejidos* on the expropriated lands. Other groups in Pajapan petitioned for use of the disputed lands and denounced the illegal sale of agrarian rights. An SRA investigation revealed that 40 parcels had been illegally sold to local ranchers for between 50,000 and 800,000 pesos per 12-hectare parcel.[82] Apolinar Hernández, a wealthy rancher and the brother of Aniceto Hernández, apparently owned five parcels while Valentino Antonio, possibly Pajapan's richest rancher, owned eight parcels as well as 100 hectares of private land in Las Choapas. Despite the land reform, land was once again concentrated in the hands of the Indian rancher class.

At first the SRA denied the claims of the hamlets, arguing that the peasants were not duly represented by a *comisariado comunal*.[83] Federal SRA officials later agreed to undertake a census of the hamlets, a first step in the creation of an *ejido*, but to no avail as the state SRA delegate in Xalapa and the president of the Communal Land Commission in Pajapan refused to co-operate with the federal land agent in charge of the census. During a General Assembly, the federal land agent spoke favorably about the distribution of land to the landless of the community but was shouted down by the *comisariado*.[84] Following these events, the state delegate and members of FCIP met separately with the State Governor to argue both sides of the conflict pitting the hamlets against the ranchers and the *comuneros*.[85] Meanwhile, ranchers continued to occupy much of the expropriated lands, in parcels of up to 50 hectares each.

Proposals and counterproposals, official agreements and government inaction, violent conflicts and political compromises followed in quick succession from the late 1980s onward. The hamlets continued to propose the creation of new *ejidos*. In support of their claim they argued that it was not possible to carry out democratic assemblies involving 905 *comuneros*. They claimed that the relatively isolated hamlets were frequently excluded from the General Assembly and denied access to agricultural credit.[86] The Communal Land Commission president sought the support of the CNC for a full restitution of the expropriated lands to the *comuneros* of Pajapan, in conformity with the presidential announcement published in the *Diario Oficial* (July 24, 1986).[87] Federal SRA officials refused to act on the grounds that the community was too unstable and that the risks to their employees were too great. They denounced the hamlets for inciting people to violence and washed their hands of the matter by claiming the conflicts were of a "cultural" nature. Inaction by state officials also reflected the uncertainty of the 1988 national presidential elections and fears of losing the electoral support of the *comuneros* of Pajapan. When peasants of Palma Real fenced in 300 hectares in the expropriated zone and El Mangal another 400 hectares, the conflict erupted into violence. Some 70 *comuneros* from Pajapan destroyed the house of a peasant in Palma Real and threatened his family. They also threatened to burn the community. Meanwhile, ranchers occupying much of the expropriated land kept a low profile in the hope that the conflict would continue unresolved for as long as possible.

The elections of 1988

By the summer of 1988 the struggle for land was momentarily displaced by another battle: the electoral struggle for power and democracy in the municipality of Pajapan and the whole of Mexico. Three formations canvassed for local electoral support;[88] (a) the PRI was represented by Simón Hernández Martínez, a bilingual school teacher living in the village of Huazuntlán located in a neighboring municipality; (b) Aniceto Hernández left the PRI (and the PPS) to represent major opposition parties united under the banner of the Partido Frente Cardenista de Reconciliación Nacional (PFCRN); the slate headed by Aniceto included Juan Pereyra Fonseca, local PSUM leader and former Communal Land President, and also Clemente Trujillo, a local merchant; (c) the PMS (Partido Mexicano Socialista, supported by FCIP) put forward its own slate headed by Bernardino Hernández who planned on forming an alliance with his brother Aniceto in the likely case of a fraudulent PRI victory.

The major objective of the two opposition parties was to challenge the hegemony of the PRI apparatus controlled by Emiliano Trujillo, the leader of the dominant Indian rancher faction, but without any commitments different from those made in the PRI campaign. Both the PRI and the PFCRN preferred not to be too specific about how the expropriated lands should be redistributed and simply promised to resolve the land conflict. The PRI candidate, a non-resident of Pajapan, encountered considerable difficulties in winning public favor. Although teachers are frequently seen as detached from rural power systems, this candidate was clearly perceived as representing the interests of the local *cacique*, Emiliano Trujillo, a rancher who had profiteered from the expropriation payments received in the early 1980s, who occupied large tracts of land in the expropriated zone and who continued to exercise excessive control over the local government process.

In order to avoid losing the elections, the PRI tried to co-opt Aniceto Hernández and other opposition candidates but without success. Prior to the election, PRI-affiliated officials (SRA, FIFONAFE, CNC, the mayor of Coatzacoalcos) went to the village on two occasions to convince Aniceto to join the PRI, in exchange for a promise to resolve the land conflict in favor of the *comuneros* of Pajapan. Aniceto declined the offer for fear that a sudden change in party affiliation would undermine his political credibility within the municipality. Also, he was personally resolved to dislodge Emiliano from the PRI.

During the campaign both the PRI organization and the opposition accused one another of corrupt electoral practices, including tampering with the ballot boxes of Minzapan and Coscapa. The final election count showed a victory for the opposition PFCRN, with 755 votes out of 1,489. The PMS and the PRI received 214 and 520 votes respectively. A week later, however, the votes were recounted in favor of the PRI! Public demonstrations and road blocks denounced the electoral fraud and an alliance with a majority of votes was struck between the two opposition parties and officially recognized. After years of struggle against the ruling PRI faction, the dissident rancher and son of Guadalupe Hernández Jáuregui took control of the local government. The Cardenista opposition also won in two neighboring municipalities, Oteapan and Chinameca, with some concessions made to them in Soteapan.

Electoral victory for the opposition, however, resulted in a weakening of local government institutions which are chronically dependent on PRI federal subsidies and bureaucracy to fulfil their electoral promises and to pursue their own administrative agenda. During Aniceto's term, little support was gained from the federal government for public works in municipal Pajapan. Nor was he in a position (as a rancher) to resolve the expropriated land conflict in favor of the *comuneros* of Pajapan. Inside sources claim that in exchange for his pledge of allegiance to the PRI party Aniceto obtained a promise from the mayor of Coatzacoalcos to improve local roads and build a bridge in Jicacal. He also attempted to take control of the local PRI organization. Both attempts failed: the influential mayor of Coatzacoalcos died suddenly and the local PRI remained under the control of his rival, Emiliano Trujillo. Aniceto finished his term in late 1991 with few credits to his name.

The expropriated land issue was finally resolved in 1992. At the insistence of the state government, FIFONAFE authorized the creation of a new *ejido* from the expropriated communal lands in an effort to blend the interests of the *comuneros* of Pajapan and the hamlets. A petition for the creation of an *ejido* from the expropriated land was developed based on a census administered by the lot administrators, a census in which each of the 905 *comuneros* of Pajapan registered a family member, usually a son (50%). About one-quarter of the *comuneros* registered their wives (Vázquez García nd), thereby obtaining access to additional land often of better quality than the parcels they already possessed. One informant, speaking of his rebel sons, argued that "if the youth had worked with the local authorities and not sought help from outsiders, the people would have supported them."[89] An additional 71 individuals, mainly sons of *comuneros* from the hamlets, were added to the census for a total of 976 petitioners. FIFONAFE granted the expropriated lands to the petitionary group, thereby creating an *ejido* with its own administrative structure known as Pajapan II. The *ejidatarios* promptly decided in a General Assembly to divide the lands into parcels of about 4 hectares each for distribution to individual members. The distribution process was tortuous, however. Ranchers (and some peasants) illegally occupying land in the expropriated zone refused to vacate and used their wealth and political power either to purchase land rights from the new *ejido* members or to thwart and delay the land distribution process, much like they did during the early 1980s. In a bizarre twist of events, a powerful rancher managed to have the new *ejido* land commission president arrested and incarcerated for distributing the *ejido* lands to their rightful owners. In a massive protest in front of the municipal palace of Coatzacoalcos (April 1992), some 1,500 Indians from Pajapan demanded the release of their representative and the expulsion of the *caciques* occupying their land. Subsequently, landholdings in excess of the legally defined *ejido* parcel (4 ha.) were reduced and the new *ejidatarios* occupied the fertile plain that had been at the center of struggles between ranchers and peasants since the 1940s.

Caciquismo, ethno-populism and factionalism

For the time being, the fathers of Pajapan who registered their wives as holders of land rights in Pajapan II in lieu of their sons have reaffirmed the ancient rule of the patrimonial domain: sons shall not inherit family property until the parents are deceased or too old to work the land. Although radically altered, the patrimonial regime is still operative in the sphere of kinship which presides over the organization of family labor and the transmission of communal land from one generation to the next. The central characteristics of traditional Gulf Nahua society will be discussed later (see Chapter 6). Suffice it to say for the moment that as a family-centered system, the patrimonial domain features a high degree of decentralization, a rule of reciprocity (acting between families, genders and generations) and also a propensity toward patriarchal inequalities; the native domain confers on men, older generations and wife-givers special rights and privileges that will not be granted to women, younger generations and wife-receivers.

Prior to the Mexican Revolution, Pajapan's kin-based regime had already been altered by prebendal colonial rule and the expansion of a mercantile hacienda economy. These early developments were followed by pressures to privatize land under the Porfiriato regime. The Revolution brought about new political and administrative institutions that further undermined native principles of patrimony, such as the authority vested in senior members of the community who controlled the lot system and the local government process. In recent decades, the Gulf Nahuas have been subjected to the growth of private business in agriculture and industry, the expansion of public property and investments administered by the federal state, and the increase of state intervention in local government affairs. The two domains ruled by capital and the state have created new divisions within native society, cleavages that have weakened the household economy and infringed upon the rights of "fathers of Pajapan" to control their resources, the produce of their labor and their mode of government as well.

Still, the power structures of state and capital have not developed without limits. The history of the Gulf Nahuas in the 1980s clearly indicates the endemic weakness and crises of the two domains in southern Veracruz. The activities of private business in this area of Mexico are severely hindered by an inefficient cattle industry highly destructive of the environment and incompatible with the productive use of land and labor and the growth of industry. As for state power, it revolves round a single-party state system crippled with debts and confronted with mounting opposition from all segments of Mexican society.

Our case study points to three phases in the changes brought by agro-industrial capital and the PRI state. The first phase, extending from the late 1940s to the late 1970s, saw the rise of PRI-rancher *caciques* to power, with the support of external agents of state and capital. The second phase lasted from 1980 to 1984, a time when the native people of Pajapan struck an ethno-popular inter-class alliance against federal government claims to the communal lowlands of Pajapan. Subsequent years witnessed a fragmentation of political positions and class interests, a "post-modern" proliferation of internal divisions that put an end to both the hegemonic rule of previous decades and the ethno-popular struggles of the early 1980s.

General conclusions regarding the dynamics of *caciquismo*, ethno-populism and factionalism are in order. Much has been written about the rule of *caciques* defined as "strong men who combine economic and political power", local chiefs who spend considerable resources in paternalistic forms of control and the symbolic legitimation of the power vested in them (e.g., through civil-religious *fiestas*).[90] Interestingly, the latter definition is an adequate description of what some theorists view as outright hegemony. Hispano-American *caciquismo*, however, involves a particular correlation of political and economic forces, one where hegemonic rule is exercised through institutional control but also through personal, informal and illegal mechanisms: paramilitary force, corruption, nepotism, patronage, and so on (Friedrich 1986; Schryer 1990: 149–50; Boege 1988: 237). *Caciquismo* is thus "a mediation phenomenon character-ized by the informal and personal exercise of power for the protection of personal and economic interests or the attainment of prestige" (Paré 1973: 22, our translation). Moreover, as pointed out by Paré, *caciquismo* is usually associated with primitive forms of capital accumulation in the countryside: for instance, the forceful dispossession of peasants from all means of production and the concentration of land in the hands of the few, as in post-revolutionary Pajapan. Finally, rural *caciques* control limited amounts of productive capital and tend to invest little in reproducing laborers through wage-labor employment. Given these limitations, their hegemonic power will typically last only as long as their interests do not clash with the growth of broader domains – with the forward march of industrial capital and state bureaucracy (Paré 1975: 36–8).

According to Friedrich (1986: 292), rural *caciques* are political middle-men (Wolf 1955) who "bridge, however imperfectly, the gap between peasant villagers and, on the other hand, the law, politics and government of the state and nation". On the whole, Friedrich's (1986: 132–76) socio-psychological approach tends to ignore structural variables that play a crucial role in what he calls the "cacical process". Our interpretation of *caciquismo* in southern Veracruz comes closer to the position adopted by Paré and Schryer who emphasize the relationship between the particular forms that *caciquismo* takes and the "changing nature of the Mexican economy and its corresponding political system" (Schryer 1990: 150, see 195–8).

Pajapan's PRI-rancher rule, which lasted for three decades, illustrates the generalizations made by Schryer and Paré regarding the history and functions of *caciquismo* in Mexico. However, our case-study also shows that a hegemonic correlation of forces (money/authority) should not be confused with the concentration of undifferentiated powers in the hands of the few. *Cacique* regimes observed in 20th-century rural Mexico do not involve a pre-capitalistic *fusion* of political and economic functions but rather an effective *conversion* of money into authority and office into wealth: one group succeeds in exercising control over both local capital and government institutions. This is to say that the two power systems remain different even when controlled by the same group. Another notion that should be dispelled is that of *caciquismo* viewed as a totalitarian regime that knows no limit. The chain of events discussed in this chapter clearly shows how the formation of a hegemonic bloc in Pajapan was faced with limitations from the start. For one thing the ruling order had to cope with tensions between the PRI administration and rival factions of Indian and mestizo ranchers. These internal problems were com-pounded by the chronic dependence of local forms of power *vis-à-vis* external agents of state and capital. Finally, *caciques* had to contend with manifestations of organized resistance from subordinate groups.

Caciques occupy political and economic positions that are fused and embedded in the kinship system. Consequently, *caciquismo* could be seen as an effect of the patrimonial domain exercised at both domestic and community levels. The characterization, however, would be misleading in that the penetration of the market economy and state bureaucracy in rural areas such as Pajapan has radically transformed the *cacique* regime. One central effect of capital and state systems on Gulf Nahua society has been to demarcate the older kinship domain from new forms of power. Although the household structure reproduces unequal relations between genders and generations, the modern rule of *caciques* hinges mostly on manipulations of money and government authority, not on customary regulations of patrimonial kinship. The possibility that Indian bosses reproduce traditional power-systems is all the more misleading as *caciques* are the first to make abundant use of the communal–Indian rhetoric. In Pajapan, appeals to customs and native identity served the *caciques'* personal agenda, which was to legitimize the control they exerted over the local economy and government process. Instead of being taken literally, the discourse should be viewed for what it is: a performative stance that plays a strategic function in contemporary Indian Realpolitik. The fact that native *caciques* appropriate the rhetoric of Indianness for their own ends does not mean that *caciquismo* is inherently traditional or even semi-Indian, however truly "native" the community may be in other important respects (see Chapters 6 and 7).

The potential weaknesses of *cacique* power in the Santa Marta highlands were brought to the fore in the late 1970s when cattle ranching activities and the expansion of the state-owned oil industry came into conflict. A marginal cattle economy using land inefficiently and little labor was no longer compatible with the growth of industry. Pajapan's fertile lowlands were expropriated to give way to a mega-industrial port project financed by PEMEX. Ranchers and peasants, local authorities and opposition groups eventually joined forces against the federal state agencies to obtain the best possible conditions of expropriation for all *comuneros* of Pajapan. Without this alliance, most segments of the native population, wealthy and poor alike, stood to lose from the expropriation. Within a few months, local politics shifted from a relatively brutal form of *caciquismo* to an ethno-popular, geopolitical confrontation of the native people of Pajapan against PEMEX and the Mexican state.

Four important lessons can be learned from this particular case of ethno-popular struggle against broader geopolitical domains. First, stories of David and Goliath do happen in real life. A powerless group can score over a powerful adversary provided that the internal alliance is a strong one and that certain external conditions are satisfied. In the case of Pajapan, two conditions had to be met. One was the availability of outside support (the media, Indian and peasant organizations, opposition parties) coupled with legal-bureaucratic channels of opposition (e.g., court injunctions) allowing subordinate groups to challenge the powers that be. Another condition was that the dominant group be playing for high stakes and be willing to make concessions to attain its own objectives (pursuing the industrial port project). Given these internal and external conditions, an ethno-popular struggle can gain its objectives even when the forces at play are not on equal terms.

Second, cases of people versus the state involve struggles that are no less significant or real than battles between capital and labor or ranchers and peasants. At the risk of repeating ourselves, the role of the state in rural areas goes beyond the contribution it makes to maintaining or attenuating existing class relations and the corresponding private property regime. The state does not content itself with extending bourgeois power to the sphere of government, nor does it simply mediate between classes with a view to salvaging the economic power system from its inherent limitations or internal contradictions. What these conceptions of the state overlook is that the state always intervenes on its own behalf in the sense of protecting its political interests and developing its own economic base (as with the oil industry in Mexico), thereby influencing the course of history. Self-interested actions of government authorities do not always meet their objectives: projects such as the industrial port planned for the lowlands of Pajapan may get cancelled after all. History rarely unfolds according to plans. Yet these government actions do have an impact on the dynamics and the final outcome of social history.

Third, studies of popular-democratic struggle should not be viewed as an alternative to class conflict analysis: one antagonism does not exclude another. However united the "native people" may have been and whatever attenuating effects the popular struggle may have had on internal class divisions, class interests did interfere with the political process throughout the struggle. As argued by Chamoux (1981), Chevalier (1982: 188–97), Schryer (1990: 228–44), Wasserstrom (1983) and others (see Chapter 2), anthropologists should be careful not to treat collective action systems such as civil–religious activities,[91] popular movements, peasant rebellions and Indian struggles as classless processes – egalitarian forces or "levelling mechanisms" pure and simple. Comments made by Stern (1983: 24) regarding the corporate peasant community apply equally well to ethno-popular fronts: "the historical origins, functions, and resilience of closed corporate communities has as much to do with internal struggles among natives ('intra-native struggles linked to new class forces unleashed by colonial rule') as they did with the survival of traditions, the desires of exploiters, or the defenses of impoverished Indians against non-indigenous outsiders."

To be sure, the popular alliance struck by the people of Pajapan against the Mexican state presented itself as a struggle of subordinate groups seeking justice from the government of Mexico. Moreover, the communal battle resulted in real gains by the poorer segments of Gulf Nahua society. This ethno-popular alliance was nevertheless fraught with internal class tensions from the start. The dominant rancher-PRI group never lost control of the alliance and the actions it took. And the battle against PEMEX brought more benefits to Indian ranchers and PRI authorities than to other segments of the native population.

Fourth, demands made by natives using an "Indian struggle" discourse are not always synonymous with "native demands" – with economic and political claims that are specific to native populations and aimed at preserving their mode of life. The principal objectives pursued by the "people of Pajapan" consisted in adequate financial payments for expropriated property (mostly for Indian ranchers) and also the parcelling of unexpropriated lands (mostly for peasants). Although these objectives may have been dressed up as requisites for the defense of Nahua culture against external threats, the real issues at stake during the few years that the battle lasted had little to do with problems of Indianness proper, let alone with the preservation of an egalitarian, closed-corporate peasant society.

There is no doubt that the people of Pajapan retain features of social organization that are distinctively Nahua. Social manifestations of "Indianness" in the Mexican countryside cannot be reduced to a creation of colonial and post-colonial history, as Pozas and Pozas (1971), Beaucage (1973) and Bonfil Batalla (1970, 1971) would have it. Having said this, the rhetoric of Indianness is "a double-edged sword" (Mallon 1983: 341), a powerful instrument that can serve different purposes, some of which may be at odds with the pursuit of community equality or the preservation of native value systems and related modes of social organization. The Indian ranchers of Pajapan who fought for the maintenance of the communal land tenure system which they controlled were upholders of tradition in appearances only; in reality they were the primary agents of capitalist penetration in Pajapan. Ethnic claims may express resistance against an unfair regime and a struggle for economic and cultural survival (Sandstrom 1991: 45, 331, 348), but they can also betray a particular group's effort to acquire cultural capital and related material and political gains.

The events of the early 1980s and the gains achieved by the *comuneros* of Pajapan against the Mexican state suggest that ethno-populism can also serve the cause of the landless and the powerless. But this is not to say that the "Indian struggle" rhetoric serves the cause of cultural preservation. In the case of Pajapan, notions of native communalism were literally imposed by the state (through legal and administrative measures) to limit Indian territoriality to its narrowest expression. Ironically, the language of communal territoriality ended up rebounding on a state domain in pursuit of more land. Indigenous peoples are not passive victims of their own Indianization; given the right conditions, Indians (or at least some of them) can turn the rhetoric of "Indianness" and "primitive communalism" against the power-holders who created the rhetoric in the first place.[92]

Pajapan's ethno-popular politics ended in 1984 when PEMEX plans to expand were cancelled: the common front dissolved as soon as it lost its *raison d'être*. Once the external threat was removed, the people of Pajapan broke up into its component parts: peasants and ranchers, *comuneros* and non-*comuneros*, Pajapan villagers and residents of smaller settlements, PRI authorities and opposition groups, pro-*ejido* (PSUM) and pro-communal (CNPI) activists. The internal divisions of Gulf Nahua society are now more visible than ever. One reason for this fragmentation is the tendency for peasants and communities to work in isolation from each other and to compete for scarce resources that are declining as the population grows. But the conflictual effects of a fragmented economy are compounded by antagonisms that have developed over the last 40 years. The Gulf Nahuas are now faced with dissension between the landed and the landless, the governing and the governed, the old and the young. The society is plagued with discord between classes, political parties and opposition groups. Cultural issues are also fought out on the religious front. Orthodox Catholics, local brotherhoods and PRI rancher politicians generally uphold the *mayordomia* tradition based on the cult of Catholic saints and related festivities. By contrast, Protestant sects, political opposition groups and the Christian Base Communities organized by the Jesuits openly denounce and boycott orthodox church activities (including traditional mass celebrations and the collection of church funds through pilgrimages).[93]

A brief phase of communal action directed against federal authorities and the oil industry has now given way to a period of factionalism. While the latter notion was initially used in anthropology as an alternative to class analysis (Nicholas 1965; Foster 1965; Gross 1973; Romanucci-Ross 1973), more recent studies of politics in the Mexican countryside have treated factionalism as a weak version of *caciquismo*, an unstable situation where the ruling powers are vying for popular support and power over wealth and government. Village factionalism is analyzed "in terms of the competition of rival upper class leaders who maintained patron–client bonds with their respective lower-class supporters" (Schryer 1990: 216).[94] In his earlier works, Schryer (1975: 291) argued that factionalism typically occurs where there is "a relatively equal distribution of land ownership (among local elite) combined with a large percentage of landless, wage-earning peasants, and an economic system which involves many isolated and autonomous productive units that are not conducive to collective action or a complex division of labor". In this perspective, factional politics result from the limited concentration of agricultural capital combined with a tendency toward the differentiation and fragmentation of the peasantry.

By and large, the conditions described by Schryer apply to the economic system prevailing in Pajapan since 1984. Such conditions, however, are not always sufficient to produce factional politics, nor is the economistic approach to factionalism entirely satisfactory. The political dynamics of a fragmented power system should also be considered. As Schryer (1990: 216, see 310) himself notes, "the task of political anthropologists is to ascertain how the political system at the national level and local class dynamics jointly determine the form of village factionalism."[95] Rivalries developing within economic classes will find an expression in the government process if and only if there are divisions instituted within the political arena (national *and* local) in the first place. Factions within a class will compete over the power to govern only if competition can be channelled through civil divisions, hence through conflicts opposing citizens against the governing body, one party or branch of government against another. Political interests are pursued and battles are fought out within their own institutional arena. Our analysis of Gulf Nahua history shows that factionalism can stem from causes other than economic class struggle. Although native Realpolitik may entail rivalries between *caciques* (Boege 1988: 60, 81) or a proliferation of intra-class disputes regarding strategies of class struggle (Schryer 1990: 216), factionalism can also result from civil divisions proper – from geopolitical conflicts over access to power and resources held in the public sphere.

As elsewhere, factional alliances in Pajapan tend to be short-lived and fluid (Schryer 1990: 216; Katz 1988: 12).[96] Conflicts that have emerged in recent years and the inability on the part of any particular Gulf Nahua group to achieve stable hegemonic power should be understood against the background of a political crisis that developed at both local and national levels and that cannot be reduced to economic class factors alone. The fiscal crisis that hit the Mexican state in the early 1980s forced PEMEX to abandon its Laguna del Ostión project and to withdraw from the Sierra de Santa Marta; federal agencies crippled with debts no longer had an interest in the region. Meanwhile, peasants had already obtained a redistribution of communal lands, at the expense of Indian ranchers. Since the land reform cut the ground from under the ranchers' feet, the local PRI-government machine was divested of one of its main functions: the administration of communal lands occupied by powerful ranchers.

Federal state agencies withdrew from municipal politics and the local government lost its power to allocate land. While the crisis weakened both state and municipal administrations, it gave an impetus to manifestations of opposition channelled through parties and peasant organizations independent of the PRI. Compared to earlier decades, local and regional struggles of the late 1980s involved greater intervention of external forces, opposition parties and pressure groups (FCIP, PPS, PSUM, CNPI) dedicated to bringing about justice and democracy in the Sierra de Santa Marta.[97] However, given the social divisions prevailing in Pajapan and the current absence of a common enemy, these counter-hegemonic groups have dispersed their activities into a number of particular struggles (for democracy, the landless, Indianness, religious pluralism) that have failed to coalesce into one overall movement.[98] In the end, factional politics in Pajapan can be attributed not only to the endemic weaknesses affecting the cattle industry and the Indian rancher class but also to the Mexican political crisis and all those divisions that pervade Gulf Nahua civil society.

This completes our discussion of political theory and the Gulf Nahua history of land tenure and government. Our analysis has shown how *caciquismo*, ethno-populism and factionalism have been molded by the active opposition of peasant labor and capital. Readers should note, however, that politics in Pajapan has never been a straightforward expression of class struggle between ranchers and peasants. Confrontations between the wealthy and the poor have always been attenuated or exacerbated by political conflicts proper – conflicts between citizens and government and between parties and spheres of authority. As argued in the next chapter, local politics have also given the local class structure its current shape.

Notes

1. Velázquez and Perales 1991; SARH 1986, 1988.

2. According to the SRA, 32 families owned 14,450 hectares of land in 1976 (with a maximum property of 1,500 ha.), hence 90% of all arable land in Pajapan. In our view, this overestimates the concentration of land in Pajapan. Our survey data indicate that a significant number of peasants (about 36% of all households) had small to medium parcels of land.

3. The estimate of the total herd and proportion owned by the 40 ranchers is based on our survey data and interviews. In our opinion, the estimate of 7,000 head of cattle made by RIGOR is too low. The 600 head of cattle figure for the year 1968 (García de León 1976) may not be all that reliable. See also ACEAX, Expediente Pajapan, December 8, 1983.

4. Similar tendencies have been observed in the neighboring municipality of Mecayapan (Velázquez 1992b).

5. Interview with Simón Antonio Hernández, Pajapan, October 7, 1987.

6. As confirmed by García de León, the peasants "in December 1967 were able to impose a municipal president favoring the majority" (García de León 1976: 130, our translation).

7. Interviews with Demetrio Bautista Hernández, Cosoleacaque, October 19, 1987; Sergio Martínez Alemán, Pajapan, September 23, 1987.

8. Interview with Enrique Cruz Antonio, Pajapan, October 6, 1987.

9. Ibid.

10. Interview with Genaro Antonio Hernández, Pajapan, September 21, 1987.

11. ASRAM, December 5, 1970.

12. ASRAX, "Informe sobre la comunidad de Pajapan (antecedentes)", July 7, 1976.

13. See articles 47, 48 and 49 of the Ley Federal de Reforma Agraria; Chávez Padrón 1987: 99–106.

14. ASRAM, Letter, December 7, 1970; Letter, January 13, 1971.

15. ASRAM, Letters of April 10, May 13, October 21 and December 15, 1972; ASRAX, February 16, 1973.

16. ASRAM, August 3, 1976.

17. Interviews with Genaro Antonio Hernández, Sixto Vargas Lorenzo, Sergio Martínez Alemán, Pajapan, September 23, 24, 26, 1987.

18. ASRAX, Telegram, April 30, 1976.

19. Interviews with Pedro Martínez Vargas and Genaro Antonio Hernández, Pajapan, September 18 and 21, 1987.

20. Interview with Pedro Martínez Vargas, Pajapan, September 18, 1987.

21. Our own research indicates that the number of large landowners in Pajapan was greater, perhaps 40 in all, but that the degree of land concentration was not as great as that indicated by the SRA report. See Chapter 4 for details of land distribution prior to the reform.

22. ASRAX, July 2 and November 24 ("Acta de posesión y deslinde definitivo total de reconocimiento y titulación de bienes comunales al poblado denominado Pajapan"), 1976; "Informe sobre la comunidad Pajapan (antecedentes)", July 7, 1976. Minor technical revisions to the mapping of the communal lands of Pajapan were carried out in late 1979 by the SRA. See ASRAM, Letters, September 11 and

November 14, 1979, and "Acta de conformidad de las autoridades ejidales del poblado denominado Pajapan", November 27, 1979. See also ASRAX, Letters, November 7, 22 and December 6, 1979, January 22, March 7 and May 6, 1980.

23. Interview with Sixto Vargas Lorenzo, Pajapan, September 26, 1987. ASRAM, Letters, July 25 and August 3, 1976.

24. Interview with Sergio Martínez Alemán, Pajapan, September 23, 1987.

25. Interview with Sixto Vargas Lorenzo, Pajapan, September 26, 1987.

26. The party was established in Pajapan in 1973 during the campaign of a PPS candidate from Coatzacoalcos for the position of federal deputy.

27. See article 44 of the Ley Federal de Reforma Agraria.

28. ASRAX, Telegram, August 31, 1978.

29. Interviews with Román and Gabriel Hernández Antonio, Pajapan, September 23 and 27, 1987; Pedro Pereyra Fonseca, Pajapan, September 28, 1987.

30. Anonymous, Archives of Pajapan, March 17, 1986.

31. Interviews with Pedro Pereyra Fonseca, Ramón Hernández Martínez and Santos Hernández Martínez, September 28, 29 and October 2, 1987.

32. Archives of Pajapan, July 2, 1979. ASRAM, Letter, October 15, 1979.

33. Interview with Gabriel Hernández Antonio, Pajapan, October 4, 1987.

34. Interview with Román Hernández Antonio, Pajapan, September 27, 1987.

35. Interview with Sixto Vargas Lorenzo, Pajapan, September 26, 1987.

36. One US sailor we interviewed in Coatzacoalcos in 1986 indicated that the port suffered from the greatest abuses in the handling of oil he had ever witnessed in over 15 years of employment on oil tankers in different parts of the world.

37. The lands to be expropriated comprised 5,153 hectares of communal land, 1,253 hectares of ejido, 2,919 hectares of private lands, 1,249 of federal lands, and 1,396 hectares of national lands (Reunión de Evalución de Programa Puertos Industriales, 1981).

38. Mexico, Programa 1981, Coordinación General del Programa de Puertos Industriales; Memoria del Programa de Puertos Industriales, 1979–82.

39. Interviews with Pedro Pereyra Fonseca and Santos Hernández Martínez, Pajapan, September 28 and October 2, 1987. See also Interviews with Ramón Hernández Martínez, Simón Antonio Hernández, Sergio Martínez Alemán, Narciso Cruz and Pablo Martínez Tino, Pajapan, September 23, 27 and October 1, 1987.

40. Representatives of seven government agencies were present including SRA, PEMEX, SAHOP, SCT, SPP and FONDEPORT. Our account of this meeting is based on 1987 interviews with Demetrio Bautista Hernández, Cosoleacaque, October 19; Francisco Morosini (ex-director of FONDEPORT office in Coatzacoalcos), Coatzacoalcos, October 14; Genaro Antonio Hernández, Pajapan, October 7; Sergio Martínez Alemán, Pajapan, September 23; Pedro Pereyra Fonseca, Pajapan, September 28; Ramón Hernández Martínez, Pajapan, September 29; and Pedro Martínez Vargas, Pajapan, September 26. See also Bouysse-Cassagne (1980: 27); Martínez and Rodríguez (1984: 12); Uno Más Uno, January 30, 31, 1980.

41. Interview with Salvador Hernández Martínez, Pajapan, September 16, 1987.

42. The draft of the expropriatory decree was prepared by the General Direction of Lands and Water of the SRA and completed on February 27, 1980. For more information on the contents of the expropriatory decree and the procedures leading to it, see ACEAX, Dictámen Positivo, Expediente 56–5471, February 27, 1980.

43. ASRAX, "Acta de Asamblea", June 29, 1980. Prior to this meeting, a letter was sent by the Governor of Veracruz to the office of the President requesting the President to guarantee future jobs for the Indians of Pajapan and to resolve the matter of the unexpropriated lands in Pajapan (ASRAM, April 29, 1980).

44. He also suggested that the expropriation money be invested in agricultural projects, a hotel, a cement factory, etc.

45. Article 130 of the Ley Federal de Reforma Agraria states that "provisional and definitive *ejidos* and communities [collective lands] will be used collectively, except when its members determine by an agreement reached during a general assembly that they will be used individually" (Chávez Padrón 1987: 161; see also article 52).

46. Archives of Pajapan, Letter, July 30, 1980.

47. Interview with Salvador Hernández Martínez, Pajapan, September 16, 1987 (our translation).

48. Interviews with Gabriel Hernández Antonio, Pedro Pereyra Fonseca and Santos Hernández Martínez, Pajapan, September 23 and 28, October 2, 1987. See also Bouysse-Cassagne (1987: 30); *Uno Más Uno*, August 15 and 16, 1980; *El Día*, August 17, 1980; and *Diario del Istmo*, August 17, 21 and 22, 1980.

49. ACNCP, "Amparo", September 18, 1980. See also Archives of Pajapan, October 10 and 14, 1980; ACEAX, October 10, 1980, and September 19, 1981; AJH, October 10 and 20, 1980.

50. On the events surrounding the expropriation, see INI film "Laguna de Dos Tiempos"; Bouysse-Cassagne (1980); Coll (1981); Lara Ovando (1987); Lara Ovando and Gutiérrez Hernández (1983); Martínez and Rodríguez (1984).

51. Interview with Sergio Martínez Alemán, Pajapan, September 23, 1987. See ASRAX, Acta de Asamblea General Extraordinaria, November 2, 1980.

52. Interviews with Genaro Antonio Hernández, Gabriel Hernández Antonio and Santos Hernández Martínez, Pajapan, September 16, 23 and October 2, 1987. Interview with Francisco Morosini (Ex-Director of FONDEPORT office in Coatzacoalcos), Coatzacoalcos, October 14, 1987. See also ASRAX, Letters, January 21, February 3, and Memorandum, March 16, 1981.

53. *El Día*, January 4 and 9, February 3 and 5, 1981; *Uno Más Uno*, January 17, 1981.

54. Interview with Lic. Ordinola, State Agrarian Sub-Delegate, Xalapa, October 22, 1987.

55. Interviews with Pedro Martínez Vargas, Genaro Antonio Hernández and Sergio Martínez Alemán, Pajapan, September 17, 21 and 23, 1987. See ASRAX, June 29, 1981. Our lot statistics are based on interviews with 17 of the 37 lot administrators, January 15–20, 1988.

56. ASRAX, Letter, February 10, 1981.

57. Based on an exchange rate of 300 pesos per US$.

58. ACNCP, "Convenio", May 7, 1981, and December 31, 1985; Acta de Asamblea, ASRAX, May 7, 1981.

59. ASRAX, November 23, 1981, February 12 and March 16, 1982; ASRAM, Letters, January 12 and February 11, 1982; Archives of Pajapan, Letters, March 18 and 25, April 25 and 29, May 1 and 26, 1982; Interviews with Genaro Antonio Hernández and Camilo Ciriaco Martínez, Pajapan, September 21 and 22, 1987.

60. ACEAX, June 23, October 7, 1982; Interviews with Gabriel Hernández Antonio and Sergio Martínez Alemán, Pajapan, September 23 and 30, 1987. One union officially registered in 1980 under the name of *Sindicato de la Construcción de la Industria* comprised 42 members.

61. ACEAX, Acta de Asamblea General Extraordinaria; AJH, Expediente Pajapan; ACNCP; Archives of Pajapan, Acta-Convenio, November 26, and Letters of December 3 and 6, 1982.

62. Many villagers invested the expropriation money into better-quality houses. Municipal Pajapan statistics indicate that the number of houses with electricity, running water and sewage facilities went up from 28%, 24% and 4% in 1980 to 67%, 65% and 30% in 1990, respectively. Although most Pajapeños were still living in one-room houses (72%) at the time of our 1986 village survey, a relatively

high proportion of houses were made of cement walls (40%) and metal roofs (49%) and had electricity (53%) and running water (49%) as well.

63. Interviews with Sergio Martínez Alemán and Santos Hernández Martínez, Pajapan, September 30 and October 6, 1987.

64. Interviews with Sergio Martínez Alemán, Gabriel Hernández Antonio, Tomás Martínez Encarnación, Juan and Pedro Pereyra Fonseca, Pajapan, September 23, October 1 and 4, 1987.

65. Aniceto was the brother of Apolinar, Municipal President from 1973 to 1976, and a son of Guadalupe Hernández Jáuregui, a powerful Indian rancher denounced by communal land authorities in the early 1970s.

66. ACNCP, Expediente Puerto Industrial de Ostión, Letter, October 19, 1984.

67. In July 1983, Abel Jímenez Hernández replaced Cipriano Yep Tiket, the former legal advisor whom many perceived as protecting the vested interests of ranchers as well as his own (interviews with Abel Jímenez Hernández, Genaro Antonio Hernández and Genaro Salas, Pajapan, September 3, 11 and 12, 1987).

68. See Archives of Pajapan, Questionnaire of the Fourth District Judge, 1983; ACEAX, Expediente Pajapan, Dictámen, December 8, 1983, and Final Report of the Evaluation, May 22, 1984.

69. AJH, Expediente Pajapan, June 4, and sentence of the Fourth District Judge, July 31, 1984.

70. AJH, Expediente Pajapan, Request for Revision, August 23, 1984; ASRAX, March 12, 1986.

71. ACNCP, Expediente Puerto Industrial de Ostión, March 31, 1982.

72. Interview with Francisco Morosini (ex-director of FONDEPORT office in Coatzacoalcos), Coatzacoalcos, October 14, 1987.

73. ACNCP, Expediente Puerto Industrial de Ostión, April 11, September 20 and 23, 1983; Interview with Narciso Cruz, Jicacal, September 27, 1987.

74. Archives of Pajapan, Handout, July 23, 1983.

75. Acciones para la reordenación intermunicipal de la cuenca de Coatzacoalcos, Government of Mexico, 1987, pp. 14–17; ACNCP, Expediente Puerto Industrial de Ostión, press summary, October 1984.

76. Excélsior, Thursday, April 23, 1992.

77. See Diario Oficial, July 24, 1986; Interview with Lic. Ordinola, State Agrarian Sub-Delegate, Xalapa, October 22, 1987. Articles 125 and 126 of the Ley Federal de Reforma Agraria state that if a project requiring expropriation is not completed within a five-year period, the land reverts to the FIFONAFE trusteeship for return to the original owners. Those who have been expropriated are not obliged to return the money paid (Chávez Padrón 1987: 154–6).

78. Interviews with Felipe Zeferino and Pedro Martínez Vargas, September 7 and 23, and with Fernando Ochoa, ex-PSUM organizer, August 29, 1987. See also ASRAX, Letters, October 28 and 29, 1987.

79. Interview with Felipe Zeferino, February 2, 1988.

80. Interview with Felipe Zeferino, October 14, 1987. The first intervention of CNPA in Pajapan was in March 1987 when they denounced the procedures used to form the Consejo de Vigilancia (i.e., without elections); see Archives of Pajapan, Letter and Report of the Audience, March 11 and June 1987.

81. Letter to FIFONAFE, from Carlos Martínez, Comisariado Comunal, February 1988.

82. See Archives of Pajapan, Proposal of El Mangal, December 1, 1986; Letter, April 8, 1987; Melitón Hernández Neri (SRA official), Investigation, April 27, 1987; List of Sellers and Buyers of Agrarian Rights and List of Landholders, May 1987; Interviews with Pedro Martínez Vargas, September 17 and 23, with Genaro Salas and Gabriel Hernández Antonio, September 12 and 23, and with Sebastián

Silvestre and Juan Pereyra Fonseca, September 19 and 20, 1987; Interview with Magdaleno Antonio, June 5, 1990; see also FCIP, Historia de la lucha por la tierra, September 1987.

83. A census update conducted in May by regional delegates of the SRA was simply ignored; in any case the official who conducted the census seems to have lumped together peasants in need of land and the Indian ranchers who had bought other *comuneros'* land rights.

84. Interview with Felipe Zeferino, Jáltipan, February 2, 1988.

85. Interviews with a FCIP organizer, October 14, and with Adrian Rosnero Cisneros, Chief of the Regional Agrarian Office in Chinameca, October 15, 1987. Archives of Pajapan, Letters, April 11, May 12, and Audience Reports, July 1987.

86. See Archives of Pajapan, Proposal to the State Governor, September 27, 1987; Interview with Pedro Martínez Vargas, September 26, 1987.

87. Interview with Carlos Martínez Cruz, October 7, 1987.

88. This section is based on interviews conducted in May and June of 1990 with Pedro Martínez Vargas, Clemente Trujillo Antonio and Genaro Antonio. See also José Luis Blanco, Interview with Bernardino Hernández, October 15, and Interview with Aniceto Hernández, October 19, 1988.

89. Interview with Genaro Salas, January 15, 1988.

90. Schryer (1980: 63). See also Schryer (1990: 37); Friedrich (1965); Alegría (1952: 313–16); Bartra et al. (1975); Kern (1973); Paré (1973); Roniger (1987). According to Paré (1975: 36) and Friedrich (1986: 292), the term comes from the Arawak word *kassiquan*, "to have or take care of a house". During the Spanish Conquest, the term was applied to Caribbean chiefs. It was later adapted by the Spaniards to designate local authorities in the conquered territories (Latin America and the Philippines). Friedrich (1970: 6) suggests that local chiefs or *caciques* supported by the Spaniards "may have represented the continuation of the pre-conquest dynasties of princes and local chiefs". F. Chevalier (1982: 30–1) mentions the following definition appearing in a Spanish dictionary of 1729: "the first of his village or the republic, the one who has more authority or power and who because of his pride wants to make himself feared and obeyed by all his inferiors."

91. Class conflict in Pajapan is partly offset by real and fictive (*compadrazgo*) kinship ties that bind the wealthy to the poor, the powerful to the powerless. The ritual *mayordomía* system operating in Pajapan also permits some redistribution of wealth among villagers. As might be expected, however, inter-class solidarities expressed through kinship play a limited role in a modern *ranchero* economy that makes little use of peasant labor. As for the levelling effects of the religious PRI-dominated *cargo* system, they are essentially symbolic. In 1986, half of the 27 religious festivities held in Pajapan were actually sponsored by peasants, not by ranchers. The total wealth spent by all *cargo* holders amounted to the equivalent of 33 head of cattle only, out of a total village herd of 7,000.

92. Given these various scenarios and possible discrepancies between discourse and native Realpolitik, lists of themes that allegedly typify Indian struggles against external domination should be used with extreme caution (Barre 1985; Mejía Piñeros and Sarmiento Silva 1987). Surface characterizations of this kind err on the side of political naivety and should never be used as substitutes for sound social and political analysis. In the words of Schryer (1990: 256), "appeals to Indianness or demands for ethnic survival in such ethnically diverse regions as Huejutla are neither inherently reactionary nor inevitably revolutionary as rival scholars would like to argue. In each case, it is necessary to examine the relationship between belief and behavior, between the official ideology and the actions of state representatives, between the rhetoric used by agrarian politicians and their personal interests and real intentions."

93. According to the 1990 census, approximately 13% of the people residing in the municipal Pajapan were Protestants (compared to less than 1% in 1960). Another 18% had no religious affiliation. The question as to how the penetration of Protestant sects in rural Mexico has affected grass-roots notions of Indian identity is open to debate. On the one hand, as Sandstrom (1991: 361) states, "a new option opened for the village poor that was completely outside the range of traditional choices. They no longer had to be either Indians or rural mestizos. They now had the possibility of being *hermanos*." The same process has been observed in Guatemala (Sexton 1989; Warren 1989). Also the struggle of Protestant sects against alcoholism, wife-beating and civil–religious hierarchies controlled by Indian *caciques* can play a progressive role in local politics. On the other hand, anthropologists should not underestimate the divisive effects that religious affiliations can have on solidarities between the village poor, as in Pajapan. Nor should they ignore the acculturation pressure created by the Christian Base Community movement, let alone the potential for conservative inter-class alliances created by the proliferation of Protestant churches and Christian organizations (such as the pro-orthodoxy Catholic Action movement) in the Latin American countryside. For a well-balanced analysis of the impact of Protestant sects on native society in Mexico, see Boege 1988: 229, 252–3, 270, 274–7, 283–5.

94. See also Schryer (1980: 101–12); (1990: 115–16, 278); Benjamin (1989: 210–12). For a discussion of patron–client politics in relation to class structure and the Mexican state, see Rothstein (1986) and Grindle (1977: 26–40). Patronage in peasant communities has its limits though and can be kept in check by the emergence of alternative political parties (or rival factions within the ruling party) and independent organizations as well. Moreover, as suggested by Greenberg (1989: 9), the "politics of patronage, though important, are only half of the village life. The other half is the politics of consensus, typically manifested in mass demonstrations or land invasions [...] Although allies try to mold a consensus through patronage, the underground currents of consensus are not easily controlled and often run counter to the elite's wishes."

95. The author, however, goes on to say that "since the Mexican political system had not changed that much since the thirties, the new forms of factionalism I encountered in Huejutla could be explained primarily in terms of changing class dynamics on the local level" (Schryer 1990: 216; see also 1980: 48).

96. For case-studies emphasizing the ability of peasant and Indian movements to form flexible alliances with the most unlikely forces, see Falcón Vega (1988: 417–47), Hu-DeHart (1988: 141–75), Reina (1988: 269–94), and Warman (1988: 321–37).

97. For a broader discussion of peasant movements and struggles for democracy in rural Mexico, see Paré (1990) and Otero (1989).

98. On the differences between counterhegemonic movements and class struggles, see Sider (1986: 119–28).

CHAPTER 4

THE ECONOMICS OF
MALDEVELOPMENT

Class structures, strictures and struggles

Three phases characterize recent Gulf Nahua politics. To each phase correspond particular forces, strategic alliances and conversions of power. The first phase revolved round the hegemonic rule established by the PRI-rancher class over communal land and political offices, to the detriment of Indian peasants forced out of agriculture and excluded from the local government process. This phase lasted from the 1950s till the late 1970s when PEMEX expropriated the fertile lowlands of Pajapan, an event that triggered the formation of an ethno-popular front of local classes and political forces against the federal state. The communal front and concessions obtained from the federal government (indemnities, land reform, roads and schools, etc.) were brought to an end by Mexico's fiscal crisis and the cancellation of the PEMEX port project in 1984. The years that followed witnessed the weakening of the local cattle industry, a reduction of state intervention in Pajapan, and an outburst of factionalism – a marked fragmentation of political positions and economic classes competing over issues of land and office. Parallel developments have occurred at regional and national levels.

The political transformations and struggles of the Gulf Nahuas over the last 40 years have shaped the current economy and class profile of Pajapan, to which we now turn. Three considerations influence our approach to class relations and productive activities in Pajapan. First, we emphasize the variable forms of exploitation in the countryside: Pajapeños now have access to land but they are exploited through means other than outright proletarianization. Second, we stress the limitations that inhere to particular forms of exploitation, such as the chronic weaknesses of ranching operations and small businesses in Pajapan. Ranching capital still remains a low-profit economy that occupies extensive tracts of land and little labor; it is destructive of its own resource base and creates no opportunity for sustainable growth (more on these issues in Chapter 5). Third, the workers' resistance to capital and peasant survival strategies are also considered. This chapter examines the impact land politics had in the early 1980s on inter- and intra-class divisions in Pajapan, and peasants' struggles to secure their livelihood. Native resistance built into economic forms ranges from subsistence production to wage-labor, petty trade, simple commodity production and small-scale ranching. We shall

124

see later that the persistence of self-employment based on subsistence and simple commodity production points to a domestic and village economy governed by kin-based rules of the patrimonial domain (see Chapter 6). Although drastically altered, native rules still govern relations between genders and generations and between human beings and spirits of the natural kingdom (see Chapter 7).

The theoretical implications of our approach to Gulf Nahua economics are outlined below. Briefly, the analysis of rural class economics presented in this chapter implies a movement away from notions of capitalism conceived as (a) *homomorphic*, governed by relations and forms of production of a single type (the industrial capital/wage-labor opposition); (b) *omnific*, able to secure all the conditions needed to satisfy requirements of maximum accumulation; and (c) *despotic*, to the point of being unperturbed by class struggle. We are not about to argue that capitalism is amorphous (as in the dependency literature), without recognizable forces and relations of production. Nor would we venture to resurrect the notion of a capitalist system planting the seeds of its own destruction wrought by class struggle. Rather, our contention is that capitalism is subject to three concurrent tendencies: the subordination of labor to capital through mechanisms that are variable and adaptable; processes of growth and maldevelopment arising from self-induced limitations; and the varied and ongoing struggle of subordinate classes against domination by capital.

The growth of capital: variable and adaptable

The economic history of Pajapan can serve to illustrate a long-standing thesis in the political economy of rural societies: the rise of agricultural capital, the dispossession of peasants from the land, and a tendency toward the differentiation of peasants into workers and owners of factors of production (Marx 1976: 879–83, 909, 950; Kautsky 1970; Lenin 1968; Bernstein 1988: 264). More specifically, the rapid development of the cattle industry in Pajapan and elsewhere in the Sierra de San Martín, particularly in the 1970s, led to the usurpation of communal property in land, the polarization of class relations within the community, and the proletarianization of a sizeable portion of the native population. Over a period of 30 years, ranchers gained control over most of the communal land, converting peasants into poorly-paid ranch peons or forcing them out of agriculture and into other sectors of the rural and urban economy. Permanent out-migration to urban centers became a major survival strategy adopted by displaced peasants and also a source of cheap labor for urban industry. The rise of agricultural capital in the countryside thus contributed labor to an expanding urban industrial complex in southern Veracruz.

Pajapan is no exception to the growing "contradictory relation between the expansion of the capitalist sector and the small peasant economy" observed throughout Mexico and Latin America (Bartra and Otero 1987: 342; see Lerda 1985). At the same time our Gulf Nahua case-study reinforces the argument made by dependency, unequal exchange, world system and structural articulation theorists alike: that land appropriation and proletarianization are only two of several forms of capitalist penetration in agriculture (A. Bartra 1979a; Bernstein 1979; Bradby 1975; Burowoy 1977; Dupré and Rey 1978; Foster-Carter 1978; Frank 1969; Long 1975; Meillassoux 1972; Mouzelis 1980; Mollard 1977; Novack 1976; Paige 1975; Rey 1971, 1973; Stavenhagen 1969; Taylor 1979; Yúnez 1988; etc.).[1] The analyses presented throughout this chapter emphasize the adaptability or "polymorphous" propensities (Amin and Vergopoulos 1974) of capital – the *variable effects and forms* of subordination of peasants to a production and exchange process based on the antagonism of capital and labor. To treat wage-work as the "essential" form of labor exploited by capital does little justice to "the immensely contradictory, complex, diverse and fluctuating phenomenal realities and experiences of 'actually existing' capitalism (vs. an ideal-typified capitalism)" (Bernstein 1988: 261).[2]

The data presented below show that not all peasants were converted into wage laborers, let alone full-time employees of local ranchers or urban employers. Some peasants managed to retain small parcels or access to land through loans or rental arrangements; many were pushed off the best land into marginal areas on the slopes of the volcano or into unsettled areas north of the communal lands. These peasants continued to produce foodstuffs to meet their family needs. Others moved into part-time or full-time craft work, petty trade or the fisheries of Jicacal and Las Barrillas. While reduced in scale and undermined as a self-sustained economy, subsistence and small-scale commodity production fulfilled a critical requirement of capital accumulation at both local and regional levels: reducing the renewal costs of the labor force hired by local ranchers or absorbed into urban industry. The subsistence economy was converted into a market-dependent sector generating human labor power, a vital commodity within the regional economy produced at no direct cost to capital (Astorga Lira 1985).

Rural workers can be exploited without the complete or definitive separation of peasants from control over some means of production. As we shall see, the redistribution of land in favor of the *comuneros* of Pajapan, an important reform implemented in the early 1980s, halted and actually reversed the trend toward a decomposition of the peasant economy. Nevertheless, the reform did not liberate the peasantry from the grip of local and regional ranchers or put an end to the subjection of the local peasantry to a predatory market economy. Although local cattle raisers suffered net losses in land and cattle, they managed to recuperate some of their losses in wealth through illegal purchases of land and the growth of a simple commodity economy involving self-employed peasants producing and renting pasture or breeding and selling calves to local ranchers. Capital can put up with some peasant ownership of land provided that there are other means of deriving concrete benefits from peasant labor (see J.M. Chevalier 1982, 1983). The extraction of surplus value from workers can operate through market relations other than wage-labor transactions. Although a central feature of modern capitalism and the world economy, the conversion of producers into "those whose only capital is their labor", to use Webster's euphemistic definition, is by no means the only mode of exploitation available to capital. As Byres (1985: 5) points out, it is misleading to think that "in a particular mode of production coherence requires that a *single* set of productive forces articulates with a *single* set of relations of production".

The process of subordination of labor to capital transforms productive relations and activities of all sorts, including subsistence and simple commodity production organized along kinship lines, into dependent branches of broader capital-dominated economies. This is to say that capitalism is far better described as a transformative process than a formal logic. It creates new classes but it also penetrates other social spaces already in existence, altering and adjusting their internal operations to meet market production requirements. Self-employed agricultural labor in Pajapan is a case in point. Although not directly purchased by capital, the labor power of peasants who produce and rent out pasture, breed small numbers of cattle or sell foodstuffs is exploited within a broader market economy controlled by ranchers. Domestic and communal patterns of production are adjusted to a commodification process governed by unequal class relations and the pursuit of profit. Once harnessed to a market economy over which natives have little control, traditional modes of livelihood cease to be self-sustainable and undergo profound transformations. In Pajapan, the end result of this process consists of plural occupational profiles, cash crop specialization (pasture, foodstuffs), an extensive use of land for grazing, and an overexploitation of all resources available within the immediate environment (soils, forest products, fauna, aquatic foodstuffs; see Chapter 5).

On the social level hinterland capitalists (ranchers) rise at the expense of rural workers. New relations emerge within the peasantry as well. An internal differentiation process develops involving market-dependent peasants, rural wage-earners and part-time urban proletarians. To this composite labor force harnessed to capital can be added another segment of the adult population: those without work and yet able to produce. Many peasants displaced from Pajapan have joined the ranks of the unemployed, a reserve army of potential workers obliged to compete with the active labor force (salaried or self-employed) for scarce work opportunities. The contribution of inactive laborers to capital resides not in the surplus value they produce as proletarians or as market-dependent peasants. The benefits accruing from the unemployed to owners of capital come rather from the downward pressure which people out of work exert on wages in rural and urban employment (Marx 1976: 781–94). Like proletarianization, unemployment in southern Veracruz is both an effect and a function of capital accumulation.

The stupid machine thesis

Although variable and adaptable, capitalism is far from the perfect machine for profit accumulation and economic production idealized by neo-conservative economists but also many theorists on the left (see Chapter 5), a machine smoothly meeting all of its requirements and attaining all profits pursued by the wealthy who control the factors of production and the mechanisms of market circulation. While the business of profit is by definition a central feature of capitalism, it is misleading to explain all observable effects of market economies by consideration of this functional requirement only. In reality capitalism is a stupid machine generating chronic effects of uneven development and outright mal-development. The so-called "logic of capital" is rife with self-induced limitations and contradictions that undermine the sustainable exploitation and maximum use of available factors of production, i.e., labor, natural resources and productive technology. Effects of maldevelopment range from crises of underconsumption (Marx 1973: 413, 422) to agricultural and industrial underproduction, from massive unemployment to the ravages of environmental destruction.

The "vicious circle" of poverty in Pajapan creates basic limitations and costs to the process of capital accumulation operating at the local and regional levels. The growth of the cattle sector was and still is highly constrained by the subordinate position local ranchers occupy within the regional structure of production and commercialization. Indian cattle-raisers (and small peasants with a few head of cattle) engage in the riskiest and most labor-intensive stages of cattle production providing outside mestizo ranchers and merchants with a steady supply of cheap, poor-quality feeder calves. These calves are raised to slaughter weight outside the Pajapan region. Dependence on outside capital has limited the ability of Indian ranchers to invest in more intensive techniques of production and in more profitable phases of the agro-industry. While Indian ranchers exercise considerable local power, they are a weak branch of regional capital with few opportunities to expand. Moreover, the industry has impoverished peasants and created few jobs and wage earnings within the village, thereby restricting the local circulation of commodities and the growth of merchant capital. As de Janvry et al. (1989) suggest, it is misleading to think that Third World capital can either proletarianize a majority of peasants or fully maximize their productivity. More realistically, the reproduction of peasant agriculture is a sign of capital's "systemic failure in providing them with sufficient employment and migration opportunities, not of success as agricultural producers" (de Janvry et al. 1989: 397).

The pre-reform concentration of land in the hands of a few Indian ranchers and the post-reform expansion of a simple commodity economy dominated by the cattle industry put hundreds of peasants out of work and degraded the immediate environment. Problems of deforestation, overgrazing, monoculture and the depletion of fish and game undermined the overall productivity of peasant agriculture and the subsistence economy as a whole (see Chapter 5). These effects are directly attributable to the inroads that capitalism has made into the local economy, but they also impose real limitations on the expansion and long-term prospects of capitalist development in the San Martín highlands. The depletion of natural resources and low levels of productivity create problems of scarcity (of fertile lands, foodstuffs for the working classes, etc.) that push all production costs upward.

The "stupid machine" argument applies to problems of unemployment as well. The usurpation of communal property by cattle ranchers forced peasants out of agriculture into urban centers in search of alternative sources of livelihood. In recent decades, similar processes have occurred in many rural areas of Mexico, resulting in a flood of workers descending on the cities of Coatzacoalcos and Minatitlán. These movements have increased the supply of labor power and reduced its market value. Capital (petro-chemical industry, construction and service sectors hiring unskilled laborers) derives significant benefits from this "reserve army" of workers in the form of low wages. But while this function is inherent to capitalism, the expulsion of labor from rural areas and its concentration in urban centers is far in excess of the needs of urban capital. Unemployment and underemployment for southern Veracruz is over 25% and as high as 40% for Mexico as a whole. This extremely large reserve army has many costly effects for the state and for capital, such as welfare expenditures and political unrest. The Mexican government provides food subsidies, hospitals and health centers, educational facilities and many other services to a population deprived of the earnings and resources needed to replenish the coffers of the state; like many other rural migrants of southern Veracruz, unemployed Pajapeños living in Coatzacoalcos or Minatitlán contribute little to state revenues. What is more, capital forgoes an opportunity to extract additional surplus value from thousands of unemployed workers and potential consumers. An oversized reserve army creates real costs symptomatic of the inability of capital fully to exploit the labor power expelled from agriculture. These effects cannot be reduced to functional requirements of capital accumulation or evidence of non-integration into the market economy.

Permanent resistance

Another inherent limitation on the accumulation of profits stems from labor's active opposition to capital. Our case-study illustrates the resistance of peasants to capitalist exploitation and their ongoing battle to increase their control over vital means of production. In contrast to studies that emphasize the stable reproduction of class inequalities, our analysis shows the continuous opposition of peasants to the ruling order and the central role they have played in shaping and transforming the local power and production system.

By peasants we mean agricultural workers, a class that excludes local native ranchers. What follows is a class analysis of the Gulf Nahua peasantry, not a romantic account of a Mexican rural tribe or rural people pitted against the state, agro-business and markets dominated by capital. Like Brass (1990), we object to neopopulist and post-modern theories of an eternal middle peasantry (family labor farms) viewed as an undifferentiated *sui generis* economic category, a subaltern mode of production or moral economy struggling to preserve its egalitarian life-world, its subsistence ethic and its Chayanovian drudgery-adverse logic (Sahlins 1972; Durrenberger 1984; Bartra and Otero 1987: 347, 350) against penetration by capital. "Classless" approaches to peasant economics fail to account for the inequalities of non-capitalist domains and also the integration of farmers into capitalist economies. They ignore the impact of modern class relations and the market economy on agricultural self-employment, hence efforts on the part of rich peasants to accumulate capital and the active striving of poorer peasants to improve their control over cash earnings, commodified factors of production and living conditions in general. Neopopulist studies of peasant economics (see Redclift 1988: 252) have in common with studies of social movements based on ethnicity, gender, religion or regionality that they risk rejecting class analysis altogether or misusing it by treating the subordinate group as forming a single class. Also, they run the risk of substituting micro-level resistance for revolutionary action and adopting a simplistic anti-state and anti-institutional (Slater 1985: 3) approach to social history. The resulting discourse is all the more dangerous as it may serve simultaneously to advance and hide the class-specific objectives of rich peasants, as was the case of Pajapan's ethno-communal rhetoric deployed by local ranchers prior to the 1980s.

The economic and political struggles of Gulf Nahua peasants have had a profound impact on the class structure of Pajapan. Active resistance to the concentration of lands usurped by the rancher class resulted in a new land tenure system, a class structure that is less polarized, and the resurgence of peasant forms of production. We shall see that the redistribution of land in the early 1980s reduced the concentration of wealth in land, cattle and merchant capital. The reform also permitted the growth of small-scale commodity production beyond the limits imposed by the former land tenure system. It halted the trend toward proletarianization by providing peasants with a minimal subsistence base from which to engage in a variety of supplementary activities (fishing, crafts, petty trade) allowing for a greater degree of economic security and autonomy. Workers continue to sell their labor power and commodities (including pasture) on the market, yet they have better control over factors of production and their livelihood as a whole.

The villagers' reversion to self-employed work has improved the overall position of the Gulf Nahua population within the market economy while also entailing more autonomy vis-à-vis capital. Peasant activities are still partly disarticulated from broader relations of production and exchange. This is a case of the peasant economy withstanding both the proletarianization process (R. Bartra and Otero 1987) and the growth of small-scale capitalism (Cook 1984; Bernstein 1988) in the countryside. Although sold, many of the goods produced by peasants and part of the wage-labor purchased locally do not enter the capital-dominated market. Rather, they are exchanged between household members or between rural workers of Pajapan. Peasants thus work in a subsistence economy that extends beyond the confines of household exchanges to include transactions between families in similar economic circumstances. This is to say that the resistance of peasants to exploitation is not only a periodic *political* struggle over land (Wolf 1969; Alavi 1979) but also a constant *economic* battle to maintain a certain degree of independence *vis-à-vis* broader markets. Subsistence and small-scale commodity production is not merely a survival strategy; it is also a daily expression of peasant labor's struggle against domination by capital (Paige 1975: 27; Rey 1973; Scott 1985). Through a combination of maximum remuneration and minimum risk, peasants struggle to make "the best use of the resources at their disposal" (Heath 1989: 280).

Analyses to follow show how class struggle over land in Pajapan has resulted in a land reform and a net loss of property and wealth controlled by the rancher class. Throughout the 1980s, herds have decreased in size and the potential for the continued expansion of ranching activities has been considerably reduced. Larger ranches have been forced to diversify their investments rather than reinvest in cattle; given the limitations of the Gulf Nahua economy, however, alternative outlets for capital investments in Pajapan are rare and yield few profits. The number of small to medium ranches has increased, yet these ranches generate few if any profits over and above their means of subsistence.

The gains obtained by the *comuneros* of Pajapan cannot be attributed to voluntarism only, a willful resistance of peasants to exploitation by ranchers. As previously argued, the strength of subordinate groups also depends on the structural weaknesses and contradictions of the power system. In order to obtain a land reform, the peasants had to rely on the intervention of an external force to challenge the hegemonic power of local and regional ranchers. They had to capitalize on divisions and conflicts emerging between a weak branch of agricultural capital and a state-owned oil industry bent on protecting and developing its own economic base. Peasants in Pajapan took advantage of the weaknesses of local capital *vis-à-vis* the state and the tensions emerging between the two industries, with a view to obtaining concessions from both domains. Local capital could not have been weakened if it had not already been weak.

The partial loss and fragmentation of agricultural capital in Pajapan has benefited the peasantry as a whole. A reallocation of land, however, cannot resolve problems of overpopulation, market accessibility, the underpricing of agricultural goods, landholding fragmentation, soil degradation and resource depletion. Moreover, recent developments in the local economy have subjected the peasantry to a process of internal differentiation. Peasants who have good land or a few head of cattle have separated themselves from those who have no cattle, poor-quality parcels or no land at all. Wage-work has also created new divisions in the local economy. This diversification of occupational activities tends to reduce the ability of the working classes to act as a front struggling against the dominant interests of PRI ranchers who continue to control local markets in foodstuffs, pasture and cattle.

The analyses that follow provide the supporting evidence for our account of class relations in Pajapan. We begin with an outline of how local inter- and intra-class divisions based on control over cattle and land have changed since the land reform of the early 1980s. This is followed by a detailed study of cattle economics over time, i.e., costs and benefits of ranching activities, variations in levels of accumulation, and the fragmentation and weaknesses of agricultural capital. We shall then address the productive profile and class position of small-scale merchants, subsistence farmers and simple commodity producers. The chapter ends with a discussion of how native wage-labor activities reflect not only peasant survival strategies but also their vulnerability *vis-à-vis* the broader market economy.

Class formation and land distribution

This section delves into the livelihoods and class structure of Pajapan, with an emphasis on the contradictory process of growth and mal-development conditioned by peasants' resistance to exploitation and struggle over land. The data presented below are based on a survey of 592 households in the village of Pajapan and surrounding hamlets (Batajapan and Tecolapa).[3] Major intra-communal divisions involving an unequal distribution of factors of production and a sectoral differentiation of productive activities are discussed.

Class typology

The population of Pajapan surveyed in the spring of 1986 consists of three composite classes: owners of capital (medium and large ranchers), small-scale commodity producers, and workers engaged in subsistence agriculture and wage-labor. Each class has a particular occupational profile combining a variety of activities including subsistence production, agriculture for the market, cattle-raising, wage-labor, petty trade, small business or craft work. The sub-classes refer to the specific combinations of these occupations within the households (see Table 4.1).

The class typology used here applies not to individuals as such but rather to families as corporate units of production and consumption, hence adult members sharing the same roof and household wealth and engaged in various productive activities. This particular approach is in keeping with the domestic character of peasant livelihood. When compared to class analyses based on individual profiles only, the household classification offers a better picture of strategies of occupational pluralism common among household groups in the Mexican countryside. Very few families devote all of their productive time to one activity only: practically all working-class households combine subsistence production with wage-work and/or simple commodity production. Subsistence activities and wage-labor in Pajapan are not full-time activities and are insufficient to meet basic household needs. By contrast, the local formation of capital is characterized by a lack of diversification in productive investments: capital tends to concentrate in one sector only, the cattle industry.

Table 4.1 Class typology

	Hlds%	Hlds[a]	Cattle	Wage-labor	Assets/Sales[b] (US$)	Trades
Subs./Wage Labor						
Wage laborers	6.4	38	< 5	> 2 d/wk	< 40 U.S. S	
Subs.-wage laborers	32.8	194	< 5	> 1 d/wk	< 40 U.S. S	
Subsistence producers	7.3	43	< 5	< 2 d/wk	< 40 U.S. S	
SCP						
Farmer-wage laborers	10.8	64	<10	> 1 d/wk	> 40 U.S. S	< 3 d/wk
Farmers	12.3	73	< 10	< 2 d/wk	> 40 U.S. S	< 3 d/wk
Petty traders	8.5	50	< 5	–	< 40 U.S. S	> 2 d/wk
Craft workers	7.9	47	< 5	–	< 40 U.S. S	> 2 d/wk
Small ranchers	7.6	45	10–24	< 2 d/wk	< 230 U.S. A	
Capital						
Small businesses	4.4	26	< 50	none	> 230 U.S. A	
Medium ranchers	1.0	6	25–49	none	< 230 U.S. A	
Large ranchers	1.0	6	> 49	none	–	

[a] Sample population (N592)

[b] A = assets; S = annual sales (including agricultural products, pasture and fish). All money values are given in US dollars based on the 1986 exchange rate of 650 pesos per dollar.

Note: These classes were arrived at using cut-off points established by the actual distribution of survey variables, coupled with observations pertaining to the economic behavior of each group. Although this analysis is based on a survey of the Pajapan village only, its findings apply to about 80% of all those living within the communal area.

The population of Pajapan is distributed in the following manner.

Subsistence and wage-working households exclusively engaged in subsistence crop production or wage-work (rural or urban), or, what is more typical, a combination of these two activities, represent almost half (47%) of the total population. By definition, these households have virtually no savings or assets of their own, and they possess fewer than five head of cattle each. This class can be divided into three discrete sub-groups:

1. Wage workers (6.4%) are those who engage in wage-labor more than two days per week and do not produce subsistence food or goods for the market. They do not work the land or sell any commodities other than their labor power.
2. Subsistence-wage laborers (32.8%) work for wages at least two days per week while also producing agricultural goods for household consumption, very little of which is sold on the market (less than US$40 per year). One third of all households in Pajapan fall into this category.
3. Subsistence producers (7.3%) have virtually no cash earnings; they do not work for wages more than one day per week and produce very little for the market (less than US$40 per year).

Small-scale commodity production represents 47% of the total household population. Their activities include small-scale ranching (fewer than 25 head of cattle), farming, fishing, craft work and petty trade, representing five sub-groups:

1. Farmer-wage laborers (10.8%) are those who sell agricultural products of their own totalling at least US$40 per year. They have fewer than ten head of cattle, they engage in petty trade or crafts less than three days per week and they work for wages at least two days per week.
2. Farmers (12.3%) have the same economic profile as farmer-wage workers except that they engage in wage-work less than two days per week.[4]
3. Craft workers (7.9%) in Pajapan include carpenters, bakers, butchers, tailors, barbers and mechanics who engage in their craft or trade more than two days a week. They sell less than US$40 per year in agricultural goods and own fewer than five head of cattle.
4. Petty traders (8.5%) buy and sell fruit, vegetables, fish, bread, pigs, beer, milk, ice cream and soft drinks during more than two days a week, they sell less than US$40 per year in agricultural produce from their own farm and they own fewer than five head of cattle. Households owning small stores with less than US$230 invested are also included in this class. The activities of these "petty commodity distributors" differ little from those of simple commodity producers, save that they are selling services of physical distribution, a productive activity not to be confused with the sphere of commercial circulation or mercantile transaction proper (J.M. Chevalier 1982: 134).
5. Small ranchers (7.6%) have between 10 and 25 head of cattle. With this number of animals, ranchers do not have to engage in wage-

work: households in this class devote less than two days a week to wage-labor. They dedicate themselves mainly to cattle-raising and meet the subsistence needs of their families. The size of their ranches is so limited, however, that they can make few investments in the development of their herds.

Capital represents a small group. Only 6% of all households in Pajapan own capital invested in cattle and small businesses.

1. Large ranchers (1%) have 50 head of cattle or more. As we shall see, these ranchers are able to increase their capital at a rapid rate and invest profits in other sectors of the local economy.
2. Medium ranchers (1%) have between 25 and 49 head of cattle. While they cannot generate significant profits for investment outside of cattle ranching, these ranchers own and sell enough cattle to meet subsistence needs and increase their capital.
3. Small businesses (4.4%) include households with businesses such as stores, taxis, cattle brokerages, restaurants and rooming houses with a minimum worth of US$230. The families may also own up to 49 head of cattle.

We now turn to a discussion of the role that the land reform of 1981 had in the development of Pajapan's class structure as observed in 1986. This is followed by a close examination of the productive profile and the overall position of each class formation within the local and regional market economy.

Land before and after the reform

By the end of the 1970s, the process of land concentration that had started in the 1940s had resulted in a sharp division between the majority landless peasants and the ranchers with large parcels of land. Survey data indicate that 61% of the local population were landless immediately before the 1981 reform while 3% controlled almost half of the arable land. The large landholders (100 ha. and more) controlled parcels averaging 235 hectares each with a maximum individual property of 800 hectares. These individuals usually held the best-quality land in the area (the lowlands) while peasants with small parcels were restricted to the poorer quality slopes of the volcano. Although the concentration of land was significant, about 36% of all households in Pajapan occupied small and medium tracts of land. About 2% had between 40 and 100 hectares, 15% between 13 and 40 hectares, and 20% less than 13 hectares (see Table 4.2).[5] While these holdings are large in comparison to the numerous *minifundios* of Mexico (less than three ha.), the land is not suited to intensive agriculture as in the central plateau.

In Chapter 3 we saw how the expropriation of 5,153 hectares of communal land for an industrial port and the subsequent land reform resulted in the loss of one-quarter of the communal land area and the division of remaining lands into 12-hectare parcels for distribution to

Table 4.2 Land distribution in the 1970s

Farm Size (ha.)	% Hlds	Total Area (ha.)	% Area
0	61	–	–
1–6	12	553	3
7–12	8	1,227	8
13–24	10	2,820	18
25–40	4	2,027	13
41–99	2	1,857	11
1–99	36	8,484	53
> 99	3	7,529	47
Total	100	16,013[a]	100

[a] An additional 3,014 hectares were communal forests on the peak of the volcano and along the shores of the lagoon. Another 131 hectares formed the urban area, for a total of 19,158 hectares of land.

905 *comuneros* (see Table 4.3). The peasantry as a whole clearly gained from the reform. Although one-fourth of the land was retained by ranchers and peasants who had land prior to the reform, about one-third of the land was redistributed to poverty-stricken peasants and peons of Pajapan. These landless workers thus moved from dependence on wage-earnings in cattle and urban industry to semi-independence as small-scale commodity producers supplying local and regional food markets. Others have moved into pasture production for local Indian ranchers or into small-scale ranching on their own.

The land reform took from the wealthy and gave to the poor. Table 4.4 indicates that the greater the wealth in land prior to the reform, the greater the loss. The 40 families with more than 100 hectares each controlling almost half of the communal land lost practically all of it through redistribution or expropriation.

The Presidential Resolution of 1968 identified 903 individuals, most of them older men, as *comuneros* with rights of access to the communal land.[6] The land reform that came 13 years later benefited some and placed others at a disadvantage. Individuals who did not appear on this list of *comuneros* could not claim rights to a 12-hectare parcel, even if they were occupying land at the time of the reform. As a result of this legal distinction between *comuneros* and non-*comuneros*, approximately 40% of all households in Pajapan remained landless even after the reform. Moreover, about 17% of the families with access to land before the reform lost all claim to the *tierras comunales*; most of them were relatively poor to begin with and had properties of less than 18 hectares (on average 8.5 ha., with a maximum of 60 ha.). They had not been included in the 1965 census of *comuneros* and lacked the political influence needed to acquire land rights during the census update.

The land reform obtained through class struggle had two opposite

Table 4.3 The redistribution of land, Pajapan

Expropriated	5,153 ha.	26.9%
Redistributed	6,054 ha.	31.6%
Retained	4,806 ha.	25.1%
Forest reserve and urban zone	3,145 ha.	16.4%
Total land	19,158 ha.	100%

Table 4.4 Land redistribution in the 1980s, Pajapan

Pre-reform Parcels		Post-reform Redistribution	
Farm size(ha.)	Total ha.	ha. lost	ha. gained
0	0		5,085
1–6	553		908
7–12	1,227		61
13–24	2,820	1,223	–
25–40	2,027	1,357	–
41–99	1,857	1,578	–
> 99	7,529	7,049	–
Total	16,013	11,207	6,054

effects on local class relations. On the one hand, it reduced the degree of *inter-class* polarization pitting ranchers against peasants: the proportion of landless villagers dropped from 61 to 40%. Nearly half (47%) of the households which received parcels of 12 hectares had possessed no land at all in the 1970s. On the other hand, the parcelling of communal property also resulted in a higher level of *intra-class* fragmentation: the more generalized access to land intensified the legal and occupational divisions prevailing within the working classes – divisions between *comuneros* and non-*comuneros*, farmers and wage-earners, petty traders and small ranchers, etc.

Class, comunero *status and land quality*

Communal property in Pajapan is no longer under the direct control of a few well-to-do families. Nevertheless, access to land is still a critical issue as it is unevenly distributed among the different classes. While 60% of the households in Pajapan presently have communal rights to land, 40% have none. The *comuneros* of Pajapan form a politically-constituted group of landholders with titles recognized by law, yet they do not form a homogeneous class at the economic level: *comuneros* belong to different classes and also engage in different occupations.

Table 4.5 Class distribution of quality parcels, Pajapan[8]

Class	Comuneros %	Soil Quality Rating	Pajapan/Lagoon %	Volcano %
Businesses, large and medium ranches	10	1.44	79	21
Small ranches, crafts	22	1.16	74	26
Subs., subs.-wage labor, farm-wage laborers	45	1.03	60	40
All land		1.14	63	37

Virtually all ranchers and owners of businesses have land rights, as do about 86% of the farmers and farmer-wage worker classes. Members of these classes tend to be the wealthiest in the village or their involvement in market agriculture and cattle-raising presupposes access to land. By contrast, only 44% of the petty traders have land as do 37% of the households in the subsistence-wage worker class and 11% of the full-time wage laborers. Given their legally limited access to land, these poorer families typically resort to petty trade and wage-labor in lieu of food production for the market to meet their family needs.[7]

The redistribution of land has reduced class polarization while also reinforcing cleavages within the working classes of Pajapan, to the benefit of small ranchers and farmers who make up both 31% of the village population and 46% of the Pajapeños with land. The new land tenure system has accentuated divisions that existed within the peasantry prior to the reform.

Another indicator of inequalities prevailing between and within rural classes in Pajapan is the uneven distribution of prime land (see Table 4.5). The large and medium ranchers and business owners have rights to land more frequently than others, and they also control the best land. These classes have better quality soil and their parcels are typically close to the village of Pajapan or in the fertile lowlands near the ocean and lagoon. Small ranchers and craft workers occupy plots with average quality soil, often located between Pajapan and the lowlands. By contrast, subsistence producers and peasants engaged in part-time wage-labor (subsistence-wage workers and farmer-wage workers) are left with the poorest quality land. These classes have parcels with poorer quality soil and less frequently located in the select areas.

Statistical findings concerning the class distribution of *comunero* status and land quality indicate that despite the reform, inter- and intra-class inequalities have not been eliminated. Ranchers and business owners are usually *comuneros* and have better quality parcels, on the average, than Pajapan's agricultural and wage-laboring classes. Moreover, the post-reform village of Pajapan is characterized by the growth of a "middle

Table 4.6 Land rental by class, Pajapan

Class	Ha. Rented	% of Rented Land
Capital	1431	58.7
Farmers	497	20.4
Subs.-wage labor	397	16.3
Other	112	4.6

peasantry" comprised of small ranchers, farmers and craft workers, sub-classes that have better access to land and better quality land than the poorer peasants. These middle peasants are better off when compared to the subsistence-wage workers and petty traders of Pajapan who represent the poorest and most vulnerable segments of the community.

Land rental, illegal purchases and the expropriated land

The division of communal property into 12-hectare plots controlled by 905 *comuneros* put an end to the concentration of land ownership by the wealthy classes while also excluding a large number of households. As a result, land rental has become important for both the land-hungry ranchers who need pasture and landless peasants who need to produce corn. An estimated 2,438 hectares, almost one-quarter (23%) of the land owned by Pajapeños, is rented to other Pajapeños. Two-thirds of this land (64%) is rented out by farmers and farmer-wage workers who play the role of land brokers to both land-hungry ranchers and landless peasants.

Ranchers recuperated some of their losses in property through illegal purchases of land rights. By 1987 about 40 parcels (480 ha.) had been bought from peasants by local ranchers, at an average cost of 200,000 pesos (US$307) per 12-hectare parcel. A few ranchers owned rights to between five and eight parcels. Land rental also made it possible for ranchers to regain partial control over the land (see Table 4.6). Ranchers and business owners rented 59% of the land area rented in 1986, usually for cattle-raising. This amounted to 13% of the total communal land area. Thus, to the 996 hectares owned directly by capital must be added another 1,911 hectares controlled by them through illegal purchases and rental arrangements. The degree of land concentration is not great in comparison to the pre-reform period: the wealthiest 14% of all households own or rent no more than 27% of the communal land. Land rental and the purchase of *comunero* rights, both of which were illegal, increased none the less throughout the 1980s and early 1990s. Recent reforms in agrarian laws will probably accelerate this process.

Overall, 89% of the land rented is used for pasture while only 11% is used for agriculture. Although relatively limited in area (268 hectares), the land rented for corn production is vital to the household economy of some peasants.[9] One-fourth of all households in Pajapan cultivate corn on land rented or borrowed from other villagers. About 80% of these are workers without land of their own, mainly subsistence-wage workers, subsistence producers and petty traders. Land rented for corn has little or no market value; three times out of four, it is paid for in kind, either in produce or in labor. This arrangement allows peasants to minimize their need for cash and their dependence on the market economy. In the few cases where agricultural land is rented with money, it is remunerated at an average rate of US$8.64 per hectare, about 5% of the value of an average corn harvest on one hectare of land. Access to good land is important to corn producers and it is often available from *comuneros* who do not use their entire 12-hectare plot.

To the issues of land rights and rental can be added another critical component in communal economics: the occupation of a lowland zone that used to belong to Pajapan and was held by the state until only recently. As already noted, 5,153 hectares of communal land were expropriated by the Mexican government in 1981 to make way for an industrial port and urban complex. The land was surveyed and the original occupants, including cattle ranchers from Pajapan, were expelled. Shortly afterward, many people returned to occupy the land and squatters have increased in numbers since the cancellation of the PEMEX project in 1984. The future of the expropriated land, the best in the community, was a hotly contested issue throughout the 1980s. In 1992 the lands were granted to a new *ejido* (Pajapan II) composed of sons and wives of *comuneros* (totalling 976 *ejidatarios*) and redistributed in parcels of 4 hectares. By 1993 ranching uses of the expropriated land had declined significantly. Pasture production and grazing continued on only one-third of the area while *milpa* production, including maize and beans accounted for approximately one-quarter of the land uses. The remaining lands had reverted to secondary vegetation.

At the time of the survey research (1986), one-quarter of the households in Pajapan made use of the *tierras afectadas*. Large ranchers occupied some 400 hectares in parcels up to 50 hectares each. Other Pajapeños occupied some 590 hectares in plots averaging 1.6 hectares each. The remaining land area in the expropriated zone was not being used, or at least not intensively. More land was not being used by the people of Pajapan and especially the ranchers because of the temporary and disputed nature of land tenure. Also, peasants resisted rancher occupation of the expropriated zone by cutting fences and rustling cattle. These lands were gradually occupied throughout the 1980s and early 1990s.

The vast majority of squatters in the expropriated area (80%) were agricultural workers and small ranchers who fell into one of two groups (see Table 4.7). Subsistence producers and subsistence wage-workers, the poorest of the village, formed the largest group (57%). These squatters occupied an average of 1.1 hectares. They usually had no land of their own: 56% and 83% of the squatters dedicated to subsistence agriculture and to subsistence-wage work, respectively, were landless. By contrast, most of the ranchers and farmers occupying land in this zone were

Table 4.7 Class distribution of lowland squatters, Pajapan

Class	Class %	Squatters %	Land Occupied %	Av. Plot ha.
Subs., subs.-wage laborers	35	57	40	1.1
Small ranchers, farmers	29	23	37	2.6

comuneros with rights to 12-hectare plots. Although they were fewer in number (23% of squatters), they occupied larger plots, typically between 2 and 4 hectares, thereby laying claim to as much occupied land as the first group. Small ranchers and farmers relied on this fertile land to expand their production and avoid rental costs. Squatting was an effective strategy used by the landless to preserve some economic independence from capital and for the middle peasantry to improve their position within the market economy.

To sum up, the parcelling of communal lands in the early 1980s resulted in a net loss of lands controlled by ranchers and reduced the polarization of local class relations. The reform obtained through class struggle, however, also gave rise to a middle peasantry in Pajapan, that is, the fragmentation of agricultural workers into landholders and landless peasants, self-employed food producers and wage-earners, peasants with a few head of cattle and those with none. The conversion of the communal tenure system into an *ejido*-like structure did not completely resolve the land question. By the mid-1980s, 40% of all households were still without land titles and had to engage in petty trade or wage-work to provide for their needs. In addition, up until the creation of the Pajapan II *ejido* in 1992, wealthier classes controlled the best available lands in the non-expropriated zone. Finally, local rental arrangements have allowed ranchers to recuperate some of their losses in land.

The land tenure system is a critical factor in the history of class relations and the rise of agricultural capital in Pajapan. Its reallocation in the early 1980s had a major impact on the distribution of wealth in cattle and also on the size, the rate of growth and the average profits of local ranches. We now turn to a more detailed discussion of the cattle industry in Pajapan, its location within the broader market economy and the transformations affecting native ranching operations following the land reform.

Cattle economics

The pre-reform cattle industry

Cattle have been part of the local landscape since the 1600s when herds from the Hacienda San Miguel Temoloapan grazed the natural savanna near the Laguna del Ostión.[10] The purchase of the current lands of

Table 4.8 Cattle sold (%) 1961–81 (Municipal Pajapan) by commercial outlet

	Pajapan		Coatza.		Jáltipan and Cosoleacaque		Others	
1961	19.3	(61.4)	42.2	(20.0)	–	–	38.4	(49.2)
1967	27.8	(71.5)	47.4	(47.4)	–	–	24.7	(68.0)
1972	22.0	(75.9)	30.1	(44.3)	–	–	47.9	(43.2)
1978	23.1	(86.1)	17.7	(38.4)	18.3	(47.6)	40.9	(91.5)
1981	29.7	(82.0)	2.7	(30.3)	32.8	(45.5)	34.8	(82.5)

Note: Figures in brackets indicate the calves sold as a percentage of all animals sold.

Pajapan in 1765 by the native inhabitants of the area was motivated in part by the need for grazing land as well as land for cultivating food crops. Individual herds probably did not exceed a few head of cattle grazed on lands not suitable for *milpa* cultivation. Elders of Pajapan report that animal stocks in the village were entirely wiped out during the Mexican Revolution by raiding bands of rebels and constitutional forces and did not begin to recover until the late 1940s. The number of cattle raised on the lands of Pajapan then began to increase rapidly, initiating a process of expansion in the cattle sector that was soon to transform the economic and political life of the native population.

A growing demand for beef in regional, national and international markets stimulated the expansion of ranching operations long established on the broad coastal flood plain into new areas of the Santa Marta highlands. Technical advances in pasture production, improved transportation services between southern Veracruz and central Mexico and state investments in credit and technical assistance for the cattle industry also contributed to the regional boom. The prime lowlands of southern Veracruz were soon covered with pasture, eradicating the last fragments of tall tropical forest on the costal plain. Pajapan, conveniently located near the city of Coatzacoalcos, was one of the first points of entry into the Sierra, an area coveted by land-hungry regional ranching interests.

In the first few decades, the growth of the local cattle industry (measured in total sales) was slow. Statistics obtained from the local Rancher Association indicate that in the 1960s fewer than 1,000 head of cattle were sold in Pajapan on a yearly basis. Close to half of the animals sold were purchased by ranchers or cattle-brokers based in Coatzacoalcos. Enrique Domínguez, a former native of Pajapan residing in Coatzacoalcos, purchased a large proportion of all cattle sold on behalf of the Sociedad Cooperativa de Producción Tablajera, a slaughterhouse owned by the regional *cacique* Guillermo Caballero. While cattle sales to these outside brokers accounted for a high proportion of all sales, transactions between residents of Pajapan increased throughout the 1960s, from 19.3% in 1961 to 27.8% of all sales reported in 1967 (see Table 4.8). This rise in internal transactions points to an increasingly fragmented industry divided

Table 4.9 Cattle sold (%) 1961–89 (Municipal Pajapan) by type

	Calves	Cows	Bulls	Total sales
1961	39.2	50.3	10.5	761
1967	59.2	30.1	10.7	885
1972	76.9	19.3	3.8	1,928
1978	72.8	25.0	2.2	3,408
1981	68.8	28.1	3.0	4,003
1989				3,369

into units of various sizes but also a tendency for smaller units to sell calves to larger ranches and cattle-brokers.

Table 4.9 also shows a growing tendency on the part of Indian ranchers to supply the regional market with immature calves as opposed to full-grown cows: from 1961 to 1967, the ratio of calves to all animals sold went up from 39.2 to 59.2% of all sales (and 71.5% of all internal sales). As the proportion of calves sold increased, fewer steers were allowed to mature, resulting in a drop in the sale of adult bulls (10.7 to 3.8% of all animals sold).

The 1970s witnessed a rapid growth in local ranching activities and the sale of calves to local and outside mestizo ranchers and cattle-brokers. Yearly sales jumped from 885 head of cattle in 1968 to 1,928 in 1972 and 3,408 in 1978. The trend already observed in the 1960s, toward a rise in the overall proportion of calves to all animals sold, continued throughout this period. In 1978, 86% all animals sold locally were calves; the corresponding figure for animals sold to merchants outside the industrial corridor of Coatzacoalcos, Cosoleacaque and Jáltipan was even higher (91.5%) (see Table 4.8). Coatzacoalcos, however, was no longer the principal outlet for calves bred in Pajapan; an increasing number of animals were purchased by ranchers and cattle-brokers from Acayucan, Cosoleacaque, Jáltipan, Perla del Golfo and San Juan Evangelista. This shift in markets reflects a decline in the hegemony exercised by Caballero (following his death in 1970) and the completion of a road from Pajapan to the Acayucan–Coatzacoalcos highway via Chinameca. The new transportation link facilitated the movement of feeder calves to the main centers of the regional cattle industry (Acayucan) and the sale of a limited number of adult animals to supply the growing urban population in the nearby industrial cities.

The impact of the land reform

In the late 1970s, only 19% of Pajapeños owned cattle in herds ranging from a few head to over 700. Of a total herd of about 9,000 animals, 84% was owned by 40 families with average herds of 189 head of cattle. The remaining 16% of the herd was distributed among households with fewer than 50 animals. Ranchers controlled a minimum of 50 hectares of land and in a few cases as much as 800 hectares.[11]

As already noted, the land reform reduced the polarization of land distribution in Pajapan while at the same time increasing the degree of working-class fragmentation. Similar changes occurred in the distribution of wealth in cattle. According to one local informant, "there were many ranchers who went down after the land redistribution. The total number of cattle decreased significantly when ranchers started to sell their cattle and put as many as possible on a small parcel of land." The total herd in Pajapan went from a pre-reform high of approximately 9,000 to 7,000, a decline of 22%. Correlatively, sales in cattle went up from 3,021 animals in 1980 to 4,003 in 1981 following the official announcement of the industrial port project and the expropriation of the lowlands of Pajapan occupied by ranchers. Close to one-third of all animals sold involved transactions between residents of Pajapan, which is the highest proportion registered since 1961; as we shall see, the port project caused not only a decline in the number of cattle but also a redistribution of wealth in cattle from large ranches to smaller ones. Sales jumped again to 4,745 in 1982, 4,380 in 1983, and 3,558 in 1984. Following the cancellation of the port project in 1984, sales in cattle declined to the pre-expropriation level of about 3,000 animals per year; the total number of yearly transactions has remained relatively stable since then.

Declines in the total herd were also accompanied by sharp drops in the size of the largest herds. Before the reform, a large herd consisted of 50 to 700 head of cattle, with an average herd of 189 head. After the reform, a large herd consisted of 50 to 200 head, with an average of 89. Without access to extensive areas of pasture, the very large herds of the 1970s could no longer be maintained. In the years since the redistribution, some ten ranchers have managed to rebuild large herds (300 animals maximum) by renting pasture from comuneros without cattle of their own and by illegally purchasing the land rights of comuneros. Nevertheless, the land redistribution has imposed severe limits on the process of land concentration and the corresponding scale of local ranching operations.

While the large ranchers were negatively affected by the reform, the number of households engaged in ranching increased from an estimated 285 units before the reform to 485 units in 1986. Ranchers who were forced to reduce their herds sold their cattle quickly and at relatively low prices. Many peasants who gained access to land and a cash settlement from the government for the expropriated property purchased cattle and established their own small herds. The parcelling of land was thus accompanied by a redistribution of wealth in cattle.

The increase in ranching units reflects a jump in the number of small herds. Ranches with fewer than 10 head of cattle rose by 80%; those with 10 to 24, by 125%. The number of medium-sized ranches (25 to 49 animals) also grew when the large herds were cut back (see Table 4.10). About 67% of the Pajapan population were and still are excluded from the cattle industry. The redistribution of land has none the less permitted many households without cattle prior to the reform to move into small-

Table 4.10 Changes in the distribution of cattle, Pajapan

Cattle	Pre-reform		Post-reform		% Difference Increase or Decrease
	Hlds	%	Hlds	%	
None	1195	81	995	67	-17
< 10	155	10	280	58	+80
10–24	60	4	135	28	+125
25–49	30	2	45	9	+50
50+	40	3	25	5	-38
All cattle owners	285	19	485	33	+70

scale cattle ranching. Two-thirds of all the households who now have between 1 and 49 head of cattle are newcomers to the industry.

The redistribution of wealth in cattle has been accompanied by greater fragmentation within the rancher class and among commodity producers engaged in small-scale ranching activities. More concretely, ranches of different sizes face various kinds of land access problems. They also vary in the profits they make and the money they require to rent pasture, hire wage workers and meet subsistence needs. The material presented below deals with observable differences in scale, profits and control over capital, variations that have important implications for the accumulation of local capital and the growth of the industry as a whole.

Cost-benefit analysis

The costs of raising cattle include labor (pasture maintenance and care of the cattle), pasture rental, supplies and medicine. In 1986, a total of $23,161 was paid in wages by cattle-raisers to both peons and ranch hands for maintaining pasture and caring for cattle.[12] This represents an equivalent of 63 full-time wage-workers, only 4% of the male labor force. For every dollar spent directly on wages by cattle ranchers, $0.67 was spent on the rental of pasture; an estimated 2,098 hectares of pasture were rented in 1986 at a total cost of $15,623. Other costs included supplies (barbed wire, nails, rope, salt) and medicine (vaccines, parasiticide, tickicide) totalling approximately $11,000.[13]

Cash expenditures represent only part of the costs of raising cattle. To the costs of wage labor, pasture rental, supplies and medicine can be added the value of the labor power of the ranchers themselves, worth about $68,468 in 1986. Considering that ranching is the main economic activity in Pajapan, total production costs are very low: approximately $118,227 for the sector as a whole. On the whole, cattle ranching contributes little to the creation of local employment or the development of local merchant capital. The cattle industry is, nevertheless, an effective means of capital accumulation. By the mid-1980s two-thirds of Pajapan's

Table 4.11 Cost-benefit analysis for the cattle industry

Head	A Value	B Sales	C Costs	B - C Sales profit	(B - C)/A Rate of sales profit	(B-C+ D)/A[a] Profits/Costs
7,000	950,600	187,329	118,227	69,102	7%	14.7%

[a] D = value of calves retained.

land was devoted to pasture production and while the reform forced a reduction in the total herd, it still numbered about 7,000 animals with a market value of almost a million dollars.[14]

Based on rates of reproduction analyzed in Chapter 5, an estimated 2,100 new calves were produced in 1986, resulting in a total herd increase of 30%. Cattle sales reported in the general survey totalled $187,329, or some 1,523 animals (22% of the herd).[15] Production costs, including the value of self-employed labor, added up to $118,227, leaving a net sales profit of $69,102 and a rate of sales profit of 7%.[16] To this modest sales profit must be added the value of the new calves retained for expansion of the herd (577 animals or 8% of the herd). Thus, the rate of capital accumulation (sales profits plus the value of the animals retained over the value of the total herd) was 14.7%, a favorable return on investment compared to other sectors of the rural economy (see Table 4.11).

Although lucrative, the cattle industry in Pajapan is faced with basic limitations on the efficient production of high value animals. The scarcity of pasture, especially since the land reform and expropriation, forces many ranchers to sell their calves shortly after they are weaned, at six to nine months of age. Many ranchers are obliged by pasture shortages to sell their calves at the onset of the dry season, when animal prices are lowest. The calves are typically underweight due to inadequate nutrition, parasites and ticks, further reducing their market value. Small-scale ranchers are particularly vulnerable to this situation; they must sell animals to larger-scale ranchers and cattle-merchants who act as cattle-brokers at critical stages in the production process. Very low levels of technical development and capitalization prevent the ranchers of Pajapan from realizing the productive potential of cattle-raising, thereby imposing significant barriers to the growth of local agricultural capital as a whole. According to calculations made by a local cattle-merchant, net profits from the production of feeder calves are low, i.e., about $108 per animal as compared to $463 for animals raised to slaughter weight. Nevertheless, only three or four ranchers in Pajapan have the resources needed to produce adult animals.

These features of the cattle industry permit cattle-merchants, large-scale producers located near urban centers and owners of transportation companies and slaughterhouses to exercise tight control over the market for calves and adult animals. The benefits to these branches of the cattle industry are significant. First, ranchers in Pajapan are restricted to breeding calves, the riskiest stage of production. Second, cattle-brokers benefit from a steady supply of immature feeder calves, often purchased at low, pre-dry season prices. These animals are transported to regional centers on the coastal flood plain where they are grown out and fattened up under more intensive conditions for resale to the slaughterhouses of Minatitlán, Jáltipan, Acayucan, and elsewhere. The final product is shipped in refrigerated trucks to markets in Mexico City, Puebla and other large urban centers. Third, quick profits can be realized from the treatment of calves weakened by malnutrition and disease. Sick calves respond quickly to veterinary medicines and gain weight rapidly when fed adequately. Some cattle-merchants in Pajapan specialize in the purchase and quick resale of recently weaned calves weakened by the dry season. Given these local conditions of production, the village of Pajapan and other communities in the mountainous areas of southern Veracruz raise fewer animals than the natural environment can potentially support and realize little of the profit of production.

Economies of scale

The costs and benefits of cattle production vary considerably for ranches of different sizes. Ranches in Pajapan can be divided into four types, each with a distinct potential for capital investment and accumulation. First, ranches with fewer than ten head of cattle (four on the average) cannot rely on cattle-raising alone for their livelihood. They must also engage in agriculture, petty trade, crafts or wage-labor. The total costs of family and wage-labor, pasture rental, supplies and medicine invested in livestock production are very low but so too are sales, leaving a very low rate of sales profit if any (see Table 4.12). Moreover, a high proportion (75%) of new calves are sold, resulting in a low rate of herd expansion (see Table 4.13). These *peasant-owned ranches* are particularly vulnerable to the loss of an animal through disease, accident or unexpected demands on savings (e.g., family illness). At best, they maintain a small herd nucleus to be used as a storehouse of wealth (Sandstrom 1991: 218f.) or savings for emergencies, thereby maximizing household security through diversified production (see Table 4.14).

The second category consists of *small ranchers* (10–24 head of cattle), units that can reduce their dependence on agriculture and dedicate themselves mainly to raising cattle. The average herd in Pajapan for this category is 14 animals, a ranch size beyond the sustainable stocking rate of a typical 12-hectare parcel of pasture (eight animals; see Chapter 5). Although small ranchers satisfy most of their labor requirements through family labor, average costs for wage-labor, the rental of pasture and the costs of supplies and medicine are higher than for smaller peasant-owned ranches. Very small profits (and limited wage equivalents) are realized by farm units of this size and a high proportion of the new calves are sold (85.7%). This puts severe limits on the expansion of the herd. By and large, these ranches need all the cash from the sale of their calves for

Table 4.12 Cost-benefit analysis by ranch size

Cattle	Rents	Wages	A Supplies	Self-empl.	B Sales	B - A Profits	Rate %
< 10	5	5	14	77	107	6	1.1
10–25	23	23	23	230	450	151	7.9
26–49	93	151	35	230	1,070	561	11.1
50 +	276	472	95	230	2,916	1,834	15.1

Note: These figures are average values per rancher in US$ for each category. *Rate* is the rate of sales profit (the net average profit divided by the total value of the average herd).

Table 4.13 Rate of herd expansion

Cattle	A New calves	B Calves sold	C Calves retained	B/A Calves % sold
< 10	1.2	0.9	0.3	75.0
10–24	4.2	3.6	0.6	85.7
25–49	11.1	8.7	2.4	78.4
50 +	26.7	23.7	3.0	88.8

Table 4.14 Herd increases and capital accumulation

Cattle	A Herd	B Profits	C Value calves retained	(B + C)/A Capital Acc. %
< 10	543	6	37	7.9
10–25	1,901	151	74	11.8
25–49	5,025	561	295	17.0
50 +	12,086	1,834	369	18.2

Note: These figures are average values per rancher in US$ for each category.

subsistence and production costs, with little left over for investment in more animals. The expansion of their herds is further restricted by the upper grazing limits of their own pasture and limited cash reserves for the rental of additional pasture. To make things worse, pasture shortages during the dry season will often oblige the owners to sell calves at unfavorable prices in order to rent pasture for their herd nucleus. Many small ranches established in Pajapan following the land reform operate under these limitations, to the benefit of large cattle-raisers and brokers who make profits from trading calves.

Medium ranchers (25 to 49 head of cattle) are independent of agriculture and other sources of income and sell enough cattle to meet both sub-sistence needs and increase their capital. Herds of this size (average 37 head of cattle) must be broken into groups and grazed on different 12-hectare parcels. Rental costs are relatively high as are wage-labor ex-penditures and costs for supplies and medicine. Day workers are hired to maintain pasture and move cattle from one paddock to another. Although they sell a low proportion of their herd, a tendency that reflects a growth strategy, these ranching units have enough capital and sell enough new calves to rent pasture, hire wage-labor, etc., and realize modest cash profits. Access to Pajapan's scarce pasture resources is not too difficult for herds of this size.

Large ranchers in Pajapan own on average some 89 head of cattle, with a maximum of 300 and a minimum of 50. The labor and pasture costs of such large herds are considerably higher than for any other ranch size. Many large ranchers hire full-time ranch hands and establish long-term land leases with *comuneros*. Arrangements of this sort in many cases amount to the illegal sale of parcels as the ranchers also assume the responsibility of maintaining the pasture. Sales of calves by these ranchers are much higher than for any other group, as is the rate of profit. High sales profits, however, reflect the limits to herd expansion imposed by local pasture shortages. Large ranchers are often forced to sell more calves than they want to and reinvest their profits in bank accounts and other businesses such as stores, trucks and taxis. Trade in calves treated for parasites and grown out for a few months on better-quality pastures also provides ranchers who have cash surpluses with a lucrative investment opportunity. Some large (and medium) ranchers manage as much as a third of their herd in the form of a rotating stock of calves they did not breed themselves.

To conclude, the cattle industry in Pajapan has adapted to the limits imposed by the land reform through mechanisms of fragmentation and diversification. Local ranches of all sizes, however, still occupy a sub-ordinate position within the broader market economy, thereby coping with low profits and high risks. The systematic transfer of profits to regional centers weakens local agricultural capital so severely it is unable to overcome technical and ecological limits on production. Low levels of production are endemic, restricting the expansion of agricultural capital in the long term. Internally, divisions have developed between classes of ranchers with varying degrees of control over the means of production. Peasants with a few head of cattle and small ranchers realize few savings from their labor. As for owners of medium and large ranches, their ability to expand is restricted by problems of access to pasture and the domination of outside mestizo ranchers and merchants. The result is a highly fragmented cattle economy characterized by a dependent peasantry and a relatively weak branch of ranching capital – an extraverted cattle economy that creates very little employment while occupying extensive tracts of land. As will be seen later, this inefficient branch of ranching industry has displaced more intensive land uses (*milpa* cultivation) and has brought about a rapid destruction of the regional rain forest environment.

Small businesses and merchant capital

The land reform and the fragmentation of agricultural capital has encouraged the development of small businesses in Pajapan. Local commercial activities, however, are still operating within an underdeveloped rural economy that permits limited concentration of merchant capital and that offers few opportunities for profitable investments.

Table 4.15 Merchant capital and petty trade, Pajapan

	N	Assets	A Circ. cap.	B Profits	B/A Rate of pr. (%)	Av. Cattle	Pre-reform ranch (%)
Cattle merchants	17	–	1,300	240	18	34	57
Taxi-owners	11	1,600	380	10	3	27	36
Small merchants	34	450	200	75	38	13	53
Petty traders	11	130	150	20	13	0	0

Note: Monthly figures in US$. Subsistence costs (wage earnings) have been deducted from the profits made by taxi-owners, merchants and store owners. > 12 ha. *Ranch* refers to land ownership prior to the reform.

In 1986, one out of every four households was engaged in a business or trading activity based on self-employment. However, the data suggest that a distinction should be made between the few small businesses which generate profits and the trading activities that provide limited cash earnings to meet household subsistence needs (see Table 4.15).

There is no large-scale concentration of merchant activity in the hands of a few well-to-do Pajapeños. Lucrative businesses consist mainly of stores, taxi services and cattle brokerages.[17] As shown below, most are owned by ranchers who cannot reinvest their profits in the cattle industry because of limited access to pasture. While the trend in the 1960s and the 1970s was for small merchants to invest in the cattle industry to increase their profits, the present trend is for ranchers to open up small businesses in lieu of increasing their herds. The development of merchant capital is nevertheless restricted by the low purchasing power of most Pajapeños and the small amount of commodities produced within the local economy.

Cattle-merchants are few in number: between 15 and 20 in Pajapan. Most of them had land and cattle of their own prior to the reform. Although one-third of them are also large ranchers, the majority own fewer than 50 head of cattle (average of 34).[18] Cattle-merchants usually buy and resell nine or ten local animals per month, transporting the animals by truck to cattle-brokers in Acayucan, Minatitlán, Jáltipan or Coatzacoalcos. Most of the cattle are calves that need to be sized and fattened on regional ranches before slaughter. Older animals which have had accidents or cows with problems of infertility are occasionally sold directly to slaughterhouses. Cattle-merchants benefit from limitations on the availability of pasture in Pajapan and the vulnerability of peasant ranchers (with fewer than ten head) to sudden cash needs. Merchants buy animals at low prices that have been weakened by the dry season or inadequate care, apply medicines to deparasite the animals and graze them until they have regained weight. The animals are then resold as healthy feeder calves. The costs of transportation are high and only a few trucks owned by the wealthiest ranchers in Pajapan are available. But the profits are also high; cattle-merchants make an average net profit of $240 per month and an 18% rate of profit on their initial investment. This is enough to increase their herds by 20 head of cattle per year or invest in other means of production. Cattle-merchants earn more profits than any other small business.

Small businesses in Pajapan include 11 locally-owned *taxis*, all of which started serving the communal area in recent years. The first taxi to operate in Pajapan appeared in 1980. The taxis circulate seven days a week and are usually driven by the owner, his son, or in three cases a peon receiving the minimum wage. The cars are worth between $1,000 and $3,000 (average of $1,600). Monthly earnings amount to approximately $440, which is barely enough to cover costs in labor ($50), fuel expenses ($180), car repairs and replacement costs ($200/mth, over a five-year period). Unlike the cattle-merchant, a taxi-owner makes little profit over time. At best he will provide for the needs of his family (or his peon) and reproduce his investment over time: i.e., a car worth approximately 12 head of cattle. Taxi owners usually have cattle as well, on average 27 head. Seven of the cars are owned by households that had little or no wealth in land or cattle prior to the reform. They purchased taxis with money earned in other sectors of the economy, usually wage-earnings from urban employment. The purchase of a taxi is often a status-seeking strategy for urbanized peasants who return to their village. The remainder of the taxi-owners reinvested their cattle and land wealth in a car following the reform.

Prior to the 1960s, there was very little commercial activity in Pajapan. In the absence of roads and bus service, villagers transported foodstuffs (corn, fruit, livestock) by horse to Coatzacoalcos and sold them in exchange for the money needed to purchase a few manufactured goods (machetes, pots and pans, etc.). The local market barely expanded during the 1970s; only two local stores currently operating in the village of Pajapan existed prior to 1978. The expansion of merchant business continued to be severely limited by the scarcity of peasant cash earnings. As a result, profits earned were usually reinvested in cattle, not small businesses.

The land reform and sudden infusion of cash into the local economy following the expropriation resulted in the proliferation of *small stores*; two out of every three stores started in the 1980s. Personal savings or the sale of one or two calves was enough to stock a small store with a few household goods imported from Acayucan: oil, soap, candles and matches, pots and pans, sugar, rice, coffee, biscuits, canned food, soft drinks, stationery, sandals, clothes, etc. By 1986 there were as many as 45 stores in Pajapan.

Some 34 stores were owned by *small merchants* with average assets ranging from $150 to $1,200, with an average of $450. These merchants bought on the average $200-worth of merchandise per month (minimum $100, maximum $600). Unlike petty traders, they generated a substantial monthly profit, around $150, a third of which was needed to provide for household needs. The maximum profit reported in our census was $300 per month (before subsistence expenses). The ratio of net profit to circulating capital is 38%, a good return on investment. Most of these stores were attended by the male owner, his wife or an adult child.

About 53% of the small merchants had cattle and more than 20 hectares of land prior to the reform. Two-thirds of these retail businesses are still owned by small ranchers who have between 10 and 24 head of cattle; some of them are owned by large cattle-raisers. For ranchers, stores are an alternative form of savings and investment in an economy where obstacles to ranch expansion are many. The large number of these stores is indicative of the weaknesses of the local economy; few alternatives exist for productive investment.

Eleven stores or *tiendas* consist of family businesses (often attended by a woman) that have less than $200 invested in merchandise (average $130) and that generate subsistence earnings but very little profit; their owners act as *petty traders* rather than small merchants. In 1986, these store-owners bought about $150-worth of merchandise per month which they sold for a total sum of $215, hence a wage-like earning of $45 and a net monthly profit of $20. None of them had cattle nor did they have land in the 1970s.

The fragmentation of merchant capital has undermined the growth of financial capital and the operation of *credit* in the local economy. In 1986, only 4% of the households in Pajapan had loans, ranging from as little as $3 to a maximum of $554. These loans added up to an estimated $4,603, virtually all of which was money loaned by individuals. The state-owned banking institutions had no presence in Pajapan. Businesses accounted for 69% of the money borrowed and had by far the highest average debt ($319). A few small ranchers, petty traders and farmers had contracted very small loans, usually less than $80.

Savings, usually in the form of money in the bank, were also rare. Approximately 11% of all households in Pajapan had savings, ranging from $15 to a maximum of $3,077. Cash savings in the local economy totalled about $72,623. Ranchers and business owners accounted for 48% of the households with savings and 60% of the total value. Large ranchers all had money in the bank, averaging some $1,616. Since levels of inflation usually exceed prevailing interest rates, returns on bank savings are less attractive than profits generated through ranching operations.

While small businesses may be the only local alternative to the cattle industry, the poverty and low population density of Pajapan are major obstacles to the growth of merchant capital and credit as well. There are few customers and their cash earnings are low. Merchants in Pajapan employ a limited number of wage workers and own little in the way of "factors of distribution" (storage facilities, pick-up trucks). Very few store-owners can afford to sell on credit or purchase agricultural goods for resale in the city. Most of what they sell consists of articles of personal consumption bought in small quantities and at higher prices from Acayucan suppliers. They compete with each other, with stores in the city, and with petty traders who make a living at retailing merchandise at the lowest possible price; as we will see, most surplus agricultural goods produced locally are handled by petty traders. As a result, the total capital accumulated over time is divided among many different stores of various sizes. The business of a village merchant remains very modest in comparison to his urban supplier. The fragmentation of rural merchant capital actually serves the interests of the urban supplier. In the words of one merchant, small store owners "don't do business; they work for Acayucan suppliers."

Subsistence and small-scale commodity production

The operations of cattle and merchant capital in Pajapan point to a history of capitalist growth and maldevelopment and to the effects of class struggle as well. The structure, strictures and struggles of Pajapan's class economy have fashioned the conditions of work and survival of the Gulf Nahuas. These conditions are the direct result of gains achieved through political and economic resistance. The gains, however, have been unevenly distributed and are still subject to a system of exploitation showing considerable resilience through time.

On the one hand, the land reform won through the struggle of peasants has resulted in a resurgence of subsistence production, reducing the peasants' dependence *vis-à-vis* the urban economy. It has also led to an expansion of small-scale commodity production. Compared to the 1970s, more peasant households are now engaged in the production of cash crops, livestock, pasture for rental, and marketable services of all sorts (petty trade, craft work). The possibility for native workers to sell commodities other than their labor power has increased their capacity to provide for their own subsistence needs, thereby improving their overall position in the market economy.

The land reform strengthened the peasantry and further weakened an already weak cattle industry. On the other hand, the economic gains accruing to peasants have been unevenly distributed and limited by existing conditions of market production and exchange. First of all, the native peasantry has undergone a process of internal fragmentation involving important differences in access to land, the use of labor power, levels of production and consumption. Second, peasants can no longer produce all of what they need to subsist. They must produce market commodities such as foodstuffs, animals and pasture for rental, articles sold at prices and under conditions they do not control. Third, through legal and illegal market mechanisms, local and regional ranchers have been able to recuperate some of the losses in land and wealth incurred in the early 1980s. Significant differences in the distribution of land and productive wealth continue to divide the community along class lines. Finally, self-employment in agriculture, fisheries, craft work or petty trade is plagued with problems of low productivity, limited markets, unfavorable prices and costly transportation services. These problems limit the peasants' capacity to provide for their needs and the total amount of surplus value that they can produce or keep from being transferred to local merchants and ranchers through market mechanisms.

Food crops and fishing

While the development of the cattle industry pushed peasants out of agriculture and into other sectors of the local and regional economy, the land reform cleared the way for a partial return to *milpa* cultivation; some 80% of the local population cultivate a small plot of corn compared to a much lower proportion prior to the reform.[19]

Involvement in corn production is greater for classes dependent upon it for family consumption. More than 90% of subsistence producers and subsistence-wage workers have *milpas*; they comprise almost half of all maize-producing units. About 82% of all farmers and farmer-wage workers are engaged in maize production as are 75% of the small ranchers and tradesmen. By contrast, only two-thirds of the business owners, large and medium ranchers produce corn; these well-to-do families are few in number and represent less than 5% of all corn producers.

The actual size and yield of a corn plot, whether per family or per hectare, also varies from class to class. The available data (466 cases of maize producers) point to three different class profiles.[20] The first group is involved in various market activities (small-scale ranching, trading, craft work, wage-labor) and as a result produces less corn on the average than the other groups. Although it comprises 63% of all corn-producing units, it accounts for barely more than half of the total land cultivated and corn harvested. It has relatively smaller *milpas* (0.64 ha.), a lower output per unit (0.97 MT), and a lower yield per hectare (1.29 MT, wet season corn only).[21]

The second group consists of subsistence producers who depend on maize production more than any other class. Their resources, however, are severely limited, a problem that accounts for only an average production profile. They represent 8% of all households that cultivate corn

Table 4.16 Total production of selected food crops

	Hlds	Ha.	M. ton	Value US	Hlds sell %	Sold %	Hlds hire %	Wages $
Beans	125	44	33	3,779	35	35	31	465
Sweet potato	43	28	101	3,108	100	74	30	170
Manioc	33	19	228	4,388	62	79	23	140
Chayote	20	5	145	3,346	100	90	13	–
Banana	22	5	–	–	37	–	0	0
Total	243	101	–	14,621	56	69	28	775

and account for 9.6% of total production and land devoted to corn. They have an average-size *milpa* of 0.87 hectares, a normal output of 1.36 MT per unit and a slightly higher than average yield of 1.48 MT per hectare (wet season only).

The last group consists of farmers, businessmen and owners of large and medium ranches who cultivate corn. These corn farmers tend to be more productive than the preceding classes. This stems from one of two reasons: either they are farmers engaged in production for the market, or they are businessmen and ranchers who possess the resources needed to work the land more effectively. They comprise 29% of all corn-producing units, yet they account for close to 40% of total corn production and land devoted to corn. They have larger *milpas* (1 ha.), a higher than average output per unit (1.61 MT), and also a higher yield per hectare (1.62 MT, wet season).

Corn is produced mostly with family labor. Households that hire workers purchase on average seven person-days per season, less than 10% of the total labor requirements for maize production (77 days). There are, however, class differences in the utilization of labor power. Wealthier families rely more heavily on wage-labor to produce corn for family needs: 81% of business owners and well-to-do ranchers hire peons to work on their *milpas* (12 person-days on the average). By contrast, only 28% of subsistence-wage laborers hire other workers to help in the production of corn (five person-days on the average).

Virtually all of the corn harvested locally is consumed by the producers themselves. The small quantity of corn sold by farmers and farmer-wage workers is purchased by other peasants directly from the producers, without the intervention of merchants.

For many peasants, the objective of the land reform was to regain access to land so as to engage in the production of foodstuffs for subsistence. While *comuneros* have attained this and while access to land through rental arrangements is probably easier for landless peasants now than it was prior to the reform, maize production is not the same for all classes. As already shown, important class differences exist in productivity and the utilization of labor power. By and large, however, the production of this vital cultivar occurs outside the sphere of capital-dominated markets.

The local land reform has made it possible for more peasants to grow a variety of food crops. In 1986, 295 households or 20% of the communal population produced some crops other than corn, including beans, sweet potatoes, chayote, manioc, plantains, fruits and other vegetables. The production profile for the main crops is given in Table 4.16. About 69% of agricultural production from these crops is sold on local and regional markets. Only 28% of the horticulturalists hire seasonal wage workers. Although precise data on the activities of peasants prior to the reform are not available, local informants report that very few households were producing and selling foodstuffs during the 1970s. Commercial crop production has increased during the last decade but it is still a relatively undeveloped sector of the local economy. The occupation of land by the cattle industry limits the total area devoted to horticulture to about 100 hectares, less than 1% of Pajapan's arable land. The total value of production (about $15,000) is negligible compared to cattle production ($1 million) or the market value of subsistence corn production ($150,000).

Beans are cultivated more frequently than any other local foodplant except for corn. Like maize, beans are cultivated mainly for household consumption: only one-third of the bean harvest is sold on the market. Subsistence-wage workers are the largest group of bean cultivators but have the lowest production: they cultivate smaller areas of land and harvest less than other classes. There are fewer farmers and farmer-wage workers producing beans but they tend to have larger bean fields and to sell a greater proportion of their harvest on the local market. Full-time farmers (who do not engage in wage-labor) are the most productive of all.

Unlike beans, 75 to 90% of the yam and the chayote harvest is produced and sold on the market by farmers and, to a lesser extent, farmer-wage workers. Few subsistence-wage workers grow yams or chayote. As for manioc and banana, production follows a dual logic: farmers harvest and sell larger than average quantities of these foodplants, whereas subsistence-wage workers tend to produce smaller quantities to meet household needs.[22]

The land reform has increased the villagers' capacity to provide for their needs. On the whole, agriculture is mostly oriented toward the production of articles consumed by the producers themselves or sold to other local peasants. The growth of the cattle industry since the 1940s has none the less caused the Gulf Nahuas to lose self-sufficiency in food. Cash crop production continues to be severely restricted by the scarcity of good agricultural land and also the absence of commercial networks for local foodstuffs. Finally, differences in levels of production have emerged between classes and among peasants as well, divisions reinforcing Pajapan's class economy and the recent trend toward a differentiation of the peasantry.

Before we turn to pasture production, a few words should be said about lagoon and ocean fishing. Although a part of the subsistence economy of Pajapan since time immemorial (García de León 1976: 119), fishing in recent decades has become an important alternative to wage-labor for peasants forced out of agriculture. Since the 1960s, an increasing number of landless peasants have turned to fishing as a means of subsistence and, in some cases, as a full-time commercial activity. The village of Jicacal was established on the shores of the lagoon by peasants from Pajapan and San Juan Volador who had been displaced by the expanding cattle industry. Despite the land reform and the return to agriculture it has facilitated, many Pajapeños continue to fish. Our 1986 survey data indicate that at least 45% of the communal households are engaged in fishing, usually one or two days per week. This represents an equivalent of 107 full-time fishers. These workers provide an important complement to the household economy of Pajapan's poor. Fishing is all the more important for those who do not have land: some 58% of fishers are landless, compared to 40% in the general population. Finally, about 58% of all households in the subsistence-wage worker class are engaged in fishing compared to only 25% of the small ranchers and none of the owners of capital.

The majority of fishing by Pajapeños is for subsistence. About 80% of the fishers in Pajapan consume all of their catch. Nevertheless, a small group of commercially oriented fishers sell on average $30 worth of fish per month during some eight months of the year. Total sales by these fishers in 1986 were approximately $29,120, more than total sales of food crops. Fishers in Jicacal, the hamlet located on the shore of the lagoon, also specialize in commercial fishing. This small but productive sector of the rural economy produces cheap, protein-rich food consumed by peasants and urban wage workers as well.

Pasture production and other livestock

The redistribution of land among peasants has made it possible for *comuneros* to engage in a new form of small-scale commodity production: the sale of pasture for grazing cattle. In 1986, at least 13% of the communal land area was rented out to cattle-raisers. The proportion has increased since then. Pasture is still in constant demand, especially during the dry season, and even the least developed of parcels can be rented out to generate some income for cash-poor peasants. Despite the scarcity of pasture, its market value does not amount to a rent: current prices are equivalent to no more than the market value of the labor power invested in producing pasture. Peasants receive about $0.75 per month for each head of cattle grazed on their pasture and on average earn some $50 per year for the rental of part or all of their 12-hectare parcels. This barely covers the labor costs of maintaining pasture. The maintenance of pasture requires labor: the *comunero* must clear shrubs, burn dead vegetation to promote regrowth and repair fences. The cost of labor and materials required to maintain a 12-hectare parcel of pasture is $36 per year, leaving a net earning of only $14 per year (1986 figures).

While pasture is a market commodity, it is remunerated at a rate equivalent to the amount of labor used in its production. The ground rent is lost to ranchers who pay only for the labor needed to produce forage. The absence of profits realized from control over land reflects the weaknesses of the local economy; most *comuneros* have few short-term alternative uses for their land beyond the few hectares needed to grow corn. Also, they lack the resources required to buy cattle or invest in commercial crop production. Many parcels located on slopes of the volcano are not suitable for crop cultivation even if the *comunero* has the capital needed to invest in production. Nor are longer-term options such as agro-forestry currently available.

Another form of commodity production is the raising of livestock other than cattle. One out of every two households owns one or two horses, in total some 613 animals. Horses are essential to the management of cattle and the harvest of maize and can be grazed on local pastures at little cost. Horses may be sold or rented locally to peasants who work as ranch hands for ranchers or who wish to establish ranches of their own. Livestock raised and sold locally in very small quantities include pigs and chickens. One out of every five households owns pigs (two to three animals each) and some 6% raise chickens (10 to 15 per household). Livestock production other than cattle has a definite class profile. The proportion of each class with horses and the number of horses owned by each household increases from the poorest subsistence-wage workers to the large ranchers. Pigs are raised by subsistence producers with surplus corn production and also by small ranchers with the financial resources needed to buy feed. Most of the households raising chickens (70%), the least costly of domestic animals, are from the poorest classes in Pajapan: subsistence-wage workers, subsistence producers, petty traders and farmer-wage workers.

Petty trading and craft work

Pajapeños no longer produce most of what they need as they did a few decades ago. Subsistence production is a vital component of their daily livelihood, yet peasants must engage in other forms of labor if they are to obtain the cash earnings required to purchase basic commodities such as food, clothing, building materials, machetes, etc. For many households, petty trading and craft work are complementary activities or alternatives to wage-work. They too are subject to limitations such as high transportation costs, small markets and low levels of production (see Table 4.17). While these problems undermine the growth of merchant capital, they also produce variations in the productive conditions of petty trading and craft work, variations that contribute to a further differentiation of the working classes.[23]

One out of five village households is engaged on a part-time or full-time basis in petty trade or semi-skilled crafts and trades. The vast majority are the poorer families of Pajapan, i.e., peasants who do not have businesses or cattle. Two-thirds of these families spend three days

Table 4.17 Average production profile of petty trading and craft work, Pajapan

	N[a]	Days/ week	Earn/ week $	Earn/ day $	Days WL[b]	Assets $	Input[c] $
Small stores	6	6.50	17.11	2.63	16.7	130	37
Cantinas	11	4.82	11.23	2.33	7.0	867	34
Petty traders	27	4.04	11.25	2.78	4.5	6	27
Fruit vendors[d]	40	3.04	17.55	5.78	9.6	0	22
Carpenters	26	4.23	12.63	2.99	16.1	39	5
Bakers	11	5.73	24.40	4.26	36.2	83	38
Butchers	8	2.42	26.15	10.81	54.9	40	76

[a] = US$ figures are based on 1986 exchange rates. Survey sample data only are presented.
[b] = Total person-days of wage-labor hired per trade.
[c] = Weekly purchases.
[d] = Horticultural labor input and land property value not included.

Table 4.18 Class profile of petty traders and craft workers, Pajapan

	Cattle	% Landed	Ha. before[a]	WL/wk[b]
Small stores	0.0	50	0.3	1.20
Cantinas	2.3	55	12.4	1.22
Petty traders	1.1	55	6.9	1.27
Fruit vendors	1.0	58	6.1	2.17
Carpenters	0.6	73	4.1	0.90
Bakers	0.3	83	5.6	0.80
Butchers	4.3	88	17.9	1.14

[a] = Hectares of land prior to the reform.
[b] = Days of wage-labor worked per household per week.

a week or more in trade-work or trading; they make up the two classes called petty traders and craft workers. The remaining cases consist of subsistence-wage workers and farmers engaged in petty trade on a part-time basis. Although acquired with fewer days of work, earnings by these workers are comparable to the wages of a full-time peon, $15 a week on the average (1986 figures). Thus, the net income of most petty traders and craft workers barely covers basic subsistence costs.

There are approximately 170 families in Pajapan that derive some earnings from retail trade. They buy and sell fruit, fish, bread, milk, baskets, canned food, oil, soap, sugar, coffee, soft drinks, beer, stationery, etc. They peddle fresh food in the village, in a neighboring community or in the city, on a daily or a weekly basis. Some of them put up a market stall, cantina or a small store in the village and buy manufactured goods from a local merchant or a supplier usually based in an urban center. They hire very little labor and purchase between $22 and $27 worth of merchandise per week on the average, most or all of which they sell for a weekly net income of $11 to $18.

Cantina and small store-owners have more expenditures and wealth invested in merchandise than itinerant vendors. Their daily earnings, however, are about the same (though for less work); the rate of return on the retailing of manufactured goods imported from city merchants is lower than for fresh foods bought in the Pajapan area and peddled in the village or elsewhere. It should be noted that the assets reported by cantina-owners (average $867) usually consist of merchandise loaned to them by beer companies rather than capital they actually own. Like the small store-keepers, they are dependent upon their suppliers. Although self-employed, they essentially work as rural distributors for city merchants and for soft drink and beer industries.

Itinerant traders work three or four days a week buying and selling fruit and fish. Since they sell perishable stock, they purchase the merchandise one to three times every week. The cost of transportation by bus to the cities and towns of the region reduces their net income by as much as 25 to 35%. Fruit vendors occasionally sell seasonal products of their own labor and land, thereby reducing their weekly purchases and increasing their net income to $17.55 a week. Compared to other vendors, they make more money with less labor (one day less a week on the average). Vendors, mostly women, go three or four times a week to one of the markets in Coatzacoalcos where they pay a fee for a sidewalk stall. They usually travel by way of Chinameca, the longer but better-serviced route, leaving at five in the morning and returning late in the afternoon. Many of these vendors are single or widowed women with few alternatives to this exhausting schedule.

Fish vendors buy 4 to 10 kilos of fresh fish or seafood from lagoon or sea-fishers in Jicacal, Playa Linda or Las Barrillas every three or four days. They salt or cook the fish before taking it to neighboring Indian communities (Tatahuicapan, Huazuntlán, Mecayapan) or sell it fresh in Pajapan. Trips are interrupted by a day or two devoted to other tasks that must be performed prior to buying more fish. The merchandise is sometimes exchanged for corn and the price may be reduced for poorer customers. Most fish vendors are women.

About 90 carpenters, bakers and butchers live and work in the village (see Table 4.18). The earnings of carpenters are not all that different from those of small store-owners and itinerant vendors of Pajapan. Woodworkers are faced with three basic problems not easily resolved: the scarcity of good quality wood (e.g., mahogany, caoba), the limited demand for furniture in Pajapan, and the high cost of transportation to the city (an expense that urban carpenters do not have). In response to these problems, a carpenters' co-operative built a workshop in 1972 with funds provided by the Instituto Nacional Indigenista, a federal agency responsible for Indian people in Mexico. However, limited demand for their products undermined the viability of the co-operative, which soon went out of business.

Bakers and butchers are better off than carpenters. The available data indicate that they make about twice as much money per week as vendors and carpenters. They usually have title to land and some wealth invested in tools, machines, or, in the case of butchers, cattle and pigs of their own. Most of the butchers are small ranchers, or used to be prior to the reform. They have now formed an association that controls entry into the trade and the price of meat sold at the local market. Butchers take turns supplying the local market, working once a month for two to three days. They generate a sizeable rate of profit (20%, or $11 per day) on what they sell. Nevertheless, the low cash earnings of peasants in Pajapan restricts the quantity of meat sold at the market and also the overall profits which are spread out between a number of butchers. Although beef is produced locally, the cost of meat in Pajapan is higher than in the city and beyond the means of most peasants. In 1986, a kilo of meat cost more than twice the daily wage paid to workers who clear the pasture and repair the fences on ranches. Peasants contribute to the production of commodities they cannot afford to buy themselves.

There are approximately 33 bakers in Pajapan, a dramatic increase over the two or three who operated in Pajapan in the 1960s. They employ wage laborers more often than the vendors and rarely work for wages themselves. They produce bread in clay ovens in their yards and may sell it to vendors who seek customers from house to house and from one village to another. Although they make bread six days a week, they earn no more than butchers earn in two or three days, i.e., about $25. Bakeries are particularly vulnerable to fluctuations in the price of flour which they buy in Acayucan. The elimination of a government subsidy on flour during the survey of 1986 was forcing many bakers to abandon the business.

Like other forms of self-employment, petty trades and craft work allow workers to maintain a degree of autonomy vis-à-vis capital. Although petty traders and craft workers depend on local market conditions for their survival, their direct contribution to capital accumulation is minimal. Many of the goods distributed by petty traders (fish, fruit, bread, meat) do not even enter the capital-dominated market: they are sold or traded to other peasants and rural workers within the local and regional economy.

Petty trade and craft work provide peasants with concrete alternatives to unemployment and to partial or full proletarianization. At the same time they introduce sectoral divisions and intra-class inequalities within the peasantry, as between peasants and non-agricultural workers, bakers and vendors, butchers and carpenters. All forms of self-employment also create new avenues of exploitation by capital. Ranchers and regional industries benefit from local pasture rental arrangements, the purchase and sale of livestock raised by peasants, and the provision of cheap foodstuffs and services that help minimize the renewal costs of labor. Peasants and non-agricultural workers are thus faced with problems of poverty, low productivity and unfavorable market conditions which they do not control (limited demand, high transportation costs, low prices for their goods and services, etc.). The surplus value extracted from self-employed labor through market mechanisms is none the less limited, subject as it is to the chronic weaknesses of the Gulf Nahua economy.

Wage-labor employment

Wage-work remains a major source of cash earnings in Pajapan, a livelihood that incorporates the Gulf Nahuas into the broader market economy. About 55% of all village households rely on the wage earnings of at least one family member. The proportion of the total labor force (measured in person-days, all adults above 15 included) engaged on a part-time or full-time basis in wage employment is close to 20%. This adds up to the equivalent of 552 full-time peons or one-third of the local male labor force.

Local wage-labor exchanges, however, do not reflect a general proletarianization process whereby self-employed workers are converted into a homogeneous class of poorly-paid wage-earners exploited by capital, as predicted by early Marxists. For one thing, the recent history of Pajapan shows a marked decline in wage-labor employment following the re-allocation of land in 1982. Also, it is not the expansion of a labor-intensive industry that forced peasants out of agriculture; the population was displaced by a cattle economy in need of land, not labor. High rates of unemployment in the lowland cities of Coatzacoalcos and Minatitlán meant that little of this cheap labor "freed" from the land could be efficiently absorbed by industry. Furthermore, wage laborers in Pajapan do not form a homogeneous class. They work in different sectors of the local and regional economy and under different conditions. A significant proportion of the wage-labor employed in Pajapan is purchased by small and middle peasants as opposed to ranchers or urban employers. Although exchanged for money under conditions determined at the broader market level, agricultural labor hired by peasants is an integral part of the village subsistence economy. The following analysis confirms this tendency toward a dual segmentation of the wage-labor force and highlights the importance of looking at all forms of wage-work, including those that fall outside the boundaries of capital.

The exploitation of peasant labor by capital is not as significant as would first appear. Table 4.19 indicates the sectoral distribution of hired labor, most of which is unskilled. About 56% of the labor is in agriculture – men working for either peasants or ranchers. Only one-third of all wage-earners are employed by cattle ranchers while some two-thirds are employed by peasants. Agricultural laborers hired by peasants work for an average of 4.2 days a week, primarily to clear, weed and plant corn plots of less than 2 hectares. As for ranchers, they employ a few peons to look after cattle, clear and weed the land for pasture and repair or put up new fences. Peons hired by ranchers work for an average of 3.7 days per week only.

Rural and urban services (shopkeepers, waiters, taxi drivers, municipal

Table 4.19 Sectoral distribution of wage-labor force, Pajapan

	% Person-days	% Laborers	Av. person-days/week
Agriculture	56.2	63.8	4.0
For peasants	37.6	40.9	4.2
For ranchers	18.6	22.9	3.7
Construction	29.0	24.0	5.5
Rural	4.4	3.8	5.2
Urban	24.6	20.2	5.5
Services	14.8	12.2	5.4
Rural	9.0	7.3	5.5
Urban	5.8	4.9	5.3

Table 4.20 Sectoral employment of wage workers, Pajapan

	Agriculture		Construction		Services		Total	
	For Peasants	For Ranchers	Rural	Urban	Rural	Urban	Person-days	%
S-WL	41.8	18.1	5.8	23.4	6.5	4.4	1,052	63.5
F-WL	42.6	18.9	1.4	24.1	8.9	4.1	270	6.3
WL	17.8	15.0	2.6	37.2	16.7	10.7	234	14.1

Note: Row percentages of total person-days, except for the last column. Other classes not included.

employees, etc.) absorb only 15% of the wage-labor force, for an average of 5.5 days a week. Construction work accounts for another 29% of all paid labor and occurs mostly in the urban centers where workers are employed for an average of five or six days per week. Most of these workers are hired for the construction of private homes in the cities of Coatzacoalcos and Minatitlán. In 1986, a skilled bricklayer employed in the city made about $4.36 per day and an assistant bricklayer $3.36. This is considerably more than the $1.53 paid to day workers in the agricultural sector. Better earnings obtained in the city, however, are offset by transportation costs and a higher cost of living. Many bricklayers would prefer to remain in the village but local work has slowed since the mid 1980s when about 200 houses were built with money received by the *comuneros* of Pajapan in compensation for the expropriated land. Since that time, the local construction industry has been steadily declining: in the summer of 1986, only 16 houses were being built in Pajapan. Employment in the urban construction sector has also declined dramatically as a result of the suspension of new petro-chemical projects and a general drop in urban economic activity.

The segmentation of the wage-labor force has given rise to different categories of wage workers in Pajapan. Nearly two-thirds of the hired labor are drawn from one class: subsistence-wage workers. The rest is equally divided between full-time wage-earners (14.1%) and farmer-wage laborers (16.3%). Table 4.20 indicates that subsistence-wage workers and farmer-wage workers are hired in the agricultural sector about 60% of the time, usually by other peasants (seven times out of ten). Given their involvement in agricultural production for the market, the farmer-wage laborers devote less time to wage-work than the two other classes. Full-time wage-earners work in urban construction 37% of the time and the service sector 27% of the time, mainly in the village. They are employed in agriculture only 33% of the time and they are hired equally by ranchers and peasants.

As with other local forms of production, the recent history of wage-labor in Pajapan points to three concurrent tendencies. First, disengagement from broader markets in wage-labor points to a peasantry resisting further integration into the capital-dominated economy. The reallocation of land obtained in the early 1980s reduced dependence on wage-labor while also incorporating wage workers into the village subsistence economy. Peasants began to hire other peasants. The successful struggle allowed rural workers to avoid full proletarianization (or chronic unemployment) and to pursue alternative strategies of subsistence and petty commodity production involving self-employment at both household and village levels. The strategy implies an internal circulation of labor, goods and money, hence commodities exchanged within the confines of a household and village economy. Second, wage-labor continues none the less to act as a mechanism of internal differentiation and effective exploitation. The gains achieved by the *comuneros* of Pajapan through the land reform have been limited and are unevenly distributed. Large segments of the local population are still obliged to sell their labor power to ranchers, urban employers and landholding peasants in order to make ends meet. Also, compared to those peasants who have land and the resources needed to employ occasional workers, the landless and the young are more dependent on wage earnings and therefore vulnerable to exploitation by capital. Finally, wage workers of Pajapan are poorly paid, unskilled and underemployed, problems indicative of the endemic weakness of a local and regional economy unable to make full use of available labor power let alone increase its overall productivity.

Conclusion

This chapter has examined the variable structure and inherent strictures of agricultural capital in Pajapan. It has also delved into the impact that peasant struggles over land have had on the local economy and class relations over time. On the matter of exploitation, we have treated the conversion of peasants into wage laborers as only one of numerous forms of capitalist subordination observed in the countryside. Land expropriation and the proletarianization process have played a central role in the rise of agricultural and industrial capital in southern Veracruz. Market economies dominated by capital, however, also derive substantial benefits from the maintenance or development of subsistence and small-scale commodity production. And while capital thrives on the incorporation of different forms of labor into the market economy, it also gains from the creation of a reserve army of unproductive workers competing with the active labor force for scarce employment opportunities.

Capitalism is variable and adaptable. It is none the less a stupid machine; it always develops a measure of irrationality, creates obstacles to growth and sets limits to its own development. In Pajapan, problems of poverty, unemployment (or underemployment), low overall productivity, loss of food self-sufficiency, limited markets, massive resource depletion and economic stagnation are effects of maldevelopment resulting from the expansion of the regional cattle industry. Although these effects are indicative of capitalist development, they also point to capital's chronic tendency to mismanage the economy. Irrational and unbalanced growth places costly restrictions on the profitability and future prospects of local and regional capital.

We have seen that the opposition of labor to capital is another endemic feature of the Pajapan economy. Our case-study shows that this opposition is constant, varied and effective (if only partially). Peasants in Pajapan engage in political battles over land, make daily efforts to improve their overall position within the market economy, and struggle to preserve some economic independence vis-à-vis capital (through household and village subsistence production). Acts of resistance have brought concrete benefits to them. Peasant struggles have had a lasting impact on the local land tenure system and the accumulation and concentration of capital. It should be pointed out, however, that gains made by peasants through the land reform of the early 1980s have been obtained under particular conditions: a weak branch of agricultural capital competing with an expanding oil industry. Also, the gains obtained through a reallocation of land were not without limits; ranchers have been able to recuperate some of their losses through alternative market mechanisms (cattle trade, rental and illegal purchases of land). Finally, the redistribution of land has given rise to inequalities emerging within the peasantry itself – divisions between the landed and the landless, the employed and the unemployed, farmers and wage earners, peasant ranchers and petty traders.

Notes

1. Although these authors agree that peasants can be effectively exploited by capital, there is no consensus within this literature regarding the role of pre-capitalist forms of production within capitalist economies, let alone the relative importance of profits accumulated through unequal exchange relations vis-à-vis capital (absolute and relative surplus value) generated in the sphere of production proper.

2. Having recognized the complexity of capitalism, Bernstein (1988: 260, 265, 268) none the less maintains the orthodox Marxian notion that simple commodity producers are petty-bourgeois and that "the essential relation of capitalism is that between capital and wage-labour; its essential categories include those of capital, wage-labour, value, surplus-value, and landed property".

3. The survey covered approximately 40% of the households living on the communal lands of Pajapan. Estimates for the total population include an adjustment to the category of large landholders.

4. This class includes seven fishermen who sell more than US$40 worth of fish or seafood per year.

5. According to the SRA, 32 families owned 14,450 hectares of land in 1976, hence 90% of all arable land in Pajapan; see ASRAX, "Informe sobre la comunidad Pajapan (antecedentes)", July 7, 1976. In our view, this overestimates the concentration of land in Pajapan. Our survey data indicate that a significant number of peasants possessed small to medium parcels of land.

6. One additional right of access to land was assigned to the school and the other to widows.

7. These contrast generalizations cover 85% of the village population. Households not accounted for consist of two smaller classes: subsistence producers and craft workers. About two-thirds of the subsistence producers are *comuneros*. Access to land allows them to engage in subsistence agriculture on a full-time basis. As for craft workers, three-quarters of them are *comuneros* with a land base of their own, yet many of them do not engage in commercial agriculture or ranching. Some tradesmen such as bakers and butchers have sizeable earnings, which allow them to avoid agriculture; other craft workers (carpenters, basket makers, midwives, woodcutters) only recently gained land from the reform and have not left their trade for agriculture.

8. Land quality is measured in two ways: a farmer-rating of soil quality (0 = poor, 1 = fair, 2 = good), and the distinction between lands from Pajapan downward (toward the lagoon, better lands) and lands on the slope of the volcano (poorer lands). See Chapter 5 for a detailed analysis of Pajapan's ecosystem.

9. Land rental has made it possible for landless peasants (non-*comuneros*) to cultivate a subsistence corn crop; peasants classified as subsistence workers rent 16.3% of the land for *milpa* cultivation. As for middle peasants, land rental has improved their access to land needed to engage in small-scale commodity production; some 20.4% of the rented land is used by farmers and farmer-wage workers who graze a few head of cattle or cultivate commercial crops.

10. AGN, Rama Tierras, Vol. 3030.

11. These estimates are based on interviews and survey data, with an undersampling adjustment made to the category of large ranches. In our opinion, the estimate of 7,000 head of cattle in 1980 made by RIGOR is too low.

12. This estimate is based on survey data using a daily wage figure of 1,000 pesos or US$1.23 and an average of 300 working days per year.

13. Cost estimates for wage-labor and pasture rental are based on the general survey. Supply and medicine costs are based on 12 case-studies for ranches of various sizes.

14. The estimate of total market value is based on a ratio of four adult cows (US$155 each) for every six calves (US$123 each). See Chapter 5 for details on herd composition.

15. Total sales are derived from the general survey, with an undersampling adjustment to the large ranches. The number of calves sold was estimated from sales data assuming an average value of $123 per calf. Animals bought and resold by cattle merchants are not included in these calculations; the total number of

cattle transactions in 1986 recorded by the local Rancher Association was approximately 3,000.

16. The rate of sales profit is the net profit divided by the total value of the herd (i.e., initial investment).

17. To this list should be added three small restaurants, two small pharmacies, one *tortillería* and a hotel (owned by an ex-rancher). Two wealthy ranchers also deliver gravel and produce cement blocks for local construction.

18. In the class typology presented earlier, cattle-merchants have been classified as business owners (43%) or ranchers (57%), depending on the importance of their trading activity relative to their wealth in cattle.

19. The survey data and interviews with local informants suggest that only about half of the population was engaged in subsistence *milpa* cultivation prior to the 1980s. Very few farmers were engaged in production for the market; Pajapan was not a net exporter but rather a net consumer of corn.

20. The findings given below are derived from our general survey (N 592) and a separate agricultural survey (N 49), both conducted in 1986.

21. Good-quality parcels are unequally distributed among the classes, but not along lines that match our analysis of corn production by class.

22. Class differences in agricultural crop production are partly influenced by environmental factors. Crops that can be preserved or harvested gradually (beans, manioc, bananas) are often used to supplement the peasants' subsistence needs while crops that must be harvested all at once and that are difficult to preserve (e.g., yams, fruit, chayote) are usually sold on the market to provide the family with cash earnings.

23. Petty trade data are based on our general survey combined with detailed interviews with petty traders.

CHAPTER 5

AGRO-ECOLOGY AND THE MEANS OF DESTRUCTION

The preceding chapter discussed the ways in which peasants are exploited by ranching capital through means other than outright proletarianization. We stressed the determining role that resistance and survival strategies played in peasants' control over land, wealth in cattle, local markets in foodstuffs and labor, and other means of livelihood. We also demonstrated the chronic inefficiency in a hinterland branch of the Veracruz ranching industry, a low-profit economy that occupies extensive tracts of land while creating little employment and few opportunities for sustainable growth.

The same threefold argument can be extended to the technical and ecological side of the Pajapan economy. In this chapter we discuss local agricultural and ecosystemic processes with a view to understanding (a) the ways in which the Santa Marta rain forest has been harnessed to a cattle economy through means other than outright industrialization; (b) peasant efforts to adapt their traditional *milpa* system; and (c) the deficiencies of current forms of production and management of cattle and pasture – i.e., their relative inefficiency and negative impact on rain forest ecology and *milpa* productivity. Changing patterns of hunting and fishing activities and related ecological problems are also examined.

Like workers, natural forces are exploited by capital in ways that are variable and exhibit a good dose of irrationality. To address issues of productivity and ecological sustainability, proper attention must be paid to labor processes and the particular ecosystems that human activities affect and are affected by. Our analysis will therefore include a description of the main features of the Santa Marta rain forest, with an emphasis on specific aspects which contribute to the complexity of the Pajapan environment. What we wish to avoid is a general characterization of principles of rain forest ecology treated as a list of natural constraints on productive activities. The specific features and incredible diversity of climatic, topographic and soil conditions found in Pajapan eschew sweeping generalizations.

Our critique of the inefficiency and wastefulness of Pajapan's cattle-driven economy raises a central issue in economic theory: the rationality or relative productivity of peasant forms of production *vis-à-vis* capitalist agriculture. We now turn to a theoretical discussion of this thorny question, followed by a brief exposition of our own threefold approach to the subject.

Theories of productivity and irrationality

Mexican theorists do not agree on the degree to which peasant labor is transformed by the development of capitalism or the relative efficiency of peasant and technologically advanced agriculture. To begin with, (a) orthodox Marxists argue that Mexican capitalism is more efficient than peasant agriculture and that the growth of agribusiness brings about a further decline in the relative productivity of peasant labor. By contrast, (b) dependency and neo-Marxian theory, building on a theory of the transfer of value from agriculture to industry, argues that peasant agriculture in Mexico is essential to the expansion of capital as a whole. Other neo-Marxists emphasize the efficiency with which the peasantry produces wage workers at no direct cost to capital. Finally, (c) proponents of the "peasant economy" school claim that the peasant way of life is apt to resist the expansion of capital and that, while negatively affected by agribusiness, peasant labor productivity still compares favorably to capitalist farming. Although different, all three arguments have one thing in common: what is never considered is the possibility that underproduction and resource depletion may be *problems endemic to capital*. An alternative explanation, to be applied to our Gulf Nahua case-study, proposes that while capitalism transforms and exploits peasant agriculture, it is also a stupid machine: a system subject to contradictions and weaknesses that limit the expansion of profits generated through changes in the labor process. As argued throughout this chapter, an important contradiction inherent to an economy based on profit maximization is the poor use and abuse of the natural resources that make production possible in the first place.

Capital decomposing the peasantry

Early Marxist analyses of agriculture claimed that the peasantry was destined to give way to the development of full-fledged capitalism. Marx argued that capitalist profit presupposes the conversion of labor-power into a commodity and the continuous development of the forces of production. In his view, the reorganization of work and improvements in the techniques and technology of production are bound to increase the productivity of labor and the amount of surplus value appropriated by capital. Advances in technology, the extension of the division of labor, and the socialization of techniques of production are not ends in themselves but rather means of increasing profit accumulation. Profits are both the impetus and the consequence of the thorough transformation of the forces of production (Marx 1976: 437).

Given these assumptions, the issue is whether or not the preservation of peasant agriculture runs contrary to the accumulation of relative surplus value by capital. Roger Bartra (1974) answers in the affirmative. Building on a Marxist–Leninist tradition, he argues that simple commodity production is associated with the early stages of the development of capitalism in agriculture. Although useful to capitalism for the purpose of breaking up landed property, the peasant economy has limited potential for exploitation by capital and is doomed to disappear under the weight of its own internal contradictions and backwardness. The disappearance of simple commodity forms of production is assured by structural limitations on the organization of peasant production. "The most important internal contradiction of the simple commodity-producing economy is its division into millions of productive units. This blocks the introduction of advanced productive forces that can only be applied given a concentration of production" (R. Bartra 1974: 94, our translation). The small-scale nature and dispersion of peasant households result in an ever-widening gap between their productive capacity and that of capitalist farms, restricting the ability of peasants to compete with capitalist agriculture in the market economy. In Hewitt's words:

> As capitalist development proceeded, that part of the total social product attributable to human labor constantly declined, while that attributable to technological innovation constantly increased. Workers on capitalist farms could produce more and more with relatively less and less effort – a trend reflected in the price structure for agricultural commodities, which tended to increase only in proportion to the average amount of labor expended in production. But family labor on peasant holdings, deprived of any meaningful possibility of increasing output through technological innovation, could not produce more without expending more effort. Therefore the relatively low prices which peasant produce could fetch in regional or national markets would not adequately remunerate producers for their effort and would force them to work ever harder in order to satisfy the minimum needs of their families. (Hewitt de Alcántara 1984: 138; see R. Bartra 1982: 101)

In a similar vein, Lerda (1985) argues that peasant labor-power does not generate as much value as labor-power employed by capitalist agriculture because it is not employed at the socially necessary level of production. The consequence of these differences in productivity is that peasant labor-power is constantly devalued in relation to the labor-power of workers employed by capitalist agriculture. Peasant agriculture is inefficiently exploited as long as its level of productivity remains below the social average. In a Marxist perspective,

> surplus value which was not created could not be transferred; and therefore the extremely labor-intensive methods of the peasantry (qua enterprise) implied no more than the donation to the wider society of an astonishing amount of human effort for which inadequate compensation was obtained – a development as deplorable as it was unjust, but which served no useful purpose for the process of capitalist accumulation as a whole. The peasantry was not, then, from this point of view, exploited in the process through which its component families invested inordinate amounts of labor to produce goods remunerated at an average level established to cover the

much less labor-intensive requirements of efficient capitalist enterprises. (Hewitt de Alcántara 1984: 139–40)

For R. Bartra and Lerda, peasant underproduction is the result of inherent limitations on labor-intensive, technology-poor agriculture, limitations that are both symptomatic of and exacerbated by the articulation of peasant and capitalist modes of production. Thus it is not surprising that the peasant economy should undergo a process of dismantling under the influence of capitalist penetration.

Capital recomposing the peasantry

Unlike early Marxist theory, the dependency approach views all forms of production, technically advanced or otherwise, as part and parcel of the world capitalist system. Underdevelopment results from the growth of capital achieved through a great variety of property relations and labor systems. Frank and other proponents of the dependency school contend that the underdevelopment of hinterland regions and satellite branches of the world system is the direct result of the development of urban and metropolitan economies. In such a scheme, the vast technological gap between the peasant and capitalist sectors of agricultural production cannot be attributed to problems of economic backwardness; rather it is a consequence of full market integration into the world capitalist economy.

The contribution of the *dependendistas* to studies of peasant agriculture should not be underestimated. The concept of dependency provided an insightful critique of bourgeois and Marxist theories of capital, both of which relied too heavily on dualistic and evolutionary interpretations of Third World rural poverty. Dependency theorists should also be credited for reassessing the role of market relations and geopolitical divisions (between industrial and Third World countries, cities and villages) in the process of underdevelopment. They thus drew attention to two central features of the world economy that were inadequately accounted for in both conservative and radical versions of unilinear economic history: the uneven growth of capitalism and its ability to incorporate various labor processes and property systems into a single world system.

Like early Marxists, however, dependency theorists believed that capital would quickly penetrate the world economy. Given this teleological reasoning, these theorists have tended to fuse three distinct concepts: the *conditions* (circumstances), *functions* (requirements) and *effects* (consequences) of capitalist exploitation. Students of dependency have tended to view the historical circumstances under which capitalism develops as system requisites and inherent effects of capitalist growth. The theory did not allow capital to expand under conditions that had developed independently of capitalism itself (feudalism, petty commodity production) and that differed from capitalist forces and relations of production proper. Nor did it consider the possibility that some of these historical circumstances could act as obstacles to the forward march of capital. Finally, the theory paid no attention to the notion of self-induced contradictions, i.e., internal effects of capitalism involving class struggle or any other unintended consequence (underproduction, resource depletion) that may limit or undermine the immediate or long-term operations of capitalist exploitation (Redclift 1987: 48).

In our view, capitalism is never in a position to secure all the circumstances and requirements of its own growth (e.g., a cheap peasant labor force). Nor are the historical conditions and effects of capitalist development (e.g., Third World agricultural underproduction) always compatible with requirements of system maintenance. Capital often destroys or fails to create what it needs to expand. It rarely meets optimum requirements for development and generates constant resistance to exploitation and a chronic wastage of human and natural resources.

In response to the deficiencies of dependency and early Marxist theories, neo-Marxists have also sought to re-examine the role of capitalism in agriculture. In a discussion of the capitalist transformation of peasant forces of production, Paré argues that peasants are increasingly tied to capitalist spheres of production. Peasant control over the labor process is lost and production is reorganized along lines compatible with capitalist agriculture. In her study of the sugar cane industry in Mexico, Paré (1977: 178) observes that "the productive process is completely organized and controlled by the sugar refinery that, with its monopoly over the purchase of sugar cane within a specific region, takes charge of the entire process, from how much to plant, on what date, when to harvest, how much will be supplied to the docks, the rate of pay for manual labor, etc." She points out that peasants tied to capital-dominated markets do not participate in the basic decision-making process and that their traditional skills and knowledge of the environment are of little relevance to production (Paré 1977: 51). Peasants may own land and other means of production, yet their work may be organized in ways similar to capitalist agriculture and be affected by technological development such as the use of agro-chemicals and machinery. Through market mechanisms and an industrialization process over which they have no control, rural workers can produce and be dispossessed of absolute and relative surplus value without ever losing ownership of the land.

Paré's work goes beyond the dependency approach in that she illustrates the close connection established by Marx between the growth of productive forces and capital accumulation in agriculture. Still, the position adopted by Paré is problematical in that she too equates what is required by capital (*functions*) with what capital actually does (*effects*). The assumption is that agricultural underproduction cannot result from capitalist development since it does not serve the interests of agribusiness. While dependency theorists argue that underproduction is a consequence and a prerequisite of capital, Paré treats the same phenomenon as an external circumstance and an obstacle to profit accumulation. The two approaches share one basic assumption: what is beneficial to capitalism must be an internal effect. *The system is never confronted with dysfunctional effects of its own creation.*

Other neo-Marxist theorists have extended Paré's line of reasoning to include all forms of peasant production that can be shown to fulfil particular requirements of the capitalist economy (beyond those of agribusiness). Armando Bartra (1979a; 1976) thus stresses the positive role peasant production plays in the expansion of agribusiness and urban industry as a whole. The author agrees that capitalism in Mexico has partially dismantled the peasant economy, yet he redefines the peasantry as a subordinate class within capitalism. If the peasantry has not been replaced altogether with wage-labor agriculture, it is because of the significant benefits that capital derives from the persistence of a large class of self-employed peasants. Unlike Roger Bartra, Armando Bartra emphasizes the mechanisms of exploitation of peasant labor by capital and also the historical relevance of peasant struggles against the predatory forces of industrial capital. Peasant demands for land and better prices for their products are compatible with the interests of the rural and urban proletariat; actually they are an integral part of a broader struggle of labor against capital.

After Vergopoulos (1979), A. Bartra claims that merchant, industrial and financial capital has much to gain from the suppression of the ground rent otherwise captured by owners of large agricultural estates (through their control over scarce land and food commodities). It gains from the reproduction of small family farms that will let the price of agricultural commodities fall well below levels acceptable to capitalist firms. The survival imperative of peasant farms implies that they sell goods below the price of production while also buying productive inputs at prices above their value (A. Bartra 1979a: 99–100). The exploitation of peasants is also achieved through gradual changes in the organization and social division of labor, changes caused by the pressures of agribusiness, the credit system and state policy. Finally, while peasant production may be less efficient than capitalist agriculture, the production of socially necessary food commodities at low costs and the transfer of value from peasant agriculture to urban industry is optimal to the development of capital as a whole. The transfer of peasant surplus value to other sectors of the economy is a constant and massive drain of value from the country to the urban centers and from agriculture to industry.[1]

The advantage of A. Bartra's account of peasant economics is that it applies not only to those peasant units that have undergone major transformations in techniques and levels of production but also to those less productive units tied to capitalist spheres of production and circulation. Our view of peasant agriculture none the less differs from that of A. Bartra and Vergopoulos. Their analysis may account for increases in peasant surplus-value production within the context of a peasant property regime, yet their argument is limited in its ability to explain observed variations in levels of productivity. Also at what point do the gains obtained from the suppression of the ground rent captured by estate-owners outweigh the drain on capital accumulation caused by restrictions on technical development associated with peasant farming? Studies of peasant economies should not underestimate the contribution that full technical development in agriculture can make to capital. Nor should

they reduce all forms of simple commodity production to purely functional moments of capitalist growth, irrespective of real variations in
levels of production, mechanization, commercialization and profit accumulation. Serious attention must be paid to issues of overexploitation,
low productivity, and the uneven development of distinct branches and
regions of the world economy – internal effects of the world system that
impose severe constraints upon capital's ability to expand its own economic base. These comments hold true especially in poverty-stricken
countries and areas such as Pajapan where the dominance of weak
branches of capital results in chronic problems of resource depletion and
agricultural underproduction.

Another variation on the view of peasant labor fulfilling the needs of
capital is a book by Astorga Lira (1985). While he agrees that peasant
economies are characterized by low levels of agricultural productivity,
Astorga Lira shares some elements with the dependency school, especially
an emphasis on the full integration of peasant production in the process
of capital accumulation. Albeit technologically unsophisticated, the
peasant economy is an efficient system that fits the requirements of
capital, which consist not in the production of food commodities but
rather the reproduction of labor-power. The fact that peasant agriculture
is of little importance to capital is confirmed by the tendency of peasants
to be net consumers of foodstuffs. Peasant forces of production can
languish in their backwardness or be partially transformed by the growth
of agribusiness without affecting the main role of the peasant economy
in the production process. That role is to produce wage-workers for rural
and urban markets. The peasant economy is a "human factory" in the
business of producing wage-workers at the lowest possible cost to capital.
"It is not the objective of the peasant economy to produce goods; these
are intermediate products whose purpose is to contribute to the feeding
and formation of other more complex final products" (Astorga Lira 1985:
84, our translation). The end-product is the worker, produced very
efficiently by the peasant household economy and exploited by rural and
urban capital with equal efficiency. The scarce resources of the peasant
economy force most peasants to engage in at least some wage-labor,
resulting in an abundance of seasonal agricultural workers, a downward
pressure on rural wages, and a rapid consumption of the human commodity as workers are exploited in ever worsening conditions.

To conclude, neo-Marxists have shown how capital appropriates surplus value from peasants through relations of unequal exchange and/or
labor markets. These insights are important to an analysis of agriculture
in Mexico. Nevertheless, the benefits to capital accruing from the peasantry should not be overestimated. Paré, A. Bartra and Astorga Lira
overstate their case when they argue that the productive or reproductive
activities of Mexican peasants create optimal conditions for the growth
of capital. In our view, problems of underproduction and resource
mismanagement continue to act as barriers to capital accumulation. The
present crisis in food self-sufficiency and the reliance of Mexico on basic
food imports is ample evidence of the inability of Mexico's current

agricultural system to provide the foodcrops necessary for continued urban development. Food shortages are compounded by an overpopulation crisis, the destruction of the environment, and a chronic underemployment of the labor force. The supply of labor provided by the peasant economy is grossly out of proportion to the needs of urban and rural capital in Mexico; a 40% rate of unemployment or underemployment as is currently the case is far in excess of the labor reserve required by capital to keep the wages below the family subsistence level. Low levels of peasant employment and productivity are not essential requirements of capital-dominated economies.

Peasant articulation and resistance

As opposed to studies that emphasize the needs of capital, proponents of Peasant Economy and Cultural Ecology have paid more attention to the internal logic of peasant production and its capacity to resist and adapt to broader production systems founded on capital. According to Wolf (1957; 1959; 1966), the peasant economy can be distinguished by its intensive use of land and labor (human and animal), its reliance on traditional skills, and its limited ability to expand productive capacity. Neo-Marxian theorists have also argued that peasant agriculture follows its own rationality (Warman 1976; Moguel 1976; Stavenhagen 1979). This argument draws on a Chayanovian view of a peasant logic oriented toward the satisfaction of subsistence needs with minimum effort, a rationale completely at odds with the pursuit of maximum profit. The aim of peasant production is to regulate the relationship between the work required to support the family and the fatigue caused by it. Although inefficient from the point of view of capital, peasant agriculture fulfils farmers' needs very efficiently.

Compared to other neo-Marxists, Warman gives greater weight to the ability of peasants to resist and influence the course of capitalist development. Instead of radically transforming peasant relations and techniques of production, market conditions will force peasants to intensify the existing forms of production. The intensive use of peasant labor and land, a central feature of the traditional economy, is thus reinforced and pushed to the limit by the growth of agribusiness and food markets. The resilience of peasant forms of production can also be illustrated by the peasants' tendency to seek out new ways of adapting to unfavorable market conditions. Contrary to the industrial model of specialization, peasants in Mexico continue to rely upon traditional skills and to diversify all aspects of household production. The introduction of some commercial crops or small-scale animal husbandry in combination with subsistence production and wage-labor, as in Pajapan, is a typical example of the peasant response to pressures of the broader market economy. The central features of a peasant economy identified by Wolf are not fundamentally altered and are initially reinforced by the growth of capital (Warman 1976: 217, 237).

Like Chayanov, most proponents of the *via campesina* view the peculiarities of agriculture as favoring small-scale forms of production organized by peasants. Chayanov argued that the specific features and technical constraints of agricultural activities account for the differences that separate the development of agriculture from urban industry. Given the skills and knowledge required on the part of farmers, surplus production can be intensified through greater deployment of labor-power without increasing the scale of organization. If "the impact of progress over time necessarily and constantly reduces the optimum size of the work-team and the optimum area of the farm, then it is improbable that the forces of production will ever be seriously held back by the ... family household farm." Thus "with rational organization, peasant property and the family farm were the form most suited to raising the level of agricultural inputs, employment and production" (Harrison 1979: 88, 327).[2]

Under capitalism, however, the efficiency of peasant production is constantly being eroded. According to Wolf (1966: 49), peasants produce significant surpluses, usually expropriated by power-holders who exercise domain over land or the peasants through various claims. More often than not the growth of capitalism entails the extortion of ever greater amounts of surplus. Broader systems of exploitation may undermine peasant livelihood, especially when social and ecological limits are exceeded. In a similar vein, Warman (1976: 236) argues that the dual trend of peasants' selective adaptation and resistance to change may gradually give way to the dominant trend of subordination to capital. In the long-term, peasant forces of production are transformed. Reliance on fertilizers, pesticides and other costly technologies are inevitable effects of the greater commercialization of peasant agriculture. Rural workers may also lose control over the types of crops, the timing of planting and other productive norms dictated by the needs of capital-dominated markets. The return to peasant labor is negatively affected by these transformations. Profit-oriented economies "attempt to renew immature ecological systems in a state of high productivity" (Redclift 1987: 18). They force peasants to overexploit the soil and extend production into ever more marginal regions in order to maintain or increase levels of production. Instead of increasing productivity, the commercialization of peasant agriculture brings about an increase in the amount of labor required to generate the same or slightly higher levels of production (Warman 1976: 299).

Cultural ecologists have treated peasant economies as systems in their own right. They have given us tools needed to understand the protracted articulation of capitalist and non-capitalist forms of production, hence the various ways in which peasant production can be dominated by capital while showing resistance and adaptability to broader market forces. Having said this, cultural ecologists have tended to romanticize the tradition of harmony prevailing between peasant society and their immediate environment and among peasants themselves. The literature also tends to lack a theory of the state[3] and to reduce the complexity of capital to simple principles (the maximization of profit). Studies of the impact of capitalism on peasant agriculture should not underestimate the variability of capitalist forces and relations of production. Nor should they treat forces and relations of production that impose limits on capital accumulation as external factors located "outside" the capitalist economy. In its own way, capitalism produces contradictions and crises that are so pervasive as never to allow the system to create optimal conditions for its own growth.

Capital decomposing itself

A common thread that runs through the arguments made so far is that peasant forces of production respond to the demands of capital-dominated markets. The thesis presented in this book differs from the articulationist and full integration arguments presented above. In our view, the debate over whether peasants produce surplus value cannot be resolved without recognizing the polymorphous structure of capitalism and also its inherent weaknesses. The first part of the argument developed below emphasizes the variable forms of subordination of peasant labor to a system of production based on the antagonism of capital and labor. The second part acknowledges the resistance of peasants to full capitalist exploitation and their struggle to maintain control over vital aspects of production. The third and final part of the argument postulates that capitalism is subject to self-induced contradictions and limitations that may undermine the full exploitation of labor and the long-term development of the forces of production and resource management system in agriculture.

The first point to be made is simply that the exploitation of peasant labor by capital can take a number of forms, i.e., whenever capital gains control over the techniques, or the instruments or the division of labor in agriculture. Interventions in the peasant labor process can range from the introduction of advanced forms of industrial technology to new administrative strategies or rudimentary improvements in tools and techniques of production. Capital may be in a position to dictate significant aspects of the labor process such as what and how to plant, when and in what quantity, how to care for the cultivates, the time and method of harvesting, etc. Through pressures coming from the market or the state, peasants may be compelled to specialize in the production of a few cash crops, to intensify production and to use labor more continuously in the production of a larger marketable surplus, with or without any change in technology. Market forces may further reduce peasant control over the quantity, quality and type of agricultural inputs used such as land, labor, chemicals and machinery (Feder 1977b: 18). Capitalist enterprises may decide where the product is marketed, the method of packaging and transportation, storage and distribution. Alternatively, capitalist control over production may result in a new division of labor where peasant farms produce animals or foodplants using rudimentary technology while agribusiness undertakes the more technically complex tasks of processing and marketing the produce. When confined to producing unprocessed foodstuffs, peasant agriculture tends to be associated with a loss of peasant skills and an increase in labor mobility between sectors of the regional or national economy. Specialization, the intensification of production, labor mobility, and the redirection of peasant agriculture to labor-intensive stages of production, all contribute to the creation of surplus value. They are forms of technical subordination that *may or may not transform the actual property regime or lead to a full-scale industrialization of peasant technology.*

Having said this, studies of underdevelopment concerned with the functions of peasant agriculture *vis-à-vis* capital are inherently teleological: great store is placed in the internal logic of capitalism and its capacity to meet its own needs. They concentrate their attention on how peasants contribute to the maximum accumulation of surplus value on the un-challenged assumption that this end is inherent to the whole system. In this perspective, capitalism always gets what it needs, either in the short term through the expansion and appropriation of peasant surplus value or in the long term through outright proletarianization. The alternative view proposed in this book is that the struggles and contradictions of capitalism may limit the production and accumulation of surplus value to less than the optimum conditions needed for the system to attain full growth. Actually, these problems are so pervasive that the minimum requirements of simple reproduction may not even be met. Thus, capital-ism is far from the perfect machine for maximum profit accumulation idealized by many theorists on the left and right. The system is better described as a contradictory combination of forces of *domination* and *resistance, growth* and *maldevelopment.*

To begin with, the peasant labor process is subject to the impact of class struggle – the second point of our argument. A. Bartra is an eloquent spokesman for a growing number of Mexican social scientists who go beyond a strictly functional conception of the exploitative logic of capital-ist relations and forces of production. In his own words:

> Various authors have demonstrated that a peasant economy sub-ordinated to the capitalist mode of production fulfils decisive structural functions and is reproduced by the system. We have also provided arguments along the line that the peasant economy is not only dismantled by capital but is also reproduced by capital. Nevertheless, we insist also on the other side of the question: the peasantry survives in capitalism because of its fight to maintain possession of at least a part of the land. However reformist the agrarian legislation may be, however populist protectionist measures of the bourgeois state may be ... the peasantry would never be saved from the rapacity of capital ... were it not for the peasants' ability to develop a permanent fight for existence, a fight which is usually expressed in the form of a movement to maintain possession of some land. (A. Bartra 1979a: 48, our translation.)[4]

While insightful, A. Bartra's active resistance thesis is limited to class action expressed through political organization and peasant demands for land. The issue of peasant resistance to domination is oddly absent from his discussion of the real subordination process. In our view, the question of struggle is also central to the analysis of peasant forces of production.

Peasant struggles against the extraction of relative surplus value can take many forms. Rural workers may develop multiple occupational strategies or conservative risk-avoiding inactions to protect themselves from increasing levels of exploitation associated with changes in the labor process that put their livelihood at risk. The effectiveness of peasant adaptive strategies presupposes the maintenance, if only partial, of non-capitalist techniques of production which allow the peasantry some control over both the physical resources and the productive activities needed to survive. "The defensive reaction of the peasants in the face of technical advances and indiscriminate modernization could be understood as a logical decision, economically suited to the better management of limited and untransferable (peasant) resources" (Warman 1983: 28, our translation). Capital may be forced by this resistance to adapt to a less than ideal productive environment, adjusting itself to limitations on the real subordination process. The frequently observed movement of peasants between subsistence production, self-employment and wage-labor and the maintenance of traditional techniques of cultivation and modes of livelihood impose real constraints on the creation of relative surplus value achieved through radical transformations in the labor process.

Our last point is that labor processes governed by capital are also subject to endemic mismanagement problems. Peasant underproduction is often explained away as a symptom of economic backwardness or a functional requirement and effect of capitalism in agriculture. In reality, low levels of surplus value production cannot be explained in isolation from the contradictory tendencies of capitalism. These include not only the struggle of peasants against all forms of domination but also the irrational use of agricultural resources by capital. Most of the perspectives reviewed above provide salient observations about the chaotic and wasteful deployment of human and natural resources resulting from the capitalization of peasant agriculture. The usual implication of these observations, however, is that capital is operating in a rational manner from the point of view of market profitability but wastefully from the point of view of either the peasantry or the critical observer. The image of capitalism is one of a perfectly functioning machine with deplorable human consequences.

Hewitt, to cite one Mexican author, concludes her study of the modernization of agriculture with a devastating critique of the path of capitalist development observed in Mexico. Her analysis shows how Mexican agriculture has involved a systematic wastage of natural resources by agricultural firms imbued with a "mining mentality". Manufactured agricultural inputs (and the foreign exchange needed to acquire them) have been managed irrationally as well, without sufficient planning, resulting in an ineffective modernization of agriculture in the irrigated areas. Profits generated by new forms of agricultural production have been squandered, without ever being plowed back into the creation of new productive enterprises. Agribusiness in Mexico has also made a poor use of human resources in general – of peasants, *colonos* and *ejidatarios* expelled from the land or confined to the least productive areas of the national territory (Hewitt de Alcántara 1978: 301).

Although legitimate, humanistic and pro-peasant critiques of the irrationalities of profit-oriented agribusiness should not underestimate the propensity of capitalism to weaken or even undermine its own productive base. A critique of capitalism "from outside" ignores the chronic problems and crises that capitalism creates for itself. Again, to the notion of capitalism as an efficient exploitative machine can be counterpoised a Janus-faced system of market growth and maldevelopment, a machine marred by imperfections, contradictions and self-induced limitations that pervade all aspects of the economy, including the labor process and the prevailing techniques of exploitation as applied to both nature and labor. Underproduction in agriculture is a case in point. The systematic transfer of profits to industrial centers may weaken agricultural capital (or the peasant economy) in some areas so severely that it is unable to overcome technical or ecological limits on the development of labor processes. Likewise, capital may force the intensification of peasant production to such a degree that deforestation, erosion and the over-exploitation of the soil and the land may threaten the natural resources that make capital accumulation possible in the first place.

Theories of peasant economics and agricultural underdevelopment have paid little attention to the internal contradictions of market economies based on the exploitation of labor and nature by capital. Marx devoted considerable attention to these endemic limitations that result in cyclical crises of capital and that create the necessary conditions for revolutionary transformations to occur. Students of rural economics can salvage these insights of dialectical materialism without falling prey to the evolutionary rhetoric of systems that "plant the seeds of their inevitable destruction". These insights point to the negative impact that capital accumulation has on the development of industry and the creation of relative surplus value, especially in Third World countries. They also point to the enormous limitations that an industry wasteful of its own resources imposes on the long-term profitability and sustainability of a world production system dominated by capital. Just as property relations based on the pursuit of unlimited profits may act as a barrier to the development of industry and productivity (as argued by Marx), so too the current system of industrial exploitation of nature may very well impair the long-term prospects of capital accumulation on a world scale.

The notion that economies based on the pursuit of profit destroy their own natural environments implies that ecosystems possess internal dynamics that are at odds with the activities of capital. This brings us to the issue of how ecosystems are dealt with in the Marxian literature. All Marxists are united by the assumption that the production of the means of subsistence is the basic fact to be taken into account in any analysis of social life. Instead of delving into natural systems and questions of rational adaptation, however, most Marxist students of agriculture in Mexico emphasize the socially determined nature of the capitalist transformation of peasant forces of production.[5] This reflects a broad rejection of the "vulgar materialism" of earlier functionalist and ecological perspectives. As a result, environmental factors are treated as isolated obstacles in the way of technical development, hence limiting factors that may explain observable variations in levels and forms of economic development.[6] As they rarely examine the internal dynamics of ecosystems, Marxists oversimplify the environmental aspects of relations prevailing between peasant systems of production and the wider capitalist economy. Ecology is reduced to a list of a few elements which set basic constraints on production, or it is passed over altogether (Redclift 1987: 8f., 47).

The study of peasant ecosystems has been the special focus of Cultural Ecologists such as Wolf, Palerm and Warman. These authors argue that peasant production must be viewed as a system of ecological adaptation consisting of specific sets of resources, instruments of production and labor processes. Wolf thus identifies specific peasant ecotypes based on the combination of elements that vary according to environmental conditions (Wolf 1966: 22). This approach takes the internal features of peasant systems of adaptation seriously, providing the basis for an understanding of the interrelationship of ecological and economic factors. The systemic features of peasant production, however, should not be derived from environmental variables only. Critics of ecological determinism point out that environmental constraints are themselves partly determined by the social forces and relations of production (Godelier 1973; Harrison 1977: 335; F. Chevalier 1982: 99). Ecological factors cannot be treated as fixed elements to which social relations must rigidly adapt. Similar environments allow for considerable variation in technical development and adaptive strategies. Variations in productive systems depend upon the complex interaction of specific environmental and socio-economic conditions, all of which require careful investigation.

Our study of problems of ecological misadaptation in Pajapan presupposes that we recognize the structural complexity of ecosystems, the socially determined character of systems of agricultural production, and the mutual interaction (sometimes dysfunctional) of social and natural factors of exploitation. Natural conditions limit the actions of people but these limits are also mediated and altered by systems of social relations that vary over time. The following Gulf Nahua case-study illustrates the latter argument, starting with a discussion of basic environmental conditions of production observed in this area of southern Veracruz. This information is all the more crucial as it allows us to understand how the Santa Marta ecosystem has affected and is affected by the current agricultural practices and the traditional *milpa* system as well.

A tropical ecosystem

Diversity's last stand

The Sierra de Santa Marta is one of two large volcanic structures comprising the Sierra de los Tuxtlas in southern Veracruz. This coastal mountain range harbors the most northern rain forest on the continent

(18° 15'N) and one of the most ancient. During the final centuries of the Tertiary era a series of tectonic events pushed sedimentary materials upwards to form the Sierra de los Tuxtlas and Santa Marta, dividing the vast coastal plain into the Tehuantepec Isthmus and the Veracruz plain (V.M. Toledo 1982). The thermostatic effects of the Gulf of Mexico provided the region with a degree of climatic stability permitting the survival of many tropical and subtropical flora and fauna during the cool-dry climatic periods of the last ice age. The Sierra was one of only a few "areas of refuge" when most rainforests in Mexico disappeared. When temperatures and rainfall increased with the beginning of the modern geological era, these and other refuge areas fanned out to reconquer the tropics of Mexico.

The climatic features of the Sierra de los Tuxtlas and Santa Marta create an island of biological diversity uncommon in the world. The sudden rise from sea level to over 1,700 meters at the highest peak transforms the moisture-laden trade winds from the Gulf of Mexico into torrential rain, over 4,000 millimeters on the northern slope. The mountain range also creates a rain shadow on the southern and eastern slopes where annual rainfall drops to as little as 1,000 millimeters. Altitudinal variations up the volcano slopes and inside the craters create a wide range of temperatures favorable to the development of varied vegetation types and animal habitats. In an area covering only 1,500 square kilometers, a vast array of biological life is concentrated.

More than 3,000 species, 607 genera and 143 families of vascular plants are present in the Sierra, representing most of the plant families found in the State of Veracruz (Andrle 1964; Paré, Blanco et al. 1992; Ramírez 1984). Some plants native to the Sierra are new to science, including a genus and species of orchid and bamboo, a fern species, five tropical shrubs belonging to the Myrsinaceae family, a herb species (*Salvia tuxtlensis*) and several others. Approximately 263 native plant species are considered medicinal by the indigenous population, 73 others are collected for food and 54 species have traditional applications for the construction of houses, furniture and tools (Paré, Blanco et al. 1992).

Approximately 1,173 animal species, 21 of which are endemic, inhabit the forests of the Sierra. An estimated 41% of Mexico's bird species, some 410 in all, depend upon the forests and mangroves of the Sierra for survival. In addition, the region provides habitat for 102 mammals, 168 species and subspecies of amphibians and reptiles, 359 bat species, 124 species of dragonflies, and 50 species of aquatic insects. Navarro (1981) argues that the regional diversity of bats is rivalled only by the lowlands of Panama and Costa Rica. Deforestation has all but destroyed this heritage: at least 140 species of fauna (mostly birds, reptiles and mammals) are at the edge of extinction.

Ramírez (1991) describes eight ecological life zones in the Sierra based mainly on climax vegetation, soils and climatic factors (see Map 6). The mountain peaks and craters are covered by various kinds of **subtropical montane forest** known to the Gulf Nahuas as *bawayoj*. At this altitude, average annual temperatures are 18° C or less and rain falls in excess of

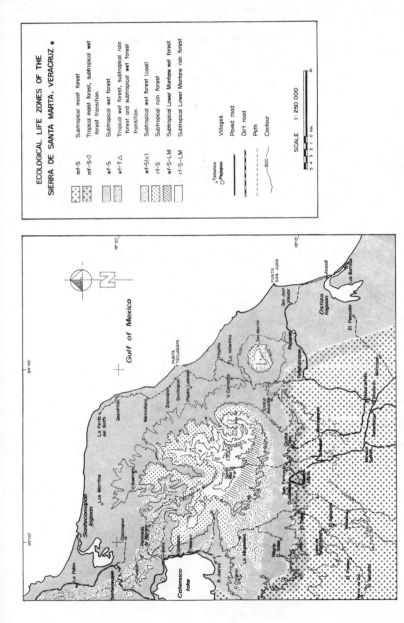

ECOLOGICAL LIFE ZONES OF THE SIERRA DE SANTA MARTA, VERACRUZ *

	mf-S	Subtropical moist forest.
	mf-S◁	Tropical moist forest, subtropical wet forest transition.
	wf-S	Subtropical wet forest.
	wf-T△	Tropical wet forest, subtropical rain forest and subtropical wet forest transition.
	wf-S(c)	Subtropical wet forest (cool)
	rf-S	Subtropical rain forest
	wf-S-LM	Subtropical Lower Montane wet forest.
	rf-S-LM	Subtropical Lower Montane rain forest.

○ Tehonca ○ Pajapan	Villages.
	Paved road
	Dirt road
	Path
300	Contour

SCALE   1 : 250 000

Map 6   Ecological life zones of the Sierra de Santa Marta, Veracruz (Ramírez 1993)

3,000 millimeters per year, providing the cool, wet conditions needed for development of these forest types. The mountain peaks are frequently shrouded in clouds, adding through condensation as much water to the local hydrology as falls in rain. The forest drips with mosses, lichens, ferns, orchids and vines. While the forest canopy reaches between 15 and 25 meters in places, on the ridges and in areas exposed to the wind the vegetation does not exceed 3 meters in height. In their most developed form, cloud forests have two strata characterized by distinct plant communities determined partly by slope and exposure to wind and sun.[7]

Montane forests are uncommon in Mexico and the world. The Sierra de los Tuxtlas and Santa Marta, El Triunfo, Sierra Madre and Sierra Norte in Chiapas and the Chimalapas in Oaxaca contain the only Mexican forests of this type. Cloud forest cover on the peak of the volcano San Martín Pajapan has been reduced by fire and clearing to only 338 hectares. This forest remains a sacred and somewhat intimidating place for Pajapeños who believe the area to be inhabited by jaguars, poisonous snakes and *chaneques*, the animal spirits. During a hike to the mountain peak the researchers saw a jaguar print that put everyone on the edge, including our native guides.

The foothills of the Sierra and much of the coastal plain are characterized by various kinds of **tropical and subtropical rain forests**. In the wetter canyons the rain forests reach as high as 900 meters above sealevel. Within this forest type, known to the Gulf Nahuas as *we bauit*, there are 14 plant associations distinguished by the indigenous population according to the most characteristic (but not necessarily dominant) species. Ramírez (Paré, Blanco et al. 1992) suggests that the tall rain forest on the southern slope of the Sierra has much in common with the primary forest of the coastal plain of southern Veracruz dominated by the tree *Terminalia amazonia*. Local informants argue that these forests are different in floral composition and structure from the forests located on the northern slope of the Sierra where the palm *chocho (Astro-carium mexicanum)* is common. This difference may be climatic in origin as the southern slope has less rainfall due to the rain shadow effect of the mountain range. The rainfall regime also distinguishes these forests from the tall rain forests of Central and South America.

The longevity of the tropical rain forests of the Sierra is a tribute to the efficiency of rain forest ecology. Constant temperatures and high humidity in the rain forest interior contribute to the rapid decomposition of forest litter and its conversion into humus by soil flora and fauna. The tiny rootlets of trees and other plants quickly recycle nutrients contained in the vegetation, returning to the living forest the remains of previous generations of plant life. This plant-to-plant recycling process is so complete that the rate of nutrients entering the system through litter, rain and dust closely balances the rate of nutrient loss through soil leaching and volatization. The rain forest derives most nutrients needed for plant growth from itself, without drawing on the limited resources of the soil. The soil remains in a state of equilibrium, serving not as a supplier of nutrients but rather as a reservoir for water and a mechanical support system for tall trees.[8]

This remarkable recycling process is aided by the closed-cover architecture of the rain forest. The tallest trees form a dense canopy at approximately 30 meters with occasional emergent trees reaching a height of 40 meters or more. This canopy completely shades the forest floor from the heat of the sun and lessens the force of the heavy rainfall. A middle stratum of trees 6 to 18 meters tall provides additional protection from sun and rain and support for a myriad of vines, orchids, mosses, mistletoes and stranglers that cling to the branches of trees. This luxuriant vegetation intercepts and absorbs a great deal of water before it strikes the ground and traps moisture for use during periods of relative drought. A lower story composed of trees, saplings, shrubs, spiny palms, and ferns completes the protective cover. The ground level of this tall forest is relatively clear and open, covered mainly by fallen trees, branches, and a thin layer of dead leaves.[9]

In addition to the conservation of biological diversity, the cloud forests and rain forests of the Sierra provide an important ecological service to the region. The vegetation captures a tremendous amount of water through horizontal precipitation (dew), perhaps as much as falls in rain (Paré, Blanco et al. 1992). This water is gradually released to lower areas throughout the year, supplying the major bodies of water in the region including the coastal lagoons Sontecomapan and Ostión, Lake Catemaco (Mexico's third largest), and numerous rivers feeding both the Coatzacoalcos and Papaloapan watersheds. Along all slopes of the Sierra, springs gush forth from the rock at major breaks in the topography, providing the basis for many human settlements (denoted through water-placenames ending with -pan). Some 80% of Coatzacoalcos' potable water, 20% of the water consumed by Minatitlán and virtually all of the drinking water of Acayucan is drawn from two springs on the southern slope of the Sierra, one near Soteapan and the other near Tatahuicapan. More than a million people in these and numerous small cities, towns and villages in the region depend upon the water captured, stored, filtered and distributed by the forest vegetation in the Sierra.

Drier conditions on the southern and eastern slopes of the Sierra create several other important ecological life zones. **Subtropical moist forest** is the primary vegetation for an area extending between 100 and 450 meters above sea-level from the western margin of the Laguna del Ostión in the municipality of Pajapan around the eastern slope of the Sierra to San Andrés Tuxtla. This relatively open forest is characterized by black oak *(Quercus oleoides)*, an evergreen tree found all the way south through Mesoamerica to Costa Rica. The forest usually reaches a height of 10 to 15 meters although under some conditions trees may grow to 30 meters. The eminent biologist Sarukhán (1968) suggests that the tropical oak forests of Mexico may have developed as a result of unique edaphic factors during the last ice age. Ramírez (1991) notes that the southern slope of the Sierra de Santa Marta where oak forests dominate is geologically older than the southern slope of the volcano San Martín Pajapan where tall rain forests are native.

The sheltered shores of the lagoons Sontecomapan and Ostión are surrounded by **mangrove forests**, a habitat rich in aquatic and land-bound life. Mangrove forests have an amphibious existence that develops in close relationship with the coastal estuary. The aerial roots of the trees disrupt water currents, enhancing "accretion of marine and stream sediments, leaf litter and other organic debris, so that soil levels within the mangrove are progressively raised" (Britton and Morton 1989: 223). Mangrove forests literally reclaim land from the sea.

The mangrove forests surrounding the Laguna del Ostión and Sontecomapan are among the most developed on the western Gulf of Mexico (Bozada and Chávez 1986; Britton and Morton 1989). Four of five Mexican mangrove species are present in these forests, arranged in bands from the shoreline to higher ground where they are replaced by other plant communities. The short, pioneer red mangrove *(Rhizophora mangle)* has colonized the intertidal shore where flooding and saline conditions are greatest. The white mangrove *(Laguncularia racemosa)* occupies a narrow band inland from the red mangroves where flooding is less frequent. These trees reach 8 to 12 meters in height (Ramírez 1984). The sedimentary accretion and build-up of leaf litter by the red and white mangroves have raised the forest floor enough to permit the establishment of the taller black mangrove *(Avicennia germinans)* further inland. This species reaches heights of 15 to 25 meters and occupies the greatest surface area within the mangrove forest. The outer fringe of the forest, seldom reached by tides, is characterized by an open forest comprising the 6-meter buttonwood mangrove *(Conocarpus erecta)*, palms and low-growing salt-marsh plants that are adapted to sandy soils. Depending upon the precise conditions of relief and soil, the mangrove forest borders on tall rain forest, swamp savanna, marsh scrub and coastal dune vegetation.

The ecology of a mangrove forest differs dramatically from that of a rain forest. Mangroves depend chiefly on incoming drainage water for a supply of nutrients, not on the plant recycling process characteristic of the rain forest. Given the superabundance of water and poor soil aeration, the litter of mangrove forests remains in the soil and is not reabsorbed by the vegetation as such (Bozada and Chávez 1986: 82; Buringh 1970: 98; Richards 1952: 216). In contrast to the closed nutrient cycles of the rain forest, mangroves "are systems open to the flux of energy and materials upon which they depend" (Gallegos 1986: 27). As a result, they are very susceptible to both marine and freshwater pollution.

The red mangroves fulfil a vital role in the ecology of intertidal waters. Britton and Morton (1989: 225) note that the red mangrove in mono-culture along the narrow band of intertidal shoreline "forms the base of one of the most productive communities on earth". An estimated 480 red mangroves can be found in a single hectare of the forest area located where the River Metzapa empties into the Laguna del Ostión (Ramírez 1991: 30). The rain of mangrove leaves falling on the forest floor initiates

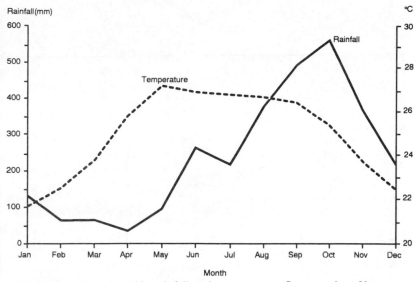

Figure 1   Mean monthly rainfall and temperature, Coatzacoalcos, Veracruz

a complex food web involving leaf shredders (small crustaceans), fungi and bacteria. These primary consumers become in turn the food of larger organisms found on the roots, stems and branches of the mangroves and in the soft bottom sediments at the base of the trees. The mangrove oyster and barnacles attach themselves to mid-tide-level mangroves. Sponges, tunicates, bryozoans, tube worms and other invertebrates are found on submerged branches and prop roots. While semiterrestrial crabs clamber over the aerial roots near the waterline, the mangrove-dominated banks of the lagoon are home to a variety of burrowing crabs including the blue-grey mud crab. Various kinds of molluscs and clams inhabit the mud on the forest floor. Transient inhabitants include bird species such as the brown pelican, the snowy egret, the little heron and tropical wading birds that feed among the shallow waters of the mangroves (Britton and Morton 1989).

The agro-ecology of Pajapan

The complex tropical ecosystem evoked above provides important ecological services to the region and the world. It also provides many opportunities and imposes specific constraints on the economic activities of the regional population.

Abundant rain and warm temperatures hold considerable agricultural promise for the farmers of Pajapan. Rainfall in Pajapan averages 2,700 millimeters per year while the annual average temperature is 25° C, ideal conditions for many tropical crops (see Figure 1). The rains are distributed bimodally, facilitating agricultural activities through much of the year.

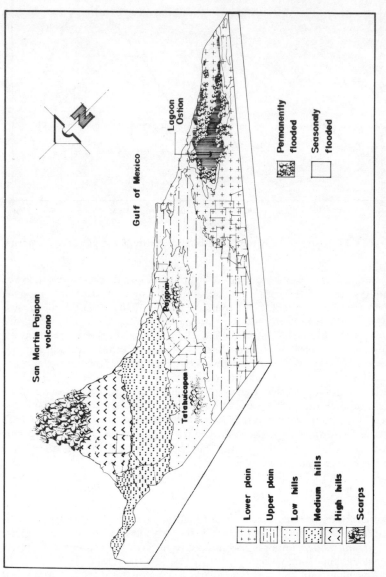

Map 7 Panoramic view of the landscape units in Pajapan (Gutiérrez 1993)

The wet season *(temporal)* lasts from June until September, a warm period with heavy downpours and night storms. The rains are briefly interrupted during the later part of August by a dry canicular spell that can have negative effects on local agriculture. A heavy drizzle and strong, cool winds from the north *(nortes)* created by tropical cyclones repeatedly strike the region from October until early March. The *nortes* bring rain that facilitates a second planting season *(tapachole)*. They also bring winds that occasionally peak at 80 kilometers per hour, knocking down maize fields and deflowering fruit trees and bean crops. A short, sharp dry season interrupting all agricultural activity arrives later as hot air masses *(suradas)* sweep in from the south from March to May. These dry winds, sometimes as strong as 40 kilometers per hour, produce clear skies and hot, dry weather that scorch the *tapachole* maize and dry out pastures.

Pajapan straddles two distinct landscapes, the coastal plain of the Tehuantepec Isthmus and the southeastern slope of the volcano San Martín Pajapan (see Map 7). The Gulf Nahua land base totals 19,158 hectares, now divided into communal lands on the upper slope and an *ejido* on the lower plain. Local soils are derived mainly from volcanic materials transformed by sun and rain into a number of soil types. Gutiérrez Martínez (1991) argues that the Pajapan environment is the most diverse in the Sierra, comprising eight distinct landscape units based mainly on edaphic and topographic factors. The **scarps** of the volcano San Martín Pajapan, located between 700 meters above sea-level and the peak of the volcano at 1,230 meters, are characterized by very steep slopes and *Orthic acrisol* soils derived from composite volcanic materials. Permanent forest is the most appropriate land use for this zone as the very steep slopes limit all productive activities.

High hills radiate out from the peak of the volcano in sharp, long ridges and deep valleys with slopes of up to 50%. These are located between 500 and 800 meters above sea-level; on the eastern side of the volcano they extend down to 250 meters. The soils, derived from composite volcanic materials and harder basalts, are also mainly *Orthic acrisols*. *Orthic andisol* and *Orthic luvisol* soils can be found on these hills in small quantities. The soils tend to be very rocky along the length of the high hills and present signs of water erosion in streambeds. Steep slopes, susceptibility to erosion and strong winds limit the productive potential of this area. Virtually all of the high hills have been deforested, making way for a tough local grass known in Nahua as *talquetzal (Paspalum virginatum)* of little value even to grazing animals. Its presence is recognized by natives as a sign of very low soil fertility.

The **medium hills** of Pajapan, located between 200 and 500 meters above sea-level, are rounded with shallow valleys. Pure basalt has given rise to the formation of *Orthic luvisol* soils which are highly susceptible to erosion but more fertile than the *Acrisols*. A wide variety of uses are possible in this zone including maize cultivation, pastures and perennial crops such as coffee and fruit trees (planted in areas protected from winds). Nevertheless, exposure to the elements has leached these soils of nutrients leaving behind red oxides. Strong winds create problems for both annual and perennial crops. Deforestation seems to be largely responsible for problems of soil degradation in this area: brown and dark soils are common on similar slopes covered by rain forest vegetation in La Valentina and Santanón Rodríguez (Stuart 1978; Paré, Blanco et al. 1992).

The **low hills** of Pajapan are located between 10 and 80 meters above sea-level on northeast and eastern slopes, between 10 and 140 meters on eastern and southeastern slopes, and as high as 300 meters on the southern side of the volcano. They consist of relatively flat tops and gentle valleys. Basalt is the principal material from which the *Chromic vertisol, Ferric luvisol* and *Chromic luvisol* soils characteristic of the low hills have been formed. While relatively flat in some parts, there is little alluvial accumulation. Chemical properties of the soils and degradation resulting from baking and leaching are limiting factors in this zone but these slopes are still (along with the plains) the most appropriate soils for crop cultivation and pastures within the communal territory of Pajapan.

The lower edge of the Gulf Nahua territory, now the *ejido* of Pajapan II, is part of the **flat plain** extending southeastward along the Gulf of Mexico. Several landscape units are found within this generic category. Unlike the medium and high hills of Pajapan, the plain consists of relatively fertile soils with good moisture retention capacity. The soils are less eroded than on the uplands and the area is partially protected from the *nortes*. Two maize crops a year can be cultivated on the plain, although the high clay content of the soils limits agricultural productivity. Archival evidence indicates that natural savannas on the plain were used in the early 1600s by Spanish ranchers.[10] Considering that human settlements in the area go back many centuries more, it is possible that the land was once covered by tall humid forest and has been permanently rendered savanna by continuous clearing and burning. This was the first area in Pajapan to be occupied by ranchers during this century. It is the best quality land in the community, hence the site of territorial competition between ranchers and peasants since the 1940s.

While volcanic activity gave birth to the basic material covering the volcano slope and plain, the lowland area near the shore of the Laguna del Ostión has been affected mainly by coastal and alluvial action. Two lowlands can be distinguished: the seasonally and the permanently **flooded lowlands**. The former is composed of *Vertic gleysol* soils derived from clay sediments capable of supporting water-resistant pastures, and *Chromic vertisol* soils black or grey in color and suitable for cultivation. *Vertisols* can be very fertile but they have a high clay content, which means they become very sticky when wet and hard when dry. These unstable soils are difficult to manage and are further limited by low water permeability, seasonal flooding (three months a year) and physical-chemical deficiencies. By contrast, the permanently flooded lowlands are composed of *Vertic gleysol* soils appropriate only for mangroves and as habitat for fish, crabs and other animals characteristic of mangrove forests. These grey, bluish and greenish soils are not susceptible to erosion.

Table 5.1 Gulf Nahua soil classification

Gulf Nahua Term	Description	Potential Land Use
Pistiktal	Black	Maize, Beans
Medio Pistiktal	Half Black	Maize
Tatahuiktal	Red, Rocky	Pasture, Maize
Gostiktal	Yellow	Maize
Istaktal	White	Maize
Teposhakio	Rocky	Maize
Xalnelijtok	Sandy	Maize, Plantain
Xaltal	Sandy	Maize, Plantain
Xalli	Sand	Watermelon
Pistiksogik	Black Mud	Plantain
Gonsogik	Mud	Pottery clay

Source: Modified from Gutiérrez Martínez (1991) and Stuart (1978), supplemented with interviews in Pajapan.

When exposed and drained, however, they lose much of their bulk and become relatively infertile, making them of little use for agriculture.

One other zone that should be mentioned is the **coastal corridor** of *Eutric regosol* soils made up of sand and medium-sized quartz particles. These soils have formed rolling dunes parallel to the coast and are suitable for pastures and crops requiring little residual moisture (watermelon, peanuts). Although the natural vegetation protects inland areas from salt spray during the season of *norte* winds, the high permeability of the sandy soils and chemical properties limit the agricultural use of this coastal corridor.

The Gulf Nahuas have a complex soil typology based on soil color, soil structure and potential for agriculture that parallels the zones identified by Gutiérrez Martínez (1991; Table 5.1). *Pistiktal*, a black soil considered the most fertile of all local soils, is associated by the Gulf Nahuas with the flat plains coveted for agriculture and cattle ranching alike. *Xalnelijtok, xaltal* and *xalli* are sandy soils mixed with varying amounts of alluvial sediments found on the coastal corridor and along riverbeds. The seasonally and permanently flooded lowlands are characterized by what the Gulf Nahuas call *pistiksogik*, black mud. One zone identified by Pajapeños is not reflected in Gutiérrez's typology: it consists of soils known as *gonsogik*, a mud sediment formed around springs, usually at points where the medium hills change to low hills.

The red and yellow soils identified by the Nahuas do not correspond directly to Gutiérrez's morpho-edaphic zones either. The color of these superficial soil horizons is the result of soil degradation processes provoked by exposure to the elements and intensive agricultural use not limited to a single zone. While *gostiktal*, a yellow soil, can be found throughout the Nahua territory, *tatahuiktal*, a red earth soil of poor quality, is increasing in land area over time, currently covering a large portion of the high, medium and low hills. Gutiérrez suggests that the soil color criterion used by the Gulf Nahuas does not capture the geological origins and evolutionary processes of the hilly land types where these soils are found.

In summation, abundant rainfall, warm temperatures and a bimodal rainfall regime make it possible to produce a wide range of tropical crops throughout most of the year. Nevertheless, strong *nortes* threaten to lodge both *temporal* and *tapachole* maize and dry, hot winds pose risks during the *tapachole*. A short, sharp dry season brings all agricultural activities to a halt in April and May. The best agricultural land in Pajapan is the plain and low hills coveted by farmers and ranchers alike while the medium and high hills are of little use for agriculture and quickly degrade after the forest cover is removed.

Climate, topography, soil, water and vegetation are all delicately balanced in a web of relationships establishing the natural constraints and potentialities of human resource exploitation in Pajapan. Natural limitations, however, have never been so rigid as to preclude important variations in modes of socially-organized adaptation. Although subject to real constraints, the environment has always allowed for important historical variations in technical development and adaptive strategies. The Gulf Nahuas lived within this environment for centuries, applying their intimate knowledge of variations in the distribution and ecology of land and water resources to exploit the natural bounty that surrounded them. They produced much of what they needed for subsistence, without recourse to the market economy or threats to the reproduction of their immediate resource base. As in other areas of Mexico (Levy and Hernández 1991), lakes, forests and abandoned fields served as a huge storehouse of high-quality protein food, firewood, timber for construction and carpentry, honey, wild fruit and medicinal plants. This original endowment was maintained in its essence by generations of Pajapeños occupying only a fraction of the territory for agricultural subsistence and leaving to the spirit world what it required to govern the universe (see Chapter 7).

The same cannot be said of the production system in the Pajapan of today. The rise of the cattle industry from the 1940s onwards has thoroughly transformed the original landscape. While population pressures under the traditional system of agriculture or the development of commercial agriculture may eventually have displaced the tropical forests and produced some degradation of soil resources, these changes would not have occurred with anything near the speed or voracity that has come to typify the modern cattle economy. As will be seen shortly, the cattle industry has been the major catalyst for profound environmental and technical transformations occurring throughout the municipal lands of Pajapan. The original rain forests have been reduced to a remnant of their past glory.

The silvo-pastoral and agricultural systems that replaced the primary ecosystems degraded the natural resource base more during the last few decades than in the previous few centuries. Soil erosion and the decline in soil fertility, pest and weed build-ups, losses in plant diversity, overfishing and the destruction of forest animal habitat undermined the ability of both the natural and social production systems to sustain themselves over time. Changing patterns of production continue to accelerate resource decline and threaten the self-sufficiency of the local food production system. In the remainder of this chapter, we offer a detailed analysis of the changes affecting the quality of the natural resource base and the performance of the cattle, *milpa* and fisheries systems upon which Pajapeños depend.

Turning forest into pasture

The cattle industry is one of the principal agents of ecological change in Latin America (Downing et al. 1992; Myers 1980; V.M. Toledo 1989). The history of cattle ranching in Pajapan illustrates the destructive role the industry has played in the conversion of tropical forests into pastures and the decline of *milpa* agriculture. Our case-study also points to the chronic weakness of an industry characterized by an inefficient and destructive use of local resources. While the rise of cattle ranching in Pajapan has contributed to the accumulation of agricultural capital, it has done so only minimally and at great cost to the growth of a regional economy dependent upon the exploitation of limited and vulnerable natural resources. The forces of production and exploitation prevailing in this remote corner of the Mexican tropics have not only consumed all competing works of nature and culture but also clumsily undermined the basis for future growth in the region.

The receding forest

In the 1930s, forest covered an estimated 70% of the Gulf Nahua territory (Ramírez 1991). Cattle introduced at that time grazed the natural savanna on the plain between the Metzapa River and San Juan Volador. The same area used to be occupied by Spanish *hacendados* in the 17th century while farmers cultivated maize and beans on the rest of the plain and low hills below the village of Pajapan. In recent decades, pastures have expanded beyond their natural boundaries on to lands left fallow by Pajapan farmers.[11] Indian ranchers, supported by outside mestizo ranchers and the local land authorities, simply fenced-in tracts of land on the plain and low hills or paid small sums to farmers for their fallow fields. Several years of brush clearing and burning of fallow fields were sufficient to induce fire-resistant grasses from wild seed blown on to the cleared areas. As the cattle population increased, the amount of land available for *milpa* cultivation on the fertile plain decreased, forcing peasants to clear forested land further up the hillside. Forest clearing in turn made way for more pasture once the fields were left to fallow. This cycle of land clearing, *milpa* cultivation and conversion to pasture pushed the forest frontier up the slope of the volcano and toward the outer limits of the Gulf Nahua territory.

Rancher-driven clearing by farmers was increased by direct clearing for pasture during the 1960s and 1970s. Guadalupe Hernández, one of Pajapan's first large-scale cattle-raisers, arranged to clear approximately 300 hectares of mature rain forest near Sayultepec on the northern edge of Pajapan's territory.[12] This was followed in the early 1970s by an intensive period of deforestation: ranchers rushed to claim remaining forested lands and establish pastures for rapidly expanding herds.[13] An estimated 1,936 hectares of tall humid forest were cut down at a rate of 215 hectares per year between 1967 and 1976 (Ramírez 1991: 9). The forests of the municipality of Pajapan were reduced from an original endowment of 15,600 hectares to 550 hectares, mainly on the upper slopes of the volcano too steep for cultivation. The mangrove forest surrounding the lagoon was also greatly reduced during this period, from 1,225 hectares in 1967 to approximately 932 hectares in 1986 (Ramírez 1991: 31). While some of the felled trees from both humid forest and mangroves were used to feed the sawmill in Tatahuicapan (operating since 1979, see E. Velázquez 1992b: 50) and to construct houses, rustic furniture and dug-out canoes, the vast bulk of exuberant vegetation was simply burned where it fell.

The retreat of primary forest from Pajapan has long-term implications for forest survival and the species composition of secondary forest. The seed of many tree species has disappeared from the local environment, effectively undermining natural reforestation. Frequent burning for the establishment of pastures and *milpa* has simplified the ecosystem, leaving behind fire-resistant grasses. Deforestation in Pajapan is permanent for all intents and purposes. While a massive reforestation effort could always be undertaken with seedlings brought from outside, such an effort presupposes that the germplasm native to the area be preserved at a regional level and that the current socio-economic conditions prevailing in Pajapan be radically changed. Unfortunately, however, cattle-led de-forestation has been repeated on a regional scale. The tropical forests of the Sierra de Santa Marta have been systematically levelled by a land-hungry cattle industry on the rise. Ramírez (1991: 1) reports that Sierra rain forests that once covered the entire region (150,000 ha.) have been reduced to less than 20,000 hectares, mainly during the 1960s and 1970s. While logging, agriculture and forest fires accounted for some of the loss, the rate of destruction fostered by ranching activities was far beyond that dictated by other forces. Almost without exception, the extensive pastoral systems that have replaced the forest ecosystems make poor use of the local resource base and are a major cause of permanent land degradation problems observed throughout the area.

As is now well understood, the destruction of tropical forests con-tributes to broader problems affecting the entire planet.[14] The loss of planetary species through tropical forest destruction has direct implica-tions for the future of agricultural and medical research dependent upon natural genetic diversity for the raw materials of invention. The extinction of countless non-human animal species in the rush to occupy all corners of the earth is another dramatic effect of modern industry. Furthermore, tropical forests are significant carbon storehouses. Burning of these forests to clear land for cattle and agriculture releases large amounts of carbon dioxide and nitrous oxide into the atmosphere, thereby contributing to global warming and the depletion of the ozone layer.[15] Climatic patterns are destabilized by the loss of forest areas that help reflect light from the earth's surface.

While deforestation in the Sierra alone has had only a small effect on global climatic transformations, the impact of the loss of forest cover on regional hydrological cycles and sedimentation processes is more apparent. The depth of the lagoon Sontecomapan has been dramatically reduced in the last 40 years through the deposition of sediments released by deforestation on to the banks of the Coxcoapan, Yahualtajapan and other rivers that empty into this body of water (Menéndez 1976; see Paré, Blanco et al. 1992). According to local fishers, similar processes have affected the water level of the Laguna del Ostión, threatening the very silt-sensitive oyster banks. The ports of Coatzacoalcos and Minatitlán, Mexico's third most important center of marine transportation, are frequently dredged at great expense to keep ahead of the massive soil deposits washed into the Coatzacoalcos watershed. As noted above, these cities also depend upon the Sierra for the supply of fresh water, an invaluable and threatened ecological service.

The intensification of underproduction

Ranching in Pajapan has gone through two distinct phases of technical development since cattle were first introduced to the area. The first phase began in the 1950s when the number of cattle and the amount of pasture increased rapidly. The receding forest frontier in Pajapan encouraged extensive grazing by large herds on unimproved pastures, a pastoral system that became the norm throughout the region. The clearing of communal forest land and second growth and the use of fire to establish grasslands were inexpensive ways of laying claim to large tracts of land and providing minimum grazing conditions for large herds. The major task of clearing mature forest had already been accomplished by peasants, and grass was an easy crop to grow. Only wild, self-seeding grasses were utilized and animals were allowed to graze freely with little handling by ranchers. The only rotation of pastures was seasonal: the plains and seasonally flooded lowlands, with their greater water retention capacity, were grazed more intensively during the dry season while the medium and high hills were more intensively grazed during the wet season. By the late 1970s, the herd grazing the communal lands of Pajapan totalled some 9,000 animals, 84% of which were owned by some 40 families with herds of between 50 and 500 head of cattle.[16] There were few small or medium-sized herds. Ranchers controlled a minimum of 50 hectares of land and in a number of cases as much as 400 hectares. A few ranchers had even larger tracts of land.

Once the humid forest was destroyed, soil resources continued to be lost through exposure to sun and rain (at least until pasture was well established). But the second phase of cattle production made things even worse. While a far cry from the ecologically stable forest systems, extensively grazed pastures are less destructive of soils and secondary vegetation than the overgrazing system that has developed in recent decades. The initial pastoral system based on deforestation and the extensive use of soil and vegetation came to a halt in the mid- to late 1970s as the last of the forested land came under direct exploitation and most cropland was converted to pasture.

Extensive grazing by large herds would have continued for some time had it not been for the events surrounding the petro-chemical port project Laguna del Ostión and the resulting changes in land tenure forced upon Indian ranchers. As discussed in earlier chapters, the expropriation of the prime coastal plain to make way for the establishment of an industrial port led to a reallocation of lands demanded by the majority landless population. The ensuing reduction of individual land claims from several hundred hectares to a uniform 12-hectare parcel per *comunero* forced ranchers to sell large numbers of cattle, in some cases to urban markets and in others to local peasant beneficiaries of the land reform. The sudden influx of cash in the form of payment for the expropriated lands partly facilitated the transfer of cattle to a greater number of small and medium-scale ranchers (see Chapter 4). While some wealthier ranchers managed to regain access to land through rental arrangements and the illegal purchase of *comunero* status and land rights, the very large herds of the 1970s were no longer possible. The largest herd in Pajapan today is probably around 200 head of cattle, compared to former herds of up to 800.

Pasture and animal management practices changed considerably following the land redistribution and proliferation of small-scale ranching units. Land use became more intensive but without any corresponding increase in productivity. Intensive management of cattle involves the improvement of grazings, reproductive performance and mortality rates. These changes contribute significantly to productivity by reducing annual fluctuations in cattle numbers and seasonal variations in liveweight (Williamson and Payne 1978: 325). Ten years after the land redistribution, cattle ranching in Pajapan falls short on all these fronts. The productivity of the industry as a whole has remained extremely low while problems of land degradation and animal and pasture mismanagement have become more severe than ever. The fragmentation of ranching capital and the subordinate position that Indian ranchers occupy within the regional economy impose significant limitations on the ability of local capital to overcome ecological and technical constraints on the development of the forces of production. As a result, the contribution to regional economic growth is far below resource potential and of questionable benefit to the long-term interests of capital accumulation in the region. This gap between resource potential and actual use is a striking feature of Pajapan's ranching sector, as shown in the following analysis.

Pasture production and management

Pasture covers about 15,326 hectares or 80% of the communal Pajapan territory. The quality is highly variable, depending upon the mix of grassy species and ranch management factors. The high and medium hills, especially on the northern and eastern slopes, are dominated by *talquetzal*, a native grass that grows spontaneously in degraded soils. *Talquetzal* has little nutritional value for cattle except when it is very young, a situation that encourages frequent burning.[17] On the low hills and plain, Guinea grass *(Panicum maximum)*, the species preferred by Indian ranchers, is dominant. It has a moderate to high nutritional value and withstands heavy grazing. However, the grass grows in bunches and has poor reseeding capability. Guinea grass is susceptible to weed invasion and does not provide complete ground cover. Sloping soils under Guinea grass are consequently subject to erosion. Small areas of African Star, an improved grass, have been planted from vegetative material by some wealthier ranchers wishing to increase the carrying capacity of their land. The grass, however, is easily damaged by overgrazing and subject to weed invasion. The seasonally flooded lowlands are dominated by a number of saline and flood-resistant natural and improved grasses. Leguminous shrubs, a high protein grazing source, are almost entirely absent from the pastures of the area.

The amount and distribution of rainfall is the single most important factor affecting the production and management of pasture for grazing animals. The abundant rainfall of coastal Veracruz favors rapid plant growth and results in higher potential pasture yields than elsewhere in Mexico (Rutsch 1984: 100). Nevertheless, pasture production in the region is severely affected by the seasonality of rainfall. Under wet season conditions, pasture tends to be underutilized, thereby causing significant losses in potential nutrients and biomass. During the dry season, plant growth slows or stops. Research in the neighboring state of Tabasco indicates an average 85–90% drop in pasture production during the dry season (Romanini 1978: 26, 40). Although dry grasses offer little nutritional value, cattle continue to graze during the dry season, often damaging the root system of the grasses. Overgrazing in turn exposes the soil to the erosive effects of the early rainy season.

In Pajapan, the months of March, April and May create severe shortages in pasture. The impact of the dry season, however, varies from one topographic zone to another. On the hills, pasture production drops off dramatically. By contrast, soils of the plain and seasonally flooded lowlands have such good water retention capacity that pastures can remain green longer into the dry season and grow faster with the June rains. This advantage places an extra premium on the plain and lowland area for dry season grazing. The lands are also preferred for maize cultivation, especially the *tapachole*. The expropriation of this area and subsequent occupation by a growing number of farmers has greatly restricted rancher access to dry season pasture land and increased pressure on poorer quality upland pastures.

Pasture in the tropics is ecologically unstable and without burning will be invaded by weeds. Ranchers in Pajapan burn pastures every year; the operation is done in the dry months of March, April or May. A corridor called a *guarda raya* is cleared around fences to prevent damage to fence posts and the spread of fire. Tall brush is slashed and the vegetation is burned. Burning kills competing plants, clears out dead vegetation and promotes rapid grass growth when the rains come. As a pasture management practice, the *quema* is cost effective in the short term but not without some long-term costs for the rancher. Annual burning destroys the organic matter in the soil and exposes the soil surface to the heavy rains of June and July, thereby contributing to soil erosion and compaction. Pasture fires are much larger than fires started to prepare an hectare or two of *milpa* and much harder to control. In 1985 pasture fires originating in Pajapan spread across the northern boundary of the communal lands, destroying the hamlet of Peña Hermosa and extensive areas of rain forest. In 1991, uncontrolled pasture fires developed again along the upper edge of the communal territory bordering on the submontane humid forest. An estimated 10% of the remaining forest on the peak of the San Martín volcano was lost, along with pasture, fallow fields, fruit trees and the *milpas* of many farmers. Forest fragments linking the high hills to the coastal plain near Peña Hermosa were irreparably damaged (Paré, Blanco et al. 1992).

The inadequacies of pasture management in Pajapan perpetuate low levels of productivity and contribute to environmental degradation as well. Despite the land redistribution, very few ranchers have divided their parcels into smaller paddocks to facilitate pasture rotation. The average grazing period on a single 12-hectare paddock is approximately six months, far in excess of optimal monthly or bimonthly rotations needed to maximize the utilization of pasture protein.[18] Soil compaction under the hooves of grazing animals increases dramatically under these conditions and many edible plants are eradicated. Long grazing periods also augment the proportion of inedible plant species unbrowsed by cattle, a situation which increases labor requirements for brush clearing and, if left unchecked, will reduce the livestock carrying capacity of an area. As already noted, much of the medium and high hill area, particularly along the northeastern slope, is dominated by the poor quality *talquetzal* grass. These degraded pastures recover slowly, even after overgrazing ceases. The soils are consequently exposed for longer periods of time to rain, wind and sun. Erosion on the medium and high hills is severe; one knowledgeable and quantitatively-minded rancher in Pajapan estimates that as much as 4 centimeters of soil are washed from steep slopes with poor quality pastures during a single heavy rainfall. Streams running through the communal lands of Pajapan are muddy during the rainy season, in contrast to the clear waters of streams in nearby areas still covered with mature rain forest.[19] Soil degradation has greatly reduced the potential for the development of more productive and sustainable land uses on these slopes.

The carrying capacity of the livestock system in Pajapan is affected by the poor quality and seasonality of pasture production and inefficient management practices. The Secretary of Agriculture and Water Resources (SARH) estimates that the annual stocking rate in Pajapan is about 2 hectares per head of cattle. Half that amount of land per animal is needed by ranchers operating on the northern slope of the Sierra (Perla del Golfo) where pastures and management practices are better. While low, the intensity of grazing in Pajapan is nevertheless higher than regional averages.[20] Easy access to water for grazing animals in the many streams that cross the communal territory makes it possible for ranchers to maintain high stocking rates even on poor quality pastures. Our survey data suggest that stocking rates in Pajapan were high during the mid-1980s in the wake of the land redistribution (i.e., 1.2 ha. per head). These rates, however, are more indicative of overgrazing than efficient pasture management practices. Stocking rates on rented land were even higher (0.8 ha. per head), suggesting a "mining" approach to the management of rented pastures.

Livestock production and management

The seasonal nature of pasture production is the most significant limitation on cattle ranching in Pajapan as it produces critical fluctuations in the growth rate of animals. Cattle in Pajapan typically experience cyclical growth patterns, losing weight during the dry season and undergoing compensatory growth during the wet season. Climatic stress depresses the appetite of the cattle. Weakened and dehydrated animals are in turn more susceptible to intestinal and pulmonary parasites. Indian ranchers estimate that weight loss incurred during the three dry-season months is in the order of 20 to 25%.[21] All of this weight can be regained within two months following the rains, provided that the affected animals are cleared of parasites and allowed to graze on new growth.

This seasonal boom and bust cycle of pasture production and animal growth reduces the productivity of cattle ranching in Pajapan. Through the use of supplementary feed during the dry season, cattle could attain adult slaughter weight within a ten-month period instead of the two to three years currently required. In response to the scarcity and higher cost of dry season pasture, ranchers are forced to reduce the animal load during the dry season. Many sell cattle at the onset of the dry season before the animals begin to lose weight. This timing of sales often does not correspond to favorable beef prices, optimal slaughter weight or the right stage in calf development. Instead of raising adult animals, most cattle-raisers in Pajapan end up selling immature calves at a time when beef prices on the regional market are lowest.

The productivity of the local cattle industry is also affected by poor animal selection and breeding practices. The utilization of cattle breeds appropriate to tropical climates is of considerable importance to the development of the industry as a whole. Severe solar radiation, high ambient air temperatures and high humidity negatively affect livestock growth and grazing behavior, the intake and utilization of feed and water, milk production and animal reproduction.[22] The ability of cattle to withstand extreme conditions differs markedly between breeds and individuals within a breed.

Ranchers in Pajapan received their initial breeding stock in the 1940s from Coatzacoalcos where dual-purpose cattle (beef and milk) are valued. Of the 7,000 head of cattle that grazed the communal lands of Pajapan in 1986, 60% were cross-breeds between the humpless temperate-type Brown Swiss and the humped tropical-type Zebu. Animals with mainly Zebu blood accounted for only 20% of the local herd, Criollo (Iberian origin) 10%, and the temperate Holandés another 10%.

Herd composition in Pajapan is not well adjusted to local conditions. Dual-purpose cattle present no advantage as there is little local demand for milk. A higher percentage of Zebu blood in the local cattle population would improve not only acclimatization and resistance to common tropical diseases and parasites but also foraging capacity in environments that lack good quality pasture. Ranchers claim that Zebu animals grow more quickly than other breeds, probably because of their greater resistance. The capacity of ranchers to improve their herds is severely limited, however, by local breeding practices. Since reproductive technology and superior quality breeding stock are not locally available, ranchers breed with bulls drawn from their own herds or rented from other cattle-raisers. Ranchers with medium to large herds can cull animals that fail to calve or that are weak or hard to handle, but small herds leave the rancher with little room for culling lesser quality animals.

Advanced animal management techniques such as castration and artificial insemination are not practised. Since bulls are costly to maintain and are only required periodically, small ranchers often do not have a mature breeding bull of their own and depend upon bulls rented or borrowed from other ranchers to inseminate cows in heat. This breeding system tends to be extremely unreliable. Even larger-scale ranchers fail to optimize breeding practices through proper timing. Bulls are kept with the cows continuously and breeding is allowed to happen at any time of the year, leading to early breeding of heifers and calving at less than optimal times (e.g., in the dry season). Indiscriminate breeding adds further dry season stress to the cows and inhibits potential calf development.[23] Since there is no internal fencing of paddocks, animals are not segregated into various types of cattle (e.g., weaned calves vs dams with calves) with distinct grazing needs.

The productivity of cattle-raising is also affected by disease. While free from major epidemic diseases, parasites are endemic among the local cattle population. Abundant rainfall and high humidity provide a favorable breeding environment for ticks, a parasite that attaches itself in great numbers to the skin of cattle. Ticks consume blood, create open sores and cause irritation that results in weight loss. They are also vectors for animal diseases such as *Piroplasmosis anaplasm*. Cattle in Pajapan suffer as well from roundworms, an internal parasite that causes gastro-enteritis resulting in diarrhoea, digestive disturbances, poor growth rates and loss of condition. Pulmonary parasites are common, especially during the dry season when fresh water is scarce. Ranchers in Pajapan attempt to control parasites by spraying with tickicide and applying anti-parasitic medicines, yet the lack of a co-ordinated effort in the region as a whole reduces the effectiveness of the treatments. Limited weight gain and retarded animal development caused by parasites result in significant economic losses.

Despite the high incidence of parasites and the stresses of seasonal malnutrition, animal mortality rates in Pajapan are not all that high (2.5% of the herd per year) in comparison to neighboring areas (10% in Coscapa) where shortages of water are greater.[24] In Pajapan, the many streams that drain the land provide cattle with the minimum conditions needed to survive the relatively short dry season. The average calving rate is in the order of 70%, although this varies considerably among ranchers.[25] Approximately 40% of the herd are cows of reproducing age, suggesting that herds increase at an average rate of about 30% per year.[26]

A striking feature of cattle ranching in Pajapan and throughout the humid tropics of Latin America is the lack of complementary interactions between livestock and crop production. While most of the nitrogen drawn from pasture is returned to the soil in the form of urine and manure, in extensive grazing systems it is spread out over a very large area, contributing little to cultivated fields or home gardens. Dry matter is relatively abundant in the humid tropics, hence crop residues are not collected for fodder but rather are burned during land preparations. In sharp contrast to drier parts of Mexico, the potential for nutrient recycling through cattle and crop interactions is not realized in Pajapan.

The lack of complementarity between cattle ranching and crop cultivation in this system becomes antagonistic from the point of view of social justice and potential land uses. Cattle ranching in Pajapan has turned ecology on its head, using the most productive lands for the least productive purposes. Ranching developed on the fertile lowlands and plain while crop production was displaced on to marginal hillsides, resulting in deforestation and soil erosion. The ecological potential of the lowlands, measured in terms of annual rainfall, temperature, solar energy and edaphic factors, is much greater than that realized by the cattle industry. The low hills and flat plain where Pajapeños once inter-cropped maize and beans produced sustainable yields in the order of 300 kilos of vegetable protein, as opposed to 50 kilos of animal protein per hectare under current ranch management practices.[27] The non-arable lands on the medium and high hills suitable for grazing were deforested for marginal crop production and subsequently degraded. Extensive areas were transformed into wastelands of little value even as rangeland and the communal lands of Pajapan as a whole became overstocked with underfed and underproductive cattle. Meanwhile, the beef produced in Pajapan at great cost to the local environment is not consumed by the majority cash-poor peasants but rather by better-off sectors of society in urban centers. Most local families consume less than a kilo of meat per week and the community as a whole consumes weekly fewer than ten animals.

In conclusion, Pajapan's ranchers have been largely excluded from technical developments and adaptive strategies appropriate to the full development of local forces of production. The demand for labor in the local cattle industry is low, a day or two a week for herds of fewer than ten head and three or four days for larger herds. The level of expertise deployed by Indian ranchers is far below industry potential. The care and handling of pasture and cattle is limited to such rudimentary tasks as annual burning of pastures, supplying salt, branding, spraying animals with tickicide, and ensuring that animals do not escape from the paddock. Traditional skills have been largely by-passed by industry developments and ranchers have not acquired the modern skills needed to manage pastures, detect animal diseases or oversee breeding. The low productivity of cattle production in Pajapan derives largely from these socially determined limitations, in sharp contrast to the natural potentialities of the local environment. The recent intensification of livestock production has exacerbated problems of soil erosion and land degradation but without the technical changes normally associated with capitalist development. As discussed in the following section, ranching has also undermined the traditional *milpa* system and limited the development of crop production in Pajapan.

The *milpa* transformed

During the 1960s and 1970s, a land-hungry cattle industry on the rise displaced farmers and undermined the traditional farming system. Pasture became the dominant land use. According to census data from the Secretary of Agriculture and Water Resources (SARH), agricultural land uses for the nine *ejidos* in the municipality of Pajapan dropped from 48% in 1950 to 24% in 1988. By contrast, the area under pasture increased from 28 to 52%. Our survey data indicate that in 1986 an estimated 1,183 hectares or 6% of the communal lands of Pajapan were devoted to *milpa* cultivation including 1,083 hectares of maize and 100 hectares of other food crops such as black beans, sweet potatoes, manioc, chayote and bananas. A few farmers grew malanga and watercress in stream beds and watermelon in sandy soils along the beaches of Jicacal. Fruit trees including mangos, oranges and hog plums were also cared for by a small number of farmers. Ramírez (1991) indicates that pastures currently represent some 80% of the Gulf Nahua territory. Agricultural land accounts for 14% of the communal land area and forests (mangroves and cloud forest), no more than 5%. This represents a dramatic shift away from *milpa* cultivation.

Total maize production dropped significantly during this period, undermining local self-sufficiency in basic foodstuffs. A *milpa* in Pajapan was on average only three-quarters of an hectare compared to 2 hectares a few decades ago. The occupation of the fertile plain by cattle ranchers has also reduced the amount of land available for the dry-season *milpa*. Only 22% of farmers produced *tapachole* maize in 1986 due to constraints on access to suitable land. Maize production for the 12-month period extending from 1985 (summer maize) to 1986 (winter maize) amounted to 1,100 metric tons of shelled maize, worth approximately US$150,000 on the local market. The total harvest and market value of other agricultural products was negligible compared to maize. Pajapan and neighboring communities went from a situation of net maize production in the 1950s to one of severe deficit in the 1990s (Paré, Blanco et al. 1992). Our survey data suggest that while 80% of all households in Pajapan produced some maize in 1986 (1 metric ton per household on average), 45% of these families purchased maize during the year, typically for a period of four to six months. Peak short-falls bordering on conditions of famine for some families occur in the months of July and August, immediately before the wet season harvest.

The creation in 1992 of an *ejido* from the expropriated lowland area is stimulating a revival of crop cultivation in Pajapan. It has also opened the possibility of agricultural alternatives to the ranching economy (see Conclusion). Nevertheless, the impact of the cattle industry on local land use patterns has radically altered the cropping system per se. As argued below, the *milpa* of today differs in many key respects from the traditional *milpa* as described by local informants and also by Stuart, an American anthropologist (Stuart 1978) who in the mid-1970s studied an isolated hamlet called Peña Hermosa composed of emigrants from Pajapan. At the time of his study the cattle industry had not extended to Peña Hermosa, external inputs were not used and land was abundant.

The agricultural cycle and labor process

A *milpa* (*milli* in classical Nahuatl) is an area of land planted in maize and other foodcrops. The term applies to a wide range of cropping systems in environments as diverse as the central valley of Mexico and the humid tropics of Central America. The *milpa* in Pajapan is a form of shifting cultivation subject to particular environmental and social conditions that have changed over time.

The agricultural year in Pajapan is divided into two maize seasons, the wet season *temporal* and the dry season *tapachole*. The *temporal*, planted in June and harvested between November and January, is the main maize crop of the year. *Tapachole* is a minor season crop planted in November and harvested between March and April. While other foodcrops play a role in the local farming system, the requirements of maize set the tone for all agricultural activities (see Figure 2). Land preparations for the *temporal* begin during the dry season when the secondary vegetation forming an *acaual* is cut down by hand with a machete and burned in the field once it has thoroughly dried. The cleared field is then planted using a dibble stick to punch a hole in the ground into which maize seeds are placed. Maize in Pajapan is planted in rows a meter apart at densities of approximately 30,000 to 40,000 plants per hectare. Since moisture is critical to the germination of maize seed, most farmers plant their maize when they feel certain that the rainy season has begun in earnest, typically by early June. While premature planting can result in

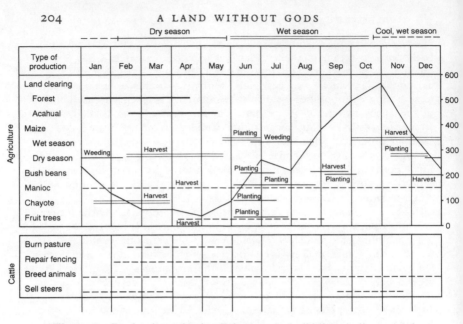

Figure 2　Production calendar, Pajapan area (solid lines indicate regular activity; broken lines, irregular activity).

crop failure due to poor germination, planting too late increases the risk of damage to the crop caused by *nortes*.

Maize is very susceptible to weed competition for nutrients, light and soil moisture. As a result, it requires relatively clear cultivation, especially during the early stages of plant development. *Milpas* are typically weeded twice during the *temporal*, in July and then in August. To weed a field, the worker proceeds down the rows of maize loosening the earth around the weeds with the tip of a machete or hoe and leaving them to dry. Manual weeding is the most time-consuming of farming operations and in recent years an increasing number of farmers in Pajapan have turned to herbicides to control weeds. The contact herbicide Paraquat is the most common, sprayed directly on the weeds between rows of maize using a back-pack sprayer. Herbicides are also occasionally used during land preparations.

The pace of plant growth is determined by plant physiology, soil nutrients, sunshine and rainfall. Virtually all farmers in Pajapan use local maize varieties requiring approximately 100 days to attain physiological maturity under the prevailing environmental conditions. Depending upon the time of planting, the first tender ears of maize may be harvested beginning in late August. By late September the maize has usually reached physiological maturity, at which point the stalks are doubled below the main ear. Rain runs off the downturned husks, thereby allowing the grain to continue drying in the field. The doubled maize plant is also less likely to break under the strong winds *(nortes)*. Thus protected,

Table 5.2 Person-days of labour for 1 hectare of Maize[a]

Task	Wet Season	Dry Season
Clearing[b]	16	12
Piling and burning	2	–
Planting	8	6
Weeding	32	10
Doubling	6	–
Guarding	2	2
Harvest and carrying[c]	7	4
Storing	4	2
Total	77	36

[a] Figures based on field data and Stuart (1978:272).
[b] Clearing task refers to a field cut from low second growth.
[c] Harvest and carrying figures assume a yield of 1,300 kg/ha. in *temporal* and 800 kg/ha. in *tapachole*.

maize can be harvested piecemeal throughout November, December and January. A horse or the back of the farmer are used to carry the harvest from the field to the home where the maize is stored on the cob, typically in the kitchen loft called a *tapanco*.

In much of Mexico, the wet season *temporal* is the only maize season. In the lowland tropics of southern Veracruz, however, periodic rainfall in the months of November, December, January and February makes it possible to grow *tapachole* maize with certain modifications to the cropping system. In the Pajapan area, *tapachole* is planted in November and harvested throughout March and April. Maize is usually planted on the same field as the previously harvested *temporal*, hence little vegetation is cleared when preparing the land. The slash produced from weeds and the stalks of *temporal* maize is not burned as in the wet season but rather is chopped and left on the field. The resulting mulch conserves soil moisture during the height of the dry season and provides the growing plants with some additional nutrients. Drier climatic conditions during the *tapachole* reduce the number of weeding operations to one as compared to the two weedings characteristic of the *temporal*. Although less labor-intensive than wet season maize, cultivation during the dry season presents other problems. The hot and strong southern winds *(suradas)* blowing in February, March and April can have severe negative impacts on yields. Also, the mulch created by crop residues provides habitat for a variety of corn-eating insects. Birds are more problematic during this season as well. These problems combined with the drier conditions reduce yields by one-third compared to wet season production (see below).

The amount of labor involved in maize cultivation is considerable, approximately 77 days per hectare during the *temporal* and 36 days per hectare during the *tapachole* (see Table 5.2).

Bush beans, the common black bean of Veracruz, is the most important secondary crop planted in Pajapan. Prior to the development of the cattle industry, bush beans were grown by Pajapeños on the plain. The area dedicated to this crop consequently declined as farming was displaced to the less fertile hillsides. The recent revival of *milpa* cultivation on the lowland has facilitated a resurgence of bean production, a potentially important cash crop (see Perales 1992).

The riskier *aventurero* crop is planted as a sole crop in June. *Aventurero* beans fetch a higher price on the market but disease problems caused by wet conditions are common. The *cosechero* planting in September involves fewer risks and less work as the beans can be intercropped in the drying *temporal* maize. Nevertheless, the strong winds and heavy rains of September and October can damage the bean flower and promote sprouting in the bean pod. The risk of wet conditions at harvest time and limited access to appropriate land limit the amount of beans planted per farmer.

Other crops grown in Pajapan include manioc and sweet potatoes on poorer quality soils, chayote and plantains on humid soils, and watermelon on the sandy soils of the coastal corridor. Fruit trees such as orange, mango and hog plum are cultivated throughout the area.

Shifting cultivation in crisis

Recent farming practices in Pajapan and throughout the Sierra de Santa Marta are increasingly breaking basic rules of shifting cultivation, at great cost to both the farmers and their immediate environment. Foremost among changes in the cropping system is the degradation of the *acaual*, the secondary forest vegetation established on fallow land. Fallow periods in Pajapan have been dramatically reduced and tree species virtually eliminated from the fallow, with grave implications for agricultural resources and system performance (see Figure 3).

Shifting cultivation in the humid tropics has frequently been characterized as a "robber economy" bent on the rapid destruction of the rain forest and the depletion of soil fertility. Forest land is cleared, cultivated for a few years and abandoned in search of a new forest and nutrient horizon. In recent years, however, science has reached a better understanding of the logic and merits of shifting cultivation. The *milpa* system practised in Peña Hermosa (observed by Stuart in the mid-1970s) was based on a plant-to-plant nutrient recycling process involving the rotation of secondary forest and cultivated fields. Shifting cultivation was circular; peasants abandoned a field when maize yields declined below acceptable levels (800 kg/ha.) and returned to the field once agricultural potential had been regained under secondary forest. Farmers in Peña Hermosa managed *acauales* as future *milpas*, noting subtle changes over time in soil characteristics, weed populations and plant species indicating the fertility status of the *acaual*. Maize fields were surrounded by *acauales* at various stages of regrowth and areas of mature forest from which natural vegetative succession on abandoned land could occur. It was a forest-linked system based on the continuous regeneration of forest species and

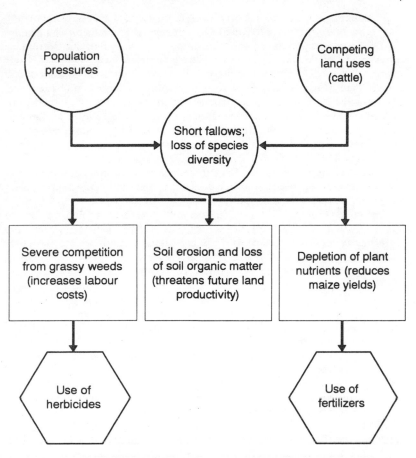

Figure 3 The decline of shifting cultivation. Although other factors contribute to the problems, only principal causes are shown (oval = cause; box = problem; hexagon = farmer adaptation).

food crops. As Redclift argues (1987: 28); "from the standpoint both of energy efficiency and the productivity of the agricultural system (in energy terms) per unit of land, the most successful systems are those which combine crop rotation and fallow with low energy inputs, such as the peasant maize-production system dominant in most of rural Mexico."

Abandoning a field to secondary forest is an effective strategy for restoring agricultural potential. In contrast to temperate environments, natural vegetation in the tropics accumulates biomass and nutrients rapidly (Romanini 1978: 16, 19). The plant species characteristic of secondary forest are well adapted to the low nutrient status of the soil and exposure to direct sunlight. They grow very rapidly in the first few years, thereby providing protection for the soil. Large amounts of biomass are accumulated in the form of trees, vines and herbaceous plants. Nutrients and organic matter depleted from the soil as a result of burning, cropping and exposure to the elements are replaced under secondary forest and imbalances in the availability of nutrients are corrected. Soils compacted and hardened under the impact of rain are softened and weeds that compete with foodcrops for plant nutrients are shaded out. The plant-to-plant recycling process is completed by slash-and-burn techniques of land preparation. Burning clears the field for planting, kills weed seeds, temporarily neutralizes acid soils and converts the abundant vegetation into a layer of nutrient-rich ash available for cultivated crops.

The time period required fully to restore agricultural potential varies greatly from one area to another depending upon rainfall, plant species composition in the *acaual,* soil type, the period of cultivation and farming techniques. In Peña Hermosa, the cropping ratio consisted of two to three years of cultivation followed by four to five years of fallow. "No informants reported having used longer fallow periods in the past, nor do they consider fallows longer than five years to be in any way superior to present fallowing periods" (Stuart 1978: 315).

Fallow periods of four to five years are much shorter than those reported for many parts of the humid tropics. Agronomists generally hold that if long-term soil impairment is to be avoided in shifting cultivation systems, two to three years of cultivation should be followed by nine years or more of fallow. The heavy rainfall of southern Veracruz does allow, however, for very rapid plant regrowth, permitting shorter periods of regrowth without impairing soil quality. Stuart's analysis of soil samples from *acauales* in Peña Hermosa indicates that regrowth of four to five years is enough to restore the nutrient status of the soil to the same levels found in mature forest conditions. He also notes that the land cultivated by the villagers of Peña Hermosa did not suffer from soil erosion or other evidence of land degradation (Stuart 1978: 311).

Under the conditions prevalent in Peña Hermosa in the early 1970s, shifting cultivation could easily avoid turning into a voracious consumer of forest species and limited soil resources. These conditions no longer hold, however, in Pajapan and throughout much of the Sierra de Santa Marta. Direct competition for land by the cattle industry and population growth have undermined the management of the *acaual.* Survey data from Pajapan indicate that two years of cultivation are typically followed by only one or two years of regrowth, less than half the fallow period used in Peña Hermosa. Frequent crop cultivation and annual burning of vast areas used for pastures have virtually eliminated the plant species associated with the traditional *acaual.* The Pajapan landscape is dominated by fire-resistant grasses, not the woody tree species, shrubs, vines and herbaceous plants characteristic of secondary forest. Some 38% of the farmers interviewed in 1986 had established their *milpas* on *zacatales,* a fallow composed entirely of grass species.

The degradation of the *acaual* has important implications for land management practices. Slashing and burning grasses cannot support crop

Table 5.3 Maize yield per hectare (Pajapan village, 1986)[a] (MT/ha.)

	Good Land	Average Land	Poor Land
Wet season	1.6	1.4	0.9
Dry season	1.2	0.8	0.5

[a] = Evaluation of soil quality made by farmers.

cultivation without drawing heavily on the limited resources of the soil. Soils subject to frequent cultivation are consequently depleted, resulting in poor crop yields and soil chemical imbalances as some nutrients are mined from the soil. The soils of agricultural land in Pajapan and neighboring communities are extremely poor in major nutrients, compared to local soils under rain forest cover.[28] Maize yields are far below historical levels (3 t/ha.). The 1985 *temporal* harvest in Pajapan averaged 1.4 tons per hectare (t/ha.) while the 1986 *tapachole* averaged 0.8 t/ha. As should be expected, variations in soil quality had a significant impact on maize yields (see Table 5.3).

Shorter fallow periods and the elimination of tree species in fallow land have also contributed to the build-up of grassy weeds in many farmers' fields. Stuart reports that weeds were not considered a major issue in Peña Hermosa. By contrast, weed control currently represents the major labor demand during the crop cycle in Pajapan and an important constraint on increases in maize productivity. Mechanical weeding is not feasible on the sloping lands of Pajapan and manual weeding is an increasingly problematic method for managing maize grown in grasslands. Farmers frequently note that weeding is a losing battle; by the time they finish weeding the *milpa* new weeds have developed where they began.

The degradation of the *acaual* threatens future land productivity in the region. The soil organic matter destroyed by frequent cultivation and burning is not replaced by short fallows dominated by grasses, thereby reducing the capacity of the soil to retain moisture and increasing the risk of soil erosion. Channel and sheet erosion have scarred the local landscape and filled the streams with sediments that not only represent a permanent loss of agricultural potential but also a threat to silt-sensitive oyster banks in the Laguna del Ostión. Soils on the medium and high hills of Pajapan have been compacted and permanently resort to *talquetzal*, a tough grass of little value even for grazing.

Farmer adaptations

The decline of shifting cultivation and the development of intensive patterns of land use have led farmers in Pajapan to adopt a number of new practices. These include the use of external inputs, reductions in the amount of land cultivated, specialization in the production of maize at the expense of other food crops and, recently, the use of green manures.

Low and declining soil fertility has been compensated for in recent years by the introduction of chemical fertilizers. In 1986, very few farmers in Pajapan used chemical fertilizers but by 1993 the practice had become more common. Subsidized credit made available to some farmers beginning in 1989 by the *Instituto Nacional Indigenista* (INI) for a package of fertilizers, herbicides, pesticides and improved varieties of maize provided a catalyst for the partial adoption of these inputs. Currently, an estimated two-thirds of the farmers of Pajapan use some fertilizer on their fields; many now believe that fertilizers must be used to obtain acceptable maize yields. Farmers have also turned to contact herbicides to ease weeding operations. While they were rarely used in 1986, by the early 1990s most farmers in Pajapan were using some herbicides during land preparations and weeding operations (Buckles and Arteaga 1993). This transition was also facilitated by INI's credit program and has been enthusiastically embraced by farmers hard-pressed to control weeds in their fields.

While fertilizers and herbicides are effective means of addressing immediate problems such as low soil fertility and weed invasion, they imply higher production costs. Many farmers cannot afford to purchase the required inputs needed to manage a full-sized *milpa* and have opted instead to use small amounts of fertilizer on particular parts of their fields. Most farmers surveyed in 1993 had used fertilizers only two or three years out of the previous five. Furthermore, the INI credit program can offer only partial coverage of the hundreds of farmers in Pajapan and is severely limited by the ongoing fiscal crisis of the Mexican state. It is unlikely that the fertilizer needs of the farming population can be met by existing credit schemes.

Learning costs and health hazards associated with greater reliance on agro-chemicals are also significant. No extension has accompanied the provision of agricultural inputs in the community, a shortcoming leading to inefficient and unsafe farming practices. Farmers do not observe standard recommendations regarding the method, rate and timing of fertilizer applications or understand the basic logic behind chemical fertilization. Paraquat, the most commonly used herbicide in Pajapan, is a highly toxic chemical that in the few years of common usage in Pajapan has caused several deaths from toxic poisoning and numerous cases of toxic shock due to improper handling. Farmers use unnecessarily high concentrations of Paraquat and commonly wash the sprayers in local streams, thereby contributing to water contamination and disturbance of aquatic life.

Farmers have a well-developed understanding of soil fertility and weed management through shifting cultivation, knowledge only partially applicable to external-input agriculture. According to Nahua farmers, cultivated land becomes tired (Sp. *cansado*) when it dries out (see Chapter 7). In ideal conditions, "soil strength" (Sp. *fuerza*) may be recovered by letting the land "rest" for seven years. The "abandoned field" (*acaual*) generates a large amount of *tasol* garbage – plant litter that "gives life to corn" by shading out weeds, rotting and keeping the soil wet, cold or fresh (*cece*). The fallow is aided by "cold" plant species such as *jonote* that produce a great deal of litter, soften the soil and "easily release the juices" of the earth. By contrast, "hot" plants such as oak dry out and harden the land, fixing soil juices in their thick bark. The leaf litter that falls on the ground during the fallow period "becomes soil", as does the ash (Nahua *banesh*, "lime made from wood") created through slash and burn. The recovery of soil fertility is perceived by Nahua farmers as a process of "healing" obtained through a balanced combination of the cold and the hot: a maize plant "does not want sun or heat only, nor does it want water or cold only" (*aguinegui niat, aguinegui tonati; aguinegui ni cece, aguinegui ni totoni*). While farmers know that dry-season mulching and plant decomposition in fallow lands will enhance the coldness or wetness of the soil, they also count on the spring burning to fertilize the soil and prevent food plants from "burning" (usually described as *chahuiste*) due to excess humidity accumulating over the wet-season cycle. It should be noted that in the native perspective, the soil is primarily a medium for these complex operations, not the source of fertility per se.

A perception of soil as process is not entirely compatible with the atomistic view of soils implicit in chemical fertilization. While resembling ash, fertilizer does not involve the alchemy of rotting and burning. The cultural memory of long fallows is fading yet there is no development of new farmer knowledge of external-input agriculture. Pajapan farmers fall back on their traditional knowledge to explain the action of new inputs. The application of herbicides, especially contact herbicides such as Paraquat, is likened to the use of fire: both techniques "burn" the vegetation. The current popularity of Paraquat is due mainly to the considerable labor savings afforded by the herbicide, but the ease of adoption also proceeds from the transparent logic of the technology. Farmer understanding of herbicides is none the less incomplete. In the native view, weed control (burning) is assumed to increase with the rate of herbicide application, a perception that partly accounts for incorrect and excessive application rates. Furthermore, the dangers to human health of a toxic chemical are not immediately apparent to the native perspective.

Land degradation and constraints on the use of external inputs have forced farmers to modify other central features of *milpa* agriculture. Farmers in Pajapan have limited competition for scarce soil fertility by favoring maize and reducing the variety and number of foodcrops in the *milpa*. Only one-fifth of all village households in Pajapan cultivate foodcrops other than maize, usually three or four staple plant species such as bush beans, manioc and plantains. These crops are simply grown in a corner of the *milpa*, not intercropped per se. Most plots are kept relatively free of weeds and even food plants that might compete with the maize. Changing weed control practices (herbicide use) have also reduced the incidence of volunteer food plants in the *milpa* such as *quilites*.

Table 5.4 Foodcrops other than Maize (Peña Hermosa and Pajapan)

	Peña Hermosa 1976 % Hlds	Pajapan 1986 % Hlds	Ha.	MT
Beans	93	8.4	44	33
Sweet potato	68	2.9	27	101
Manioc	71	2.2	19	228
Chayote	46	1.4	5	145
Banana	93	1.5	5	–

Sources: Peña Hermosa: Stuart 1978; Pajapan: survey data.

The paucity of foodcrops in Pajapan contrasts sharply with the traditional *milpa* system observed in Peña Hermosa (see Table 5.4). Stuart reports that in Peña Hermosa maize was widely planted in rows and inter-seeded with other crops at various times of the year. Most plots contained from three to 10 additional crops. Vine and bush beans, sweet potatoes, squash and dasheen were intercropped in the maize while sugar cane, bananas and manioc were planted in a section or along the edge of the *milpa*. Volunteer quilites and chiles were allowed to grow scattered in the maize field. Other plants grown by some farmers in Peña Hermosa include rice, tannia, chayote, yam bean, annato, papaya, pineapple, garlic, pigeon pea and sesame, crops virtually absent from the Pajapan farming system (Stuart 1978: 147).

The diversity of foodcrops found in the *milpas* of Peña Hermosa presents a significant advantage over mono-cropping. In a field interseeded with many foodcrops, plants of the same species are relatively isolated from each other by plants of another species, a feature inhibiting the spread of some pests and plant diseases. The various species grow at different rates and root at different levels in the soil, making wide use of available soil nutrients and rainfall. Stumps of burned trees, an occasional living tree and perennial plants such as bananas and fruit trees protrude through the main crop, creating a partial upper canopy of sun-protecting vegetation and a wind break. Vining, low-lying plants such as squash and sweet potato provide additional ground cover. This planting strategy lessens the erosive force of the rain, provides shade to the soil and helps conserve soil moisture. It also offers greater food security against the failure of staple crops.

Farmers in Pajapan have specialized in the production of maize but without fully adjusting the cropping system to monoculture. Maize plants remain widely spaced, leaving the soil relatively unprotected and lowering the land productivity of the *milpa*. Pesticides and fungicides have not been introduced to compensate for reduced biological control. The particular variant of *milpa* cultivation in Pajapan is plagued by weed control problems and increasing dependence on external inputs. In short, the traditional *milpa* has been displaced by an unproductive and unsustainable cropping system that neither maximizes the potential of new technology nor retains important adaptive features of the traditional cropping system.

Recent developments in the cropping system of Pajapan are more promising. Diagnostic work by the authors and other members of the Sierra Santa Marta Project (SSMP, see Conclusion) identified a low-input technology indigenous to the region based on the leafy legume velvet bean (*Mucuna sp.*). Farmers in Soteapan and Mecayapan first experimented with velvet bean as a natural fertilizer several decades ago, noting its ability to smother weeds and improve maize yields on degraded lands. The notion of "improving the fallow" was a small step for farmers keenly aware of natural processes of soil fertility decline and recovery through shifting cultivation. By broadcasting velvet bean seed into abandoned fields, farmers can reduce fallow periods from five years to two. The legume is also used as a rotation crop for *tapachole* maize and, increasingly, as an intercrop in *temporal* maize. Researchers from the SSMP have given experimentation with green manures a boost in Pajapan by making farmers aware of diverse management options already tried in the area and introducing several improvements on the technology (Buckles and Perales 1995).

Hunters and fishers of diversity

Analyses of farming systems in the tropics must consider the role of non-agricultural foodstuffs in the maintenance of the food production system as a whole (see Roosevelt 1980; Gross 1975). In the Pajapan area limitations on the production of beans and other food plants implies that adequate dietary protein cannot be provided from agriculture alone. Minimum standards of nutrition require that land and marine animal protein also be included in the diet of farming families. Stuart notes that the major sources of protein in the diet of villagers in Peña Hermosa are corn (41%), meat and poultry (17.5%), fish (15.8%) and beans (14.9%).

Prior to the development of the cattle industry, few Pajapeños engaged in hunting and fishing on a full-time basis. These sources of livelihood were a complement to farming, particularly during slack periods in the agricultural cycle and for underemployed family members. As shown below, the land crisis created by the expansion of cattle ranching in Pajapan has brought major changes in both activities. For one thing, the cattle industry pushed many peasants out of farming and into other sectors of the rural and urban economy, including fishing. The village of Jicacal, settled in 1970, is composed almost entirely of ex-farmers engaged in fishing on a full-time basis or working as fish vendors and small restaurateurs. While in the traditional setting farmers fished for subsistence and sold surplus catches, some 90% of fishers in Jicacal presently sell most of what they produce and consume the poorer quality surpluses. This is in sharp contrast to fishers in Pajapan, who produce mainly for home consumption. As for hunting activities, the cattle economy has destroyed much of the forest, resulting in a dramatic decline in rain forest fauna. Population growth and commercial overhunting further hastened the trend toward local extinction of wild animal species.

Hunting for protein

In the 1970s hunting provided about 70% of the meat and 13% of the total protein consumed by the villagers of Peña Hermosa (Stuart 1978). Up until very recently, some 15 species of animals considered potential food sources were known to inhabit the tropical rain forest surrounding the village. The brocket deer, paca, agouti and armadillo were killed and eaten regularly while two species of iguana, peccaries, tapirs, raccoons, freshwater turtles and several species of birds were taken occasionally.

Hunting in the rain forest is difficult and brings limited returns. Animal populations are small and dispersed in search of scarce food resources among the largely unpalatable woody plant species. They can easily escape human predators by climbing into the forest canopy. Most of the animals killed in Peña Hermosa were not encountered in the forest but rather in or near maize plots where they came in search of food. Pacas, brocket deer and raccoons were attracted from the forest to the *milpa* during the late spring and early summer when the maize is young and again in late summer when the ears form. They were hunted by villagers before dawn with firearms or a bow and arrow. Iguana and some species of birds were killed as farmers walked to and from their *milpas*. Since animals were encountered during the course of normal agricultural activities, hunting occupied little time. Night hunts in the forest by small parties of men with dogs were undertaken only occasionally (Stuart 1978).

In addition to hunting for food, some wild animals were and are still killed for their pelts by petty traders travelling through the rain forest to remote villages. Ocelot, margay and jaguarundi encountered along jungle trails are shot and their pelts sold to a few fur buyers in Coatzacoalcos. Olive-throated parrots are occasionally captured on the upper slopes of the volcano and sold in the city as are young spider monkeys. The hunting of forest animals for sale in urban markets contrasts with the traditional use of the forest fauna as a source of protein for human consumption.

Constant predation and the loss of habitat resulting from the development of the cattle industry has greatly reduced the local animal population. A few years after Peña Hermosa was settled, tapirs and peccaries were hunted to local extinction. Animals that venture beyond the forest edge on to cultivated land or animals such as white-tail deer that thrive in second growth are overhunted by a peasant population deprived of access to land and adequate food resources. The result is the local extinction of many species of tropical fauna and the loss of a traditionally significant source of protein essential to human nutrition. Presently, only a few individuals in Pajapan hunt.

The lagoon and freshwater fishery

The Laguna del Ostión is a semi-enclosed coastal body of water in which fresh water continuously dilutes sea water. Numerous rivers originating in the mountain peaks of San Martín Pajapan and Santa Marta flow into the lagoon, creating saline conditions that vary from one season or point in the lagoon to another. These unique saline conditions allow a wide variety of aquatic species to co-inhabit the lagoon. The most distinctive and productive of the lagoon inhabitants is the tropical mangrove oyster which gave this body of water its Spanish name. Hard substrata at different points throughout the lagoon originally provided the oysters a cultch upon which to settle. Later generations of oysters attached themselves shell to shell, gradually building oyster reefs. Numerous small estuarine fishes seek shelter on the oyster reefs and colonies of clams cover the lagoon mud bottom.

Gulf Nahua fishers identify at least 12 oyster and clam reefs in the lagoon. Their abundance and exact location, however, are influenced by sedimentation, changes in water salinity and overexploitation. Fishers report that during the 1950s the oyster fishery fell into complete decline due to a sharp fall in the salinity of the lagoon waters. Wave action moved the narrow passage between the lagoon and the ocean further from the main body of the lagoon, thereby reducing the influence of ocean tides. Oyster productivity declined until 1965 when a work party of villagers from Pajapan and San Juan Volador was organized to open a new passage between the lagoon and the sea. Because of their high fecundity and rapid growth, the oyster reefs recovered quickly. In recent years, however, problems of low salinity, overexploitation and pollution have undermined the survival of the oyster banks.

Many species of ocean and fresh-water fish are transient beneficiaries of the lagoon waters and mangroves where they seek food and protection from predators. Snook, an ocean fish, comes into the lagoon to deposit its eggs in the mangroves near the mouth of the Huazuntlán and Tecolapan rivers. Great numbers of striped mullet also enter the lagoon from the ocean to spawn. Ocean shrimp enter the lagoon at an early stage of their development; they can grow quickly in the protected and nutrient-rich intertidal waters of the mangroves before venturing once again into the ocean. Odum and Heald estimate that 80–90% of the fish in the Gulf of Mexico are linked to food chains originating in mangrove forests along the shore of coastal lagoons and river estuaries (see Gallegos 1986). Thus the 1,304 hectares of Pajapan's lagoon waters and 932 hectares of mangrove forest that make up this coastal estuary are vastly more important ecologically than their small area would suggest. The impact of the transformation of this ecosystem by human activity extends far beyond the immediate environment.

As with hunting, the exploitation of aquatic resources is fraught with uncertainty. With the exception of the oyster and clam banks, fish and crustaceans inhabiting the lagoon and local streams are mobile, scattered and therefore difficult to locate and capture. Also, the abundance of fish

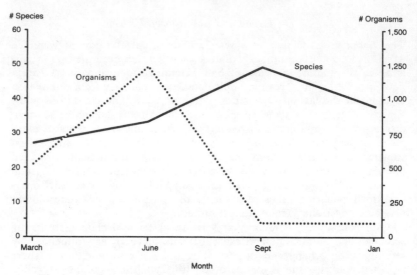

Figure 4 Seasonal variations in the number of aquatic species and organisms, Laguna del Ostión. *Source*: Bonada and Chávez 1986.

and crustaceans varies both seasonally and annually (see Figure 4). Crayfish in the tropical streams and estuaries are available only during the dry season when they migrate downstream to spawn. The peak fishing season in the lagoon occurs during the dry season, followed by a short season in August for the shrimp fishery and in December when sea mullets enter the lagoon to spawn. North winds striking the coast in September, October and November create turbulence, making it difficult to harvest oysters, clams and some fish.

The seasonality and mobility of aquatic resources restrict the concentration of the fishing labor force and the application of large-scale technology. A survey of lagoon fishers undertaken by the researchers in 1984 indicates that between 200 and 300 individuals engaged periodically in the lagoon fishery, usually in crews of one to three people. Approximately 80 fishers were present on the lagoon during the main fishing seasons. Some 16% of these fishers were women, mainly from Jicacal and San Juan Volador. All lagoon fishers used canoes made from the trunks of mangrove trees or simply fished from the shore.

The vast majority of fishers (69%) were divers. Oysters and clams were and still are collected by divers equipped with face-masks, flippers and a knife for locating clams in the muddy bottom. Most of these fishers are young men with the stamina to dive to depths of up to 8 meters. Although each man retains his own catch, divers usually work in groups of two or three to a canoe, sharing the ownership or rental of the canoe. Divers other than young men (women, children and older men) collect small oysters by hand in the shallow waters and among the roots of the mangrove trees, locating them with their feet and hands. The introduction of face-masks and flippers in the early 1950s allowed divers to collect oysters and clams from the deeper banks and also to harvest shallow water banks more effectively. In 1984, divers collected on average 63 clams and 6.5 liters of oysters in a six-hour day, far more than would have been possible without these simple tools.

One-quarter of the lagoon fishers surveyed in 1984 utilized a cast net, woven from lightweight monofilament fishing line and hung with lead weights, to capture small and medium-sized fish feeding or spawning in the lagoon. Fishers typically work in pairs, one person poling a dugout canoe from the back while the other casts the net from the front. Although fishers utilize their intimate knowledge of tidal flows and seasonal variations to concentrate their efforts in certain areas at specific times, cast nets are used to exploit much of the lagoon surface. Fishers with cast nets average approximately 5 kilos of fish during a six-hour day, mainly small ocean snook, bass and sea mullets.

The great variety of marine species requires a parallel development of specialized technologies with narrow, seasonal applicability (Breton and Estrada 1989). Freshwater crabs are captured in simple baited hoop traps. Land crabs are speared when forced to the surface of their burrows along the banks of the lagoon following heavy rains. Purchased spear-guns, face-masks and flippers are used by a few fishers to seek out large fish in the deep, fast-moving water at the mouth of the lagoon. Hand-held, home-made spears launched with a heavy rubber band can also be used in combination with gill nets to spear fish trapped in an enclosed area. Fishers anchor large branches of mangrove trees in the shallow waters of the lagoon, thereby providing shelter to attract small and medium-sized fish normally scattered throughout the lagoon. These sites are then enclosed with a net and the trapped fish speared by swimming fishers.

Only two fishers still use the traditional bow and arrow to capture large fish such as the ocean snook hidden among the aerial roots of the shoreline mangroves. To accomplish this, two fishers canoe to the edge of the mangrove forest or to one of the rivers entering the lagoon and enclose a section of shoreline with a gill net. The bowman climbs into a tree overlooking the water while the other fisher slaps the surface to startle fish feeding or resting among the roots of the mangroves. The fish is then shot with an arrow and collected in the canoe.

Numerous freshwater streams originating on the upper slopes of the volcano flow through the communal land and empty into the lagoon and Gulf of Mexico. The Gulf Nahuas exploit these resources using fish poisons, crayfish traps and hand-held spears. The most common practice is to capture crayfish using a circular hoop-net about three-quarters of a meter in diameter called a *matayahuale*. Fishers stand in the shallow waters and use the hoop to scoop crayfish moving downstream. Most of these fishers are women who combine fishing with wood-collecting activities and the delivery of food to men in the fields. Young boys armed with hand-held spears and equipped with face-masks hunt small fish and crayfish in the streams, partly as a recreational activity. A few fishers set conical traps of about 1.5 meters long to capture migrating crayfish. Stuart (1978) mentions that fishers used to dam small streams and to throw poison made from barbasco roots and vines into the water to stun fish and collect them. By the mid-1970s, this practice had been abandoned for lack of barbasco.

Traditional fishing technology severely limited levels of exploitation of both lagoon and freshwater resources. Only the manatee, a mammal with a very low rate of reproduction, seems to have suffered local extinction during the first half of this century. The introduction of a few simple tools such as diving gear and cast nets during the 1940s and 1950s made it possible for fishers to exercise more control over marine resources. Many more species of fish could be readily exploited and a much larger area could be fished. The technology could also be used at times of the year when traditional methods such as the bow and arrow proved ineffective, thereby extending the fishing season.

The intensification and diversification of lagoon and freshwater fishing has been accomplished without radically altering the scale and type of production. There has been no mechanization of either the fish catching technologies or fishing vessels. The new tools of production are still artificial extensions of the person, controlled directly by the fisher. Although some of the technologies involve a more active and mobile approach to locating and capturing aquatic resources than was traditional, the unit of production has remained small and the division of labor is still very limited. Traditional knowledge concerning the ecology of fishing has been preserved and may even increase as fishers are required to understand the movements of a greater variety of fish species.

The development of lagoon fishing techniques does not reflect the real subordination process theorized by Marx, a process whereby the labor force is concentrated into fewer but larger units of production using a more complex technology. Nor has there been a systematic differentiation between the conception and manual execution of labor and the corresponding deskilling process. Having said this, changes in fishing technology have allowed many more people to enter the fishery, partly in response to land pressures and the increase in demand for marine products that occurred during the 1970s and 1980s. These changes have resulted in severe problems of overexploitation affecting the lagoon fishery. Equipped with simple but effective technologies, a growing population of fishers excluded from agriculture have literally mined the oyster and clam banks into oblivion. Fish such as *constantino* and *sabalo* are now extinct in the lagoon while several species of snook are greatly diminished. These and other ocean fish species are also heavily fished beyond the boundaries of the lagoon by coastal fishers. Finally, an intensified shrimp fishery threatens the local reproduction of the species as lagoon fishers harvest adult shrimp moving from the ocean to intertidal waters to spawn. These developments have severe implications for the economy of local fishers and the nutritional status of Pajapeños, many of whom depend upon marine products for protein.

Contamination by the petrochemical and sulfur industries located along the Coatzacoalcos watershed has also undermined the ability of the lagoon and local rivers to support aquatic life. The Coatzacoalcos River is one of the most polluted in the world and the coastline for many miles on either side of the port city is polluted with residues from oil exploration and drilling in the Gulf of Mexico. The beaches of Pajapan are periodically washed with crude oil and urban refuse that enters the lagoon with the tides. Lagoon waters also suffer influxes of sulfur originating from factories near Jáltipan via the Chacalapa and Huazuntlán rivers. These contaminants could eventually pose a grave threat not only to many aquatic species that use the lagoon during part or all of their life cycle but also to the health of the human population that consumes them. To make matters worse, the lagoon is directly affected by black waters generated by the growing regional population upstream. Contamination from fecal matter and also from pesticides and herbicides (Lindano, BHC, Aldrin, Dieldrin, Endrin, Heptacloro) is greater in the lagoon than in the Coatzacoalcos River (Gutiérrez Martínez 1991).

The coastal fishery

The traditional coastal fishery in Pajapan has also undergone dramatic transformation. García de León reports that fishers from San Juan Volador used to construct platforms raised on poles erected beyond the surf in two or three meters of water. Large fish such as *sabalo*, sharks and mackerel were speared from the platforms as they swam by. Smaller fish were caught with a hook and line from the platform or the rock out-croppings at the Punta de San Juan or Peña Hermosa. These coastal shore fishing techniques were practised until the late 1960s when water contamination by the oil industry forced the large fish further from the shore and overfishing beyond the Gulf Nahua territory reduced their numbers.

On a larger geographic scale, coastal fishing throughout Veracruz was dominated during much of this century by beach seining operations involving two or more *piraguas*, 10–12 meter wooden vessels with oars manned by crews of 30 to 40 individuals. A net one kilometer or more long was let out in a wide arc stretching from one point beyond the breakers to another further along the shore. The two ends of the net were then brought together and hauled ashore by the beach crew. Schools of fish such as Spanish mackerel and mullet migrating up the coast were blocked by the net and guided into a large bag at the center point. Only a few individuals in each crew needed to be skilled in the art of locating fish and directing the work. The rest of the labor force was composed mainly of temporary workers supplying rowing and hauling power.

Beach seining was very destructive of marine life as all fish above a certain size were captured in the sweep of the net. Many fish fry and species with little commercial value were killed and left on the beach. Stuart (1978: 192) reports that in the mid-1970s the residents of Peña Hermosa assisted crews of beach seiners from neighboring communities, collecting non-commercial species as pay.

In the mid-1970s, coastal fishing in the Gulf of Mexico was transformed by the widespread introduction of small fiberglass boats, outboard motors and a package of fishing technologies including various types of gill nets and longlines (Breton and Estrada 1989). Most of this technology was of Japanese design and manufactured in Mexico under licence. Many more species of fish could be captured with this technology which also allowed fishers to be more selective than the wasteful methods of beach seining. Weather became less problematic and greater mobility of the fishing craft facilitated the exploitation of a much wider area. Fishing crews were reduced to three or four individuals, one person skilled in the location of fish, a *motorista* and one or two additional crew. By 1984 three such crews were operating out of Jicacal, one of which was the local fishing co-operative. Most coastal fishing in the area was organized by mestizo fishers living in Las Barrillas where 14 boats and crews were based. Many of the crew members were originally from San Juan Volador while the boat-owners had migrated to the area from Alvarado and other fishing communities near the Port of Veracruz. These fishing operations utilized the full range of net and longline fishing gear to catch fish as far as 2 kilometers from shore. Virtually all of the product was purchased by one fish merchant supplying markets in Coatzacoalcos and Mexico City.

Coastal fishing production was mechanized, miniaturized and adjusted to smaller units of production. As a result, productivity improved significantly. The fractionalization of coastal fishing units differs radically from technical processes that characterize many other primary resource sectors. The history of Mexican coastal fisheries demonstrates that a decentralized organization of labor is none the less compatible with the intensification and diversification of commodity production, hence with the capitalist development of productive forces geared to the growth of broader market economies. But it also shows how the aquatic environment imposes clear limits on the development of resource productivity. Unlike agricultural resources, the supply of marine resources is regulated by natural reproductive cycles and cannot be readily improved through the application of labor and technology. Fishers can capture only what nature provides. While this limitation can be reduced through fish farming techniques, the marine environment has by and large frustrated human attempts to increase resource productivity.

Conclusion

This chapter has examined the effects of land concentration and land redistribution on ranching, crop agriculture, hunting and fishing. The analysis shows that the capitalist transformation of peasant activities has taken forms other than the large-scale industrialization process observed in some branches of agriculture. It also shows how the conversion of mature forest into pasture has destroyed the rain forest environment and with it the abundant supply of water and the fauna and flora that used to play a vital role in the native subsistence economy. While fishing once offered some compensation for the loss of hunted animal protein, the fisheries too have suffered serious declines due to over-fishing and contamination. The great diversity of a native environment characterized by many different ecosystems, vegetation types and soil variations has been replaced by a relatively uniform farming system based mainly on extensive grazing of poor quality pastures. Stable patterns of land use based on the pursuit of food security (rather than market profit) have given way to an extensive pastoral system that violates the essence of *milpa* cultivation in the tropics.

The redistribution of land in the early 1980s allowed many Gulf Nahua peasants to resume *milpa* cultivation, yet cattle ranching remains the dominant activity. An agricultural system originally devoted to the production of a wide variety of foodstuffs has been reoriented toward the production of specialized surpluses (beef) exported from the local economy. Under such conditions, the expansion of cattle ranching was bound to affect the traditional system of shifting cultivation. The amount of fallow land available for crop rotation in Pajapan has been greatly reduced, resulting in a severe agricultural crisis affecting soil resources and weed management practices. Agricultural production has become more specialized (mainly beef and corn), and the total amount of land dedicated to food agriculture and the size of individual *milpas* have declined, resulting in the loss of local food self-sufficiency. All in all, the productivity of the *milpa* system as a whole has fallen dramatically and many of the adaptive features of *milpa* ecology have been lost, without any compensatory development of new agricultural knowledge and technology.

The forces of production that have emerged in Pajapan do not conform to the narrowly defined logic of technical advances normally associated with capitalist development. While intensifying production, the division of land into parcels and the restriction of cattle to many smaller paddocks has not resulted in the concentration of energy output. On the contrary, the data indicate that problems of inefficient land use, animal mismanagement and low productivity have been exacerbated for both large and small ranches alike. Local maldevelopment is none the less a direct offshoot of developments in the broader world system. The Gulf Nahua economy has been systematically harnessed to the outside accumulation of agro-capital produced at the expense of native peasants, their subsistence livelihood and their immediate environment. What is more, the new ranching economy has been so destructive of its own resource base as actually to undermine all long-term prospects for sustainable production in Pajapan. The local beef industry is far from being an efficient source of productive exploitation and commercial profit. Cattle ranching in Pajapan has been relegated to a very poorly managed stage of breeding while outside capital-intensive operations control the more profitable processes of fattening for slaughter, transportation and commercialization. The integration of native cattle ranching activities into the wider market economy has resulted in a chronic underdevelopment of local forces of production; the result is a highly constrained pastoral economy serving a shortsighted process of capital accumulation in privileged sectors of the regional and national economy.

Notes

1. See A. Bartra (1979b); Paré (1982); Barkin and Suárez (1985); Díaz-Polanco (1982); Esteva (1980); Feder (1977b); Goodman and Redclift (1981); Hewitt de Alcántara (1978); Moguel et al. (1981); Rama and Rello (1979). A. Bartra adds that agribusiness would not let the prices fall were it able to meet all of its food needs. Even the most marginal or inefficient peasant production is socially necessary. The author rejects the concept of marginality in so far as it suggests that the economy can dispense with inefficient farm units. Thus the conditions of production under the influence of world-wide competition so evident in industry do not apply in the same way to agriculture. Given the material limits to agricultural production and the scarcity of food commodities, not even the poorest land or least productive units could be abandoned without affecting the global market.

2. Although Chayanov did not foresee the development of large-scale agricultural machinery and other applications of science to agriculture, the general thrust of his argument is still supported within some circles in Mexico. This is reflected in an increasing interest in traditional techniques of agriculture, and an appreciation of the diversity of natural environments and peasant farming systems. The latter approach is meant to counterbalance research priorities that emphasize the development of technologies suited to specialized and large-scale capitalist agriculture on the untested assumption that this is the best way to improve agricultural outputs. As noted by Redclift (1980: 499), the research priorities of the *via campesina* would "include developing crop strains as used by *campesinos*, devising fertilizers and insecticides which can be used by small producers, and finding ways of improving production which both absorb labor and improve yields, thus raising *campesino* living standards". The *via campesina* literature suggests that the problem is not the inefficiency of peasant agriculture but rather its neglect.

3. *Campesinistas* argued that the neglect of peasant agriculture could be righted by the judicious use of state intervention in the areas of land redistribution, credit, technical assistance, etc. The most outspoken proponent of this approach, Gustavo Esteva (1980), has devoted a great deal of attention to the possible role of the Mexican government in the promotion of a peasant-centered model of agricultural development. Not surprisingly, his optimistic concept of a "benevolent" state has been widely criticized by theorists on the left (A. Bartra 1979a: 17–21; Redclift 1980; Warman 1980). Otero (1980) has strongly criticized not only the *campesinistas* but also many of the neo-Marxists studying the Mexican peasantry for the absence of a theory of the state in their analysis.

4. See also Grammont (1986); Terán (1976); Otero (1980); Moguel et al. (1981).

5. See Barkin and Suárez (1985); Astorga Lira 1985; Hewitt de Alcántara (1978); de la Peña (1981).

6. These limits are often thought to be very different in agriculture and industry. Obstacles posed by the environment can be taken as a point of departure for understanding the formation, rhythm of development and characteristics of agrarian capital, including the formation of rent. Marxian considerations relating the specificity of agriculture to environmental conditions include questions of climate, the slow growth of plants, the perishability of foodstuffs, variations in the distribution and resource endowment, the ecological disadvantages of specialization, and the fact that land is not reproducible in the same way as capital.

7. For a description of plant communities in the Sierra, see Andrle (1964) and Ramírez (1991).

8. For details on the nutrient cycles of tropical rain forest see Richards (1952); Buringh (1970); Fearnside (1986); Forsyth and Miyata (1984).

9. For more details on the architecture of the tall rain forests of the Sierra see Stuart (1978: 64–7) and Andrle (1964).

10. See Títulos Primordiales de Pajapan, AGN, Rama Tierras, Vol. 3030.

11. Interviews with Genaro Antonio, February 14, 1991 and Simón Antonio, May 12, 1986.

12. Interviews with Santos Martínez, May 19, 1990 and Genaro Antonio, May-20, 1990. The cleared area, still surrounded by mature rain forest, can be seen in aerial photos from 1971.

13. Interview with Andrés Martínez, June 10, 1986.

14. For a discussion of rain forest ecology and the global implications of deforestation, see Myers (1980); Gómez-Pompa et al. (1972); Fearnside (1987); and McNeely et al. (1990).

15. Readers are reminded, however, that the burning of fossil fuels, mainly in the industrial world, is by far the most important source of global warming and ozone depletion.

16. The estimate of herd size is based on survey data and has been corroborated by data collected by SARH and also by interviews with Andrés Martínez, Simón Antonio and other native ranchers.

17. Talquetzal is also used as roofing material for the traditional mud and lattice huts characteristic of Pajapan.

18. This average six-month figure is based on a survey of 12 ranchers. Andrés Martínez (interview June 11, 1990), a native rancher, estimates that 12-hectare parcels with good pasture cover and access to water can support 20 head of cattle for a period of 30–40 days, followed by 45 days of fallow. Such rotations could be sustained indefinitely. Agronomists recommend monthly rotations (Williamson and Payne 1978; Romanini 1978: 26).

19. Stuart (1978) made a similar observation in 1975.

20. Rutsch (1984: 94). Average annual stocking rates in Central America are higher than Mexican averages in similar climatic conditions: i.e., 1.8 hectares per head of cattle for smallholdings and 2.2 hectares per head of cattle on large holdings (Williamson and Payne 1978: 227).

21. Interviews with Andrés Martínez, June 10, 1990, and Gustavo Antonio, June 8, 1990.

22. For details on animal physiology see Williamson and Payne (1978: 10–19).

23. See Williamson and Payne (1978:132).

24. This average rate of animal mortality is based on a survey of 12 ranchers with a total of 203 head of cattle. The figure has been corroborated by Indian ranchers (Andrés Martínez, May 16, 1986 and June 10, 1990; Gustavo Antonio, May 28, 1990).

25. The effects of economies of scale on the process of cattle expansion and capital accumulation are discussed in Chapter 4. Moises de la Peña reported in the 1940s that calving rates in Veracruz were 80%. SARH, however, estimates that calving rates in the Pajapan region are in the order of 50–60%. Our own estimate of 70% may be slightly higher than they should be due perhaps to a bias in our sample toward medium and larger-scale ranchers. Incidentally, calving rates reported for Africa average 45–50% (Williamson and Payne 1978: 332).

26. De la Peña (1980: 559) found that in the 1940s herds increased at a rate of 18–20% on "poor" ranches and 25% on "better" ranches.

27. Calculations based on maize yields of 2 MT/ha. and 1 MT/ha. of intercropped beans, with a crude protein content of 8% in maize and 25% in beans.

28. Based on soil analyses conducted at the International Maize and Wheat Improvement Center (CIMMYT) in 1992.

CHAPTER 6

DYNAMICS OF THE PATRIMONIAL DOMAIN

Kinship and process theory

In earlier chapters, we saw how political economic forces of Gulf Nahua history (Chapters 2 and 3) shaped the local class economy, and we examined how the native peasants of Pajapan are dominated by broader domains and exploited through an unequal distribution of the factors of production (land, cattle) and the returns of labor (Chapter 4). In Chapter 5, we showed how the same forces have profoundly transformed the way the rain forest ecosystem is exploited, i.e., through an inefficient branch of the cattle industry bent on divesting the San Martín area of its natural riches and subsistence production potential. These transformations, however, have not been so radical as to wipe out all previous relations and forces of production. The chronic weaknesses of local agents of capital and the struggles waged by peasants have allowed the Gulf Nahuas to maintain some technical and social patterns of subsistence production. Older economic practices associated with the *milpa* system (slash-and-burn cultivation, family farming) have been preserved, if only in part.

While severely affected by the growth of the market and cattle economy, traditional family relations have not been completely destroyed. Native family solidarities play a key role in current forms of Gulf Nahua adaptation to broader market forces and the rain forest environment. The local economy is still dependent on kin-based power and exchange relations that pervade all aspects of Pajapan society. This brings us to the patrimonial domain,[1] a system mentioned in previous chapters whose characteristics and evolution need to be explored in greater depth. To this domain corresponds a particular view of bonds among humans and between nature and culture as conveyed through narrative discourse, to be explored later. We now turn to a detailed discussion of this patrimonial domain, with a view to answering two questions: what are the actual rules that govern family life in Pajapan, and to what extent do these rules still operate?

In this chapter we attempt to answer the latter questions using a threefold strategy. First, we examine the traditional system of kin relations, with an emphasis on norms and patterns of social organization. These patterns include a particular construction of relations of affinity and descent (bilateral, ego-centered, nucleated, male-biased, with five generations) conveyed through native kin designations. We have been careful, however, not to separate the question of how relatives are classified in language from practical aspects of the domestic economy: that is, the household composition (mostly nuclear) and authority structure (patrimonial), the division of labor (based on sex and age) and the rule of inheritance (male ultimogeniture). The analysis includes an ethnographic discussion of prevailing patterns of residence (patrilocal, semi-neolocal), the institution of marriage (monogamy and polygyny), the division between wife-givers and wife-receivers and related customs of brideservice and brideprice.

By and large, kinship in Pajapan contains a good dose of eccentricity: as with the prehispanic Nahuas (Lockhart 1992: 73), the family system is decentralized, both from a genealogical and economic perspective. We shall see, however, that the eccentric ordering of Gulf Nahua society does not preclude bonds of reciprocity (within and between households) or relations of inequality. Although without corporate clans or lineages, the kinship system involves vital exchanges between men and women, the old and the young, blood relatives and affines – alliances governed by native principles of authority and hierarchy favoring men and older generations. As with the Mazatecs, exchanges between genders and generations have in common with interchanges between culture and nature that they occur between unequals (Boege 1988: 109, 112, 129, 157).[2]

Second, Gulf Nahua kinship must also be understood dynamically, as a system in motion that leaves room for all sorts of tensions, variations and calculations affecting the individual or household trajectory. Households share certain common denominators, but they also display important variations in size, sexual composition and age. Differences in family profiles occur by chance and also from the process of aging and the family life cycle – "systematic changes that occur in household structure and composition as members pass through stages of their lives" (Sandstrom 1991: 178f., see 182). The available data show that the household cycle has important economic implications: to each phase of family life corresponds a particular ratio of consumers to producers and a mean rate of agricultural productivity as well. Moreover, kinship dynamics involve strategic calculations reflecting practical concerns, points of dispute and exceptions to the rule. Risks and problems exist that simple rules cannot solve: for example, choosing the right spouse, negotiating the best possible marriage arrangement, having more than one wife, leaving a violent father or an alcoholic husband, claiming compensation for a "kidnapped" daughter (eloped), etc.

Third, the dynamics of Gulf Nahua kinship must be understood from a broader perspective, i.e., against the background of wider forces affecting local forms of household organization based on descent and marriage, gender and age. A close examination of demographic data for Pajapan, from the 1900s to the late 1980s, allows us to address the question of changing patterns of marriage, inheritance, residence and household composition – changes in population structure and kin relations caused by the growth of the cattle and oil industries in southern Veracruz. Kin relations and differences in family profiles are conditioned by the sectoral fragmentation of the market economy (agriculture, petty trade, etc.) and also by the class inequalities that have developed between ranchers, peasants and landless wage workers.

A close examination of Pajapan's kinship system confirms the feminist political economic assumption that patriarchy is a widespread phenomenon, not to be confined to capitalist society alone. This should not come as a surprise. Students of Aztec history have shown that gender-based inequalities already existed in the prehispanic era.[3] Like Taggart's (1983: 4, 6) analysis of Puebla Nahuat society, our case-study clearly departs from romantically idealized conceptions of gender equality in native society.[4] Stress points ranging from inter-generational conflicts to sibling rivalries and the domination of women by men result not only from externally-induced factors such as shortages of land (Sandstrom 1991: 182–8, 340) but also from internal features of the patrimonial domain. Patriarchy, however, is a vague concept that should not be used in such ways as to preclude a careful investigation of specific historical and cultural situations (Amos and Parmar 1984; Mohanty 1991: 64ff.). As argued by Jaggar (1983) and Morgen (1990), the ethnic dimension is particularly critical in this respect as it impacts on all aspects of gender and determines the practical meaning that can be assigned to such basic concepts as the household, labor, sex and reproduction.[5] In this chapter, we are careful to specify the exact ways in which native women are subordinated to men (and the young to the old). We situate these inequalities against the background of a complex kinship system involving particular patterns of descent, marriage, residence, inheritance and domestic organization (household composition, division of labor, authority structure). These family practices are reducible neither to ideology (the "sphere of culture") nor to biology (the "sphere of reproduction");[6] rather they constitute a comprehensive web of relations that are both material and meaningful, embedded as they are in all aspects of Gulf Nahua society and history.

The Latin American literature that debates native gender issues usually emphasizes one of two things: relations of reciprocity or systems of patriarchal subjugation. While functionalist studies of native kinship may be accused of romanticism, feminist analyses that deny features of reciprocity to Indian societies err on the side of naivety as well. In reality, principles of reciprocity and domination are not entirely incompatible. Although rhetorically effective, notions of patriarchy that know no limit are misleading. As with capitalism and feudalism, a kin-based mode of social organization can impose and sustain a hierarchical regime provided that certain conditions be met. The exercise of power must respond to not only basic reproduction needs but also on-going struggles and rules of legitimation that determine the concrete parameters of any regime. The actual conditions under which patriarchy functions, and limits to the concentration of gender-based power, must be carefully investigated lest the analysis lapse into anti-patriarchal rhetoric.

What follows is an exercise in the processual analysis of Gulf Nahua kinship. Family life is an ensemble of "orderly processes" – a system of positions and relations governed by native rules of reciprocity and social hierarchy. Kin relations, however, are also the site of transformational and confrontational processes, hence strategic actions, cyclical changes, tensions and exceptions that escape a purely static (functional or structural) approach to social organization. These dynamic effects of the patrimonial domain create important variations in the household economy while also responding to broader "historical processes", such as the formation of class relations and the differentiation of the peasantry in contemporary Veracruz history. While the market economy has altered the kinship organization, the impact of capitalism varies also according to the family system already in place: pre-existing relations "affect the processes through which capitalist relationships are deepened and spread" (Wilson 1985: 1024).

Descent, marriage and the household economy

Kin terminology

The Gulf Nahua kin terminology is bilateral, without any distinction made between relatives on the mother's side and those on the father's side, or between descendants from a son and those from a daughter (as among the neighboring Zoque-Popolucas and the Aztecs as well; see Baez-Jorge (1973: 145–58); Rodríguez-Shadow (1991: 37); Lockhart (1992: 73, 82); Sandstrom (1991: 158f.). All adults of the grandparental generation are lumped into the same categories distinguished by sex, i.e., 'old fathers' and 'old mothers'. The suffix -weh implies old age. Gendered terms for uncle and aunt as distinct from father (-tah) and mother (-ye) apply to siblings of both parents; these terms are also used for senior siblings (see Baez-Jorge 1973: 150). The root word for sibling is -iknin, to which can be added a word marking gender (-ogich is the base for a male, -soa for a female) or distance (-wehka); cousins are "distant siblings". Special terms for cross and parallel cousins are lacking. Younger brothers and siblings are called notsoyo and notetso; as with other terms, the prefix no- or n- acts as a possessive pronominal, first person singular ("my"). There are distinct terms for son (nochogo) and daughter (notago). The base for child is pil, and the diminutive tsin can be used as a suffix to denote a grandson (nopiltsin), with -soa added for the granddaughter (nosoa:piltsin). All nephews and nieces are defined as "distant children" (nowehkapiltsin). Finally, the base for son-in-law is -mon. The words for female, father or mother (nan) are combined with -mon to signify a daughter-in-law (nosoa:mon), a father-in-law (nomontah:) or a mother-in-law (nomonan), respectively. Nosoa:t is my wife, and notawial, my husband. As in the prehispanic era (Lockhart 1992: 74, 77), terms used to designate in-laws of ego's generation are nowehpol (of ego's opposite sex), notex (a man's same-sex in-law), and nowes (a woman's same-sex in-law).[7]

The kin terminology reconstructed above (see Figure 5) points to several important features of Gulf Nahua social organization. First, kin designations used in Pajapan have retained important features of the

	MALE			FEMALE	
+2	NOTAHWEH			NO:YELA:	
+1	NA:CH \ NOTAH			NOYE / NOPI:H	
OLDER		NA:CH NOTAYAGANTOK	NOPI:H		
EGO	NOWEHKAIHNIN	NOGICHIKNIN	NOTETSO / NOSOA:IKNIN	NOWEHKAIKNIN	
YOUNGER		NOTSOYO			
-1	NOWEHKAPILTSIN	NOCHOGO	NOTAGO: / NOPILOA:N	NOWEHKAPILTSIN	
-2		NOPILTSIN	NOSOA:PILTSIN		

LATERAL		LINEAL	LATERAL
-tah	father	-a:ch	uncle, older brother
-ye	mother	-tayagantok	older brother
-la(:mah)	old, female	-pi:h	aunt, older sister
-weh	old, male	-wehka	distant
-ogich	male	chogo	boy
-soa	female	-tago	girl
-iknin	sibling	-piltsin	male descendant
-tetso	younger sibling		
-tsoyo	younger brother	no-, n-	my

Figure 5   Gulf Nahua kin terminology (*Source*: García de León 1976: 135)

prehispanic system (Lockhart 1992: 82, 85) in that they are still founded on a bilateral, ego-centered conception of descent: no distinction is made between relatives on the father's side and those on the mother's side. Each individual is at the center of his or her own kindred consisting of close and distant relatives, all of whom add up to a network of ego-related kin, not a corporate clan or lineage dominated by a common ancestor. One immediate result of this ego-centered system is that kin terms always have a possessive prefix governed by the reference point, without ever appearing in the free form. Also, personal genealogies tend to be relatively shallow:[8] all adults of the second ascending generation are lumped together as grandfathers and grandmothers, all cousins as "distant siblings", and all nephews and nieces as "distant children".

Second, nuclear family terms (father and mother, brother and sister, son and daughter, husband and wife) are demarcated from all other kinsfolk who are simply treated as distant nuclear-like relatives (without sexual distinction in the case of cousins, nephews and nieces). Nuclear family members are one's immediate relatives, those with whom one shares the same house and domestic resources for a lengthy period of time (though not for life), thereby forming a corporate group, the basic unit of production and reproduction. As Lockhart (1992: 75) and Sandstrom (1991: 159–66, 224) point out, this bilateral system of prehispanic origin is flexible in that it centers on an Eskimo-like nuclear family formation (without naming it) while also permitting a Hawaiian extension of lineal kin terms to collateral relatives (distinguished by generation) – an extension mechanism compatible with the existence of large extended families.

Third, although involving obligations of reciprocity, nuclear family solidarities are not particularly egalitarian, without vertical distinctions. The words that people use to classify their relatives already convey a principle of seniority based on criteria of age and sex. On the whole the terminology emphasizes vertical age-group divisions, hence intra-generational solidarities as opposed to large lineal group formations (Sandstrom 1991: 165; Lockhart 1992: 83, 89). It creates five distinct generations (+2, +1, ego, -1, -2), to which can be added a threefold categorization of siblings: older brothers and sisters (who are like uncles and aunts), younger siblings, and those of one's own age group. A privileged position is also granted to males. The term used for an older brother who looks after his siblings (*tayagantok*, from *yacana*, occasionally applied to the oldest sister) implies leadership and authority. Moreover, the system provides a designation for the younger brother (*notsoyo*) but none for the younger sister. The term for grandson (*-piltsin*) is applied to all descendants, lineal or lateral (preceded by *-wehka*); female descendants are specified by adding *-soa*.

Fourth, the kin terminology establishes no equation between parents-in-law and any class of uncles and aunts, nor does it equate one's spouse with any special category of cousins (e.g., cross-cousins). In other words, the language of genealogy leaves the question of whom one should marry unanswered. As we shall see, factors other than kinship relations intervene in the formation of alliances between spouses and their respective families.

Lastly, words denoting parents- and children-in-law revolve around the son-in-law (*nomon*) who acts as the prototypical affine, hence the base for all derivative in-laws (*nomontah, nomonan, nosoa:mon*). This is in keeping with the male bias operating within the terminology as a whole and also the role of the son-in-law as the outsider par excellence, the one who takes the daughter away from her original family.

The nuclear family

The nuclear family, composed of parents and their dependent children living under the same roof, lays the foundations of the Gulf Nahua economy and society, a system centered on household dependencies and solidarities. As in other rural areas of Mexico and Latin America, nuclear domestic groups also act as units of production and biological reproduction. Peasant households basically resemble one another and follow general organizational rules. However, while similar in many respects, these units also vary considerably in that they are subject to constant internal differentiation. Family relations form a system of differences based on sex and age, two factors that lend themselves to variations in household composition and that have a direct bearing on all aspects of the household economy.

The sexual division of labor is central to the domestic economy. Men and women engage in complementary productive activities. While both spouses fetch wood and collect fruit and food from the *milpa*, men are generally responsible for clearing the land, tending the crops and the field animals (horses, cattle), and carrying out all construction works, private and communal. They do the hunting and the fishing (except for freshwater crayfish collected mainly by women, and oysters which men and women collect jointly or separately). Women do almost all the childrearing and related chores such as cooking, housekeeping and washing. They fetch water, look after fruit trees and domestic animals (chicken, turkeys, pigs), and may participate in the harvesting of corn and beans, or sell farmyard animals, fruit and other foodstuffs on the local or regional market.

Children are breast-fed till age three or until other children are born. They are expected to help their parents from a young age, especially the girls; boys are said to play longer and be less interested in working or helping their parents. Girls fetch water on a daily basis from the age of five and, as they grow up, help their mothers do the laundry, house cleaning and cooking. By the age of eight girls are already familiar with much of the work they will be expected to do as young women. Boys aged six and older are asked to fetch wood (for household consumption or local sale), tend the animals, guard the crops against rodents, and do some *milpa* work under their fathers' supervision. Boys and girls work on their own, without close parental supervision, from the age of 12.[9]

While fathers can be affectionate and often play with their children, they can also demand unquestioning obedience from wives and children and use force to uphold their authority. Gulf Nahua men can be very strict and violent, especially when drunk or succumbing to fits of jealousy or sheer impatience: "they do not speak with words", as one female informant put it. They have the final say in most family matters, including who their daughters will marry, the use of contraceptives by wives, or even when the mother should breast-feed the child.

The relationship between mother and son turns formal when the latter reaches the age of six. Sedeño and Becerril (1985: 53–7) suggest that this sudden rupture between a caring mother and her young son is the origin of men's aggression toward the opposite gender. After weaning, children are disciplined by their mothers, their grandparents and their older siblings, all of whom may act as substitute parents if need be – if the mother or the father has gone or if both parents are busy working. Grandparents often play an important role in raising children and have a say in matters of marriage and also child custody when parents divorce or separate. Older children look after their younger brothers and sisters and exercise considerable authority over them as well; in the parents' absence, the older *tayagantok* brother or sister is the one literally in charge. An older brother can come down in favor of or against a suitor asking for his sister's hand in marriage. More work and discipline is usually expected of children from former marriages and orphans adopted by relatives.

Although designed to ensure an equitable distribution of land rights at the village level, property relations within the family place women in a vulnerable position. As Vázquez García (nd) notes, a woman's relationship to property in land and its produce is almost always mediated by men – her father when she is young, her husband when she marries, and her son when she turns old or when the husband dies. When they marry, daughters are usually given no more than bedding and cooking equipment and a few farmyard animals from their parents; they are also entitled to some of their deceased mother's personal belongings (jewellery, clothing). Women cannot inherit their fathers' land rights; since their responsibility is to look after children, not after land, they are not considered to be legitimate heirs (*"no tienen validez"*). By contrast, all sons will receive financial assistance from their fathers at marriage (wedding costs mostly) and are likely to inherit part of their father's property as they establish independent households. The inheritance may include a piece of fallow land, a house or some building materials, and also a few head of cattle (or horses), depending on the father's wealth. The youngest son is usually the principal benefactor: he inherits his father's house, herd (if any) and communal land rights. The rights of the youngest son, however, are associated with real obligations, such as supporting his parents in their old age and assuming the cost of their funerals.

Local inheritance laws are partly attributable to Mexican state policies *vis-à-vis* land. While land in the prehispanic era could be passed on from parent to daughter and from sibling to sibling, inheritance laws prevailing since the colonial era have consistently privileged the transfer of property in land from male household head to adult son with widows acting as custodians of property inherited by non-adult sons. Article 97 of the agrarian legislation passed in 1927 decreed that *"ejido* members shall be Mexican nationals, males over the age of eighteen, or single women or widows supporting a family". In 1971 the agrarian code was finally changed with articles 45, 76 and 78 giving women equal rights to land and establishing full equality between male and female *ejidatarios*. Because of customary inheritance laws, illiteracy problems, women's exclusion from legal and public transactions and their confinement to household activities, this progressive legislation became a dead letter. In 1984, only 15% of *comuneros* and *ejidatarios* living in rural Mexico were women. (Arizpe and Botey, 1987: 70f; Vázquez García nd).

In 1967, rights of access to the communal lands of Pajapan were given to eight widows (mothers of young sons) who "defended themselves" with the support of La Güera, a literate native woman who grew up in the city of Coatzacoalcos. The 1981 census update transferred these rights to sons and male relatives of the widows, but it also granted 4.1% of all land rights to 40 widows of *comuneros* who had died or left the area since 1967. At the insistence of state officials and in accordance with article 103 of the Federal Law of Agrarian Reform of 1971, one parcel of land was assigned to 12 widows for their own use. The women initially farmed the land but abandoned it six years later because of poor soil conditions and inadequate resources (Vázquez García nd).

As Vázquez García shows, the creation of the Pajapan II *ejido* in 1992 allowed a considerable number of women to gain legal access to tillable land. In an effort to settle claims over the expropriated lands and resolve conflicts between the 905 *comuneros* of Pajapan, their landless sons and other peasants living within the communal area, an agreement was reached stating that 4-hectare parcels would be assigned to one adult son or wife per *comunero* (and 71 new individuals as well). As a result, women make up one-third of the current *ejidatarios* of Pajapan II. The legal gains obtained by these *ejidatarias*, however, should not be over-estimated. After all, the local understanding is that women will eventually transfer land rights to their youngest sons in keeping with local tradition. Also, *comuneros* simply used the names of their wives (and a few un-married daughters in the case of ranchers) to gain legal access to lands in the expropriated zone; very few parcels (5%) were assigned to widows and single women. Wives were thus registered as a way of preventing rebellious sons from taking control of the land.

Residence and marriage

A relatively simple division of labor and property system based on sex and age governs the traditional Gulf Nahua economy. It also accounts for the prevailing rule of residence, which involves a sequence of patri-locality and semi-neolocality (moving out of the father's house but not too far). After marriage, a young man usually brings his wife to live in his father's house (or the kitchen if the house is too small); the daughter-in-law is treated like another member of the family and will be "raised a little more" by her parents-in-law if still young. The newly-wed couple remain there until they have a child or can afford to build a house of their own, preferably near the father's house or within the same patrilocal compound (consisting of parents, their sons and families forming an adjoining household group).[10]

Prior to the expansion of the market economy and the cattle industry in the Santa Marta highlands, the Gulf Nahuas practised a strict rule of temporary, pre-nuptial uxorilocality (moving to the house of the bride's father) as part of the brideservice institution. Informants recall the days when a young man had to work with his father-in-law and be at his service for up to a year before he could receive the daughter in marriage. Cases of brideservice performed according to tradition are still reported in Pajapan.[11] Marriage in Pajapan is still defined as a man giving his daughter away to another man and his patrilocal family. The alliance involves a young woman moving out of her father's house and joining her husband and his family, both of whom are expected to return the "gift" with payments in kind (all wedding expenses) and cash as well. In the spring of 1991 the total cost of a wedding following a proper marriage proposal added up to about US$1,000[12], with one-third of the amount given in cash and two-thirds as payments in kind for the nuptial celebrations.

The brideprice – what the girl *bien pedida* ("well proposed") will cost to the husband and his father – is never seen as a market transaction. Nor is it defined as material compensation for the loss of a woman's productive labor-power. Although these considerations may not be absent from the transactions leading up to a marriage, the stated purpose of the brideprice and the older brideservice institution is to provide the girl's father with a tangible proof of his son-in-law's good will, his sense of responsibility and marital commitment, hence his capacity to look after the needs of his future wife and children. If a young man is given a bride free of charge, there is fear that he may not "appreciate" the woman, abandon her or fail to take proper care of her. If he abandons or mistreats her, the girl's father can always use the money he received at the wedding day to look after his daughter's needs. Some informants also speak of the brideprice as a *gratificación para la crianza*, i.e., compensation for the expenses incurred in raising a daughter.[13]

The marriage and related transactions are preceded and conditioned by several ritualized meetings between parents and representatives of the future bride and groom.[14] The detailed prescriptions of visits and ritual proceedings associated with marriage vary from one Nahua village and native informant to another. Basic rules, however, remain constant. At marriage fathers, sons and brothers try to maintain residential and economic ties, whereas women are expected to sever all connections with their family of origin. The rule of inheritance is predominantly patrilineal, with an emphasis not on the usual rule of primogeniture (Taggart 1983: 24; Sandstrom 1991: 173f.) but rather ultimogeniture (favoring the last son) and the obligation of the youngest son to look after his parents in their old age. The dominant pattern of residence is patrilocal. This form of residence was traditionally preceded by a period of uxorilocal brideservice, and then followed by what might be called patri-neolocality – the couple moving out of the husband's father's house but not too far.

Village endogamy is the norm, though not by social requirement. Marriage between first-degree cousins is generally prohibited. Most marriages are monogamous. As in Aztec society (Rodríguez-Shadow 1991: 202, 207–16; Lockhart 1992: 80), however, polygynous unions between one man and two (or more) women who may be sisters are by no means uncommon. In the words of one informant, polygyny "is not a vice, it's a custom". In principle, the first wife must be informed and preferably consulted when the husband enters into a second (common-law) marriage. Unions with second wives or concubines do not require full wedding rituals; they involve relatively simple negotiations between the husband and the woman's father and much lower costs. Although they sometimes reside within the same compound, the wives normally live in separate houses. The first wife is usually treated as the principal spouse and is granted some degree of authority over secondary wives.

While male infidelity is merely criticized, female infidelity or suspicions thereof can easily result in separation or acts of violence. Stories of jealous husbands beating their wives or killing their wives' lovers are not rare. A woman should never accept more than one "engagement" (*com-*

promiso) lest she should lose all credibility as a virtuous bride or a reliable wife; village gossip will tarnish her reputation and reduce her marriage prospects in no time. Her long-term economic security and the material support she and her children can expect from her husband depend on her compliance with rules of proper female behavior.

Divorce or separation also follow certain customary rules. According to some informants, the children of a broken home used to end up living with parents of the opposite gender; while girls would look after their father's household needs, boys would stay with the mother and work the land. The rule still applies today and tallies with the sexual division of labor generally prevailing in Pajapan. Grandparents on both sides and the municipal syndic or judge play a key role in settling all matters of child custody (in the absence of a family agreement).[15]

Kinship hierarchy, variability and strategy

Kin relations in Pajapan are largely centrifugal. To use the Durkheimian concept, Gulf Nahua social organization is based on mechanical rules of solidarity: domestic units are similar to one another and self-sufficient in many respects. The society, however, amounts to more than the sum of all interchangeable and unchanging households sharing the same territory and norms of conduct. Although highly decentralized, the observed system involves particular forms of power stratification, important demographic variations, and constant transactions within and between the household units. These are vital issues of anthropology that tend to escape observation when using a purely functional or structural approach to kinship.

First, kinship is a power structure. As already noted, elements of hierarchical organization are built into Gulf Nahua rules of descent, marriage, residence and inheritance. These elements add up to an indigenous version of the patrimonial domain, a ruling order that vests men, wife-givers, older generations and youngest sons with special rights and privileges not granted to women, wife-receivers, younger generations and first sons. At the village level, there is no *consejo de ancianos* that presides over communal affairs, yet land, offices and the government process are under the effective control of male family heads. Prior to the rise of ranching activities in Pajapan, authority was vested in male elders acting as government officers and lot administrators protecting the village land base against external threats.

Second, kinship is also a variable structure. Household units are internally differentiated along gender and generational lines, and they are subject to important variations in size, age and sexual composition. Inter-family variations based on demographic factors (number of births and deaths, age and sex profile, migrations) have a direct bearing on critical matters such as the household ratio of consumers to producers and of household members to resources under their immediate control. Each family profile directly affects the unit's capacity to meet its subsistence needs at any time. Differences in family profile result in part from unpredictable factors such as the number of children born, the proportion of boys to girls, the life expectancy of household members, their state of health and potential productivity, etc.

The patrimonial domain and the household economy are subject to the vagaries of family and community histories. Still, factors that create variations in household composition are not entirely unpredictable: family changes follow certain patterns. This brings us to the process of aging and the life cycle of domestic relations in Pajapan. Because engaged in both productive and reproductive activities, the nuclear household involves an essentially cyclical economy. A unit is formed at marriage, it gradually detaches itself from the patrilocal unit and expands as children are born. It then transforms itself as children marry and add new members to the household or the immediate compound. Eventually the larger patrilocal unit disintegrates once more as parents die and children age and leave. As we shall see, to each phase of the nuclear patrilocal family cycle corresponds a mean production profile based on average membership, age distribution, and the ratio of consumers to producers.

Third, kinship is a site of strategic exchanges within and between units. Households are never entirely self-sufficient. Material exchanges between blood relatives extend beyond the household unit. Important transfers of wealth and exchanges of labor occur between closely related household heads, i.e., between a father and his youngest son who has just married, or between brothers living in separate houses, each with their own wife and children. The same rule of inter-household dependency applies to relations of affinity: the incest taboo compels the offspring of each unit to seek spouses from outside the immediate family and to form new units. Adults depend on non-relatives to maintain both productive and reproductive activities. Practically all marriages involve "transfers" of women and wealth moving in opposite directions, i.e., between households that give daughters and those that give wealth (or labor).

Transactions between household units are not performed merely according to rule. Decisions and actions are not simply pre-determined by the prescriptions and interdictions of customary law. Rather they are adjusted to the particular trajectory of each person or household. Men and women are constantly confronted with choices related to marriage, residence and inheritance, choices that involve real concerns and practical risks as well. Although governed by laws of their own, the daily lives of Pajapeños are subject to variable circumstances that require strategic adjustments. Moreover, their lives are not without disputes and manifestations of resistance to the ruling order. The universe of family relations in Pajapan is thoroughly politicized: it is governed by the laws of tradition but also by strife and negotiations between the old and young, husbands and wives, blood relatives and affines.[16]

For example, issues of brideprice are open to decisions and transactions, claims and counterclaims, hopes and fears that form an integral part of the political economy of Gulf Nahua marriage. A father intent on getting his son married may hesitate about what to promise his future in-laws; the son may not want to pay more than the minimum brideprice and may reject the idea of a civil marriage proposed by the bride's family because too binding. Given these difficulties, the young woman may simply decide to marry against the wish of her father, who will immediately claim compensation from the girl's husband and his father. Alternatively, a poor man may opt to bypass the brideprice obligations by marrying a "widow" or a woman whose father is gone or deceased. If the bridegroom's parents are deceased, the young man may ask the hand of another man's daughter without being able to meet all the economic requirements of a normal wedding. The father-in-law may be impressed by the young man's reputation as a hard-worker (or worry about his daughter's chances of getting married) and either go along with a simple and inexpensive wedding or ask that payments be made in kind (labor) or in cash over time. Moreover, once married, the couple and their families may have second thoughts about earlier decisions. A girl may regret not having followed her parents' advice to marry at a later age. The man she married may prove to be irresponsible toward her and their children after all. Meanwhile her husband may feel that he was pressured to marry too quickly (his girlfriend took refuge in his house after being beaten by her father) and feel justified in going regularly to the brothel, having a mistress or planning to leave his wife and children.

People can also opt for special trajectories that are allowed by custom without actually representing the norm: for instance, celibacy or homosexuality, both of which may permit some adults (healers, midwives) to free themselves from obligations of the patrimonial domain (see Boege 1988: 173). The practice of polygyny is another special case. Under certain circumstances, a man may consider that the benefits of polygyny, material and emotional, will outweigh the costs and responsibilities of having more than one wife, and children from more than one marriage. The benefits may be more attractive if the second wife is young and hard-working, compensating for a first wife who may be ill, pregnant, too busy looking after children and hence unable to do *milpa* work or engage in petty trade. As for the principal wife, she may feel that she is not in a position to question her husband's decision. Or she may welcome the prospects of another woman's company and help in looking after the needs of husband and children. Alternatively, she may force the husband to choose between wife and mistress; cases of women threatening to leave or abandoning their husbands for reasons of adultery or bigamy are not uncommon. The woman may fear the prospects of cohabiting with her husband's second wife, especially if she is of the same age or a few years older or simply not inclined to accept orders from the principal wife. If the wife accepts the new marital arrangement, she may insist that her own children receive better treatment from their father than their half-siblings.

The second wife, too, may have doubts about her decision to marry a polygynous man. The experience might prove stressful, especially if she does not get along with the principal wife and is mistreated by her. Alternatively, she may have lost her virginity or been abandoned by her husband and, for lack of economic security and other opportunities to remarry, agree to become another man's secondary wife. Experience may have convinced her that a wealthier polygynous man whom she trusts has more to offer than a poorer monogamous husband who lacks any sense of family responsibility.

Whether monogamous or polygynous, marriages may be terminated through separation or divorce. A wife may commit adultery or leave her husband because he is too violent, frequently absent, addicted to alcohol or downright lazy. She may decide to live on her own, unless she appeals to her father or older brother to provide her and her children with material assistance and lodging. If no agreement is reached on questions of child custody, the grandparents may intervene and try to convince the village syndic or judge that their son- or daughter-in-law is not responsible enough to look after the children. If children stay with the mother, as is usually the case, then the grandparents may insist that the mother refrain from living with another man until her own daughters are fully grown and married. Otherwise, there is fear that daughters will be sexually abused by their stepfather without the mother being able to do anything (for fear of being abandoned herself).[17]

Patterns of residence also experience variations and tensions that elude a simple application of customary laws of patrilocality and patri-neo-locality. Young men do not always reside with their fathers or brothers. The decision to follow or break the normal rule of residence depends on a number of factors: the occupation of the father and brothers, whether or not the father has access to land, the number of sons who are already working or living together, the space available within the immediate compound, whether or not the son and his wife are on good terms with other family members, etc. Moreover, there are circumstances where uxorilocality is the preferred option for all parties. For instance, while a father may refuse to support a lazy son, the young man's father-in-law may have no son he can count on to work and inherit the land and support him and his wife in their old age. If so, the bride's father may invite the son-in-law to join his house. People will criticize the young man for living at the expense of his father-in-law, who will in turn be accused of stealing another man's son; yet both parties may benefit from this arrangement and be willing to put up with village gossip.

Similar comments apply to the domestic division of labor. Although men and women are generally assigned different tasks, exceptions to the rule are not rare and deviations from the prevailing norms will occur without anyone taking offence. For instance, women will not fell trees and put up fences, but some peasant wives, especially those from poorer families with children at school, are accustomed to working in *milpa* doing such chores as planting, burning, weeding and harvesting. Widows and women separated from their husbands occasionally perform all the tasks usually reserved for men. A woman is exempted from fetching firewood if she is pregnant or if she is married to a jealous husband who will not let his wife wander alone in the forest. As for men, they may find themselves in situations where they have to do a woman's job. Some may spend considerable time looking after children and doing house chores because their wives are pregnant or sick, because they have no female relative to replace the mother, and because they lack the resources to hire a woman to do the wife's work. Mention should also be made of the daily bickering, claims and tensions associated with the application of rules of household organization. Just as men are known to complain about their wives' inefficiency, many women reproach their husbands for working too little, wasting cash earnings and lacking any sense of family responsibility. Just as parents insist that young and old children pull their own weight, children may occasionally blame parents for their failure to meet their basic needs and support their aspirations in life.

Although clearly favoring the last son, rules of household inheritance also allow for variations and deviations. Moreover, these rules can be contested. As noted by Stuart, the rule of ultimogeniture is flexible and will be adjusted to the particular circumstances of families. For example, if the father dies when some of the children are still young, then the eldest son living in the household inherits his father's property and responsibilities. Alternatively, older brothers may work the land until the youngest brother is old enough to make use of the parcel received from his father; this assumes that the younger man is willing to engage in farming activities and to look after his parents in old age, which is not always the case. As can be expected, resentment and conflict between the youngest son and his oldest *tayagantok* brother over questions of inheritance are not uncommon. If the father has daughters only or if sons are not interested in cultivating the land and providing for their parents' needs, then a son-in-law may move in and inherit home and land rights.[18]

Finally, provided that she asserts her rights, a widow may become a *comunera* if her deceased husband has no male heir or brother to claim his land rights or if his only son is too young to make productive use of the land: in the latter case, parents or brothers of the deceased *comunero* will insist that the woman not remarry (until the son is able to inherit) for fear that the family property be passed on to her new husband instead of her son. While only eight widows obtained *comunero* rights in the 1967 Pajapan census, 40 widows became full-fledged *comuneras* in 1981. For reasons already discussed, women also make up one-third of the *ejidatarias* of the lowland Pajapan II *ejido* founded in 1992. About 10% of these *ejidatarias* are widows or single mothers with young children; politicized by ten years of land struggles, many of these women asserted their rights through active participation in communal and official census assemblies (Vázquez García nd).

Six cases of inheritance were discussed in detail with informants in Pajapan. All of them followed the patrilineal rule. Daughters never inherit their fathers' parcels of land or house plots; they have access to land through husbands only. Four cases out of six observed the right of the youngest son (or the only son) to inherit the family property in land. The two other families broke the rule. In one case, the oldest son inherited because the youngest son had already left his father's house. The other case involved a property of 250 hectares that the father owned before the land reform and that was divided among five sons. When the local land tenure system was changed in the early 1980s, the third son received his father's rights in addition to his own; he in turn intends to divide his two parcels between his two sons.

Gulf Nahua kinship follows patterns and rules that involve important variations amongst the household units and complex transactions between family groups and household members. Family life becomes even more complicated when viewed against the background of forces of modern history. Native patterns of domestic organization based on sex and age have suffered radical alterations under the expansion of capital and state. These changes can be attributed to broader developments such as immigration and colonization, the growth of industry and urbanization, and the expansion of markets in land, labor and foodstuffs. To these factors can be added the intervention of state bureaucracy in the distribution of authority, land, subsidies for public services, marriage contracts, educational services, etc.

The analyses that follow deal with the impact of broader forces on Gulf Nahua society. Each period of local history will be analyzed in terms of demographic trends that reflect prevailing economic tendencies and their effects on local population structures and related patterns of household organization. Field data collected in the 1980s will be used to provide a more detailed account of current variations in household structures and production profiles, variations that respond to differences in class position and family cycle as well. Although still operative, the rules of Gulf Nahua society have suffered important shifts and transformations that point to both the vulnerability and adaptability of Pajapan society *vis-à-vis* the outside world.

Demographic history

General trends

Pajapan's patrimonial domain and domestic economy have not been completely destroyed by the expansion of rural and urban capital. Although the general trend is toward an effective subordination, distortion and dissolution of native forms of social organization, all indications are that the Gulf Nahuas have adjusted their way of life to the new ruling order. The historical evidence also suggests that tendencies toward integration and subordination have developed unevenly through time: important shifts in the relative weight of traditional and non-traditional practices have occurred throughout the century. These fluctuations are no surprise given the erratic growth of a regional primary-sector economy based on the production of lumber, cattle and oil, mostly for export.

Before we delve into fluctuations of the local population structure, a few words should be said about general trends that have marked contemporary Gulf Nahua history, especially from the 1940s till the end of the 1970s.[19] Since they involve a partial reversion to older patterns, trends observed in the 1980s will be discussed later. Pajapan's integration into the regional oil and cattle economy has been achieved mostly through the concentration of communal lands and government authority by the rancher class, the out-migration and proletarianization of landless peasants, and the growth of commodity production and exchange within the local economy. These developments have directly affected kinship and household practices in Pajapan. Primarily, relations of interdependence between genders and generations have been seriously eroded. Most goods and services are no longer produced and exchanged within the boundaries of the household and the village. Nor are critical decisions regarding the allocation of land and wealth channelled principally through household and family connections. Customary differences and interchanges between the old and the young, men and women, blood relatives and affines have given way to divisions between buyers and sellers, laborers and owners of capital (agricultural, mercantile, industrial), government authorities and native citizens, the literate (especially school teachers) and the illiterate (about 50% of current Pajapan villagers compared to 90% in 1960).

Traditional dependencies based on age, sex, marriage and descent brought elements of hierarchy together with requisites of reciprocity. Although exercising power, men and older generations had to assume obligations and responsibilities toward women and younger adults whom they depended on to meet their own needs. Since the early 1950s, however, the role of elders has been severely eroded by the rise of Indian rancher *caciques* to power and the increasing intervention of school teachers and the literate youth in local government activities (Velázquez 1992b). The process of capital accumulation and the intrusions of state authority have tended to pit power-holders against the poor and the powerless: in the case of Pajapan, ranchers against peasants (with and without land), urban merchants against poverty-stricken villagers, employers against unskilled wage laborers, agents of the state and local *caciques* against native people. A cattle economy that makes little use of peasant labor or produce represents an extreme version of domains that create hierarchy without reciprocity. While industrial employers must reproduce the labor force in order to exploit it, Pajapan ranchers represent a particularly ruthless class in that they have no vested interest in meeting the survival needs of peasants or turning them into agricultural wage workers. When a ranching economy usurps virtually all the available land and prospers without having to exploit labor, as in Pajapan (from the 1950s to the 1980s), the rule of hierarchy turns into despotism.

Until the late 1970s, the expansion of the cattle economy and the control over land exercised by local *caciques* rendered the rule of patrilineal inheritance virtually inoperative. Peasants dispossessed of their land no longer had property to give by inheritance. Very young and very old peasants were severely affected by these developments: young adults could no longer count on older generations to secure access to land, nor could the latter trust landless sons to look after their needs in old age. Inheritance became a function of class: only ranchers could bequeath property in land or animals. Furthermore, those who owned large herds and sizeable tracts of land have tended to break the rule of ultimogeniture by dividing property among sons. The wealthiest ranchers could even afford to leave wealth to their wives, mistresses and daughters; all three women who have *comunero* rights in Pajapan are widows of wealthy Indian ranchers. The more estate a man owns, the greater the difficulty in resolving problems of inheritance and the greater the pressure on the man to name his wife and older children in his will or to give them cattle or real estate on the occasion of their marriage or before his death. Pajapeños recognize that fathers can bequeath property as they wish and break the rule of patrilineal ultimogeniture, provided that they do so of their own free will.

The domestic and village economy has been severely disrupted by the proletarianization of landless peasants emigrating to the city and the involvement of all households in the market economy. Prior to the 1930s, a very large proportion of articles that were part of Gulf Nahua livelihood (food, clothes, lodging) were produced and used by the household group. The returns of male and female labor were mostly in kind, shared by all family members, and they were in excess of immediate needs: foodstuffs could be preserved and stored against future use. The market economy introduced entirely different rules of wealth management: the labor power and produce sold by workers on the local or regional market was converted into money, hence personal wealth that could be disposed of by the *individual* controlling it. The proceeds of a wage worker or a simple commodity producer were for all intents and purposes "his", and they could be spent in all sorts of ways and without delay. In most cases, cash earnings were barely sufficient to meet short-term family needs and might be wasted on articles other than subsistence goods.

These days, wealth in cattle and most cash earnings circulating in Pajapan are in the hands of the male population, leaving women more vulnerable than ever. While they can rely on stored foodstuffs to meet future needs, women have no guarantee that men's cash income will suffice or that it will be used adequately; husbands are known to waste much of the family income on non-subsistence commodities such as alcohol. Owners of cattle are in a better position to look after their family needs, yet the capital invested in ranching operations belongs to men only and is theirs to save, use, sell or bequeath as they see fit. From men's vantage point, money and agricultural capital reduce their dependence on their wives' subsistence labor and their daily commitment to family life and the household economy. In some cases the income derived from wage-labor or petty commodity production is so limited that men spend all of it trying to meet their own basic needs, without being able to sustain the family they have started or are planning to start.

In short, with the market economy, property and wealth have become vested in classes and individuals as opposed to kin groups and positions within the patrimonial domain. The resulting fragmentation of family solidarities is partly reflected in current uses of kin terms. The adoption of Spanish designations for cousins, grandchildren, nephews and nieces indicates a tendency to abandon the broader family model based on the extension of nuclear family terms (brother and sister, son and daughter) to distant blood relatives, in favor of a more narrow view of family life. The tendency to add "a more thorough distinction between lineal and collateral kin" as a result of Spanish influence (Lockhart 1992: 85) is further reinforced by the current abandonment of native terms for same-generation in-laws and their replacement by Spanish terms (*cuñados, concuñados*). With the exception of polygynous families, kinship solidarities are increasingly reduced to their narrowest expression: unstable biological families and nuclear households consisting of parents and their dependent children.

The break-up of the patrimonial domain is also reflected in shifts in Gulf Nahua marriage practices. Problems of landlessness and unemployment spell ruin for a household and village economy based on the sexual division of labor, the marriage alliance and the practice of brideservice and brideprice. For landless wage-earners, marriage and family life has become more a costly venture and less a productive investment: having many children is *puro gasto* ("pure spending"). Nor does brideprice paid in cash or in kind (labor, foodstuffs) make sense in a context where the union no longer promises the creation of a new family farm. Thus the brideservice institution is rapidly disappearing. Bridegrooms and their fathers are still expected to settle all engagement and wedding expenses, including the brideprice. Available data suggest, however, that the bride-price has declined over the years (except for a few short inflationary periods). Most youths complain that the payments are higher than before, yet these statements do not reflect real increases in the cost of marriage but rather a net decline in the economic returns of family life. Given this devaluation of the household economy, many young men prefer to minimize the cost of marriage by "kidnapping" the bride, a pejorative term for elopement. Elopements are viewed as weddings gone secret and private, without a sense of public commitment *vis-à-vis* the institution of marriage. Even when performed according to rule, wedding negotiations are reduced to their simplest expression: two or three visits spanning a short period of time. Finally, all indications are that families are more unstable than ever: as we shall see, couples separate and remarry more often than before.

Couples and youths in general have been partially freed from the customary exigencies of brideservice and from family dependencies in matters of material livelihood. Some women, especially the *viajeras* or *mujeres de empeño* self-employed in the service sector (mostly as petty traders), have achieved a certain degree of autonomy *vis-à-vis* men. These women can now travel by themselves, they can earn money to meet their needs and those of their children, they have access to contraceptives that give them greater control over their bodies, and they are more inclined than ever to bring husbands who are violent or alcoholic before the local court. Unlike older women, the young Nahua woman *"no se deja"*, as the local expression goes; she doesn't let herself be pushed around. According to one female informant, while unfaithful women used to "pay [for] their vulgarity" at great cost, a woman can now have a lover provided she is discreet and that she does not let herself be bullied by her husband or father. Women now have the means to "defend themselves" and are not as much afraid of men as they used to be.

Although important, these gains have been offset by the many problems that poverty-stricken men and women face when uprooted from their kin-based mode of livelihood and subjected to a broader market economy over which they have no control. The new regime has resulted in chronic problems of poverty, alcoholism, social conflict and cultural alienation affecting all segments of the Gulf Nahua population, including women. Gender and family relations have been partially commodified through the introduction of a class-based economy geared to cash earnings and the accumulation and concentration of profits in the hands of the few. Traditional rules of marriage and family organization have survived but not without profound distortions. Older informants thus point out that brideprice in the form of cash payments was not practised prior to the expansion of the cattle industry in Pajapan. They are critical of the institution and view exchanges of money for wives as "men buying women".

Stories are told of girls aged from 12 to 15 who have been sold against their will to foreigners or local ranchers, to be deflowered and then abandoned when pregnant. Although vulnerable to village gossip, fathers have been known to ask exorbitant payments from future bridegrooms.[20] The impact of money on marriage transactions is so pervasive that even female virtue has acquired an exchange value: virgins are worth considerably more money than 'widows', a euphemism for women who have been abandoned or who are no longer virgin. Furthermore, to the extent that they have been commodified, female sexuality and marriage alliances are now subject to fluctuations in markets (foodstuffs, labor) and the intrusion of broader economic forces. Thus the local brideprice tends to rise in periods of rapid urban growth when more money and market commodities circulate within the village economy. As we shall see, fluctuations in brideprice respond to shifts in broader economic conditions and related population indices: i.e., the degree of male out-migration and the ratio of marriageable girls to single men residing in the village.

Marriage arrangements are subject to variations in class position. For example, children of well-to-do ranchers tend to intermarry, and the price paid for marrying the daughter of a wealthy cattle-raiser tends to be higher than for the daughter of a poor peasant. While class endogamy tends to be the norm, class exogamous marriages involving wealthier men and poorer women occur more frequently than unions between the male poor and wealthier-class women (see Boege 1988: 63; J.M. Chevalier 1982: 289). In those few cases where a poor peasant succeeds in marrying the daughter of a wealthier family, the bride's father may decide to waive the brideprice and meet his daughter's wedding expenses himself. These unions are potentially costly for the bride's father but advantageous for the propertyless bridegroom. The latter may be ridiculed by others for not meeting his normal obligations, but the immediate and long-term implications of such a marriage far outweigh the short-term cost to his personal reputation. Class factors also intervene in the practice of male polygamy which has become very common, if not generalized, amongst wealthy ranchers and merchants. The number of polygynous marriages has not declined over time, yet the function and social correlates of polygamy have been radically altered under the impact of Pajapan's class economy. While women cohabiting with polygynous men used to spend most of their time in subsistence activities together with their rural-poor husbands, they now tend to live with ranchers who rely on the labor of their first or second wives to attend various ranch or small commercial businesses (stores, restaurant, bakery, etc.).

Patterns of residence and the population structure of Pajapan have also changed. Initially, pressures from outside mestizo ranchers and urban populations forced many natives to concentrate in the central village and communal lands of Pajapan. The appropriation of lands by Indian ranchers in a context of increasing population density eventually resulted in the out-migration of young Gulf Nahua men to the city or to peripheral areas of the municipality in search of land. Many young single women, "widows" and daughters of single mothers have left the village, either permanently or for lengthy periods to work as domestics in the city (see Vázquez García nd), but an even greater number of young men have out-migrated. Migratory losses suffered over the years undermined the traditional practice of patrilocality and village endogamy. These losses have altered the sex ratio of young adults residing in the village and introduced a measure of uxorilocality at the community level: while women leave their family at marriage, more men abandon the village without having married, leaving behind a surplus of young female adults (with or without children). Unlike their husbands and adult sons, women have been increasingly confined to a domestic and village economy geared to subsistence production, petty trade and family reproductive activities. At the same time, the local ratio of producers to consumers has declined at both the household and village levels, to the detriment of the peasants' capacity to meet their subsistence needs. A crisis in the village economy was bound to ensue from this destruction of family life suffered in a context of declining access to land. The crisis was further exacerbated by improvements in the rates of birth and overall longevity experienced by the Gulf Nahuas since the 1940s, changes that reduced the proportion of middle-aged cohorts representing the more productive segments of the native population.

This completes our overview of major trends affecting traditional patterns of social organization in Pajapan. We now turn to a more detailed analysis of Gulf Nahua social and demographic history spanning the century.

The Pre-cattle era (1830–1940)

With the exception of the 1920s, the period extending from 1860 to 1940 witnessed a gradual concentration of natives of the San Martín area in the village of Pajapan (see Table 6.4).[21] By the end of the 1930s,

Table 6.1 Net population losses, (%) by cohort, municipal Pajapan, 1900–40

Cohort aging from	1900–30	Cohort aging from	1930s
0–4 to 30–34	-61.9	0–4 to 10–14	-34.5
5–9 to 35–39	-53.9	5–9 to 15–19	-57.3
10–14 to 40–44	-56.4	10–14 to 20–24	-24.2
15–19 to 45–49	-55.6	15–19 to 25–29	2.9
20–29 to 50–59	-66.3	20–29 to 30–39	-32.4
30+ to 60+	-83.3	30–39 to 40–49	-61.6
		40–49 to 50–59	-50.5
		50–59 to 60–69	-58.6
		60+ to 70+	166.0
Total	-65.1		-38.3

Note: Out-migration and mortality statistics are not available for municipal Pajapan. This makes it impossible to measure each factor separately. This table, however, gives us a partial view of population losses per cohort, i.e., deficits incurred by each cohort from one census to another due to both mortality and out-migration factors.

Table 6.2 Household size and marital status by sex, municipal Pajapan, 1831–1940 (row %)

	Hld size	% Married			% Single			% Widowed[a]		
		Men	Women	Total	Men	Women	Total	Men	Women	Total
1831		90.8	62.8	74.2	6.1	10.6	8.8	3.1	26.6	17.0
1900	4.03	64.8	51.2	57.2	26.0	31.5	29.1	9.2	17.3	13.7
1930		79.1	68.7	73.5	16.2	15.1	15.6	4.7	16.2	10.9
1940	4.05	79.1	69.7	74.1	18.3	18.4	18.4	2.5	11.9	7.5

[a] The term "widow" is often used in Pajapan to denote a woman 'abandoned' by her husband.

the village represented 65% of the total municipality. From a population of 2,474 in 1900, the municipality grew by 24% over the first two decades of this century and by another 22% during the 1920s, following the Mexican Revolution. During these three decades, Nahua villages suffered moderate population losses to neighboring cities such as Coatzacoalcos. Local population losses were due mostly to epidemics, low standards of living and death by natural causes. The economic crisis of 1907, the Mexican Revolution and the collapse of the trans-isthmic railway following

Table 6.3 Rates of population growth, 1930–90

	Coatzacoalcos		Veracruz	Municipal Pajapan		Pajapan village	
	Pop.	Increase (%)	Increase (%)	Pop.	Increase (%)	Pop.	Increase (%)
1930	12,271			3,741		2,307	
1940	21,816	77.8		3,554	-5.0	2,299	-0.3
1950	28,347	29.9	26.0	5,540	55.9		
1960	53,148	87.5	33.7	5,714	3.1		23.7
1970	109,588	106.2	39.8	6,364	11.4	2,844	45.5
1980	186,129	69.8	33.9	8,548	34.3	3,701	30.1
1990	232,314	24.8	14.7	11,432	33.7	5,384	45.5

the opening of the Panama Canal in 1914 acted as major obstacles to the economic and demographic expansion of Coatzacoalcos and southeastern Veracruz. These barriers to growth protected municipal Pajapan from the usual effects of large-scale urbanization, industrialization and the market economy.

But the process of urban growth was soon to mark all future developments in southern Veracruz. In 1900 the urban population of Coatzacoalcos (4,487) was less than twice the size of Pajapan; the proportion of Mexicans living in the countryside was still very high. Coatzacoalcos, however, increased by 35% between 1900 and 1920 and by as much as 61% and 78% during the 1920s and the 1930s, respectively.[22] From 1930 to 1940, Pajapan lost about 5% of its municipal population (see Tables 6.1 and 6.3). Of those living in Pajapan in 1930, only 62% remained in 1940 – a result of death or out-migration.

The urbanization process created a tendency for young Nahua men (aged 15 to 24) to leave the municipality. Demographic shifts due to this young male out-migration phenomenon can be inferred from sex distribution statistics available for Pajapan. The 1900 census registers an equal proportion of males and females (see Table 6.9).[23] The sex ratio, however, varies from one age-group to another. As in later censuses, more males are born in Pajapan than females and men live longer than women. In spite of this, there is a higher proportion of females between 15 and 24, probably because of young men leaving the village in search of wage earnings outside the rural municipality. During the 1930s, a period of economic depression followed by urban growth, the young male out-migration took on larger proportions: 57% of those aged five to nine in 1930 were no longer residing in the municipality ten years later.

The young rural male out-migration phenomenon resulted in a lower fertility rate and an aging population.[24] The "local fertility rate" (the number of children between zero and four divided by the number of women between 15 and 45) actually fell from 0.95 in 1900 to 0.85 in

Table 6.4 Municipal population distribution, 1920–90 (%)

	Pajapan village	Minzapan	San Juan	Hamlets
1920	69.9	9.0	13.7	7.4
1930	61.7	18.1	11.0	9.2
1940	64.7			
1960	50.4			
1970	44.7	15.0	13.3	27.0
1980	43.3	17.6	13.3	25.8
1990	47.1	13.6	12.4	26.9

Table 6.5 Local fertility rate, municipal Pajapan, 1900–90, number of children between 0 and 5 by number of women between 15 and 45

1900	1930	1940	1950	1960	1970	1980	1990
0.95	0.85	0.66	0.73	0.92	0.98	0.87	0.78

1930. Pajapeños below the age of 20 dropped from 60 to 56% during this period.[25] The decade that followed exacerbated these trends. By the end of the 1930s the local fertility rate had fallen to an all-time low of 0.66. Children between zero and four appear to have been the hardest hit by the depression. Their numbers declined by 24% over the decade. By 1940, they comprised only 15.3% of the total population, 3.7% less than in 1930 (see Table 6.7). This downward trend may have resulted from a higher incidence of infant mortality, a declining fertility rate in the second half of the 1930s, or a greater number of young couples migrating to the city (the absolute number of Pajapeños aged 15 to 19 fell by 7.7%).

The cattle and oil era (1940–80)

The second half of the 20th century brought about profound transformations in Gulf Nahua economy and society. By and large, this was a period of rapid urban and industrial growth in the south of Veracruz, trends that stimulated the expansion of the cattle industry (centered in Acayucan and Minatitlán) and the concentration of land in the hands of Indian and non-resident mestizo ranchers, all at the expense of the Gulf Nahuas. Peasants, especially the younger men, were forced out of the village of Pajapan, moving either into the city or to remote corners of the municipality in search of land.

In-migration is negligible in the municipality of Pajapan and virtually non-existent in the communal area.[26] Important movements within the

Table 6.6 Fertility rates in municipal Pajapan, 1960–90

	Ratio mothers/women				Average children			
	1960	1970	1980	1990	1960	1970	1980	1990
15–19	37.2	31.5	27.1	31.5	1.32	1.58	1.62	1.44
20–24	72.0	76.3	74.0	78.1	2.40	3.02	2.53	2.45
25–29	80.7	84.3	83.2	91.4	3.97	4.71	3.94	3.75
30–34	85.8	94.4	85.7	88.1	5.01	6.08	5.32	4.73
35–39	87.5	92.9	89.4	96.6	4.89	7.39	6.55	5.80
40–49	80.4	89.1	85.3	94.3	4.95	7.99	7.02	6.66
50+	74.2	79.7	82.8	93.8	4.90	7.60	6.15	6.60
Total	71.1	74.9	71.1	79.1	3.93	5.57	4.80	4.74

Table 6.7 Age distribution, municipal Pajapan (% of total population, 1900–90)

	1900	1930	1940	1950	1960	1970	1980	1990
0–4	19.3	19.0	15.3	16.2	19.4	19.4	17.4	16.1
5–19	40.6	37.0	39.6	40.8	39.8	40.2	40.9	42.6
20–59	37.3	41.4	42.8	39.4	37.7	36.4	37.0	37.0
60+	2.8	2.6	2.3	3.6	3.1	4.0	4.7	4.3

municipality, however, have taken place in recent decades. From the 1870s until the 1940s, the village of Pajapan comprised between 60 and 70% of the municipal population. Prior to the 1950s and the development of the cattle industry in the area, few Pajapeños (less than 10%) lived outside of Minzapan, San Juan and the village of Pajapan. Since then, however, Pajapan has been declining in size compared to other settlements located within the municipality. Landless peasants have either gone to the city or moved to remote settlements of the *municipio*. The village of Pajapan accounted for 44% of the municipal population in 1980. The proportion was 7% higher in 1960. By contrast, the smaller hamlets and ranches scattered around the three major settlements have increased in number (from less than five in 1930 to about 15 in 1980) as well as in size (see Table 6.4).[27]

Net migratory losses and low rates of growth suffered by the people of Pajapan have been partly compensated for by a reduction in infant mortality (Revel-Mouroz 1980: 72), hence a shift toward a higher birth rate and a younger population. The rate and value of marriage and the average household size have none the less fallen over the years, indicating the impact of the market economy on local kin relations. Family life has

Table 6.8 Net population losses, municipal Pajapan, % by cohort, 1940–90

Cohort aging from	1940s	1950s	1960s	1970s	1980s
0–4 to 10–14	42.6	-18.3	-26.1	-9.2	11.0
5–9 to 15–19	-13.7	-45.8	-42.0	-21.5	-12.6
10–14 to 20–24	16.0	-36.6	-23.0	-14.2	-12.8
15–19 to 25–29	63.9	-21.7	-7.2	2.8	-10.0
20–29 to 30–39	-12.8	-36.7	-35.4	-13.4	-10.3
30–39 to 40–49	-25.9	-38.3	-31.3	-4.0	- 9.1
40–49 to 50–59	-12.2	-38.7	-26.5	-18.8	-23.9
50–59 to 60–69	10.9	-49.1	-32.6	-16.6	-20.1
60+ to 70+	0.0	-69.1	-47.5	-23.8	-49.4
Total	4.6	-35.7	-30.0	-12.6	-10.4

Table 6.9 Sex ratio, municipal Pajapan, male%–female%, 1900–90

	1900	1930	1940	1950	1960	1970	1980	1990
0–14	4.1	0.77	2.11	2.08	1.58	4.97	0.53	1.05
15–24	-3.68	-3.31	-0.28	-2.11	-1.44	-0.53	-0.34	0.20
25–39	0.28	1.87	-0.68	0.09	-0.72	-0.39	0.11	-0.67
40+	-0.97	0.37	-0.31	1.03	0.96	0.96	1.49	0.80
Total	0.44	-0.30	1.46	1.08	0.38	5.00	1.78	1.40

been severely affected by a propensity for young men to move out of the municipality and for men and women to rely less on each other and the subsistence economy to provide for their livelihood.

Although accurate, the general trends summarized above do not reflect important fluctuations that marked particular decades, such as the 1940s and the 1970s. As pointed out by Revel-Mouroz (1980: 72, 74f.), the colonization of southern Veracruz has not been a continuous process: rather it has alternated between periods of rapid expansion and years of stagnation or slower growth. The latter fostered a return to the land and to peasant strategies of survival. Even though foreign oil companies were nationalized in 1938, the oil boom and rapid expansion of cities such as Coatzacoalcos and Minatitlán did not occur until the late 1940s and early 1950s. Statistics available for the 1940s actually show a much lower rate of population growth for Coatzacoalcos compared to municipal Pajapan. Similarly, the 1970s show a declining rate of urban expansion and the corresponding shift in Pajapan statistics, toward a higher rate of population growth combined with an aging population and falling birth

Table 6.10 Household size and marital status by sex, municipal Pajapan, 1940–90, (row %)

	Hld size	% Married			% Single			% Widowed		
		Men	Women	Total	Men	Women	Total	Men	Women	Total
1940	4.05	79.1	69.7	74.1	18.3	18.4	18.4	2.5	11.9	7.5
1950	5.49	71.3	68.6	69.9	24.9	19.3	22.0	3.8	12.1	8.1
1960	5.05	64.3	67.4	65.9	31.7	24.6	28.2	4.0	8.0	5.9
1970	4.82	–	–	–	–	–	–	–	–	–
1980	4.86	61.7	67.2	64.4	35.4	24.6	30.2	2.9	8.2	5.4
1990	4.94	57.8	61.2	59.5	39.5	29.8	34.7	2.7	9.0	5.8

rates (possibly due to the introduction of family planning). As shown below, the average household size and the ratio of men to women aged above 24 tend to increase in periods of rural expansion (1940s, 1970s) and decrease in times of rapid urban growth (1950–70).[28]

The demographic history of Pajapan has been directly conditioned by fluctuations in the regional economy: on the whole, urban gains result in lower rates of rural expansion. During the 1930s Pajapan's population deficit was a contribution to urban growth in Coatzacoalcos, a city whose net migratory gains for the period were as high as 44%. This trend was completely reversed in the 1940s. From a 78% increase in the 1930s, Coatzacoalcos grew by 30% in the 1940s, the lowest rate since the Mexican Revolution; its net migratory gains fell to 4%. By contrast, municipal Pajapan increased by 56%, the highest rate recorded in this century (see Table 6.3). Table 6.8 suggests that many of those who had left the municipality in the 1930s, especially the younger families, came back to Pajapan in the 1940s; by the end of the decade, the population born prior to 1940 and living in Pajapan had actually increased by 4.6%.[29] The age profile of Pajapeños shifted accordingly, toward a higher birth rate, a younger population and larger households (up to 5.5 per dwelling in 1950).[30] Given the greater importance granted to family farming activities, the cost of marriage rose moderately, from the equivalent of 80 days'-worth of wage-labor in 1938 to 200 person-days ten years later.

The 1950s and the 1960s saw further expansion of the urban petrochemical complex of Minatitlán and Coatzacoalcos, the development of the cattle industry and the concentration of land in communal Pajapan. Coatzacoalcos thus resumed its expansion and grew by as much as 286% from 1950 to 1970 (with net migratory gains of 11,237 in the 1950s only). Meanwhile, the population of municipal Pajapan increased by only 15% and suffered enormous cohort deficits. While the birth rate continued to increase, the household size actually shifted in the opposite direction, decreasing to five in 1960 and 4.8 in later censuses. The Gulf

Table 6.11 Value of corn, Pajapan village, labor and marriage, 1940–91

Year	F% - M% 15–24	Married %	Corn kilo $	Daily wage $	Brideprice $	In P-D
1940	+0.28	74.1	–	–	–	–
1946	–	–	0.15	0.40	40	100
1948	–	–	0.20	0.50	100	200
1950	+2.11	69.9	–	–	–	–
1951	–	–	0.40	0.50	500	1,000
1954	–	–	0.30	0.50	400	800
1956	–	–	0.40	0.90	400	444
1958	–	–	0.40	1.50	300	200
1960	+1.44	65.9	–	–	–	–
1963	–	–	0.25	6	400	67
1966	–	–	0.35	10	300	30
1968	–	–	0.40	7	350	50
1970	+0.53	–	–	–	–	–
1971	–	–	–	30	7,000	233
1973	–	–	–	60	7,000	116
1975	–	–	25	85	6,000	70
1978	–	–	18	300	12,000	40
1980	+0.34	64.5	–	–	–	–
1982	–	–	30	300	20,000	67
1984	–	–	40	500	20,000	40
1986	-1.13	68.0	90	1,000	50,000	50
1991	–	–	–	10,000	1,000,000	100

Note: Values given in unadjusted pesos. P-D = person-days.

Nahuas reverted to smaller household units as in the early decades of this century (see Table 6.10). The fact that families became larger while households became smaller suggests better living conditions but also a fragmentation of kin relations, as a result of male migration and the greater autonomy of men and women engaged in the market economy.

The 1970s witnessed yet another shift: while the rate of growth rose to 34% in Pajapan, it fell to 70% in Coatzacoalcos.[31] As a result, rates of mortality and out-migration have decreased considerably in Pajapan since 1970. In fact, in the 1970s, the trend reverts to an aging population and a lower birth rate, as in the 1930s. All indications point to Pajapan following lower fertility trends observed in Veracruz and Mexico.[32]

Further evidence of a social fragmentation process marking the second half of this century can be inferred from the statistical distribution of married, unmarried and widowed adults registered from 1940 onwards. Table 6.10 shows that the proportion of married people has steadily declined since 1940 (though at a decreasing rate). Men are largely responsible for this change in marital patterns: from 1940 to 1980 the percentage of single men has nearly doubled. Unmarried adults comprised one-third and one-fourth of the men and the women residing in Pajapan

in 1980, respectively. Celibacy is none the less a typically female phenomenon: there has always been at least twice as many "widows" (husband
dead or simply gone) in Pajapan as "widowers", a pattern reflecting the
greater size of the female population aged 15 to 39 compared to men.

This declining marriage rate corresponded to a devaluation of the
household economy based on the sexual division of labor, a long-term
tendency that was bound to bring the brideprice down (measured in
wage earnings). At first, greater involvement in the market economy
(urban wage-labor, ranching, simple commodity production, petty trade)
and the rise of class inequalities within the Gulf Nahua population
resulted in marriage costs peaking in the early 1950s (see Table 6.11).
From 1951 and 1966, however, the price of marriage fell by as much as
97%; the corresponding figure for the 1970s is 83%. Excluding a few
exceptional years,[33] the period from 1950 to 1978 can be characterized
by rural depopulation and urban proletarianization, the forced exodus of
peasants from their native land, and a devaluation of agricultural commodities relative to wage-labor.

Pajapan society in the 1980s

Pajapan's population growth (and other demographic shifts) throughout
the 1970s resulted not so much from positive changes that could have
occurred in the countryside (e.g., ranchers losing their monopoly over
land) as from the slackening of industrial activity and the rise in unemployment in Coatzacoalcos and Minatitlán. The decade that followed
began with a major economic and fiscal crisis that forced the government
of Mexico to abandon its mega-industrial port project planned for the
Pajapan area. For the Gulf Nahuas, however, the crisis became a blessing
in disguise. The community obtained a major reform that allowed peasants
to reappropriate the communal lands controlled by the rancher class. To
these concessions were added major improvements in Pajapan's educational and health services subsidized by the federal state.

By and large, changes in the local economy that resulted from these
events reinforced the socio-demographic trends already observed in the
1970s. From 1980 to 1990, the municipal population increased by another
34% (compared to 14.7% for the whole of Veracruz), as in the previous
decade. The village of Pajapan is largely responsible for this growth.
Census data suggest that the population residing in the village increased
by as much as 45.5% from 1980 (3,701 inhabitants) to 1990 (5,384),
hence during the economic crisis and land reform implemented by the
government. For the first time since 1940, the size of communal Pajapan
relative to other settlements located within the municipality increased,
from 43.3 to 47.1%.

The local fertility rate continued to fall and reached 0.78 in 1990 (see
Table 6.5). As in the 1970s, the population is aging: the overall proportion
of young children aged below five has further declined, from 17.4% in
1980 to 16.1% in 1990 (see Table 6.7).[34] The ratio of males to females
aged below 24 is once again on the increase (see Table 6.9), a tendency

suggesting declining rates of out-migration. During the 1980s, young men between 15 and 24 stayed in the village in greater numbers than at any other time during the 20th century. Men of this age group now outnumber females, a fact that clearly reflects the effects of the land reform and urban unemployment on young Nahua men's migratory behavior.

Recent years have seen a shift in the local economy, back to a subsistence and simple commodity strategy and corresponding investments in household and village solidarities. The redistribution of land and the integration of a greater number of young males in local productive activities have boosted the domestic economy based on marriage and the sexual division of labor. The land reform has resulted in the proliferation of small ranching units, hence the broadening of a local cash economy involving a greater number of peasant families investing their savings in a few head of cattle.[35] Despite the economic crisis prevailing at national levels, more money is thus available within the village to cover wedding expenses; adults are still marrying in fewer numbers, but they are investing more of their personal wealth in weddings.

Household structure and family cycle

Relations between genders, generations, blood relatives and affines have changed greatly over time. Customary rules of social hierarchy and exchange have suffered the impact of a market economy and a class society. As already shown, the transformations affecting family relations touch all aspects of native life: where individuals live and with whom, their chances of marrying and under what conditions, how many children they have, what they inherit, their life expectancy, and so on.

Having said this, Gulf Nahua kinship continues to play a crucial role in the livelihood of present-day Pajapeños. The domestic economy based on native patterns of organization constitutes a central ingredient of Pajapan society. Thus we have shown how household units conform to rules of marriage, residence and descent that are specifically Nahua. These rules, however, are not static. They are open to variations that point to a central aspect of the domestic economy: its internal dynamics. Although sharing common features, native households change over time. Families display important variations in size, sexual composition and age, differences that result from the idiosyncrasies of each family trajectory but also from the process of aging and the life cycle built into Gulf Nahua society. The analyses that follow offer a detailed account of current household dynamics involving cyclical changes in productive and repro-ductive activities, changes affecting and affected by class relations and the market economy. Three issues shall be addressed: (a) differences in household structure based on the age cycle and family composition (nuclear family, single-parent households, etc.); (b) the impact of these household variations on levels of agricultural productivity; and (c) the relationship between household organization and class position.

To capture the internal dynamics of the domestic economy, careful

Table 6.12 Household typology and profile, Pajapan village, 1986

	Hld %	Father av. age	Mother av. age	Children < 20	Adult dependents	Size
Nuclear	66.0	37.6	31.2	3.10	–	5.12
Nuclear + adult	13.0	49.2	41.9	3.64	1.43	7.07
Husband + wife	7.8	36.9	29.8	–	–	2.00
Single mother	3.4	–	39.5	2.60	–	3.60
Single father	2.2	42.5	–	0.69	–	1.69
Mother + adult	2.0	–	38.8	2.17	1.08	4.25
Father + adult	5.6	26.1	–	0.57	1.21	2.78

attention must be paid to variations in household formations. In order to do this, two simple questions must be asked: who lives under the same roof, and at what stage of the family cycle are they? Consider first the prevailing patterns of household composition, starting with the most typical unit, the nuclear family (see Table 6.12).

Nuclear households Two-thirds of all households in Pajapan consist of simple nuclear families, i.e., two parents and at least one child below 20, with an average of 3.1 children residing in the same house. This is in keeping with both native and non-native norms of household residence (nuclear, neolocal). Other domestic units described below are either larger or smaller. As we shall see, many of these anomalous households approximate the nuclear family composition (or an extended version thereof) while also following the customary rule of patrilocality. Other household formations are the product of changes in family structure caused by a subsistence economy in decline.

Nuclear households with adult dependent(s). About 13% of all households are formed by couples sharing the same roof with at least one dependent adult (married or above 19). This is the largest and the oldest household on average. Half the dependents are sons, usually unmarried and in their early twenties. The other half comprise young daughters, mothers and sons' wives. Most of these extended nuclear households conform to the native rule of patrilocality.

Couples living alone. Couples living alone, about 7.8% of all households, are much younger or older than the average; they are at the beginning or at the end of the normal family life cycle. A majority of these neolocal couples are below 30 (60% of the spouses); while there is a higher proportion of women below 20, men are usually in their twenties. As expected, elderly couples are overrepresented in this category.

Single-parent families, without adult dependents. Single mothers and fathers living without adult dependents are older and have fewer children than nuclear household parents. Single female household heads are greater in

Table 6.13 Household cycle typology, Pajapan village, 1986

Husband	Wife	N	%	Nucl. hlds	%	Av. ch. (A)	Ch.+ dpdts	Av. size (B)	Ratio[a] (B-A)/B
15–20s	14–19	50	8.4	23	5.9	0.68	1.18	2.90	0.77
20s	20s	131	22.1	95	24.3	1.77	2.07	3.93	0.55
30–50	20s	94	15.9	83	21.2	2.77	2.84	4.84	0.43
30s	30s	93	15.7	59	15.1	3.65	3.85	5.60	0.35
40–60	30s	71	12.0	57	14.6	3.83	3.97	5.97	0.35
40–60	40s	77	13.0	44	11.2	3.57	3.77	5.63	0.36
50+	40+	76	12.8	30	7.7	2.35	2.47	4.33	0.46

[a] = Ratio of adults to dependent children.

number than their male counterparts; they also have four times as many children. Their age is 8.3 years above the average reported for nuclear household women (4.9 years in the case of men); only one single mother is less than 30 years of age. Although few in numbers (5.6%), single-parent households point to the fragmentation of kin relations and the vulnerability of women *vis-à-vis* the market economy.

Single-parent families, with adult dependents (7.6%). By contrast, most of the single parents cohabiting with an adult dependent are men in their twenties or younger, with few children on average. Their dependents include a number of younger siblings aged 19 and less and an even greater number of women who are single or widowed: i.e., mothers and a few sisters and daughters, all of whom provide domestic assistance to the single men who support them.[36]

Patterns of household composition observed in neighboring communities are remarkably similar. Nuclear families (including young couples temporarily without children) represent the norm: i.e., 79% in Pajapan, 75% in Peña Hermosa, and 69% in Soteapan (Stuart 1978: 32; Baez-Jorge 1973: 177). Women typically look after their young children when separated from their husbands, and men typically look after their parents when in need. Uxorilocal households (men living with their parents-in-law) are the exception.[37]

Households can also be classified according to age, using the family cycle criterion. Table 6.13 describes the distribution and composition of households headed by parents of different age-groups; the typology takes the age of both parents into account. Figure 6 shows the relationship between the age of parents, household size and the average number of children of different ages. As should be expected, household size and the proportion of children to adults increase from youngest couples to middle-aged families (H40–50 & W30, husbands in their forties and fifties married to women in their thirties) and then gradually decline.[38]

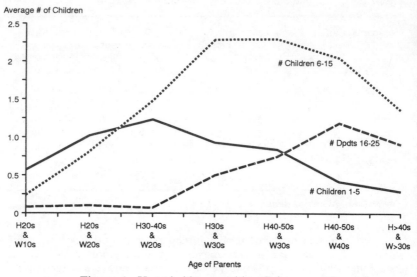

Figure 6 Household composition, Pajapan, 1986

Although static, typologies based on household composition and family cycle can be used to achieve a better understanding of the internal dynamics of the domestic economy. As argued below, levels of productivity, occupational strategies and class positions are partly conditioned by non-market factors such as household structure. But first a few observations should be made with regard to the age differential observed between husbands and wives in Pajapan and built into our household cycle typology. Married women tend to be younger than married men (see Table 6.14). The average age difference between a husband and wife is about 6.69 years. Of 514 couples appearing in our 1986 survey, 92.4% comprise older men and younger wives (minimum one year difference). Moreover, the older the male cohort is, the greater the average difference.

Several factors account for this age differential between spouses. First, women marry at a younger age than men; while girls may marry as soon as they can reproduce, men can start a family only when ready to produce, i.e., when given access to land or an opportunity to work for money. Second, men live longer and many of them leave the village before they reach the age of 30; as a result, Pajapeños in search of wives tend to be older than Pajapeñas in search of husbands. Third, older men tend to be wealthier than young men and can offer more material security to young women in the prime of their productive and reproductive years. Where marriage is concerned, older women and younger men are clearly at a disadvantage *vis-à-vis* other marriageable adults (see the single parents' age profile). Four, the widespread practice of polygyny favoring older and wealthier men limits the number of women available to young male peasants, forcing many of them to marry at an older age. Finally,

Table 6.14 Couples' age differential, Pajapan village, 1986

Age	Couples	Average difference
15–19	5	1.6
20–24	44	2.5
25–29	99	3.8
30–34	64	4.5
35–39	86	5.6
40–44	55	6.3
45–49	52	8.7
50–54	31	8.2
55–59	25	9.6
60–64	15	15.7
65–69	19	16.6
70–74	8	19.0
75+	7	21.9
Total	510	6.7

marriages between older men and younger women are congruent with the Gulf Nahua propensity to grant more authority to men and the old compared to women and the young (see Taggart 1983: 26).

Family production and class position

The relationship between class and household profile shows partiality against women (especially single mothers), the young in general and the very old. Composite households (nuclear family + adult dependents) are formed mostly where there is wealth to be shared, hence amongst the wealthy. These tendencies point to a domestic economy governed by native divisions of gender and generation, patrimonial disparities that are affected by an expanding market economy but that cannot be reduced to mere effects of broader domains.

Table 6.15 describes variations in household age profile by sectoral **occupation** and class position. Briefly, cattle ranching families are the oldest in Pajapan, while those engaged in wage-labor (and fishing) are the youngest. On the average, simple commodity producers (small farmers, craft workers) are older compared to families involved in small-scale commerce. The available data indicate that enlarged nuclear households are more often engaged in commercial or cattle ranching activities than all other family units; simple nuclear families, in wage-labor and subsistence production (especially when wives are young). Finally, single mothers are overrepresented in petty trade.

The household age variable also influences the actual distribution of communal land. In the 1970s, the **amount of land** owned or occupied

Table 6.15 Household age and class structure, Pajapan village, 1986. Column % (where overrepresentation only)

Husband	Wife	Ranchers	SCP	Subs.	Commerce	Wage-Labor Farm	Subs.	% Total
1. 15–20s	14–19						14.3	8.4
2. 20s	20s							22.1
3. 30–50	20s				19.5	26.2	31.6	15.9
4. 30s	30s	25.0			24.7			15.7
5. 40–60	30s	17.9	16.7					12.0
6. 40–60	40s	25.0		18.6				13.0
7. 50+	40+	17.9	20.0	23.2	20.8			12.9
Av. household age		5.0	4.8	4.7	4.2	3.9	3.2	

Table 6.16 Land distribution by household age, Pajapan village, 1986

Husband	Wife	Comuneros %	Ha. in 1970s	Soil quality	Upland %
1.	15–20s	14–19	36.0	1.59	2.18	50.0
2.	20s	20s	33.6	2.84	1.77	37.5
3.	30–50	20s	58.5	3.94	1.76	40.4
4.	30s	30s	66.7	5.77	1.82	34.6
5.	40–60	30s	78.9	7.54	1.83	36.2
6.	40–60	40s	77.9	16.00	1.90	37.2
7.	50+	40+	59.0	14.36	1.97	18.4

in Pajapan increased with age. In the 1980s, the percentage of landholding *comuneros* again correlates with the family age factor. The oldest couples are an exception in that they were and continue to be disadvantaged in this respect compared to middle-aged units (men between 40 and 60). As might be expected, only one of every four households headed by single mothers holds a *comunero* status. Our survey findings suggest that the youngest have the poorest soil-quality ratings and the highest proportion of plots situated near the volcano. As for other household age groups, average soil quality (self-rated from 1 to 3) decreases with age. Single-parent families (especially single mothers) have the poorest land, on average.

Tables 6.17 and 6.18 describe the relationship between **cattle ranching** and the household age factor. The first table shows that ranchers are generally older than those who own no cattle. While those with less than 25 head (97% of all cattle-owning households) get older as their herd increases, the average age of wealthier ranchers declines with ranch size. The second table demonstrates again that the older the family is, the

Table 6.17 Ranch size by rancher's/household age, Pajapan village, 1986

Herd	Hlds	Rancher's age	Household age[a]
No cattle	414	34.9	3.65
0–4	57	39.5	4.07
5–9	47	40.8	4.79
10–24	54	43.8	4.93
25–49	8	38.4	4.43
50+	6	33.8	4.00

[a] The average household age is based on our household age classification (7 categories, see Table 6.18).

Table 6.18 Household age and ranch profile, Pajapan village, 1986

Husband	Wife	With cattle (%)	Herd	With rental costs (%)	Av. yearly rental costs	Av. yearly wage costs	Av. yearly sales
1.15–20s	14–19	20.8	9.3	20.0	3.20	2.50	47.43
2. 20s	20s	16.8	7.0	27.3	10.96	9.86	105.65
3.30–50	20s	23.4	11.1	27.3	16.10	51.84	209.29
4. 30s	30s	38.7	14.4	41.7	26.35	41.12	246.94
5.40–60	30s	35.2	11.6	28.0	7.71	21.46	144.67
6.40–60	40s	40.3	13.4	12.9	5.70	10.10	179.00
7. 50+	40+	43.4	9.1	21.2	10.12	0.33	86.07

Note: Costs and sales are in Mexican pesos (thousands)

greater the likelihood it will own some cattle. Ranch size, however, reaches its peak amongst middle-aged families. On the whole, couples in their thirties have the largest herd and the highest yearly costs (in labor and land rental) and sales on the average; the younger and the older households own and sell the least. About 57% of all enlarged nuclear households have cattle, by far the largest percentage for all households; they also have the highest average expenditures in wage-labor and pasture rental. Composite families thus tend to be formed amongst the wealthy.

Our 1986 survey statistics also show a strong connection between **corn production** and the household cycle. The older the couple is, the greater the likelihood the household will grow wet-season corn, the larger the *milpa* plot will be and the average harvest as well. The only predictable exception to this rule involves the last phase of the family cycle where there is a decline in production. Average production per hectare is at its highest with the third household category, i.e., men in their thirties or forties married to women in their twenties. Couples at opposite ends of the age spectrum have the lowest rates of productivity. The same

Table 6.19 Household age and corn production, Pajapan village, 1986

	Husband	Wife	Av. MT	Av. Ha.	MT/Ha.	Wet-season Corn %	Dry-season Corn %
1.	15–20s	14–19	0.717	0.547	1.311	74.0	10.0
2.	20s	20s	0.806	0.618	1.304	75.9	12.2
3.	30–50	20s	1.070	0.702	1.524	83.0	14.9
4.	30s	30s	1.086	0.793	1.369	69.9	16.1
5.	40–60	30s	1.276	0.904	1.412	85.9	15.5
6.	40–60	40s	1.317	0.953	1.382	84.4	22.1
7.	50+	40+	1.009	0.812	1.243	77.6	22.4

Table 6.20 Household age, fishing and trade, Pajapan village, 1986

	Husband	Wife	% Small businesses	Fruit Days/week	Petty trade Days/week	% Fishing Hlds
1.	15–20s	14–19	18.0	3.00	2.00	46.0
2.	20s	20s	19.8	3.37	3.33	61.1
3.	30–50	20s	17.0	–	5.00	52.1
4.	30s	30s	26.9	4.12	6.67	53.8
5.	40–60	30s	28.2	4.00	2.00	52.1
6.	40–60	40s	33.8	2.60	3.00	40.3
7.	50+	40+	32.9	2.83	3.60	30.3

bellshaped frequency distribution is observed for dry-season corn cultivation by household age.

Involvement in corn production is also conditioned by variations in household composition.[39] About 80% of all two-parent households, with or without children or adult dependents, cultivate wet-season maize, compared to 61% and 45% for single-father and single-mother households, respectively. Single parents cohabiting with an adult dependent fall in between. A similar pattern applies to *milpa* size and wet-season corn productivity. Two-parent households and single fathers have larger *milpas* (from two-thirds of an hectare to 1 ha.) and produce from 1.0 to 1.12 MT of corn on the average. By contrast, single mothers living alone or with an adult dependent produce no more than 0.5 and 0.62 MT, respectively; also they have the smallest *milpas* (0.36 to 0.44 ha.).[40]

The household cycle factor determines to some extent the family's involvement in fishing, small-scale commerce and trades. Excluding the youngest couples, the frequency of **fishing** tends to decline with family age (see Table 6.20). A third of the fishers in Pajapan are either very young or elderly women not fully employed in domestic work or in the care and feeding of children. The population of male fishers is mainly composed of boys and young men with the stamina and condition to cast nets and dive for commercially valuable clams and oysters. The technique used varies according to age. While near-shore fishing and the use of bows and arrows are typical of younger fishermen (average 29), fishing with hook and line tends to be practised by older men (average 38). Spear and net fishing entails greater costs (spear guns, nets, dugout canoes) and tends to be practised by average-aged fishers (i.e., 34) and their sons. Although women do not practise any of these techniques, they spend considerable time collecting oysters, clams or shrimps with a small circular net called a *matayahuale*; about 15% of all married women (usually aged below 40) do so.

Unlike fishing, the proportion of families engaged in **trades and petty trade** increases with household age (excluding the well-to-do, middle-aged cattle-merchants and taxi-owners). Although variations in cash income are not significant, weekly expenditures in merchandise and salaries tend to rise with age with the exception of the oldest families. By and large, carpenters, butchers and petty traders are the poorest and the youngest. Owners of bakeries, cantinas and small stores are older than cattle-merchants and taxi-owners who tend to be middle-aged and to rank among the wealthiest in the village. About half of all single mothers sell fruit or engage in some form of petty trade; they devote more time per week to this activity than other fruit vendors and petty traders.

Most adults engaged in **wage-labor** are young men. The younger a man is, the more likely he is to work in the construction and service sector, especially in the countryside (the most labor-intensive sector), as opposed to agriculture. It should be noted that ranch hands tend to be younger than peones working for peasants. Finally, single women who are household heads derive very few earnings from wage-labor; the opposite is true of enlarged nuclear households and single fathers living with an adult.

The tendency for middle-aged families to produce and own more than younger and older households seems to confirm the Chayanovian rule which says the smaller the working capacity of the household is, the more its members will work (see Sahlins 1972: 87–92, 110–21). Some of the data presented above show that the investment of labor in productive activities (e.g., corn cultivation) increases with the number of dependents within the household. But the analysis also points to other factors intervening in the domestic economy, factors that are not limited to the working potential of household members and the ratio of producers to consumers. These factors revolve around the unequal distribution of wealth (cattle and land) and the sectoral division of labor based on age and sex. As Sahlins notes (1972: 87, 93, 110), the Chayanovian model applies to households that have access to land, that produce most of what they consume (and consume most of what they produce), and that are unimpeded by the larger structures of society. These conditions are no longer characteristic of the San Martín area. The Gulf Nahua economy is now governed by class differences that directly affect relations of production and property between genders and generations, to the detriment of women, the young and the old.

Schooling and the civil–religious hierarchy

Class divisions and conflicts over land and office in Pajapan are partly attenuated by real and fictive (*compadrazgo*) kinship ties that bind the wealthy to the poor, the powerful to the powerless. The *mayordomia* system so typical of Mesoamerican villages is also operative in Pajapan, permitting the ritual sharing of wealth amongst villagers. The levelling effects of the religious *cargo* system, however, is more apparent than real. In 1986, the residents of Pajapan celebrated 27 religious events, half of which were financed by peasants, not ranchers. Compared to peasant-sponsored *fiestas*, rancher-sponsored events cost slightly more on average (US$475 vs $ 325).[41] The total money spent by all *cargo* holders, however, added up to US$4,071 only. This is the equivalent of 33 head of cattle, out of a total village herd of 7,000 and yearly sales of 3,000 animals.

A few words should be added concerning the impact of schooling and literacy on relations between genders and generations. Compared to wealth in land and cattle, literacy is a value that tends to be more evenly distributed amongst the Gulf Nahuas. According to the 1990 census, 50% of those residing in the municipality and aged above five are literate (compared to 10% in 1960) and 57% are going or have gone to primary school. The ability to count, read and write allows peasants to look after their own interests when engaging in market transactions and public activities such as elections and political representations to the press, the state government and the federal bureaucracy.

The benefits of literacy in Pajapan, however, should not be over-estimated. Only 20% and 9% above the age of 14 have completed their primary schooling and received post-primary education, respectively. In 1990, as many as 42% of those aged 6 to 14 were not attending school. Also with schooling come certain social and cultural costs. As elsewhere in rural Mexico, schools have been the agents of cultural assimilation for the Indian population, to the detriment of languages, views of the world and ways of life that pre-date the hispanic era. Given the importance of speaking Spanish and the pejorative associations of Indianness in Mexico, many adults in Pajapan make no effort to teach their children the native language and often forbid them to speak the dialect at home. As a result, only 5.3% of the municipal Pajapan population speaks Nahua only; 27% are unable to express themselves in the local dialect (or deny any knowledge of the dialect to census-takers).

Schooling has also contributed to a radical transformation of family relations in Pajapan. Like commodities, schooling is a personal asset with an exchange value that falls outside the control of families and household groups. Those who have received full primary school education have a much better chance of moving out of their village and making a living in the city, without having to count on a parent or a spouse to provide for their personal livelihood (as in the traditional domestic economy). Moreover, the few opportunities afforded by education have not been distributed equally. By and large, schooling has been made available to men and the young. Although the discrepancy is decreasing

Table 6.21 Literacy (%) by sex and age-group, municipal Pajapan, 1990

	15–9	20–4	25–9	30–4	35–9	40–4	45–9	50–4	55–9	60+	Total
Men	88.9	83.4	72.8	72.2	60.1	55.5	57.1	48.5	55.3	37.5	69.7
Women	66.1	52.0	35.1	23.8	15.4	9.4	8.7	6.9	2.5	1.3	33.3
M/W	1.3	1.6	2.1	3.0	3.9	5.9	6.6	7.0	22.1	28.8	2.1

over time, men are twice as likely to be literate as women; about two-thirds of those who have gone to high school are men (see Table 6.21). Also the younger the age-group, the higher the rate of literacy. As they constitute the least educated segment of Pajapan society, women above the age of 50 are the least bilingual of all groups: according to the 1990 census, 22% of them speak Nahua only, compared to 5.3% for the overall municipal population. In short, the unequal distribution of schooling and literacy has both undermined the authority vested in the elders and increased women's overall marginality within native society, confining them to a vulnerable household and village life stripped of its customary solidarities between genders and generations.

Conclusion

This completes our analysis of Pajapan's kinship system, its internal variations and dynamic interaction with broader economic conditions and fluctuations observed throughout this century. Relations instituted within and between native household formations are founded on divisions and struggles of gender and generation eluding the grasp of broader domains. In general, local patterns of domestic organization display cyclical dynamics that play a crucial role in the sphere of production. At the same time, the analysis shows the many ways in which patrimonial relations based on customary rules of residence, marriage and inheritance respond to differences in class position, thereby adjusting to the development of new power relations linked to an expanding market economy.

The patrimonial domain is a key ingredient and malleable component of native culture and history. On this question of native culture, readers should note that we have been careful to treat the Nahua dimension of life in Pajapan as a critical aspect of all social relations observed in the field, a dimension subject to important changes occurring over time. Culture has not been confined to a particular set of variables, a fixed sub-system of extant practices (language, religion, kinship) salvaged from the ravages of modern history. We have not equated the cultural with the symbolic or the discursive, as distinct from the practical or the material, the political or the economic. Unlike Moore (1988: 36) or Bourque and Warren (1981), we do not believe that ideological practices can be demarcated from other aspects of social life and then combined with political economy to produce a comprehensive view of society. However, this is not to say that symbolism expressed through discursive practices (narrative, ritual) is of little importance or cannot be treated as a distinct object of anthropological enquiry. As we are about to see, customary interactions between genders and generations and between human beings and their environment must be situated against the background of a much broader discourse: the Gulf Nahua views on relations and problems that govern all life forms dwelling in the universe.

Notes

1. According to Lockhart (1992: 174), the colonial Spanish *patrimonio* denoted either an inherited family estate in toto or an individual share of the estate, to be preserved by the owner but also disposed of according to his free will. In this book, we use the same term in a more general sense to denote a regime of property and authority vested in men.

2. Many features of Gulf Nahua social organization are also operative in Mazatec society: i.e., gerontocracy, patrilocality, male ultimogeniture, polygyny and the brideservice institution (Boege 1988: 38, 62, 64, 168, 173, 226).

3. See Antón (1973), Soustelle (1974), Nash (1980), Vaillant (1980), López Austin (1980), Krickeberg (1982), Morgan (1983) and Rodríguez-Shadow (1991).

4. Rothstein (1982) argues that pre-industrial gender relations in Mexico were egalitarian. Anthropologists who have emphasized gender equality in Aztec society include Meza (1975) and León-Portilla (1980). See Ródriguez-Shadow (1991).

5. See also Phillips (1990), Benería and Roldán (1987).

6. On the concept of reproductive relations and activities, see Harris and Young (1981), Benería and Sen (1982), Roberston and Berger (1986).

7. See García de León (1976: 134); Sandstrom (1991: 164ff). Terms used by a man or a woman to refer to his brother's wife (*nowehpol* or *notex* for a male speaker, *nowehpol* or *nowes* for a female speaker) are not entirely clear. In any case, these terms seem to be falling into disuse in Pajapan.

8. The same comment applies to the Nahuas of northern Veracruz (Sandstrom 1991: 159).

9. Field observations and interviews with Juana Martínez, Pajapan, May 14–17, 1991. See also García de León (1976: 130, 133); Law (1960: 94, 96, 119, 124, 162ff).

10. Similar patterns of patrilocal residence amongst other Nahua groups have been observed by Taggart (1983: 25) and Sandstrom (1991: 166f., 173, 179f.).

11. Interviews with Juana Martínez, Pajapan, May 14–17, 1991. See also Stuart (1978: 34); García de León (1976: 134); Martínez Morales (1983: 34, 40); Law (1960: 122–7, 138–9); González Cruz et al. (1983: 27–30, 57).

12. This figure is based on an exchange rate of 2,900 pesos per US$.

13. Interviews with women (anonymous) in Jicacal and Pajapan and with Juana Martínez, Pajapan, May 1991.

14. When asked if she is willing to "work" with a man, the girl will suggest that the matter be discussed with her father. The suitor will then break the news to his own father, and both of them will look for a *parcial*, an unrelated elderly man who will represent the young man and his family during meetings with the other party. The visits which the suitor, his father or representative will pay to the girl's family can last between three months and a year. The first proposal visits involve the suitor, his father or representative going to the house of the girl's parents, with alcohol (aguardiente, beer) and cigarettes. Traditionally the proposal took a rhetor-

ical form, evoking the suitor's desire to capture a white dove or flower in bloom seen in the man's house. At the end of the first meeting, the girl's father asks the visitors to come back in a week or two. Although some men consult their wives and daughters, it is not uncommon for the father's decision to be forced on the daughter. The father's decision is communicated to the other party at the second meeting, at which time parents of the young couple become *compadres*. The suitor's father and *parcial* must pay two other visits to the girl's father and provide him with the liquor needed to approach the man chosen to represent his family (usually the girl's godfather, her *-gojkol*) and also to invite close relatives to the official engagement ceremony.

The second phase starts with a list of requests that are presented by the girl's family via her representative. These include a money payment and all the foodstuffs and services needed to celebrate the wedding: one or two animals to be sacrificed, alcohol, musicians, etc. In the mid-1980s, the prevailing brideprice varied between US$30 and $80 (650 pesos per dollar); additional wedding expenses could add up to anywhere between $150 and $230. However, final decisions concerning the wedding are not made till the official engagement ceremony, which occurs several weeks after the fourth visit. The suitor, his party (parents, godparents, *parcial*), the girl and her immediate family, her godparents and relatives, all are present at the engagement ceremony held in the girl's house. The suitor's party is expected to bring gifts in kind to be shared with their hosts and also a *mesa de juramento*, a table serving as a marriage pledge or love-oath altar. Advice is given to the young couple sitting at the table by godparents and senior relatives of the bride. The suitor's *parcial* acts as the master of ceremony in charge of negotiating the brideprice and the official wedding date. Once an agreement is reached, the young man is free to visit his fiancée on a regular basis.

The wedding is normally held several months after the engagement. The wedding feast starts on Saturday morning, with a meal hosted by the groom's father. In the afternoon, the groom and his party proceed to the girl's house in the company of musicians and with all the gifts to be offered to the other party. Traditionally the groom was expected to stay at his father-in-law's house for the whole day and do errands for his in-laws. The official marriage, civil or religious, is performed the following morning. Each family hosts a separate feast; male guests assist their host by fetching wood while women do the cooking. At midday, the young man and his party proceed to the girl's house where the bride will once more be dressed by her godmothers. The couple sit again at the oath table and receive advice from the girl's grandparents. The bridegroom's *parcial* will eventually ask that his party be given the bride so that she can be "transferred" (*trasladar*) to her new family's house. The couple and relatives of the bridegroom return to the husband's parents' house with the bedding and cooking equipment received by the bride from her own parents. When in her father-in-law's house, the bride goes to the kitchen to help her mother-in-law prepare food. The feasting continues for another night while the marriage is consummated by the young couple. The following day the two fathers will ask the groom to confirm the girl's virginity. If not confirmed, the marriage may be annulled and compensation can be claimed by the husband's family for all the expenses incurred by the marriage, especially the money payment (see Garcia de León (1976: 133); Martínez Morales (1983: 8–18, 20–36); Law (1960: 121–5); González Cruz et al. (1983: 21–3, 33–9, 41–57); Interviews with Juana Martínez, Pajapan, May 14–17, 1991).

15. Field observations and interviews with Juana Martínez, Pajapan, May 14–17, 1991.

16. The ethnographic illustrations of the general points offered in this section are based on field observations, numerous informal discussions with men and

women (anonymous) in Jicacal and Pajapan, and interviews with Juana Martínez, Pajapan, May 14–17, 1991.

17. According to village gossip, a woman who had remarried decided to give away her 12-year-old daughter in marriage for fear that she become her husband's mistress; although well-intentioned, the mother's decision to marry her daughter at such a young age earned the woman considerable criticism from neighbors and relatives. Since the young bride had allegedly lost her virginity, her husband became an object of ridicule and eventually left both his wife and their new-born child. The young girl came back to her mother's house and became her stepfather's mistress, a situation that brought further reproach to both the girl's mother and her husband.

18. See Stuart (1978: 32–5); García de León (1976: 133); Martínez Morales (1983: 6); Martínez Morales et al. (1982: 16); Law (1960: 193–4).

19. There is little recorded information on the Nahuas of the San Martín highlands from the colonial era (1521–1821) up until the 1940s. We shall therefore concentrate on changes that occurred in recent decades, using census statistics and ethno-historical data collected in the field by ourselves and other anthropologists.

20. In one particular case, the so-called *gratificación* amounted to US$4,600 (1986 exchange rates), and not a peso was spent on wedding celebrations: the bride's father happened to be a member of a Protestant sect opposed to Catholic fiesta traditions. The man conveniently converted both his paternal authority and religious beliefs into sizeable cash earnings obtained through brideprice. Monetary considerations have led another man to arrange a marriage between his 16-year-old grandson and his younger wife's 9-year-old daughter (from a former marriage), thereby avoiding the costs of wedding celebrations and the brideprice altogether.

21. The people of San Francisco Minzapan, a village located on the plain near the Laguna del Ostión and ancestral village of Pajapan, formed a municipality in the 1820s and then gradually declined throughout the 19th century. Pajapan was established by mid-century and grew quickly, forming a separate municipality in the 1860s. Large numbers of residents of San Francisco Minzapan moved to Pajapan in 1869 and the early 1870s while others established the new Minzapan in its present location, a village eventually annexed to municipal Pajapan. By 1886 the village of Pajapan was double the size of Minzapan; its population went from 921 in 1886 to 2,138 in 1920 (eight times the size of Minzapan) and 2,307 in 1930. The respective population figures for Pajapan and Minzapan are 263 and 686 in 1869, 817 and 469 in 1870, 913 and 517 in 1873, 1,035 and 542 in 1878, 921 and 441 in 1886.

22. Rates of growth for the state of Veracruz and Mexico in the 1930s are 17.6% and 19%, respectively.

23. In 1831 the female population of Minzapan represented 60% of all municipal residents. It was mostly female children (244 vs 211) and also single women (20 vs 8) and widows (50 vs 4) that outnumbered their male counterparts. The proportion of widows over all adult women (26.6%) was particularly high. These observations probably reflected high rates of male out-migration and mortality, losses possibly caused by the establishment of new colonies in Coatzacoalcos (from 1828 to 1834) and the ravages of epidemics spreading during this period of southern Veracruz history. By 1870, the ratio of males to females had gone from 40 to 61%, a shift that may have resulted from large population movements involving a majority of male adults going from Minzapan to Pajapan.

24. The age profile of the native population of Minzapan and Pajapan remained relatively stable throughout the 19th century. About 59% of the Minzapan population described in the 1831 census were children (age limits undefined); in 1900 the proportion of natives below the age of 20 was virtually the same (59.9%).

25. When compared to all other cohorts, children aged up to four in 1900 have incurred the highest losses over these years (61.9%, cf. Table 6.1).

26. According to the 1990 census, less than 1% of all those living in municipal Pajapan were born elsewhere or were living elsewhere in 1985.

27. Most of the smaller settlements established within municipal Pajapan were founded between 1945 and 1975, usually by young landless peasants originating from the more densely populated communities such as Pajapan and San Juan Volador (and to a lesser extent Minzapan and Coscapa). Available data on age distribution show how young these hinterland populations are when compared to Pajapan (Stuart 1978: 31–2; Martínez Morales et al. 1982: 7).

28. Compared to their female counterparts, the proportion of males above 24 tends to increase in times of rural population expansion (1940s, 1970s). Those who enter the decade in their late teens while residing in Pajapan, young women mostly, are the most sedentary of all; they experience the lowest rate of attrition from one census to another. Children who are below 15 early in the decade suffer much higher losses, and those between five and nine are the most likely to migrate before the end of the decade.

29. The cohorts aged 10 to 14 and 15 to 19 in 1940, those in their twenties at the end of the decade, expanded by 16% and 64%, respectively. Their children (between 10 and 14 in 1950, parents minimally in their late twenties) also grew in number, from 542 to 773, representing a 42.6% increase over the decade. All other cohorts (except those above 50 in 1940) fell in size during this period but at a much slower rate in comparison with the 1930s. As in the 1930s, the middle-aged (30–39) and children aged five to nine suffered the highest losses.

30. The local fertility rate steadily rose from 0.66 in 1940 to 0.98 in 1970. In the 1960s the ratio of mothers to women went up from 71.1% to 74.9%, and the number of children per mother, from an average of 3.93 to 5.57. The zero to 19 age-group rose from 55% of the municipal population in 1940 to 59.6% in 1970 (see Tables 6.6, 6.7, 6.8).

31. By 1980, the municipality of Pajapan (306 km²) had a population density of 28 inh./km², which is quite low when compared to Coatzacoalcos (96 inh./km²). The population density is the same for Soteapan, a neighboring municipality where commercial coffee production and wage-labor prevail. The *municipio* of Mecayapan has a slightly lower population density (18 inh./km2) and a subsistence economy that is relatively more intact. Statistics indicate that 56% of all Veracruzanos live in villages of Pajapan's size or less, hence below 5,000 inhabitants; the corresponding figure for Mexico as a whole is 40%.

32. The 0–19 age-group grew by 30.8% in the 1970s compared to 36% for those between 20 and 59 and 56.6% for the elderly (above 59). Young children (zero to four) had the lowest rate of increase (19.5%) and their proportion has declined significantly, from 19.4% in 1970 to 16.1% in 1990 (compared to 13.6% for Veracruz as a whole; see Table 6.7). The 1980 census also shows that the number of children born per mother and the proportion of women who gave birth declined during the 1970s, inverting the trend observed in the 1960s (see Table 6.6). The percentage of women aged 15 to 19 who have had at least one child was smaller than in 1960.

33. This deflationary trend was interrupted in the late 1960s when the brideprice rose from 300 to 7,000 pesos in the span of three years. This period, ending in 1971, was marked by a relative shortage of young women coupled with high population growth in Coatzacoalcos and an urban boom similar to that of the early 1950s.

34. The corresponding figure for the state of Veracruz in 1980 is 13.6%.

35. In the 1980s the local economy also expanded under the impact of the wage-labor opportunities originally created by the industrial port project and the influx

of public subsidies and private indemnities granted by PEMEX and the federal government.

36. Mothers heading similar households have more children on the average and tend to be older; their overall profile is closer to the nuclear family norm. They cohabit with nuclear kinsmen (four sons, two fathers, one brother) more often than their male counterparts: half of them do so.

37. There is no single-mother household reported in Stuart's analysis; this reflects the pioneering nature and subsistence orientation of his peripheral Gulf Nahua population.

38. There are only a few anomalous husband/wife age combinations that do not fit in the typology (21 out of 592 cases). Single-parent households have been categorized according to the age of the parent actually residing with the children. These families are not evenly distributed among the household categories; by definition, they are excluded from those domestic units that show an age differential between husbands and wives (i.e., categories 3 and 5, both of which comprise two-parent families only). The first household type includes 14 single-parent families, the highest proportion observed for all household categories.

39. About half of the total land dedicated to crops other than corn and pasture (mostly beans, fruit trees and sweet potato) is cultivated by 35% of all households: i.e., units headed by couples in their twenties and, more importantly, middle-aged couples (men in their forties or fifties married to women in their forties). Although single-parent families (with or without adult dependents) comprise 13.2% of all households interviewed in 1986, they account for only 5.1% of the land (913 ha.) devoted to food plants other than maize.

40. Households that cultivate dry-season corn comprise mostly nuclear families living with or without an adult dependent. In comparison to simple nuclear households, however, enlarged units produce dry-season maize (*tapachole*) more frequently (28.6% vs 18.2%), on larger plots (0.85 ha. vs 0.78 ha.) and in greater quantity per unit (0.91 MT vs 0.58 MT) and per hectare (1.07 MT vs 0.75 MT).

41. Compared to peasant *mayordomías*, the rancher-sponsored *mayordomías* involved intra-communal "pilgrimages" of holy statues that gathered more church donations on average (US$15 vs $8). On the whole, the money gathered through local *peregrinaciones* is negligible.

CHAPTER 7

SEEDS, SEX AND THE AZTECS

The laws and tensions of the patrimonial domain touch all aspects of life in Pajapan. Native myths are no exception: they too wrestle with problems of authority, subsistence and reproduction affecting men and women, the old and the young. Actually Gulf Nahua myths deliberate two sets of questions simultaneously: interchanges between genders and generations, and the ways in which humans interact with the land and all other forms of life, including plants, animals and spirits of the natural world. Folk narratives ponder on the mutual dependencies and power struggles that pervade family life and the entire universe.

In this chapter, we illustrate the latter thesis through an in-depth analysis of a central Gulf Nahua myth: the story of the "corn-god-child" known as Sintiopiltsin. To the Gulf Nahuas, maize is not merely a staple food satisfying biological needs, a plant exploited by humans bent on harnessing nature to survive. Corn is not simply a "use-value" or a material commodity that may be exchanged for money. Rather, the maize plant is a godly figure that plays a crucial role in the Mesoamerican view of linkages between nature and culture and between humans themselves (Boege 1988: 31). The story of Sintiopiltsin's journey through life places humans within a web of life involving plant gods, animal spirits, and all other forces of nature. The narrative also extends to the universal problems of power, production and reproduction that form an integral part of the patrimonial domain. Through mythical discourse, the tensions and dynamics of a native political economy based on gender and age are transposed to a much broader system, the cosmos.

The story as told to García de León in 1967 is summarized below. To this summary we have added a transcription of the original Nahua narrative. We then proceed to a general discussion of how our semiotic excursion into native mythology links to other analyses developed throughout the book. Our close reading of the text is also preceded by an outline of the interpretative method chosen for this exercise. The chapter ends with a brief discussion of how folk tales respond to the social and ecological crises that plague modern native history.

Our Gulf Nahua reference myth revolves around the corn child's pilgrimage to the burial ground of his father and his quest for immortality. The story begins with an old man and his wife discovering two eggs in a *milpa*, eating one (the female) and preserving the other. A young boy is born from the egg and grows up to become *Sintiopiltsin*, the "venerable son of the corn god", also known as *Tamakastsin*, "the little priest",

Plate 1   Homshuk, Isla de Tenaspi, Lake Catemaco

Itamatiosinti, the "wise maize god", Homshuk in Soteapan (Blanco 1992), or San Isidro Labrador in the village of Zaragoza (García de León 1966, 1991: 35; see egg-shaped corn god monolith, Plate 1). One day the child goes to fetch water for his adoptive father and meets with a few iguanas who make fun of him and tell him where his real father is: in *Tagatau-atzaloyan*, the "land-where-men-are-dry". The boy eventually catches one animal by the tail but then lets his prey go. The child grows in age and decides one day to join some old men who undertake a journey to Oaxaca, toward the land of his father. Two incidents occur along the way to the boy's destination: ants eat the hero's flesh, and a rock swallows the boy. In each case the child is attacked while sleeping and is abandoned by the Pilgrim Fathers. He delivers and restores himself to life by catching one ant with his hair and by peeing on his own chest. He then arrives in the land of his father where he sees an old woman sleeping under a sapodilla heavy with fruit. The boy climbs up the tree and throws fruit at the woman. After climbing down from the tree the boy learns from his mother that his father has died. He decides to resurrect his father but warns his mother not to cry or hug her husband lest the old man turn into a wild animal. The mother fails to comply with this recom-mendation, and the story ends with the father transforming himself into a deer that flees into the forest.

The following text is the story transcribed by García de León (1976) in its original dialect.

Hi:n gihtoa yeh onoya se we:wehtsin wa:n ila:mahtsin. Pero até gipiaya ni se inpiloa:ntsitsin. Sente we:whetsin wa:n la:mahtsin. Pero gipiayah inmiltsin, yahah gitegipanoayah inmilpan, tamiáh. Un

día gitechóah o:me pioteksis, wehwe:y pioteksis. "Bieha, tiaweh
tikwiatih hi:n pioteksis. Tiaweh tapacholtitih topió iga matigitagan
te:yawi poniti." Y ke wa:lak ichan gitapacholtih ipió, se gipacholtihkeh
ipió wa:n se gimangeh giba:hkeh; ba:hkeh ho:n pioteksis wa:n
durante unos dias gipacholtihkeh pió. Bak gigák nemi-ya poni ho:n-
ya pioteksis se go:ne:tsin, se chogotsin; malmirarohkeh-ya la:mahtsin
wa:n we:wehtsin. "Karamba, tikpolohkeh tikba:hkeh se, sino anga
naseroayah el par, anga ho:n tago:tsin gatka. Pero en esto pues se
giba:hkeh-ya. Y mas agimatiáh te:gatka ho:n chogotsin, ho:n si:ntio-
piltsin gatka.
We:yak-ya, we:yaltih-ya chogotsin. We:wehtsin ginentiaya *milpan*,
gimaga magibiti a:ta:pan. Wa:n onok bagetspalimeh ompa, gipiniah-
tiahkeh, pinahtiayah chogotsin, gihliagih "elun, elun nagastanpepel,
ta:gatawatsaloyan ompa onok motah." Wa:laya ginotsaya chogotsin.
Pues agimatia la palabra ke gihgiáh, gihliáh-san "elun, elun nagastanpepel ta:gatawatsaloyan ompa onok motah."
Después gitahtagetskeh itah we:wehtsin. "Buelito, nepa esos
animales wi:tseh moburlaroah de neha; ne:chihliagih estas palabras.
Xine:chi:wili se nopi:chawan, nia nigintsonwiti wa:n se noma:megat."
"Hon nia nikchi:ati." We:wehtsin lo ke gichí:w al otro dia, gichi:wilih
chogotsin ipi:chawan. Te:moilih sera iga yawi gitsonwiti bagetspalimeh. Entonses yahki chogotsin a la ora.
Ompa sehpa wi:tseh "elun, elun nagastanpepel, ta:gatawatsaloyan
ompa onok motah." "Anda kabrón, nia nimitsonwiti." Gichí:w
gitogatih ipi:chawan "tras"; gilpilih ikola, yahki, wa:lak sió. Gilipilih
sehpa-gok iyikxi, bueno gigiskih, wa:n bueno gimegawitek.
"Tes tiwi:ts tinehpinahtigeh, até niwa:lak mamawiltigo moá:n.
Neh niwa:lak ne:chohmák notahwé:h manikbiligi a:t iga a:tanegi
nemi tamiá *milpan*. Xah-ya iga mas nehpinahtia iga nia niname:-
chilpiti. Un dia niname:chilpia, hamah niname:chmahka:wati. Nia
niname:chwiati wa:n notahwé:h wa:n yawi namé:chba:ti." Bueno
ginmohmotih, yahkeh, aikate-ya wa:layah, wehka-san gitsahtsiliáh.
We:yak chogotsin ihkó:n, durante años we:yak chogotsin. Ke los
biehitos de antes gita:lihkeh un biahe a wahaka pero a pie. Gichi:hkeh
intotopochtsitsin, intaxkal, yahkeh-ya akél biahe. Pero chogotsin
no:gimati akeyos señores yaweh al biahe. Komo tamatia si:ntiopiltsin,
gimatk iga ho:n lugar ompiga onok itah. Momák de kuenta y después
gihliagi itahwé:h. "Welito, neh no: nia al biahe kon esos señores."
"Pero te:tikbiti nopiltsin." "Neh nia ompiga nipaxaloti inwa:n." Tia-
wach, manimichi:wili-wach moa:tsitsin iga ho:n yaweh wehka. Pero
teh até tikpia motaxkal yeh tikba:ti ompiga." "Neh ompiga apoliwi
te: nia nikba:ti, totál neh nia inwa:n." "Bueno, xah." Bueno por
tanto gitasohta we:wehtsin ichogotsin, gimahká:w yahki al biahe
kon akeyos señores.
Después asitoh un lugar, gihliagi los biehitos agimatia anga si:ntio-
piltsin. "Nigah xixtega achi baxiwit, ximopehpe:chti miak, porke
nigah te:ba: arierra." Adióh nigah gitek yei baxiwit gen gita:lih
agita:ih. Motegak, gochik. Bak yahki taneisto até masi, san-ipet-
somiotsin onok. Mochi giwigiliah arrierohmeh, giba:hkeh. Después
los biehitos gihliagi: "Ya bes (chogotsin bibo), los konsehos atikrero,

manimitsihliaya xiktega miak baxiwit iga te:ba arriera. Poko baxiwit tikta:lih wa: aman ya bes gen tonok." "Bueno, nehka:wagan, neh nikmati te: nikchi:ati. Anyaweh, xagan. Nenga nimitstechoa pa oh." Bueno ompa gahtehkeh, yehameh yahkeh, segirohkeh ohti. Kuando menos wa:lak se arriero nemi gitegilia mas inagayo. Chogotsin gibik se itsongal gitahkoilpih. "Gen tikmati, tinehsaloilia nonagayo gen-san tinehtegilih o nimitstahkoteponoti wa:n notsongal." "Karamba, pero aiki ne:chapretaro mas iga tinehtahkowiltegiti." "A la buena tinehsaloilia nonagayotsin ta seguro nia nimitstahkowiltegiti wa:n hi:n notsongal." "Bueno, nehmahka:wi manigihliti notayaganga iga matimisaloiliahwach monagayo." "Bueno, xah."

Mahká:w, arrierahtsin yahki. Al kabo rrato ompa wi:ts se tsintanah arrieroh weh. "Te: pasaro?" "Nigah anehsaloiliah nonagayo gen-san anehtechohkeh o gen agimati sino anyaweh mal." Bueno pues ni modo, mandarohya hi:n tayaganga magisasaloiliah inagayo. Gisasaloilihtiahkeh sehpa. Total gita:lihkeh perfektamente komo gen-san onoya primero (kuerpo intero). Bueno mahkew chogotsin yahki iteposta ajeyos señores, yahyahkehya, nemi yaweh al biahe. Bak al menos yahki gitsinwitek se we:wehtsin gan yawi pa oh. Gihliagih: "Gen timorremediaroh?" "Neh nosabiduria, niginobligaroh sehpa manehsaloilia nonagayo."

Segirohkeh ohti, yahkeh. Asitoh en otro lugar gan gochitoh-ya sehpa. Gihliagih we:wehtsitsin chogotsin: "Teh gexka tigochiti?" "Neh nigah nigochiti pan hi:n tet, yekmonso hi:n tet, nigahsan nia nimotegati." "Amó xigochi pan tet iga nigah te:ba: tet." "Adióh neh anikte:moa mas lugár, nigah yekmonso onok hi:n tet, nigah nia nigochiti."

Ke motegak pan tet. Bak tane:sik, nochi-ya gitoloh tet. Sanitsontegontsin ne:si, pero tahtohtok bibo. Gihliagih se we:wehtsin: "Pues ya bes atikrero los konsehos. Pues aman si ompa tiga:wi. Gen timogopinati, mitstoloh-ya tet?" "Nehkla:wagan, anyaweh xagan, manigita te: rremedio nikchi:ati." Ke segirohkeh ohti we:wehtsitsin, ompa gigahtehkeh.

Después al kabo rrato iga gisak akeyos señores. Wa:lak se to:totsin. "Melaxixa chogotsin, melaxixa chogotsin." "Ke será rremedio iga nimelaxixa, nehmahka:wati tet?" To:totsin gihliaya sehpa: "Melaxixa chogotsin, melaxixa chogotsin." Chogotsin lo ke gichi:w gibik iya:xixtsin, mela:xixak. Bak al rrato gimahká:w tet.

Adióh gisegiroh sehpa ohti. Nenga gintechoto we:wehtsitsin. Mas we:wehtsitsin agimatigeh ke tirada giwia. Yeh gite:mohtia itah porke gihlih-ya bagetspalimeh iga ta:gatawatsaloyan ompa onok itah. Después asitiahkeh-ya del lugár, modespediroh-ya de we:wehtsitsin. "Xawan ompa-gok mobiahe. Neh nigah nia, nigah wi:ts, nigah nehga:wi." "Ihkó:n gen wel titechoch rresponsable. De rregreso amó xasiti toá:n." "Até pasaroh nité, neh nikmati lo ke nikchi:a."

Bueno gitagih onok de birtú chogotsin ompa gigahtehkeh, yehameh yahkeh. Gimatik pan ho:n lugár onok itah. Asitiaya yohyo:lik, gitak ompa se rrancho. Enfrente de ho:n gahli ompa onok se chigotsapobawit, taktok di alma. Gitak iye:la:mahtsin ompa tampa ho:n chigotsapobawit. Ompa nemi tahkiti, nemi gihkiti se beyi.

Después yeh gogochtok la:mahtsin nemi tahkiti. Yeh manin yahki tehkaw ahko chigotsapot. Gite:moh-ya yohyoksik nemi-ya giba:k chigotsapot. Bak ahko-ya nemi gimotilih se la:mahtsin pan iyitkat gan nemi tahkiti. La:mahtsin isak, gipehpen chigotsapot. Gitak bakyoksik, gipartiroh giba:. "Malaya siók gatka. Te:dióh gixini hi:n chigotsapot san-yoksik?" Agimati iga chogotsin onok ahko. Después chogotsin gimahka:wili siók, la:mahtsin mas isak-ya. Gitahkopartiroh siók, giba:k o:me. Ihkí:n giba:k eyi. Bagón ginotsak: "Mamasita si tiknegi mas niktegi mas, nigah onok yokyoksik." "Teh aha:ga tiwa:lak, teh a:k?" "Neh fulano." "Xitemo: manimits:xmati, anga tinopiltsin, pero neh animitsi:xmati. Anikmati ni gan tinaseroto a:k mitskriaroh. Xitemo:." Temoh chogotsin wa:lak.

Tahtagetsatia wa: iye:. "Bueno, notah gan yahki." "Mopapá gipia mas de años mik. Mas palante ompa onok isepultura." "Notah nia nigixititi, san-nehne:xtiliti notah gan gisepultaroto. Nia nikkopinati wa:n nia nigixititi." "Ihkó:n nia nimitsne:xtiliti." Giwiak iye:la:-mahtsin gine:xtilito gexka gisepultaroh."

"Aman xah para tochan, neh nia nikkopinati notah wa:n nia nigixititi." La:mahtsin yahki. "Nia nimitsrreko-mendaroti a la ora ke tia tigitati notah kuidáh tichoga, kuidá tikchihchimi porke si tiwi:ts tichihchimigi o tichoga, notah atiaweh tiktechotih. Notah yawi mobepati un animal del kampo."

Iye:la:mahtsin agikreroh gihtoagi: "Te: gimati ho:n?" Yahki ichan, si:ntiopiltsin gichí:w lo posible, witek itah girrebibiroh. Bak isak-ya, aya gikompletaroa anga irresurrekción. Gen se tawan nemi giwia ichan. Ke la:mahtsin bak gitak ompa-ya giwahlia iwe:wehtsin. Embés moawantaroskia amó machoga tsatsiwe:tsik choga. Yahki nemia ginapalo iwe:wehtsin. Ihuela, mas ke mobepak se masat: "huííí, huííí, huííí." Gibik a:gawahlo, yaya. Gixitih itah pero agiserbiroh para nada. Ompa tamik ho:n kuento.

Other regional variants of this myth were collected by García de León (1968) in Zaragoza and San Juan Volador, by Culturas Populares in Hueyapan de Ocampo (López Arias 1983), and by Law in Mecayapan (Law 1957; Campos 1982: 163–70). Two Zoque-Popoluca variants from the community of Soteapan have also been published by Foster (1945; see Münch 1983: 163–9). We recorded a Spanish variant of the same myth in Pajapan in 1987. García de León (1991: 35) encountered a dozen variants of this myth in native villages extending from the Papaloapan Valley to la Venta. The actual origin of this myth is uncertain. The classical Nahuatl story concerning the discovery of maize has only a few motifs in common (e.g., the ant) with our Gulf Nahua reference myth (León-Portilla 1980: 166–71; Taggart 1983: 93). The myth may have been borrowed by the Gulf Nahuas from their Zoque-Popoluca neighbors following the invasion of Nahua speakers migrating from the Central Plateau in the 9th century (García de León 1976: 10–14). Parts of the story are indeed suggestive of Maya mythology as recorded in the Popol Vuh and in recent Mayan ethnographies (Foster 1945: 194f.).[1]

Be that as it may, the myth is now an integral part of indigenous cultures native to the Santa Marta area. In Pajapan, events surrounding the life of Sintiopiltsin are told in the Nahua idiom, through words and motifs that activate a host of associations and evocations that convey a particular vision of life and related perceptions of the universe. Our analysis is not so much concerned with the origin of the myth as with the Nahua world constructed through narrative discourse.

The social and the mythical

Before we delve into the detailed symbolism of Sintiopiltsin's story, a few general remarks should be made as to how the narrative relates to other analyses developed throughout this book. To begin with, the story illustrates several points we have made in Chapter 2 regarding the absence of a process of institutional differentiation operating within traditional Gulf Nahua society. Our exegesis of the corn narrative will show how Nahua mythology succeeds in weaving together a multitude of themes ranging from sex and procreation to consumption and production, domination and subordination, sacrifice and retribution. Mythical imageries will not let themselves be pigeon-holed into natural history (botanical, zoological, etc.), nor can they be sub-divided into government, market, church and family themes. Although concerned with a divided world that needs attention, the story does not separate economic activities from issues of authority, family or spirituality. Considerations of the private sphere are never marked off from public matters, physical objects from human subjects, the material from the mental or spiritual dimensions of life. The myth speaks rather to all aspects of reality joined in one narrative plot.

Events surrounding the corn child's journey through life conjure up visions of authority radically different from institutional expressions of state, class and church power. For one thing the language deployed in the myth precludes a class discourse based on a polarized distribution of factors of production treated as commodities. The story lacks the words needed to speak of material use-values that can be measured, contractually exchanged, or privately owned. On the political plane, the myth portrays fathers and old men playing powerful roles in the lives of both gods and natives of the land. Although problematical in their own way, Nahua principles of patriarchy and gerontocracy are none the less at odds with the tensions and conflicts of civil government and state authority and also with the rhetoric of collective representation reflecting class, national or communal interest groups. Senior members of the community accede to power not because of their ability to "represent" their constituencies but rather by virtue of their gender, age and personal reputation – attributes that mark them off from the rest of society. Finally, powers are vested in spirits and sorcerers who mediate between humans and gods, yet the traditional Nahua view of religious activity (involving sorcerers constantly at war with one another) never burdens itself with problems of centralized church power. Pajapan's narrative account of the world precludes supranatural spirits and ecclesiastics being placed above the lay, the secular and the profane.

The story of the Corn Master will serve to illustrate the central features of patrimonial kinship discussed in the preceding chapter. In its own way, the narrative reflects on domestic practices eluding the institutional control of state, capital and church. This is not to say that the tale of Sintiopiltsin projects a world of family ties based on principles of social equality, a universe governed by simple measures of unity and harmony (so Bonfil Batalla 1991: 137–40; Argueta 1991: 38). On the contrary, the myth busies itself with basic divisions and problems inherent to the patrimonial domain. In addition to relations between humans, plant and animal spirits, the myth reflects on inequalities and tensions that exist between the young and the old, the male and the female. The story deploys a language that confirms the centrality of male characters and the authority vested in senior father figures. As we shall see, the story deliberates family life, a kin-based regime where men and the old are granted privileges and exercise real power vis-à-vis women and younger generations. To these expressions of patriarchy the narrative adds a vertical view of relations between nature and culture. Creatures of nature may be mastered by humans who must eat plants and animals in order to live, yet humans must ultimately defer to natural gods and spirit animal-owners who control the resource base and livelihood of native people (García de León 1969: 306).

In the preceding chapter, we saw that the patrimonial domain is repressive yet subject to internal disputes, hence manifestations of resistance to a ruling order governed by elderly men. Similar comments apply to the corn myth: it too suggests a vision of authority exercised within certain limits. First, the powers vested in the hands of ruling fathers have always left room for eccentricity. The relative autonomy of nuclear families vis-à-vis broader power systems allows for some dissemination of authority. The story of Sintiopiltsin revolves around a son, a daughter and their immediate parents (adoptive and real, human and botanical). The story confines itself to a narrowly-defined expression of family life and pays no attention to broader group relations that may prevail between generations or genders, between chiefs and followers, between natural spirits and the human species as a whole.

Second, the exercise of patrimonial power is limited by all the mutual dependencies and cyclical changes that preside over relations between the young and the old, men and women. Ranchers do not need peasants to accumulate capital, urban employers can make profits without reproducing the unemployed labor force, and male wage laborers can make a living without having wives and children or looking after their needs. By contrast, in an economy based on relations of gender and generation, men and elderly parents depend on women and their adult children for their survival. Although hierarchical, native forms of organization require measures of "reciprocity between unequals" (Boege and Barrera 1991: 94), vital exchanges based on rights and obligations that holders of power must satisfy lest they undermine their own household authority.

Our reading of gender imageries deployed in the narrative will speak to female attributes of power, womanly forces that men must reckon with when dealing with problems of life and death on earth. As with women, the young can also oppose the power vested in fathers. As pointed out in Chapter 6, native family ties are constantly severed and reorganized as new members are added and others leave to form new households. Under such conditions, the power exercised by male household heads is never irreversible. The story of Sintiopiltsin illustrates the point. The corn god is a child dependent on humans and older plant generations that fathered him. Yet the story starts at a critical phase of family life: the final stage of life when children are no longer living with their parents (save the youngest son). Power vested in the parental couple will not last forever. The story features a boy growing in age, asserting himself and becoming his own master. Sintiopiltsin overcomes his enemies and achieves autonomy (if not superiority) towards his adoptive parents and the Pilgrim Fathers who accompany him on his journey. The corn child actually ends up reviving his own father, thus inverting his relationship to the man who gave him life.

Third, the exigencies of reciprocity also apply to vertical relations between nature and culture. To be sure, spirits, plant gods and _chaneque_ masters of the universe possess special attributes that men, women and children will always fear and envy. Humans are dominated by forces of nature endowed with will, forces that may either assist humans in satisfying their needs or inflict harm on the greedy and the disrespectful: e.g., hunters and fishers who kill more than they need, peasants who overcultivate without letting the land rest, people who collect plants without paying tribute to the spirit-owners, men who display their wealth without sharing it, etc. All the same, the dominion that natural spirits hold over humans is not of the tyrannical kind, a universe where "human existence hangs on the whim of indifferent spirits that require continuous ritual attention" (Sandstrom 1991: 257). As we are about to see, the corn myth speaks to the mutual dependencies that tie natural spirits to the human species (Megged 1991: 19). Peasant families may be at the mercy of Sintiopiltsin, yet the opposite is also true: mythology makes it abundantly clear that the corn god can only reproduce himself through peasant labor (López Austin 1990: 100). The story of the god's journey through life is a reflection on the web of life – on creatures that feed on one another through cycles of production and reproduction.

Fourth, obligations of reciprocity assigned to nature and culture, men and women, the old and the young, are couched in a particular idiom that sets bounds to all forms of power: the moral of self-sacrifice. This brings us to lessons of ascetic naturalism based on the cult of nature and the tragic ways of self-denial, narrative teachings that will be illustrated at length. Briefly, the Gulf Nahua version of Mesoamerica's "sacrificial geography" (Boege 1988: 283) is expressed by way of a hero's journey through life and his response to a series of narrative invitations: the perilous attractions of the iguana tail and mocking tongue, the _megat_ snare (belt, lover) and _guetzal_ mode of speech, the comfortable bed of leaves and soothing waters-of-life, etc. The corn child's response to temptations of the good life procured without abnegation will serve to exemplify an obligation shared by humans and plant gods alike, which is to serve the other forms of life one needs to reproduce. In spite of some hesitations, the corn boy ends up making the right choices. His decision to walk in the footsteps of his father, toward the burial land of *Tagatauatzaloyan*, is taken with resolve. He too will die so as to reproduce his seed and feed human beings as well. Animals and humans who fail to follow in the hero's footsteps are given due warning: for lack of merit, they shall lose all the powers and blessings they seek or possess.

Humans depend on the cyclical sacrifice of earth and maize for their own livelihood. While the earth must be reduced to ashes so as to produce food (Soustelle 1982: 108–9), the corn god must dry and die so as to feed peasants and the children who look after them in their old age. But the god's sacrifice is also self-serving. If Sintiopiltsin were to refuse to give himself to humans, presuming that it were in his power to do so, then there would be no one to attend to the needs of children of the corn god, sowing and cultivating the seed of father plants. As in Aztec mythology, while macehual humans are born from a divine sacrifice, the sacrifice of men harnessed to the land is also necessary for the deserving gods (León-Portilla 1983: 184ff., Boege 1988: 150).

Imageries of self-denial uphold a native version of the Law of the Father, a patrimonial domain that grants privileges to the father figure, at great cost to women and the young. Narrative precepts of self-discipline can legitimate the power vested in men and spirits whose authority has been attained through model gestures of self-sacrifice. Having said this, there is more to the native ideals of sacrifice than mere rhetoric. The moral of self-renunciation applies to people and creatures occupying all avenues of life, the powerful and the powerless alike. The law of self-mastery makes no exception, limiting the powers vested in natural forces, men and the old. The corn god will grow and achieve the power to regenerate his seed only if he bears the cost of reproduction, hence drying, feeding humans and losing his own life. On the social level, measures of self-denial are imposed on power-holders who must obey the law (or at least feign to do so) lest they undermine their material livelihood and claims to authority. If they do not work towards meeting the needs of women, children and the community, fathers may put their own well-being at risk and be compelled to use sheer force to maintain themselves in power. The latter strategy, i.e., coercion without cooptation, hierarchy without reciprocity, may work for ranchers who exploit peasants with little concern for their survival.[2] However, the use of unrestrained force is ill-suited to a kin-based peasantry that combines patrimonial measures of domination with the mutual dependencies and cyclical transformations of family life.

The tale of Sintiopiltsin deliberates basic rules and tensions of traditional Gulf Nahua social organization. The story, however, does not address problems of colonial and post-colonial history, hence the profound alterations suffered by this kin-based society following the expansion of class, state and church institutions (discussed in previous chapters). Other tales told in Pajapan give us a better idea of how myths may account for the ravages of modern history. Some of these tales are briefly discussed at the end of the chapter.

The interpretive method: rudiments of scheme analysis

The semiotic method applied throughout the chapter should be explained. To begin with, our analysis of Gulf Nahua symbolism produces findings that are partly compatible with those of Sedeño and Becerril. In *Dos Culturas y una infancia: psicoanálisis de una etnia en peligro*, these anthropologists offer a detailed examination of ethnographic data gathered in two Nahua villages of municipal Mecayapan. Their analysis emphasizes tensions between genders and generations, hence a patrimonial domain founded on a native version of the Law of the Father. Briefly, the authors show how the ethnographic material collected in Mecayapan and Tatahuicapan converges on stories of brothers, fathers and sons competing for the attentions of the nurturing mother, a highly repressive system where the father succeeds in imposing his despotic rule, at great cost to women and the young. By exercising excessive power over his own children and wife, the father seeks to compensate for the love he was denied as a child while at the same time giving vent to his feelings of self-depreciation and also anger and resentment toward the female gender. Although embedded in traditional family life, these sentiments of male inadequacy are aggravated by the expansion of broader domains which weaken the authority vested in native fathers and undermine the customary mechanisms of social control. Problems and tensions played out in Gulf Nahua society are exacerbated by the subjection of Indians to alien forces governed by the rule of might, giving way to rampant alcoholism, violence and strife within the family (wife-beating, incest, disputes over land). Broader systems of domination produce deep-seated feelings of hostility and guilt and a chronic inferiority complex *vis-à-vis* the outside world (Sedeño and Becerril 1985: 82–114).

With the tools of psychoanalysis, the authors proceed through a maze of symbolic details that confirm their claims regarding the Gulf Nahua personality structure and its transformations over time. Their study avoids a surface description of culture, it goes beyond the clichés of natives living in social harmony, and it moves away from a purely cognitive approach to symbolling, toward an understanding of tragedy emerging from family life and social history.

Our analysis of the corn myth none the less departs from their approach in several ways. First, we lay more emphasis on linkages between nature and culture, fundamental relations that are not reducible to Oedipal projections of genders and generations interacting within the family circle. Second, our analysis addresses the issue of morality, or the customary teachings of "ascetic naturalism" revolving around the cult of nature and the exigencies of sacrifice. These teachings point to traditional morals of self-mastery, a way of life applicable to all segments of native society and to all forms of life as well. Native ethics impose limits on the

Law of the Father: the ideals expressed through narrative discourse and family life suggest that women and the young are never fully subordinated to their husbands or fathers. Through discourse and family politics, men are pressured to comply with basic norms of reciprocity, if only to secure their own authority and material livelihood. By raising these issues, we try to avoid a brand of psychoanalytic feminism that pays little attention to the specificity of each and every culture, treating all of them as so many illustrations of the Oedipus complex. Our goal is also to go beyond theories that reduce women to passive subjects that are forever subjected to the Law of the Father and that never act on their own social conditions of existence.

Finally, our reading of the corn myth is based on the premise that ethics and worldviews are coded through sign systems. Whether compatible with the Oedipus complex or not, semantic connections attributed to particular imageries hinge on associations that are constructed within the realm of language and that require careful investigation. In our view, interpretations based on universal frames of reference that elude the complexity and variations of language and culture are bound to impose arbitrary connections on their own object of study.[3]

The order of similarities and differences

This brings us to the question of the semiotic strategy developed within our own analysis. Our approach to the story of Sintiopiltsin centers on the motions of time and desire in the act of coding (J.M. Chevalier 1990). First, our analysis is an exercise in decoding. The notion of a sign structure is a *sine qua non* of any interpretive practice that pays attention to the orderly aspects of symbolling. Thus each scene of the corn child myth will be accounted for by translating the imageries into similarities, oppositions and mediations governing the material at hand. Special attention will be paid to relations in space and time, axes that revolve around geographic and calendrical divisions evoked or implied by terms used in the narrative. To these two axes will be added three other pivotal codes. They include the construction of sexual and anatomical relations in language, the botanical and agricultural ordering of relations between plants and humans, and the political economy of signs of production and consumption, wealth and poverty, domination and subordination.

Insights into the coding process require knowledge of the language that generates the myth. Unlike Lévi-Strauss, we view the particular idiom used to relate a story as a key ingredient of the code. Accordingly, our interpretation of narrative symbols is based on extensive ethno-semantic interviews in Pajapan, the village where García de León originally collected the myth. Ethno-linguistic connections suggested throughout our reading come mostly from denotations and connotations assigned to the words by our Pajapan informants (or by García de León, the author of a short Gulf Nahua dictionary). To this material we have added references to entries appearing in the classical Nahuatl dictionary compiled by Rémi Siméon, originally published in 1885. The purpose of these excursions into classical Nahuatl is not to explain Gulf Nahua mythology through Aztec culture. Rather our intention is to suggest that some of the themes explored through our reference myth are variations on linguistic usages dating back to prehispanic times.

In Nahua, root words are combined in such complex ways that special knowledge is needed to understand how the terms are "linguistically engineered" (León-Portilla 1983: 56). To avoid making arbitrary connections, most of the etymological interpretations offered in the analysis are based on Siméon's dictionary which contains extensive information on word formation by agglutination. Readers are asked to bear in mind that the idiom spoken by the people of Pajapan corresponds to the "t" dialect of Nahua, as opposed to the "tl" variant spoken by the Aztecs. In pages to follow, words or expressions currently used in Pajapan will be both italicized and underlined (e.g., _megat_). By contrast, Nahuatl terms recorded by Siméon will be simply underlined (mecatl). So as not to distract the reader from the main points of our analysis, we shall footnote these secondary references to classical Nahuatl as often as we can. Words appearing in italics only are in Spanish.[4]

A few remarks concerning the agglutinative features of the Gulf Nahua dialect are in order. The Nahua idiom spoken in southern Veracruz comprises simple and composite words. The former are few in number and can be shortened, extended, duplicated (through syllabic repetition), or compounded to produce new words. Composite nouns, consisting usually of two terms (sometimes more), constitute the majority of words used by Nahua speakers. New meanings are encoded through the juxtaposition and agglutination of simple substantives, adjectives, verbs and adverbs, to which can be added a number of prefixes and suffixes. In addition, root words have meanings that vary from one context to another. Given these features, the language creates no illusion of "things" or proper "identities" (locations, people) that can be denoted univocally, without compositional devices. Every word is a coded sentence pointing to the relational aspects of objects and actions that constitute the real world.

The semantic information encoded in signs can be gathered by researching the lexical, colloquial and etymological effects conventionally assigned to them. The implications of each and every sign can also be explored by looking at connections made explicit in other variants of the same myth or in other manifestations of Gulf Nahua culture: rituals, folklore, popular beliefs, etc. Our interpretive reading of the reference myth takes into account ethnographic observations concerning the practical usages, perceptions and knowledge associated with signs deployed in the narrative (e.g., how iguana snares are made and used). All of this information collected either by ourselves or by other anthropologists is used to decode narrative symbols while situating them in their proper cultural context.

Codes are bundles of homological and oppositional relations organized into systems of similarities and differences. The relational aspects of language imply the existence of logical connections that can be established not only between words *but also between the multiple meanings that can be activated by a single word.* As Bakhtin (1981: 276) puts it: "no living word relates to its object in a singular way: between the word and its object, between the word and the speaking subject, there exists an elastic environment of other, alien words about the same object, the same theme." For instance, the Gulf Nahua term *megat* lends itself to all sorts of evocations that are not strictly botanical (see Beaucage 1987). If used erotically, the word can signify a string or liana viewed as an amorous or a procreative tie, hence a lover or an umbilical cord (*xicmegat*), the kind that used to be attached to a larger lineage (mecayotl). Given these positive evocations, lianas may serve as doors opening on to sacred sites inhabited by the underworld spirits (García de León 1969: 295). When associated with the anal or phallic tail imagery, however, the same term can be given a filthy twist, as in the vulgar "backside handle" motif (*tzinmegayo*). When turned against one's prey, the string image becomes a fishing line (*mamegat*), a cord or a lasso designed to shoot, snare (mecauia, mecayotia) or flog (*mogauitegui*) an animal; in classical Nahuatl a mecapallo is a slave. Finally, the string may denote a belt tightened around one's own body or a whip to flog oneself with, hence a sign of self-discipline.

In our analysis of the iguana scene, we argue that the *megat* lasso is to the iguana *tzinmegayo* tail what a belt is to the body, or what a mistress is to her lover. Having said this, there is more to structural analysis than a mere listing of correlations of binary oppositions (as constructed between words or the various meanings conveyed by them). Although codes carve up reality into its component parts, language also works to attenuate the contradictions of its own making, thereby restoring some unity to reality. Unity is achieved through measures of mediation that vary from one context to another and that are carried out with uneven success. Some mediators are more powerful than others. The narrative unfolding of the code is subject to variations in levels of mediation ranging from admissions of discord to effects of harmony verging on absolute unity.

The iguana snared by the corn child is a case in point. The animal is a powerful mediator in that it moves freely between water, earth and sky. The creature has the tail and scales of a reptile, it walks with four legs, and it swims like a fish. It also behaves like a bird in that the lizard lays lots of eggs and dwells in trees. All in all, the iguana rivals the corn god in its ability to counter the afflictions and divisions of human reality. Given these powers, the *bagetspalin* can make fun of the young Sintiopiltsin who lives with the constant fear of drowning in water or drying in the sun. And yet great weakness lies in the lizard's strength. As a gluttonous creature and a corn-eating parasite, the animal lacks what earthlings need to reconcile the good life with the requirements of productive labor and reproductive travail. Unlike the corn god, the lizard cannot address the paradox of life and death on earth. Accordingly, Gulf Nahua mythology assigns basic limitations to what the iguana can do to resolve problems of the human condition.

The logic of desire

The act of decoding is a first step toward an understanding of the narrative process. When excluding other interpretive methods, however, structuralism oversimplifies the complexities of *la parole*. Logical accounts of symbolism neglect a fundamental property of the sign system: the fact that some signs are given greater attention than others. The *megat* snare composition discussed above is heavily biased toward the aggressive side of the Nahua string imagery. Erotic and ascetic usages of the *megat* motif (lover, belt) are prevented from entering the surface scene; they have an impact on the composition only by way of exclusion or deferment. As in all acts of speech, some meanings are bracketed while others are brought to the fore. If properly explored, this unequal treatment of narrative signs gives us access to the interplay between the overt and the covert, between express imageries and remote signs acting at a distance from the surface narrative, *in absentia* so to speak.

Our reading of the *imagines mundi* of Sintiopiltsin pays equal attention to both aspects of the sign process: the schemes and the schemings of semiosis, hence the "complex play of light and shadow the word enters" (Bakhtin 1981: 277). The plotting of signs can be understood through a threefold method that disassembles each scene as follows. First, readers are invited to probe the surface narrative for the moral teachings of the composition at hand and the dominant signs chosen in preference to other meanings. To use the iguana snare example again, the *megat* motif cannot be used simultaneously in all possible ways, without a sense of verbal and ethical direction informing the text. In the iguana scene, the string is used as a hunting instrument that precludes a literal reading of erotic or ascetic meanings into the *megat* motif. The warlike ways of men chasing animals or women are visibly preferred over alternative usages of the *megat* sign. In the long run, however, the ascetic moral of Sintiopiltsin's journey through life is bound to prevail against the teachings of conquest; like the corn plant "doubled" and tied at the waist at autumn, humans must learn to turn the *megat* against themselves and tighten their belt if they are to survive and enjoy a life of plenty. Given his sacrificial mission, the corn god ranks above and wins against the lizard. Both the literal and ethical preferences of the narrative point to what might be called the rank-ordering of signs, a twofold measure that provides language with a sense of rule – normative rulings as to how signs should be read and as to how all creatures should behave.

Second, signs repressed from the surface story form the underside of the narrative, a secret plot comprising all the anxieties subsumed in the text. Sintiopiltsin's treatment of the *megat* string as a snare to capture his enemy requires that both erotic and ascetic evocations of the same imagery be reduced to silence, if only for a while. These evocations are hidden with good reason. On the erotic side of things, the young hero captures his prey and yet dreads the sexual powers vested in the iguana. He lets go of the powerful tail in his possession for fear of becoming like the animal itself, a creature loaded down with signs of phallic lechery.

The move is understandable, given that the hero is too young to chase and tie himself to the *megat* woman of his desire (typically encountered at a well, which is where the iguana makes fun of his immaturity). On the ascetic side of the narrative, the corn boy shows equal timidity in that he dares not turn the string imagery against himself, i.e., in the form of a belt tightened around his body, an expression of reproduction achieved through abnegation. Although he masters the iguana and shows wisdom by releasing its tail, the corn child is not accepting the costs of growth and reproduction, issues that must be confronted sooner or later.

Third, a ban can be placed on secret implications of the narrative provided that the text signifies the unsaid in a roundabout way, by means of implication, deferment or distortion. In the iguana trap scene, two things are coded while being unsaid: the fear that the child will misbehave but also the hope that he will comport himself heroically. On the one hand, there is the fear of transgression conveyed through a *megat* snare acting as a lustful "be-longing", an instrument that points to what the young hero is searching for, something he is not allowed to possess. The snare consists of a lasso which is akin to a noose or a net but also a mistress. The string is tied to a bamboo stick resembling the spinal column and backside appendage of the powerfully-tailed lizard. The snare thus embodies all the trappings of the good life on earth, the kind foolishly enjoyed and lost by the prolific, long-tailed iguana. On the other hand, the snare creates moral expectations as well. Since the child chooses not to keep the trap and the prey in his possession, readers may be hopeful (but not certain) that the hero's journey through life will set an example of virtue. As we shall see, these hopes of ascetic behavior may be expressed through the *megat* imagery, i.e., by turning the string motif against the hero who is expected to tighten the string around himself (at autumn) or pull it like hair from his head (at harvest) so as to reproduce.

The schemings of narrative time

When viewed synchronically, signs act as elements within systems of static differences. Variations occurring through time can be explored through comparison, by searching for the similarities and differences that lie between one speech sequence and another. In our view, this synchronic approach to the sign process does little justice to the dynamic motions of language – to the wheelings and dealings of time that govern the politics of narrative attention. Far from being an immediate presence of the mind, the order of attention is a command to the senses to be ready for what is deferred; it disposes the senses to respond to words that are not yet spoken or that are no longer uttered. The attentions of language thrive on memories of the past and also a constant disposition to wait and see: *l'attente*. Desires at work in the process of symbolling are subject to the hermeneutic principle of *distentio* (Ricoeur 1984: 22), a tension between recollections and expectations of signs of distant times (past or future) that haunt the narrative present. This principle is the obverse of what may be called the logic of *contentio,* lapses of memory and fears of contentious events apprehended at all moments of narrative time.

The interplay between layers of codified attention (the explicit, the implicit, the illicit) is not purely synchronic. Signs of the overt and the covert converge on a temporal experience of language, a fearful and hopeful experience that "contains" – at once conveys and withholds – the moving scenes of a plot. "Forming itself in an atmosphere of the already spoken, the word is at the same time determined by that which has not yet been said but which is needed and in fact anticipated by the answering word. Such is the situation in any living dialogue" (Bakhtin 1981: 280).

The secret implications of the Gulf Nahua story of a corn child catching the iguana and breaking its tail serve to illustrate the point. As already suggested, the moral weaknesses of the mighty-tailed lizard account for the punishment inflicted on the animal. More importantly, its demise at the hands of the corn child produces *pre- and post-figurative effects that serve to keep the narrative plot in motion.* For one thing the battle reminds listeners of several things that the corn child should not forget: his immaturity, the danger of a good life procured without abnegation, and the many enemies and obstacles in the way of reproduction and growth. Although Sintiopiltsin masters the iguana, the scene lays the ground for a more durable resolution of these problems: it invites listeners to place their hopes in the sacrificial ways of the mature corn god. It does so pre-figuratively though, well before the hero's arrival to the "land-where-men-are-dry", while also doing it indirectly, through the breaking of the lizard's back and the child releasing the animal tail. As we shall see, the mutilation suffered by the iguana announces the corn plant "doubled" at autumn, a story of backbreaking sufferings that beg to be told. The story is about the corn god's sacrifice performed at the end of the maize cultivation cycle, a time when ears of corn tied at the waist join father plants that have already dried (so as to feed humans and produce new seed). The correction applied to the iguana gives the listener a pre-text to invest hope in the re-enactment of stories of human and plant survival achieved through self-sacrifice.

Although apparently without a sense of the dramatic (as Foster claims, cf. 1945: 243), the corn myth follows a plot. All scripts play games with the passing of time. "Movement is symbolism for the eye; it indicates that something has been felt, willed, thought" (Nietzsche 1967: 551). Every discourse has a story to tell and does so with its sense of development, a "speculative" operation that adds interest to the code. The story of the Nahua corn god has its own mode of speculation on time. Each scene makes compositional moves that convey and withhold signs of the future along with memories of the past. This chapter is structured in such a way that readers may keep close track of Sintiopiltsin's progression through time, toward maturity, death and reproduction in the "land-where-men-are-dry". Our reading of the myth will thus proceed along lines set by the story itself, from one sequence to another, starting with the beginning: i.e., an old couple and two eggs in a *milpa,* to which we now turn.[5]

An old couple and two eggs in a *milpa*

It is said (*gihtoa*) that there was an old man (*wewehtsin*) with his old woman (*ilamahtsin*) but they did not have children (*inpilo-antsitsin*). There was only the man and the woman. However, they had a *milpa* (*inmiltsin*) and they went to work (*gitegipanoayah*) in their *milpa*, weeding (*tamiah*).

The Nahua corn myth starts with an old childless couple. The scene conveys the male-centered division between man and woman: the couple (a man "with his woman") revolves around the male figure, a bias that prefigures the father planting his male seed in the *milpa* and killing the corn god's sister-egg. With this primordial couple comes the old age motif (*ue*) and the affliction of human sterility: the couple is described as being without *pilhuatsitsin* offspring (*piltia*, to be born).[6] *Pilli* signifies child and used to stand for nobility and purity, gentleness and grace. Sadly, our humble couple is bereaved of all such blessings; the life of an aging man and his elderly wife is not being rejuvenated or honored with the blessings of youth. Signs of hardships to come are planted in the inaugural imagery of our corn myth.

These negative implications are softened by the evocation of a *milpa* cultivated by the couple. The absence of children is compensated by the ownership of a seed plot (Sp. *sementera*). The suffix *tzin*, commonly used as a diminutive and a mark of affection, respect and protection, is assigned to this piece of land, the couple and the children (emphasized by way of repetition). Likewise, the prefix *ue* is assigned to the old man, a term that connotes distance in time (old age) or in space (i.e., high; large is *-ueyac*, far is *-uehca*). It may also imply a measure of growth and superiority in rank, as in *-ueya* and *-ueica*. All in all, the *milpa*, the suffix and the prefix suggest that, although infertile, the couple is by no means deprived of social standing and wealth in land. Ownership (*tego*) means security for their old age.

But the ownership of a *milpa* without young children to inherit places the old couple in a vulnerable position: who will serve them and look after their property when they are no longer able to work the land? To make matters worse, the elderly couple are low-status peasants working the land without anyone's help. The narrative confirms that the landowner is but a humble peasant (*miltagat*) condemned to labor and serve (*tequi-panoa*), the male counterpart of a woman "doing housework" (*teguicha*).[7] The low-status attributes of the peasantry are strengthened by the root word *tegui*, which implies work and the burden of function, servitude and tribute. *Teguit* also denotes collective work (*faena*) organized by the communal authorities and the municipal *teguiwa* president, the one in charge of distributing or "speaking" on matters of work and taxes (*teguitatoa*); in Pajapan, the term *teguio* refers to someone who holds a public office.[8] The scene does not develop the negative associations of peasant labor and tribute, yet it suggests that the couple has ample reason to labor and to *teguipachoa* – to suffer discontent and to be preoccupied with their immediate future.

What kind of work are they doing? The narrative describes the old couple weeding (*tamiah*) the *milpa*. This time-consuming activity usually occurs in the month of July, some 30 days after planting maize. The task is accomplished when maize plants are knee-high, with leaves open but still without flowers or ears. Weeding is a critical field operation as yields suffer greatly from weed competition. The plot is cleared of weeds so that corn can develop under the combined action of rain and sun. Weeding is usually performed with a machete or a small *chahuaste* or *xawak*, instruments of male agricultural labor: in Mecayapan, the tool is given to the newborn boy in the hope that he become a hard-working man (González Cruz et al. 1983: 11). Thus the man is the one who cuts, peels, shaves, fells or destroys (*xima, xini, xixini*) unwanted plants that compete with the young maize for soil "strength' (Sp. *fuerza*). These terms, however, can also denote the action of fruit being thrown on the ground (as in a later scene) or a man pouring or spreading the seed of life (*xinachtia*). Could it be that a father aging and without a tree-like family is uprooting plants with a view to cultivating the earth and letting his own seed flourish in watered (*xixintok*) soil? If so, the imagery would converge on the paradox of life and death, spending and saving, consumption and production. More on this symbology later. For the moment, suffice it to say that death will prove to be a basic requirement of life, and destruction (or sexual consumption) a condition of reproduction.

Issues of youth and age, fertility and sterility, femininity and masculinity, plant production (seeding) and consumption (cutting), honor and servility, are prefigured and problematized through an unsettling dominance of second terms. For reasons to be seen, the inaugural imagery also conveys an earth-focus excluding all references to the sun above and the water below (López Austin 1990: 180), two vital requirements of earthly existence. There are, however, promising indications of deference, land ownership and the imminent renewal of the botanical sustenance of life on earth. The narrative is about to deliver on these promises in the simple form of two stone-like eggs lying in the *milpa*.

Eggs and twins, sex and corn

One day they found (*gitechóah*) two chicken eggs (*ome pioteksis*), two large (*wehwey*) eggs. "Old woman, let's take (*tikwiatih*) these eggs and have our hen (*topió*) sit on them (*tapacholtitih*) and see (*matigitagan*) what they lay (*poniti*)." So they went to their house (*ichan*) and had the hen sit on them. The hen sat on one egg and they took (*gimangeh*) the other and ate it (*gibahkeh*). They ate the egg. The hen sat on the other egg for a few days. When it hatched, it laid a boy (*gonetsin*), a male infant (*chogotsin*). The old man and the woman were surprised. "Caramba, we lost (*tikpolohkeh*) an egg, the one we ate; if not maybe (*anga*) the couple would have been born; the other was probably a girl (*tagotsin*). But we already ate it." Moreover, they didn't know (*agimatiáh*) who the little boy was. He was "the venerable son-god-ear-of-corn" (*Sintiopiltsin*).

One day the old couple came across two large *pioteksis* eggs, like stones in a field. *Pio* and *teksis* are of unknown origin. The first term means chicken and may come from pillotl, which stands for childhood, nobility and descent (*nopiloán* in Pajapan). In Nahuatl, a chicken is called a totolin, and an egg is a toto-tetl, hence a bird-stone.[9]

In Pajapan, the egg or bird-stone motif is a metaphor for testicle while the *totot* bird is synonymous with both the penis (like the English cock) and the newborn child. The notion that the bird embodies the principle of male fertility is confirmed in such derivative expressions as *totomigui* (bird-dead), to be impotent. The egg scene thus brings together all the blessings of masculine fertility: the phallic bird, the stone-testicles and the childlike eggs of noble descent. Although childless, the old couple is blessed with the discovery of two large eggs lying in their seed plot, eggs effortlessly procured from heaven like fruit nesting in trees.[10]

The egg scene extends the rule of harmony to gender relations as well. Although associated with the phallus, the stone-egg can easily turn into a womb-like house (*gahli*) or uterine enclosure. To the Gulf Nahuas, a *gagash* (from *gahli*) is a bird-cage. The stone-container function can also be attributed to a mountain inhabited by dwellers of the earth. *Tepet*, from *tet* (stone), means a mountain, a country or a locality, hence a portion of the mother earth sheltering people, water and spirits. The word *altepet* (water-mountain) is still used in Pajapan to denote a community.[11] Finally, stones lying in a corn plot are reputed to keep the soil humid and fertile and are closely associated with the growth of calabash.

In short, the stone-egg motif brings opposites together on several planes. It acts as a mediator between signs of maturity (phallic) and immaturity (infantile) and also between the masculine organs and the feminine vessels of life on earth. It is as if two lifeless stones of the field had been turned into testicle-like seeds and womb-like containers of life – two eggs laid by a female, cock-like bird and freely granted to a couple otherwise childless and aging.

Terms of mediation between the two genders are an integral part of the Gulf Nahua discourse on human sexuality. Words that designate various parts of the reproductive organs point to an intertwining of gender attributes, a blending of masculinity and femininity written over both sexes from the moment of birth. Consider first the language of female anatomy.[12] Unlike the phallus (*tepol*), organs of female reproduction are assigned the predictable uterine vessel imagery. According to Siméon, the uterus used to be called tepilquaxicalli, the "head-calabash of a child-mouth" (vulva): from tentli (mouth), pilli (child), quaitl (head, extremity), and xicalli (calabash). In Pajapan, the last word (*xigal*) stands for the vulva and also the local *tortillera* shaped like a bowl (*gomit*) and made from the *tegomat* or *tegon* calabash. In classical Nahuatl, when preceded by the word for wood, the same word denoted a bowl to keep the hearts of sacrificed victims (quauhxicalli). Another Gulf Nahua equivalent of the uterine-calabash connection is the *chayoh*, a thorny, calabash-like fruit equated with the vulva; *taguihlo* is thus a chayote, a fruit that hangs, or the vulva. In the Zoque-Popoluca variant of our corn myth (López Arias 1983), the ashes of the vagina of the ogress Chichiman are sown by the hero to produce calabash and chayote.

All indications are that the uterus, the head and the calabash have something in common. What would that be? The answer is that they all contain _at_, a Gulf Nahua term denoting not only water but also the sinciput, the brain and the infant – a human being with a brain that is "still water" and with a spiritual life force dipped in baptismal head-water (_bategui_, "head-washed"). The word for water also stands for urine expelled from the _xiton_ bladder, or the vulva known as _axix-tegon_, the urine vessel or "water calabash".[13]

While waters of the womb are at the root of life, too much water can cause death. There is a common belief among the Gulf Nahuas that the child's head contains water immediately above the forehead, a part of the body that should not be touched lest the waters break and the child drown. Midwives move the head of the newborn immediately after birth in such a way that the excess water is expelled through the nostrils. Water accumulated in the mouth of the newborn may cause the infant to suffocate and die. In Soteapan a pregnant woman should not worry about anything lest the pressure exerted on her own brain result in a difficult delivery (Foster 1945: 188). It is also recommended that expectant fathers refrain from getting drunk at night lest the child's brain-water "rise" and the infant drown in foam coming out of its mouth. This symbiotic relationship between fluids of the infant and the father is reinforced by the belief that a father may experience cerebral nauseas during his wife's pregnancy (González Cruz et al. 1983: 11, 13). Finally, healing rituals establish a direct connection between the waters of life, the sinciput and the egg-like head. Local and regional healers treating patients from a loss of _tonal_ spirit caused by fright (_espanto_) will often place an egg against the person's sinciput so as to extract the illness or the foreign body invading the patient's "headwaters" of life (García de León 1969: 283).

To sum up, female anatomy is constructed through evocations of heads, vessels and calabashes that contain children assimilated to water, urine and brains. But the womanly organs can also produce bird-like children and _teksis_ eggs that stand for the opposite sex, the masculine. The same paradox applies to the phallus, a complex sign that contains its own female side. Gulf Nahua words denoting the male organs refer to cranial vessels, fluids and calabashes that hark back to the feminine gender. First, the head container imagery belongs as much to the male sex as to the female. According to our informants, _tzontegonxipin_ is the word for the prepuce. It literally means the penis (_xipin_) head-vessel separated from its body. Second, in classical Nahuatl, the penis-head has lips and is a pipe that carries "water" (= urine = child). This is to say that both men and women have reproductive canals emitting fluids of life.[14] Third, the notion that water (child, brain) and calabash (womb, head) are central ingredients of the phallic imagery is confirmed by the Gulf Nahua word for semen or any fluid secreted from the body, _tepolayol_; _ayol_ means water, juice or liquid (_ayoh_ is juicy), and _ayo_ stands for the calabash. Thus semen is penis calabash-like juice.[15]

The semantics of Nahua anatomy suggest that each sex partakes of the attributes of the opposite gender. When viewed on the female side, the egg evoked in the opening scene of the corn myth contains albumen in the same way that the womb contains the child or that the gourd vessel, the breast and the head contain water, milk and the human brain, respectively.[16] Similar tropes apply to the phallic domain – to the water-stones, milky secretions, hollow tubes and head-like organs of manly procreation. Words of anatomy signal both the effects and the prospects of man and woman becoming one flesh, hence "no more twain". The question is whether or not the promises of sexual commerce, fertility and harmony conveyed through eggs in a *milpa* shall be delivered in scenes to follow. That the couple found two eggs rather than a single one or even a multitude points to an answer in the negative. Non-identical twins appearing at the beginning of our narrative herald in a primordial unity about to be broken.

The seed and fruit of discontent

The twin-egg motif saves the couple from problems of old age and childlessness. It also saves them from hunger. Two large eggs found in a *milpa* can be assimilated to seed planted in a plot but also fruit nesting in a tree. In its own way the narrative transforms seeds of agricultural production into fruit of the good life on earth – food procured without labor. Both categories of food, the raw and the cooked, the natural and the cultural, play an important role in reproducing life. As we are about to see, they are like the oldest and the youngest in a family, the first seed and the last fruit of man's flesh. But the relationship between fruit and seed, the first son and the last, raises new difficulties: the two ingredients of family reproduction are not created equal in the eyes of man, nor are they fully compatible. Basic dualities such as these will not let themselves be resolved through a simple twin-sibling imagery.

In a previous chapter, we have seen that tensions of the patrimonial domain preside over relations between the old and the young, the first-born and children of the rising generation: in other words, between the first-seed and later fruits of human reproduction. In Pajapan *ach* (achtli, a seed, a grain) stands for an uncle or an older brother, hence the son who comes first (*achto*).[17] When combined with *xini* , to fall and fell but also to sow and spread, the latter word can denote seed plentiful as mites, hence *xinach*.[18] A closely-related usage recorded in Siméon's dictionary is ayoachtli, the calabash water-seed, *yolayo* to the Gulf Nahuas, from *yol*, the eye, the heart or a seed. The genealogical rendering of the first-seed motif points in turn to the word *tayagantok*, from the nose (*yac*), denoting an older brother holding power within the household while also looking after the welfare of his siblings.[19] These terms and their derivatives converge on the rank-ordering of sons within the patrimonial family. They also suggest that the authority vested in the older brother is not without cost, for the first son is obliged to attend to the needs of his siblings, as if he were their "humble servant" (achtli in Siméon).

By contrast, the youngest son (_chogotsin_, xocoyotl) has no authority. But he is the one who inherits the land. With this privilege comes also the duty of serving one's parents in their old age: there is no authority or property without family responsibility. The word used to designate this last son is a derivative of _xocot_, a cherry fruit; _xogoyo_ is to bear fruit. Unlike corn and beans, fruit include things that taste sour (_xogok_, _xogomigui_) and are a source of drunkenness (xocomiquiliztli), pleasures collected like eggs in trees without toil. Though they enjoy eating them, the Gulf Nahuas do not consider fruit (all sweet fruits, bananas, plantains, root crops, sugar cane, squash, green maize on the cob) to be suitable for a main meal. Raw fruit are to be distinguished from real food consisting of _taxcal_ (tortillas), hot _tamal_ and _tabal_, or side dishes cooked and eaten with tortillas (soup, stew, broiled meat; Stuart 1978: 234ff.).

The young son stands to the old as the fruit of luxury stands to the first grain seed and the sustenance of life procured through labor. The two sources of food are both important but not of equal value. Nor are the oldest and the youngest son on an equal footing in real life. The opposition between sons of different ages could always be resolved by having twins born like eggs (fruit, seed) in a _milpa_. The word for twin or friend in Pajapan is _coate_, from _goat_ or coatl, hence a snake. In classical Nahuatl, the word is synonymous with the dibble stick used for planting (González Torres 1985: 84) and also the umbilicus and the stomach (_xicti_, _ihti_ in Pajapan). This imagery has many positive associations. The twin–serpent–umbilicus association bears witness to the close relationship that exists between human beings, such as between a mother and a child or between twins. It can also evoke the tie that binds a man to the female earth, or any person to his or her native land. The umbilicus, like the corn plant, ties the motherland and the parent plant to all the lives they feed: i.e., human beings and the navel-like germs or "sons" (_ixictayol_) of the corn plant. Moreover, like plants pulled out of the earth at harvest time, the umbilicus must be cut at birth. Both the umbilicus and the corn plant express the paradoxical requirements of the cycle of life on earth, those of rooting and severance.[20]

As serpent-like creatures, twins can none the less bring life to a premature end. The imagery harks back to Ciuacoatl (also Quilaztli), the Aztec goddess portrayed as the woman-serpent, mother of twins and the human species as a whole. Her reign implied a two-faced life force that may lapse into the rule of death. Given these associations, the lady's twin offspring cannot be expected to embody the rule of unity. Our narrative is about to describe the two fledglings as brother and sister born at the same time. Twins may represent the rule of unity obtained by way of likeness bordering on sameness. The reality of twins, however, is that one can live without the other: the two individuals are similar but not interdependent. In Gulf Nahua society, twins are viewed as abnormal creatures and are not usually welcome; some women will breast-feed one child and let the other die (González Cruz et al. 1983: 7). Although two eggs imply more food and life than a single offspring, a scene of _coate_ eggs born at the same time is disturbing.

Two eggs laying in a *milpa* lack what is needed to help the story move beyond the principle of duality (once ruled by Ometeotl), toward the reign of harmony attained through complementarity, as between genders and generations (Münch 1983: 161; León-Portilla 1983: 92, 153–63, 172–6). For the moment, the twin offspring is but a pale reflection of what the myth is searching for: an answer to problems of life and death, feasting and fasting, consumption and production, domination and subordination. All indications are that the corn myth is hatching an evil plan from the start: destroying the weaker egg, the female, while attending to the needs of the old couple and their male seed.

Covering the male, eating the female

Eggs containing the fluid of life produced by a winged creature are found on earth, in a corn plot, midway between culture and nature, neither in a human dwelling nor in a bird's natural forest habitat. The old couple bring the eggs home (*chan*) where they use one egg as food for human consumption, hence both a loss (*poloa*)[21] and a requirement of life.[22] The other is treated as offspring to be covered by a hen, the fertile counterpart of an old man's aging and sterile wife. The corn boy is kept alive by the domestic fowl but without being allowed to enter the house of his surrogate parents.[23]

The male egg is preserved against death. As with corn seeds, one egg is consumed whereas another, the stronger, is wisely put aside for future needs. Moderation is a guarantee of survival. But there is a price to be paid for the preferential treatment accorded to the male seed. Sons nurtured by their parents are trapped into serving their masters. While the act of brooding (*tapachoa*, wrapping, encircling) performed by the hen and the old couple implies protection, it also suggests a measure of domination. In Nahuatl, a "person that broods" (tlapacho) is someone with authority, a household head, one who governs, administers property, etc.[24] A creature that broods can be suspected of holding another in captivity. Wittingly or not, one creature nurturing and folding another in its arms may end up crushing it, "covering it with stones" (*tepachoa*) as it were.[25] In retrospect, the male egg-seed protected by the corn-eating hen is vulnerable.[26] The male egg or corn seed is to the hen what the hen, daughter or wife is to the *milpa* master: a dependent in need of protection but also a servant and a source of food that will perish when consumed.

The vulnerability of a boy born in the *milpa* is at the heart of a story that speaks of a male plant that must die and be consumed in order to reproduce. The egg is referred to as *gonetsin*, a term used by women to denote a child of either sex. The narrative immediately adds another word, *chogotsin*, from xocotl, a fruit, also the youngest son of the family, the one who inherits the land and the obligation to look after his parents when too old to provide for their own needs. The boy, however, is more than an egg-like fruit: he is also a staple plant. This is the story of *Sintiopiltsin*, the corn-god-child: from *sinti*, a dry ear of corn, the grain-bearing spike or head of the plant; *tio*, a god or a goddess; and *piltsin*, a child (in Nahuatl, a lord). The maize plant is here defined as a male creature;[27] at the beginning Sintiopiltsin did have a sister, but she was taken away by lightning (García de León 1966: 5). In anatomical terms, the "son of maize" is the name assigned to the umbilicus (*ixictayol*) or germ of the kernel taken from a large, dry ear of corn. The narrative thus assimilates the male egg found in the *milpa* to the germ of the corn seed surrounded with albumen.

As in the prehispanic era,[28] the Gulf Nahuas have a particular name for each stage of maize development.[29] Sintiopiltsin is corn at an early stage of a growth process that ends in death. While the seed and the young plant require water to grow, the mature plant must dry out and sexually exhaust itself in order to produce seeds for future generations (Sedeño and Becerril 1985: 107). The father plant must wither if it is to produce seed corn that will inherit its portion of the earth. The best ears of the dry-season *tapachol* harvest (April or May) must be put aside and cared for (*tapachoa*) so as to be later used to seed the wet-season *temporal* (planted in June, harvested in November).

The twin-egg imagery announces a two-sided strategy: while the male child is protected, the female is devoured. The scene ends on an ambivalent note. The dying and the living are portrayed as separate characters, as if they were travelling on different roads. The couple laments the sister's fate, yet her death is not recuperated through some meaningful lesson that could save her loss from sheer narrative absurdity. Since he is preserved from death, the male seed could always be seen as rescuing the scene from a gloomy ending. The problem though is that his survival implies certain costs that have yet to be faced. The young "water-like" Sintiopiltsin is a god destined to dry and die under the heat of the sun and to be eaten by human beings – by the *milpa* masters who hold the deity in captivity. The narrative has barely begun its journey toward a fully-developed illustration of signs of self-denial embedded in natural cycles of life. Like eggs and chickens that the Gulf Nahuas will sacrifice to restore health and growth to humans and plants (García de León 1991: 30; Boege 1988: 118, 143–5, 193), the corn boy will have to be killed and devoured so as to feed new generations of men and maize alike.

The mocking iguanas incident

A father in need of water

The young boy grew and grew (*weyakya*). The old man was going to the *milpa*, and he "gave him" (*gimaga*) to fetch (*magibiti*) water from the fountain (*atapan*).

In a Zoque-Popoluca variant of our corn myth (López Arias 1983), a son whose father had died was crying so much that his mother decided to grind him on a *metate* rock and to throw the mantilla head-covering containing his remains into the river. She disposed of the son like fruit wrapped in clothing. The poor boy was then transformed by God into an egg and placed on a liana. While going to the river, a cannibal sorceress named Chichiman saw the egg reflected in the water. With the help of her sorcerer husband, she tried in vain to pull the egg out of the river until the man looked above and saw the egg in the liana. They brought it down for the sorcerer to eat, but the old woman said they should cover the egg to see what was in it. After seven days a little boy broke out of the egg crying. The woman thought she recognized her son. The old man told his wife they should raise him and eat him. After seven days the boy was already tall and the sorceress sent him to fetch water from the river.

This story brings out some of the implications of the symbols deployed in the introductory scene of our Gulf Nahua reference myth. Associations between birth, water and head (child wrapped in a head-covering) are explicit. The water-of-life motif is conveyed through the infant's tears, the child bathing in the river and then fetching water for his surrogate mother. The fruit-child wrapped in clothing (tlaaquillotl) is synonymous with the chayote known as _taguihlo_ in Pajapan, also a term for any fruit that hangs and the vulva as well. Chayote grows on vines that climb around tree trunks. Given these connections, it is only logical that a fruit or child placed in a vulvar garment and dropped into the water-of-life should grow back into a chayote-child nesting in a liana.[30]

The seed and fruit of life grow in water. In our Gulf Nahua myth, the child's task after birth is to grow with the beneficial rain "watering the head" of Sintiopiltsin in due season, immediately after planting (May–June) (see Foster 1945: 194).

The prefix _ue_ has now turned into a verb (_ueyak_) denoting growth rather than age or the size of the eggs laying in the _milpa_. The water fetched by the boy reinforces this growth imagery. The fluid implies a fountain (_apan_, or _amel_, "water-flow") of blessings. The surrogate father asks the corn son to fetch water while he is working in the _milpa_, attending to the needs of his maize plants. The corn god is drawing water (_atabi_) from the underground to feed humans who return the favor by pouring water-like seeds into the ground and looking after the plants. Signs of life, fertility and growth conveyed through watering augur well for the immediate future of both the child and his adoptive father.[31]

All the same, few textual alterations would be needed to turn the well scene in the opposite direction, toward memories of evil and trials suffered on earth. First, water may be a harbinger of doom. When poured without measure, the fluid can destroy plant life just like heat or fire. The corn son must be raised well above water, away from the beginnings of life, if he is to grow and reproduce. He must avoid drowning in tears or in water that comes from his brain, a _malviento_ or a north wind blowing at harvest time.[32] Second, the plant child's birth in water implies the death of the father plant, as in the Zoque-Popoluca variant, or the aging of his surrogate parents who are in need of water and food; life given to the young is taken away from the old. Third, the imagery of a boy "taking" (_bi_, _bilia_, _cui_) water from the well lends itself to pejorative speculations.

The act is synonymous with stealing and sexual abuse: to rape a woman (*guiguizki*, cuitiuetzi) is to take something away with haste, a gesture implying an act of cutting, removing or grasping (*guizki*, cuicui).[33] Accordingly, falling into water (atoyauia) conjures up the vision of a moral fall, of man lapsing into sin by letting too much of his own "water fall" (*auetzi*, to ejaculate) through sexual activity. Unless the proper measures are taken, readers can expect water poured or consumed in excess (*atoloani*) to turn into a waste product (*at* = water = urine): come the right moment in time, the corn boy will be required to pour urine on his own breast.[34]

The well scene shows latent signs of unbridled sexuality, crimes of thievery and the flooding of plant life and humans alike. In spite of its positive associations, a well is to be feared. The Gulf Nahuas commonly view springs, fountains and rivers as dangerous sites where human souls can be stolen through fright, i.e., *espanto* (*nemotil*, from *momohtia*). If plunged into aquatic surroundings, men's shadow-like souls can suffer sickness or death, just like maize plants. When in water, humans can lose the solar life forces (*tonal*) that dwell in their bodies, souls that are pale reflections of *tonati totahtsin*, our father the sun, the supreme being who makes plants sprout and men "live", "inhabit" or "walk" (*nemi*) the earth.[35]

Wells threaten souls that can be taken captive by otherworldly spirits known as *chane* or *chaneques*, from *chan* or *chanti*, a house. These spirits are central to the Gulf Nahua view of relations between humans and spirits and between humans themselves. Native beliefs and rituals pertaining to these ancient gods can serve to illustrate a principle that pervades our reference myth: the moral notion that the good life recoils on those who indulge in it while being granted to those who renounce it. Self-destruction awaits all creatures who attempt to reproduce (food, children) without self-denial.

The *chaneques* are funny little creatures that wear no clothes and never engage in sex, at least not between themselves. They dwell (*chantia*) in mountains, ruins, caves, water caverns (*atiopan*, water-god-site) or any body of water. They have holes instead of noses and are particularly attracted by humans and their noses. They are in the habit of catching human souls and feeding on human flesh; like the prehispanic tlaloque, they are particularly fond of children's souls (González Torres 1985: 137). Water-chaneques (achanes, taneko) can take the form of ferocious alligators or "water-lizards" (acuetzpalin), cousins of the "forest-lizard" iguana (*baguetspalin*) who is about to make his entry at the well scene. Alternatively, the spirits are said to use alligators as boats and to live at the bottom of marshes, in houses guarded by man-eating alligators, or in rooms that equal the segments of an iguana tail.[36]

The *chaneques* and the lower world they inhabit embody the good life. Their chthonian houses are accessible through doors shaped like tiger mouths or through deep tunnels located underneath *amate* trees, below the seaside Campanario Rock and the San Martín volcano.[37] The latter trees serve as a medium between humans and water spirits: they grow near rivers and are the source and the synonym of paper used anciently for "writing" (*ihbilo*, *cuiloa*). Creatures living under their "wing" or "foliage" (*amatlapalli*) are by definition wealthy. Sacred doors and paper trees give access to houses that form part of an underworld known as *Talogan*, an Edenic universe lying on the other side of a river full of blood or yellow pus (*temal*); a black dog accompanies those who cross the river. The houses are guarded by fearsome serpents and jaguars and are full of precious stones and money, fruit and honey, flowers and food in abundance, tall *chicozapote* trees, beautiful women, countless animals and human souls held in captivity. All wild animals and fish are said to be owned by the *chaneques* and each animal species has its *tayaganga* master.[38]

Access to these spirits and their subterranean riches is regulated by movements of the solar body and the maize cultivation cycle. Encounters with *chaneques* are more likely to occur at Easter, around the time of the vernal equinox and the harvesting of dry-season ears of corn (used to decorate the church on Holy Friday; some informants consider that Christ and the sun are one and the same divinity; see Sandstrom 1991: 248). The date corresponds to the end of the Christian Lent, a four-week period during which present-day healers collect and prepare medicinal plants growing in the forest. Contacts with the other world also occur typically around the time of the summer solstice, on the night of the June 24. This period of the year extending from early March to the summer solstice (known in Spanish as the *tiempo de figuras*) is a time when important religious festivities are held and when most medicinal plants are collected, apprentice healers are trained, and maize seeds begin to sprout.[39]

Under certain conditions, *chaneques* will allow courageous sorcerers and "men of vision" to enter their world and even marry a female *chaneca*.[40] The spirits can grant special healing powers to plants and herbs collected by healers, they can give fishers and hunters the catch they need to feed themselves and their families, and they can restore a spirit to its human body (via the innocuous appearance of a butterfly, a spider, a grasshopper). They can do all of this provided that certain rules be followed. First, the patient, the healer, the hunter or the fisher must fast and abstain from sexual activity or physical contact with their wives or other women. Hunters and fishermen who give part of their catch to their mistresses or use the money obtained from their produce to buy the services of prostitutes will move the spirits to anger. Chances are that they will suffer an accident and lose access to the wild animals owned by the *chaneques*. Men chasing after wives or women on the game are condemned never to catch food.[41]

Men who fall in love with *chanecas* must abstain from having sex or physical contact with their wives lest they be deprived of the life of plenty found in *Talogan*. On this matter of sexual fasting, it bears mentioning that old persons, virgins and youths below the age of puberty are specially suited to certain ritual tasks such as collecting and grinding medicinal flowers and plants, perfuming a fishing net with incense (*sahumar*), or carrying saints in processions. Also, friendship with the spirits may be reinforced by the ritual burning of a cotton wick. Cotton and agave threads (_ishcat_) are associated with the weaving of clothes to protect female modesty; they stand for the virginity (ichpochtli) of women behaving like young hens or chicks (_ishposh_) that are given in sacrifice to the underworld _chaneques_. In its own way the ritual evokes the burnt offering of female sexuality.[42]

Second, when given access to chthonian riches, men should not take more than one precious object less they be denied everything they see.[43] The same logic applies to men's daily lives: humans should never kill more fish or animals than is strictly needed. They should be careful not to hurt animals needlessly. _Chaneques_ are responsible for treating and healing animals that have been harmed by careless hunters. Likewise, broken ears of maize should not be kept as it would prolong the agony of the Corn Master. Nor should grains of corn be thrown away or wasted lest the whole harvest be lost.[44] The crime amounts to a deicide: in the words of one healer, the corn plant "is a god and there would be no life if he did not exist".

The third rule concerning the _chaneques_ is that "humans must constantly placate spirit entities with offerings in order to set things right" (Sandstrom 1991: 313). Vigils and gifts must be offered to the spirits or the healer acting on their behalf: i.e., flowers, perfume, aromatic water, _copal_ incense, holy palms, or a chick, to be given in exchange for the soul or "shadow" lost by a frightened child. Healing can be performed with water and stones taken from the site where the trauma occurred. Alternatively, the healer may treat his patient with the use of plants, dry corn silk, ears of corn (with seven kernels), holy water, images of saints, or pig fat. Finally, a ranch egg may be placed against the sinciput so as to pull out and receive the illness or foreign body sapping the patient's strength.[45]

More should be said about the importance of the flower symbolism in Gulf Nahua language and religion. The native word for flower is _xochit_, a term that embodies all things beautiful and the good life on earth. To the Aztecs, perfume was xochiocotzol, "flower-resin" that smells as good as the _copal_ incense obtained from the xochicopalquauitl tree. When combined with terms for water or house (xochatl, xochicalli), the term used to signify rose-water and a bath house, respectively. Paradise on earth was xochitlalpan, a land adorned with lots of trees that bear fruit, a place where people are well treated and have every reason to laugh, rejoice (xochimati) and make jokes (xochuia).[46] Similar tropes are found in present-day Pajapan. Joking is what trickster-like _chaneques_ covered with flowers (_xochipontoc_) are reputed to do. Some of these joyful spirits live in a "water-temple" or sacred _atiopan_ cave located near Pajapan, by a river known as _Xochat_. As they live in a world of flowers, they are described as xochtic, i.e., small, young and pretty, like infants that do not speak. They are thought to eat meat and corn like gluttons (xochtlaquani) and to attract, charm or seduce (_xochiuia_, _xochixinia_) human beings who wish to become like them. They are as powerful as the xochitonal flower-spirit or alligator guarding their subterranean abode, the cousin of a mocking iguana about to enter the scene. Like most prehispanic gods and the iguanas discussed below, they are in a position to laugh and amuse themselves at the sight of humans struggling to survive (León-Portilla 1983: 200ff.).

This floral and water symbology points to the blessings of a better life filled with laughter. The blessings, however, can turn into a nightmare if pursued without abnegation. Feasting without fasting – gluttony without sacrifice – spells ruin for men who aspire to live in a land of plenty. If unrestrained, the outpouring of water and the fluids of life gives way to a flood of tears caused by destruction, rape and theft. Souls caught delighting themselves at springs and wells are likely to be lost at the hands of chthonian spirits who have it in their power to divest men of food, health and the solar life force that dwells in them. To avoid losing everything they crave for, humans must show respect toward nature and deprive themselves of the good life through dietary practices (sexual and alimentary) and offerings to the maize god (Foster 1945: 180). Otherwise they will not be able to produce staple plants to meet their needs, and their efforts to conquer the women and the animals they chase will come to naught. As in prehispanic days, humans must show self-control in matters of food and sex (León-Portilla 1983: 131, 135, 142ff., 222f., 238). They must renounce pleasures of the flesh, make floral offerings to the *chaneques* and emulate these asexual child-like spirits if they wish to be like them – to find laughter and walk in the nude in the underworld paradise. Unless they behave like subterranean infants deprived of noses, they shall never attain the power of the mighty *tayangaga* (from *yagat*, nose) spirits, "big brothers" reputed to control the *chaneques* and all the riches hoarded in *Talogan* (García de León 1969: 292, 296).

In the scene that follows, more is said about the moral of asceticism and the role of the mocking iguana *vis-à-vis* humans, plants and spirits of the lower world. The narrative has reached a point where a central notion can rise to the surface: life must keep a certain distance from water, the origin of life and all things wet, if it is to grow and reproduce.

The mocking iguanas

And there were iguanas (*bagetspalimeh*) there who were making fun (*pinahtiayah*) of the boy. They said "*elote, elote*, cut ears (*nagastanpepel*), your father is over there, in the land where men are dry (*Tagatawatsaloyan*)." They came to inform (*ginotsaya*) the boy. He didn't know (*agimatia*) what they were saying. They were just saying "*elote, elote*, cut ears, your father (*motah*) is over there, in the land where men are dry."

The *elote* boy is mocked by iguanas. The animals make fun of his "cut ears" (drooping, hairless)[47] and tell the boy where his real father is, in the "land-where-men-are-dry". An *elote* is maize after three months of growth, beyond the immature *xiloti* stage, with leaves of husk that have begun to dry. Though still in the milk stage and not dry enough to be harvested or to produce seeds for future generations, the _elote_ grains are already formed and can be eaten on the cob or be ground to produce fresh-maize _tamales_ or _tortillas_. This growth stage is normally reached just before the arrival of the heavy rains of September and October brought by tropical storms in the Gulf of Mexico and Caribbean (followed by the cold, gusty _nortes_ blowing from October through March). In order to promote drying and protect _elote_ ears against wind and water, the stalks are bent over or "doubled" below the lowest ear once the corn has reached maturity. The upper part of the stalk is usually tied to the lower with the maize leaves. The iguanas seem to be laughing at the sight of the corn child's "doubled ears".

In a Zoque-Popoluca variant (López Arias 1983), the corn boy identifies himself as _clavito y a la vez dobladito_, i.e., nail-like yet "doubled". The plant boy is standing up but also bowing down before the mighty winds and rains of the high sea. Corn-eating birds (pigeons and grackles) also make fun of his red hair and threaten to eat him. The red-hair attribute assigned to the hero converges again on signs of immaturity. The plant creature feeding on water and light (_tauil_) partakes in the redness (_tlauhyo_, _tatahuic_) of the morning sun rising at "dawn" (_tlauizcalli_, "light-house"), literally "lighting up" while ascending through the "red house" to the east or the southeast (_tlauhcopa_), beyond the sea.[48]

The corn boy has yet to reach full maturity. He is torn between the beginnings of life in water and the requirements of heliotropic growth. His surrogate father faces the opposite problem in that the old man experiences thirst while working. A dry mouth indicates that someone is "dying of thirst" (_amigui_) and is in a state of want.[49] Logically, a man who is aging, moving away from life-that-begins-in-water, will suffer from thirst. The corn child's real father suffers a similar fate in that he dwells in _Tagatauatzaloyan_, the "land-where-men-are-dry". The term combines the word for man, _tagat_, with _uatza_, to dry, to become weak or to drain oneself sexually; _tauatzal_ denotes something that has been tanned or dried (_uaktok_). According to García de León (1969: 303–4; 1976: 138), the mythical land in question is of prehispanic origin and is located in the highland Papaloapan valley, west of Pajapan. The site corresponds to _galagui tonati_, "the house where the sun enters", hence the sun aging and disappearing beyond the mountains at the end of the day. The sun's westerly house lies far away from the sea, opposite from _guiça tonati_, which is "where the sun comes out" or "begins".[50]

In short, the young corn child is to his father what the wet lowland is to the dry upland, the east to the west, the morning light to the evening darkness – what the reign of life is to the rule of death. Both characters can be mocked as they lack the ability to reconcile opposite moments in time and locations in space.[51] By contrast, the trickster-like iguana or "forest lizard" (_baguetspalin_) has no problem in reuniting land and water, the high and the low. The iguana moving freely between water, earth and sky, has every reason to make fun of the corn child.[52] It walks on earth with four legs yet also lives near water and mangrove swamps and is a good swimmer. Like a fish or a serpent, it has a body covered with scales and a powerful tail to punish or protect itself from its enemies (García de León 1991: 30); rumor has it in Pajapan that the reptile possesses ophidian flesh due to mating with snakes. The animal also resembles a bird: it lays lots of eggs (30 to 50), dwells in trees and eats fruit, insects and eggs.[53] In its own way, the iguana embodies the good life: it is not only good to eat but also a prolific begetter and a voracious eater, a glutton (cuetzpal). The boy is disgraced by the fact that he is no match for the iguana. Although born from an egg-like seed and feeding on water and sun, the young plant is doomed to grow with the fear (tepinaualiztli)[54] of drowning in water or drying in the sun.

And yet great weakness lies in the powers of the iguana. The corn son has to receive education (tlacauapaualiztli, human aging, strengthening) from his father but he will not get this from the iguana who, in spite of its massive tongue, or perhaps because of it, is unable to speak the human way, that is, with caution and modesty (tlacatlatoa). The iguana puts the boy to shame by calling him and his father names; in Gulf Nahua notza is to call a person by his name and nohnotza, to criticize or insult.[55] Given its evil tongue, the iguana deserves to be silenced or forced to shout, as in the next scene. In the Zoque-Popoluca variant (López Arias 1983), the iguana has a bad cough and is unable to deliver an important message. A small lizard takes over from the iguana but ends up saying exactly the opposite of what the corn boy meant to tell his mother. Because of the lie told by the lizard, the narrative goes on to say, human beings are no longer immortal. To punish the animal, the corn god cuts its tongue in half, which accounts for the forked tongue characteristic of the small cowixin lizard.

The iguana's ability to move freely between water, earth and sky and the corresponding forms of life can also be held against it. Powers acquired at no sacrificial cost will not last; they cannot be preserved because they are never deserved. An earthly creature of the flesh (gluttonous and well-fed yet edible and mortal) rising above the earth without sacrificial intent can be suspected of rising above (ahco) and therefore against (acomana) the godly powers that be. Accordingly, the animal should be punished, condemned to have its feet tied or to walk slowly, as in another scene and in other variants of the same story.

In order to avoid suffering the same fate as the iguana, the corn boy must be taught the ascetic way of life. Lowering the immature corn ear is a good start. The downward position (tani) is bound to produce some humiliation or "downfall" (tlanitlaça). The plant, however, can turn its fall to advantage by transforming it into a sacrifice. Through doubling and drying, the hero will grow, mature and reproduce life, his own and the lives of men as well. The corn son is thus in a position to emulate the plant that gave him life.

Life is torn between the blessings of the sunny life and death caused by the heat of the tonati sun. On the one hand, ancient Nahuatl and current Gulf Nahua derivations of the root verb tona are evocative of not only food and the sustenance of life (tonacayotl) in general but also dry-season corn (tonalmil) and everything else that grows "under the sun" (_tonayan_), in the heat (_tonalli_) of the summer season (_tonallan_). Accordingly, in Pajapan, the _tonal_ denotes one's portion or lot in life, hence the soul, shadow, spirit or life force of the human body.[56] On the other hand, the drying process (_tonaluagui_) is a requirement of plant reproduction, a sacrificial offering (_tonaltia_) built into the cycle of life and death on earth. Corn ears must be dried, shelled (_taoya_) and cleansed of all impurities to produce edible food or seed for planting, hence dry _tayol_ grains.[57] To dry under the sun is to move closer to the moment of death and to gather the strength needed to reproduce. The rule applies to humans, soils and plants alike. Just as a man advancing in age is growing both thin and strong (_chigac_, _pipiktik_), so too a plant or a plot that dies under the action of sun or fire has gained in maturity (_yoksik_) and may serve to reproduce life.[58]

Our solar father (_totahtsin_) that feeds all plant life is subject to the same fate. In order to grow and rise out of water to the east, he must ascend to the dry southern sky and then die in arid western mountains at the end of each day, thereby joining the corn child's father who lies in _Tagatauatzaloyan_. The father of life must disappear at the end of each day and temporarily cease "to be" (_ag_) if he is to accede to a new dawn. The sun is thus subject to native images of "being" (_tagat_, man, the "one who is") that speak to the complementarity of life and death, a cyclical regime where signs of absence or "non-presence" (_ayag_) are never a pure waste: being thrives on non-being. The interpenetration of being and non-being is already inscribed in the root word _ag_ which can be used to describe not only the "one who is" (_tagat_, man) but also the sun that is no longer – the solar father that "hides and falls into a house" at night (_galagui tonati_). In the latter expression, the verb _agui_ implies that the male sun is penetrating, entering, planting, wearing or deceiving (_agui_, _tahaguilia_) the earth, just like a man seducing a woman or making love to her while she sleeps (_tetlan aqui_).[59] In the final analysis, man and sun can count on enjoying the light of life as long as they hide themselves and their shameful parts in clothes, darkness, the earth and the womb.[60]

The iguana snare

Narrative references to the growth, the doubling and the drying of the maize child suggest that the hero has begun his journey toward full maturation. Sintiopiltsin can start moving in the direction of his father and the sun who rest beyond mountains to the west, away from the earth, waters of the womb and pleasures of the flesh. Unlike the iguana, the hero must suffer trials that will give him the strength needed to grow and to feed human beings and new plant generations with his own life. The mocking iguana scene is but one step toward a full-fledged illustration of the teachings of asceticism. As argued below, the boy's encounter with the mocking iguana at the site of a well gives our young hero a first opportunity to set a good example by emulating the child-like spirits (_chaneques_) dwelling in _Talogan_. Given the right conduct, the maize child can triumph over an iguana known for its long tail and loose tongue, a frivolous creature unable to secure the blessings of wealth and laughter found in the underworld paradise.

The narrative describes Sintiopiltsin's victory over his iguana enemy in the following manner:

Later the boy spoke (_gitahtaguetskeh_) to his elderly father (_itah wewehtsin_). "Grandfather, the animals over there come to make fun of me; they come to tell me (_nechihliagih_) these words. Make me an iguana snare (_nopichawan_), I'll lasso them (_nia nigitsonwiti_) with my string (_nomamegat_)." "This I'll do for you (the grandfather said)." The next day the old man made the child an iguana snare; he looked (_temoilih_) for wax.

(The iguanas come again and repeat the same words.) "Come on you ruffian (_anda cabrón_), I'm going to lasso you (said the boy)." He followed (_gitogatih_) them with his snare and _tras_, he caught one (_gilpilih_) by the tail ... and the tail broke (_postek_). It came back again (_walak siók_) and he caught it (_gigiskih_) once more if only by the foot (_iyikxi_) and hit it with the string (_gimegawitek_).

"Why do you come to mock me? I didn't come to play (_mamawiltigo_) with you. I came because my grandfather (_notahwéh_) sent me (_nechóhmak_) to fetch (_manikbiligi_) water (_at_), because he gets thirsty (_atanegi nemi_) when he clears the _milpa_. Go away, and if you mock me once more I'll lasso you. One day I'll lasso you and I'll never let you go (_ninamechmahkawati_). With my grandfather I'll take you (_ninamechwiati_) and he'll eat you up." So he frightened them (_ginmohmotih_) and they went away and never came back. They only shouted at him (_gitsahtsiliah_) from afar (_wehka_).

The scene revolves around the impressive tail and tongue of the mocking iguana, appendages that raise basic issues regarding language and sexuality. Consider first the loose-tongue motif. The iguanas are guilty of indiscretion, of letting words escape from their careful attention. Such ill-spoken creatures are not worthy of admiration (_mauizoa_) and deserve to be silenced or reduced to shouting and crying (_mahmauitzatzi_, _tzohtzi_, _tzatzatzi_) while fleeing. In the Zoque-Popoluca variant, the lizard's tongue is cut in half because of the animal's failure to tell the truth. The animal stands accused of treating words like rumors, mockeries and lies that spread too quickly, changing their meaning through misinterpretation. Fish poking fun at the boy's red hair suffer a similar fate; the boy retaliates by catching a few fish with a line and hook and then passing a string through their mouth. The iguana, the lizard and the fish are punished where they have sinned: through mouth and tongue.[61]

While the iguana indulges in frivolous language,[62] the conversation the corn god entertains with his grandfather (_gitahtaguetskeh_) takes the form of the ancient tlatlaquetzalli, a tale but also a jest, from quetzalli or _guetza_, terms that illustrate the powers of Gulf Nahua speech.[63] The root verb, _guetza_, implies narrative elegance and the telling of a tale (_tataguetza_) designed to set an example. But the word can also serve to raise other issues having to do with tails, feathers and sex. In classical Nahuatl, quetza stands for things and people of great value: jewelry, a son or parent, a protector or leader, a generous soul (quetzalyollotl). All of these are as precious and beautiful as the green tail-feather of the quetzaltototl (*Pharomacrus mocino*), a trogon bird brilliant green above and red below, with long streaming tail-feathers in the male. In keeping with these feather-tail associations, the verb quetza means to rise, to erect, to stand up. Finally, the root word lends itself to evocations of sensual activity and mating. The term signifies to unite, to create harmony, to embrace, to support (as with a *taguetzal* pillar or post). The symbology applies to a couple about to marry: the Gulf Nahuas speak of a *tauialquetzal* fiancé, a shining feather, and his *soaguetzal* bride.[64]

Tails are the site of great power and blessings envied by all. Although all species have tails (cuitlapilli), some have longer appendages than others. The quetzal bird and rats (cuitlapilhueyac) are well endowed in this regard, as is the iguana. The reptile has such a long rear end that it is reputed to mate with serpents and to possess ophidian flesh; its tail is so massive and strong that the Gulf Nahuas believe it will continue to live even when cut, as if it were a serpent. Also *chaneque* spirits are said to inhabit the bread-like buttocks (*tzintamal*) of the iguana. They use the animal tail to flog hunters who hurt animals needlessly or kill them to feed their mistresses (García de León 1969: 294, 306).[65]

All in all, the iguana and the corn boy occupy different positions vis-à-vis issues of sexuality conveyed through the guetza language and tail-feather imagery. Although growing rapidly and speaking with elegance, the ear of corn is still without the reproductive powers of the iguana and the ability to reunite water, earth and sky. Nor do his leaves or stalk compare all that favorably with the tail of the iguana, a green appendage as impressive as the quetzalli tail-feather. In the tail (and the tongue) of the iguana, however, lies a great weakness, a lack of restraint that points to the superiority of the corn spirit.[66] Too big a tail spells ruin for the wealthy, the potent and the powerful. The inferior backside part is all the more perishable as it can be linked to material that rots, hence excrement, *bitat* in Pajapan, a term synonymous with money, fault and filth.[67] Finally, the lizard is guilty of making fun (*auiltia*) of the corn boy, hence playing or toying (*auilnemi, ahauil*) with the root verb *auia*, a term implying a wastage of one's wealth.[68] The animal deserves to lose its appendage.

The animal is chastised according to the rule of proportional retribution, a rule whereby evil returns to cause its own destruction. An excess of phallic might results in castration. The boy insults the iguana by calling it *cabrón*, a male goat that stands for a cuckold but also a paramour, a ruffian or a pimp. The insult suggests a conversion, from cock to cuckold. Moreover, the hero catches and mutilates his prey. One iguana is caught by the rear end, producing the sound *tras*, an onomatopoeia and the word for behind (*tzin, el trasero*). The corn boy cuts the tail of the animal and frightens (*mahmaui*, cuitla-pammauhtia) the iguana away. The gesture is the equivalent of denigrating (mauizpoloa) and reprimanding (_postegui_) the culprit, breaking the animal's back, shoulders or loins.[69] The iguana becomes spineless and shoulderless. It is condemned to flee, to "turn a shoulder" and "run with fear".[70] The imagery implies emasculation: the captured tail is a "bottom-stick" (_tzinbayo_), a staff or stalk that suffers from impotence when dead (tzinmicqui) or broken (_postequitzinbayo_). Actually the punishment is so severe as to affect all bodily extremities: not only the phallus but also the tongue, the tail and the foot. The long-tailed, firm-footed and loose-tongued animal is unmanned and silenced, put down and trampled (_icxipechtia_). The narrative ties the animal by the tongue, the tail and the foot (_icxiilpia, iximegauia_). It silences and slows it down with the appropriate string (_iximegat_), if only to confirm its inclination to self-debasement and laziness (icximiqui, dead feet).

The hero's victory over the iguana is complete. Losses suffered by the iguana are our young hero's gains. Sintiopiltsin's plan to catch the mighty-tailed iguana is a pretext to rob the animal of its inherent powers. He does this with a solid bamboo stick with a string (_megat_) at one end to pull a lasso fixed at the other extremity. The cord is twisted (_malinah_) like a liana or climbing plant (_bamegat, bamegayo_) and is covered with beeswax to make the noose slide. Interestingly, the trap is so constructed as to prefigure the catch itself.[71]

The lasso bears close resemblance to the animal prey falling into the trap (mecauia). On the surface level, the string resembles a belt, a _mamegat_ fishing line, a twisted cord to shoot arrows with (mecayotia), or a handle (_megayo_) attached to a utensil or tool. But a _megat_ carries associations other than the literal string serving as a lasso. If used to carry heavy loads, the string (_megapal_) becomes the mark of a slave (mecapallo), a creature flogged (_megauitegui_) by his master. The mastery procured through this imagery applies to the sexual domain as well. The connection is threefold. First, the _megat_ snare used by the hero is a stronger version of the iguana _tzinmegayo_ tail or vulgar "backside handle": the hunter's line triumphs over the lizard's phallic tail. Second, the noose or net used in this scene stands for the greatest prey of all: a _megat_ lover.[72] The lasso-at-the-well imagery suggests that the boy is trying to put someone else's head in the noose (ilpiacayotl) in the sense of binding or attaching (_ilpia_) another life to his own, confining an attractive creature to a prison-like (teilpilcalli) trap. Third, if converted into a matrimonial tie, the string can turn into an umbilical cord (_xicmegat_); the conversion points to the germ-son of corn (_ixictayol_) and the linkages of a family, a genealogy, or a lineage (mecayotl).

In short, the _megat_ and derivatives thereof denote not only the means (snare, lasso) to conquer something or someone but also the object conquered or possessed (lover, slave, family ties). Ascetic usages of the string imagery, however, suggest that objects of desire and means to possess them cannot be mastered and preserved against the enemy if never renounced.

The corn boy can master his prey through a show of self-denial, an exercise that requires the _megat_ string to be made of hair plucked from the child's head. As with Samson, the strength of our hero lies in his hirsute head, in his ability to lasso (*tzonguia*, *tzonuia*) his enemy with his hair (*tzonti*), catching it with his *tzongal* hair-house turned into a deadly snare (tzouaztli). In order to obtain this snare and conquer his prey, however, the maize boy must be made bald. This is to say that he can obtain victory by attaining maturity, the kind that results in a *pixca* harvest, from pi, to tear or pull a plant or a person's hair. Like the iguana hanging by the string or the fish caught with hook and line, the plant must be pulled by the head and then husked with a wooden tool called *pixcon*. In Pajapan, this husking device is a euphemism for the penis, and the husking, peeling and plucking imagery (*xipia*), the equivalent of a man losing his virginity.[73] The powers of reproduction shall be granted to the hero provided that the boy resign himself to being deflowered, losing his hair or head, hence bowing the head down. He must refrain from "raising his hair" (*tzohmioguetza*), becoming angry and rebelling against what life has in store for him. In the long run, a head that bows down is the only head that can sow (*tzontoctoc*, from *tzonti* and *toga*, to sow). Death by hair-cutting (*tzontegui*, also "to cut oneself") or decapitation (*geshtzontegui*) heralds in a new life.

The fact that the corn god masters the iguana augurs well. But the boy has yet to demonstrate his valor and achieve maturity by turning the string and tail imagery against himself. Unless he flogs or disciplines (*megauitegui*) himself and atones for the crimes of others (cuitlatzacuilia), his victory will be as short-lived as the powers enjoyed by the foolish iguana. If the boy refuses to break down and bend (*doblar*, beloa) under the heavy rains, he will suffer the fate inflicted on his father, as in another variant of the myth: he will be whipped by the winds of autumn and be destroyed by lightning and thunder (*tatibini*) from the north. In order to reproduce, the boy must tighten a belt (cuitlapicayotl) of leaves around his body, gird up his loins (cuitlalpia), and then bow (cuitlacaxxoa) or fall to the ground, be shelled, beaten and chastised (*uitegui*). The secret of immortality lies precisely in the corn god's ability to withstand all such trials, which are unknown to the iguana. As made clear in the Zoque-Popoluca story, Sintiopiltsin will live forever and triumph over his natural enemies as long as he agrees to dry up, spread his seed and serve as food for men.[74]

To catch the iguana, the corn boy had to follow (*toga*, *togatia*) or search for (*temoa*) his prey. The actual catch results in a riddle: the hunter appropriates an animal tail while also finding fault with it. Wisely enough, the narrative chooses to remove the appendage from the boy's grip. Instead of playing along with the foolish animal, the hero persists in his task, which is to fetch fresh water for his grandfather. In doing so, he secures and gives up the source of life (and the iguana flesh) for the sake of his adoptive father, all in anticipation of an even greater sacrifice: the corn god offering itself as food for men.

The pilgrim fathers, the ant and the rock

Having given up life that begins in water to the east and mastered the iguana, the hero is empowered to move between water, earth and sky, closer to his father in the highlands, west of Pajapan.

> Thus grew the boy during many years. The old ones organized (_gitalihkeh_, from _tlalilia_) a trip to Oaxaca, by foot though. They prepared roasted food (_totopitos_) and their tortillas (_taxkal_). The boy knew they were leaving. He knew that he was the Master of Corn and that his father was there. He went to tell (_gihliagi_) his grandfather. "Grandfather, I too am going on a trip with these men." "But what will you bring, my son?" "I am going to wander (_nipaxaloti_) with them." "Go then, so that I may prepare (_manichiwili_) your water (_moatsitsin_), for they are going far (_wehka_). But they do not have tortillas for you to eat over there." "I will not lack (apoliwi) anything to eat there, so I am going with them." "Well, go then." The old man loved (_gitacohta_) his son (_ichogotsin_) so much that he let him go.

While steps are taken to reunite the high and the low, movement occurs through time as well. The child has grown and his journey to the headwaters of the Papaloapan River, from sunrise to sunset, from light to darkness, is undertaken in the company of Pilgrim Fathers substituted for his adoptive grandfather. Although by no means resolved, the opposition between old age and the motions of youth is attenuated by a boy growing older in the company of elderly men on the move.

The trip-to-Oaxaca scene is full of signs of the good life procured through abnegation, i e , saintly behavior associated with devotional voyages, the drying process and the lowering of the head. While on their way to Oaxaca (and perhaps Guatemala), the Pilgrim Fathers will leave the corn boy in the land of his father assimilated to the Señor de Otatitlán, a dark-skin father figure of the highland Papaloapan valley reputed to have survived his own decapitation (Münch 1983: 258).[75] The sanctuary of Otatitlán attracts pilgrims from Pajapan and from all parts of Mexico during the first week of May. This time of the year coincides with the clearing of plots before the rainy season and the planting of corn and calabash (García de León 1969: 302). The Señor de la Salud and la Santa Cruz, protector of merchants (anciently travelling to Guatemala via Tabasco and Chiapas), are also celebrated in early May, in memory of Christ ascending to heaven. Shortly thereafter, a visit is made to the Virgen de Carmen in Catemaco with a view to encouraging the rains and a good harvest in return for the sacrifices and offerings made to God and the Virgin.[76]

These pilgrimages are all the more important as they occur immediately before the early days of July, a period characterized by a shortage of corn, poor hunting and fishing, hence times of sickness and death (Stuart 1978: 212). Then comes the drying process. The corn boy growing in July and August must be doubled over and bow before the heavy rainfalls and storms blowing at autumn. When transposed to issues of moral behavior, the story implies that life and food cannot grow without gestures of lowliness and renunciation. The boy's adoptive father must give up the son he appreciates (_tasohta_) and let the food of his life go if it is to mature and reproduce. As for the boy, he feeds the life of others with little concern for his own needs; he gives fresh water to his adoptive father and loses part of himself in the form of food (_taxkal_, tortilla, and _totopito_, cooked food) fed to the Pilgrim Fathers. The corn master is a thriving plant that grows, yet he chooses to uproot himself from his native soil, after the manner of the Pilgrim Fathers who renounce the comfort of their native land.

As in real life, father and son depend on one another to survive. This relationship of mutual complementarity, however, is not likely to last. After all the corn boy is undertaking a journey toward full botanical maturity, toward his own death by drying and the regeneration of life that comes after. The narrative holds many trials in store for the young hero, including separation from the Pilgrim Fathers who will repeatedly abandon Sintiopiltsin while travelling on the way to the "land-where-men-are-dry".

The boy devoured by ants

The next scene is set in the summer season, between the moment of planting and the full maturation of corn plants obtained through doubling and drying. Danger awaits the hero and the pilgrims as they attain the mid-point of maize growth, midway between the lowland and the highland. The danger takes the shape of leaf-cutters, i.e., harvester ants known as _arrieras_ in Spanish, from the word for mule drivers. The insects are large red ants that attack maize plants from the moment of sprouting to the appearance of ears, two months after planting. It is from these creatures that Quetzacóatl received the gift of maize (Münch 1983: 177; León-Portilla 1983: 107).[77]

> Later they arrived (_asitoh_) in a place, the old ones say (_gihliagi_) – they didn't know he was the Master of Corn. "Spread (_xiktega_) here a few leaves (_achi baxiwit_), prepare (_ximopehpechti_) it (your bed) well (_miak_), for here there are leaf-cutter ants that eat men (_teba_)." He cut (_gitek_) three leaves, like he was spreading (_gitalih_) and not spreading (_agitaih_) them. He lay down (_motegak_) and fell asleep (_gochik_). When he woke up (_tanesito_) he was no longer there (_até masi_), there were only his bones (_ipetsomiotsin_). The leaf-cutters took everything away (_giwigiliah_) and ate it. Later the old ones said to him (_gihliagi_) (the boy was alive): "You see, you didn't believe the advice we gave you (_manimitsihliaya_), that you should spread many leaves on account of the leaf-cutters that eat men. You spread (_tiktalih_) few leaves and now you see what has become of you." "Well, just leave me (_nehkawagan_), I will know what to do. You go (_aniaweh_, _xagan_), I will catch up with you (_nimitstechoa_) on the trail (_pa oh_)." So they left him (_gahtehkeh_) there and went their way.

Great danger lies in the decision to lie down and fall asleep while rising at the height of the summer season. *Tega* is to lay (e.g., leaves on the ground), to lie down. In prehispanic times, however, the word also meant to have sex, to sow discord, to dishonor; a *tetecani* was a slanderer and a man who had sex with a woman. As for the resting motif, it differs little from our notion of sleeping (*gochi*), the opposite of vigilance. Someone who sleeps a lot (*gochca*) neglects (*cochcaua*) things that need attending, indulges in sex, and sleeps with women or possesses them in dreams or in their sleep (*cochuia*). Little does the lazy man know that while he "dreams in silence" (*gochtemigui*) he also courts death (*gogochi*, *gochmigui*, sleep-death).[78]

Sintiopiltsin is told to make his bed. In Nahua the act of preparing a bed (*pehpechtia*) or a seat is akin to hitting an animal of burden, beating it like a rug or mattress, using it for support, treating it like a *pehpech* blanket or saddle. The bed scene implies that the Mother Earth and her leaf-blanket are mounted or saddled by the corn boy. *Talia*, another term used to denote the act of spreading leaves on the ground, is also synonymous with "sitting" and "mounting". Someone climbing into a bed of leaves can thus be likened to a man climbing on an animal for transportation, on a woman for purposes of copulation (*tailia*), or on another creature with domination in view.[79]

The story leaves no doubt as to how the tension between the Corn Master and the Mother Earth should be resolved: at the expense of Sintiopiltsin. Given his inclination to rest, the leaf-cutters get the better of the Corn Master. Albeit small and easily trampled, the devouring ants (*tzigat*) behave like man-eating *chaneques*, tigers (*tebani*), serpents (*tequancoatl*), hence the "offspring of a venomous serpent" (*tebangonet*).[80] The insects inspire as much fear as their queen mother and her kindred spirit, the monstrous *tzicatl inan* ("ant mother") or *nauayaca* fer-de-lance, a serpent dwelling in *arriera* ant-hills and appearing as a beautiful woman to any sorcerer rolling himself in the nude over the ant-hill (Münch 1983: 208; García de León 1969: 286). In lieu of possessing the earth and the woman of his dream, the corn boy ends up being buried in an ant-hill (*tzicatpotzal*), bitten and devoured by a host of servants in the train of an all-powerful queen ant.

The earth consumes his flesh. Why though? Why can't the Corn Master enjoy a good night's rest and the good life that comes with it? The answer lies in his *tapesh* bed or, better said, in his *ahcotapesh* deathbed, the corn loft where maize plants stripped of life and leaves are stored away to be protected from insects. The secret of a peaceful rest lies in those leaves carried and devoured by the ants, leaves that should have been cut in greater number by their owner, the corn child. On the one hand, the Pilgrim Fathers tell the corn boy to cut a few (*achi*) leaves to make his bed, with the implication that he should not cut too many. That would spell ruin for him in that he would lose his green foliage and with it his ability to grow and reproduce. On the other hand, the narrative makes it quite clear that he should cut more than just a few leaves, if not a lot (*miagueh*). Herein lies his fault: his refusal to let go of more than three leaves.

Because he doesn't cut enough leaves, the corn boy is cut into pieces and ends up somewhere between life and death. He wakes up (*taneci*), literally making himself manifest, showing his face and coming to light like the sun appearing (*neci*, *nextia*) in the morning. At the same time he disappears from everybody's sight. He is not entirely there: *até maci*, "he was no longer complete", from *aci*, to arrive, to reach (*acic* is perfect). The child has lost his cheeks (*ixnagayo*) and corn-bread buttocks (*nagatamal*). He has been deprived of all flesh (*nagat*), the source of physical mobility, potency and descent, food and the festive life (nacaqua).

The corn boy is reduced to bones (omit). The fact that the Corn Master is deprived of his flesh entails a loss of vital strength, but it can also be turned into a mark of sacrifice, the source of a renewed strength. In order to feast on the flesh men must first abstain from eating meat, a restriction usually accompanied by a ban on sex. Moreover, having lost his flesh, the hero can count on his bones to recover what he lost through laziness. Good health comes from bones that are kept united (omiquetza). Provided that he renounces all carnal pleasures, the young boy could use his own bones as awls (omitl) to cut or open (*tapani*) the flesh. He could thus become a powerful nacapanca (nacatl + tlapana) butcher, a flesh-killer (*nagamictia*) but also a food provider that helps life sprout or burst forth from its shell (tlapana).

The Pilgrim Fathers reproach the corn boy for not having followed their advice. The boy's reaction is one of independence and self-confidence: "Well, just leave me, I will know what to do … I will find you on the trail." Instead of putting himself in the hands of the old men, he dismisses them, as if he no longer needed their protection. As we are about to see, the trials of Sintiopiltsin are a blessing in disguise. Once abandoned, the hero will be able to grow in sacrificial strength. He will find salvation in his own fall – in the loss of his flesh and the weakening of his enemy falling prey to temptations of gluttony.

Belting the ant and kicking the old man

Instead of tightening its belt and making do with the provisions obtained from its victim, one gluttonous ant comes back to cut more flesh. Like the long-tailed iguana in the well scene, the insect shows no restraint. The creature deserves to be punished where it has sinned: the belly. The episode is said to account for a central feature of ant anatomy: a thin waist separating the frontal sections of the insect from its large abdomen and the ovipositor at the end.

> Then came a leaf-cutter to cut more of his flesh (*inagayo*). The boy grabbed (*gibik*) one of his hairs (*istongal*) and tied it [the ant] by the middle (*gitahkoilpih*). "You know, you give me back (*tinehsaloilia*) my flesh just like it was when you cut it or I will cut you (*nimitstahko*) in half (*teponoti*) with my hair." "Caramba, don't squeeze me more, you'll make my waist burst (*tinehtahkowiltegiti*)." "Good, you give me back my flesh, because if not, I will cut you in half

with my hair." "Let me loose (*nehmahkawi*) so that I can tell (*manigihliti*) my leader (*notayaganga*) to give you back your flesh." "Go."

He let her go (*mahkaw*), the leaf-cutter went away. Soon after an ant with a "big behind" (*tsintanah*) came. "What happened?" [she said] "You give me back my flesh here and now, just like you found it (*anehtechohkeh*), or you'll be in trouble." The leader ordered that he be given back his flesh, and they gave it back. They put it back just like it was at first, the whole body. The boy got up (*mahkew*) and went behind (*iteposta*) the men who had gone away, on their journey. When they least expected it (*yahki*) he kicked the behind (*gitsinwitek*) of an old man on the trail. They told him: "How did you remedy your situation?" "With my wisdom I forced them to give me back my flesh."

Since he is deprived of flesh, Sintiopiltsin can take advantage of his weakness: through self-sacrifice, he can turn the string or belt imagery against his enemy. The hero plucks one hair (*tzonti*) from his head, a gesture resembling the *pixca* harvest and the act of husking, stripping the ear of its blond tassel hair (*xilot, xilotzonti*) or silky headdress. Given that hair (*tzongal*, hair-house) and head are synonyms, the hair-cutting gesture implies decapitation, or the separation of upper and lower parts of the body.[81] Death by beheading corresponds to what happens to the *elote* boy at autumn, a time when stalks are doubled, bent over and fastened at the waist: the upper part is tied to the lower with the use of leaves forming a belt. Measures of self-sacrifice can also be obtained by cutting something or oneself in half (*tahcotegui*).[82] Since *tahco* also means shoulder, the action amounts to breaking someone's back (*tahcopostegui*) or his column (*tahcoomio*). This backbreaking imagery has already been discussed, in reference to the iguana tail and the doubling of corn at autumn.[83]

The child regains the strength needed to take revenge against his enemies: the hair string plucked from his head gives him an instrument of domination, a cord to lasso (*tzonuia*) his enemy, tying (*ilpia*) the victim and making it fall into a snare. Great power lies in acts of self-mutilation, including the power to recover from thinness and death and to master one's enemy. The hero converts his pitztli bones and the thinness (*pitzac*) of his middle body (*tahco*) into a *pitzauayan* snare, a *tahcoilpia* belt (*cuitlalpia*) tightened around the enemy's waist.[84]

As in the iguana scene, however, the boy's victory over his predator must not end in sheer destruction. Domination is but a means toward an end, which is to get his flesh back. The ant goes to fetch the *tayaganga* queen ant, from *yagat*, the nose, a mark of seniority and superiority. The ruling ant restores the corn boy to his former condition. Having mastered the ant, the hero must let his prey loose. Were he to rob the insects of their lives and tie (*ilpia*) or possess the fat-bellied queen ant, the corn child would become like his enemy: a gluttonous creature in need of a reprimand. As with the iguana, the Corn Master must let go of his prey and her large oversized behind – her massive buttocks (*tzintanah*) shaped like a large _tanah_ straw bag.⁸⁵ If not her body will put temptation in Sintiopiltsin's way.

The Gulf Nahua word to describe the action of catching an animal by the tail is _tatzinbi_, from _tzin_, for behind, and _cui_, to take something or to possess a woman. In Nahuatl, the word is synonymous with shelling maize. This is precisely what the ants are accused of, a crime that the Corn Master should not replicate. By biting into the hero the ants behaved like humans shelling the corn boy and depriving him of his flesh or bread-like buttocks (_tzintamal_), cutting the plant at the base (_tzintan_). All of this material can be translated into sexual behavior, into an erotic possession of the corn plant treated like a female prey: a broken back evokes a man seducing, spoiling or raping a woman (_tzintzayana_).⁸⁶

The ant episode ends with the boy quickly getting up on his feet, guarding himself against the enemy (_eua_). The boy succeeds in recovering his flesh, yet he refuses to sit on his laurels, saddle or seat (_icpal_, tzinicpalli), renouncing the carnal pleasures that lie in a bed of leaves. The Corn Master treats the bed of leaves and the pedunculated ants like bottoms and refuse that must be abandoned (teputzcaua). The new strength gathered by the hero compensates for what he leaves behind (euacayaotl). This strength is manifested through the boy's aggressive treatment of the Pilgrim Fathers, a scene rife with anal and sexual imagery. The hero is said to catch up with the Pilgrim Fathers and kick (_uitegui_) an old man in the butt (_tepoz_). In Pajapan, the word used to describe the boy finding and joining (_techoa_) the pilgrims is a euphemism for having sex.⁸⁷ The boy rising and catching up with the Pilgrim Fathers behaves like a man pursuing or chasing after a woman (_tepostoga, tohtoga_), a hunter and his _tahtoga_ dog about to fall on a prey.

But why should the old men deserve such a rude treatment? Why should disrespect be shown towards men who embody the ancient teputze father figure, a parent or chief endowed with strong shoulders (_teposta_) and a sturdy back? Could it be that the boy is turning the anal imagery against the Pilgrim Fathers who "left him behind"? The act of hitting (_uitegui_) or kicking (_tiliksa_) is a reprimand and a mark of rebellion. "Hitting" is also the word used for felling or shelling. Having been shelled by ants, the Corn Master repays those who are disloyal to him in kind.

By castigating a human father, however, the narrative endangers the future of the dependent corn seed and child. After all, the reproduction of Sintiopiltsin hinges on humans looking after the corn plant. The corn boy must continue to feed those who adopt him, thereby turning the "kick" against himself and accepting to be husked. Images of self-flagellation (uitecoca) have yet to be substituted for expressions of aggression directed against natural enemies and disloyal men who threaten the reproduction of corn.

The deadly rock and pissing boy episode

The corn child has not ridden himself of his inclination to seek rest and comfort while travelling. In the scene that follows, the young hero chooses to sleep on a comfortable rock, reverting to the uterus as it were. As a result, the narrative transforms the stone-vessel into a man-eating rock, a chthonian womb turned into a belly as destructive of plant life as the ant-hill. As in the previous episode, the unwatchful boy is consumed by the earth.

> They went their way and left. They arrived at another place where they slept again. The old men told the boy: "Where are you going to sleep?" "I will sleep here on the rock (_tet_), this is a very nice (_yekmonso_) rock, here only I will lie down." "Don't fall asleep on this rock, for here the rocks eat men." "I will not look (_temoa_) for another place, the rock here is very nice, and I will sleep here."
>
> So he lay down on the rock. When he woke up, the rock had completely swallowed him (_nochi-ya gitoloh_). Only his head (_itsontegontsin_) appeared (_neci_), but he was talking (_tahtohtok_) alive. One old man told him (_gihliagih_): "You see, you didn't believe the advice [we gave you]. Now (_aman_) you're here to stay (_caua_). How are you going to get out (_copina_)? The rock has already swallowed you." "Leave me alone, go away, so I can see (_ita_) what remedy I will use (_nikchiati_)." They went their way and abandoned (_cauhteua_) him there.
>
> After the old men had gone a bird (_tototsin_) came [and said]: "Piss on your chest (_nimelaxixa_), boy!" "Will it cure me if I piss on my chest? Will the rock let go of me?" The bird said again: "Piss on your chest, boy! Piss on your chest!" What the boy did was to grab (_gibik_) his urine (_iyaxixtsin_) and piss on his chest. And the rock let him loose immediately. He went his way and caught up with the old men.

The notion that the corn boy should be devoured by a rock and yet preserve his head and powers of speech augurs well for the boy: the hero's death is neither complete nor irreversible. The boy can still treat his suffering as a sacrifice, a step toward resurrection. Our hero resembles the beheaded Lord of Otatitlán: like him, he has to have his head (hair, leaves) cut off and his body lowered and humbled if he is to hold his head high (_baneci_) again. The sacrifice will earn him the blessings of life after death, life that "wakes up" or "shows itself at dawn" (_taneci_).[88]

To master the rock, the Corn Master must avoid behaving like a gluttonous (_tlatoloani_) rock losing its head over food – "bending the head" as it swallows (_toloa_) its prey. Rather, he must embrace the humble ways of the lifeless stone lying in the wasteland, a stone cast away and acting as an obstacle in the way of movement and growth. Provided that he abstain from indulging in the good life and mould himself in the shape of his prison, assuming the lifeless attributes of a solitary rock, the child can pull himself out (_copina_) of the rock.[89]

The young god can put the rock imagery to ascetic usage in other ways, through gestures of self-degradation. A bird (= penis) appears on the scene to save the boy swallowed by the rock. He advises the hero to pee (_axixa_, "water-defecate") on his chest. The narrative casts the prey in the mould of his predator, letting him become his stone-shaped enemy. The equation assimilates the corn boy to the rock motif and derivatives thereof: i.e., the water-stone, head or testicle (_atetl_) that "makes water" (urine, brain, child), hence the egg that gives birth to the bird and the infant. The bird advises the boy to act like a water-stone letting the "fluid of life fall" (_auetzi_, ejaculate), thereby forming a new organism, re-creating his own body and flying away like a magnificent bird (as in the Zoque-Popoluca variant). The narrative, however, is quite explicit as to how the scene should be understood: as an act of self-abasement, not of self-fertilization or uterine impregnation (_itetia_). The boy does not recover his body by using his _el_ chest as a reproductive "inside" cavity (_ihti_, itetl). Rather he transforms the belly or womb (_eltana_) into a bladder-vessel (_axixtegon_), a stomach, an intestinal container (eltzaccatl). The hero is revived through a decomposition of life, treating himself as waste matter, the refuse that Pilgrim Fathers have left behind.

In the final analysis, the boy's downfall is like any original Fall, a _felix culpa_ acting as a blessing in disguise. The secret of Sintiopiltsin's power and of life after death lies in cyclical expressions of self-ablation or abnegation, gestures that are required to feed the lives of men who return the favor by reproducing corn. In the Zoque-Popoluca story, God said to the corn spirit that he would never die since he would always serve as food for men. "So the young boy knew it was because of this that he had power: because he was the spirit of corn. And he also understood that they were going to eat him" (López Arias 1983).

Waking the mother and resurrecting the father

The corn child has matured to the point that he can travel on his own. The Pilgrim Fathers bid the corn god farewell, confident that he knows (_mati_) what he is doing.

> He took to the road again and caught up with the old men. They didn't know (_agimatigeh_) that he was looking for his father because the iguanas had told him that his father was in _Tagatawatsaloyan_. After they arrived at the place, he bid farewell to the old men. "You go your way and continue your trip. This is where I go, you leave me here." "We feel (_wel_) responsible for you. When we come back you will not be with us." "Nothing will happen and I know what I am doing."
> Seeing that the boy was "of virtue", they left him there and went their way. He knew that his father was there. He approached the place (_asitiaya_) slowly (_yohyolik_) and saw a ranch. In front of the house (_gahli_) there was a chicozapote bearing a lot of fruit (_taktok_). He saw an old woman (_iyelamahtsin_) below the chicozapote tree. There she was weaving (_tahkiti_).

The wisdom (tlamatiliztli) shown by a god of maize known as *Itamatiosinti* allows our hero to come closer than ever to his father who dwells in the "land-where-men-are-dry". The land signals the stage when mature corn plants are doubled and protected against predators and the heavy rains of autumn. When dry enough the plants are harvested, the grain is transformed into food and seeds are preserved for future planting. The drying process (*uatza*) implies a weakening of the plant body ending in death, a requisite of plant reproduction. In spatial terms, the boy's journey to his fatherland is from east to west, sunrise to sunset, light to darkness, summer solstice to autumn equinox. The further our hero moves above and out of his homeland and the lowland waters that gave him life, the more likely he is to enter the house where the aging sun-father enters (*galagui tonati*) at the end of each day.

This last episode portrays the boy coming to a ranch, a house, a sapodilla heavy with fruit, and beneath the tree, an old woman weaving a dress. A Gulf Nahua word that captures this arrival scene is *agui*, a term applied to the solar father entering his house to the west (aquian). The evening sun entering or wearing (*agui*) the earth bears all the vitality of a man planting a seed in arable land (aquiloni) or seducing and penetrating a woman at night (tetlan acqui). Without the sun suffering this small death, no man (*tagat*) would ever exist (*ag*), nor would the sun ever see another day (tlacatli).[90]

The *agui* motif accounts for the narrative imagery of a *tahaguilo* tree, a tree "covered" with fruit hanging from the tree top (aqui, *taktok, taguih*), from its hairy-house head (*tzongal*). The derivative word *taguihlo* denotes the *chayote*, a fruit known to bear a lot, to grow on *megat* lover vines, to resemble the vulva and to originate from the vagina of the Chichiman witch burnt to ashes. By extension, the term applies to any mature fruit that drops from a tree, reproducing itself by covering itself up with earth. These signs tally with the particular tree species appearing in this scene, i.e., the tall wild-forest *xigotzapot*, the *chicozapote* or sapodilla. In classical Nahuatl, a tzapotquauitl is a tree that bears fruit (tzapoyo), and tzapoquauhtla, an orchard. In Nahua, *tzapot* is the generic term for sweet fruit.[91]

In keeping with the image of a tree "dressed" (*tahaguilo*) with fruit, the sapodilla scene includes a woman weaving a dress. While echoing the twisted lover-vine imagery, the verb for interlacing means to fold a garment, to roll a thread or a sheet of paper, to wrap in baby clothes.[92] The old mother is weaving a *beyit* dress that goes around the body like fruit in a nest or in a piece of cloth (tlaaquillotl), hence children dressed in clothes or wrapped in the womb. The material combines signs of erotic commerce and procreative activity.

The sapodilla bears signs of fertility and plentiful food. Phallic attributes can also be assigned to this tree known to produce a milky substance and tough hardwood valued for construction (columns, posts, handles); in Pajapan a *tzapot* (= banana) stands for the penis. Having said this, life under the prolific sapodilla is marred with problems of the human condition. For one thing all trees are loaded with signs of sexual

domination. In Pajapan, the words *bauit* (quauitl) and *tzinbayo* (tzin-
quauhyotl) denote not only the phallus but also a tree, a beam, a stick
used for beating. Derivative terms suggest the act of beating someone on
the head (*bauitegui*) or stabbing him with a stick (*bauia*). If done from
behind (*tzinbauia*), the latter gesture produces a reprimand and evokes
anal sex. In classical Nahuatl, quauhtilia means to have an erection
(*baguetza* to the Gulf Nahuas) or to show firmness when inflicting
punishment. In short, the tree imagery carries both signs of erectness
and chastisement, as if an exercise of phallic power entailed physical
correction and discipline.

To these indices of sexual domination can be added signs of life
coming to an end. Although standing beneath a tree bearing fruit, the
old mother can no longer bear children and is approaching the end of
her life. A *chicozapote* going through its reproductive stage announces the
felling of trees and the exhaustion of Mother Earth lying at its feet, a
tired (*batia*, turn into wood) old lady falling asleep (quauhtenuetzi)
and about to turn into an ogress (García de León 1991: 34). As for the fruit
and seed borne by the tree, they can develop into new plants only if
fallen, buried into the ground, or hiding in the *bayo* forest (*batahaguia*),
after the manner of the solar body going to rest, falling and "wearing"
the earth at night.

Although he may be "given a house" (*gahlotia*) like a fledgling lodged
in a nest or a shell (*gahlot*, totoltecacalli), the boy has good reason to
approach the house calmly and slowly (*yolic*), as when danger lies ahead.
That caution is needed makes sense if we consider that the house arrival
scene is loaded with images of sexual interment. The boy's entry into a
house or grave-like hole (*axapota*) is akin to an act of sexual penetration
(xapotla) that can be turned against the hero. Caution is in order as
Sintiopiltsin is entering a dangerous zone, going through a mouth-door
(*itengahli*) and falling into the inside-stomach (*ihti*) of a voracious enemy.[93]
Actually death awaits the corn boy drawing near the house, destined as
he is to become dry grain stored in the corn loft or the *ahkotapesh*
deathbed situated above the kitchen fire.[94] The boy's fate is to be stripped
of his shuck, thereby losing his virginity and wooden-house bark (*bagahlo*),
which is the only way he can enter someone else's bodily habitat and
reproduce.[95] The maize child is condemned to be husked, stored in bags
and swallowed by man. He will then go through all the digestive "houses"
located inside the human body: the *bitaxcol* intestine-bag, the *axixtegon*
bladder-vessel, and the *xigal* vulvar house (also a *tortillera* made of *tegon*
wood).[96] This small death imagery tallies with the boy's previous burial
in an ant-hill and a stone turned into a funeral "bone-rock-house"
(tepetlacalli, omicalli).

The corn boy throwing fruit at his mother

The hero is closer than ever to experiencing both the afflictions and the
blessings of a small death. He is on the verge of discovering the secret
of life after death, a process of human and plant reproduction that

reunites the male and female, the young and the old, water and sun, the earth and the sky. The child's journey toward full maturity meets with success essentially because of all those sufferings born during the voyage, ordeals such as plant doubling and the drying of grain seed, to be poured and planted into the earth like bones buried in a tomb or food swallowed by the stomach. The trials endured by the hero imply most of all a battle against the temptations of gluttony and lechery, as exemplified by the long-tailed iguana, the fat-bellied ant, and the devouring rock. Having passed these tests, the boy is now in a position to reproduce, throwing fruit to the ground and reawakening the old Mother Earth.

The old woman fell asleep. The boy immediately (*manin*) climbed up (*tehkaw ahko*) the *chicozapote*. He found fruit that were ripe (*yoyoksik*) and was eating *chicozapotes*. When he was above he threw (*motilih*) a fruit at the old woman, on the threads (*iyitkat*) where she was weaving. The old woman woke up (*isak*) and picked up (*gipehpen*) a *chicozapote*. She saw that it was ripe, cut it and ate it. "May there be more! Who on earth is throwing (*gixini*) *chicozapotes* as ripe as these?" She didn't know that the child was above. The boy threw (*gimahkawili*) another fruit and the old woman woke up even more. She cut it and ate two (*ome*). And thus she ate three (*eyi*). That's when he called her (*ginotsak*). "Mamacita, if you want (*tiknegi*) I will cut (*niktegi*) more, there are some that are very ripe here." "You are someone who came. Who are you (*ak*)?" "I am so-and-so." "Come down (*xitemo*) so that I may know you (*mati*). Perhaps you are my son. But I don't know you. I don't know where you went when you were born nor who raised you. Come down." The boy came down and got closer (*walak*).

But there is a problem. Inasmuch as he is replenishing the earth mother, Sintiopiltsin is replacing his father. The scene is rife with signs of masculine erection and insurrection. The hero goes up the tall tree (*batehcaui*) and reaches the highest point in his journey to the sun-drenched land of *Tagatauatzaloyan*.[97] A mature corn boy climbing (*ahcobi*) into a house or a tree and shedding fruit or seed from above evokes a state of erection (*baguetza*, "wooden stick standing") and also grain seed stored in an "upper-house" loft (*tlecopa*) located beneath the *ahcogalli* roof. The maize son can be suspected of rising against the father plant originally stored in the loft. Thus, in the Zoque-Popoluca story, the corn loft is where the boy kills the surrogate father who planned on eating his son's flesh; the man's head is cut off while trying to catch the boy hiding in the roof.

An incestuous connection is developing between mother and son. The boy throws fruit at the mother. Four verbs are used in the narrative to describe the act of fruit picking and throwing: *mota*, *xini*, *mahcaua*, and *tegui*. The first term, *mota*, means to touch, to encounter, but also to throw or to hit with stones. While *tamota* describes the action of throwing or hunting, *amota* is to throw water, a verb that applies to a man ejaculating (or a woman "getting wet"). *Mahcaua* is to let go from one's hand, a gesture harking back to the corn boy taking his distance from his predators turned into prey (the iguana, the ant, the rock). The other terms have already been explored. All terms converge on the principle of "propagation by cutting", on acts of reproduction performed through expulsion and severance.[98]

Semen and seeds of life (xinachyotl) must be thrown and scattered (xini) in order to be gathered and propagated.[99] Trees have in common with the phallus that they must spread their seed and suffer the fall if they are to reproduce. Having frequent sex with a woman is thus comparable to the act of pruning a tree (quauhtequi, quauhtzatzayana), hence to punish, to throw on the ground (quauhtlaça).[100] Death by decomposition is another requisite of life. The connection between the rotting and the reviving of life points in turn to the tahcalli motif. While the word can be used to signify reproduction, as in tatahcalli, to lay an egg, it can also mean to defecate. The word comes from icali, to attack, or tlacali, to knock someone down; batahcalli is to fell trees. As with all forms of life, fruit and trees must fall down and decompose if they are to propagate and multiply.[101] The green tasol litter rotting (palaktik) on the soil surface plays an important role in that it preserves humidity and "gives life to maize", as one informant put it; it allows the soil to rest (ceui), keeps it fresh (cece) and soft, hence fertile (yamani).

But why should the fruit be thrown on the woman's yarn woven into a beyit dress? The answer lies again in the process of reproduction. The dress covers the woman in the same way that her body and uterus contain the human embryo, or that the earth shelters the plant seed and the sun at night. While ish is the word used for thread or fiber, ishcat is a sheep, and ishposh, a hen starting to lay eggs and a model of virginity (ichpochyotl). Given these equations, fruit and seed thrown on the female yarn (to be woven into baby clothes) imply an act of procreation that brings a woman's virginity to an end.

The woman plays along with the incestuous boy. She picks up the fruit, eats it, and gradually wakes up (iça, ixitia, to resuscitate), as if she were coming back to life. In the Nahua idiom, a woman selecting and gathering scattered fruit behaves like a mother adopting and raising a child or giving food to patio chicks (pehpena). As for the downward movement of fruit falling from a tree, toward the soil and a woman at rest, it conjures up images of son-like seeds planted in the earth mother and also food going down through the stomach (temua). The fruit-seed falling from the sapodilla are ripe (yoyoksik) enough to be planted and eaten by the mother, as if they were hot or cooked (yoksik). While reducing plants and animals to waste, the act of eating serves a repro-ductive function comparable to sexual intercourse. The imagery confirms that the son is now able to reproduce and to feed humans. The more the grain-seed approaches death, the closer it gets to entering both the human stomach and the earth-mother lying in a state of sleep. The boy's journey has resulted in a movement from wet to dry, from water to fire, from cold to hot, from raw to cooked, from sprouting to eating and planting – from productive growth to the consumption of food and sex.

Instead of reproaching (*nonotza*) his mother for abandoning him at birth, the orphan speaks and reconciles (*notza*) himself with her.[102] The seed of the father comes nearer (*ualah*) the mother who receives him (*namigui*) like an *ix namicti* (face-together) spouse, someone who suits her, a man she can marry (*namicti*). In the Zoque-Popoluca variant the mother actually mistakes her son for her husband who died before the child was born. The boy is usurping his father's role as he spreads his fruit, seed or fluid of life on earth. This incestuous reunion scene, however, is countered by the mother's failure to recognize (*mati*, to become fond of, to seduce) the boy. The woman maintains her son at a distance. The Corn Master will have to do the same. In lieu of replacing his mother's husband, the mature boy must maintain his independence and persist in his task, which is to shed his seed and regenerate the lives of those who feed him, including a human father to adopt and look after his seed.

Through his voyage the boy has gone a long way in illustrating the teachings of self-sacrifice. He was deprived of a father and gave water to the man who adopted him. He released his long tailed enemies from his grip, abandoned his homeland and lost his flesh and leaves. He cut his hair, pissed on his breast, broke his back and tightened his belt (through doubling). He dried up and gave fruit to his mother. All the same, the narrative is not about to let the hero rest on his laurels: although reunited with his mother, the boy must pursue his quest for life after death through self-denial.

A father turned into a deer

In the last episode, Sintiopiltsin resurrects his father, pulling him out (*copina*) from the earth like a seed. The boy attempts the impossible: substituting the principle of immortality for the natural cycle of life. The attempt is bound to fail. Corn has no other choice but to wear itself out regenerating the lives of humans who continue to plant and nurture new generations of maize. Likewise fathers cannot attain full independence from plants, women and the young, nor can they avoid the obligation of dying so as to feed those they need to reproduce. Just as resting and dreaming (*temigui*) at night permits the body to rise or resurrect (*ixitia*) at dawn, so death (*miguiliz*) is a vital ingredient of the reproductive cycle of humans and plants alike.

The boy was talking with his mother. "Well, where did my father (*notah*) go?" "Your father died (*migui*) many years ago. His tomb is further ahead." "I will resurrect (*ixitia*) my father, just show me (*nextia*) where they buried him. I will pull him out (*copina*) and I will revive him." "In that case I will show you." His mother took him and showed him where they buried him.

"Now go to your house (*tochan*) so that I can pull out my father and resurrect him." The old woman went away. "The only thing I would recommend is that when you see (*tigitati*) my father you do not cry (*choga*), and be careful not to grab him (*tik-chihchimi*). For if you grab him or cry, we will never find (*techo*) my father again. My father will be transformed (*mobepati*) into an animal of the field."

His mother did not believe him. "What does he know?" she said (*gihtoagi*). She went to the house. The Corn Master did what he could: he hit (*uitek*) his father and revived him. When he woke up (*isak*), his resurrection was still incomplete. He brought him to his house, like a drunkard (*tawan*). When she saw that he was bringing the old man, the old woman fell shouting (*tsahtsiwetsik*) and weeping instead of refraining from crying. She was hugging (*ginapalo*) the old man. Son of a ... (*ihuela*), and he turned into a deer (*masat*): "*huiii, huiii, huiii.*" He took to a field (*acaual*) and went away. He resurrected his father but it was all in vain. The story ends (*tamik*) there.

All mortal creatures depend on others for their reproduction and survival. Were the deceased father able to keep his wife at a distance, he might achieve self-sufficiency and immortality. Before resurrecting his father, the hero advises his mother to go home, to abstain from weeping or shouting when she sees her husband alive, and also to refrain from grabbing or embracing the man. In the Zoque-Popoluca variant, the woman is told neither to laugh nor to look at her husband straight in the face. The wife must keep her distance in all possible ways, physically and emotionally, lest her husband run away like an animal fleeing into the forest.

If grabbed by his wife, the man will be weakened. The word for grabbing (*chihchimi*) comes from *chichi*, to suckle but also to suck, to dispossess little by little (*chichina*),[103] an image echoing the ogress *Chichiman* adopting the corn boy with a view to devouring him. While to suckle an infant is to give it the food it needs[104], the action also creates a dependency, treating the child as a subordinate creature. It can also cause a foreign fluid or substance to enter the child's body, provoking a dizziness[105] or an illness that healers (*tachichina*) can remedy through ritual suction or smoking performed with caution: the illness should be extracted without contaminating the healer or milking the patient of all his strength.[106]

The imagery suggests a fundamental riddle: how can the narrative allow the real father to be reborn as a child-like creature under female protection while at the same time preserving his male adult strength? How can the hero search for (*ixtemoa*, "to want children" in Nahuatl) and revive the whole father figure without the father becoming a weakling, a nursling to be taken in a woman's arms (*napaloa*), someone to educate, to protect, to govern (like a tlanapalolli godchild). How can the old man return to life without depending on his wife and son?

Although reborn, man "manifesting" (*ixmahtia, ixneci*) himself like the sun reappearing at dawn is forever subject to the dependencies and weaknesses of real life, which include sex. Accordingly, expressions of the mother's face (*xayac, ix*) and eyes (*ixtololo*, face-ball, *ixtauil*, eye-light) undermine the vigor of a father coming back to life. The woman must be careful not to rob the man of his newly-gained strength. Were she to smile or laugh (_ixuetzca_, to make fun), she might end up showing disrespect toward the man and depriving him of his fatherly authority (Sedeño and Becerril 1985: 61). Also, while seeing (_ita_, _ittaa_) is a sign of recognition, the woman cannot look at her husband straight in the face, welcome him or come near him (_taixco_, _ixnamiqui_). The gestures are tantamount to having sex and getting married – to extracting vital fluids and services from the man.[107] When sexually united (_necpanoa_), hence interlacing or weaving (ixnamictia, _ixnecpanoa_) their lives and bodies, men and women are obliged to wear themselves out giving one another what they need to survive and reproduce; true immortality requires no such sacrifice. Lastly, were the old woman to cast her eyes on her child-like husband, she could scare the life out of him, causing his "soul strength" to come out through the eyes, an illness known as _ixkogoyal_ (García de León 1969: 284).

Nor should the woman cry. Tears are a face-juice (_ixayot_) secreted by round-stones-of-the-face (_ixtololo_), eye-holes or house-like sockets (_ixapoyo_, ixcallotl) filled with sadness. Fluids of sorrow are secreted from the _ixpan_ forehead and from eyes that resemble seeds (_iyol_). Tears are thus comparable to semen issued from the male eggs or water-stones of life that begins in water (= brain = child).[108] They are signs of the process of reproduction in its painful stage. Were the woman to cry at the sight of her husband's rebirth, she would behave as a woman in travail, a mother breaking her waters and giving her son the source of life. She would treat her husband as her _iyol_ seed or eye, the apple of her eye (ixteotl, eye-god) – a dependent son obliged to repay his mother for the life received. Immortality implies no such pain let alone the mortgaging of a man's future life.

The woman refuses to obey the Corn Master. As a result, the resurrection granted to Sintiopiltsin's father implies just another life, a new beginning that replicates basic problems of life on earth. In lieu of becoming immortal, the resurrected father behaves as a suckling or a newborn child. He is barely walking on his two feet and is not fully resurrected or woken up (_iça_). He has all the appearances of a drunkard (_ixtauan_), a _bahbatauan_ wandering in the forest, a crazy man whose head is filled with saliva or beer (_bachissyoh_). The _ixbixin_ drunkard is not as yet a responsible man (_ixguetza_, face-elevate), one who can control his thirst for pleasures of the flesh. Actually the man can be suspected of having a spotted (_bixin_) face, pimples or moles (_ixgogo_, _ixtamal_) hurting like thorns in the flesh or an _ahwayo_ itch, a yearning to have sex.[109] Sintiopiltsin's father is so feeble as to lose face and head all at once.[110]

Sintiopiltsin's journey finds its conclusion in the "land where men are dry", a mountainous area inhabited by the Mazatecos, the deer-people (García de León 1966: 5; Boege 1988).[111] Accordingly, the father turns into (_papalotia_, _pata_, _bepa_) a _masat_, a brocket deer (_Mazama americana_), a locally-important motif of great antiquity (see Plate 2). He is transformed into a wild animal of second growth and brushy country. He becomes a "savage man" (tlacamaçatl, man-deer) who flees through a field lying fallow (_acaual_), a land of weeds and grasses gone lazy (_tatziui_)

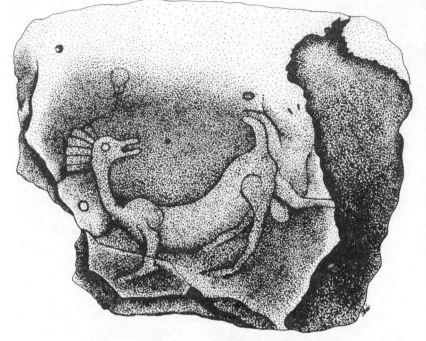

Plate 2   Monolith No. 1, Mirador Pilapa, Soteapan

and reverting to the wilderness (<u>maçauacan</u>, *bata* or <u>*bayo*</u>).[112] Human beings will never accede to the blessings of immortality. The boy's effort to resurrect his father, however, was not entirely in vain. The transformation contains an act of partial restoration: through reincarnation (<u>patillotia</u>), the father is healed, i.e., <u>*pahtia*</u>, to be cured or to be covered with mud, hence to reproduce (<u>*sogit*</u> and <u>*sokwia*</u>).[113]

This reincarnation scene extends to the dead the mutual dependencies that prevail between human beings and between all life forms, whether human, animal or botanical. On the one hand, the father is transformed into a savage deer-man roaming about the forest, a creature that feeds on plants growing in the *milpa*. In the words of one informant, the deer must be allowed to eat corn, for "they have to eat too" (Stuart 1978: 165). Inasmuch as he treads on man's corn, the animal ancestor is comparable to an elderly father served by his children and planning on devouring the maize son he adopted (as in other variants of the story).[114] The herbivorous deer-father will take every opportunity he has to eat the corn grown by men. On the other hand, the deer-father is a prey hunted for its flesh and owned by forest *chaneques* as part of their livestock.[115] Deers are killed when caught eating corn and beans in the *milpa* or sleeping in the forest. This is to say that the corn-father-deer must flee as he risks being eaten by the men he fed.[116] Like a man or a plant that wears itself out fathering a new life, the deer must die and serve as food for men.[117] Although immortality is out of men's reach, the life cycle of corn and man-the-farmer, both feeding on each other, is now extended to the relationship between the deer and man-the-hunter – a model for exchanges between the living and the dead, the young and the old. The story ends with the paradox of life and death transposed from the agricultural domain to the hunting field and the cult of the dead.

Warnings of the plumed serpent

The narrative material explored above speaks to life in society and the universe as constructed through traditional Gulf Nahua mythology. But times have changed. The story remains silent on all matters of recent history, including the partial loss of native language and culture (native dress, shamanic rituals, kinship practices) and the hegemonic expansion of Western culture and the powers of state and capital. The story of the corn child offers no response to the proliferation of religious sects that undermine the shamanic cult and related visions of the universe, confining all things sacred to life in heaven (Boege 1988: 283–4). Nor does the corn myth address the tyrannical rule of cattle ranchers. It does not speak to pressing problems of deforestation, the raising of animals that "eat up the forest", or landless men who abandon village life and land cultivation altogether. Although concerned with gender relations and family life, the narrative does not reflect on husbands who dispose of their cash earnings as they wish or fathers who give their daughters away in exchange for money.

Some local tales, however, establish direct connections between the demise of traditional gods and the changing conditions of life experienced by the Gulf Nahuas. The gods have been exiled and can no longer be counted on to sustain the lives of native inhabitants of the Santa Marta highlands. The powerful Mono Blanco (White Monkey) spirit worshipped by sorcerers and healers throughout the region is thought to have moved away from the Cerro Pelón in Pajapan to Piedra Labrada in the neighboring municipality of Soteapan, and then to Catemaco and abroad. There are also stories of an Olmec monument that was taken from the San Martín mountain to a state museum in 1962 (Soustelle 1983: 19; García de León 1969: 285, 295). Like Sintiopiltsin who left his native hearth, the Corn God statue and Master of the Animals (*Dueño de los Animales*) has left the land. The statue was taken in exchange for schools, roads and public services. Local informants recall that the stone statue was facing the rising sun and had a grinding stone (*metate*) and utensils of its own. The god used to receive offerings from the local population and was responsible for protecting corn crops against lightning and winds striking from the north (responsible for the death of the corn child's father in the Pajapan variant recorded in 1987). As long as it was there, the Nahuas could count on good harvests and sufficient rains as well. The land fed large herds of wild animals and produced all the food that was needed. People never had to steal.

The statue, however, was taken away and the winds began to blow. Some informants say that the god was angered by men's frequent use of powerful firearms and chose to hide himself and the animals under his protection in the underworld _Talogan_ (García de León 1969: 305–6). As a result the Nahuas can no longer provide for their needs; they can no longer hunt and must buy corn and other products from outside. Communal lands have been converted into a large ranch owned by a few _caciques_. These men are believed to have received their first animals from San Antonio who owned the Old Minzapan ranch. Instead of thanking the gods for what they received, the _caciques_ let the animals "move into and eat the forest", as one informant put it. With the expansion of the cattle industry, men who used to be hunters and farmers have turned into idle people who have neither land nor jobs. Others have formed herds of dirt-poor peons paid to work like beasts of burden held captive in their own land.

The worst mythical scenario has come true. Like their prehispanic ancestors and other Nahuas of modern-day Mexico (León-Portilla 1983: 69, 113, 124, 167, 379; Taggart 1983: 55), the Gulf Nahuas view the _cemanauac_ world as a flat surface surrounded by water and supported by four volcanos, one at each corner of the land. When angered by men, the gods use hurricanes and earthquakes produced by these volcanos to track them down, pushing them into the sea to trap them in their huge oceanic corral. This is precisely what has happened in recent history. With the help of _caciques_, winds of destruction have trapped the people of Pajapan and driven them to the edge of the sea. Until the corn god and the "alternative civilization" (Bonfil Batalla 1987) it stands for is restored to the Gulf Nahuas, poverty and misery await a native population dwelling in a barren land and on the verge of falling into the sea.[118]

The people of Pajapan recognize the destructive nature of cattle ranching for subsistence agriculture and the environment. They wonder how it is that gods who used to guard all riches of the world have let themselves be captured and despoiled without retaliation. The _chaneques_ are now reduced to hiding and crying in holes of the chthonian earth while forests are burned down and animals in tears flee from the land. Life that began in water (León-Portilla 1983: 106) suffers in a land turned dry, a portion of the earth exploited without the slightest concern for new cycles of growth. Human beings no longer show respect for the multitude of life forms inhabiting the earth, disregarding the imperatives of conservation and the laws of nature upheld by ancient spirits of the _cemanauac_ universe.

Informants speak of a male plumed serpent discovered in 1985 in a highland spring near the Yuribia water plant that supplies some 80% of Coatzacoalcos' potable water. The plant is controlled by the State Water Commission and is guarded by soldiers whose task is to prevent the people of Tatahuicapan from closing the water valves and demanding local services from the federal government. Like children snatched by evil strangers or male peasants expelled from village life (Paré 1992), the beast was separated from its female companion who remained in the spring. The 20-meter and several-ton serpent is said to have been taken by a truck to the Museum of Anthropology in Mexico. The man driving the bulldozer who spotted the plumed serpent died a few months after the discovery together with two other workers. The gods will not let humans rob the land of its water and its riches with impunity. Three men died and, to make matters worse, the people of Pajapan are now running out of water and their soils are less fertile than ever. Springs and rivers flowing from the Santa Marta highlands are no longer protected by the forest cover. The urban population of Coatzacoalcos and Minatitlán is also faced with prospects of severe water shortages that add to the general ecological crisis prevailing in southern Veracruz. Unless these cities and the country as a whole bring profound changes to hinterland resource management, they too will fall into the sea. In the long run, warnings of the plumed serpent will be given the last word.

Notes

1. In its own way the myth inverts this ancient migratory movement, from highlands to the Gulf coast; through myth the Nahuas are reverting to their Central Plateau origins as it were.

2. In Pajapan, well-to-do ranchers are sometimes thought to have sold their souls in exchange for wealth. The Mazatec view of the power exercised by outsiders over their own lives also points to the demonic implications of a repressive system exercised without reciprocity (Boege 1988: 122, 125).

3. To give one example, Sedeño and Becerril argue that the rule prohibiting children to look at "our father the sun" implies the fear of castration associated with the sight of the father's penis (Sedeño and Becerril 1985: 61, 68). We shall see that this visual taboo is imposed on the corn child's mother at the end of our reference myth. A close examination of the facial imagery used in this scene and in Gulf Nahua language shows that sexual connotations can be attributed to a face-to-face reunion between man and woman. When situated in its proper linguistic and narrative context, however, the imagery has to do with a sexual encounter between genders, not between generations (involving the primal scene of the phallus). Another telling example concerns the rule against male masturbation. In our view, the rule must be situated against the background of the native *xima* "seeding" imagery (see our analysis), a complex symbology that has little to do with feelings of maternity-envy arbitrarily invoked by Sedeño and Becerril (1985: 63, 97). While pervasive, sexuality cannot be understood through universal equations that will exempt the analyst from delving into the unconscious manipulations of each and every language.

4. The narrative material examined in this chapter is based on our own translation of García de León's Spanish version of the myth. A direct transcription of the native terms originally used by the informant is given in parentheses; to avoid useless repetition, native terms will not appear more than once in the text. As with other Nahuatl dialects (Sandstrom 1991: xxv), there is no standardized system for transcribing Gulf Nahua words. Our spelling of classical Nahuatl and Gulf Nahua words follows the conventions adopted by Siméon (with the exception of the full-length narrative collected by García de León, as transcribed below, using García de León's spelling conventions).

5. Because of the complexity of the interpretive method outlined above, we have chosen to apply this diachronic mode of reading to the corn myth only. Other

variants of the myth and closely-related observations of Nahua culture are taken out of their own narrative context and made to gravitate round the tale of Sintiopiltsin.

6. In Nahuatl, pilhuatia is to procreate and pilhua is someone who has many children. The Zoque-Popoluca variant of our corn myth mentions that the old couple "had never had any children" (Foster 1945: 191).

7. To the Aztecs, a tequipane was someone hired on a weekly basis, and tequipanilhuia (or tequitilia) was to work for someone else. All indications are that labor came with the primordial creation of man and woman (León-Portilla 1983: 181).

8. Unlike *faena* work, tapalewi denotes co-operative labor between relatives, neighbors or friends.

9. Amongst the Gulf Nahuas, totolteksis means a turkey egg, large by definition, as in the narrative. For other mythical references to the bird–rock association, see Foster (1945: 196). The classical Nahuatl word tetia means to become hard like a rock but also to spawn or to lay eggs. Tetl was also a suffix for numbers referring to round things (eggs, melons, etc.).

10. The prefix uei is used in this scene to denote the promising size of the eggs in lieu of the earlier old-age motif.

11. As in other languages, the stone and uterine rock symbolism can also be applied to the destruction of life. While in Nahuatl tepantia is to build a house, the same word can be used in Pajapan to indicate the action of throwing stones at someone, hence to accuse. Likewise, tetia means to amass building stones and to lay eggs but also to become solid and hard as a lifeless rock (*tetic*, *tetia*). While excluded from the surface narrative, these negative usages of the stone imagery loom large in deeper layers of the narrative. Other inauspicious usages mentioned by Siméon include the word tepeouican ("dangerous mountain"), which stands for a precipice or the abyss. Accordingly, tepexiuia is to throw oneself or someone into the pit, to commit a serious fault, or to chastise and destroy a country that is badly governed. The sufferings of human beings end with the tepetlacalli burial, a funeral "rock-mountain-house" or earth-womb turned solid and lifeless. Finally, when associated with the tree motif (quauitl), stones can serve to chastise.

12. In classical Nahuatl, organs of "male-flesh" (oquich-nacayotl) are distinguished from organs of "female-flesh" (ciua-nacayotl); the penis (tepulli) from the vulva or vagina (tepilli); and male secretions (*tepuayotl*) from female fluids (ciua-ayotl).

13. *Maxixa* is to urinate, and *axixti* is urine. The head–calabash–vessel imagery is made explicit in the *Popol Vuh* (Foster 1945: 195; López Austin 1990: 104). On the prehispanic ritual of baptism, see León-Portilla (1983: 195).

14. The Nahuatl language used to emphasize the birth-orifice function of female organs. Unlike the phallic tepulli, the female tepilli was an amalgamation of two terms: pilli for child, and tentli for lips or mouth ("word" and "memory" by extension). The vagina is a mouth that gives birth. Likewise, the glans penis is a tepul-qua-xipeuhcatl, a penis-head-peeled, a head-like vessel with its own mouth orifice; the glans has lips known as tepulcamapiccatl, tepul for penis, camatl for mouth or lips, and piccatl for the female *labia*. Tepulacayotl is the penis viewed as a urinary conduit. Acayotl means the urethra and, by extension, the penis; when preceded by ciuatl (woman), the same word designates the vaginal tube. Another word for prepuce is xipintzontecomatl, and the man's foreskin is xipintli, or tepuleuayotl, the penis-skin.

15. In Siméon's dictionary, aloyotl (origin unknown) is the word for scrotum; the calabash is ayotli. To complete this imagery, Siméon informs us that a testicle is a water-stone, a-tetl, an image echoed by a "water-mountain" community (*altepet*)

and a rock-mountain (tepetl) secreting spring water (tepeat). The calabash has in common with the testicle that it too is a juicy-stone, an ayo-tetl. Hence, the pouring of sperm secreted from male stones resembles emissions of calabash juice and seeds substituted for real children. Incidentally, Siméon lists the turtle as another meaning for the ayotl juice; the reptile is known as galapa in Pajapan and is synonymous with the vulva, apparently because of its shell shaped like a bowl.

16. For ethno-semantic evidence confirming the association between breast and calabash and also between milk, semen and saliva, see our discussion of the last scene of the Gulf Nahua reference myth. See also Boege's discussion of Mazatec myths that combine imageries of twins, eggs, testicles and the dual constructions of sex (male/female), age (young/old), space and time (diurnal sun/nocturnal moon) (Boege 1988: 95, 109–10, 129).

17. The Nahuatl term achcautli signifies a high priest, a supreme judge, a chief, a first son, or anything deemed to be superior. Teachton is someone's past, and achtoitoani, the one who spoke first (a prophet). In Pajapan, the expression teachto pano refers to "what happened first". For an interesting discussion of the ach motif as used by the Nahuas of northern Puebla, see Beaucage (1987).

18. In Pajapan xinach denotes a large quantity of mites or anything resembling it, hence seed by extension. Xinachtia is to be attacked by mites, unwanted insects dwelling in a talxinach termitary and competing with human beings for plant food (García de León 1976: 101). When translated into classical Nahuatl, the seed-pouring imagery suggests that man possesses the power to reproduce life by spreading (xinachoa) the grain seed (xinachtli) or semen of life (xinachotl) on the ground, sexual acts that lead to adultery when unrestrained (see xima in Siméon 1977). Men must put some of their seed apart (xinachtia) and destroy trees and weeds if they are to grow maize and survive. Thus a xinqui is someone who saves and puts some seed apart (xinachtia) for future needs – someone who refrains from eating peeled fruit (taxin, from xima) only. An excessive consumption of pleasures of the flesh would bring a loss of manhood, of man's generative strength. Accordingly, xinach-tlatlacolli, from vegetable seed (xinachtli) and fault (tlatlacolli), is the greatest crime of all, the original sin. Ximoayan is the "site of the fleshless", hence the land of the dead (León-Portilla 1983: 395). For a discussion of "seed spirits" (xinaxtli) ruled by the Mother Earth (Tonantsij) and worshipped by the Nahuas of northern Veracruz, see Sandstrom (1991: 244).

19. In Nahuatl, tlayacayotl (or yacapantli) is primogeniture.

20. These connections are made explicit through birth rituals. In Mecayapan, the umbilicus of the newborn is held against an ear of corn when cut; the midwife wraps it in leaves and buries it in a corner of the house. The gestures convey two wishes: that the child experience good luck in life (plentiful corn) and that he or she remain in the village when grown up. Life that grows and flourishes thrives on both operations of planting and cutting (González Cruz et al. 1983: 10, 62).

21. Life must either "conquer" (poloa) its prey or die. By definition, acts of conquest and consumption imply the loss, wastage or destruction of what is edible (qualoni), hence what is good (qualli), beautiful (qualnezcayotl), magnificent (qualneci), or simply appropriate (qualcan). The satisfaction of man's appetite ends therefore in sadness, for it is incompatible with the preservation of food (tlaqualli) and all that is valuable and worth praising (qualitoa), including the human virtues of moderation (quallotl) as expressed through fasting and dieting (tlaqualizcaua). See also León-Portilla (1983: 387).

22. The consumption of female flesh (the egg-sister, the hen) is an essential ingredient of the good life, yet it is also a threat to its preservation obtained through female reproduction. A female egg that disappears and cannot bring new life to light is reminiscent of the lunar body going into eclipse (qualocayotl) when

swallowed up by darkness. Pajapeños refer to a lunar eclipse as _nemi balo toyetsin_, "our mother is being eaten" (presumably by the sun-father; see Foster 1945: 217). The term _balo_ is "to be eaten" and also "to suffer". When socially transposed, a woman lost to (or eaten by) another man is compensated by food received at a daughter's wedding feast. Whether received or given, possessed or lost, female creatures "consumed" through marriage are a source of nourishment to man.

23. The scene is reminiscent of a ritual accomplished by parents on the occasion of a real birth. When a Gulf Nahua child is born from a mother who has lost children and fears another death, the newborn is sometimes taken out of the house and left in the yard where the birth occurred, as if it were unwanted. The ritual is thought to increase the child's chances of staying alive and growing in good health; the good are thought to die young when spoiled with love (González Cruz et al. 1983: 9).

24. In Nahuatl, a pacholoni is a person nestling against another, i.e., in a position of inferiority and subordination. The term tlapachouaztli denotes a net for catching birds, and the word for feeding, qualtia, means to punish.

25. The amnion or chorion membrane surrounding the egg or the fetus used to be a cone-matlatl, literally a child-net.

26. In her own way, the daughter nestling against her husband and his family has also been caught, captured as she is by a son-in-law behaving like a trap: the word montli used to mean both a son-in-law (_monti_ in Pajapan) and a trap for mice and rats, creatures that feed on other people's corn.

27. This male-centered conception of the maize plant is not without scientific validity. The physiology of maize is indeed dominated by its male part which will take precedence over the female ear in times of stress (drought, infertile soils, nutrient deficiencies). It does so by putting its energy into the flower and the production of pollen at the expense of the female grain, which may be aborted or simply fail to grow.

28. Anciently the corn divinity had several names that corresponded to different stages of growth as well. Tzinteotl, from tzinti, to begin, is the origin and first phase of corn life. Xilonen comes immediately after. She is the goddess of corn ears that are edible though still at the milk stage, hence "starting to form themselves" (_xiloti_) and growing their own hair (_xilot_, _xilotzonti_). Corn that grows and sprouts (nenepiltia) produces offspring of its own, "children from the vulva" projected like a tongue (_nenepil_, the "vulva-child') from the mouth. The corn goddess used to be celebrated in the seventh month, from about June 22 to July 11. She was also known as Tonantzin ("our mother"), serpent-woman (Ciuacoatl), mother of twins and goddess of the earth. Tonantzin is from nantli, for mother. In Pajapan, -monan (_monti_, in-law + _nan_) means a mother-in-law.

29. The terms listed below, all followed by ya nomil ("my _milpa_"), are taken from Stuart (1978: 150) and have been checked and corrected with the assistance of our own Nahua-speaking informants.

Wechome: maize "sprouting" with no leaves, one week from planting (June–July)
Isuayo (or xrigo)pontok: 4 inches, "with leaves" about to open (the word izcallo means to have a stalk, a "guide")
Maxintok: when the leaves open (11 to 12 days after planting), with "arms extended"
Totamba: when the maize is "knee-high", about one month old
Batepompolitia: 1.5 months old, above tree stumps, above "small-heads-lost"
Punti aroti: with "flower tips", will flower soon (1 month, 25 days)
Nemia pone: with flowers starting to open
Nemia xilotia: small ears beginning to form, two months old
Tomakxrilot: ears well started, hence getting "fat", 2 months 10 days
Etzal: first leaves of husk beginning to dry, 2 months 20 days

Celik elot: young ears ready to pick for eating on cob
Elot: kernel beginning to harden, though still in milk stage (time to make fresh
  maize tamales). An *elote* is a green ear with grains already formed, while an
  olote is a shelled ear
Elot taxkaja: kernel slightly harder, time to make fresh maize tortillas
Sinti: maize
Niaya postagitik: time to bend over or "break" the stalks
Sagik ya sinti: dry and ready for harvest; *sintia* is said of a plot that "gives maize"
Nisia nik pixkati: all harvested

30. We shall see later that a liana (*megat*) equals a womb and also a mistress. In
Foster's variant of the corn myth, the corn boy and fish are taken out of water
with a fish net and a sombrero, respectively (Foster 1945: 191).

31. In classical Nahuatl, water stands for a child, the first era of humanity
(atonatiuh, "sun of water"), the food of life (atl tlaqualli), and also fertile land
(atacpan) exposed to rainfall, riverine flooding or irrigation. Moreover, water marks
the site of territorial ownership: aua is the owner of water, and aua tepeua, the
owner of water and mountain, hence a dweller of the land. In Pajapan, *altepet*
(water-mountain) is a community. On the prehispanic notion of altepetl, see
Lockhart (1992: 14–28).

32. González Cruz et al. (1983: 13); Trujillo Jáuregui et al. (1982: 19); Interviews
with anonymous sorcerer, notes p. 88. Nahua healers and sorcerers often attribute
the cause of various illnesses to evil *ehegat* spirits (see Sandstrom 1991: 252).

33. The Nahuatl cuitia verb implies the recognition of someone's property, yet
the same term suggests an admission of guilt, confessing to envying the other
man's possessions. In the same vein, cuicuilia is to steal, to fail to meet one's
obligations (especially a woman's), or to investigate into someone's behavior. While
the word cui denotes the recovering of one's strength (or a man sobering up), it
also connotes a man having intercourse with a woman; a stallion breeder is thus
a tlacuini. If combined with water, the same motif (atlacui, *atabi* in Pajapan)
signifies to take or steal water out of a well, a spring or a fountain. But when
applied to the male gender, the act of taking water implies castration or mutilation,
hence atecui, literally the removal of water-stones. See also cui, cuilia, cuicuitiuetzi
and cuitiquiça in Siméon (1977).

34. Abuses of water can rebound on men who thirst for pleasures. Evocations
of wicked behavior may result in a flood (atlatlac) befalling evil men and their land
ruined or destroyed by means of "liquidation" (atitlanaquia).

35. See García de León (1969: 283); Interviews with anonymous sorcerer, notes
p. 59. In Nahuatl, although the sun gives life (nemiltia) to all dwellers and animate
creatures (nemilice) of the land, only God possesses the secret of immortality. On
the prehispanic god known as Tonatiuh, see León-Portilla (1983: 394).

36. Interviews with anonymous sorcerer, notes pp. 9, 126; García de León (1969:
290, 292, 294, 299; 1976: 77; 1966: 16); Trujillo Jáuregui et al. (1982: 23); Foster
(1945: 181); Münch (1983: 174f.); Sedeño and Becerril (1985: 169ff., 186ff.). In
one particular variant of the corn myth collected in Pajapan, an alligator ate the
Corn Master while he was travelling to Oaxaca; the boy cut his way out of the
animal's belly with an obsidian knife.

37. This symbology and many of the anatomical features of *chaneque* spirits are
reminiscent of the famous colossal heads and other sculptures of the ancient
Olmecs: i.e., "baby faces" with flat noses and thick lips, their smile, their nudity
and asexuality, the emphasis on the head imagery (= brain = water = infant) and
the jaguar–mouth–door motif. See Winfield Capitaine (1991: 14–18); Soustelle
(1983: 33, 43, 47, 53).

38. Culturas Populares No. 17 (1982: 24); Hernández et al. (1981: 24); Interviews with anonymous sorcerer, notes pp. 15, 32–3; Interviews with Pajapeños; García de León (1969: 299; 1976: 10, 79, 84); Foster (1945: 181); Münch (1983: 160, 173ff.); Sedeño and Becerril (1985: 32, 165); Beaucage (1990). On prehispanic images of Tlalocan inhabited by Tlaloque gods, see García de León (1969: 294); and León-Portilla (1983: 131, 135, 206f.).

39. Culturas Populares No. 27 (1982: 32); Münch (1983: 206, 244, 253); García de León (1969: 284).

40. Culturas Populares No. 17 (1982: 7–11, 24); Interviews with Pajapeños.

41. Culturas Populares No. 9 (1981: 45, 55); Culturas Populares No. 27 (1982: 32); Trujillo Jáuregui et al. (1982: 13–14, 17); García de León (1976: 32, 78); Interviews with anonymous sorcerer, notes pp. 81, 110, 133, 136; Foster (1945: 181); Münch (1983: 178, 199ff., 206, 230, 247); Beaucage (1990).

42. Culturas Populares No. 9: 55; Culturas Populares No. 27 (1982: 43); Trujillo Jáuregui et al. (1982: 14, 23); García de León (1969: 289, 296; 1976: 78); Münch (1983: 199ff.); Boege (1988: 170–3)). The classical Nahuatl term telpochtli denotes a youth (León-Portilla 1983: 389).

43. Interviews with Pajapeños.

44. Trujillo Jáuregui et al. (1982: 19–20); García de León (1969: 294); López Austin (1990: 162).

45. Native healers can predict the fate of a patient with the use of copal incense thrown into a glass of water: death awaits those whose copal sinks to the bottom of the glass. García de León (1991: 30); Culturas Populares No. 27 (1982: 24–7, 31, 40, 56, 62, 65, 71–2); Trujillo Jáuregui et al. (1982: 24); Interviews with anonymous sorcerer, notes p. 65; Culturas Populares No. 9 (1982: 43). Offerings to the chaneques have also been reported by Foster (1945: 201). For similar ritual practices observed among the Mazatecs, see Boege (1988: 118, 143–6).

46. Other ancient derivations of the flower motif include milk-like or resin-like honey (xochinecutli, xochi-memeyallotl), fat (xochiotl), sweets (xochitlaqualiztli), and all fruits defined as "edible flowers" (xochiqualli). To this floral material could be added the terms for adorning (xochiota), treating well (xochimati), trees that bear fruit (xochiquaquauitl), glowing (xochicueponi), good memories (xochititiuh), and praise (xochiyotia) .

47. The word nagastanpepel appears to be a combination of nagaz for ear, and penaga, to be naked, or pepetlaua, to strip (nimopepeci means "I undressed myself"). To the Aztecs, a person who has large or sharp angular ears (nacace, nacazueyac in Pajapan) is by definition a wise person. As should be expected, the corn child is without wisdom. He is without honors or power (nacaztia, referring to "ears sticking out" in Pajapan) in that, unlike a tenacaz, he represents no one. Alternatively, the narrative may suggest that the corn ear is without hair, another sign of powerlessness and immaturity. The young plant is deprived of the silk-hair needed to carry pollen to each seed for fertilization. In lieu of having "rock-like hair on his ears" (nacatzontel), of being proud and rebellious, the boy is punished and humiliated (nacazana). That is, his ears are mutilated, bent or cut (nagaztegui). As a result, the boy is unable to understand the words uttered by the iguanas, as if "hard of hearing" (nacaztepetla) or stone-deaf (nacatzatzatl, denoting a "sticky substance" in Pajapan). Still, we shall see that mutilated ears can be turned to advantage; after all, the imagery can serve as a sign of sacrificial behavior, as among the Aztecs (González Torres 1985: 102).

48. Tauiltia is to set fire (tai in the case of a maize plot). On these ancient associations between redness, water, the alligator and the east, see León-Portilla (1983: 111, 122).

49. When preceded by and pronounced separately from the privative prefix a,

the word _migui_ denotes immortality. When pronounced as one word, _amigui_ (_at_ + _migui_) implies death from thirst.

50. _Içatok_ is to be alive, and _içaçan_ means early. The east is also where the full moon appears, a good time for sowing and cutting wood (Münch 1983: 157). According to León-Portilla (1983: 111, 114, 122), the west used to be viewed as not only the sun's house but also the land of the moon at sleep and of women in general. Classical Nahuatl expressions echoing the Gulf Nahua solar imagery are tonatiuh iaquian and tonatiuh iquiçayan. Similar expressions are used by the Nahuas of Puebla (Taggart 1983: 57).

51. Nor can this upland-father and lowland-son imagery cope with problems originating from the "upper" north (_para ahko_) or the "lower" south (_para tani_), directions associated with winds that blow at different times of the year. In Spanish the _norte_ denotes the north but also a "cold wind" (_cecekehegat_) or rain storm coming from the Gulf coast. Gulf Nahua _milpa_s and villages can be protected from north winds issued from the mouth of a mythical serpent by placing a cross at each corner of the plot or the community (Trujillo Jáuregui et al. 1982: 8, 19; on prehispanic connections between death and the cold north, see León-Portilla 1983: 111, 122). As for the _suradas_ (_tonalehegat_), they are strong "sun-winds" that blow from the south during the dry season. Destructive winds (_yualehegat_) from the south also blow in August. Winds that damage maize crops are a reminder that sun and water, two vital ingredients of life, can be quite deadly. Unless flames are put out to "rest" (_ceuia,_) or protection is found in the shade (_gan ta ceui_), the sun can cause creatures to die of heat (_tonalmigui_). Water without light and warmth can be equally lethal: rain and dew (_cekti_) are inherently cold (_cecec_), they may freeze into ice (_cetl_), or they can turn into cold water (_cecegat_) and fearsome storms descending from the north.

52. The black iguana is locally known as _bauisbinti_; it is smaller than the green _baguetspalin_ (or _quauhcuetzpalin_) and lays its eggs in tree holes. In Nahuatl, the cayman alligator is called acuetzpalin, the water-lizard.

53. The relevance of the iguana egg motif is made explicit in another Gulf Nahua variant of the corn myth (collected by the authors in 1987) which compares the corn child to a ball of dough, a ball shaped like an egg and placed in an iguana nest perched in a tree.

54. The animal laughs at the red-haired _elote_ boy, making him go red and blush to the roots of his hair, as if the redness of the dawning sun were turned against our inexperienced hero. _Pinahtia_ is to grimace, to humiliate or blame; the word is from _pinah_, to be ashamed, to go red in the face, to be saddened (also tlauia).

55. The root word can be used to denote the act of advising, informing, be-friending or talking with someone. Tenonotztli is a story and nonotzalalizmachtia, the art of speaking, an art which the iguana does not truly possess. This paradox and the sexual implications of this scene of shame (as they relate to tepinauiz, the shameful parts) are discussed later. As we shall see, a man who mixes and has too much sex with women (ciuauia, ciuanotza) is subject to exhaustion (ciuanotzaliztli), the loss of his male energy and therefore his virility.

56. _Tonalelot_ is a green ear growing in the dry season. Something that grows in the summer was called tonallacayotl. To the Aztecs, a summer fruit was tonaltzapotl, tonalxocotl or tonalxochiqualli. Closely related words produce a vision of earthly fertility and abundance (tonacati), life in a garden of delights (Tonacaquauhtitlan, "food forest"). The close connection between the soul (_tonal_), the sun (_tonati_) and the east (_tonayan_) finds an echo in the Mazatec asean motif discussed by Boege (1988: 142, 173, 184). See also Sandstrom (1991: 247f., 258, 276).

57. Anciently, the act of casting seeds of corn (tlaolchayaua) was a way of determining men's lot on earth.

58. Overexposure to solar heat can none the less kill. The sorcerer emulating the powers of the sun was once known to cast spells (tonalitlacoa) by shooting arrows and rays of light (tonalmitl) that are destructive of plant life. Closer to the Gulf Nahuas and their corn myth, there is the action of the sun or the hot wind (tonalehegat) rising to the south or the east (tonayan), causing men to sweat (itonil) and ears of corn to die through drying (tonalmigui).

59. Similar connections made explicit by the Nahuas of Puebla are discussed by Taggart (1983: 58f.). In classical Nahuatl, the same meanings are conveyed by the words aqui, aquia, actiuh and actitlaça. Older derivatives of the root word ag suggest that even when absent, the sun continues to regenerate (agui) the fruit and days (tlacatli) of all human beings (tlacatl) born (tlacatitilia; in Pajapan, tagatilia is "to be made a man") from their mother's womb (tlacatcayotl) and living a life of chastity, moderation and generosity (tlacayotl).

60. Provided the male sun covers itself up at night, the mother earth can count on receiving water and sunlight from the east in due time. Having been properly watered, she can give birth to her new maize son who will in turn spread his array over the land, replacing the original cover lost through slashing and burning (Boege 1988: 127, 149–50).

61. A Gulf Nahua verb that could be used to describe the reproachable behavior of the iguanas is cahcayah (cayaua), to entertain and seduce but also to lie and deceive. In Siméon's dictionary, the action of "letting words escape" (by way of rumor) is tlatolchitoniliztli. Mockeries, lies and faulty interpretations are tlatolpinauhtia, tlatolpictli and tlatolpapaçolli (or tlatolcuepaliztli).

62. The moral importance attributed to language is reflected in classical derivations of itoa, to speak. The latter can serve to evoke men of noble descent (tlatocamecayotl) such as kings, lords, princes, governors, ambassadors and mediators (tlatoani). These are men who speak (tlatoa, tahtoa) for others and distinguish themselves by their heroic deeds (tlatocatlachiuhtli) and the palaces (tlatocan) they live in. More importantly, they can be recognized by their manner of speech (tlatoliztli), their ability to sing or express themselves with persuasion (tlatolmaca), eloquence and dignity (tlatocayotl), if not poetry (tlatolchichiualiztli). They master the discourse of history (tlatollotl) and writing (tlatollacuiloliztli) as well. Perfection and purity of speech is at the origin of all the powers that the noble possess, including the capacity to command others (tlatocatlatoa) and to make their will manifest (tlatoltica). Great value lies in words (tahtol) that deserve to be spoken (tlatoloni).

63. The powers of seduction are an integral part of the nahuat language, an idiom resembling a dance (naua) performed with a sense of rhythm and harmony. Native utterances "sound" (nauati, nauatilia) as clever as the speech of a diviner or a sorcerer (naual), a cunning thief (tenaualpoloani) or a spy (nauallachiani). Words uttered in this idiom involve a good measure of enchantment, seduction and prostitution, concealment and deceit. The language also implies humor, as in naualaua, laughing at the imperfections of others. Given these derivations (see Siméon), anyone embracing (naua, nauatequi) or mastering the language can be suspected of laying a trap for his enemy, waiting for his victim like a viper coiled up (naualihtoc) in a lair, an evil wind, or a sorcerer transformed into a tiger and about to descend on its prey. For more on sorcerers, winds and tigers in Gulf Nahua culture, see Münch (1983: 190f., 202) and García de León (1969: 287). On ancient nahual sorcerers, see León-Portilla (1983: 86).

64. In Pajapan, tzinguetza is to bow down, to have anal sex. Talguetzal is "feather of the earth", a particular kind of grass used for thatch. In classical Nahuatl, quequeça was the word applied to birds mating. An animal in heat (quetztlani) was a quetzallani, and tequetzani, a breeding stallion.

65. To use the classical Nahuatl imagery, an appendage of robust flesh (cuitlananacatic) is all that is needed for someone to prosper (cuitlapiltia). The creature who possesses it is likely to grow a bigger belly (cuitlatecomatl). Riches of the earth shall accrue to powerful men endowed "with shoulders" (cuitlapane), creatures who have spinal columns, behinds (cuitlapampa), buttocks (cuitlaxacayatl, "the backside face") and trunks prolific as a corn ear (cuitlapanxilotcayotl), strong as an arrow or a shinbone (cuitlapanteputzchichiquilli).

66. The connection between tail and tongue is made explicit in the Zoque-Popoluca story of a hunter who pretends to admire the tail of an alligator and then throws a stone in the mouth of the careless animal and cuts off its tongue (Foster 1945: 199).

67. For the money–excrement connection, see Culturas Populares No. 14 (1982: 9). Older derivatives of the tail motif can be used to denote a wound, ripeness verging on decay (cuitlacucic), hence the act of sullying someone's reputation (cuitlayoa) or sowing discord (cuitlacpeua). When transposed to humans, the tail stands for a vulgar person, a peasant, a worker, a beast-like slave. Finally, the buttocks and the tail point to creatures that are fat and walk slowly (cuitlananacatic), immature individuals who have no sphincter control (tzinbita in Pajapan), hence the weak, the sleepy and the lazy (cuitlapan, also for latrines). Thus a deformed corn ear is cuitlacochin, maize that sleeps.

68. The iguana may be suspected of indulging (auia) in the consumption of fresh (auic) food that tastes (auiac) and smells good, excessive drinking (auiliuinti), frivolous words (auillatoani), carnal lust and related services procured from prostitutes (auianiti) trained to seduce (auilpauia). All of these are vain (auillatoani) pleasures that will lead the beast to vice and corruption (auilquiçaliztli), self-degradation (auiloa, auilquiça) and self-destruction (auiliui). On the relationship between playing and making fun, see Boege (1988: 115) and López Austin (1990: 161).

69. Current and ancient verbs denoting the cutting of a tail are tzintegui, tzinteponoa, cuitlapilana or cuitlapiltequi. Tzinpostegui (cuitlauitequi, cuitlapuztequi, cuitlapantli) is to break a creature's back, shoulders or loins.

70. The corresponding words are cuitlacuepa and mauiztlaloa. The animal suffers from the kind of terror that causes bowel movements (mauhcaaxixa) or even disembowelment (cuitlatzayani).

71. The snare is made of parts deviously stolen from the animal. It includes a bamboo stick that looks like an arrow, a spinal column or the animal's back. The word for trap (pitzauayan) designates the narrow or central part of a hole or a body, hence the belt or the waist to which tails are attached, an important motif to be developed in the arriera ant episode. Finally, there is wax (xicocuitlatl, bee-excrement, honey), a substance akin to tallow fat (xicocuitla-icpayollototl) and evoking the fatness and sweetness of a land of plenty. Stories of underworld creatures caught with honey are common in Pajapan (García de León 1969: 297; 1976: 84–6). For older connections between honey and sex, see León-Portilla (1983: 238).

72. The fact that a prey should be chased at a fountain or well makes sense if we consider that courtship between Gulf Nahua men and women typically occurs on the way to the well or brook. A boy growing up and taking water from an atlacui well is a prelude to a man pouring his own fluids (auetzi) and having sexual intercourse (cui).

73. Similarly, the word used to speak of a woman who becomes pregnant is piloa, to fish or to hang. When combined with tzon (for head), the term means to "bow the head", which is what the corn boy must do if he is to mature. In Nahuatl, pilchiua is to sin. Pil is from piloa, to fall, to hang, to fish, to bother or

to cling to someone. <u>Pipiloa</u> is to hang something, to climb into a bed, to seduce a woman.

74. López Arias (1983); Foster (1945: 192). On the cyclical view of time in classical Nahuatl philosophy, see León-Portilla (1983: 47, 97, 111) and Soustelle (1940: 85).

75. Popular belief holds that three statues of Christ were commissioned by Felipe II in the year 1595. The first was given to a marquis residing in Santiago Tuxtla, near the lake of Catemaco. The second went to Chalma in the highland Papaloapan valley, and the third to Esquipulas in Guatemala. The *imágenes* were given indigenous features, i.e., dark skin, almond-shaped eyes and oriental traits, after the pre-Columbian god of merchants, Yiacatecuhtli. In 1931 conflicts between the church and the state caused an incident involving the Christ of Otatitlán: the head was cut and an attempt was made to burn it, without success. The head was eventually recovered and placed at the foot of the original statue. The Christ of Otatitlán is related to six "images" of the Lord of Health (Señor de la Salud) worshipped in Santiago Tuxtla, Oteapan, Mecatepec, Pajapan, Coacotla and Cosoleacaque. In Pajapan the *mayordomía* of the Virgen del Carmen is in charge of organizing pilgrimages to both Catemaco and the Cristo Negro de Otatitlán (García de León 1976: 137; Münch 1983: 255ff.).

76. The Virgin, protector of seamen and women in labor, is said to have appeared to an Indian fisherman on the shore of Lake Catemaco. Like pilgrims bathing in the Papaloapan River, those who visit the Catemaco shrine purify and rejuvenate their body in waters of the lake (Münch 1983: 244–64).

77. *Arriera* ants can strip a plant by cutting sections roughly one square centimeter from the leaves. Soldier ants may reach a length of 1.5 centimeters Their nests can cover an area of 50 square meters or more. When peasants select a *milpa* site they will avoid the nests if they can, but the ants can travel over long distances (100–200 m) (Stuart 1978: 160).

78. Thieves and seducers (<u>tecochtecani</u>) lull their victims to sleep with the use of charm or sorcery (<u>cochtlaça</u>). See León-Portilla (1983: 204) on death and dreaming.

79. Derivatives of <u>talia</u> suggest an exercise of authority: witness the old men who decreed (<u>gitahlikeh</u>) that a trip be made to Oaxaca.

80. See García de León 1969: 294. The classical Nahuatl term for <u>tebani</u> is <u>tequani</u> (see León-Portilla 1983: 105).

81. See García de León (1966: 5). In Pajapan, the hair-pulling imagery is synonymous with soul theft (García de León 1969: 290). For classical Nahuatl expressions of this imagery, see <u>tzoncotona</u> in Siméon; the word means to cut or harvest, to kill or sacrifice something, reducing it to bare bones, making it thin as bone. Closely-related words include <u>tzontepeua</u>, <u>tzontepoloa</u>, and <u>tzontlaça</u>.

82. <u>Tlacouia</u>, <u>tlacoitta</u>, <u>tahcotzayana</u> and <u>tahcotzononia</u> are Nahuatl synonyms of the Gulf Nahua <u>tahcotegui</u> motif. In Pajapan, <u>tahcouia</u> is to carry something on the shoulder.

83. To use the older Nahuatl hair-and-head rhetoric, the humble and the meek should bow to the noble (<u>tetzon</u>) who attain peaks of power (<u>tzonyotl</u>, <u>tzonixua</u>) lest they lose everything they cherish. By definition humility is a virtue that goes against the vice of disobedience and stubbornness associated with heads and hair hard as rock (<u>tzonteti</u>, <u>tzonteyotl</u>, <u>nacatzontetl</u>). The humble know better than to rebel against those "forming the head" (<u>tzontecontia</u>, <u>tzontegontia</u>) of the body social.

84. Through self-mutilation, the Corn Master obtains the kind of string or snare (<u>tequammecatl</u>, <u>tequammatlatl</u>) required to catch the devouring beast.

85. See <u>tzintlan</u>, <u>tzintlantli</u> and <u>tzintli</u> in Siméon.

86. While *xipia*, to peel, can be said of a man losing his virginity, the word for "tearing" or "slicing" (*tzayana*) applies to a woman being deflowered. When sold, the bottom becomes a sign of prostitution (*tzinnamaga*).

87. *Acitiuitz*, to rapidly catch up, is another term that captures the scene and that tallies with the conflictual implications of the *eua* imagery. In classical Nahuatl, the term means to chase or fall on the enemy, to get angry at someone. The word is an amalgamation of *uetzi*, to fall, and *aci*, to arrive, to reach, to join; in Nahuatl, the latter term also means to have sex with a woman (hence to lie down, *uetztok* in Pajapan). A closely related term is *cuitiuetzi* (*cui*, to recover, to possess a woman), which means to fall on someone, to attack or rob, to seduce or rape.

88. By virtue of his sacrifice, the corn-god-child can enjoy a new day appearing with a splendor that equals the "magnificence" of things that are "good to eat" (*qualneci*). He can recover his head (*tzoncui*) and with it the powers of speech and the rock-like strength to rebel (*tzontetia*) against his enemy and to avenge his own death.

89. The hero is condemned to stay and be abandoned (*caua*) at the site of the rock. The solitary implications of the *caua* imagery are exemplified by Nahua words denoting men and women widowed or "abandoned", i.e., *ogichcaual* and *soagaual*.

90. The fall of the solar body at dusk is a small death impregnating a new moon rising to the west (Trujillo Jáuregui et al. 1982: 29). In classical Nahuatl, the sun wears the cloak of darkness and surrenders (*calaqui*) to its rule, all in the hope of ascending once again to the sky through the red house (*tlauizcalli*) at dawn.

91. See Culturas Populares No. 27 (1982: 92); Hernández et al. (1981: 24); López Arias (1983); and Stuart (1978: 93, 197, 234-8, 390). In Spanish the word *xicotzapot* (*Manikara sapota*, of the star-apple family) is pronounced *chicozapote*, a term referring to *chictli* or *tzictli*, the green gum obtained from the milky juice of the sapodilla and used in the making of figurines and the manufacture of chewing gum. The sapodilla plum is an edible apple-shaped fruit, brown and rough-skinned with a sweet, yellowish to reddish pulp. The plums reach maturity at the same time that dry-season corn is planted, in May and June. In Pajapan, the word *tzapot* came to mean banana or plantain, as in *tzapot taxcal*, the banana tortilla eaten in times of maize shortage as a substitute for the main meal *masa tortilla*. The well known *zapote mamae* (*batzapot*, *quauhtzapotl*, *Calocarpum sapota*) also grows in the mature forest. The tree is taller than the *chicozapote*, yet its wood is more fragile and less useful. Its fruit surrounds a large oily seed called *pisti*. In Pajapan, *pistik* is black, the color of fertile soil (*pistiktal*), and *pisti* (also a horse's hoof) is the oil derived from the pit (*piztli*) and used as a hair and skin dressing or as medicine to heal wounds and fractured bones (García de León 1969: 283). The seed can also be cooked and ground with maize to make *pozol* or *tortillas*. *Tiltzapot* is the black sapodilla.

92. Few alterations would be needed to transform this scene into a reproductive play, i.e., an erect man whirling and twisting a stick with his feet, hence *quauhtlatlaça*, a classical Nahuatl derivative of *quauhtlaça*, to have frequent intercourse with a woman and also to fell trees. The verb *quauilacatzoa*, to play with sticks or to interlace plants, conveys similar connotations. The term comes from *quauitl*, a stick, and *ilacatzoa*, to coil round a tree trunk. Similar images can be applied to a woodland motif viewed as a planting field (*quauhtica*), a web of scrubs, thorns, weeds, vines and other creeping plants (*quauhmatlatl*, *bauizmegat*) interwoven and forming a huge trellis (*quauhtecpantli*) of botanical life.

93. Since the land surrounding the house is described as a corral, the hero could be turned into an animal kept in captivity. The classical Nahuatl term denoting an animal enclosure is *tepancalli*, from *tetl*, a rock, *pantli*, a wall (row, line), and *calli*,

a house. The site is built (tepantia) with stone walls delimiting the property in land, buildings and animals owned by the family.

94. See López Arias 1983. In Nahuatl, a corn loft is a place that "compares to a house"' (calnepanolli).

95. In his attempt to enter the female flesh or sex (betax), the hero may lose his own skin, cloak or hide (betaxo).

96. In the same vein, an axixcalli was a urine-house, and yollocalli, a bowel-house.

97. The Gulf Nahua verb for "going up" is tehcaui, to take something up, tleco in classical Nahuatl. Although from a different origin (tetl, fire), the term tleco also means "in the fire". When brought together, these two meanings suggest that to go up is to get closer to the solar father burning in the sky.

98. Plants can be propagated in a seedplot by cuttings or layering (quauhxinachtli, tree-fall-seed). This is done by bending a twig, a shoot or a "tree freshly started" (quauitl itzincelica) and covering it with earth until it roots. Another term for propagation by cuttings is quauhtoca, to plant or bury trees. The Gulf Nahua equivalent of this word is batoga; it describes the action of forcing someone's head to bow, after the manner of corn plants doubled at autumn.

99. A closely-related term appearing in Siméon's dictionary is quauhxiuhcotona, to cut branches or leaves, from cotona, to collect fruit.

100. In the Zoque-Popoluca story, the Maize Child triumphs over messengers of the god of lightning by proposing a wager. The spirit of corn cuts the trees halfway through and traps the tiger and the bull into putting their hands into the crack. The bull stays caught for about five days and loses weight. As for the god of lightning, his hand is trapped in a hole in the middle of the sea. The hero agrees to free the god on the condition that he pour rain over the corn boy and bathe him in water year after year so that the boy may survive and grow. Although thickly textured, the imagery betrays a simple moral: the wager between life and death is won by those like the corn plant who break their back building themselves a gahli house (= gahlot, shell, husk = bagahlo, bark), away from life that begins in water. While building a house for himself, no mention is ever made of the boy actually felling the trees or penetrating the house he builds, gestures evoking the full sexual act. By contrast, enemies of the corn plant are punished as they commit the error of penetrating the wooden or watery habitat and letting the tree and seed of life fall, at their own expense.

101. Trees must be cut down and felled if the land is to be quauhtlalli, soil fertilized with disintegrated wood, excellent for corn production.

102. According to León-Portilla (1983: 197f., 385), the word notza used to evoke the moral of self-discipline achieved through "self-reproach".

103. Sorcerer and witches (techichinani) are known to extract blood from their victims through sucking. In Mecayapan, a woman having a miscarriage is said to be full of blood and the fetus is thought to be a demonic creature sucking the life out of the mother (González Cruz et al. 1983: 6–7; Sedeño and Becerril 1985: 97).

104. Chichih means to suck at the mother's chichihual breast, and chichitia, to suckle a baby. Milk is synonymous with semen (tepolecheh-yo), or breast-juice (chichiualliayotl) in classical Nahuatl. To the Aztecs, a woman with big breasts was a breast-water-calabash vessel (chichiualaapilo, chichiualatecomatl).

105. Breast-feeding is like spitting (chihcha, or chichi + piaçoa, to urinate); thus the word for saliva or spit is chixti. When botanically transposed, the action of spitting produces corn beer (chihcha); in Pajapan chichic stands for beer or anything bitter. A person getting drunk with beer is like a head full of saliva (bachissyoh), a head that turns crazy.

106. Healers of Pajapan report that the practice of extracting foreign bodies

through sucking is no longer performed because too dangerous (Interviews with anonymous sorcerer, notes p. 127; see García de León 1969: 284).

107. Siméon defines the term namictli as meaning both a spouse and an enemy, someone to fight with. In Pajapan, however, the verb namictia, to marry, does not imply quarrelling. Although very similar, mamictia is the term used by the Gulf Nahuas to denote a "hand-fight".

108. On the yollotl life force in classical Nahuatl philosophy, see León-Portilla (1983: 122, 191, 396).

109. The scene of a woman's face expressing her feelings (ixyoyomocpol) implies a manifestation of carnal desire, an itch to have sex (yomoni). Her husband can also be accused of succumbing to weaknesses of the flesh. His propensity to wander aimlessly betrays an uncontrolled longing to possess the women he desires (ixeleuia), an "itch" to chase (ixami), seduce, deceive and mock (ixcuepa) the women he meets along his path.

110. Although resurrected, the father is a pale reflection of his former self. To use the facial imagery, the man has no "personality" (see León-Portilla 1983: 67, 81, 191, 229, 384). He resembles an evil-faced (ixtlaueliloc) character who shows audacity but also a lack of moderation, sobriety, and caution. The old man is the opposite of a clever person with a head on his shoulders (ixe, ixpanca), someone who is careful and astute (iximati, ixmoquetza).

111. As in classical Nahuatl symbology, the deer motif is associated with the sun setting to the west (León-Portilla 1983: 122). Like many other imageries appearing in our Gulf Nahua reference myth (eggs, twins, a child gaining strength and overthrowing his father after a long voyage), the deer-father motif plays an important role in Mazatec culture (Boege 1988: 95, 109–12, 129, 205). The Nahuas of northern Veracruz also speak of the death and resurrection of the corn spirit and a corn-child god (piltsintsij) fathered by a deer (Sandstrom 1991: 245f., 292).

112. The father is condemned to wander like a fool (maçayauh) on the path of evil (maçaotli) and to be hunted for his flesh until he falls into a snare (maçamecatl).

113. The Gulf Nahuas believe that every deceased person is reincarnated through a domestic animal (horse, dog, pig, bull) or a child born within the same family. When someone dies, measures are taken to help the deceased move on to another life. One measure consists in throwing out the household trash of the deceased, in the direction of the rising sun. The dead are thought to depart from this world like the solar sphere ascending to the sky at dawn. The departure, however, is not a full rupture. Sun-like souls (tonal) are known to wander after death, especially at night, and to visit their relatives during their sleep. They also spend a whole day feasting with their relatives around the time of the autumn equinox and the wet-season corn harvest, on the occasion of All Souls' Day. In other words, the departed behave like the sun returning to the earth at night, or the maize plant fathering the seed of a new life at autumn. See Hernández et al. (1981: 1, 20); Interviews with anonymous sorcerer, notes pp. 30, 47, 51, 87; Münch (1983: 269). For a discussion of concepts of reincarnation in classical Nahuatl philosophy, see León-Portilla (1983: 207).

114. The deer is reminiscent of the tlacuache (sp. Didelphis) father-figure of Mazatec and prehispanic mythology (Boege 1988: 115–116, 129; López Austin 1990).

115. These spirits are said to dwell underneath the Campanario Rock facing the Gulf of Mexico, at the foothills of the San Martín volcano. The sacred site consists of a seaside rock serving as an entry to an underworld inhabited by immortal animals and herds of cattle led by a magnificent bull wearing horns of gold. The "enchanted cattle" is the property of San Antonio, a saint celebrated on June 13, a week before the summer solstice and the ritual visits that healers and sorcerers pay to the animal-masters living beneath the volcano. The cattle is said to have

been stolen a long time ago by the Spaniards who took the animals to Spain and kept them in a corral. The livestock, however, was eventually freed by four birds and brought back to the Campanario Rock where they disappeared, as if "enchanted" and swallowed by the earth. In Chiapas mythology (López Austin 1990: 104–5), chthonian spirits are responsible for converting gold obtained from the sun into sun-colored grains of corn. See García de León (1969: 292; 1991); Culturas Populares No. 17 (1982: 30); Interviews with anonymous sorcerer, notes p. 90; Münch (1983: 298ff.).

116. The male figure behaves like a female _chaneca_ transformed into a golden-horned deer and chased for her tender flesh at the site of a brook or a spring (Culturas Populares No. 17 1982: 7–11). Because resurrected by his son and pursued by his wife, the man may lose both his parental and masculine attributes in one narrative stroke.

117. The same sacrificial logic applies to the mother figure. In the Zoque-Popoluca story, the man's wife, the ogress Chichiman, dies in a tree set on fire by the hero. The ashes of the genitalia are then transformed into plant food, i.e., calabashes and chayote (López Arias 1983: 11–12).

118. Interviews with anonymous sorcerer, notes pp. 32, 90; Trujillo Jáuregui et al. (1982: 36); Sedeño and Becerril (1985: 220); Münch (1983: 169).

CONCLUSION: THEORY
AND PRAXIS

Outline of a theory of process

The preceding analyses raise issues ranging from the role of the state to rain forest ecology, underdevelopment, kinship and gender relations, native semiotics and the narrative process. The book reflects an inter-disciplinary approach to social phenomena, one that brings together various "regions" or aspects of society distinguishable in theory but not isolated in reality. To a large extent the material is integrated through historical generalizations establishing connections between social processes. General concepts, however, are also needed to bring out the assumptions underlying particular explanations and to broaden their scope, thereby avoiding the juxtaposition of theories that are hermetically sealed off from one another, "a deliberately cultivated diversity of theoretical standpoints" (Giddens 1987: 31).

What follows is an outline of the basic assumptions that have guided us throughout the research. While we have borrowed concepts from different disciplines and perspectives, we have made an effort to develop a framework that brings various theories together, one that stresses the *processual* nature of social phenomena. Although limited in its actual use, the term "process" can be applied to a heteroglossic reading of social reality. First of all, the concept of process raises the question of order, or the orderly "procedures" of social life. A process is a method of doing things in society, whether it be a narrative tradition, a family structure, a way of livelihood, or a mode of government. These interactive procedures should not be defined too rigidly. As argued below, attention must be paid to the indeterminacy and variability of all forms of social behavior lest we reduce history to its simplest expression. Secondly, by process we also mean a set of actions to defend or impose a right or claim, hence a power struggle involving a confrontation of classes and parties, genders and generations, gods and humans compelled to "serve a process" on each other. Thirdly, the term process also alludes to the passing of time in human activity. Accordingly, our case-study offers a dynamic understanding of the time factor built into native politics, economics, kinship and mythology, hence a critique of history conceived as "context" – external forces acting mostly in the background.

All social processes are driven by people confronting pressing problems. Our closing comments thus shift from issues of general theory to a discussion of our own praxis – the contribution of the Sierra Santa Marta Project (SSMP) to promoting the claims and rights of native

peasants and their natural spirits struggling to survive in the highlands
of southern Veracruz.

Process: division and variable order

Each activity examined in this book has been viewed as a process simply
defined as a course of action or method of doing things in society,
whether it be attaining or exercising a political office, producing subsistence goods or commodities for the market, tracing descent or contracting
a marriage, or telling the story of a plant god's journey on earth. Our
task consisted in identifying the established ways of carrying on the
business of a government, an economy, a kinship system and a mode of
discourse. The exercise implies that we explore dispositions or propensities
to act in certain ways (Bourdieu 1990: 90), hence the usual manners of
proceeding in culture and society and the resulting patterns of social
activity. While carried on by people, these procedures cannot be reduced
to unit acts or simple operations (such as consumer choices) performed
by single individuals. Far from being the total sum of its constituent
acts, life in society is a web of interaction, a "relational totality" (Giddens
1987: 80-7) or arrangement of elements so divided and related as to
form complex "fields of action". By fields we mean "historically constituted areas of activity with their specific institutions and their own
laws of functioning" (Bourdieu 1990: 87).

The notion of orderly process was applied to all aspects of Gulf Nahua
society. In the first chapters of this book, we examined the Gulf Nahua
political process, a body politic consisting of divisions and relations
established between geopolitical formations, organized parties and the
government, officials and citizens, branches of bureaucracy and spheres of
authority. In Chapter 4, we treated the local economy as a class-interactive
structure – the domination and subordination of classes occupying unequal
positions *vis-à-vis* the labor process and property in land and cattle. This
was followed by an in-depth discussion of local processes of resource
management and ecological adaptation. Chapter 6 was concerned with
rules governing the native system of descent, marriage, residence and
inheritance, a kinship process generating basic divisions and transactions
between genders and age-groups. Finally, the last chapter delved into
semantic patterns of native mythology and the teachings of ascetic
naturalism as expressed through sign-relations and the narrative process.

Each process is a web of orderly relations. It is also a divisive and
transformative activity. Distinctions in society and in language are not
static effects of logical typologies and actors neatly classified into groups.
Social life is a complex production process generating all those distances
and interchanges that tie one group or class to another: a civil government
to a body of citizens, owners of capital to wage laborers, men to women,
wife-givers to wife-receivers, the old to the young, gods to humans.
Actors, classes and signs interact to create differences in society and
produce tangible effects, processing one thing into another: i.e., natural
resources into commodities and capital, electoral support (real or con-

trived) into government authority, communal membership into access to land, brideservice into marriage, images of plants and animals into narrative lessons of sacrifice.

Transformative processes should not be treated as lawful operations, mechanical and uniform. Throughout this book, we emphasized the malleability of observed rules of social activity, hence the vagueness and indeterminacy of social practice (Bourdieu 1990: 77f.). Our analysis of capital and state in southern Veracruz allowed for important variations and contingencies in the ways that private business (property regime, labor process) and government affairs (party formation, political co-alitions) are actually carried out. These variations and adaptations are an integral part of what capitalism and state regimes mean in history. Similar comments apply to the kinship and narrative material examined in later chapters. The analyses brought out the playful expressions of Nahua asceticism conveyed through native mythology, and also the pliable applications of patrimonial kinship – variations stemming from the process of aging and the cyclical transformations of household structure.

In short, each process is a web of orderly relations that are both transformative and transformable. But how do we know that one process can be distinguished from another, say family life from economic activity? The question is not as simple as it may seem. One danger with the multi-regional research strategy outlined above is that we start with an a priori list of the processes or fields of social activity to be found in all societies and to be investigated with the proper scientific tools, those of economics, ecology, political science, kinship analysis or semiotics. In reality, these divisions should not be taken for granted and spread around the world, as in the Althusserian literature (Althusser and Balibar 1970: 316). They exist only by virtue of a particular history, our own. This brings us to the *institutionalization* phenomenon, *a higher-order process* establishing basic differences between spheres of activity (family, church, market, government) and related rules of interaction in modern society (Godelier 1972: 77, 302; Sahlins 1976: 37-9; Clifford 1988: 303, 323). The institutional-ization phenomenon is particularly important for anthropologists who deal with non-industrial societies struggling with a modern world that divides public affairs from private business (domestic, commercial), material activity from the spiritual aspects of life. As with other native populations of the Americas, life in Pajapan has been radically affected by the dislocation of political, economic, domestic and religious activities. Given these transformations, anthropologists are obliged to reflect on the specificity of each division, recognizing that all practices are relatively autonomous from one another as the Althusserian expression goes.

Having said this, we also argue that the autonomy possessed by each institution is relative at best. From a cultural perspective, Western forms of organization have important elements in common: for instance, the notion of a contractual agreement that binds a husband to a wife, a wage laborer to an employer, a body of citizens to a representative government. Moreover, institutions are so closely interwoven that no process can ever be separated from other institutional effects, say capital accumulation from state formation. Relations in one area will affect other spheres of activity. Although distinguishable both in theory and in practice, institutions are not separate domains free from mutual influence. Interactions between institutions provide much of the stuff out of which modern social history is made. Under certain conditions, exchanges observed in Pajapan are held across institutional boundaries: money is converted into office, office into capital, capital into wives, women into money. Although performed within limits, these multi-level conversions reduce the distance that separates one field of activity from another.

As with all processes, the institutionalization phenomenon is open to all sorts of variations. The relationship between the property regime and the government process in Pajapan involves particular arrangements that cannot be deduced from general theories of state and capital. Gulf Nahua society is all the more complex as it combines Western institutions with prehispanic forms of patrimonial organization. These complex syncretic "realities of cultural change, resistance, and translation" (Clifford 1988: 303) have been discussed at length, with a view to capturing the articulations that have evolved between native and non-native forms of political and economic organization, family life and religious discourse in Pajapan. The specifics of Pajapan's island of history have been understood against the background of local cultural structures (Sahlins 1985: 72). The diversity of local histories is such that anthropologists must reject either-or approaches to native history, hence stories of savages either frozen in a primitive state or tragically fallen from grace due to the ravages of modern history.

Process: domination and resistance

Social life proceeds according to plans. Processes for doing things in society, however, often imply an exercise of power. Fields of action are invested with "interests" (Bourdieu 1990: 87) that are variable and conflictual: purposive behavior "is merely the consequence of the will to power manifest in all events, an order of rank" (Nietzsche 1967: 552). Although simple enough, these remarks have three implications for social theory. First, each course of action entails a process understood in the old sense of a "proclamation", a formal declaration that serves to establish an authority structure involving a ranking of social forces (classes, spheres of government, forms of speech) and the corresponding interests. Second, the rules of conduct in society are the site of one force struggling against another, hence the terrain of actors "serving a process" on each other, employing the methods or measures at their disposal to proceed or launch an attack against competing interests. The struggles are of two types: procedures of domination designed to maintain the regime, or strategies of resistance aimed at weakening or dislodging the powers that be. Third, it is important that we avoid seeking in social practices more logic than they actually contain. Not that too much logic would render human behavior inflexible and impractical, as Bourdieu suggests (1990: 79). More to the point, tensions inherent in social life are bound to create problems for the ruling order, divisions and contradictions that may undermine the laws of social conduct. As with legal systems, conflicts, loopholes and inconsistencies built into the laws of society can create so much inefficiency they weaken or threaten the established order. Rules and laws are subject to manipulation; they can be disputed and quibbled over (Fr. *processif*) to the point of being turned against themselves and diverted from their original ends, producing unintended consequences of all sorts (Giddens 1987: 8–11).

This book explores measures of domination and resistance that have shaped the history of the patrimonial domain and the expanding powers of state and capital in Pajapan. Our analysis showed how broader domains interconnect with local systems of micro-control produced through patrimonial kinship and the ascetic prescriptions of Nahua discourse. To avoid espousing too rigid a view of principles of social hierarchy, we also made a point of stressing the uneven distribution, limitations and contradictions of powers controlled by the ruling interests. These restrictive conditions include the on-going struggles of subordinate groups against all forms of domination. They also include confrontations between dominant groups. On the political level, our case-study spoke to the rivalries and clashes that exist between officials and levels of government, public and private business, geopolitical divisions and spheres of authority. As with capital, state power is unevenly developed, conflict-ridden and crisis-prone. While power does not disperse evenly or at random, without centers of institutional control, its exercise is never simply unified through measures of absolute hegemony. Authorities are vulnerable to internal divisions and weak alliances, conflicting actions and resource limitations, external imponderables and sheer miscalculations. All of these problems entail disruptive effects that introduce elements of unpredictability and irrationality, social risk and speculation into all spheres of life.

Chapters 4 and 5 dealt with the subordination of Gulf Nahua peasants and the rain forest environment to the rule of capital. In these chapters, however, we also paid attention to the battle of subordinate classes against exploitation and the impact their struggle had on local land tenure and the pursuit of profit in agriculture. The broader conditions under which peasants resisted hinterland ranchers and the oil industry were explored in detail, together with the limitations on gains achieved. Finally, the analysis addressed the self-induced limitations of capitalist development in rural Veracruz. Far from being the all-powerful system it is often made out to be, capitalism remains an inherently stupid machine, an exploitative process that creates limits to its own growth. Problems of unemployment, underproduction, resource depletion, loss of food self-sufficiency, all point to a system bent on mismanaging the factors of production at its disposal. These problems impose costly restrictions on the actual profitability and future prospects of local and regional capital. Obstacles to growth result not from imperfect market conditions but rather from intrinsic features of capitalism: the uneven distribution of wealth and power, production for capital accumulation, and the wasteful pillage of natural resources.

Our discussion of the patrimonial domain followed similar lines. Chapter 6 addressed relations of inequality based on sex and age, and the impact of global power systems on local kinship patterns. At the same time the patrimonial domain was shown to include struggles and strategic actions emerging from negotiations between genders and generations interacting through family life.

The last chapter transposed concepts of process analysis to a detailed account of the corn god's pilgrimage to the land of his deceased father, *Tagatauatzaloyan*, the-land-where-men-are-dry. When applied to the symbolic domain, the notion of "process for doing things in society" points to the manufacturing of signs interacting within the order of speech defined as a variable code. What has been said about the ranking effects of classes in struggle, however, applies equally to the narrative process. We view discourse as a war of words, an arrangement of signs geared to the active production and imposition of a moral order or "unitary language" (Bakhtin 1981: 271): in the case that concerns us, the Nahua teachings of patrimonialism and ascetic naturalism. Viewed from this angle, the narrative process is a *procès-verbal*, a report of authorized statements concerning the appropriate or inappropriate conduct of moral beings, human and natural, earthly and godly. Each narrative deploys complex procedures toward the investigation and correction of a crime; the powers of speech busy themselves carrying a judgment into narrative effect. At the same time a processual approach to symbolling implies that we explore the subversive potentialities of discourse, hence the heteroglossic manipulations and deviations of language. It requires that we pay attention to the transgressive ways of *la parole* (J.M. Chevalier 1990). In the words of Bakhtin (1981: 276), "any concrete discourse (utterance) finds the object at which it was directed already as it were overlain with qualifications, open to dispute, charged with value, already enveloped in an obscuring mist – or, on the contrary, by the 'light' of alien words that have already been spoken about it. It is entangled, shot through with shared thoughts, points of view, alien value judgments and accents."

Process: time and history

A process implies both order and conflict, as in hearings of the court. When applied to social analysis, however, the concept of process is usually advocated simply as an alternative to structural or functional notions of synchrony – to social phenomena viewed as the end-product of systems frozen in time. Activities "in process" allude to the unfolding of time in social life. Our preceding discussion suggests that this dichotomy between process and structure may be quite misleading: the two concepts are by no means incompatible. As already argued, the notion of process lends itself to an understanding of both order and conflict; the time factor does not exhaust the subject matter of a process-oriented view of social activity. Commonplace notions of "historical processes" are none the less a reminder of the crucial role that history plays in social activity.

These implications are to be retained, provided of course that we expel all connotations of uniform progression from our understanding of narrative stories and social history.

Throughout this book we avoided treating changes over time as illustrations of principles of linear evolution. But we also eschewed the opposite temptation, which is to reduce historical processes to mere context, a hodgepodge of conjunctural information that may serve to capture the particular background of systems fixed in time. No single chapter was used to present the general context of our analyses. Rather our strategy consisted in reconstructing the historical dynamics emerging from each regional analysis. Thus our discussion of the body politic dealt with changes that occurred from one government regime to the next, from one set of procedures to other laws and administrative actions that came after. On the economic plane, we examined the various phases that marked the history of resource management, property relations and market activities in Pajapan. Moreover, the analysis addressed cycles of production and rates of capital accumulation in agriculture and local commerce. All of these constitute the micro- and macro-dynamics of economic history. The patrimonial domain has its own dynamics as well, subject as it is to constant changes in kin relations based on the process of aging and the cyclical motions of family life. Similar comments apply to the passing of time in the realm of speech. Our reading of the corn myth proceeded from one series of events to another, thereby following the logic of mythical history proper. In order to avoid a purely sequential account of mythical time, we also paid attention to what Ricoeur (1984: 20) calls the "dialectic of expectation, memory, and attention", hence the interplay of pre- and post-figurative imageries within the narrative present, signs of distant times that keep the narrative plot in motion.

Each process has its own story to tell, a time factor built into the activities that fall under its jurisdiction. Throughout this book we discussed the internal dynamics of capital, state and the patrimonial regime (domestic and mythic). But we also emphasized the impact that events and cycles occurring in one field had on other field histories. For instance, Chapter 6 showed how kinship patterns in Pajapan responded to the economic transformations of the early 1980s, changes that stemmed in part from political changes at the local and national levels. Although never identical, the histories of divergent fields do interact. Social processes will intersect to produce correspondences between economic periods, government eras, patterns of family life, and phases of religious history. These interconnections can be brought together within a *longue durée* story (Braudel 1980: 25ff.) reflecting major trends governing a particular social formation:

But histories are not bound to proceed strictly according to plans: time is never so rigid as to imply absolute regularity. Processes rarely unfold mechanically, directly from past trends to plans of the immediate future. Even when applied to native society, metaphors of cultural continuity make a mockery of the "complex historical processes of appropriation, compromise, subversion, masking, invention, and revival"

(Clifford 1988: 338). Actually there are three factors that may upset the lawful proceedings of micro- and macro-history. First, social life is composed of a plurality of processes and field histories, a complex range of stories that follow divergent paths, disparate events and cycles that meet but never merge into one linear trajectory (Clifford 1988: 341). Rather than producing a synthetic *longue durée* story, the overdeterminations of social activity (processes affecting one another) can have the opposite effect, which is to compound the stresses and strains suffered in each field of activity. That is, in lieu of coming together into one general history, regional histories can clash or produce uneven results. For instance, in the early 1980s, the oil industry of southern Veracruz grew at the expense of ranching activities in Pajapan, causing a local economic crisis but also greater stability in family life; meanwhile, religious practices and church activity were unaffected by these events.

Second, social processes are never so fully structured as to regulate all internal matters, resolving all of them through proper rules of social life and narrative history. Given the uncertainties of human praxis and the contribution that human agents make to their own fate (Ricoeur 1984: 182), questions unsettled by the ruling order will always produce "partially indefinite" solutions to problems raised in society or in language. As Bourdieu argues (1977: 9), social analysis must substitute the concept of strategy for that of rule, thus reintroducing the ingredients of time and risk in our understanding of the probabilistic nature of social laws.

Third, readers are reminded of the case we make for systems rife with limitations, variations and contradictions – elements of uncertainty that form an integral part of state politics, capitalist economics, patrimonial kinship and native mythology alike. The same comment can be extended to methods of doing things through time: all courses of human action involve unforeseen crises and inconstancies that elude simple laws of linear history. Even when dealing with structural phenomena, social history is to be understood as "both the product of previous struggles to transform or conserve the structure, and, through the contradictions, tensions and power relations that constitute that structure, the source of its subsequent transformations" (Bourdieu 1990: 42).

This completes our discussion of a process-oriented approach to social history. We now turn to a personal expression of what praxis means to the authors of this book: our commitment to furthering the cause of equity and sustainable development in the Pajapan area.

The Sierra Santa Marta project

What will life be like in Pajapan some 20 or 30 years from now? Recent history suggests that cattle ranching will continue to dominate the local economy and that the process of land concentration temporarily halted by the land redistribution of 1981 will once again gather momentum. Recent reforms to land tenure legislation in Mexico legalize the current practice of land rental and sale of agrarian rights, allowing native ranchers in Pajapan to continue acquiring larger tracts of land. While new federal taxes on land are a burden to cash-poor peasants engaged in subsistence cultivation, new inheritance laws facilitate the conversion of disputed land into a market commodity. These and other reforms are bound to stimulate a process of land concentration as better-off ranchers and farmers buy land from impoverished peasants (A. Bartra 1991; Paré 1991a). The transfer of land is proceeding especially in the new *ejido* Pajapan II, the lowland area where the interests of ranchers and peasants have always clashed. To make matters worse, there is little indication that the land-extensive techniques of cattle production will change in the near future. Pajapan's ranchers will by and large remain a weak link in a chain of breeding and marketing of poor-quality beef in national markets. While subsistence maize production may provide a survival strategy for many peasants in Pajapan, current trends of land degradation offer little hope for improvement in productivity.

But Gulf Nahua history also suggests that the interests of native ranchers can clash with predatory forces far more powerful than local capital. Mexico's current neo-liberal policies (privatization of collective lands, price deregulation, dismantling of state corporations, entry into GATT and the North American Free Trade Agreement between Mexico, Canada and the United States) are an invitation to exploit the countryside (A. Bartra 1991; Paré 1991a; Oswald Spring 1992). The prospect of foreign investment in *ejidos* and agrarian communities, once unthinkable, is now a real possibility. The North American pulp and paper industry is a case in point, one that is particularly relevant to our Gulf Nahua case-study. Driven by a weakening supply of industrial pulp for paper, international paper companies have initiated tree plantation projects in many developing countries including Mexico, Thailand, India, Brazil, Chile, Uruguay and Indonesia. Tropical tree plantations present many advantages over temperate sources of pulp, including the low costs of land and labour and the rapid growth of tropical species such as the Australian eucalyptus (Paré, Buckles et al., 1992). These developments have particular importance for Mexico's Indian people and peasants as some 75% of the forest lands belong to agrarian communities and *ejidos*. As fortune would have it, Pajapan was selected by the transnational Simpson Investment Company for a massive plantation project that has embroiled the community in a national debate concerning eucalyptus plantations, forest ecology, foreign investment and the future of the *ejidos*.

In a masterful use of ecological rhetoric, the first version of the eucalyptus plantation proposal defined itself as a project for environmental regeneration and reforestation, an alternative to the current wasteland of cattle production. A close examination of the proposal tells a different story (Paré, Buckles et al. 1992). First of all, the lands proposed for the plantation are not the degraded upper slopes of the volcano where even pastures are of poor quality. Rather, the company is planning to use the prime lowland area previously claimed for the industrial port project and only recently reconquered by peasants for the cultivation of maize and beans. Second, evidence from many countries shows that extensive areas of eucalyptus can lower the water table and eliminate local fauna. Third, chemical substances released by the eucalyptus suppress other forms of vegetation, thereby threatening the long-term diversity of local plant species. Fourth, monoculture plantations such as the one proposed for Pajapan are susceptible to pest and disease problems that require agrochemical control, eventually leading to problems of water and soil contamination. Finally, the plan to use the Laguna del Ostión as a waterway for rafts loaded with tree trunks would do irreparable damage to the lagoon aquatic environment and undermine the recovery of currently degraded oyster banks.[1]

While the ecological implications of the Simpson Investment Company plan are disastrous, the economic terms offered to the owners of the land are scandalous. Although direct land purchases by foreign companies are still prohibited in Mexico, the recent reforms permit the development of joint ventures between foreign companies and *ejidos*. Companies are expected to provide the capital and technical skills while *ejidos* provide land and labor. The Simpson Investment Company has proposed such a structure to the agrarian community of Pajapan with a minimum required commitment of 10,000 hectares for a period of 30 years. The company offers capital for which high interest is charged back to the joint venture. While the company and the community would each have three votes on the administrative board, the company would have the power to veto all major decisions affecting the project. The rent offered to landholders is extremely low, approximately US$50 per hectare per year, an amount that barely matches what landholders can expect from the rental of poor quality pastures. Increased local employment, one of the key arguments put forward by the company, is equally misleading; peasant employment during all operations would amount to between five and ten days per hectare per year, much less than the level of labor currently employed on the same land area.

The Simpson Investment Company proposal, and the industrial port project before it, illustrate a basic weakness of underdeveloped regions: drained of resources and power, peasant communities can do little more than react to outside initiatives that show little concern for problems of local poverty and environmental destruction. Although vigorous reactions may change the course of events in ways unforeseen by the dominant powers, they rarely offer alternative visions of regional development. In an effort to remedy this problem, the authors and the Mexican anthropologist Luisa Paré initiated in 1990 an applied research project sensitive to peasant views on major regional problems and aspirations for the future. With funding from the International Development Research Center (IDRC, Canada), a multi-disciplinary team that includes the authors has developed an analysis of regional issues and broad development guidelines drawing on the knowledge and expressed needs of the local population (Paré, Blanco et al. 1992). In contrast to conservation-oriented projects, guidelines developed by the Sierra Santa Marta Project (SSMP) promote a sustainable resource-use strategy for resolving problems of poverty and ecological degradation. The project relies on a thorough analysis of current ecological and economic conditions and on local participation in problem identification as well. It promotes ecologically sound production alternatives that are compatible with "a multiple-product, regional, near-subsistence economy, the participation of native people using indigenous knowledge, technologies that evolved in the tropics, together with formal and informal risk sharing" (Redclift 1987: 78).

One important accomplishment of the SSMP to date is a careful revision of the plantation project developed by the Simpson Investment Company. At the invitation of the state government, members of the SSMP participated in inter-institutional meetings to examine the potential impact of the project in the region. The main contribution of the SSMP in this forum was to elucidate the terms and conditions of the project from an ecological point of view and from the perspective of the local population as well. While the eucalyptus project received considerable support in principle from government agencies at all levels, official assurances following this review process emphasized the need for a thorough environmental impact study and full, informed support from the affected communities. Analysis by Pajapeños of all aspects of the project (facilitated by the SSMP) makes their support for the project unlikely.

On a more general level, the SSMP has contributed to a debate concerning the establishment of legal norms for the use and protection of the remaining forest in the region. In 1980, some 82,000 hectares of the Santa Marta highland forest were formally declared a protected area. Six years later, both the Mexican government and the United Nations (UNESCO) recognized the area as a Special Biosphere Reserve. These declarations, however, remained virtually unknown to the local population and to many government agencies as well. Major land use projects such as Simpson's and land redistributions by the Secretaría de Reforma Agraria proceeded without paying the slightest attention to these official conservation policies (Paré 1991b). The SSMP has identified numerous land tenure anomalies and inconsistencies affecting the remaining fragments of the regional forest, prompting government authorities to strengthen the implementation of the reserve principles.

State government agencies recently launched the Programa de Desarrollo Integral de los Tuxtlas, an inter-institutional land-use planning committee for the sierra with local representation from *ejidos* and municipalities. At the behest of the SSMP, the Sierra de Santa Marta, the larger of the two regional volcanic formations, was included in this program. An initial development plan published by the state government and the University of Veracruz was prepared for both Los Tuxtlas and Santa Marta, with considerable input from the SSMP (Gobierno del Estado de Veracruz and Universidad Veracruzana 1992).

The SSMP has confronted externally-controlled development projects and helped catalyze conservation efforts. Measures to protect both the forest and the local population from further impoverishment do not preclude, however, alternative development strategies based on the sustainable use of resources. To this end, the SSMP has initiated a series of applied research and extension projects to combat poverty and thus reduce human pressure on the remaining forested areas. Farmer participatory research with cover crops and green manures was built on a locally developed technology capable of improving maize yields, reducing weed populations and lessening erosion (Buckles and Perales 1995). This technology was subsequently introduced to more than 3,000 farmers in the region through an extension campaign featuring local farmer-extensionists (Buckles and Arteaga 1993). Farmer-to-farmer communication has been reinforced through the development of a network of farmer-extensionists using workshops, slides, video and simple written materials to convey information on a wide range of issues including fire prevention techniques, soil conservation practices, maize seed selection and developments in national agricultural policies.

Conservation of forested areas also requires concerted efforts to develop alternative uses of forest resources, and the organizational structures needed to implement these measures. The SSMP has been instrumental in the development of a regional association of vanilla producers and made progress in the formation of village groups to establish norms for the harvest of palm from the rain forest and to negotiate prices with regional palm merchants (Paré, Blanco et al. 1992).

These and other projects are guided by the recognition that successful development depends upon local participation in the definition of problems and priorities and in the development of alternative strategies. Local participation in development must be extended, however, to include the development of the institutions needed to sustain local initiatives and demand outside resources. Recent government legislation calling for the establishment of municipal ecology committees was reinforced by the SSMP through technical support to municipal governments interested in addressing specific ecological problems. For example, a committee was struck in Pajapan to petition the state government and federal authorities for the opening of a new entrance to the Laguna del Ostión, an action needed to recover declining oyster banks. The committee, supported by municipal authorities, now organizes periodic collection of oyster shells in the villages of Pajapan and San Juan Volador so they can be returned to the lagoon, thereby enhancing oyster reproduction. These committees, while still in their infancy, are new vehicles for articulating local needs and demanding outside support.

The future in store for the Santa Marta highlands and its native population will emerge from these and other local initiatives as well as regional, national and international efforts to counter current trends of social and ecological impoverishment. As in the story of Sintiopiltsin, custodians of the land are not powerless to explore alternative endings to their dreaded passage through the "land-where-men-are-dry".

Note

1. Faced with these criticisms, the company has now distanced itself from the rhetoric of born-again ecologists by admitting that the eroded slopes of the volcano would entail lower potential yields and greater transportation costs as well.

BIBLIOGRAPHY

Primary sources

Public and private archives

Archives of Pajapan. (Various anonymous individuals).
Archives of the Local Rancher Association. Pajapan.
Archivo de la Comisión Agraria Mixta. Expediente Nos. 1860, 14, 3403, Pajapan and San Juan Volador. Xalapa, Veracruz. (ACAM)
Archivo de la Comisión Nacional Coordinadora de Puertos. México. (ACNCP)
Archivo de la Reforma Agraria (formerly Departamento de Asunto Agrarios y Colonización, DAAC). Expediente 276.1/2414. México. (ASRAM)
Archivo de la 14ta. Delegación de la Secretaría de Reforma Agraria. Expediente C-26 Bis. Xalapa, Veracruz. (ASRAX)
Archivo del Comisariado Comunal, Titulos Primordiales. Pajapan, Veracruz.
Archivo del Centro de Estudios Agrarios. Xalapa, Veracruz. (ACEAX)
Archivo del Instituto de Antropología. Díaz de Salas, M. Diario de Campo, Nahuas de Pajapan, Veracruz. Xalapa: Universidad Veracruzana.
Archivo del Licenciado Abel Jímenez Hernández. Coatzacoalcos, Veracruz. (AJH)
Archivo General de la Nación. Rama Presidentes. México. (AGN)
Archivo General de la Nación. Rama Tierras, Vol. 3030, No. 1. (AGN)

Government publications

México. Gaceta Oficial. Vol. CXXII, No. 20, February 14, 1979. Vol. CIX, No. 139, November 19, 1973. Vol. CXV, No. 143, November 27, 1976. Vol. CXXI, No. 142, November 27, 1979.
— Diario Oficial de la Federación. May 19, 1978; January 28, 1980; July 10, 1980; July 24, 1986.
— Diagnóstico Regional. Acayucan, 1986. Centro Coordinador Indigenista, Instituto Nacional Indigenista.
— Veracruz, Cuaderno de Información para la Planeación. México: Secretaría de Programación y Presupuesto (SPP).
— X Censo General de Población y Vivienda, 1980. Estado de Veracruz. México: SPP.
— Diagnóstico de los condiciones de salud en la microregión de Coatzacoalcos, nd. México: SPP.
— Un estudio de los requerimientos de personal calificado, nd. México: SPP.
— Memoria preliminar del deterioro del ambiente, nd. México: SPP.
— Agenda Monográfica y Estadística Distrital, 1986, Distrito de Desarrollo Rural No. 174, Jáltipan. Xalapa: Secretaría de Agricultura y Recursos Hidráulicos (SARH).
— Agenda estadística. Distrito de temporal No. 8, 1978. México: SARH.
— Plan de desarrollo agropecuario y forestal. Diagnóstico global del distrito de temporal No. 8, 1978. México: SARH.
— Programa de desarrollo rural integral del estado de Veracruz, 1985–1988 (Anexo Estadístico). México: Veracruz.
— Primer informe de la Coordinación General del Programa de Puertos Industriales, 1982. México: Coordinación General del Programa de Puertos Industriales, Secretaría de Comunicaciones y Transporte (SCT).

349

— *Segundo informe de la Coordinación General del Programa de Puertos Industriales, 1982.* México: Coordinación General del Programa de Puertos Industriales, SCT.

— *Programa, puertos industriales, 1981.* México: Coordinación General del Programa de Puertos Industriales, SCT.

— *Memoria del programa de puertos industriales, 1979–82.* México: Coordinación General del Programa de Puertos Industriales, SCT.

— *Demanda de vivienda y suelo para Coatzacoalcos, (Laguna del Ostión), 1980.* México: Secretaría de Hacienda y Obras Públicas, (SAHOP).

— *Propuesta para la planificación del desarrollo urbano regional de la zona de Coatzacoalcos–Villahermosa–Salina Cruz, 1978.* México: SAHOP.

— *Programa de Puertos Industriales, Declaratoria de Zona Industrial, Estado de Veracruz, Municipio de Coatzacoalcos y Pajapan, 1979.* México: SAHOP.

— *Proyecto de planificación regional: consideraciones en torno a la planificación de los transportes de la región sureste de México, 1980.* México: Secretaría de Programación y Presupuesto /Organización de Naciones Unidas, (SPP/ONU).

— *Programa de Puertos Industriales: consideraciones en torno a su congruencia con la planeación nacional y regional, 1980.* México: SPP/ONU.

— "Región Coatzacoalcos - Minatitlán, informe de trabajo de campo, 1978." D.G.A.H.O.P.

Veracruz. *Plan parcial de desarrollo urbano. Laguna del Ostión, Coatzacoalcos, Veracruz, 1980.* Xalapa, Veracruz: Gobierno del Estado de Veracruz.

Veracruz and Universidad Veracruzana. *Los Tuxtlas, plan para su conservación y desarrollo integral, 1992.* Xalapa: Gobierno del Estado de Veracruz y Universidad Veracruzana.

Maps

Anonymous. *The Village of Minzapa [later Pajapan] and Laguna de Minzapa [later Ostión], 1605 [copy made in 1880].* Archives of the Comisariado Comunal, Pajapan, Veracruz.

Anonymous. *Communal lands of Pajapan, 1981, showing five lots created in 1884.* Archives of the Comisariado Comunal, Pajapan, Veracruz.

Coordinación General del Programa de Puertos Industriales. *Proposed Industrial Port Laguna del Ostión, 1981.* 1:250,000. Mexico City, 1981.

Gutiérrez Martínez R. *Panoramic view of the Landscape Units in Pajapan, 1993* 1:50,000. Xalapa: Proyecto Sierra de Santa Marta, 1993.

Ramírez R., F. *Ecological Life Zones of the Sierra de Santa Marta, Veracruz, 1993* 1:250,000. Xalapa: Proyecto Sierra de Santa Marta, 1993.

Secretaría de Reforma Agraria, Departamento de Asuntos Agrarios y Colonización, *Communal Lands of Pajapan, showing the five lots created in 1884.* 1:40,000. Xalapa, 1968.

Newspapers

Diario del Istmo (Coatzacoalcos), *Elcélsior (Mexico City)*, *El Día* (Mexico City), *La Jornada* (Mexico City), *Uno Más Uno* (Mexico City)

Secondary sources

Alavi, H. (1982) "State and Class Under Peripheral Capitalism." In *Introduction to the Sociology of Developing Societies.* Edited by H. Alavi and T. Shanin. London: Macmillan, 289–307.

— "Peasants and Revolution." In *Peasant Struggles in India.* Edited by A. R. Desai. Delhi: Oxford University Press, 671–718.

Alegría, R. T. (1952) "Origins and Diffusion of the Term 'Cacique'." In *Selected Papers of the XXIX International Congress of Americanists*. Edited by Sol Tax. Chicago: University of Chicago Press.

Althusser, L. and E. Balibar (1970) *Reading Capital*. Translated by B. Brewster. London: New Left Books.

Amin, S. and K. Vergopoulos (1974) *La question paysanne et le capitalisme*. Paris: Editions Anthropos.

Amos, V. and P. Parmar 1984 "Challenging Imperial Feminism." *Feminist Review* 17: 3–19.

Andrle, R. R. (1964) "A Biogeographic Investigation of the Sierra de Tuxtla in Veracruz, Mexico." Unpublished Ph.D. Dissertation. Louisiana State University.

Antón, F. (1973) *La mujer en la América antigua*. México: Ed. Extemporáneos.

Antonio Hernández, S. (1979) "Historia que se labora con motivo de los principios del Partido Revolucionario en el Municipio de Pajapan." Unpublished Manuscript. Pajapan: Local PRI Committee.

Argueta, A. (1991) "Pueblos indios y recursos naturales." In *Nuevos enfoques: para el estudio de las etnias indígenas en México*. Edited by A. Warman and A. Argueta. México: UNAM, 13–46.

Arizpe, L. and C. Botey (1987) "Mexican Agricultural Development Policy and Its Impact on Rural Women." In *Rural Women and State Policy in Latin America*. Edited by C.D. Deere and M. León de Leal, Boulder: Westview Press, 67–83.

Asaola Garrido, E. (1982) *Rebelión y Derrota del Magonismo Agrario*. México: SEP 80.

Astorga Lira, E. (1985) *Mercado de Trabajo Rural en México*. México: ERA.

Baez-Jorge, F. (1980) "Pajapan, los indios y el desarrollo industrial." *Punto Aparte* (October 9): 16–17.

— (1973) *Los Zoque-Popolucas*. México: Instituto Nacional Indigenista.

Bakhtin, M. M. (1981) *The Dialogical Imagination*. Edited by M. Holquist. Translated by C. Emerson and M. Holquist. Austin: University of Texas Press.

Barkin, D. and B. Suárez (1985) *El Fin de la Autosuficiencia Alimentaria*. México: Oceano.

Barre, M.-C. (1985) *Ideologías indigenistas y movimientos indios*. México: Siglo Veintiuno.

Barry, T. (1987) *Roots of Rebellion. Land and Hunger in Central America*. Boston: South End Press.

Bartra, A. (1991) "El 27." *Cuadernos Agrarios* 3: 24–9.

— (1985) *Los Herederos de Zapata: movimientos campesino posrevolucionarios en México*. México: ERA.

— (1979a) *La Explotación del Trabajo Campesino por el Capital*. México: Editorial Macehual/ENAH.

— (1979b) "El panorama agrario en los '70s." *Investigación Económica* 38: 179–235.

— (1976) "La renta capitalista de la tierra." *Cuadernos Agrarios* 2: 5–78.

Bartra, A. et al. (1991) *Los nuevos sujetos del desarrollo rural*. México: ADN Editores.

Bartra, R. (1982) *Campesinado y Poder Político en México*. México: ERA.

— (1974) *Estructura Agraria y Clases Sociales en México*. México: ERA.

Bartra, R. and G. Otero (1987) "Agrarian Crisis and Social Differentiation in Mexico." *Journal of Peasant Studies*, 14 (3): 334–62.

Bartra, R. et al. (eds) (1975) *Caciquismo y Poder Político en el México Rural*. México: Siglo Veintiuno.

Bates, R. H. (1978) "People in Villages: Micro-level Studies in Political Economy." *World Politics* 31: 129–49.

Beaucage, P. (1975) "¿Modos de producción articulados o lucha de clases?" *Historia y Sociedad* 5: 37–58.

— (1973) "Anthropologie économique des communautés indigènes de la Sierra

Norte de Puebla (Mexique): les villages de basse montagne." *Revue Canadienne de Sociologie et d'Anthropologie* 10: 114–33 and 289–307.

Beaucage, P. and Taller de tradición oral (1990) "Le bestiaire magique: catégorisation du monde animal par les Maséhuals (Nahuas de la Sierra Norte de Puebla, Mexique)." *Recherches Amérindiennes au Québec* XX (3–4): 3–18.

— (1987) "Catégories pratiques et taxonomie: notes sur les classifications et les pratiques botaniques des Nahuas (Sierra Norte de Puebla, Mexique)." *Recherches Amérindiennes au Québec* XVII (4): 17–36.

Benería, L. and M. Roldán (1987) *The Crossroads of Class and Gender: Industrial Homework, Subcontracting and Household Dynamics in Mexico City.* Chicago: University of Chicago Press.

Benería, L. and G. Sen (1982) "Class and Gender Inequalities and Women's Roles in Economic Development: Theoretical and Practical Implications." *Feminist Studies* 8 (1): 157–76.

Benjamin, T. (1989) *A Rich Land, A Poor People: Politics and Society in Modern Chiapas.* Albuquerque: University of New Mexico Press.

Bernstein, H. (1988) "Capitalism and Petty Bourgeois Production: Class Relations and Divisions of Labour." *Journal of Peasant Studies* 15 (2): 258–71.

— (1979) "African Peasantries: A Theoretical Framework." *Journal of Peasant Studies* 4: 431–43.

Binford, L. (1985) "Political Conflict and Land Tenure in the Mexican Isthmus of Tehuantepec." *Journal of Latin American Studies* 17: 179–200.

Blanco, J. L. (1992) "Tierra ritual y resistencia entre los popolucas de Soteapan." In *Agraristas y agrarismo.* O. Domínguez Pérez et al. Xalapa: Gobierno del Estado de Veracruz, 270–304.

— (1991) "Políticas de desarrollo en la Sierra de Santa Marta." Unpublished Manuscript. Xalapa: Proyecto Sierra de Santa Marta.

Blanke, B. et al. (1978) "On the Current Marxist Discussion of Analysis of Form and Function of Bourgeois State. Reflections on the Relationships of Politics to Economics." In *State and Capital: A Marxist Debate.* Edited by J. Holloway and S. Picciotto. London: Edward Arnold.

Blom, F. and O. La Farge (1926) *Tribes and Temples.* New Orleans: Middle American Research Series 1.

Boege, E. (1988) *Los mazatecos ante la nación: Contradicciones de la identidad étnica en el México actual.* México: Siglo Veintiuno.

Boege, E. and N. Barrera (1991) "Producción y recursos naturales en los territorios étnicos: una reflexión metodológica." In *Nuevos enfoques: para el estudio de las etnias indígenas en México.* Edited by A. Warman and A. Argueta. México: UNAM, 91–119.

Bonfil Batalla, G. (1991) "Las culturas indias como proyecto civilizatorio." In *Nuevos enfoques: para el estudio de las etnias indígenas en México.* Edited by A. Warman and A. Argueta. México: UNAM, 121–42.

— (1987) *El México profundo.* México: SEP-CIESAS.

— (1971) "El concepto del indio en América: una categoría de la situación colonial." In *La situación actual de los indígenas en América del Sur.* Edited by G. Bonfil Batalla et al. Montevideo: Tierra Nueva.

— (1970) "Del indigenismo de la revolución a la antropología crítica." In *De eso que llaman antropología mexicana.* Edited by A. Warman et al. México: Nuestro Tiempo, 39–65.

Bourdieu, P. (1990) *In Other Words: Essays Towards a Reflexive Sociology.* Translated by M. Adamson. Stanford: Stanford University Press.

— (1977) *Outline of a Theory of Practice.* Translated by R. Nice. Cambridge: Cambridge University Press.

Bourque, S. C. and K. B. Warren (1981) *Women of the Andes: Patriarchy and Social Change in Two Peruvian Towns.* Ann Arbor: University of Michigan Press.

Bouysse-Cassagne, T. (1980) "Le bruit de la lagune, histoire de le création d'un port industriel chez les Nahuas de Veracruz." Unpublished Manuscript. Paris: Centre de Recherche et Documentation sur l'Amérique Latine, Institut des Hautes Etudes de l'Amérique Latine.

Bozada, L, and Z. Chávez (1986) *La Fauna Acuática de la Laguna del Ostión*. México: Centro de Ecodesarrollo.

Bradby, B. (1975) "The Destruction of the Natural Economy." *Economy and Society* 4: 127–61.

Braudel, F. (1980) *On History*. Translated by S. Matthews. Chicago: University of Chicago Press.

Bravo Garzón, R. (1972) "Un efecto regional del desarrollo económico de México: Veracruz, 1940–1970." *Dualismo* 1 (2): 9–49.

Breton, Y. and E. Estrada (1989) "Ciencias Sociales y desarrollo de las pesquerías: modelos aplicados al caso de México". México: Instituto Nacional de Antropología e Historia.

Breton, Y., E. Lopez, G. Coté and D. Buckles (1985) *Pescadores y Desarrollo Nacional: Hacía una valorización de la dimensión social de la pesca en México*. Québec: Université Laval/Universidad Autónoma de México.

Britton, J. C. and B. Morton (1989) *Shore Ecology of the Gulf of México*. Austin: University of Texas Press.

Brockett, C. D. (1988) *Land, Power, and Poverty: Agrarian Transformation and Political Conflict in Central America*. Boston: Unwin Hyman.

Buckles, D. (1989) "Cattle, Corn and Conflict in the Mexican Tropics." Unpublished PhD Dissertation. Ottawa: Carleton University.

Buckles, D. and L. Arteaga (1993) "Extensión campesino a campesino de los abonos verdes en la Sierra de Santa Marta, Veracruz, México." In *Gorras y sombreros: caminos hacía la colaboración entre técnicos y campesinos*. Edited by D. Buckles. Mexico City: CIMMYT.

Buckles, D. and J.M. Chevalier (1992) "Ejido *versus* bienes comunales: historia política de Pajapan." In *Agraristas y agrarismo*. O. Domínguez Pérez et al. Xalapa: Gobierno del Estado de Veracruz, 231–48.

Buckles, D. and H. Perales (1995) "Farmer-based Experimentation with Velvetbean: Innovation within Tradition." Unpublished Manuscript Mexico City: CIMMYT.

Buringh, P. (1970) *Introduction to the Study of Soils in Tropical and Subtropical Regions*. Wageningen, Netherlands: Centre for Agricultural Publishing and Documentation.

Burowoy, M. (1977) "The Functions and Reproduction of Migrant Labour: Comparative Material from Southern Africa and the United States." *American Journal of Sociology* 81: 1050–87.

Byres, T.J. (1985) "Modes of Production and Non-European Pre-Colonial Societies: The Nature and Significance of the Debate." *Journal of Peasant Studies* 12 (2–3): 1–18.

Campbell, H. (1989) "La COCEI: cultura y etnicidad politizadas en el Istmo de Tehuantepec." *Revista Mexicana de Sociología* 51 (2): 247–63.

Campos, J. (1982) *La Herencia Obstinada*. México: Fondo de Cultura Económica.

Cancian, F. (1965) *Economics and Prestige in a Maya Community*. Stanford: Stanford University Press.

Caouette, D. (1988) "Rural Politics and the Struggle for Land in Mexico: a Case Study." Unpublished MA Dissertation. Ottawa: Carleton University.

Carmack, R. M. (1981) *The Quiché Maya of Utatlán*. Norman: University of Oklahoma Press.

Carmona, F. (1982) "Estado y capitalismo en México: imbricación creciente con la sociedad civil." In *El Estado Mexicano*. Edited by J. Alonso. México: Editorial Nueva Imagen, 17–48.

Caso, A. (1953) *El pueblo del Sol*. México: Fondo de Cultura Económica.

A LAND WITHOUT GODS

Chamoux, M. (1981) *Indiens de la Sierra: La Communauté Paysanne au Mexique.* Paris: Editions L'Harmattan.

Chance, J. K. and W. B. Taylor (1985) "Cofradías and Cargos: An Historical Perspective on the Mesoamerican Civil–Religious Hierarchy." *American Ethnologist* 12: 1–26.

Charlton, T. H. (1991) "Land Tenure and Agricultural Production in the Otumba Region, 1785–1803." In *Land and Politics in the Valley of Mexico: A Two Thousand Year Perspective.* Edited by H. R. Harvey. Albuquerque: University of New Mexico Press, 223–63.

Chávez Padrón, M. (1987) *Ley Federal de Reforma Agraria – Ley de Fomento Agropecuario.* *Exposición de motivos, antecedentes, reformas, comentarios y correlaciones.* México: Editorial Porrúa.

Chevalier, F. (1982) "The Roots of Caudillismo." In *Caudillos: Dictators in Spanish America.* Edited by M. Hamill. Norman: University of Oklahoma Press, 27–41.

— (1963) *Land and Society in Colonial Mexico: the Great Hacienda.* Berkeley: University of California Press.

Chevalier, J. M. (1990) *Semiotics, Romanticism and the Scriptures.* Berlin and New York: Mouton de Gruyter.

— (1983) "There is Nothing Simple About Simple Commodity Production." *Journal of Peasant Studies* 10 (4): 153–86.

— (1982) *Civilization and the Stolen Gift: Capital, Kin, and Cult in Eastern Peru.* Toronto: University of Toronto Press.

CIMMYT (1991) "Análisis de los ensayos regionales de agronomía, 1990." Programa regional de maíz para Centro América, Panamá y el Caribe, México.

Clarke, S. (ed.) (1991) *The State Debate.* New York: St Martin's Press.

Clifford, J. (1988) *The Predicament of Culture: Twentieth-Century Ethnography, Literature and Art.* Cambridge, Massachusetts: Harvard University Press.

Clifford, J. and G. E. Marcus (1986) *Writing Culture: The Poetics and Politics of Ethnography.* Berkeley: University of California Press.

Cobarrubias, M. (1980) *El Sur de México.* México: Instituto Nacional Indigenista.

Cohen, J. (1983) *Class and Civil Society. The Limits of Marxian Critical Theory.* Oxford: Martin Robertson.

Coll, T. (1981) "Desalojo. Desaperacerán tres pueblos: Jicacal, Mangal, Las Barrillas," and "Tierras de la nación en venta." *Revista Por Esto*, July 2 and July 9.

Collins, H. (1982) *Marxism and the Law.* Oxford: Clarendon Press.

Colmenares, F. (1982) *Petróleo y Lucha de Clases en México, 1864–1982.* México: Ediciones el Caballito.

Cook, S. F. (1984) "Peasant Economy, Rural Industry and Capitalist Development in the Oaxaca Valley, Mexico." *Journal of Peasant Studies* 12 (1): 3–40.

— (1971) "Human Sacrifice and Warfare as Factors in the Demography of Pre-Colonial Mexico." In *Ancient Mesoamerica,* Selected Readings. Palo Alto: Peek Publications, 279–98.

Corrigan, P. (1980) "Towards a History of State Formation in Early Modern England." In *Capitalism, State Formation and Marxist Theory: Historical Investigations.* Edited by P. Corrigan. London: Quartet Books, 27–48.

Corrigan, P. and D. Sayer (1985) *The Great Arch: English State Formation as Cultural Revolution.* Oxford: Basil Blackwell.

Corrigan, P., H. Ramsay and D. Sayer (1980) "The State as a Relation of Production." In *Capitalism, State Formation and Marxist Theory: Historical Investigations.* Edited by P. Corrigan. London: Quartet Books, 1–125.

Cruz Martínez, F. (1991) *Pajapan: El litigio por sus tierras.* Unpublished Manuscript. Cosoleacaque.

Culturas Populares (1982) *Historia de los tres hijos.* Acayucan, Cuadernos de Trabajo 14.

— (1982) *Leyendas Nahuas.* Acayucan, Cuadernos de Trabajo 17.

— (1982) *Medicina tradicional*. Acayucan, Cuadernos de Trabajo 27.

— (1982) *Rituales y creencias de los Zoque-Popolucas*. Acayucan, Cuadernos de Trabajo 9.

Dehouve, D. (1984) "Las separaciones de pueblos en la región de Tlapa (siglo XVIII)." *Historia Mexicana* 33: 397–404.

de Janvry, E. Sadoulet and L. Wilcox Young (1989) "Land and Labour in Latin American Agriculture from the 1950s to the 1980s." *Journal of Peasant Studies* 16 (3): 396–424.

de la Peña, M. (1980) *Veracruz Económico*, Vol. I and II. Xalapa: Gobierno del Estado de Veracruz.

de la Peña, S. (1981) *Capitalismo en Cuatro Comunidades Rurales*. México: Siglo Veintiuno.

Díaz, J. (1986) *Tierra Fría, Tierra de Conflictos en Michoacán*. Zamora: Colegio de Michoacán.

Díaz-Polanco, H. (1982) *Formación Regional y Burguesía Agraria en México*. México: ERA.

— (1977) *Teoría Marxista de la Economía Campesina*. México: Juan Pablos Editores.

Domínguez Pérez, O. et al. (1992) *Agraristas y agrarismo*. Xalapa: Gobierno del Estado de Veracruz.

Dow, J. (1977) "Religion in the Organization of a Mexican Peasant Economy." In *Peasant Livelihood: Studies in Economic Anthropology and Cultural Ecology*. Edited by R. Halperin and J. Dow. New York: St Martin's Press, 215–26.

Downing, T. et al. (eds) (1992) Development or Destruction: the Conversion of Tropical Forest to Pasture in Latin America. Boulder: Westview Press.

Ducey, M. T. (1992) "From Village Riot to Regional Rebellion: Rural Protest in the Huasteca, Mexico, 1750–1870." PhD Dissertation. University of Chicago.

— (1989) "Tierras comunales y rebeliones en el norte de Veracruz antes del porfiriato, 1821–1880: El proyecto liberal frustrado." *Anuario* 6: 209–30.

Dupré, G. and P.-P. Rey (1978) "Reflections on the Relevance of a Theory of the History of Exchange." In *Relations of Production: Marxist Approaches to Economic Anthropology*. Edited by D. Seddon. London: Frank Cass, 171–208.

Durand, P. (1975) *Nanacatlan, Société paysanne et lutte de classes au Mexique*. Montréal: Presses de l'Université de Montréal.

Durrenberger, E.P (ed.) (1984) *Chayanov, Peasants, and Economic Anthropology*. London: Academic Press.

Eckstein, S. (ed.) (1989) *Power and Popular Protest: Latin American Social Movements*. Berkeley: University of California Press.

Esteva, G. (1980) *La Batalla en el México Rural*. México: Siglo Veintiuno.

Estrategia (1986) "Coatzacoalcos-Minatitlán: una región petrolizada." *Estrategia* 70: 59–70.

Evans, G. (1986) "From Moral Economy to Remembered Village: The Sociology of James C. Scott." *Working Paper* 40, Le Trobe University, Sociology Department.

Falcón Vega, R. (1988) "Charisma, Tradition, and Caciquismo: Revolution in San Luis Potosí." In *Riot, Rebellion, and Revolution: Rural and Social Conflict in Mexico*. Edited by F. Katz. Princeton: Princeton University Press.

— (1977) *El Agrarismo en Veracruz: la etapa radical 1928–1935*. México: Colegio de México.

Farris, N.M. (1984) *Maya Society Under Colonial Rule: The Collective Enterprise of Survival*. Princeton: Princeton University Press.

Fearnside, P. M. (1987) "Deforestation and International Economic Development Projects in Brazilian Amazonia." *Conservation Biology* 1 (3): 214–22.

— (1986) *Human Carrying Capacity of the Brazilian Rainforest*. New York: Columbia University Press.

Feder, E. (1977a) "Campesinistas y descampesinistas: tres enfoques divergentes (no incompatibles) sobre la destrucción del campesinado." *Comercio Exterior* 27 (12): 1439–46.

— (1977b) *El Imperialismo Fresa: una investigación sobre los mecanismos de dependencia de la agricultura Mexicana.* México: Editorial Campesina.

— (1971) "Latifundia and agricultural labour in Latin America." In *Peasants and Peasant Societies.* Edited by T. Shanin. Harmondsworth, Middlesex: Penguin Education.

— (1970) "Counterreform." In *Agrarian Problems and Peasant Movements in Latin America.* Edited by R. Stavenhagen. Garden City: Anchor Books.

Flores Lúa, G., L. Paré and S. Sarmiento (1988) *Los voces del campo: Movimiento campesino y política agraria 1976–1984.* México: Siglo Veintiuno.

Florescano Mayet, E. (1984) *Origen y Desarrollo de los Problemas Agrarios de México.* México: ERA.

Forsyth, A. and K. Miyata (1984) *Tropical Nature.* New York: Charles Scribner's and Sons.

Foster, G. (1965) "Peasant Society and the Image of the Limited Good." *American Anthropologist* 47: 293–315.

— (1945) "Sierra Popoluca Folklore and Beliefs." *American Archaeology and Ethnology* 42 (2): 177–250.

— (1942) *A Primitive Mexican Economy.* New York: American Ethnological Society, No. 5.

Foster-Carter, A. (1978) "The Modes of Production Controversy." *New Left Review* 107: 47–77.

Fowley, M. W. (1991) "Agrarian Conflict Reconsidered: Popular Mobilization and Peasant Politics in Mexico and Central America." *Latin American Research Review* 26 (1): 216–38.

Frank, A. G. (1969) *Latin America: Underdevelopment or Revolution.* New York and London: Monthly Review Press.

Friedrich, P. (1986) *The Princes of Naranja: An Essay in Anthrohistorical Method.* Austin: University of Texas Press.

— (1970) *Agrarian Revolt in a Mexican Village.* Englewoods Cliffs, New Jersey: Prentice-Hall.

— (1965) "A Mexican Cacicazgo." *Ethnology* 4: 190–209.

Gallegos, M. (1986) *Petróleo y Manglar.* México: Centro de Ecodesarrollo.

García de León, A. (1991) "Paraíso perseguido." *Ojarasca* No. 2. México: Pro México Indígena.

— (1976) *Pajapan: un dialecto Mexicano del Golfo.* México: Instituto Nacional de Antropología e Historia, Colección Científica, No. 43.

— (1969) "El universo de lo sobrenatural entre los nahuas de Pajapan, Veracruz." *Estudios de Cultura Náhuatl* VIII: 279–311. México: UNAM.

— (1968) "El dueño del Maíz y otros relatos nahuas del sur de Veracruz." *Tlalocan* V (4): 349–57.

— (1966) "Semana Santa en Zaragoza, Veracruz." Unpublished Manuscript.

Giddens, A. (1987) *Social Theory and Modern Sociology.* Stanford: Stanford University Press.

Godelier, M. (1973) *Perspectives in Marxist Anthropology.* Cambridge: Cambridge University Press.

— (1972) *Rationality and Irrationality in Economics.* Translated by B. Pearce. London: New Left Books.

Gollas, M. and A. García Rocha (1973) "El desarrollo económico reciente de México." In *Contemporary México.* Latin American Studies Series, Vol. 29. Edited by J. W. Wilkie, M. C. Meyer and E. Monzon de Wilkie. California: UCLA Latin American Center.

Gómez-Pompa, A. , C. Vázquez-Yáñes and S. Guevara (1972) "The Tropical Rain Forest: A Nonrenewable Resource." *Science* 177: 762–65.

González Casanova, P. (1970) *Democracy in Mexico*. Translated by D. Salti. New York: Oxford University Press.

González Cruz, G. et al. (1983) *Ciclo de vida de los Nahuas*. Acayucan: Dirección General de Culturas Populares.

González Torres, Y. (1985) *El sacrificio humano entre los Mexicas*. México: Instituto Nacional de Antropología e Historia.

Goodman, D. and M. Redclift (1981) *From Peasant to Proletarian: Capitalist Development and Agrarian Transitions*. Oxford: Basil Blackwell.

Gordillo de Anda, G. (1988) *Campesinos al asalto del cielo: de la expropriación estatal a la expropriación campesina*. México: Siglo Veintiuno.

Grammont, H. (1986) *Asalariados Agrícolas y Sindicalismo en el Campo Mexicano*. México: Juan Pablos Editor.

Greenberg, J. B. (1989) *Blood Ties: Life and Violence in Rural Mexico*. Tucson: University of Arizona Press.

— (1981) *Santiago's Sword: Chatino Peasant Religion and Economics*. Berkeley: University of California Press.

Grindle, M.S. (1977) *Bureaucrats, Politicians, and Peasants in Mexico: A Case Study in Public Policy*. Berkeley: University of California Press.

Gross, D. R. (1975) "Protein Capture and Cultural Development in the Amazon Basin." *American Anthropologist* 77 (3): 526–49.

— (1973) "Factionalism and Local Level Politics in Rural Brazil." *Journal of Anthropological Research* 29: 123–44.

Guerrero, J. (1979) "La diferenciación interna del campesinado mexicano." In *Polémica sobre las clases sociales en el campo mexicano*. Edited by L. Paré. México: Editorial Macehual.

Gutelman, M. (1974) *Capitalismo y Reforma Agraria en México*. México: ERA.

Gutiérrez Martínez, R. (1991) "El medio físico en la Sierra de Santa Marta: caracterización regional." Unpublished Manuscript. Xalapa: Proyecto Sierra de Santa Marta.

Habermas, J. (1987) *Theory of Communicative Action*, Vol. 2. *Lifeworld and System: A Critique of Functionalist Reason*. Translated by T. McCarthy. Boston: Beacon Press.

— (1974) *Theory and Practice*. Translated by J Viertel. Boston: Beacon Press.

Hall, J, A (1986) "States and Economic Development: Reflections on Adam Smith." In *States in History*. Edited by J. A. Hall. Oxford: Basil Blackwell, 154–76.

Hamilton, N. (1982) *The Limits of State Autonomy: Post-revolutionary Mexico*. Princeton: Princeton University Press.

Hansen, R. (1973) "PRI Politics in the 1970s: Crisis or Continuity." In *Contemporary Mexico*. Latin American Studies Series, Vol. 29. Edited by J. W. Wilkie, M. C. Meyer and E. Monzon de Wilkie. California: UCLA Latin American Center.

Harner, M. (1977) "The Ecological Basis for Aztec Sacrifice." *American Ethnologist* 4 (1): 117–35.

Harris, M. (1964) *Patterns of Race in the Americas*. New York: Walker.

Harris, O. and K. Young (1981) "Engendered Structures: Some Problems in the Analysis of Reproduction." In *The Anthropology of Pre-capitalist Societies*. Edited by J. S. Kahn and J. R. Llobera. London: Macmillan, 109–47.

Harrison, M. (1979) "Chayanov and the Marxists." *Journal of Peasant Studies* 7 (1): 86–100.

— (1977) "The Peasant Mode of Production in the Work of A.V. Chayanov." *Journal of Peasant Studies* 4 (4): 323–36.

Harrison, R. and F. Mort (1980) "Patriarchal Aspects of Nineteenth-Century State Formation: Property Relations, Marriage and Divorce, and Sexuality." In *Capitalism, State Formation and Marxist Theory: Historical Investigations*. Edited by P. Corrigan. London: Quartet Books, 79–109.

Heath, J.R. (1989) "The Dynamics of Mexican Agricultural Development: A Comment on Bartra and Otero." *Journal of Peasant Studies* 16 (2): 276–85.

Heidegger, M. (1968) *What Is Called Thinking?* Translated by J. G. Gray. New York: Harper and Row.

Herbert, J.-L., C. Guzmán Bochler and J. Qan (1972) *Indianité et lutte des classes*. Paris: Union Générale d'Editions.

Hernández, E. et al. (1981) *Los Nahuas y la muerte*. Acayucan: Dirección General de Culturas Populares.

Hewitt de Alcántara, C. (1992) "Introducción: Restructuración económica y subsistencia rural." In *Restructuración Económica y Subsistencia Rural*. Edited by C. Hewitt de Alcántara. México: Colegio de México.

— 1984 *Anthropological Perspectives on Rural Mexico*. London: Routledge and Kegan Paul.

— 1978 *La Modernización de la Agricultura Mexicana, 1940–1979*. México: Siglo Veintiuno.

Hill, R.M. and J. Monaghan (1987) *Continuities in Highland Maya Social Organization: Ethnohistory in Sacapulas, Guatemala*. Philadelphia: University of Pennsylvania Press.

Hindess, B. (1983) *Parliamentary Democracy and Socialist Politics*. London: Routledge and Kegan Paul.

Hirsch, J. (1978) "The State Apparatus and Social Reproduction: Elements of a Theory of Bourgeois State." In *State and Capital: A Marxist Debate*. Edited by J. Holloway and S. Picciotto. London: Edward Arnold.

Hirst, P.Q. (1980) "Law, Socialism and Rights." In *Radical Issues in Criminology*. Edited by P. Carlen and M. Collison. London: Martin Robertson.

— (1985) "Socialism, Pluralism and Law." *International Journal of the Sociology of Law* 13: 173–90.

Hodges, D. and R. Gandy (1979) *Mexico 1919–1976: Reform or Revolution?* London: Zed Press.

Holloway, J. (1991) "The State and Everyday Struggle." In *The State Debate*. Edited by S. Clarke. New York: St Martin's Press, 225–59.

Holloway, J., and S. Picciotto (eds) (1978) *State and Capital: A Marxist Debate*. London: Edward Arnold.

Hu-DeHart, E. (1988) "Peasant Rebellion in the Northwest: The Yaqui Indians of Sonora, 1740–1976. In *Riot, Rebellion, and Revolution: Rural and Social Conflict in Mexico*. Edited by F. Katz. Princeton: Princeton University Press, 141–75.

Iglesias, J.M. (nd) *Acayucan en 1831*. Xalapa: Colección Suma Veracruzana, Universidad Veracruzana.

INIREB (Instituto Nacional de Investigaciones Sobre Recursos Bióticos) (1980) "Ecoplan del puerto industrial de Laguna del Ostión: diagnóstico y pronóstico del ecoplan." Xalapa, Veracruz.

Jaggar, A. M. (1983) *Feminist Politics and Human Nature*. Totowa, NJ: Rowman and Allanheld.

Jessop, B. (1990) *State Theory: Putting the Capitalist State in its Place*. Cambridge: Polity Press.

— (1987) "Economy, State and Law in Autopoietic Theory." Essex Papers in Politics and Government No. 42. Colchester: Department of Government, University of Essex.

Katz, F. (1988)"Introduction: Rural Revolts in Mexico." In *Riot, Rebellion, and Revolution: Rural and Social Conflict in Mexico*. Edited by F. Katz. Princeton: Princeton University Press, 3–17.

Kaustky, K. (1970) *La question agraire*. Paris: Maspero.

Kern, R. (ed.) (1973) *The Caciques: Oligarchical Politics and the System of Caciquismo in the Luso-Hispanic World*. Albuquerque: University of New Mexico Press.

Knight, A. (1985) *The Mexican Revolution*. Cambridge: Cambridge University Press.

Krickeberg, W. (1982) *Las Antiguas Culturas Mexicanas*. México: Fondo de Cultura Económica.

Labra, A. (1982) "El estado y la economía." In *El Estado Mexicano*. Edited by J. Alonso. México: Editorial Nueva Imagen, 49–64.

Laclau, E. (1977) *Politics and Ideology in Marxist Theory*. London: New Left Books.

Lara Ovando, J. J. (1987) "La resistencia indígena de Pajapan ante la construcción del puerto industrial Laguna del Ostión." Unpublished Manuscript. México: Facultad de Ciencias Políticas y Sociales, Naucalpan, UNAM.

Lara Ovando, J. J., and L. Gutiérrez Hernández (1983) "Pajapan, el impacto de la penetración capitalista." Unpublished Manuscript. México: Facultad de Ciencias Políticas y Sociales, UNAM.

Law, H. (1960) "Mecayapan, Veracruz: An Ethnographic Sketch." Unpublished MA Dissertation. University of Texas.

— (1957) "Tamákatzi, a Gulf Nahua Text." *Tlalocan* III (4): 344–60.

Lenin, V.I. (1968) *The Development of Capitalism in Russia*. Moscow: Progress Publishers.

León-Portilla, M. (1983) *La filosofía nahuatl estudiada en sus fuentes*. México: UNAM.

— (1980) *Toltecayotl: aspectos de la cultura náhuatl*. México: Fondo de Cultura Económica.

Lerda, F. (1985) *Agricultura, campesinos y transferencias de valor: mitos fisiocráticos del siglo XX*. México: UNAM.

Levy, D. C. and G. Székely (1987) *Mexico, Paradoxes of Stability and Change*. Boulder and London: Westview Press.

Levy, T. and E. Hernández X. (1991) "Sucesión secundaria vegetal y su manejo." In *Modernización de la Milpa en Yucatan: Utopia o Realidad*. Edited by D. Zizumbo et al. Mérida: CICY-DANIDA-CP.

Lockhart, J. (1992) *The Nahuas After the Conquest: A Social and Cultural History of the Indians of Central Mexico, Sixteenth Through Eighteenth Centuries*. Stanford: Stanford University Press.

Long, N. (1975) "Structural Dependency, Modes of Production and Economic Brokerage in Rural Peru." In *Beyond the Sociology of Development: Economy and Society in Latin America and Africa*. Edited by I. Oxaal et al. London: Routledge and Kegan Paul.

López Arias, M. (1983) "El espíritu del maiz." In *El espíritu del maíz y otros relatos zoque-popolucas*. Acayucan: Dirección General de Culturas Populares.

López Austin, A. (1990)*Los mitos del tlacuache*. México: Alianza Editorial Mexicana.

— (1980) *El cuerpo humano e ideología: las concepciones de los antiguos nahuas*, 2 vols. México: UNAM.

McBride, G. (1923) *The Land Systems of Mexico*. New York: American Geographical Society.

McLeod, M. (1972) *Spanish Central America: A Socioeconomic History, 1520–1720*. Berkeley: University of California Press.

McNeely, J. A. et al. (1990) *Conserving the World's Biological Diversity*. Gland, Switzerland, and Washington, D. C.: IUCN, WRI, CI, WWF-US, the World Bank.

Maison, H. and C. Debouchet (1986) *La colonización francesa en Coatzacoalcos*. México: Universidad Veracruzana.

Mallon, F. E. (1983) *The Defense of Community in Peru's Central Highlands*. Princeton: Princeton University Press.

Mann, M. (1986) "The Autonomous Power of the State: Its Origins, Mechanisms and Results." In *States in History*. Edited by J. A. Hall. Oxford: Basil Blackwell, 109–36.

Martínez, A. and H. Rodríguez (1984) "La lucha de los campesinos de Pajapan y el proyecto del puerto industrial de la laguna del Ostión." Unpublished Manuscript. Xalapa: Facultad de Sociología, Universidad Veracruzana.

Martínez Hernández, S. (1982) *Tiempos de Revolución*. México: La Red de Jonas.

Martínez Lorenzo, I. et al. (1981) *Medio Ambiente y Economía de los Nahuas de Veracruz*. Acayucan: Dirección General de Culturas Populares.

Martínez Morales, E. (1983) *El Matrimonio Nahua*. Acayucan: Dirección General de Culturas Populares.

Martínez Morales, E. et al. (1978) *Las Clases Sociales en Pajapan*. Acayucan: Dirección General de Culturas Populares.

— (1982) *Sociedad e historia de los Nahuas de Veracruz*. Acayucan: Dirección General de Culturas Populares.

Marx, K. (1973) *Grundrisse*, trans. and with a foreword by M. Nicolaus. Harmondsworth: Penguin Books and New Left Review.

— *Capital: A Critique of Political Economy*, Vol. 1. Introduced by E. Mandel. Translated by B. Fowkes. New York: Vintage Books.

Medick, H. (1987) "Missionaries in the Row Boat? Ethnological Ways of Knowing as a Challenge to History." *Comparative Studies in Society and History* 19 (1): 76–98.

Megged, N. (1991) *El Universo del Popol Vuh: Análisis histórico psicológico y filosófico del mito quiché*. México: Editorial Diana.

Meillassoux, C. (1972) "From Reproduction to Production: A Marxist Approach to Economic Anthropology." *Economy and Society* 1: 93–105.

Mejía Piñeros, M. C., and S. Sarmiento Silva (1987) *La Lucha Indígena: un reto a la ortodoxia*. México: Siglo Veintiuno.

Melgarejo Vivanco, J. L. (1980) *Historia de la ganadería en Veracruz*. Xalapa: Ediciones del Gobierno de Veracruz.

— (1960) *Breve historia de Veracruz*. Xalapa: Ediciones Gobierno del Estado de Veracruz.

Mendoza Neri, J. (1982) "Ganadería y otras actividades económicas en el sur del Estado de Veracruz-Llave (notas de una estancia del campo en la región)." Unpublished Manuscript. México: Antropología Social, Universidad Autónoma Metropolitana-Ixtapalapa.

Menéndez, F. L. (1976) "Los manglares de la Laguna de Sontecomapan, Los Tuxtlas, Veracruz." Unpublished Dissertation. Facultad de Ciencias, Biología, UNAM.

Meza, O. (1975) *Breve estudio sobre la mujer mexihca*. México: Dirección General de Perfeccionamiento Profesional del Magisterio.

Michaels, A. and M. Bernstein (1973) "The Modernization of the Old Order: Organization and Periodization of Twentieth-Century Mexican History." In *Contemporary Mexico*. Latin American Studies Series, Vol. 29. Edited by J. W. Wilkie, M. C. Meyer and E. Monzon de Wilkie. California: UCLA Latin American Center.

Migdal, J. S. (1974) *Peasants, Politics, and Revolution: Pressures towards Political and Social Change in the Third World*. Princeton: Princeton University Press.

Mitchell, W. P. (1991) *Peasants on the Edge: Crop, Culture, and Crisis in the Andes*. Austin: University of Texas Press.

Moguel, J. (1976) "Notas sobre el problema campesino, lucha económica y lucha política en el campo: la asociación en la producción como una forma de lucha." *Cuadernos Agrarios* 3: 5–44.

Moguel, J. et al. (1981) *Ensayos Sobre la Cuestión Agraria y el Campesinado*. México: Juan Pablos Editor.

Mohanty, C. T. (1991) "Under Western Eyes: Feminist Scholarship and Colonial Discourses." In *Third World Women and the Politics of Feminism*. Edited by C. T. Mohanty, A. Russo and L. Torres. Bloomington: Indiana University Press, 51–80.

Mollard, A. (1977) *Les paysans exploités*. Grenoble: Presses Universitaires de Grenoble.

Moore. B. Jr. (1966) *The Social Origins of Dictatorship and Democracy: Lord and Peasant in the Making of the Modern World*. Boston: Beacon Press.

Moore, H. L. (1988) *Feminism and Anthropology*. Mineapolis: University of Minnesota Press.

Morgan, M. I. (1983) *Sexualidad y sociedad entre los aztecas*. México: Nuestro Tiempo.

Morgen, S. (1990) "Conceptualizing and Changing Consciousness: Socialist-Feminist Perspectives." In *Women, Class and the Feminist Imagination*. Edited by K. V. Hansen and I. J. Philipson. Philadelphia: Temple University Press, 277–91.

Mouzelis, N. (1980) "Modernization, Underdevelopment, Uneven Development: Prospects for a Theory of Third World Formations." *Journal of Peasant Studies* 7: 353–74.

Münch, G. (1983) *Etnología del Istmo Veracruzano*. México: Universidad Nacional Autónoma de México.

Murphy, R. (1971) *Dialectics of Social Life (Alarms and Excursions in Anthropological Theory)*. New York: Columbia University Press.

Murra, J. V. (1975) *Formaciones económicas y políticas del mundo andino*. Lima: Instituto de Estudios Peruanos.

Myers, N. (1980) *Conversion of Tropical Moist Forests*. Washington, DC: National Research Council.

Nahmad, D. (1989) "Pajapan: historia y economía política de una comunidad campesina." Unpublished Dissertation. Iztapalapa: UAM.

— (1987) "Notas de historia política." Unpublished Manuscript. Veracruz: Instituto Nacional de Antropología e Historia.

— (1985) "Desarrollo industrial y grupos de poder en el sur de Veracruz." Unpublished Manuscript. Veracruz: Instituto Nacional de Antropología e Historia.

— (1984) "Pajapan, tenencia de la tierra y política local." Unpublished Manuscript. Veracruz: Instituto Nacional de Antropología e Historia.

— (nd) "La región y sus contornos." Unpublished Manuscript. Veracruz: Instituto Nacional de Antropología e Historia.

Nash, J. (1980) "Aztec Woman: The Transition from Status to Class in Empire and Colony." In *Women and Colonization: Anthropological Perspectives*. Edited by E. Mona and E. Leacock. New York: Praeger Special Studies.

Navarro, D. (1981) "Mamíferos de la estación de Biología Tropical Los Tuxtlas, Veracruz." Unpublished Dissertation. Facultad de Ciencias, Biología, UNAM.

Needler, M. C. (1982) *Mexican Politics: The Containment of Conflict*. New York: Praeger.

Nicholas, R. (1965) "Factions: A Comparative Analysis." In *Political Systems and Distribution of Power*. ASA Monograph 2. London: Tavistock.

Nietzsche, F. (1967) *The Will to Power*. Translated by W. Kaufmann. New York: Vintage Books.

Nolasco, M. (1980) "El sistema urbano de los paises subdesarrollados: el caso de Coatzacoalcos-Minatitlán." In *Conflicto entre ciudad y campo en América Latina*. Edited by I. Restrepo. México: Nueva Imagen.

Novack, G. (1976) "The Law of Uneven and Combined Development and Latin America." *Latin American Perspectives* 3: 100–6.

Offe, C. (1975) "The Theory of the Capitalist State and the Problem of Policy Formation." In *Stress and Contradiction in Modern Capitalism*. Edited by L. N. Lindberg et al. Massachusetts: Lexington Books, 125–44.

— (1984) *Contradictions of the Welfare State*. London: Hutchinson.

Orlove, B. S., M. W. Fowley and T. F. Love (eds) (1989) *State, Capital, and Rural Society*. Boulder: Westview Press.

Oswald Spring, U. (1992) "El campesinado ante el Tratado de Libre Comercio." *Cuadernos Agrarios* 4: 42–59.

Otero, G. (1989) "The New Agrarian Movement: Self-Managed, Democratic Production." *Latin American Perspectives* 63, 16 (4): 28–59.

— (1980) "Lucha de clases, estado y campesinos." *Revista del México Agrario* 11 (4): 51–66.
Paige, J. M. (1975) *Agrarian Revolutions: Social Movements and Export Agriculture in the Underdeveloped World*. New York: Free Press.
Paré, L. (1992) "Cuando se llevan a los dioses." *Ojarasca* 11: 48–50.
— (1991a) "¿Rezago agrario o rezagados del agro?" *Cuadernos Agrarios* 3: 30–37.
— (1991b) "La tenencia de la tierra en la Sierra de Santa Marta: análisis regional." Unpublished Manuscript. Xalapa: Proyecto Sierra de Santa Marta.
— (1991c) "¿Es conveniente sembrar eucaliptos en el sur de Veracruz?" *El Jarocho Verde 1*.
— (1990) "The Challenges of Rural Democratization in Mexico." In *The Challenge of Rural Democratization: Perspectives from Latin America and the Philippines*. Edited by J. Fox. London: Frank Cass, 79–96.
— (1982) "La política agropecuaria 1976–1982." *Cuadernos Políticos* 33: 59–72.
— (1977) *El Proletariado Agrícola en México: ¿campesinos sin tierra o proletarios agrícolas?* México: Siglo Veintiuno.
— (1975) "Caciquismo y estructura de poder en la Sierra Norte de Puebla." In *Caciquismo y Poder Político en el México Rural*. Edited by R. Bartra et al. México: Siglo Veintiuno, 31–61.
— (1973) "Caciquisme et structure du pouvoir dans le Mexique rural." *Revue Canadienne de Sociologie et d'Anthropologie* 10 (1): 20–43.
Paré, L. (ed.) (1979) *Polémica sobre las clases sociales en el campo mexicano*. México: Editorial Macehual.
Paré, L., D. Buckles, J. Chevalier and F. Ramírez (1992) "Las plantaciones comerciales de eucalipto: ¿un nuevo modelo para comunidades indígenas del trópico húmedo?" Unpublished Manuscript. Xalapa: Proyecto Sierra de Santa Marta.
Paré, L., J.L. Blanco, D. Buckles, J. Chevalier, R. Gutiérrez, A. Hernández, H. Perales, F. Ramírez and E. Velázquez (1992) "La Sierra de Santa Marta: hacia un desarrollo sustentable". Unpublished Manuscript. Xalapa: Proyecto Sierra de Santa Marta.
Pashukanis, E. B. (1978) *Law and Marxism: A General Theory*. Translated by C. Arthur. London: Ink Links.
Pearce, J. (1986) *Promised Land: Peasant Rebellion in Chalatenango, El Salvador*. London: Latin American Bureau.
Perales Rivera, H. (1992) "Caracterización y valorización del autoconsumo en la agricultura de los Popolucas de Soteapan, Veracruz." Unpublished MSc Dissertation. Colegio de Postgraduados, Botánica, Montecillo, México.
Phillips, L. (1990) "Rural Women in Latin America: Directions for Future Research." *Latin American Research Review* 25 (3): 89–107.
Pierson, C. (1984) "New Theories of State and Civil Society: Recent Developments in Post-Marxist Analysis of the State." *Sociology* 18 (4): 562–71.
Popkins, S. L. (1979) *The Rational Peasant: The Political Economy of Rural Society*. Berkeley: University of California Press.
Poulantzas, N. (1978) *L'état, le pouvoir, le socialisme*. Paris: PUF.
Pozas, R., and I. de Pozas (1971) *Los Indios en las Clases Sociales de México*. México: Siglo Veintiuno.
Programas de Desarrollo Integral en el Estado de Veracruz (1991) *Los Tuxtlas: propuestas para su conservación y desarrollo integral*. Xalapa: Gobierno de Veracruz.
Proyecto Sierra de Santa Marta (1991) "La ganadería en la Sierra de Santa Marta, Veracruz: una primera aproximación." Unpublished Manuscript. Xalapa: Proyecto Sierra de Santa Marta.
Rama, R. and F. Rello (1979) "La agroindustria mexicana: su articulación con el mercado mundial." *Investigación Económica* 147: 99–125.
Ramírez, F. (1991) "Vegetación y uso del suelo en la zona Pajapan". Unpublished Manuscript. Xalapa: Proyecto Sierra de Santa Marta.

— (1984) "Plan conceptual para el manejo y desarrollo de una Reserva de la Biósfera en la Sierra de Santa Marta, Veracruz". Unpublished Manuscript. Xalapa: Instituto Nacional de Investigación sobre Recursos Bióticos.

Redclift, M. (1988) "Introduction: Agrarian Social Movements in Contemporary Mexico." *Bulletin of Latin American Research* 7(2): 249–55.

— (1987) *Sustainable Development: Exploring the Contradictions.* London and New York: Routledge.

— (1980) "Agrarian Populism in Mexico: the 'Via Campesina'." *Journal of Peasant Studies* 7 (4): 492–502.

Reina, L. (1988) "The Sierra Gorda Peasant Rebellion, 1847–1850." In *Riot, Rebellion, and Revolution: Rural and Social Conflict in Mexico.* Edited by F. Katz. Princeton: Princeton University Press, 269–94.

Reina, R. E. (1966) *The Law of the Saints.* Indianapolis: Bobbs-Merrill.

Rello, F. (1982) "La política del estado y la lucha campesina." In *El Estado Mexicano.* Edited by J. Alonso. México: Editorial Nueva Imagen, 181–8.

Revel-Mouroz, J. (1980) *Aprovechamiento y colonización del Trópico Húmedo Mexicano: la vertiente del Golfo y del Caribe.* México: Fondo de Cultura Económica.

Rey, P.-P. (1973) *Les alliances de classes.* Paris: Maspero.

— (1971) *Colonialisme, néo-colonialisme et transition au capitalisme. L'exemple de la "Comilog" au Congo-Brazzaville.* Paris: Maspero.

Richards, P. (1952) *Tropical Rain Forest.* Cambridge: Cambridge University Press.

Ricoeur, P. (1984) *Time and Narrative,* Vol. 1. Translated by K. McLaughlin and D. Pellauer. Chicago: University of Chicago Press.

RIGOR (1981) "Estudio Socio-económico de la comunidad de Pajapan." Unpublished Manuscript. México.

Roberston, C. and I. Berger (eds) (1986) *Women and Class in Africa.* New York and London: Africana Publishing Company/Holmes and Meier.

Robles, R. and J. Moguel (1990) "Agricultura y proyecto neoliberal." *El Cotidiano* 34: 3–12.

Rodríguez-Shadow , M. J. (1991) *La mujer azteca.* México: Universidad Autónoma del Estado de México.

Romanini, C. (1978) *Agricultura tropical en tierras ganaderas: alternativas viables.* México: Centro de Ecodesarrollo.

Romanucci-Ross, L. (1973) *Conflict, Violence and Morality in a Mexican Village.* Palo Alto: National Press Books.

Roniger, L. (1987) "Caciquismo and Coronelismo: Contextual Dimensions of Patron Brokerage in Mexico and Brazil." *Latin American Research Review* 22 (2): 71–99.

Roosevelt, A. C. (1980) *Parmana: Prehistoric Maize and Manioc Subsistence along the Amazon and Orinoco.* New York: Academic Press.

Rothstein, F. (1986) "The Class Basis of Patron-Client Relations." In *Modern Mexico: State, Economy and Social Conflict.* Edited by N. Hamilton and T. F. Harding. Beverly Hills: Sage Publications, 300–12.

— (1982) "Two Different Worlds: Gender and Industrialization in Rural Mexico." In *New Directions in Political Economy: An Approach for Anthropology.* Edited by M. B. Leons and F. Rothstein. Westport, Connecticut: Greenwood Press, 249–66.

Rubio, B. (1987) *Resistancia campesina y explotación rural en México.* México: ERA.

Rutsch, M. (1984) *La Ganadería capitalista en México.* México: Editorial Linea.

— (1981) "El sistema alimentario mexicano y la ganadería bovina de carne." *Nueva Antropología* V (17): 89–110.

Rzedowski, J. (1978) *Vegetación de México.* México: Limusa.

Sahlins, M. (1985) *Islands of History.* Chicago: University of Chicago Press.

— (1976) *Culture and Practical Reason.* Chicago: University of Chicago Press.

— (1972) *Stone Age Economics.* Chicago: Aldine.

364 A LAND WITHOUT GODS

Salamini, F. (1971) *Agrarian Radicalism in Veracruz, 1920–1938*. Lincoln: University of Nebraska Press.
Saldana, E. M. and J. Juárez Sánchez
— (1972) "El Istmo de Tehuantepec: un análisis preliminar." *Dualismo* 1 (2): 301–33.
Sam, M. (1991) "Resumen de datos demográficos de la Sierra de Santa Marta." Unpublished Manuscript. Xalapa: Proyecto Sierra de Santa Marta.
Sanderson, S. (1986) *The Transformation of Mexican Agriculture: International Structure and the Politics of Rural Change*. Princeton: Princeton University Press.
Sandstrom, A. R. (1991) *Corn Is Our Blood: Culture and Ethnic Identity in a Contemporary Aztec Indian Village*. Norman: University of Oklahoma Press.
Sarukhán, J. (1968) Estudio sinecológico de las selvas de Terminalia amazonia en la planicie costera del Golfo de México. Unpublished MSc Dissertation. Colegio de Posgraduados de Chapingo.
Schryer, F. (1990) *Ethnicity and Class Conflict in Rural Mexico*. Princeton: Princeton University Press.
— (1987) "Class Conflicts and the Corporate Peasant Community: Dispute over Land in Nahuatl Villages." *Journal of Anthropological Research* 43 (2): 99–120.
— (1986) "Peasants and the Law: a History of Land Tenure and Conflict in the Huasteca." *Journal of Latin American Studies* 18: 283–311.
— (1980) *The Rancheros of Pisaflores: The History of a Peasant Bourgeoisie in Twentieth Century Mexico*. Toronto: University of Toronto Press.
— (1975) "Village Factionalism and Class Conflict in Peasant Communities." *Canadian Review of Sociology and Anthropology* 12: 290–302.
Scott, J. (1976) *The Moral Economy of the Peasant: Rebellion and Subsistence in Southeast Asia*. New Haven: Yale University Press.
— (1985) *Weapons of the Weak: Everyday Forms of Peasant Resistance*. New Haven: Yale University Press.
Sedeño, L., and M. E. Becerril (1985) *Dos culturas y una infancia: psicoanálisis de una etnia en peligro*. México: Fondo de Cultura Económica.
Séjourné, L. (1957) *Pensamiento y religión en el México antiguo*. México: Fondo de Cultura Económica, Col. Breviarios 28.
Seler, E. (1963) *Comentarios al Códice Borgia*, 3 vols. México: Fondo de Cultura Económica.
Sexton, J. D. (1989) "Protestantism and Modernization in Two Guatemalan Towns." *American Ethnologist* 5 (2): 280–302.
Shanin, T. (1982) "Class, State, and Revolution: Substitutes and Realities." In *Introduction to the Sociology of Developing Societies*. Edited by H. Alavi and T. Shanin. London: Macmillan, 308–31.
Sheridan, T. E. (1988) *Where the Dove Calls: The Political Ecology of a Peasant Corporate Community in Northwestern Mexico*. Tucson: University of Arizona Press.
Sider, G. M. (1986) *Culture and Class in Anthropology and History*. Cambridge: Cambridge University Press.
Siemens, A. H. (1964) "The Character and Recent Development of Agricultural Settlement in Southern Veracruz, Mexico." Unpublished PhD Dissertation. University of Wisconsin.
Siméon, R. (1977) *Diccionario de la lengua Nahuatl o Mexicana*. Translated by J. Oliva de Coll. México: Siglo Veintiuno.
Skerrit, D. (1987) "El trabajo rural en un municipio veracruzano alrededor de 1920." Anuario IV. Centro de Investigaciones Históricas-Instituto de Investigaciones Humanísticas, Universidad Veracruzana.
Skocpol, T. (1985) "Bringing the State Back In: Strategies of Analysis in Current Research." In *Bringing the State Back In*. Edited by P. Evans et al. Cambridge: Cambridge University Press.
— (1979) *States and Social Revolutions: A Comparative Analysis of France, Russia, and China*. Cambridge: Cambridge University Press.

Skocpol, T. and E. K. Trimberger (1978) "Revolution and the World-Historical Development of Capitalism." In *Social Change in the Capitalist World Economy*. Edited by B. H. Kaplan. Beverly Hills: Sage Publications.

Slater, D. (ed.) (1985) *New Social Movements and the State in Latin America*. Amsterdam: CEDLA.

Smith, G. (1989) *Livelihood and Resistance: Peasants and the Politics of Land in Peru*. Berkeley: University of California Press.

Sorj, B. (1983) "The State, the Bourgeoisie and Imperialism in the Light of the Peruvian Experience." In *Military Reformism and Social Classes: The Peruvian Experience 1968–1980*. Edited by D. Booth and B. Sorj. London: Macmillan, 185–204.

Soustelle, J. (1983) *Los Olmecas*. Translated by J. J. Utrilla, México: Fondo de Cultura Económica.

— (1982) *El universo de los aztecas*. Translated by J. L. Martínez and J. J. Utrilla. México: FCE.

— (1974) *La vida cotidiana de los aztecas en vísperas de la conquista española*. México: Fondo de Cultura Económica.

— (1940) *La pensée cosmologique des anciens mexicains*. Paris: Hermann et Cie.

Spalding, K. (1984) *Huarochiri: An Andean Society under Inca and Spanish Rule*. Stanford: Stanford University Press.

Spores, R. (1984) *The Mixtecs in Ancient and Colonial Times*. Norman: University of Oklahoma Press.

Stavenhagen, R. (1979) *Problemas Etnicos y Campesinos: Ensayos*. México: Instituto Nacional Indigenista.

— (1969) *Las Clases Sociales en las Sociedades Agrarias*. México: Siglo Veintiuno.

— (1965) "Clases, colonialismo y aculturación." *América Latina* 6: 63–104.

Stephen, L. (1991) *Zapotec Women*. Austin: University of Texas Press.

Stern, S. J. (1987) "New Approaches to the Study of Peasant Rebellion and Consciousness: Implications of the Andean Experience." In *Resistance, Rebellion and Consciousness in the Andean Peasant World, Eighteenth to Twentieth Centuries*. Edited by J. Stern. Madison: University of Wisconsin Press, 3–25.

— (1983) "The Struggle for Solidarity: Class, Culture, and Community in Highland America." *Radical History Review* 27: 21–45.

— (1982) *Peru's Indian People and the Challenge of Spanish Conquest*. Madison: University of Wisconsin Press.

Story, D. (1986) *The Mexican Ruling Party: Stability and Authority*. New York: Praeger.

Stuart, J. (1978) "Subsistence Ecology of the Isthmus Nahuat Indians of Southern Veracruz, Mexico." Unpublished PhD Dissertation. University of California.

Taggart, J. M. (1983) *Nahuat Myth and Social Structure*. Austin: University of Texas Press.

Tannenbaum, F. (1968) *The Mexican Agrarian Revolution*. Hamden, Conn: Archon Books.

— (1950) *Mexico: The Struggle for Peace and Bread*. New York: Alfred A. Knopf.

Taylor, J.G. (1979) *From Modernization to Modes of Production: A Critique of the Sociologies of Development and Underdevelopment*. Atlantic Highlands, New Jersey: Humanities Press.

Taylor, W. B. (1972) *Landlord and Peasant in Colonial Oaxaca*. Stanford: Stanford University Press.

Teichman, J. (1989) "The State and Economic Crisis in Mexico: Restructuring the Parastate sector." Paper presented at the Annual Meeting of the Canadian Association for Latin American and Caribbean Studies, October 1989.

Terán, S. (1976) "Formas de conciencia social de los trabajadores del campo." *Cuadernos Agrarios* 1: 20–36.

Thompson, E.P. (1978) *The Poverty of Theory and Other Essays*. London: Merlin Press.

— (1977) "Eighteenth-Century English Society." *Social History* 3 (2): 133–65.
— (1975) *Whigs and Hunters: The Origin of the Black Art*. London: Allan Lane.
Thompson, R. (1984) "Conflictos campesinos e intervención estatal en torno a la explotación petrolera en el sureste." *Boletín de análisis e información agraria*. Universidad Nacional Autónoma de México.
Tilly, C. (1985) "Models and Realities of Popular Collective Action." *Social Research* 52 (4): 717–47.
Toledo, A. (ed.) (1982a) *Petróleo y Ecodesarrollo en el Sureste de México*. México: Centro de Ecodesarrollo.
Toledo, A. (1982b) *Cómo Destruir el Paraíso: el desastre ecológico del sureste*. México: Océano/Centro de Ecodesarrollo.
Toledo, V. M. (1989) *Naturaleza, producción, cultura: ensayos de ecología política*. Xalapa: Universidad Veracruzana.
— (1982) "Pleistocene Changes of Vegetation in Tropical Mexico." In *Biological Diversification in the Tropic*. Edited by G. T. Prance. New York: Columbia University Press.
Trujillo Jáuregui, S. et al. (1982) *Rituales y creencias Nahuas*. Acayucan: Dirección General de Culturas Populares.
Tucker, W. P. (1957) *The Mexican Government Today*. Minneapolis: University of Minnesota.
Tutino, J. (1988) "Agrarian Social Change and Peasant Rebellion in Nineteenth-Century Mexico: The Example of Chalco." In *Riot, Rebellion, and Revolution: Rural Social Conflict in Mexico*. Edited by F. Katz. Princeton: Princeton University Press, 95–140.
— (1986) *From Insurrection to Revolution in Mexico: Social Bases of Agrarian Violence 1750–1940*. Princeton: Princeton University Press.
Urban, G. and J. Sherzer (eds) (1991) *Nation-States and Indians in Latin America*. Austin: University of Texas Press.
Urias Hermosillo, M. et al. (1987) *Coxquihui, Chumatlán y Zozocolco: tres municipios totonacos del Estado de Veracruz (historia y realidad actual 1821–1987)*. Veracruz: Instituto Nacional Indigenista.
Urry, J. (1981) *The Anatomy of Capitalist Societies: The Economy, Civil Society and the State*. London: Macmillan.
Vaillant, G. (1980) *La Civilización Azteca*. México: Fondo de Cultura Económica.
Van Young, E. (1981) *Hacienda and Market in Eighteenth-Century Mexico: The Rural Economy of the Guadalajara Region, 1675–1820*. Berkeley: University of California Press.
Vázquez Garcia, V. (nd) PhD Dissertation in Progress. Ottawa, Carleton University, Department of Socioloy.
Vázquez Peña, B. (nd) "Estudio de la Comunidad Nahuatl de Pajapan, Veracruz: período 1978–1979." Unpublished Manuscript. Pajapan: Centro de Salud.
Velázquez, E. (1992a) "Reforma agraria y cambio social entre los nahuas de Mecayapan." In *Agraristas y agrarismo*. Edited by O. Domínguez Pérez et al. Xalapa: Gobierno del Estado de Veracruz, 249–68.
— (1992b) "Política, ganadería y recursos naturales en el trópico húmedo veracruzano: El caso del municipio de Mecayapan." *Relaciones: Estudios de Historia y Sociedad* 50: 23–64.
— (1991) "La cuestión política en el municipio de Mecayapan." Unpublished Manuscript. Xalapa: Proyecto Sierra de Santa Marta.
Velázquez, E. and L. Paré (1991) "Tenencia de la tierra y recursos naturales en la Sierra de Santa Marta: el caso de Mecayapan, Veracruz." Unpublished Manuscript. Xalapa: Proyecto Sierra de Santa Marta.
Velázquez, E. and H. Perales (1991) "Autosuficiencia de maíz en la Sierra de Santa Marta." Unpublished Manuscript. Xalapa: Proyecto Sierra de Santa Marta.

Vergopoulos, K. (1979) "El papel de la agricultura familiar en el capitalismo contemporáneo." *Cuadernos Agrarios* 9: 33–42.

Warman, A. (1988) "The Political Project of Zapatismo." Transl. by J. Brister. In *Riot, Rebellion, and Revolution: Rural and Social Conflict in Mexico*. Edited by F. Katz. Princeton: Princeton University Press, 321–37.

— (1983) "La nueva polémica agraria: invitación al pleito." *Nexos* 71: 25–31.

— (1980) *Ensayos Sobre el Campesinado en México*. México: Nueva Imagen.

— (1976) *Y Venimos a Contradecir. Los Campesinos de Morelos y el Estado Nacional*. México: Ediciones de la Casa Chata.

Warren, K. B. (1989) *The Symbolism of Subordination: Indian Identity in a Guatemalan Town*. Austin: University of Texas Press.

Wasserstrom, R. (1983) *Class and Society in Central Chiapas*. Berkeley: University of California Press.

Wells, D. (1981) *Marxism and the Modern State: An Analysis of Fetichism in Capitalist Society*. Sussex: Harvester Press.

Williamson, G. and W. J. A. Payne (1978) *An Introduction to Animal Husbandry in the Tropics*. London and New York: Longman.

Wilson, F. (1985) "Women and Agricultural Change in Latin America: Some Concepts Guiding Research." *World Development* 13 (9): 1017–35.

Winfield Capitaine, F. (1991) *Las Culturas del Golfo*. Xalapa: Graphos.

Wolf, E. (1986) "The Vicissitudes of the Closed Corporate Peasant Community." *American Ethnologist* 13 (2): 325–9.

— (1969) *Peasant Wars of the Twentieth Century*. New York: Harper and Row.

— (1966) *Peasants*. Englewoods Cliffs, New Jersey: Prentice-Hall.

— (1959) *Sons of the Shaking Earth*. Chicago: University of Chicago Press.

— (1957) "Closed Corporate Communities in Mesoamerica and Java." *Southwestern Journal of Anthropology* 13 (1): 1–18.

— (1955) "Types of Latin American Peasantry: A Preliminary Discussion." *American Anthropologist* 57 (3): 452–71.

Yúnez N., A. (1988) "Theories of the Exploited Peasantry: A Critical Review." *Journal of Peasant Studies* 15 (2): 190–217.

Závala de Cosío, M. E. (1985) "El petróleo y la petroquímica en el sur del estado de Veracruz." *Márgenes 1*. Departamento de Sociología, Universidad Veracruzana.

Zeitlin, M. (ed.) (1980) *Classes, Class Conflict, and the State*. Cambridge: Winthrop Publishers.

INDEX